WRITERS' AND ARTISTS'
YEARBOOK 1979

Writers' & Artists' yearbook 1979

SEVENTY-SECOND YEAR OF ISSUE

A Directory for writers, artists, playwrights, writers for film, radio and television, photographers and composers

ADAM & CHARLES BLACK · LONDON

© 1979 A. & C. BLACK (PUBLISHERS) LTD.

35 BEDFORD ROW, LONDON WC1R 4JH

ISBN 0 7136 1903 1

Writers' and artists' yearbook:
   1979: seventy-second year of issue.
   1. Literature - Directories
   808′.02′025   PN12
   ISBN 0–7136–1903–1

PRINTED AND BOUND IN ENGLAND BY
HAZELL WATSON AND VINEY LTD
AYLESBURY, BUCKS

contents

theatre, tv radio, agents

art, music prizes, clubs

copyright
tax, services

preface

This year, as in every previous year, the *Writers' and Artists' Yearbook* has been thoroughly revised and updated. At the same time we have taken one stage further the changes which were initiated two years ago, and which were designed to make the book easier to use whilst at the same time providing the detailed and up-to-date information which is the basis of the *Yearbook*'s reputation.

New design The book is divided into five sections with page markers; on the back cover, for easy reference, is a summary of contents. In a book of this kind, which has grown steadily over many years, it is not possible to provide completely self-contained sections. We hope, however, that the changes which we have made, coupled with use of the index and contents list, will make it possible to find information more readily than hitherto.

Annual revision Annual revision of the *Yearbook* ensures that the market sections, which give details of journals and publishers, are carefully checked, each entry being referred to the relevant editor or publishing house. All addresses, requirements, rates of payment and other details are therefore up-to-date at the time of going to press. Similarly, all the many other features of the *Yearbook* have been revised for the benefit of contributors to newspapers and magazines, writers of books, and those who aim to find a market in the theatre, films, radio or television, as well as freelance artists, designers and photographers. This edition includes a completely new article on Income Tax.

Vanity publishing Every edition of the *Yearbook* in recent years has contained a strong warning that the author who pays for the publication of his work is almost invariably making an expensive mistake. It has been suggested that several distinguished poets have found it necessary to underwrite their first books in order to establish themselves, and in this respect the cautionary note on "vanity publishers" on page 216 has been mildly modified; but unhappily there is still ample evidence that an emphatic general warning is necessary.

It should be repeated, too, that the publishers of the *Yearbook* cannot provide an advisory service, and that to rely on an out-of-date edition is to invite inevitable difficulties and disappointments.

newspapers & magazines

WRITING FOR NEWSPAPERS, MAGAZINES, ETC.

More than five hundred journals are included in the British Journals section of the *Yearbook*, almost all of them offering opportunities to the writer. Some 200 leading Commonwealth and South African journals are also included, and while some of these have little space for freelance contributions, many of them will always consider outstanding work. Many journals do not appear in our lists because the market they offer for the freelance writer is either too small or too specialised, or both. It is impossible to include all such publications in the *Yearbook*, for the benefit of only a small proportion of its purchasers, without substantially increasing its price. Those who wish to offer contributions to technical, specialist or local journals are likely to know their names and can ascertain their addresses; before submitting a manuscript to any such periodical they are advised to write a preliminary letter to its editor.

Magazine editors frequently complain to us about the unsuitability of many manuscripts submitted to them. Not only are the manuscripts unsuitable, but no postage is sent for their return. In their own interests, writers and others are advised to *enclose postage for the return of unsuitable material*.

Before submitting manuscripts, writers should study carefully the editorial requirements of a magazine; not only for the subjects dealt with, but for the approach, treatment, style and length. Obvious though these comments may be to the practised writer, the beginner would be spared much disappointment if he studied markets more carefully (though he must not expect editors to send him free specimen copies of their magazines). An article or short story suitable for *Woman's Own* is unlikely to appeal to the readers of *The New Statesman*. The importance of studying the market cannot be over-emphasised. It is an editor's job to know what his readers want, and to see that they get it. Thus freelance contributions must be tailored to fit a specific market; subject, theme, treatment, length, etc., must meet the editor's requirements.

A number of magazines and newspapers will accept letters to the editor, paragraphs for gossip columns, and brief filler paragraphs, and will pay for these sums up to £5. For a list of these journals see the Classified Indexes at the end of the *Yearbook*.

The Classified Indexes provide a rough guide to markets. They must be used with discrimination, and it is always desirable to examine a copy of a journal if you are not familiar with it, and are submitting a MS. to the editor for the first time. For list of recent journal merges, changes of title, and terminations, also see end of the *Yearbook*.

A list of British magazine publishers, with their addresses, will be found on pages 90–92.

Writers and artists, and others, are advised not to accept from editors less than a fair price for their work, and to ascertain exactly what rights they are being asked to dispose of when an offer is made.

It has always been our aim to obtain and publish the rates of payment offered for contributions by journals and magazines. Certain journals of the highest standard and reputation are reluctant, for reasons that are understandable, to state a standard rate of payment, since the value of a contribution may be dependent not upon length but upon the standing of the writer or of the information he has to give. Many journals when giving a rate of payment indicate that it is the "minimum rate", others, in spite of efforts to extract more precise information from them, prefer to state "usual terms" or "by arrangement".

Writing for markets outside the UK The lists on pages 93–118 contain only a selection of the journals which offer some market for the free-lance. To print, and to keep up-to-date, a complete list for each English-speaking country would increase the extent and cost of the *Yearbook* quite disproportionately to the value of such enlargement. For the overseas market for stories and articles is small, and editors often prefer their fiction to have a local setting.

The larger newspapers and magazines buy many of their stories, as the smaller papers buy general articles, through one or other of the well-known syndicates, and a writer may be well advised to send printed copies of stories he has had published at home to an agent for syndication overseas.

Most of the big newspapers depend for news on their own staffs and the press agencies. The most important papers have permanent representatives in Britain who keep them supplied, not only with news of especial interest to the country concerned, but also with regular summaries of British news and with articles on events of particular importance. While many overseas journals have a London office, it is usual for MSS. from free-lance contributors to be submitted to the headquarters' editorial office overseas.

Bangladesh and Pakistan are now omitted from this section because of uncertainty regarding the continuity of periodicals in those countries and the rates of payment of those which still exist.

India is still retained, though would-be contributors must be prepared for disappointment and not infrequently to hear no more of MSS. submitted to publications in that country.

When sending MSS. abroad it is important to remember to enclose International Reply Coupons. These cost 25p each and can be exchanged in any foreign country for stamps representing the minimum postage payable on a letter sent from that country to this country.

UNITED KINGDOM JOURNALS AND MAGAZINES

Aberdeen Evening Express, R. Smith, Lang Stracht, Aberdeen, AB9 8AF *T.* 690222.
7p. D.—Lively evening paper reading. *Payment:* by arrangement. *Illustrations:* mainly half-tone.

(Aberdeen) The Press and Journal (1748), Peter Watson, Lang Stracht, Aberdeen, AB9 8AF. *T.* 690222. London Office, Greater London House, Hampstead Road, London NW1 7SH.
9p. D.—Contributions of Scottish interest. *Payment:* by arrangement. *Illustrations:* half-tone.

Accountancy (1889), Geoffrey Holmes, City House, 56–66 Goswell Road, London, EC1M 7AB *T.* 01-628 7060.
80p. M.—Articles on accounting, financial, legal and other subjects likely to be of professional interest to accountants and businessmen. *Payment:* £30 per 1000 words. *Illustrations:* half-tone and colour. Cartoons.

Achievement, World Trade House, 50 London Road, Riverhead, Sevenoaks, Kent, TN13 2DE *T.* 0732 58144.
40p. M.—Lively articles relating to British business achievements of direct interest to American company presidents. *Illustrations:* first-class photographs. *Payment:* by arrangement.

Administrative Accounting (incorporating **Book-keepers Journal**) (1920), Derek Bradley, The Institute of Administrative Accounting, 418–422 Strand, London, WC2R 0PW *T.* 01-240 3106.
50p post paid. Q.—Articles on accounting and general business practice. *Length:* 1000–2000 words. *Payment:* by arrangement. *Illustrations:* offset litho.

Aeromodeller (1935), Managing Editor: R. G. Moulton, Editor: M. B. Cowley, Model and Allied Publications Ltd., P.O. Box 35, Bridge Street, Hemel Hempstead, Hertfordshire, HP1 1EE. *T.* Hemel Hempstead 2501.
35p. M. (£5.75 p.a.).—Articles and news concerning model aircraft and radio control of model aircraft. Suitable articles and first-class photographs by outside contributors are always considered. *Length:* 750–2000 words, or by arrangement. *Payment:* about £5.00 to £8.00 per page. *Illustrations:* photographs and line drawings to scale.

Aeroplane Monthly (1973), Richard T. Riding, IPC Transport Press Ltd., Dorset House, Stamford Street, London SE1 9LU *T.* 01-261 8108. *T.A.* Bisnespres, London SE1. *Telex.* 25137.
50p. M.—Articles relating to aviation in general, and with particular emphasis on historical aspects. *Length:* up to 2000 words. *Payment:* varies according to contribution. *Illustrations:* half-tone, line, colour. *Payment:* £20 per 1000 words; photographs £3.00 minimum.

Agenda, William Cookson, 5 Cranbourne Court, Albert Bridge Road, London, SW11 4PE *T.* 01-228 0700. Associate Editor: Peter Dale. *T.* 01-644 3424. £3.00 p.a. ($9.00 in U.S.A.). Q.—Poetry and criticism. *Payment:* £3.00 per poem or per page of poetry, occasionally higher. *Illustrations:* half-tone. Contributors should study the journal before submitting MSS.

Air Pictorial, The Dial House, 6 Park Street, Windsor, Berks, SL4 1UU *T.* Windsor 69777.
40p. M.—Journal with wide aviation coverage. Many articles commissioned, and the Editor is glad to consider competent articles exploring fresh ground or presenting an individual point of view on technical matters. *Payment:* £7.35 per 1000 words standard. *Illustrations:* half-tones and line drawings; new photographs of unusual or rare aircraft considered.

Alive, Derek McEwen, Parkdale, Dunham Road, Altrincham, Cheshire, WA14 4QG *T.* 061-928 0793.
25p. M.—Articles on nutrition and alternative lifestyles. *Payment:* by arrangement. *Illustrations:* photographs of foods, crops, relevant events, nature studies, etc.

AMA, The (Journal of the Assistant Masters Association), Peter Smith, 29 Gordon Square, London, WC1H 0PT *T.* 01-388 0551–2.
30p. 8 times a year.—Features, articles, comment, news about secondary education. *Payment:* £15 per 1000 words (minimum). Cartoons, illustrations, photographs.

Amateur Gardening (1884), P. Wood, King's Reach Tower, Stamford Street, London, SE1 9LS *T.* 01-261 5180.
15p. W.—Articles up to 1000 words about any aspect of gardening. *Payment:* by arrangement. *Illustrations:* line or half-tone.

Amateur Photographer (1884), Martin Hodder, Surrey House, Throwley Way, Sutton, Surrey, SM1 4QQ *T.* 01-643 8040.
25p. W.—Original articles of pictorial or technical interest, preferably illustrated with either photographs or diagrams. *Length preferred:* (unillustrated) 400 to 800 words: cine articles up to 1500 words; (illustrated) 2 to 4 pages. *Payment:* by negotiation. Illustrations unaccompanied by text will be considered for covers.

Amateur Stage (1946), Roy Stacey, 1 Hawthorndene Road, Hayes, Bromley, BR2 7DZ *T.* 01-462 6461.
30p. M.—Articles on all aspects of the amateur theatre, preferably practical and factual. *Length:* 600–2000 words. *Payment:* minimum of £3.00 per 1000 words. *Illustrations:* photographs and line drawings, *payment* for which varies.

Ambit (1959), Dr. Martin Bax, 17 Priory Gardens, Highgate, London, N6 5QY *T.* 01-340 3566.
75p. Q.—Poems, short stories, criticism. *Payment:* by arrangement. *Illustrations:* line and half-tone.

Angler's Mail, John Ingham (IPC Magazines Ltd.), King's Reach Tower, Stamford Street, London, SE1 9LS *T.* 01-261 5000.
15p. W.—Features, cartoons and news items about sea, coarse and game fishing. *Length:* 850 to 1500 words. *Payment:* £11.25 (basic) per 750 words and pro-rata. *Illustrations:* Colour transparencies £8.50 (basic). Black and white £3.00 (basic). Half-tones, colour transparencies, line and wash drawing. (Web offset litho printing).

Angling (1959), (incorporating **Creel**), Brian Harris, 30–34 Langham Street, London, W1N 5LB *T.* 01-580 6972.
40p. M.—Angling articles and photographs. *Length:* 550; 2000 words. *Payment:* £10 per 1000 minimum. *Illustrations:* line and half-tone; colour transparencies.

Angling Times (1953), Bob Feetham, EMAP, Bretton Court, Bretton, Peterborough, PE3 8DZ *T.* Peterborough 266222.
14p. W.—Articles, pictures, news stories, on all forms of angling. *Payment:* £13.00 per 1000 words. *Illustrations:* colour, half-tone, line.

Anglo-Welsh Review, The (1949) (formerly **Dock Leaves**), Gillian Clarke, 1 Cyncoed Avenue, Cyncoed, Cardiff, CF2 6ST *T.* 755100. *Publisher:* H. G. Walters (Publishers) Ltd., Knowling Mead, Tenby, Dyfed, SA70 8EE.
£2.50 p.a. Three times a year.—Short stories, plays, poetry, satire, and articles on literature, the arts, history, travel, education, having some relation to Wales. Reviews of books in English by Welsh authors, and with a Welsh setting. *Payment:* by arrangement. *Illustrations:* eight pages of blocks or photographs.

Animal Ways (1935), Thelma How, RSPCA, Causeway, Horsham, Sussex, RH12 1HG *T.* Horsham 64181.
15p. 5 per annum. The animal world for the younger generation. Fiction and factual notes concerning animals and animal welfare. *Length:* 350–1000 words. All MS must be typewritten. *Readership:* children between 7 and 11. *Payment:* according to value. *Illustrations:* line and half-tone; some colour transparencies used.

Animal World, Thelma How, RSPCA, Causeway, Horsham, Sussex, RH12 1HG T. Horsham 64181.
15p. 5 per annum. Fiction and factual notes concerning animals and animal welfare. *Length:* 350–1000 words. All MS. must be typewritten. *Readership:* young people between 12 and 17. *Payment:* according to value. *Illustrations:* line and half-tone; some colour transparencies used.

Annabel (D. C. Thomson & Co. Ltd.), 80 Kingsway East, Dundee, DD4 8SL, and 185 Fleet Street, London, EC4A 2HS.
25p. M.—Colour gravure monthly for the modern woman with wide interests. Personal experience stories, biographical stories of well-known personalities, family and parenthood topics, fashion, cookery, knitting, fiction. Art *illustrations* and photographs in full colour and black-and-white. *Payment:* on acceptance.

Antique Collector (1930), David Coombs, Chestergate House, Vauxhall Bridge Road, London, SW1V 1HF *T.* 01-834 2331.
75p. M.—Practical and fully illustrated information for those interested in extending their knowledge and enjoyment of all aspects of antiques and art. *Illustrations:* fine black and white and colour photographs.

Antique Dealer & Collectors Guide, The, Alison Brand, City Magazines Ltd., 1–3 Wine Office Court, Fleet Street, London, EC4A 3AL *T.* 01-353 4060.
65p. M.—Articles on antique collecting. *Length:* 1000–2000 words. *Payment:* £23.00 per 1000 words. *Illustrations:* line and half-tone colour. *Payment:* £2.00 for black and white, up to £15 for colour transparencies.

Antiques (1963), Tony Keniston, Old Rectory, Hopton Castle, Craven Arms, Salop, SY7 0QJ *T*. 05474 356.
50p (£2 p.a.). Q.—Articles on antiques and of interest to antique dealers and serious collectors. *Length:* 600 to 2000 words. *Payment:* £1.50 per 100 words published. *Illustrations:* line and half-tone.

Antiquity, Glyn Daniel, St. John's College, Cambridge, CB2 1TP *T*. 61621. Publisher: Heffers Printers Ltd., Kirkwood Road, Kings Hedges Road, Cambridge, CB4 2PQ *T*. Cambridge 51571.
£3.00. Q. (£7.50 p.a.).—General articles on archaeology of all parts of the world. *Length:* 2000 to 5000 words. *Payment:* free offprints supplied. *Illustrations:* half-tones and line blocks.

Apollo (1925) (Apollo Magazine), Editorial: Denys Sutton, 22 Davies Street, London, W1Y 1LH *T*. 01-629 3061.
£2.00. M.—Knowledgeable articles of about 2500 words on art, ceramics, furniture, armour, glass, sculpture, and any subject connected with art and collecting. *Payment:* by arrangement. *Illustrations:* colour and half-tone.

Aquarist and Pondkeeper, The (1924) (The Buckley Press, Ltd.), The Butts, Half Acre, Brentford, Middlesex, TW8 8BN *T*. 01-568 8441. Editor: Laurence E. Perkins.
35p. M.—Illustrated authoritative articles by professional and amateur biologists, naturalists and aquarium hobbyists on all matters concerning life in and near water. *Length:* about 1500 words. *Payment:* by arrangement. *Illustrations:* photographs and line.

Architect, The, David Crawford, 4 Addison Bridge Place, London, W14 9BR *T*. 01-603 4567.
Controlled circulation. M.—Articles of interest to architects. *Length:* 1500 to 2500 words. *Payment:* by arrangement.

Architects' Journal, The (1895), Leslie Fairweather, R.I.B.A., 9 Queen Anne's Gate, London, SW1H 9BY *T*. 01-930 0611.
32p. W.—Articles (mainly technical) on architecture, planning and building accepted only with prior agreement of synopsis. *Payment:* by arrangement. *Illustrations:* photographs and drawings.

Architectural Design (1930), 7–8 Holland Street, London, W8. *T*. 01-737 6996.
£1.50. M.—Articles on architecture and allied subjects, with illustrations. *Payment:* by arrangement. *Illustrations:* half-tone and colour.

Architectural Review (1896), Lance Wright, R.I.B.A., 9 Queen Anne's Gate, Westminster, London, SW1H 9BY *T*. 01-930 0611.
£1.50. M.—Contains articles (up to 3000 words in length) on architecture and the allied arts. Must be thoroughly qualified writers. *Payment:* by arrangement. *Illustrations:* photographs, drawings, etc.

ARELS Journal (1972), Kate Topham, Association of Recognised English Language Schools, 125 High Holborn, London, WC1V 6QD *T*. 01-242 3136–7.
£4.00 p.a. post free. 3 times a year.—Articles on teaching of English as a foreign language. *Length:* 1000–2500 words. *Payment:* by arrangement. *Illustrations:* half-tone and line.

Army Quarterly and Defence Journal, Major-General C. H. Stainforth, C.B., O.B.E., 1 West Street, Tavistock, Devon *T.* 0822-3577. *T.A.* Books, Tavistock.
£3.35. Q. (£12.00 p.a.).—Devoted to all matters connected with the Army and defence. Articles should deal with international, current and historical military topics in the light of tactics, strategy, administration and political consciousness; they should be from 2000 to 5000 words. Articles from the younger generation of officers are particularly welcome. *Payment:* by arrangement. *Illustrations:* maps if essential.

Art and Antiques Weekly (1968), Anne Morley-Priestman, 181 Queen Victoria Street, London, EC4V 4DD *T.* 01-248 3482.
45p. W.—Expert articles on antiques. *Leight:* 800–3000 words. *Payment:* £2.00 per 100 words printed. *Illustrations:* line, half-tone, colour.

Art and Artists (1966), John George, Hansom Books, P.O. Box 294, 2 & 4 Old Pye Street, off Strutton Ground, Victoria Street, London, SW1P 2LR *T.* 01-222 4475.
£1.00. M.—Articles on art, sculpture and architecture. *Length:* 2000 words with photographs. Commissioned articles only accepted. *Payment:* by arrangement. *Illustrations:* line, half-tone and colour.

Art and Craft in Education (1946), Henry Pluckrose (Evans Brothers Ltd.), Montague House, Russell Square, London, WC1B 5BX *T.* 01-636 8521.
35p. M.—Articles must be of a practical nature and deal with the various phases of art and craft in Primary and Secondary Schools. *Payment:* by arrangement. *Illustrations:* line, half-tone.

Artist, The (1931), Peter John Garrard, 7 Carnaby Street, London, W1V 1PG *T.* 01-437 8090.
60p. M.—Instructional articles relating to every branch of fine and commercial art. Articles are mainly commissioned from artists of highest repute. *Length:* 1500 to 2000 words. *Payment:* by arrangement. *Illustrations:* must relate to articles. Line, half-tone, and colour.

Arts Review (1949), Eaton House Publishers Ltd., 1 Whitehall Place, London, SW1A 2HE *T.* 01-839 2041.
45p. F.—Art criticism and reviews. Commissioned work only. *Illustrations:* half-tone and line.

Author, The (1890), Richard Findlater, 84 Drayton Gardens, London, SW10 9SD *T.* 01-373 6642. *T.A.* Auctoritas, London.
50p. Q.—Organ of The Society of Authors. Commissoned articles from 1000 to 2000 words on any subject connected with the legal, commercial, or technical side of authorship. *Payment:* by arrangement. (Little scope for the freelance writer: a preliminary letter is advisable.)

Autocar (1895), Raymond Hutton, Dorset House, Stamford Street, London, SE1 9LU *T.* 01-261 8273. *T.A.* Autocar, Bisnespres 25137, London, Telex.
25p. W.—All aspects of cars, motoring and motor industries. Articles, general, practical, touring, competition and technical. *Payment:* varies; mid-month following publication. *Illustrations:* tone, line (litho) and colour. Press day news: Monday.

Balance (1934), Prisca Middlemiss, The British Diabetic Association, 3–6 Alfred Place, London, WC1E 7EE.
7½p. Bi-M.—Articles on diabetes or related topics; articles of general interest written by diabetics or their relatives. *Length:* 1000–2000 words. *Payment:* £10.00 per 1000 words. *Illustrations:* line, half-tone, colour.

Ballroom Dancing Times (1956), Alex Moore, Editorial Adviser, Mary Clarke, Executive Editor, 18 Hand Court, High Holborn, London, WC1V 6JF *T.* 01-405 1414.
20p. M.—Dealing with ballroom dancing from every aspect, but chiefly from the serious competitive, teaching and medal test angles. Well informed free-lance articles are occasionally used, but only after preliminary arrangements. *Payment:* by arrangement. *Illustrations:* web offset; action photographs preferred.

Banker, The (1926), Robin Pringle, Editorial Office: Minster House, Arthur Street, London, EC4R 9AX *T.* 01-623 1211.
£1.00. M.—Articles on economic policy, finance and banking, home and overseas, 1500 to 3000 words. Outside contributions are accepted on banking and general economic subjects. *Payment:* by arrangement. *Illustrations:* half-tones of people, buildings.

Bankers' Magazine, The (1844), Margaret Thoren, Holywell House, Worship Street, London, EC2A 2EN *T.* 01-247 5400.
75p. M.—Articles of from 200–2000 words. *Payment:* by arrangement.

Baptist Times (1855), Geoffrey Locks, 4 Southampton Row, London, WC1B 4AB *T.* 01-405 5516. *T.A.* Preacher, London, WC1.
10p. W.—Religious or social affairs matter, 800 words. *Payment:* by arrangement. *Illustrations:* half-tone.

Battle for Wargamers (1974), R. A. Gee, Model and Allied Publications Limited, P.O. Box 35, Bridge Street, Hemel Hempstead, Hertfordshire, HP1 1EE *T.* Hemel Hempstead 63841.
35p. M.—Articles and features on wargaming and boardgaming in all scales and periods.

Battle Picture Library (1961), IPC Magazines Ltd., King's Reach Tower, Stamford Street, London SE1 9LS *T.* 01-261 5000.
12p. Eight each month.—All picture war stories. Artists and authors invited to submit sample work to the Editor.

Beano, The (D. C. Thomson & Co. Ltd.), Courier Place, Dundee, DD1 9QJ, and 185 Fleet Street, London, EC4A 2HS.
5p. W.—Picture paper for young folk. Comic strip series, 12–22 pictures. *Payment:* on acceptance.

Bedfordshire Magazine (1947), Betty Chambers, 50 Shefford Road, Meppershall, Shefford, SG17 5LL *T.* Hitchin 813363.
25p. Q.—Articles of Bedfordshire interest. *Length:* up to 1500 words. *Payment:* £1.05 per 1000 words. *Illustrations:* line and half-tone.

Beezer, The (D. C. Thomson & Co. Ltd), Courier Place, Dundee, DD1 9QJ, and 185 Fleet Street, London, EC4A 2HS.
7p. W.—Picture paper for children. Stories told in pictures in 14–20 panels per instalment. Also comic strips in series, 6–15 pictures each number. Interest drawings—history, geography, general—suitable for full colour reproduction. *Payment:* on acceptance.

(Belfast) News Letter (1737), John Trew, Donegall Street, Belfast, BT1 2GB *T.* 44441. 7p. D.—Unionist.

Big Farm Management, George Macpherson, Northwood House, 93–99 Goswell Road, London, EC1V 7QA *T.* 01-253 9355.
80p. (12 issues per year).—Management and marketing aspects of large scale farming; articles and photographs with authoritative and informative captions. *Payment:* by arrangement. *Length:* 1000–2000 words. *Illustrations:* line and half-tone.

Birds and Country Magazine, Hockley Clarke, Managing Editor, 79 Surbiton Hill Park, Surbiton, Surrey. *T.* 01-399 7809.
35p. (£2.00 p.a.). Q.—Original observations on bird life and natural history subjects all over the world, occasional outside articles up to 1000 words. *Payment:* by arrangement. *Illustrations.*

Birmingham Evening Mail (1870), D. H. Hopkinson, Colmore Circus, Birmingham, B4 6AY *T.* 021-236 3366 (30 lines). *Telex:* 337552. London Office: 23–27 Tudor Street, London, EC4Y 0LA *T.* 01-353 0811.
8p. D.—Ind. Features of topical Midland interest considered. *Length:* 400–800 words.

Birmingham Post, The, N. J. Reedy, P.O. Box 18, 28 Colmore Circus, Birmingham, B4 6AX *T.* 021-236 3366.
8p. D.—Authoritative and well-written articles of industrial, political or general interest are considered, especially if they have relevance to the Midlands. *Length:* up to 1200 words. *Payment:* by arrangement.

Blackwood's Magazine (1817), David Fletcher, 32 Thistle Street, Edinburgh, EH2 1HA *T.* 031-225 3411.
60p. M.—*Original and high quality* work of all kinds: fiction, adventure, travel, history, poetry, and biography; as well as miscellaneous articles treating in a fresh manner any unhackneyed subject of general interest. Emphasis is placed on material coming from personal experience or original research. Not illustrated. *Length:* 2000–9000 words. *No preliminary letter* is required, but would-be contributors are advised to study the magazine before submitting material. A pamphlet for the guidance of authors is available on request. Return postage or International Reply coupons must accompany all MSS. *Payment* is good and is made on publication.

Blue Jeans (D. C. Thomson & Co. Ltd.), Courier Place, Dundee, DD1 9QJ *T.* 23131; and 185 Fleet Street, London, EC4A 2HS *T.* 01-242 5086.
12p. W.—Colour gravure magazine for teenage girls. Picture love stories. True experience text stories up to 3000 words. Pop features and pin-ups. General teen interest features. Fashion and beauty. *Illustrations:* pop and boy/girl transparencies and black and whites, picture story artwork, humorous illustrations. *Payment:* on acceptance.

Bolton Evening News and Lancashire Journal Series (1867), T. H. Cooke, Mealhouse Lane, Bolton, Lancashire, BL1 1DE *T.* Bolton 22345. *T.A.* Newspapers, Bolton. London: 23–27 Tudor Street, EC4.
8p. D. and W. —Articles, particularly those with South Lancashire appeal. *Length.* up to 700 words. *Illustrations:* photographs; considered at usual rates. *Payment:* on 15th of month following date of publication.

Book Collector, The (1952) (incorporating **Bibliographical Notes and Queries**), Editorial Board: Nicolas Barker (Editor), J. Commander, T. Hofmann, M. Hunter, D. McKitterick, P. H. Muir, The Collector Ltd., 3 Bloomsbury Place, London, WC1A 2QA *T.* 01-637 3029.
£9.00 p.a. ($24.00). Q.—Articles, biographical and bibliographical, on the collection and study of printed books and MSS. *Payment:* by arrangement.

Books and Bookmen (1955) Sally Emerson, Hansom Books, P.O. Box 294, 2 & 4 Old Pye Street, off Strutton Ground, Victoria Street, London, SW1P 2LR *T.* 01-222 3533.
£1.00 M.—Articles on authors and their books; reviews; only commissioned material accepted. *Payment:* by arrangement. *Illustrations:* line, half-tone.

Bookseller The (1858), David Whitaker (J. Whitaker and Sons Ltd.), 12 Dyott Street, London, WC1A 1DF *T.* 01-836 8911.
£12.50 p.a. W.—The organ of the publishing and bookselling trades. While outside contributions are always welcome most of the journal's contents are commissioned. *Length:* about 1000 to 2000 words. *Payment:* by arrangement.

Brewing & Distilling International (1865), Bruce Stevens, 5–7 Southwark Street, London, SE1 1RQ *T.* 01-407 6981.
M.—This journal is devoted to the interests of Brewers, Maltsters, Hop Growers, Barley Growers, Distillers, Soft Drinks Manufacturers, Bottlers and Allied Traders, circulating in over 100 countries.   Contributions (average 2500 words) accepted are technical and management articles written by authors with a special knowledge of the subjects dealt with. Such articles may be illustrated by line drawings and photographs. *Payment:* by arrangement.

Bristol Evening Post (1932), G. B. Farnsworth, Temple Way, Bristol, BS99 7HD *T.* Bristol 20080.
7p. D.—Articles up to 800 words with strong West-country interest. *Payment:* at recognised rates.

British Chess Magazine (1881), B. P. Reilly, 9 Market Street, St. Leonards-on-Sea, East Sussex, TN38 0DQ *T.* Hastings 424009.
55p. Annual subscription £6.60 post free. M.

British Deaf News, The (1950), Editorial Board of the British Deaf Association, 38 Victoria Place, Carlisle, CA1 1HU *T.* Carlisle 20188.
20p. Bi-M.—Articles, news items, letters dealing with deafness. *Payment:* by arrangement. *Illustrations:* line and half-tone.

British Esperantist, The (Journal of the British Esperanto Association) (1905), W. Auld, 140 Holland Park Avenue, London, W11 4UF *T.* 01-727 7821. 25p+postage. (£2.50 p.a. post free). M.—Articles in English or Esperanto, by arrangement, on the applications of the International Language, Esperanto, to education, commerce, travel, international affairs, scouting, radio, television, literature, linguistics, etc. *Illustrations:* photos by arrangement. *Payment:* by arrangement.

British Farmer and Stockbreeder (1971), Montague Keen, Surrey House, 1 Throwley Way, Sutton, Surrey, SM1 4QQ *T.* 01-643 8040.
12p. Fortnightly.—Photographs or cartoons of farming interest. Very occasional articles (400–500 words) of interest to farming people and photographs of country subjects for the Home Pages. *Payment:* from £20.00 per 1000 words or more, illustrations, £3–£5 for reproductions. More for special assignments and for exclusive pictures.

British Journal of Photography, The (1854), G. W. Crawley, 24 Wellington Street, Strand, London, WC2E 7DH *T.* 01-836 0731–4.
20p. W.—Articles on professional, commercial and press photography, and on the more advanced aspects of amateur, technical, industrial, medical, scientific and colour photography. *Payment:* by arrangement. *Illustrations:* in line, half-tone, colour.

British Medical Journal (1840), Stephen Lock, M.A., M.B., F.R.C.P., British Medical Association House, Tavistock Square, London, WC1H 9JR *T.* 01-387 4499.
80p. W.—Medical and related articles.

British Naturism (1964), Bob Caldwell, 3 Berwyn Grove, Loose, Maidstone, Kent, ME15 9RD *T.* Maidstone 43062.
40p. Q.—Articles on any aspect of the sun and holiday movement in Britain and overseas. *Length:* 600 words. *Payment:* by arrangement. *Illustrations:* line and half-tone. Cartoons and photographs welcomed.

British Printer (1888), Andrew Parker, 30 Old Burlington Street, London, W1X 2AE *T.* 01-437 0644.
£8.40 p.a. M.—Articles on technical and aesthetic aspects of printing processes and graphic reproduction. *Payment:* by arrangement. *Illustrations:* offset litho from photographs, line drawings and diagrams.

British Racehorse, The (1949), Michael Seth-Smith, 55 Curzon Street, London, W1Y 7PF *T.* 01-499 4391.
£1.60. March, June, August, September, November. Preliminary letter essential. Articles on breeding of racehorses and ancillary subjects by recognised experts.

British Ski Magazine, Pixie Maynard, Piggery Hall Cottage, Piggery Hall Lane, West Wittering, West Sussex, PO20 8PZ *T.* West Wittering 2294. Publishers: Ocean Publications Ltd., 34 Buckingham Palace Road, London, SW1W 0RE *T.* 01-834 3430.
40p. M (September to February).—Articles, instructive and informative, on ski-ing and winter sports in all parts of the world. Winter travel articles, news items, etc. *Length:* 500 to 3000 words, preferably illustrated. *Payment:* by arrangement. *Illustrations:* Photographs.

British-Soviet Friendship (formerly **Russia To-day**) (1927), 36 St. John's Square, London, EC1V 4JH *T.* 01-253 4161.
12p. Every two months.—An illustrated magazine on British-Soviet relations. Good photographs and well-informed news items and articles up to 900 words (on Soviet Union and British-Soviet relations). *Payment:* for articles and photographs only by special arrangement.

British Weekly (1886), David Coomes, 146 Queen Victoria Street, London, EC4V 4EH *T.* 01-248 2124-5.
10p. W.—A Christian inter-denominational journal of news and comment, and relating Christianity to social, political and economic questions. Uses commissioned work mostly, but always welcomes articles of topical interest and importance, news items, etc. Study of paper desirable. *Payment:* £4.00 per 1000 words.

Broadcast, Julian Graff, Communications Software, Ltd., 111A Wardour Street, London, W1V 3TD *T.* 01-439 9756.
40p. (£22.50 p.a.). W.—News and authoritative articles designed for all concerned with the British broadcasting industry and with programmes and advertising on television and radio. *Illustrations:* line and half-tone. No cartoons. *Payment:* by arrangement.

Brownie, The, Official Magazine of The Girl Guides Association, Mrs. J. V. Rush, 17–19 Buckingham Palace Road, London, SW1W 0PT *T.* 01-834 6242.
8p. W.—Short articles for Brownies (girls 7–10 years). Serials with Brownie background (500–700 words per instalment). Puzzles, Line Drawings, "Things to make," etc. *Payment:* £10.00 per 1000 words. *Illustrations:* line and half-tone.

Buckinghamshire and Berkshire Countryside (1961), E. V. Scott, Wm. Carling & Co., Market Place, Hitchin, Herts, SG5 1EA *T*. Hitchin 59657.
25p. M.—Articles of interest to Buckinghamshire and Berkshire. *Length:* approximately 1000 words. *Illustrations:* half-tone and line.

Building (formerly **The Builder**) (1842), Cornelius Murphy, The Builder House, Pemberton Row, EC4A 3BA *T*. 01-353 2300.
30p. W.—A magazine covering the entire professional, industrial and manufacturing aspects of the building industry. Articles on architecture and techniques at home and abroad considered, also news and photographs. *Payment:* by arrangement.

Building Societies Gazette, The (1869), Steve Short, Franey & Co., Ltd., Burgon Street, London, EC4V 5DP *T*. 01-236 0855 (5 lines).
80p. (£10.40 p.a. pre-paid). M.—Articles on matters of interest to building societies, financial rather than on house construction. *Length:* up to 2000 words. *Average payment:* £20.00 per 1000 words. *Illustrations:* line and half-tone.

Built Environment, Peter Hall and Tom Hancock, Kogan Page Ltd., 120 Pentonville Road, London, N1 9JN *T*. 01-837 7851.
£2.50. Q. (£8.50 p.a.).—Articles about architecture, planning and the built environment. *Length:* 1000 to 3000 words. *Payment:* by arrangement. *Illustrations:* photographs and line drawings. A preliminary letter is advisable.

Bullet (D. C. Thomson & Co., Ltd.), Courier Place, Dundee, DD1 9QJ, and 185 Fleet Street, London, EC4A 2HS.
8p. W.—Picture-stories, in line, for boys. Subjects—adventure, sport, war, mystery. Instalments of 2 to 4 pages; 8 to 10 frames per page. *Payment:* on acceptance.

Bulletin of Hispanic Studies (1923), Geoffrey Ribbans, School of Hispanic Studies, The University, P.O. Box 147, Liverpool, L69 3BX *T*. 051-709 6022. Published by the Liverpool University Press, 123 Grove Street, Liverpool, L7 7AF.
£3, £10 p.a. (£8 individual subscribers). Q.—Specialist articles on the languages and literatures of Spain, Portugal and Latin America, written in English, Spanish, Portuguese, Catalan or French. *No payment* made.

Bunty (D. C. Thomson & Co. Ltd.), Courier Place, Dundee, DD1 9QJ, and 185 Fleet Street, London, EC4A 2HS.
7p. W.—Picture-story paper for young girls of school age. Vividly told stories in picture-serial form, 16–18 frames in each 2 page instalment; 27–28 frames in each 3-page instalment. Comic strips and features. *Payment:* on acceptance. Special encouragement to promising script-writers and artists.

Bunty Library (D. C. Thomson & Co., Ltd.), Courier Place, Dundee, DD1 9QJ, and 185 Fleet Street, London, EC4A 2HS.
9p. M.—Stories told in pictures for schoolgirls; 64 pages (about 140 line drawings). Ballet, school, adventure, theatre, sport. Scripts considered; promising artists and script-writers encouraged. *Payment:* on acceptance.

Burlington Magazine (1903), Benedict Nicolson, Elm House, 10–16 Elm Street, London, WC1X 0BP *T*. 01-278 2345. *T.A.* Rariora, London, WC1.
£2.00. M.—Deals with the history and criticism of art. Rate of *payment:* £3.15 per page. Average length of article, 500 to 3000 words. The Editor can use only articles by those who have special knowledge of the subjects treated, and cannot accept MSS. compiled from works of reference. Reviews and a monthly chronicle. No verse. *Illustrations:* almost invariably made from photographs.

Buses (1949), John F. Parke, ASSOC. C.I.T., Terminal House, Shepperton, Middlesex, TW17 8AS *T.* Walton-on-Thames 28950.
40p. M.—Articles of interest to both road passenger transport operators and bus enthusiasts. *Illustrations:* half-tone, line maps. *Payment:* on application.

Business Credit and Hire Purchase Journal, Quaintance & Co. (Publishers) Ltd., 24A Chertsey Street, Guildford, Surrey, GU1 4HD *T.* Guildford 67965.
Subscriptions £8.00. M.—Articles on any aspect of Credit, preferably by contributors with practical or professional experience. *Length:* 1500 to 2500 words. *Ilustrations:* half-tone or line.

Business Scotland (1947), Roderick Martine, Allander House, 137 Leith Walk, Edinburgh, EH6 8NS *T.* 031-554 9444.
30p. M.—Articles on industry, politics, economics and oil.

Buster (1960), King's Reach Tower, Stamford Street, London SE1 9LS *T.* 01-261 5000.
8p. W.—Juvenile comic. Comedy characters and adventure stories in picture strips. For boys and girls ages 6 to 12. Full colour, and black-and-white.

Busy Bees' News, R. I. Cookson, P.D.S.A. House, South Street, Dorking, Surrey, RH4 2LB *T.* 0306-81691.
15p. Bi-M. (60p p.a.).—Short stories (max. *length* 700 words) and factual articles (max. *length* 700) about animals suitable for children up to eleven; also puzzles and cartoons. *Payment:* by arrangement, on acceptance. *Illustrations:* line and half-tone, black-and-white.

CTN (Confectioner, Tobacconist, Newsagent, incorporating **Smiths Trade News),** Len Bright, IPC Consumer Industries Press Ltd., 40 Bowling Green Lane, London, EC1. *T.* 01-837 3636.
10p. W. (£8.00 p.a.).—Trade news and brief articles illustrated when possible with photographs or line drawings. Must be of live interest to retail confectioner-tobacconists and newsagents. *Length:* Articles 600–800 words. *Payment:* news lineage rates, minimum of £1.50 per 100 words, articles at negotiated rates.

Cage and Aviary Birds (1902), J. P. Read, Surrey House, 1 Throwley Way, Sutton, Surrey, SM1 4QQ *T.* 01-643 8040.
15p. W.—Practical articles on aviculture and ornithology. First-hand knowledge only. *Payment:* by arrangement. *Illustrations:* line and photographic.

Camera User Magazine, Rex Hayman, Link House, Dingwall Avenue, Croydon, Surrey, CR9 2TA *T.* 01-686 2599.
25p. M.—Technical articles, with accompanying illustrative material, about all aspects of photography. *Length:* 2000–4000 words. *Payment:* Mono £10 per page; Colour £15 per page. *Illustrations:* line, half-tone, transparencies. *Payment:* £2–£15 depending on size.

Campaign, Bernard Barnett, Regent House, 54–62 Regent Street, London, W1A 4YJ *T.* 01-439 4242.
40p. W.—News and articles covering the whole of the mass communications field, particularly advertising in all its forms, marketing, newspapers and publishing, public relations, television and printing. Features should not exceed 2000 words. News items also welcome. Press day, Wednesday. *Payment:* above NUJ rates.

Camping (1961), Philip Pond, Link House, Dingwall Avenue, Croydon, CR9
2TA *T*. 01-686 2599. *T.A*. Aviculture, Croydon.
40p. M.—Articles based on real camping experiences, all aspects, illustrated with photographs if possible. Practical articles welcomed. *Length:*
1000 to 2000 average. *Payment:* by arrangement. *Illustrations:* line and
half-tone.

Candour (1953), R. de Bounevialle, Forest House, Liss Forest, Hants, GU33
7DD *T*. 073082-2109.
20p. M.—Politico-economic articles with a national and Commonwealth
appeal. *Length:* 1200–1500 words. *Payment:* £5 per 1000 words.

Canoeing (1960), Mike Clark, 19 Main Street, Hemington, Derby, DE7 2RB.
Published by Ocean Publications Ltd., 34 Buckingham Palace Road, London, SW1W 0RE.
30p. M.—Short articles on canoesport or canoe camping, racing, wild
water or international canoesport. *Illustrations:* half-tone and line.

Car (1962), Mel Nichols, 64 West Smithfield, London, EC1A 9EE *T*. 01-606
7836.
40p. M.—Top-grade journalistic features on car driving, car people and
cars. *Length:* 1000–2500 words. *Payment:* £25.00 per 1000 words minimum. *Illustrations:* black-and-white and colour photographs to professional standard.

Car Mechanics, Tony Bostock, Mercury House, Waterloo Road, London, SE1
8UL *T*. 01-928 3388. *T.A*. Sysmaga, London, SE1.
35p. M.—Practical articles on car maintenance and repair for the non-
technical motorist with limited facilities. *Length:* Average 1500 words of
hard fact. *Payment:* £22.00 per 1000 words; pictures £2.90 each (minimum).
Illustrations: line and half-tone. *Preliminary letter outlining the article is
necessary.*

Caravan, The (1933), A. W. Bradford, Link House, Dingwall Avenue, Croydon,
CR9 2TA *T*. 01-686 2599.
40p. M.—Lively articles based on real experience of touring caravanning,
especially if well illustrated by photographs. General countryside or motoring material not wanted. Payment: usually £10.00 per 1000 words, and
higher for commissioned technical work.

Caravanning Monthly (1950), Barry Williams, Link House, Dingwall Avenue,
Croydon, CR9 2TA *T*. 01-686 2599.
35p. M.—Authoritative articles on any aspect of touring caravanning.
Length: 1500 words ideal, but no limit either way so long as well written
and informative. *Payment:* by agreement. *Illustrations:* half-tone, two
colour line, and line monotone; full colour cover.

Catering & Hotel Management (1928), Harry Stone, Link House, Dingwall
Avenue, Croydon, CR9 2TA *T*. 01-686 2599.
30p. M.—Illustrated features of technical interest to management and
executive staff in hotel, restaurant, industrial or welfare catering establishments. *Payment:* by arrangement on publication.

Catering Times (1963), Miles Quest, Elm House, 10–16 Elm Street, London,
WC1X 0BP *T*. 01-278 2345.
15p. W.—News items and authoritative feature material on all aspects of
the food service and hospitality industries, written in crisp concise style.
Payment: by arrangement. *Illustrations:* photographs.

Catholic Education Today (1967), James McGibbon and W. T. Glynn, St. Mary's College, Strawberry Hill, Twickenham, Middlesex, TW1 4SX *T.* 01-892 0051, ext. 282.
75p. Q.—Articles on all aspects of educational theory and practice, particularly the teaching of religion. *Payment:* by arrangement. *Illustrations:* half-tone and line.

Catholic Fireside (1879), P. Charles Walker, 24 Spencer Hill, London, SW19 4NY *T.* 01-947 6687.
12p. W.—Combines instruction, information and amusement for home reading. Short stories, serials, brightly written articles on subjects of Catholic interest, travel, etc. Should be from 1500 to 3000 words. Illustrated articles always given preference. *Payment:* by arrangement, on publication. *Illustrations:* half-tone and line.

Catholic Herald, The, Richard Dowden, 63 Charterhouse Street, London, EC1M 6LA *T.* 01-253 7973.
12p. W.—An independent newspaper covering national and international affairs from a Catholic Christian viewpoint as well as Church news. Articles 600 to 1100 words. *Payment:* £5 to £20. *Illustrations:* Photographs of Catholic and Christian interest.

Catholic Pictorial (1961) Norman Cresswell, 12 Prescot Road, Liverpool, L7 0LQ *T.* 051-263 9551–2–3.
10p. W.—News and photo features of Lancashire interest.

Centre Point (London Teacher) (1883), Managing Editor: Fred G. Smith, 81 Hamilton Road, Cockfosters, Barnet, Herts, EN4 9HD *T.* 01-449 1720.
45p p.a. 3 issues per year.—Organ of the Inner London Teachers' Association (NUT). Contributions of interest to teachers in London considered. *Illustrations:* Educational cartoons and photographs.

Certified Accountant, Peter Muldoon (Association of Certified Accountants), 29 Lincoln's Inn Fields, London, WC2A 3EE *T.* 01-242 6855.
50p. Bi-M.—Articles of accounting and financial interest. *Preliminary letter* to Editor before submitting MSS.

Cheshire Life (1934), Leslie N. Radcliffe, The Whitethorn Press Ltd., Thomson House, Withy Grove, Manchester, M60 4BL *T.* 061-834 1234.
35p. M.—Articles of county interest only. No fiction. *Length:* 800–1500 words. *Payment:* £8.00 per 1000 words minimum. *Illustrations:* line and half-tone, 4-colour positives for cover. Photographs of news value and definite Cheshire interest. £1.05 minimum payment.

Chest, Heart and Stroke Journal, The (1976), Tavistock House North, Tavistock Square, London, WC1H 9JE *T.* 01-387 3012.
35p. Q.—Medical articles of up to 2500 words on the nature, causes, prevention and treatment of all aspects of chest, heart or cerebrovascular illnesses by qualified contributors only. *Payment:* by arrangement.

Child Education (1924), Annie Smith (Evans Brothers, Ltd.), Montague House, Russell Square, London, WC1B 5BX *T.* 01-636 8521. *T.A.* Bryonitic, London, WC1. *Telex:* 8811713.
40p. M. Also 4 Quarterly Numbers, 35p.—For teachers, social workers and parents concerned with children aged 3–7. Articles by specialists on practical teaching ideas and methods, child development, songs, stories and poems. *Length:* 800 to 1200 words. *Payment:* by arrangement. Profusely illustrated with photographs and line drawings; also large pictures in full colour.

China Quarterly, The, Dick Wilson, Contemporary China Institute, School of Oriental and African Studies, Malet Street, London, WC1. *T.* 01-637 2388. £2.50. Q. (£10 p.a.).—Articles on Contemporary China. *Length:* 8000 words approx. *Payment:* on specially commissioned articles only.

Christian Herald (1866), South Wharf, Aldrington Basin, Portslade, Brighton, BN4 1WP   *T.* Brighton 413088.
10p.   W.—Contributions, about 1200 words, should be bright, accompanied by photographs if possible. Topical articles should be received at least a month in advance of date concerned. Christian serial stories with plenty of movement, 20,000–40,000 words, will be considered, also short stories, 1250 words. The paper is strictly evangelical and definitely upholds the Reformed Faith. *Payment:* varies according to length and interest.

Christian Record (Interdenominational Weekly) (1969), David Coomes, 146 Queen Victoria Street, London, EC4V 4EH   *T.* 01-248 2124–5.
10p.   W.—Emphasis on news of evangelistic enterprise. Mostly commissioned feature articles; no fiction. *Length:* 1000 words maximum. *Payment:* £4.00 per 1000. *Illustrations:* photographs.

Church of England Newspaper (1894), David Coomes, 146 Queen Victoria Street, London, EC4V 4EH   *T.* 01-248 2124–5.
10p.   W.—The newspaper contains articles relating the Christian faith to everyday life. Study of paper desirable. *Length:* 1000 words maximum. *Payment:* £4.00 per 1000. *Illustrations:* photographs.

Church of Ireland Gazette (1885, New Series 1963), Rev. R. S. J. H. McKelvey, 48 Bachelor's Walk, Lisburn, Co. Antrim, BT28 1XN   *T.* Lisburn 75743.
10p.   W.—Church news, articles of religious and general interest. *Length:* 600 to 1000 words. *Payment:* according to length and interest.

Church News (1948), 1 Abbey Precincts, Bury St. Edmunds, Suffolk. *T.* 0284-3530.
4½p.   M.—An Illustrated Church magazine inset. Articles of popular Church interest (500 to 800 words); occasional short stories and verse. *Illustrations:* photographs and line drawings of religious and ecclesiastical subjects. *Payment:* by arrangement.

Church Times (1863), 7 Portugal Street, London, WC2A 2HP   *T.* 01-405 0844.
10p.   W.—Articles on ecclesiastical and social topics are considered. Usual *length:* 750 to 1500 words. No verse or fiction. *Payment:* £5.00 per 1000 words minimum. *Illustrations:* news photographs.

Churchman, The (1879), 7 Wine Office Court, Fleet Street, London, EC4A 3DA   *T.* 01-583 1486.
95p.   Q. (£4.00 p.a. inc. postage).—A quarterly journal of Anglican theology, evangelical in emphasis. Articles on subjects of current interest and significance in theology and church life. *Length:* 2000 to 8000 words. No illustrations.

Civil Engineering (incorporating **Public Works Review**) (1906), Chris Gosselin, Morgan-Grampian (Professional Press) Ltd., 30 Calderwood Street, London, SE18 6QH   *T.* 01-855 7777.
Controlled circulation and subscription £8.00 p.a. UK, $24 p.a. USA.   M.—Contains in-depth reviews and technical articles of current interest to Civil Engineers. 1000–3000 words. *Payment:* by arrangement. *Illustrations:* line drawings and photographs germane to article. *A preliminary letter is essential.*

Clergy Review, The, Revd. M. Richards, S.T.L., B.LITT., M.A., Heythrop College, 11–13 Cavendish Square, London, W1M 0AN   T. 01-580 6941.
£6.90 p.a., USA $15.00.   M.—A journal of information, dialogue and research for Catholics of the English-speaking countries. *Length* and *payment* by arrangement.

Climber and Rambler (1962), Walt Unsworth, c/o Holmes McDougall Ltd., 12 York Street, Glasgow, G2 8JL.   Official Journal of the British Mountaineering Council.
40p.   M.—Articles on all aspects of mountaineering and hill walking in Great Britain and abroad and on related subjects. *Length:* 500 to 3000 words, preferably illustrated. *Payment:* according to merit. *Illustrations:* photographs and line drawings.   Study of magazine essential.

Club Secretary (1953), D. Kennedy, UTP House, 33–35 Bowling Green Lane, London, EC1.   T. 01-837 1212.
£8.80 p.a.   M.—Feature articles and news items aimed at informing people concerned with the management of registered and licensed clubs of every type. *Payment:* by arrangement. *Illustrations:* line and half-tone.

Coins and Medals (1964), Richard West, Link House, Dingwall Avenue, Croydon, CR9 2TA   T. 01-686 2599.
40p.   M.—Articles of high standard on coins, tokens, paper money and medals. *Length:* up to 1300 words. *Payment:* by arrangement. *Illustrations:* line and half-tone.

Commando (D. C. Thomson & Co. Ltd.), Albert Square, Dundee, DD1 9QJ   T. 0382 23131 and 185 Fleet Street, London, EC4A 2HS.
9p.   Eight each month.—Fictional war stories of World War II told in pictures.   Line drawings.   Scripts should be of about 140 pictures, 63 pages.   Synopsis required as an opener.   New artists and writers encouraged. *Payment:* on acceptance.

Commercial International, P. Stephens, 69 Cannon Street, London, EC4N 5AB   T. 01-236 2675.
45p.   M.—Authoritative outside contributions are accepted on commercial and industrial subjects. *Payment:* by arrangement. *Illustrations:* half-tone. *Preliminary letter essential.*

Commercial Motor (1905), Iain Sherriff, IPC Transport Press Ltd., Dorset House, Stamford Street, London, SE1 9LU   T. 01-261 8484.
20p.   W.—*Payment:* varies for articles (technical and road transport only), maximum length 2000 words, drawings, and photographs.

Community Care (1974), Mark Allen, Surrey House, 1 Throwley Way, Sutton, Surrey, SM1 4QQ   T. 01-643 8040.
20p.   W.—Feature articles of professional interest to local authority social workers. *Length:* 1000 to 2500 words. *Payment:* £24 per 1000 words. *Illustrations:* half-tone and line.

Computer Survey (1962), 33–35 Bowling Green Lane, London, EC1.   T. 01-837 1212.
£30.00 p.a. inland; Swiss Francs 172.00 overseas.   Bi-M.—Devoted mainly to surveys of the digital computer industry in Britain. *Payment:* by arrangement. *Illustrations:* line and half-tone.

Computer Weekly (1966), M. Peltu, IPC Electrical-Electronic Press Ltd., Dorset House, Stamford Street, London, SE1 9LU   T. 01-261 8000.
Controlled circulation.   W.—Specialised news and features on computer subjects. *Payment:* £2.00 per 100 words published. *Illustrations:* line and half-tone.

Connoisseur, The (1901), William Allan, Chestergate House, Vauxhall Bridge Road, London, SW1V 1HF *T.* 01-834 2331.
£2.00. M.—Articles on all subjects interesting to art and antique collectors are considered, but a *preliminary letter* should be sent. *Length:* Articles about 2000 words. Writers are held responsible for all dates and facts mentioned. *Payment:* £75. *Illustrations:* photographs suitable to subjects dealt with. Good quality illustrations are essential.

Contemporary Review (incorporating the **Fortnightly**) (1886), Editor: Rosalind Wade. Literary Review: A. G. de Montmorency. Editorial Advisers: Sir Herbert Butterfield and Professor Esmond Wright. Fine Arts Correspondent: Ernle Money. Music Correspondent: David Fingleton, 61 Carey Street, London, WC2A 5JG *T.* 01-242 3215.
50p. M.—Independent, but slightly left of centre. A review dealing with all questions of the day, chiefly politics, theology, history, literature, travel, poetry, the arts. A great part of the matter is commissioned, but there is scope for free-lance specialists. Articles submitted should be typewritten and should be about 2000 to 3000 words. If refused, articles are returned, *if a stamped envelope is enclosed. Payment:* £3.00 per 1000 words, 2 complimentary copies. Intending contributors should study journal before submitting MSS.

Contributor's Bulletin see Freelance Press Services on p. 451.

Control & Instrumentation (1958), Andrew Bond, M.A. (Morgan-Grampian (Process Press) Ltd.), 30 Calderwood Street, Woolwich, London, SE18 6QH *T.* 01-855 7777.
£15.00 p.a. M.—Authoritative main feature articles on measurement, automation, control systems, instrumentation, and data processing. Also export, business and engineering news. *Payment:* according to value. *Length of articles:* 750 words for highly technical pieces. 1000 to 2000 words main features. *Illustrations:* half-tone and photographs and drawings of equipment using automatic techniques, control engineering personalities.

Cornhill Magazine (1860), 50 Albemarle Street, London, W1X 4BD T. 01-493 4361 Publication has been temporarily suspended.

Cosmetic World News (formerly **International Perfumer**) (1949), M. A. Murray-Pearce, Caroline Marcuse, 130 Wigmore Street, London, W1H 0AT *T.* 01-405 3960 and 0189. *Telex:* 817133.
£20.00 p.a. M.—International news magazine of perfumery, cosmetics and toiletries industry. World-wide reports, photo-news stories, articles (500–1000 words) on essential oils and new cosmetic raw materials, and exclusive information on industry's companies and personalities welcomed. *Payment:* by arrangement. Minimum 3p. per word. *Illustrations:* black and white photographs or colour separations.

Cosmopolitan (1972), Deirdre McSharry, Chestergate House, Vauxhall Bridge Road, London, SW1V 1HF *T.* 01-834 2331.
35p. M.—Short stories, articles. Commissioned material only. *Payment:* by arrangement.

Country Gentlemen's Magazine, The (1901), Country Gentlemen's Association, Icknield Way West, Letchworth, Herts, SG6 4AP   *T.* Letchworth 2377. £7.00 per annum.   M.—Journal of the Country Gentleman's Association. Practical and authoritative articles of general country interest.   From 500 to 1500 words.   *Payment:* varies: from £10.00 per 1000 words.

Country Life (1897), Michael Wright, King's Reach Tower, Stamford Street, London, SE1 9LS   *T.* 01-261 7058. 40p.   W.—An illustrated journal, chiefly concerned with English country life, social history, architecture and the fine arts, natural history, agriculture, gardening and sport.   *Length of articles:* about 900, 1350 or 1800 words; short poems are also considered.   *Payment:* according to merit.   Press day, Thursday.   *Illustrations:* mainly photographs.

Countryman, The (1927), Crispin Gill, Editorial Office: Sheep Street, Burford, Oxford, OX8 4LH   *T.* Burford 2258. 55p.   Q.—Every department of rural life and progress except field sports. Party politics and townee sentimentalising about the country barred.   Copy must be trustworthy, well written, brisk, cogent and light in hand.   Articles up to 1500 words.   Good paragraphs and notes, first-class poetry, and skilful sketches of life and character from personal knowledge and experience. Dependable natural history based on writer's own observation.   Really good matter from old unpublished letters and MSS.   *Payment:* £12.00 per 1000 words and upwards according to merit.   *Illustrations:* black and white photographs and drawings, but all must be exclusive and out of the ordinary, and bear close scrutiny.   Humour welcomed if genuine.

Country Quest, Gwyn Jones, Centenary Buildings, King Street, Wrexham   *T.* 55151. 35p.   M.—*Illustrated* articles on matters relating to country-side of Wales and Border counties.   *Length:* 1000 to 1500 words.   No fiction.   *Payment:* by arrangement.   *Illustrations:* half-tone and line.

Country-Side (1905), Anthony Wootton, 40 Roundhill, Stone, Nr. Aylesbury, Bucks, HP17 8RD   *T.* Stone (029 674) 768. £2.50 p.a.   Published every 4 months.   Official organ of The British Naturalists' Association (B.E.N.A.).   Original observations on wild life and its protection, and on natural history generally, but not on killing for sport. *Payment:* not usually made.   *Illustrations:* photographs and drawings. *Preliminary letter* or study of magazine advisable.

Courier and Advertiser, The (1816 and 1801), (D. C. Thomson & Co., Ltd), 7 Bank Street, Dundee, DD1 9HU   *T.* Dundee 23131.   *Telex:* DCThom 76380; and 185 Fleet Street, London, EC4A 2HS   *T.* 01-242 5086. 7p.   D.—Independent.

Coventry Evening Telegraph, K. Whetstone, Corporation Street, Coventry, CV1 1FP   *T.* Coventry 25588.   London Office: 14 Bride Lane, EC4Y 8EE. 7p.   D.—Illustrated articles of topical interest, those with a Warwickshire interest particularly acceptable.   *Maximum length:* 800 words.

Creative Camera (1964), Colin Osman, Coo Press Ltd., 19 Doughty Street, London, WC1N 2PT   *T.* 01-405 7562. 50p.   M.—Illustrated articles and pictures dealing with creative photo-graphy.   *Payment:* by arrangement.   *Illustrations:* black-and-white gravure.

Cricketer, The (1921), David Frith, 6 Curling Vale, Onslow Village, Guildford, Surrey, GU2 5PJ.
40p. M.—Cricket articles of topical or historical interest. *Payment:* £10 to £20 per 1000 words. *Illustrations:* line, half-tone, colour.

Criminologist, The (1966), Nigel Morland, Forensic Publishing Co., P.O. Box 18, Bognor Regis, West Sussex, PO22 7AA.
Controlled circulation. £1.00 post free or £4 p.a. Q.—Specialised material designed for an expert and professional readership. Covers nationally and internationally criminology, the police, forensic science, the law, penology, sociology and law enforcement. Articles (2000 to 4000 words) by those familiar with the journal's style and requirements are welcomed. *A preliminary letter* with a brief résumé is preferable. *Payment:* is wholly governed by the nature and quality of manuscripts. *Illustrations:* line and photographs.

Critical Quarterly (1959), C. B. Cox and A. E. Dyson, The University, Manchester, M13 9PL *T.* 061-273 3333.
£1.00. Q.—Literary criticism, poems. *Length:* 2000–10,000 words. *Payment:* by arrangement. Interested contributors should study magazine before submitting MSS.

Crusade (1955) John Capon, 19 Draycott Place, London, SW3 2SJ *T.* 01-581 0051.
25p. M.—News on activities and events within the Christian world, including evangelism, social issues and missionary work; information about people active in the Christian sphere; photographs of prominent personalities; various major features (after discussion with the editor). *Payment:* on publication.

Cumbria (1951), W. R. Mitchell, Dalesman Publishing Company, Ltd., Clapham, via Lancaster, LA2 8EB *T.* Clapham (Lancaster) 225.
22p. M.—Articles of genuine rural interest concerning Lakeland. Short *length* preferred. *Payment:* according to merit. *Illustrations:* line drawings and first-class photographs.

Custom Car (1970), Colin Gamm, Link House, Dingwall Avenue, Croydon, CR9 2TA *T.* 01-686 2599. *T.A.* Aviculture, Croydon.
40p. *Payment:* by arrangement. *Length:* 1000–2000 words.

Cycling (1891), Ken Evans, IPC Specialist and Professional Press Ltd, Surrey House, 1 Throwley Way, Sutton, Surrey, SM1 4QQ *T.* 01-643 8040.
25p. W.—Touring, technical, and short humorous articles not exceeding 2100 words are invited. Topical photographs and a limited amount of fiction with a pronounced cycling interest also considered. *Payment:* by arrangement.

Daily Express, Derek Jameson, Fleet Street, London, EC4P 4JT *T.* 01-353 8000; Great Ancoats Street, Manchester. *T.* Manchester (061) 236 2112.
8p. D.—Exclusive news: striking photographs. Leader page articles, 600 words; facts preferred to opinions. *Payment:* according to value.

Daily Mail (1896) (Now incorporating **News Chronicle** and **Daily Sketch**), David English, Northcliffe House, London, EC4Y 0JA *T.* 01-353 6000.
8p. D.—Highest payments for good, exclusive news. Leader page articles, 500–800 words average. Ideas for these welcomed. Exclusive news photographs always wanted.

Daily Mirror (1903), M. Molloy, Holborn Circus, London, EC1P 1DQ *T.* 01-353 0246.
8p. D.—Top payment for exclusive news and news pictures. Few articles from free-lances used, but ideas bought. Send only a synopsis. "Unusual" pictures and those giving a new angle on the news are welcomed.

Daily Record, B. Vickers, Anderston Quay, Glasgow. *T.* 041-248 7000. *Telex* 778277. London: 33 Holborn, London, EC1P 1DQ *T.* 01-353 0246.
8p. D.—Web off-set with full colour facilities. Topical articles of from 300 to 700 words. Exclusive stories of Scottish interest and exclusive photographs.

Daily Telegraph, The (1855), William Deedes, 135 Fleet Street, London, EC4P 4BL *T.* 01-353 4242.
9p. D.—Independent. Authoritative articles, 600 to 1400 words, arising out of current topics are welcome. *Illustrations:* topical photographs.

Dairy Farmer, David Shead, Wharfedale Road, Ipswich, IP1 4LG *T.* Ipswich 43011.
Controlled circulation. M.—Authoritative articles dealing in practical, lively style with dairy farming. Topical controversial articles invited. Well-written, illustrated accounts of new ideas being tried on dairy farms are especially wanted. *Length:* up to 2500 words. *Payment:* according to merit. *Illustrations:* half-tone or line.

Dairy Industries International (1936), 33 Bowling Green Lane, London, EC1. *T.* 01-837 1212.
£11.90 post free; Overseas £22. M.—Covers the entire field of milk processing, the manufacture of products from liquid milk, and ice cream. Articles relating to dairy plant, butter and cheese making, ice cream making, etc. *Payment:* by arrangement; special lineage rates. *Illustrations:* glossy prints and indian ink diagrams.

Dalesman, The (1939), W. R. Mitchell, Dalesman Publishing Company Ltd., Clapham, via Lancaster, LA2 8EB *T.* Clapham (Lancaster) 225.
23p. M.—Articles and stories of genuine rural interest concerning Yorkshire. Short *length* preferred. *Payment:* according to merit. Colour reproductions, line drawings and first-class photographs.

Dance and Dancers (1950), Editor/Art Director: Peter Williams, Hansom Books, P.O. Box 294, 2 & 4 Old Pye Street, off Strutton Ground, Victoria Street, London, SW1P 2LR *T.* 01-222 3779 and 4670.
50p. M.—Articles and photographs on classical ballet, modern dance and national dancing in theatre, films and television. Only commissioned material accepted. (No ballroom or competitive dancing.) *Payment:* by arrangement.

Dancing Times (1910), Editor: Mary Clarke, Editorial Adviser: Ivor Guest, 18 Hand Court, Holborn, London, WC1V 6JF *T.* 01-405 1414–5.
40p. M.—Dealing with ballet and stage dancing, both from general, historical, critical and technical angles. Well informed free-lance articles are occasionally used, but only after preliminary arrangements. *Payment:* by arrangement. *Illustrations:* web offset, occasional line, action photographs always preferred.

Dandy, The (D. C. Thomson & Co., Ltd.), Courier Place, Dundee, DD1 9QJ, and 185 Fleet Street, London, EC4A 2HS.
5p. W.—Comic Strips for boys and girls, 6–15 pictures per strip. Stories told in pictures (12–20 frames each instalment.) Promising script writers and artists encouraged. *Payment:* on acceptance.

Data Processing (1959), Tony Rand, IPC Electrical-Electronic Press Ltd., Dorset House, Stamford Street, London, SE1 9LU *T.* 01-261 8404. *T.A.* Bisprs G London. *Telex:* 25137.
£2.00 10 issues p.a. (£15.00 p.a., $39.00 in US and Canada).—Articles on data processing methods and machines including descriptions of new computers and peripheral equipment, the application of computers in business and industry, software developments, and computer-based management techniques. *Length:* 2000 to 5000 words. *Payment:* by arrangement. *Illustrations:* Half-tone and line.

Data Processing Practitioner (1967), Derek Bradley, The Institute of Data Processing, 418–422 Strand, London, WC2R 0PW *T.* 01-240 3106.
50p post paid. Q.—Articles on all aspects of data processing and business applications of computers. *Length:* 1000–2000 words. *Payment:* by arrangement. *Illustrations:* offset litho.

Data Systems, Clare Smythe, Embankment Press Ltd., 59 GEC Estate, East Lane, Wembley, Middlesex. *T.* 01-904 2246.
75p. M. (£12 p.a.).—Authoritative, well-written articles, addressed to senior businessmen, company directors, managers, accountants, systems analysts, programmers, etc., on aspects of business information technology, e.g. cybernetics, operations research and data retrieval. A very high standard is required. *Length:* 1760 words and upward. *Payment:* by arrangement, normally £30.00 per 1000 words. *Illustrations:* line and 120 screen half-tone.

Debbie and Spellbound (D. C. Thomson & Co. Ltd.), Courier Place, Dundee, DD1 9QJ, and 185 Fleet Street, London, EC4A 2HS.
7p. W.—Picture-story paper for schoolgirls. Stories in serial or series form, told in pictures. 2- and 3-page instalments, 9–10 frames per page. Editorial co-operation to promising scriptwriters. *Payment:* on acceptance.

Debbie Library (D. C. Thomson & Co. Ltd.), Courier Place, Dundee, DD1 9QJ, and 185 Fleet Street, London, EC4A 2HS.
9p. M.—Stories told in pictures, for schoolgirls; 64 pages (about 140 line drawings). Adventure, animal, mystery, school, sport. Scripts considered; promising script-writers and artists encouraged. *Payment:* on acceptance.

Delta, a Literary Review (1953), Michael Launchbury, Geoffrey Pawling, 54 West Fen Road, Ely, Cambridgeshire CB6 1AN *T.* Ely 3316.
50p. 3 times p.a.—Poetry, short stories, reviews of contemporary literature. *Payment:* by arrangement.

Derbyshire Life and Countryside (1931), Lodge Lane, Derby, DE1 3HE *T.* Derby 47087–8–9.
30p. M.—Articles, preferably illustrated, about Derbyshire life, people, and history. *Length:* 1200–1600 words. Short stories set in Derbyshire accepted, but verse not used. *Payment:* according to nature and quality of contribution. *Illustrations:* photographs of Derbyshire subjects.

Design (1949) Mark Brutton, Design Council, The Design Centre, 28 Haymarket, London, SW1Y 4SU *T.* 01-839 8000.
75p. M.—Articles on industrial design, architecture, interiors, and engineering at home and abroad; case-histories of new products and company design policy (by arrangement with the editor). *Payment:* by arrangement. *Illustrations:* line, half-tone and drawings.

Dickensian, The, Andrew Sanders, B.A., M.LITT., Birkbeck College, Malet Street, London, WC1E 7HX.
£3.00 p.a. 3 times a year.—Published by The Dickens Fellowship. Welcomes articles on all aspects of Dickens' life, works and character. *No payment.*

Digests with one or two exceptions are not included since they seldom use original material, but reprint articles previously published elsewhere and extracts from books. But see **The Reader's Digest.**

Dog News and Family Pets (1975), Joan Palmer, 92 High Street, Lee-on-the-Solent, Hants, PO13 9DA *T.* 551811.
25p. Bi-M.—Articles on breeding, showing and training of dogs; also features on cats and other domestic pets. *Length:* 1000 to 1500 words. *Payment:* about £6.50 per 1000 words. *Illustrations:* line and half-tone.

Do It Yourself (1957), Tony Wilkins, Link House, Dingwall Avenue, Croydon, CR9 2TA *T.* 01-686 2599. *T.A.* Aviculture, Croydon.
30p. M.—Authoritative articles on every aspect of do-it-yourself in the house, garden, workshop and garage. Leaflet describing style, requirements, available on request. *Payment:* by arrangement. *Length:* up to 1000 words unless negotiated. Press 3 months ahead.

Dorset—the county magazine (1967), Rodney Legg and Colin Graham, Knockna-cre, Milborne Port, Sherborne, Dorset, DT9 5HJ *T.* 0963 32583.
45p. M.—A campaigning regional magazine specialising in reports on threats to the environment. Subject matter exclusively about Dorset. Major historical features also used with *payment* by arrangement depending on *length* (preferably over 3000 words) and *illustrations.* £2 each paid for black and white photographs put on file and later used separately in the magazine. £15 paid for striking 2¼″ square (or larger) colour transparencies of Dorset for front cover use. Line drawings not used except with features. This magazine deals exclusively with controversial stories from both the present and the past and *has no use for either* short stories or poetry.

Downside Review, The, Dom Daniel Rees, Downside Abbey, Stratton on the Fosse, nr. Bath, Somerset. *T.* Stratton-on-the-Fosse 232 720.
£1.10. Q. (£4.40 p.a.).—Articles and book reviews on theology, metaphysics and monastic history. *Payment:* by arrangement.

Drama (1919), Executive Editor: Walter Lucas, 9 Fitzroy Square, London, W1P 6AE *T.* 01-387 2666.
80p. Q.—A magazine of the theatre. Articles, 1000 to 3000 words. *Payment:* by arrangement. *Illustrations:* photographs.

Drapers Record (1887), Gerald Saunders, Knightway House, 20 Soho Square, London, W1V 6DT *T.* 01-734 1255.
25p. W.—Matter should be of special interest to the retail and wholesale fashion and textile trade. *Length* of articles from 500 to 1000 words. *Payment:* by arrangement. *Illustrations:* drawings or photographs.

Dundee Evening Telegraph and Post (D. C. Thomson & Co., Ltd.), Courier Place, Dundee, DD1 9QJ. *T.* Dundee 23131. *Telex:* DCThom 76380; and 185 Fleet Street, London, EC4A 2HS *T.* 01-353 2586.
7p. D.

Early Music (1973), J. M. Thomson, Oxford University Press, Ely House, 37 Dover Street, London, W1X 4AH *T.* 01-629 8494.
£2.00 (£7.50 p.a.). Q.—Lively, informative and scholarly articles on aspects of performing medieval, renaissance and baroque music. *Payment:* £15 per 1000 words. *Illustrations:* line, half tone; colour on cover.

East–West Digest, Geoffrey Stewart-Smith, 139 Petersham Road, Richmond, Surrey TW10 7AA *T.* 01-948 4833.
£5 p.a. Fortnightly—News stories and authoritative articles on subversion, the Communist world, international affairs, defence, political warfare, and East–West relations. Articles and reviews are accepted on their merits. *Payment:* by arrangement.

Eastern Daily Press (1870), G. B. Nunn, Prospect House, Rouen Road, Norwich, NR1 1RE *T.* Norwich 28311; London Office, Aldwych House, WC2.
8p. D.—Independent. Limited market for articles of East Anglian in terest not exceeding 850 words.

Eastern Evening News (1882), R. Walker, EEN, Prospect House, Rouen Road, Norwich, NR1 1RE *T.* Norwich 28311; London Office, Aldwych House, Aldwych, WC2.
7p. Independent.

Ecologist Quarterly, The, Edward Goldsmith, 73 Molesworth Street, Wade-bridge, Cornwall, PL27 7DS *T.* Wadebridge 2996–7.
£1.00. Q.—Articles on the philosophical, scientific, ideological and eco-logical implications of the post industrial society. *Length:* Up to 6000 words. *Payment:* by arrangement.

Economic Journal (1891), J. S. Flemming, Nuffield College, Oxford, OX1 1NF *T.* 0865 48014
£20.00 p.a. (Free to members). Q.—The organ of the Royal Economic Society. The kind of matter required is economic theory, applied economics and the development of economic thinking in relation to current problems. *Payment:* none. Statistical and economic diagrams. Reviews of new books and other publications.

Economica (1921) New Series, 1934), Editors: R. Jackman, Dr. A. Shorrocks, Dr. A. Smith, London School of Economics and Political Science, Houghton Street, London, WC2A 2AE *T.* 01-405 7686.
£8.50 p.a. (U.K.), £12.00 or $24.00 (Overseas). Q.—A learned journal covering the fields of economics, economic history, and statistics.

Economist, The (1843), 25 St. James's Street, London, SW1A 1HG *T.* 01-930 5155.
50p. W.—Articles staff-written.

Edinburgh Evening News, Ian A. Nimmo, 20 North Bridge, Edinburgh, EH1 1YX *T.* 031-225 2468. London Office, Thomson Regional Newspapers, Ltd., Greater London House, Hampstead Road, London, NW1 7SH.
8p. D.—Independent. Features on current affairs, preferably in relation to our circulation area. Women's talking points, local historical articles; subjects of general interest.

Education (1903), Tudor David, 5 Bentinck Streeet, London, W1M 5RN *T.* 01-935 0121.
30p. W.—Special articles on educational administration, all branches of education; technical education; universities; school building; playing fields; environmental studies; physical education; school equipment; school meals and health; teaching aids. *Length:* 1000 to 1500 words. *Payment:* by arrangement. *Illustrations:* photographs and drawings.

Education and Training (1959), Derek Bradley, A.B.E. Publications, 10 Dryden Chambers, 119 Oxford Street, London, W1R 1PA *T.* 01-240 3106.
£1.00.· M.—Authoritative articles of 1000–2000 words on all aspects of further education, commercial and industrial training. *Payment:* by arrangement. *Illustrations:* offset litho.

Electric Living (1978), 25 Fouberts Place, London, W1V 2AL.
15p plus postage. 3 times p.a.—Articles on domestic electricity and electrical appliances as well as home ideas features and recipes. *Length:* 1000–1500 words. *Illustrations:* Black and white photographs and line.

Electrical Review (1872), T. C. J. Cogle, B.SC.(ENG.), M.I.C.E., F.I.E.E. (Editor), A. H. Crawford (Engineering Editor), IPC Electrical-Electronic Press Ltd., Dorset House, Stamford Street, London, SE1 9LU *T.* 01-261 8430/8736. *T.A.* Review, 25137, BisPrs-G, Telex.
25p. W.—Articles on electrical engineering and international trade; outside contributions considered. Electrical news welcomed. *Illustrations:* photographs and drawings.

Electrical Times, The (1891), G. A. Jack, Dorset House, Stamford Street, London, SE1 9LU *T.* 01-261 8494. *T.A.* 25137 Bisprs G.
12p. W.—Technical articles about 1000 to 1500 words, with illustrations as necessary. *Payment:* by arrangement. *Illustrations:* line and half-tone.

Embroidery, de Denne Ltd., 161 Kenton Road, Kenton, Harrow, Middlesex, HA3 0EU *T.* 01-907 5476.
65p. Q. (£3.20 p.a. including postage. Overseas: £3.20 p.a. and $12 including postage).—Articles dealing with embroidery, lacemaking, and macramé; contemporary, historical, foreign. *Payment:* by arrangement. *Illustrations:* line and half-tone.

Emma (D. C. Thomson & Co. Ltd.), Courier Place, Dundee, DD1 9QJ, and 185 Fleet Street, London, EC4A 2HS.
8p. W.—Picture-story magazine for girls. Scripts in series or serial form (7–8 frames per page. Also personality features—cinema, TV, pop, sport —appealing to young schoolgirls. Encouragement to promising artists and writers. *Payment:* on acceptance.

Encounter (1953), Melvin J. Lasky and Anthony Thwaite, 59 St. Martin's Lane, London, WC2N 4JS *T.* 01-836 4194.
80p. M.—Reportage, stories, poems. *Length:* 3000–5000 words. *Payment:* £10 per 1000. Interested contributors should study magazine before submitting MSS.; s.a.e essential for return if unsuitable.

Engineer, The (1856), John Mortimer, M.SC., C.ENG., M.I.MECH.E., M.R.AE.S., 30 Calderwood Street, London, SE18 6QH *T.* 01-855 7777.
£20 p.a. W.—Outside contributions paid for if accepted.

Engineering (1866), Roy Dodd, Design Council, 28 Haymarket, London, SW1Y 4SU   *T.* 01-839 8000.
75p.   M.—Contributions considered on all aspects of engineering, particularly design.   *Payment:* by arrangement.   Photographs and drawings used.

Engineering Materials and Design, D. H. Fears, C.ENG., M.I.MECH.E., A.M.B.I.M., IPC Industrial Press Ltd., Dorset House, Stamford Street, London SE1 9LU   *T.* 01-261 8788.
Controlled circulation.   Technical articles on engineering design and on materials and components.   *Payment:* by arrangement.   *Length:* from 1000 words.   *Illustrations:* line and half-tone.

English, the Journal of the English Association, Martin Dodsworth, 59 Temple Street, Brill, near Aylesbury, Bucks.
£2.00.   Three times a year.—Articles on literature and teaching of English at University level, reviews of books, and poetry.

English Historical Review (1886), Dr. G. Holmes and A. Macintyre, Longman Group, Journals Division, Longman House, Burnt Mill, Harlow, Essex, CM2O 2JE   *T.* 0279 26721.
£12.00 p.a.   Four times a year.—This journal contains high-class scholarly articles (such as are usually found in quarterlies), documents, and reviews. Contributions are not accepted unless they supply original information and should be sent direct to Dr. G. A. Holmes, Editor, E.H.R., St. Catherine's College, Oxford.   *No payment.*

Entomologist's Monthly Magazine (1864), Dr. B. M. Hobby and others, 7 Thorncliffe Road, Oxford, OX2 7BA   *T.* Oxford 58976.
£7.50 p.a. 3 times p.a.—Articles on all entomological subjects, foreign and British.   *No payment.*

Esperanto Teacher, The (Journal of the Esperanto Teachers Association), Bryn Purdy, 6 Mount Road, Tettenhall Wood, Wolverhampton, WV6 8HT.
£1.00 p.a.   3 times a year.—Articles and news items, in English or Esperanto, concerning the teaching of Esperanto in schools, colleges of education, universities.   *Illustrations:* photographs.   *Payment:* by arrangement.   Intending contributors should contact the editor in advance.

Essex Countryside (1952), E. V. Scott, Wm. Carling & Co. Ltd., Market Place, Hitchin, Hertfordshire, SG5 1EA   T. 59657.
35p.   M.—Articles of county interest.   *Length:* approximately 1200 words. *Illustrations:* half-tone and line.

European Plastics News (1929), Tom Tebbatt, Dorset House, Stamford Street, London, SE1 9LU   *T.* 01-261 8000.   *T.A.* Bisnespres, London, SE1.   *Telex:* 25137.
£1.00.   £12.00 p.a.   M.—Technical articles dealing with plastics and allied subjects.   *Length:* depending on subject.   *Payment:* by arrangement.   *Illustrations:* half-tone blocks 120 screen, line.

Evangelical Quarterly (1929), F. F. Bruce, D.D., The Crossways, Temple Road, Buxton, Derbyshire SK17 9BA   *T.* 3250.   Published from Paternoster House, 3 Mount Radford Crescent, Exeter, Devon, EX2 4JW   *T.* Exeter 58977.
90p.   Q.—A Theological review, international in scope and outlook in defence of the historic Christian faith.   Articles on the defence or exposition of Biblical theology as exhibited in the great Reformed Confessions. *No payment.*

Evening Chronicle (Newcastle), Geoffrey L. Baylis, Newcastle Chronicle and Journal, Ltd., Thomson House, Groat Market, Newcastle upon Tyne, NE99 1BO *T.* 0632-27500. London: Thomson Regional Newspapers, Greater London House, Hampstead Road, London, NW1 7SH *T.* 01-387 2800.
8p. D.—News, photographs and features covering almost every subject which are of interest to readers in Tyne Wear, Northumberland and Durham. *Payment:* according to value.

Evening News (1881), L. Kirby, Carmelite House, London, EC4Y 0JA *T.* 01-353 6000.
8p; Saturday 10p. D.—Independent. Exclusive news stories and pictures. Short stories, 1100 words.

Evening Post, New Hythe Lane, Larkfield, Kent, ME20 6SG *T.* Maidstone 77880.
7p. Monday to Friday.—Local news covering the Medway towns, Gravesend, Dartford, Swale and Maidstone. Also national news. Paper with emphasis on news and sport, plus regular feature pages. *Illustrations:* line and half-tone.

Evening Post (Reading) (1965), Peter Hiley, 8 Tessa Road, Reading, RG1 8NS *T.* Reading 55833.
6p. D.—Topical articles based on current news. *Length:* 1000 to 1200 words. *Payment:* £4.20 to £15.00 per 1000 words. *Illustrations:* half-tone.

Evening Standard (1827), Simon Jenkins, Shoe Lane, London, EC4P 4DD. *T.* 01-353 8000. *Telex:* 21909.
10p. D.—Independent. Articles of general interest considered, 1000 words or shorter; also news, pictures and ideas.

Exchange and Mart (1868), Link House, West Street, Poole, BH15 1LL *T.* Poole 71171. *Telex:* 417109.
15p. W.—No editorial matter used.

Expedition—The International Exploration & Travel Magazine (1970), Kathy Lambert, World Expeditionary Association, 45 Brompton Road, London, SW3. *T.* 01-937 1923. *T.A.* Wexas London, SW3.
£6.00 p.a. Q.—Entertaining, informative, well-illustrated features for the actual or armchair traveller. Articles on adventure travel, expeditions, field research and exploration of all kinds—natural history, anthropology, ecology, archaeology, zoology. Subjects most in demand are adventure, animals, underwater, primitive peoples. Also 'tips' sections by experts. *Length:* 1500–2000 words. Leaflet with full details of requirement on application to the Editor. *Payment:* £16 per 1000 words. *Illustrations:* high quality colour transparencies and 8″×10″ black and white prints to accompany articles. *Payment:* colour photographs £5.00 each; black and white prints £4.00 each; cover photographs (colour) £10.00 each.

Fab 208 (1964), Betty Hale, King's Reach Tower, Stamford Street, London, SE1 9LS *T.* 01-261 5886.
14p. W.—Short stories (about 2000 words) with boy/girl themes aimed at girls 15–16 years, £36.00; also emotional short-short stories about 1000 words £27.50. Serials about 3000 words per instalment, £48.40, basically love stories but with real life situations and interesting backgrounds, specially written for this particular age group. A strong emotional content is very important. Submit first instalment and synopsis of follow-up. "Emotional" features about actual teen-age girls. *Payment:* approx £40 according to length and arrangement. *Illustrations:* black-and-white photographs and colour; also drawings in line, tone and wash.

Faith and Freedom: A Journal of Progressive Religion (1947), Manchester College, Oxford. Editor: E. Shirvell Price, M.A., Chalice Lodge, Aldbourne, Marlborough, Wilts, SN8 2DD   *T*. Aldbourne 618.
£1.50 ann. sub., 3 issues (Oct., Feb., June).—Articles on philosophy and religion from free, non-dogmatic point of view, 3000 to 5000 words. *No payment.*

Family Circle, Christine Brady, Elm House, Elm Street, London, WC1X 0BP *T*. 01-278 2345.
25p.   M.—Service features of all kinds, homecraft ideas, occasional human interest, 500–1500 words. *Payment:* by arrangement. *Illustrations:* colour, black-and-white.

Family Law (1971), A. J. Chislett, O.B.E., Little London, Chichester, Sussex, PO19 1PG   *T*. Chichester 83637. *T.A.* Juslocgov.
£1.00 8 issues p.a. (£8.50 p.a.).—Articles dealing with all aspects of the Law as it affects the Family, written from a sociological or legal point of view. *Length:* 1000 words plus. *Payment:* £5 per column. *No illustrations.*

Far East Week by Week, 27 Leinster Square, London, W2 4NQ   *T*. 01-221 6590.
£40.00 p.a.   W.—Business and finance items concerning trade with Asia, including China, Newsleads, Projects and Developments, Contracts and Orders, Guidelines. *Payment:* for original material of high news value: £5.25 for up to 250 words, if suitable.   No *illustrations.*

Farmers Weekly (1934) (Agricultural Press Ltd.), Travers Legge, Surrey House, 1 Throwley Way, Sutton, Surrey, SM1 4QQ   *T*. 01-643 8040.
25p.   W.—Articles on agriculture from freelance contributors will be accepted subject to negotiation.

Fashion Forecast (1946), Nina Hirst, 33 Bedford Place, London, WC1B 5JX *T*. 01-637 2211.
$5.00 in U.K., $6.00 overseas, $10.00 airmail. Twice p.a. (May, November).—Factual articles on fashions and accessories with forecast trend. Articles on textiles, promotion, export markets, etc. *Length:* 800 to 1000 words. *Illustrations:* half-tone and line.

Fashion Weekly (1959), George White, IPC Consumer Industries Press (Ltd.), 40 Bowling Green Lane, London, EC1R 0NE   *T*. 01-837 3636.
12p.   W. (£9.00 p.a. post free).—News and features of interest to women's and children's wear manufacturers and retailers. *Payment:* on publication. *Illustrations:* line and half-tone.

Field, The (1853), (incorporating **Land and Water** and **The County Gentleman),** 8 Stratton Street, London, W1X 6AT   *T*. 01-499 7881. *T.A.* Field Newspaper, London.
25p.   W.—Specific and informed comment on the British countryside and country pursuits, including natural history, field sports, gardening and farming.   Overseas subjects are considered but opportunities for such articles to appear in *The Field* are limited.   No fiction or children's material.   Articles, *length* 800–1200 words, by outside contributors are considered, and there are occasional openings for brief news items. *Payment:* on merit. *Illustrations:* photographs, some colour if sufficiently high standard.

Films and Filming (1954), Robin Bean, Hansom Books, P.O. Box 294, 2 & 4 Old Pye Street, off Strutton Ground, Victoria Street, London, SW1P 2LR   *T*. 01-222 3779 and 4670.
50p.   M.—Articles on serious cinema, preferably with illustrations. Only commissioned material accepted. *Payment:* by arrangement.

Filtration & Separation (1964), W. G. Norris, 1 Katharine Street, Croydon, CR9 1LB *T*. 01-686 6330.
£1.75. Bi-M.—Articles on the design, construction and application of filtration and separation equipment and dust control and air cleaning equipment for all industrial purposes; articles on filtration and separation and dust control and air cleaning operations and techniques in all industries. *Payment:* by arrangement. *Illustrations:* line and half-tone.

Financial Times (incorporating **The Financial News**) (1888), M. H. Fisher, Bracken House, 10 Cannon Street, London, EC4P 4BY *T*. 01-248 8000.
15p. D.—Articles of financial, commercial, industrial, and economic interest from 800 to 1400 words. *Payment:* by arrangement.

Fire (1908), Harry Klopper, L.I.FIRE.E., A.I.L., Unisaf House, 32–36 Dudley Road, Tunbridge Wells, Kent, TN1 1LH *T*. Tunbridge Wells 23184–6.
45p. M.—Principal aim: Promotion and propagation of fire engineering, fire prevention, fire extinction, and fire salvage. Original technical articles, personal paragraphs and suitable photographs accepted. *Payment:* at editor's valuation. *Illustrations:* drawings or photographs.

Flight International (1909), J. M. Ramsden, Dorset House, Stamford Street, London, SE1 9LU *T.A*. Flight, Bisnespres LDN 25137, London, Telex.
30p. W.—Deals with aviation in all its branches. Articles operational and technical, illustrated by photographs, engineering cutaway drawings, also news paragraphs, reports of lectures, etc. *Payment:* varies; cheques month following publication. *Illustrations:* tone, line, occasionally two- and four-colour. News press day: Monday.

Forensic Photography, incorporating **Medico-Legal Photography** (1972), Nigel Morland, P.O. Box 18, Bognor Regis, Sussex, PO22 7AA.
£1.00 p.a. Q.—Though this journal goes only to subscribers and is not sold through retail channels, the editor is always interested in articles (illustrated or not) concerned with photographic techniques slanted to the professional and concerned with any aspect of the journal's title. *Payment:* by arrangement. *Illustrations:* line or half-tone.

Freelance Report see **Freelance Report Market Research,** p. 451.

Freelance Writing & Photography (1965), Arthur Waite, 67 Bridge Street, Manchester, M3 3BQ *T*. 061-832 5079.
£1.75 p.a. Q.—Articles and market news of interest to the freelance writer and photographer. *Payment:* £5.00 per 1000 words. *Illustrations:* line and half-tone.

Friend, The (1843), David Firth, Drayton House, Gordon Street, London, WC1H 0BQ *T*. 01-387 7549. Publishing: Headley Brothers Ltd., Ashford, Kent.
17p. W.—A Quaker weekly paper. Matter of interest to the Society of Friends, devotional or general, considered from outside contributors. No fiction. 1200 words maximum length. No *payment*.

Fruit Trades' Journal (1895), David Shapley, 430 Market Towers, New Covent Garden, Nine Elms Lane, London, SW8 5NN *T.* 01-720 8822. *Telex:* 915149.
24p. W.—Articles dealing with above trades on the marketing aspects of production but particularly importing and distributing sides; articles should average 500–700 words, and are paid for at 50p. a (2¼ in.) column inch, or by arrangement. *Illustrations:* half-tone or line blocks.

Gambit (1963), John Calder (John Calder (Publishers) Ltd.), 18 Brewer Street, London, W1R 4AS *T.* 01-734 3786.
£1.25, £4.50 p.a. (U.S.A. and Canada $3.00, $11.00 p.a.). Q.—Plays by contemporary writers, neglected authors, translations of foreign works. Full length and short. Also articles and interviews on theatre, opera, films. Reviews. *Payment:* by arrangement. *Illustrated.*

Gamekeeper and Countryside (1897), Edward Askwith, Gilbertson & Page Ltd., Corry's, Roestock Lane, Colney Heath, St. Albans, Herts, AL4 0QW *T.* Bowmans Green (0727) 22614.
30p. M. (£3.60 p.a.).—Informative articles of from 300 to 1000 words on field sports, country lore and natural history. *Payment:* by arrangement. *Illustrations:* camera-ready art work, monochrome only.

Games & Puzzles (1972), David Pritchard, 1 Hanway Place, London, W1A 4XF *T.* 01-636 8278.
50p. M.—Authoritative articles on proprietary, traditional or original board, card, tile or pencil-and-paper games (but not indoor sports). *Length:* 1000–3000 words. Also original puzzles, including crosswords. *Payment:* Articles £10 per 1000 words; puzzles £1.50. *Illustrations:* line and half-tone. Preliminary letter advisable.

Games and Toys (1914), H. Richard Simmons Ltd., Central Buildings, 24 Southwark Street, London, SE1 1TY *T.* 01-403 3033. *T.A.* Appressolo, London, SE1.
40p. M.—A trade journal specialising, as its name implies, in everything to do with games and toys. *Length:* 800 words. *Payment:* £4.00 per 800 to 1000 words, or according to the value of articles accepted. *Illustrations:* photographs, accompanying articles.

Garden News (1958), Peter Peskett, Park House, 117 Park Road, Peterborough, PE1 2TS *T.* Peterborough 63100.
15p. W.—Gardening news and human features on gardeners and their methods of success. *Payment:* £20.00 per 1000 words. Higher rate for good short pieces suited to our style. *Illustrations:* line, half-tone and colour.

Gas World (1884), G. W. Battison (Benn Brothers Ltd.), 25 New Street Square, London, EC4A 3JA *T.* 01-353 3212.
£1.20. M. (£15.00 p.a.).—Full news coverage and technical articles on all aspects of the gas and associated industries. *Length:* from 1500 to 4000 words. Pictures and news items of topical interest are paid for at standard rates. *Payment:* by arrangement.

Gay News (1972), Denis Lemon, 1A Normand Gardens, Greyhound Road, London, W14 9SB *T.* 01-381 2161.
30p. F.—Short stories up to 3000 words; articles up to 4000 words; poetry. *Payment:* by arrangement. *Illustrations:* line and half-tone; cartoons.

GC & HTJ, Barry Hutton, Regent House, 54–62 Regent Street, London, W1A 4YJ   *T.* 01-439 4242.
20p.   W. (£12.15 p.a.).—A practical horticultural journal for the trade and public parks staff.   Outside contributions considered and, if accepted, paid for; they should contain from 500 to 1500 words.   No fiction.   *Payment:* by arrangement.   *Illustrations:* in half-tone and line.

Gem Craft (1974), Evelyn Barrett, P.O. Box 35, Hemel Hempstead, Herts, HP1 1EE   *T.* 0442-2501 and 63841.
50p.   M.—Factual articles on lapidary, jewellery, enamelling and allied crafts.   *Payment:* £5.00 per page minimum.   *Illustrations:* half-tone.

Gems (1969), Richard Lambert, 84 High Street, Broadstairs, Kent.   *T.* 0843 64083.
40p.   Bi-M.—Articles about minerals, semi-precious stones, lapidary, jewellery making, metalwork and enamelling.   *Length:* up to 800 to 1000 words.   *Payment:* by arrangement.   *Illustrations:* line and half-tone.

General Practitioners, Journal of the Royal College of (founded as the Journal of the College of General Practitioners in 1954), Dr. D. J. Pereira Gray, M.A., F.R.C.G.P., 9 Marlborough Road, Exeter, EX2 4TJ   *T.* 0392-57938.
£20.00 p.a.   M.—Articles relevant to general medical practice.   *No payment.* *Illustrations:* half-tone and colour.

Geographical Journal (1893), Royal Geographical Society, Kensington Gore, London, SW7 2AR   *T.* 01-589 5466.
£5.00 (post free).   3 times a year (£12.00 p.a.).—Papers read before the Royal Geographical Society and papers on all aspects of geography or exploration. *Length:* 5000 words.   Edited by Sir Laurence Kirwan.   *Payment:* for reviews.   *Illustrations:* photographs, maps and diagrams.

Geographical Magazine, The, Derek Weber, 1 Kensington Gore, London, SW7 2AR   *T.* 01-584 4436.
50p.   M.—Informative, readable, well-illustrated, authentic articles, from 1500 to 2000 words in length, dealing with people and their environment in all parts of the world; modern geography in all its aspects; kindred subjects such as hydrology, meteorology, communications, civil engineering, space, etc.; man's control of the environment in which he lives, works and plays; travel, exploration, research; plant and animal life in their relationship with mankind.   A *preliminary* letter is recommended.   *Payment:* from £25.00 per 1000 words.   *Illustrations:* of high technical and artistic quality.   Photographs unaccompanied by articles can be considered.   *Payment:* colour, from £10.00 upwards, covers by negotiation; black and white, from £5.00 upwards, depending on size of reproduction.

Geological Magazine (1864), Mr. W. B. Harland, Dr. C. P. Hughes, Dr. G. A. Chinner, Cambridge University Press, 200 Euston Road, London, NW1 2DB   *T.* 01-387 5030.
£24.00 p.a.   Bi-M. (January etc.).—Original articles on general and strati-graphical geology, petrology, palaeontology, mineralogy, etc., containing the results of independent research by experts and amateurs.   Also reviews and notices of current geological literature, correspondence on geological subjects—illustrated.   *Length:* about 5000 words; maximum 10,000 words. *No payment* made.

Gifts, Vhairi Pearson (Benn Publications Ltd.), 25 New Street Square, London, EC4A 3JA   *T.* 01-353 3212.
£10.00 p.a., £15.00 p.a. overseas.   M.—News of gifts industry—products, trends, shops.   *Articles:* retailing, exporting, importing, manufacturing, crafts (U.K. and abroad).   *Payment:* by agreement.   *Illustrations:* products, news, personal photographs.

Glasgow Evening Times (1876), C. M. Wilson, 70 Mitchell Street, Glasgow, G1
3LZ   *T.* 041-221 9200; London Office: 1 Jerome Street, London, E1 6NJ   *T.*
01-377 0890.
8p.   D.—Welcomes well-written short topical articles.   500–700 words.
Illustrations: half-tone and line.

Glasgow Herald (1783), Alan R. Jenkins, 70 Mitchell Street, Glasgow, G1 3LZ
T. 041-221 9200; London Office: 1 Jerome Street, E1 6NJ   *T.* 01-377 0890.
8p.   D.—Independent.   Articles up to 1000 words.

Gloucestershire and Avon Life, J. Hudson, 10 The Plain, Thornbury, Avon,
BS12 2AG   *T.* Thornbury 413173.   *Publisher:* Whitethorn Press Group.
30p.   M.—Articles of interest to the counties concerned based on first-hand
experience dealing with the life, work, customs and matters affecting welfare of town and country.   *Length:* articles 500 to 1500 words.   *Payment:*
by arrangement.   Photographs also by arrangement.   *Illustrations:* preference given to articles accompanied by good photographs relating to subject.

Golf Illustrated (1890), Bill Robertson, 8 Stratton Street, London, W1X 6AT   *T.*
01-499 7881.   *T.A.* Golfirst, London, W1.
20p.   W.—Articles on golf and of interest to golfers.   *Payment:* by arrangement.   *Illustrations:* photographs of golfers and golf courses.

Golf International (1969), Editor: Chris Plumridge, Publisher: Mark H. McCormack, 183–5 Askew Road, London, W12 9AX   *T.* 01-743 7501.
30p.   W.—Profiles of great players, hard news, tournament coverage,
feature articles of 1200 or 600 words.   *Payment:* £30 per 1000 words.   *Illustrations:* colour, black-and-white.

Golf Monthly (1911), Percy Huggins, 256 West George Street, Glasgow, G2
4QP   *T.* 041-248 4667.
50p.   M.—Original articles on golf considered (not reports).   *Payment:* by
arrangement.   *Illustrations:* colour transparencies for cover.

Golf World (1962), Sean Pryor, Millstream House, 41 Maltby Street, London,
SE1 3PQ   *T.* 01-237 3011.
50p.   H.—Expert golf instructional articles, 500–3000 words; general interest articles, personality features 500–3000 words.   Little fiction.   *Payment:*
by negotiation.   *Illustrations:* line, half-tone, colour.

Good Housekeeping (1922), Charlotte Lessing, Chestergate House, Vauxhall
Bridge Road, London, SW1V 1HF   *T.* 01-834 2331.
35p.   M.—Articles of 1000–2500 words from qualified writers are invited on
topics of interest to intelligent women.   Domestic subjects covered by staff
writers.   Short stories and humorous articles also used.   *Payment:* good
magazine standards.   *Illustrations:* mainly commissioned.

Good Motoring (1935), R. O. Howell, 352 Lewisham High Street, London SE13
6LE   *T.* 01-690 6651.
15p.   M.—Articles on all motoring subjects.   *Length:* varies.   *Payment:* by
arrangement.   *Illustrations:* half-tone and line.

Gramophone, Malcolm Walker, 177–179 Kenton Road, Harrow, Middx., HA3
0HA   *T.* 01-907 4476.
45p.   M.—Outside contributions are occasionally used.   Features on
recording artists, technical articles, and articles about gramophone needs.
1000 or 1500 words preferred.   *Payment:* by arrangement.   *Illustrations:*
line and half-tone.

Great Outdoors, The (1978), Roger Smith, Allander House, 137–141 Leith Walk, Edinburgh, EH6 8NS *T.* 031-554 9444.
40p. (£5.80 p.a.). M.—Articles on walking or camping in specific areas, or about walking generally, preferably illustrated. *Length:* 1500–2500 words. *Payment:* £10 per 1000 words. *Illustrations:* half-tone and line.

Grocer, The (1861), A. de Angeli, 5–7 Southwark Street, London, SE1 1RQ *T.* 01-407 6981.
10p. W.—This journal is devoted entirely to the trade. Contributions accepted are articles or news or illustrations of general interest to the grocery and provision trades. *Payment:* by arrangement.

Grower, The (1923), Peter Rogers, 49 Doughty Street, London, WC1N 2LP *T.* 01-405 0364.
25p. W.—News and practical articles on commercial horticulture, preferably illustrated. *Payment:* by arrangement. *Illustrations:* photographs, line drawings.

Guardian, The (1821), 119 Farringdon Road, London, EC1 *T.* 01-278 2332 and 164 Deansgate, Manchester, M60 2RR *T.* 061-832 7200.
15p. D.—Independent. The parts of the paper for which outside contributions are chiefly desired are the feature pages. Articles should not normally exceed 1200 words in length. *Payment:* from £46.00 per 1000 words. *Illustrations:* news and features photographs.

Guideposts (1966) (U.S. edition: 1946), Raymond W. Cripps, Guideposts, Marlborough Lane, Witney, Oxon, OX8 7DZ *T.* Witney (0993) 3981–2.
20p. Every two months.—Concentrates almost entirely on true, first person, narrative-style stories, with a strong, spiritual "take-away thought" with which readers can identify. Close study of the magazine is advised. *Length:* 200–1400 words. *Payment:* £10 to £50; more by arrangement. *Illustrations:* line and half-tone.

Guider, Official Organ of the Girl Guides Association, Mrs J. V. Rush, 17–19 Buckingham Palace Road, London, SW1W 0PT *T.* 01-834 6242.
25p. M.—Short articles of interest to adult youth leaders, 500–1500 words, mostly by experts in the wide range of training subjects. Cartoons about Guide Movement. *Payment:* £10.00 per 1000 words. *Illustrations:* line and half-tone.

Hampshire—The County Magazine, Dennis Stevens, 13 Portland Street, Southampton, SO1 0EB *T.* Southampton 23591.
30p. M.—Factual articles concerning all aspects of Hampshire and Hampshire life, past and present. *Length:* 500-1500 words. *Payment:* £5.25 per 1000 words. *Illustrations:* photographs and line drawings.

Harpers & Queen (1929), Willie Landels, Chestergate House, Vauxhall Bridge Road, London, SW1V 1HF *T.* 01-834 2331.
75p. M.—Features, fashion, beauty, art, theatre, films, travel, interior decoration, mainly commissioned. *Illustrations:* line, wash, full colour and two- and three-colour, and photographs.

Health Education Journal (1943), Freddie Lawrence, Health Education Council, 78 New Oxford Street, London, WC1A 1AH *T.* 01-637 1881.
£3.00 p.a. Q.—Matter on mental and physical health, health education and social well-being; reports of surveys of people's knowledge of health: educational method and material; anthropology; nutrition; educational psychology and preventive psychiatry. Book reviews. *Length:* 1500 to 3000 words. *No payment. Illustrations:* half-tone and line blocks are used when required.

Hearing (official journal of the Royal National Institute for the Deaf), Antony Burton-Brown, 105 Gower Street, London, WC1E 6AH   *T.* 01-387 8033. 25p.   Bi-M.—Articles dealing in a bright and intelligent way with deafness. Special consideration given to deaf or hard-of-hearing contributors. *Payment:* by arrangement. *Illustrations:* photographs and line.

Heredity: An International Journal of Genetics (1947), D. R. Davies, The John Innes Institute, Colney Lane, Norwich, NOR 7OF   *T.* Norwich 52571. £25.00 (two volumes each of three parts yearly).—Research and review articles in genetics of 1000 to 15,000 words with summary and bibliography. Book reviews and abstracts of conferences. *No payment. Illustrations:* line, half-tone and colour.

Here's Health, Beaver House, York Close, Byfleet, Weybridge, Surrey. *T.* Byfleet 49123. 40p.   M.—Articles on nutrition; dieting; slimming; health foods; diet reform; natural food cookery; natural health and healing therapies; pollution; organic husbandry. *Length:* 750–2200 words. *Payment:* by arrangement. Preliminary letter advisable.

Hers (1966), Jack McDavid, King's Reach Tower, Stamford Street, London, SE1 9LS   *T.* 01-261 6385. 30p.   M.—Stories in first-person fictionalised form reflecting human problems and situations. To have strong appeal to women readers. *Length:* 2000 words upwards. *Payment:* by arrangement.

Hertfordshire Countryside (1946), E. V. Scott, Wm. Carling & Co., Market Place, Hitchin, Hertfordshire, SG5 1EA   *T.* 59657. 30p.   M.   Articles of county interest, 1000 to 1500 words. *Illustrations:* line and half-tone.

Heythrop Journal, The (1960), Rev. Dr. Robert Murray, Heythrop College, University of London, 11 Cavendish Square, London, W1M 0AN   *T.* 01-580 6941. £1.55 including postage. Q. (£5.00 p.a., U.S.A.,$14.00).—Articles (5000–8000) in: philosophy, theology speculative and positive, scripture, canon law, church relations, moral and pastoral psychology of general interest but of technical merit. *Payment:* Authors receive 24 offprints.

Hi-Fi News & Record Review (1956), John Crabbe, Link House, Dingwall Avenue, Croydon, CR9 2TA   *T.* 01-686 2599.   *T.A.* Aviculture, Croydon. 45p   M.—Articles on all aspects of high quality sound recording and reproduction; also extensive record review section and supporting musical feature articles.   Audio matter is essentially technical, but should be presented in a manner suitable for music lovers interested in the nature of sound. *Payment:* from £20 per 1000 words. *Length:* 2000 to 3000 words. *Illustrations:* line and/or half-tone; cartoons.

History (1916), Professor K. G. Robbins M.A., D.PHIL., Editorial, Department of History, The University College of North Wales, Bangor, Gwynedd, LL57 2DG. Business: 59A Kennington Park Road, London, SE11 4JH *T*. 01-735 3901.
£7.00 p.a. Three times yearly.—Published by the Historical Association. Historical articles and reviews by experts. *Length:* usually up to 8000 words. *No payment. Illustrations:* only exceptionally.

History Today (1951), Peter Quennell and Alan Hodge, 5 Bentinck Street, London, W1M 5RN *T*. 01- 935 0121.
50p. M.—History in the widest sense—political, economic, social, biography, the social scene, relating past to present; World history as well as English. *Length:* about 3500 words. *Payment:* by agreement. *Illustrations:* prints and original photographs.

Home and Country (1919), Peggy Mitchell, 11A King's Road, Sloane Square, London, SW3. *T*. 01-730 0307.
17p. M.—A good deal of the material published relates to the activities of the National Federation of Women's Institutes, whose official journal it is, but articles of general interest to women, particularly country women, of 800 to 1000 words are considered. *Payment:* by arrangement. *Illustrations:* photographs and drawings.

Home Science (1964), Arthur J. Fearon, Church Lane, Dagenham, Essex. A. J. Fearon & Associates. *T*. 01-592 2033.
25p. M.—Articles on home, food, nutrition, cooking, hygiene, textiles, grooming, home management, furnishing, domestic appliances, laundry. *Length:* 1000 words. *Payment:* by arrangement. *Illustrations:* line, half-tone, colour.

Home Words (1870) (incorporating **Church Standard, Church Monthly** and **The Sentinel**), P.O. Box 44, Guildford, Surrey, GU1 1XL *T*. Guildford 33944.
M.—An illustrated Church magazine inset. Articles of popular Church interest (400 to 500 words). *Illustrations:* photographs of religious and ecclesiastical subjects. *Payment:* by arrangement.

Homemaker (1959), Robert Tattersall, King's Reach Tower, Stamford Street, London, SE1 9LS *T*. 01-261 6969.
30p. M.—Practical features on all aspects of homemaking and inspired do-it-yourself. *Illustrations:* colour, half-tone, line. *Payment:* by arrangement.

Homes and Gardens (1919), Mrs. Psyche Pirie, King's Reach Tower, Stamford Street, London, SE1 9LS *T*. 01-261 5678.
25p. M.—Fiction of the highest quality and articles of domestic and general interest to every intelligent woman. *Length:* articles, 900–3000 words; stories, 2000–5000 words. *Payment:* generous, but exceptional work required. *Illustrations:* all types.

Honey (1960), Mary Anderson, King's Reach Tower, Stamford Street, London, SE1 9LS *T*. 01-261 5240.
35p. M.—Aims at the intelligent 18–25-year-old girl. Features mostly commissioned, but fiction bought from free-lance writers. Contributors are advised to study the magazine carefully before submitting mss.

Horse and Hound, M. A. Clayton, King's Reach Tower, Stamford Street, London, SE1 9LS *T*. 01-261 6315.
30p. W.—Special articles, news items, photographs, on all matters appertaining to horses, hunting.

Horse + Pony (1971), Scottish Farmer Publications Ltd., 39 York Street, Glasgow, G2 8JL   *T.* 041-221 7911.
35p.   M.—All material relevant to equestrian interests.   No fiction.   *Payment:* items paid on value to publication rather than length.   *Illustrations:* black-and-white, with a strong story line.

Horticulture Industry (formerly **Commercial Grower**), H. G. Warr (Benn Brothers Ltd.), Sovereign Way, Tonbridge, Kent.   *T.* 0732-364422.
60p.   M.—(£8 p.a.).—Trade and news pictures and practical informative articles on production and distribution for those engaged in fruit, flower and vegetable growing on a commercial scale, both outdoors and under glass. *Length:* 1000 to 2000 words. *Payment:* by arrangement. *Illustrations:* half-tone or line.

Hot Rod & Custom UK (1979).) Ian Penberthy, Link House, Dingwall Avenue, Croydon, Surrey, CR9 2TA   *T.* 01-686 2599.   *T.A.* Exchmart, Croydon.
50p.   M.—Technical and non-technical features on street rodding, customising, drag racing.   *Payment:* £25 per 1000 words.   *Illustrations:* half-tone and colour.

Hotel, Catering and Institutional Management Association Journal (1971), Nan Berger, O.B.E., 3 Estelle Road, London, NW3 2JX   *T.* 01-485 7988.
Journal of the Hotel Catering & Institutional Management Association.
50p.   M.—Articles on welfare and commercial catering, the hotel industry, restaurant practice, hospital and university domestic administration, school and university catering.   *Illustrations:* photographs and line.   *Payment:* by arrangement.

Hotspur, The (D. C. Thomson & Co., Ltd.), Courier Place, Dundee, DD1 9QJ, and 185 Fleet Street, London, EC4A 2HS.
7p.   W.—Picture-stories for boys—adventure, sport, war, school and mystery.   Line drawings only.   Instalments 2 to 4 pages, 8 to 10 frames per page.   *Payment:* on acceptance.

House & Garden, Robert Harling, Vogue House, Hanover Square, London, W1R 0AD   *T.* 01-499 9080.
50p.   M.—Articles (always commissioned), on subjects relating to domestic architecture, interior decorating, furnishing, gardening, household equipment.

House Builder and Estate Developer, The, Andrew Deg, 82 New Cavendish Street, London, W1M 8AD   *T.* 01-636 6575.
60p.   M.—A technical journal for those engaged in house and flat construction and the development of housing estates.   The Official Journal of the House-Builders Federation.   Articles on design, construction, and equipment of dwellings, estate planning and development, and technical aspects of house-building.   *Length:* articles 500 words and upwards, preferably with illustrations.   *Preliminary letter* advisable.   *Payment:* by arrangement.   *Illustrations:* photographs, plans, constructional details.

Housecraft, Official Journal of the Association of Teachers of Domestic Science, Laurie MacLennan, Hamilton House, Mabledon Place, London, WC1H 9BB *T.* 01-387 1441.
46p. plus postage.   M. (£4.60 p.a. plus £1.60 postage).—Articles on the teaching of home economics, including needlecrafts, and social and technical background information for teachers.   *Length:* 1000–1500 words.   *Payment:* approx. £10.00 per 1000 words.   *Illustrations:* line and half-tone. Most articles are commissioned from teachers.

Ideal Home (1939), Terence Whelan, King's Reach Tower, Stamford Street, London, SE1 9LS   *T.* 01-261 5000.
35p.   M.—Specialised home subjects magazine, and articles usually commissioned. Contributors advised to study editorial content before submitting material. *Payment:* according to material. *Illustrations:* usually commissioned.

Illustrated London News (1842), James Bishop, Elm House, 10–16 Elm Street, London, WC1X 0BP   *T.* 01-278 2345.
50p.   M.—A news monthly dealing chiefly with current and cultural affairs of British and international interest.   Stories for the Christmas number are usually accepted only from authors of established repute.   Interesting articles dealing with politics, social issues, science, art, archaeology, ethnology, travel, exploration, are particularly acceptable. *Payment:* for illustrations at the usual rates, or by special arrangement; special prices for exclusive material.   Photographs (especially exclusive).

Impact of Science on Society (1950), Unesco, Place de Fontenoy, Paris, 75700.
T. 577 16.10.   *T.A.* Unesco, Paris.
96p.   Q.—Articles and original studies on the social, political, economic, cultural aspects of science.   A *preliminary letter* to the Editor is requested. *Length:* 4500 words. *Payment:* up to £125 on acceptance. *Illustrations:* photographs, tables, graphs and drawings. Intending contributors are advised to study the magazine.

In Britain (1930), Bryn Frank, The British Tourist Authority, 239 Old Marylebone Road, London, NW1 5QT   *T.* 01-262 0141.
35p.   M. (£5.75 p.a.).—Features magazine about events and places in Britain.   Short pieces (maximum 150 words) sometimes accepted.

Incorporated Linguist, The, The Institute of Linguists, 24A Highbury Grove, London, N5 2EA   *T.* 01-359 7445.
£1.10.   Q. (£4 p.a.).—Articles of interest to professional linguists in translating, interpreting and teaching fields.   Articles usually contributed, but *payment* by arrangement.   All contributors have special knowledge of the subjects with which they deal. *Length:* 3000–3500 words. *Illustrations:* line.

Index on Censorship (1972), Michael Scammell, 21 Russell Street, London, WC2B 5HP   *T.* 01-836 0024.
£1.25 (£7.00 p.a.).   Bi-M.—Articles up to 5000 words dealing with political censorship, book reviews 750–1500 words. *Payment:* Articles £20 per 1000 words, book reviews £10.

Indexer, The, Journal of the Society of Indexers, of The Australian Society of Indexers, and The American Society of Indexers (1958), L. M. Harrod, c/o Barclays Bank, 1 Pall Mall East, London, SW1Y 5AX.
Free to members (subscription rates from 26 Golders Rise, Hendon, London, NW4 2HR).—Twice yearly.—Articles of interest to professional indexers, authors, publishers, documentalists. *Payment:* by arrangement.

Industrial Management, Chris Phillips, Building 59, GEC Estate, East Lane, Wembley, Middlesex.   *T.* 01-904 2246.
£1.25.   M. (£15.00 p.a.).—News based features on industry. *Length:* 1000 to 3000 words. *Illustrations:* line, half-tone, four colour.

Industrial Participation (1884), Ian Gordon Brown, 78 Buckingham Gate, London, SW1E 6PQ   *T.* 01-222 0351.
£3.00 p.a. post free.   Q.—Journal of the Industrial Participation Association. Articles on participation and involvement in industry, employee shareholding, joint consultation, the sharing of information, labour-management relations, workers participation, and kindred industrial subjects from the operational angle, with emphasis on the practice of particular enterprises, usually written by a member of the team involved, whether manager or workers, and with a strong factual background.

Industrial Safety (1955), Charles Micklewright (United Trade Press Ltd.), 33–35 Bowling Green Lane, London, EC1.   *T.* 01-837 1212.
£14.00 p.a.   M.—Devoted to the interests of industrial safety, health and welfare, including safety equipment and protective clothing. Technical and general articles on all aspects of industrial accident prevention, industrial fire prevention, factory safety organisation, etc. *Payment:* by arrangement. *Illustrations:* high-quality photographs and drawings.

Industrial Society (1918), Chloë Mailer, Denise Granatt, The Industrial Society, Peter Runge House, 3 Carlton House Terrace, London, SW1Y 5DG   *T.* 01-839 4300.
£6.00 p.a., £10 p.a. overseas.   M.—Articles, news items, photographs on developments in industry and commerce in five inter-related areas: effective leadership, productive management-union relations and participation, practical communication, relevant conditions of employment and working environment and the development of young employees. *Length:* 1000–2000 words. *Payment:* £20 per 1000 words or by negotiation. *Illustrations:* half-tones and line drawings.

Inquirer, The (1842), Rev. Fred M. Ryde, 1–6 Essex Street, London, WC2R 3HY   *T.* 01-240 2384.
10p. Fortnightly.—A journal of news and comment for Unitarians. Articles 700 to 1100 words of general religious, social, cultural, and international interest. Religious articles should be liberal and progressive in tone.

Insurance Brokers' Monthly (1950), Brian Susman, 34 Lower High Street, Stourbridge, West Midlands, DY8 1TW.
60p.   M.—Articles of technical and non-technical interest to insurance brokers and others engaged in the insurance industry. Occasional articles of general interest to the City, on finance, etc. *Length:* 1000 to 1500 words. *Payment:* from £5.00 per 1000 words on last day of month following publication. Authoritative material written under true name and qualification receives highest payment. *Illustrations:* line and half-tone, 100–120 screen. Cartoons with strong insurance interest.

Intermedia (1970), John Howkins, International Institute of Communications, Tavistock House East, Tavistock Square, London, WC1H 9LG   *T.* 01-388 0671.
£1.50.   Bi-M. (£7.50 p.a. individuals; £10.00 p.a. Institutions, excluding postage.).—International journal concerned with policies, events, trends and research in the field of communications. *Preliminary letter* essential. *Payment:* by arrangement. *Illustrations:* black and white line.

International Affairs (1922), Wendy Hinde, Royal Institute of International Affairs, Chatham House, St. James's Square, London, SW1Y 4LE.   *T.* 01-930 2233.
£2.00.   Q. (Annual subscription: £7.50 in this country; $22.00 in U.S.A., £9.50 elsewhere).—Serious long-term articles on international affairs. *Length:* average 5000 words. *Illustrations:* none. *Payment:* by arrangement. *A preliminary letter is necessary.*

International Broadcast Engineer, J. G. Newman, 50 High Street, Eton, Berks. *T.* Windsor 62515.
£1.00. M.—Articles of interest to television, radio and audio engineers on new techniques and developments. Circulates to over 119 countries and international aspect is stressed. Preliminary letter advisable. *Illustrations:* line and half-tone. *Payment:* by arrangement.

International Construction, A. J. Peterson, Surrey House, 1 Throwley Way, Sutton, Surrey, SM1 4QQ *T.* 01-643 8040. *Telex:* 944546.
M.—Articles dealing with new techniques of construction, applications of construction equipment and use of construction materials in any part of the world. *Length:* maximum 1500 words plus illustrations. *Payment:* from £6.00 per column, plus illustrations. *Illustrations:* half-tone and line. Some two-colour line illustrations can be used.

Inverness Courier (1817), Miss Eveline Barron, O.B.E., M.A., P.O. Box 13, 9–11 Bank Lane, Inverness, IV1 1QW *T.* 0463-33059. *T.A.* Courier, Inverness.
5p. Bi-W.—Short articles (no stories or verses) of Highland interest. *Payment:* by arrangement. No *illustrations.*

Investors Chronicle, M. J. L. Brett, Greystoke Place, Fetter Lane, London, EC4A 1ND *T.* 01-405 6969.
50p. W.—The leading journal for finance, investment and business concentrating on U.K. development. Only occasional outside contributions are accepted. *Payment:* by negotiation.

Jackie (D. C. Thomson & Co., Ltd.), Courier Place, Dundee, DD1 9QJ *T.* 23131; and 185 Fleet Street, London, EC4A 2HS *T.* 01-242 5086.
8p. W.—Colour gravure magazine for teenage girls. Complete picture love stories. Type stories up to 2000 words dealing with young romance. Pop features and pin-ups. General features of teen interest—emotional, astrological, humorous. Fashion and beauty advice. *Illustrations:* transparencies, picture story art work, colour illustrations for type stories. *Payment:* on acceptance.

Jazz Journal International (1948), Sinclair Traill, 7 Carnaby Street, London, W1V 1PG *T.* 01-437 8090. Published by Billboard Ltd. by arrangement with Novello & Co. Ltd.
55p. M.—Articles on jazz. *Illustrations:* photographs; line drawings of jazz subjects.

Jewish Chronicle (1841), Geoffrey Paul, 25 Furnival Street, London, EC4A 1JT *T.* 01-405 9252.
12p. W.—Authentic and exclusive news stories and articles of Jewish interest from 500 to 1500 words are considered. There are weekly children's, women's and teenage sections. *Payment:* by arrangement. *Illustrations:* of Jewish interest, either topical or feature.

Jewish Telegraph (1950), Frank Harris, Telegraph House, 11 Park Hill, Bury Old Road, Prestwich, Manchester, M25 8HH *T.* 061-740 9321 (4 lines) and 2a Mexborough Street, Chapeltown Road, Leeds, LS7 3DS *T.* 0532-620934.
5p. W. Articles of Jewish interest, especially humour. Exclusive Jewish news stories and pictures, national and local. *Length:* 1500–2000 words. *Payment:* by arrangement. *Illustrations:* half-tone and line.

Journal The, G. C. Stanton, Thomson House, Groat Market, Newcastle upon Tyne, NE99 1BO *T.* Newcastle 27500. London Office, Greater London House, Hampstead Road, London, NW1 7SH *T.* 01-387 2800.
8p. D.—Independent. No fiction, but topical articles of north-country interest.

Journal of Park and Recreation Administration, Kenneth L. Morgan, Managing Editor, Lower Basildon, Reading, RG8 9NE   *T.* Goring-on-Thames (049 14) 3558.
15p.   M.—Articles on park, recreation and horticultural subjects. *Payment:* £7 per 1000 words (according to type of material). *Illustrations:* line and half-tone.

Journalist, Ron Knowles, Acorn House, 314 Gray's Inn Road, London, WC1X 8DP   *T.* 01-278 7916 and 0223-891071.
10p.   M.—Official organ of the National Union of Journalists. Relating to journalism, journalists, and general conditions in the newspaper industry. Mainly contributed by members, and outside work is not paid for.

Judy (D. C. Thomson & Co., Ltd.), Courier Place, Dundee, DD1 9QJ, and 185 Fleet Street, London, EC4A 2HS.
7p.   W.—Picture-story paper for schoolgirls. Stories in pictures, line drawings, as serials or series, 8–9 frames per page. Also stories (in type) written to appeal to girls of school age. *Payment:* on acceptance. Encouragement to young artists and writers of promise.

Judy Library (D. C. Thomson & Co., Ltd.), Courier Place, Dundee, DD1 9QJ, and 185 Fleet Street, London, EC4A 2HS.
9p.   M.—Stories told in pictures, for schoolgirls; 64 pages (about 140 line drawings). Ballet, school, adventure, theatre, sport. Scripts considered; promising artists and script-writers encouraged. *Payment:* on acceptance.

Junior Age (1936), Su Pearce, Link House, Dingwall Avenue, Croydon, CR9 2TA   *T.* 01-686 2599.   *Telex:* 947709.
35p.   M. (£6.50 p.a. post free).—Articles, news, etc., appertaining to children's clothes and equipment. *Length:* 1000 words, or short paragraphs. *Payment:* by arrangement. *Illustrations:* photographs.

Junior Bookshelf, Marsh Hall, Thurstonland, Huddersfield, HD4 6XB   *T.* Huddersfield 21467.
60p.   Six issues p.a. (Annual sub., £3.00 inland, £3.60 ($10.00) overseas).—Articles on children's books and authors. *Length:* about 1200 to 1500 words.

Junior Education (1976), Annie Smith (Evans Brothers Ltd.), Montague House, Russell Square, London, WC1B 5BX   *T.* 01-636 8521.   *T.A.* Byronitic London WC1   *Telex:* 8811713.
45p.   M.—For teachers, social workers and parents concerned with children aged 7–13. Articles by specialists on practical teaching ideas and methods, the politics and philosophy of eduuation. *Length:* 800 to 1200 words. *Payment:* by arrangement. Profusely *illustrated* with photographs and line drawings; also large pictures in full colour.

Justice of the Peace (1837), B. T. Harris and P. J. Morrish, Little London, Chichester, Sussex, PO19 1PG   *T.* Chichester 87841.   *T.A.* Justlocgov, Chichester
35p.   W.—Articles on magisterial law and associated subjects including Children and Young Persons, Criminology, Medico-Legal matters, Penology, Police, Probation (length preferred, under 1400 words). Short reports of Conferences, Meetings, etc. Rate of *payment:* articles minimum £3.00 per column except when otherwise commissioned. *Preliminary letter welcomed although not essential.*

Karate and Oriental Arts Magazine (1966), Paul H. Crompton, 638 Fulham Road, London, SW6. *T.* 01-736 2551.
45p. Bi-M.—Accounts of eastern dancing, body development, body training systems: Yoga, Karate, fencing, etc. Photographs of men and women with brief notes on same. *Payment:* £5.00 per 1000 words. *Illustrations:* half-tones, line.

Kent Life (1962), F. J. Nixon, 109 Week Street, Maidstone, Kent, ME14 1RB *T.* Maidstone 671269.
40p. M.—All articles must have a Kent connection. *Length:* 300 to 1000 words, sharp black-and-white pictures with articles. *Illustrations:* half-tone or line-drawings; colour on cover. *Payment:* by arrangement.

Kent Messenger, Messenger House, New Hythe Lane, Larkfield, Kent, ME20 6SG *T.* Maidstone 77880. Branch Offices: Ashford, Chatham, Gravesend, and Suite 511 International Press Centre, 76 Shoe Lane, London, EC4A 3JB.
15p. Friday.—Articles of special interest to Kent and referring to Kent. *Length:* up to 1000 words. *Payment:* state price. Articles dealing with film, stage, radio, or TV stars who are in any way connected with Kent. *Illustrations:* all types, line and half-tone are used.

Labour Monthly (1921), Pat Sloan, 134 Ballards Lane, London, N3 2PD *T.* 01-346 5135.
45p. M.—A Magazine of International Labour. Well-informed special articles, 1200 to 3000 words, or shorter news items. *Preliminary* letter desirable. No *payment* is made.

Labour Weekly (1971), Donald H. Ross, Transport House, Smith Square, London, SW1P 3JA *T.* 01-834 9434.
10p. W.—Political articles. *Payment:* £1.50 per 100 words. *Illustrations:* half-tone.

Lady, The (1885), Joan L. Grahame, 39 and 40 Bedford Street, Strand, London, WC2E 9ER *T.* 01-836 8705.
20p. W.—British and foreign travel, countryside, human-interest, animals, cookery, careers, historic-interest and commemorative articles (a preliminary letter is advisable for articles dealing with anniversaries). *Length:* 800–1850 words. Viewpoint: 800 words. *Payment:* by arrangement, averaging £18 per 1000 words for first British Serial Rights only, plus varying *payments* for *illustrations* (drawings, photographs).

Lancashire Evening Post, Barry Askew, 127 Fishergate, Preston, PR1 2DN *T.* 54841.
8p. D.—Topical articles on all subjects. Area of interest Wigan to Lake District and coast. 600 to 900 words. *Payment:* by arrangement. *Illustrations:* half-tones and line blocks.

Lancashire Evening Telegraph (1886), Ian A. Jack, Telegraph House, Blackburn, Lancashire, BB1 5BA *T.* Blackburn 55291.
8p. D.

Lancashire Life, William Amos (The Whitethorn Press, Ltd.), Thomson House, Withy Grove, Manchester, M60 4BL *T.* 061-834 1234.
40p. M.—Articles of county interest; no fiction. *Length:* 1000 words. *Payment:* £9.00 per 1000 words minimum. *Illustrations:* line and half-tone; four-colour positives on cover. Photographs of news value and definite Lancashire interest. £1.05 minimum payment.

Lancet (1823), I. Munro, M.B., 7 Adam Street, Adelphi, London, WC2N 6AD *T.* 01-836 7228.
£1.00. W.—Mainly from medical profession.

Liberal News, Terence Wynn, 1 Whitehall Place, London, SW1A 2HE *T.* 01-839 4092.
10p. (£7.50 p.a.). W.—The official newspaper of the Liberal Party. Political and social features. *Payment:* nominal, unless specifically agreed otherwise.

Library, The (1889), P. Davison, Department of English, St. David's University College, Lampeter, Dyfed, SA48 7ED *T.* Lampeter 422351. For the Bibliographical Society.
£1.35 net. Q.—Articles up to 15,000 words, as well as shorter Notes, embodying original research on subjects connected with bibliography. *Illustrations:* half-tone and line.

Library Review, W & R. Holmes (Books), 30 Clydeholm Road, Whiteinch, Glasgow, G14 0BJ *T.* 041-954 2271.
£4.00 p.a. Q.—Concerned with information transfer, conservation and exploitation. Papers of 2,500–5,000 words considered. Line *illustrations.* Publication of contributions accepted, after referring, is regarded as conferring distinction to which *payment* is irrelevant.

Life and Work: Record of the Church of Scotland, 121 George Street, Edinburgh, EH2 4YN *T.* 031-225 5722.
10p. M.—Articles and news not exceeding 1200 words. *Illustrations:* photographs and line drawings. Seldom uses poems or stories. Study the magazine. *Payment:* on publication: up to £15.00 per 1000 words, or by arrangement.

Light Horse (1950), Michael Williams, 47 Moreton Street, London, SW1V 2NY *T.* 01-821 0546.
35p. M.—A sophisticated magazine covering all forms of equestrian activity at home and abroad. Good writing and technical accuracy essential. *Length:* between 750 and 1600 words. *Payment:* by arrangement. *Illustrations:* photographs and drawings, the latter usually commissioned.

Listener, The, George Scott, BBC, 35 Marylebone High Street, London W1A 4LG *T.* 01-580 5577.
25p. W.—Articles based on, or relating to BBC and Independent television and radio broadcasts. General articles on broadcasting. Poems, book reviews and reviews of the arts. *Payment:* at market rates. *Illustrations:* half-tone and line.

Liverpool Daily Post (1885), Norman Cook, P.O. Box 48, Old Hall Street, Liverpool, L69 3EB *T.* 051-227 2000. London: Wine Office Court, 146 Fleet Street, London, EC4A 2BU *T.* 01-353 7656.
9p. D.—Independent. Takes articles of general interest and topical features of special interest to North West England and North Wales. *Payment:* month following publication: according to value. News and feature photographs used. No verse or fiction.

Liverpool Echo, John Pugh, P.O. Box 48, Old Hall Street, Liverpool, L69 3EB *T.* 051-227 2000.
9p. D.—Articles of up to 600–800 words of local or topical interest. *Payment:* according to merit; special rates for exceptional material. Independent. This newspaper is connected with, but independent of the **Liverpool Daily Post.** Articles not interchangeable.

Living (1967), Vera Segal, Elm House, Elm Street, London, WC1X 0BP   *T.* 01-278 2345.
25p.   M.—General interest and human interest features.   *Payment:* by arrangement.

Local Council Review, The (The Official Journal of the National Association of Local Councils), Campbell Nairne, 100 Great Russell Street, London, WC1B 3LD   *T.* 01-636 4066.
£1.60 p.a. post free.   Q.—Articles on the law and practice of local government especially in relation to rural parishes; on charitable and benevolent activities in the countryside; on co-operation between statutory authorities and voluntary organisations and on any matters which may affect the well-being of the rural elector.   *Length:* 400–2500 words.   *Payment:* from £12.00 per 1000 words.   *Illustrations:* photographs, drawings, cartoons.

Local Government Chronicle (1885), Crispin Derby, 11–12 Bury Street, London, EC3A 5AP   *T.* 01-623 2296.   *T.A.* Together, London.
20p.   W.—Technical articles relating to financial, legal and administrative work of the local government and public service officer.   *Payment:* by arrangement.   *Illustrations:* half-tone.

Local Government Review (until 1971, part of **Justice of the Peace,** 1837). R. S. B. Knowles, Little London, Chichester, West Sussex, PO19 1PG   *T.* Chichester 87841–2.
30p.   W.—Articles on local government law and practice, including administration, finance, environmental health, town and country planning, rating and valuation (*length* preferred, 1200–1400 words).   Short reports of Conferences, Meetings, etc.   Rates of *payment:* articles minimum £3.50 per column except where otherwise commissioned.   *Preliminary letter welcomed although not essential.*

Local Historian, The (formerly **The Amateur Historian**), (1952). David Dymond, Grundle House, Stanton, Bury St. Edmunds, Suffolk, IP31 2DK   *T.* 0359 50363.   Standing Conference for Local History, 26 Bedford Square, London, WC1B 3HU.
70p.   Q. (£2.50 p.a. post free).—Articles, popular in style but based on knowledge of research, covering methods of research, sources and background material helpful to local and family historians—histories of particular places, people or incidents *not* wanted.   *Length:* maximum 3000 words.   *Payment:* none.   *Illustrations:* line and photographs.

London Magazine: A Review of the Arts (1953), Alan Ross, 30 Thurloe Place, London, SW7 2HQ   *T.* 01-589 0618.
96p. (£10.00 p.a.).   M.—Poems, stories, literary memoirs, critical articles, features on art, photography, theatre, cinema, music, architecture, events. Self-addressed envelope necessary.   *Payment:* by arrangement.

London Mystery Magazine (1949), Norman Kark, Norman Kark Publications, 268–270 Vauxhall Bridge Road, London, SW1 1BB   *T.* 01-834 8851.
50p.   Q.—Macabre, ghosts and whodunits.   Must be strong and novel in plot.   *Length:* maximum 4000 words.   *Payment:* by arrangement.   *Illustrations:* line.

Look and Learn (1962), King's Reach Tower, Stamford Street, London, SE1 9LS   *T.* 01-261 5000.
20p.   W.—Weekly educational magazine, that informs as it entertains. Educational articles, particularly science, literature and history written in an exciting yet informative style and suitable for children 9–15.

Look Now (1972), Richard Barber, 27 Newman Street, London, W1P 3PE *T.* 01-637 9671.
30p. M.—Romantic short stories, features and articles, personality interviews slanted towards young women between the ages of 16–20. *Payment:* by arrangement. *Illustrations:* line.

Love Affair (1971), Jack McDavid, King's Reach Tower, Stamford Street, London, SE1 9LS *T.* 01-261 6510.
15p. W.—Romantic short stories, written in first person. *Length:* 1250–6000 words. *Illustrations:* half-tone and colour. *Payment:* by arrangement.

Love Story Picture Library (1952), IPC Magazines Ltd., King's Reach Tower, Stamford Street, London, SE1 9LS *T.* 01-261 5000.
Six issues every month, 12p each.—Picture stories of 130–140 frames with minimum wordage. Bright, light, romantic themes presented from point of view of modern young heroine.

Loving (1970), Alison Mackonochie, IPC Magazines Ltd., King's Reach Tower, Stamford Street, London, SE1 9LS *T.* 01-261 5970.
14p. W.—First person real-life stories with strong love content for teenage and early twenties readership. *Length:* 2000 to 5000 words. Features of emotional or practical interest for the young market. *Length:* 1000–2500 words. *Payment* by arrangement.

Magic Comic (D. C. Thomson & Co. Ltd.), Courier Place, Dundee, DD1 9QJ, and 185 Fleet Street, London, EC4A 2HS.
9p. W.—Picture stories, puzzles and comic strips for younger children. Drawings in line or colour for gravure on children's subjects. *Payment:* on acceptance. Special encouragement to promising writers and artists.

Manchester Evening News, Doug Emmett, 164 Deansgate, Manchester, M60 2RD *T.* 061-832 7200.
8p. D.—Feature articles of up to 1000 words, topical or general interest and illustrated where appropriate, should be addressed to the Features Editor. *Payment:* on acceptance.

Mandy (D. C. Thomson & Co. Ltd.), Courier Place, Dundee, DD1 9QJ, and 185 Fleet Street, London, EC4A 2HS.
7p. W.—Picture-story paper for schoolgirls. Serials and series in line drawings. 2 and 3 page instalments, 9–10 frames per page. Editorial co-operation offered to promising scriptwriters. *Payment:* on acceptance.

Mandy Library (D. C. Thomson & Co. Ltd.), Courier Place, Dundee, DD1 9QJ, and 185 Fleet Street, London, EC4A 2HS.
9p. M.—Stories told in pictures, for schoolgirls; 64 pages (about 140 line drawings). Adventure, animal, mystery, school, sport. Scripts considered; promising script-writers and artists encouraged. *Payment:* on acceptance.

Mankind Quarterly, Dr. R. Gayre of Gayre, 1 Darnaway Street, Edinburgh, EH3 6DW *T.* 031-225 1896.
£1.50. Q. (£5.00 p.a.).—Articles on ethnology, human heredity, ethno-psychology, anthropo-geography. *Payment:* £1.05 per printed page. *Illustrations:* line and half-tone.

Manx Life (1971), Valerie Roach, Hill Street, Douglas, Isle of Man. *T.* Douglas 3074.
35p. Bi-M.—Factual articles on historical or topical aspects of the social, commercial, agricultural or cultural activities and interests of the Isle of Man. *Payment:* £6.00 per 1000 words on publication. *Illustrations:* black-and-white, half-tone and line.

Marine Week, Simon Timm, Dorset House, Stamford Street, London, SE1 9LU
T. 01-261 8608.
50p. W.—International journal covering commercial and technical stories
in shipping and shipbuilding worldwide. Articles aimed primarily at a
readership of shipowners on any facet anywhere likely to interest them are
paid on lineage. Half tone or line drawing welcome. The readership is
knowledgeable and the writer should be confident enough to match that. A
preliminary phone call is welcome. *Illustrations:* line and half tone, black
and white.

Market Newsletter (1965), John Tracy, Focus House, 497 Green Lanes, London,
N13 4BP T. 01-348 4463.
£9.50 p.a. M.—Current information on editorial requirements of interest
to writers and photographers

Masonic Square (1975), B. P. Hutton, Terminal House, Shepperton, Middlesex,
TW17 8AS T. Walton-on-Thames 28950.
40p. Q. (£2.00 p.a.).—Biographies, history, symbolism, news items all of
relevance to Freemasonry or affiliated subjects. *Length:* 1000 to 1500
words. *Payment:* £4.00 per 1000 words. *Illustrations:* black and white,
line and half-tone.

Matrix (1973), Carol Burns, The City Lit. Centre for Adult Studies, Stukely
Street, Drury Lane, London, WC2B 5LJ T. 01-242 9872.
30p. Twice a year.—Experimental fiction, poetry, interviews, documentary
articles. *Payment:* by arrangement. *Illustrations:* line and half-tone.

Media Reporter, The (1976), James Brennan, 39 Legh Road, Sale, Cheshire, M33
2SU T. 061-973 0041.
£1.00. Q.—Articles on media studies and practice (press, radio, television).
Payment: by arrangement. *Illustrations:* half-tone.

Melody Maker, Richard Williams, IPC Specialist and Professional Press Ltd.,
24–34 Meymott Street, London, SE1 9LU T. 01-261 8000.
15p. W.—Technical, instructional and informative articles on jazz and pop
music. *Payment:* by arrangement. *Illustrations:* half-tone and line.

Methodist Recorder (1861), W. E. Pigott, 176 Fleet Street, London, EC4A 2EP
T. 01-353 4748.
8p. W.—This journal is devoted to the interests of World Methodism.
Articles which have some bearing on religion, particularly in the ecumenical
field, up to 600 words. Paragraphs, notes on subjects of Methodist interest.
A *preliminary letter* is necessary. Ordinary *payment:* £5.00 per column.
Special terms by arrangement. Photographs used. Press day, Tuesday.

Mid Kent Gazette (Kent Messenger Group), New Hythe Lane, Larkfield, Maidstone, ME20 6SG T. Maidstone 77880.
15p. W.—Personal and local news covering Maidstone and mid-Kent.
Pictorial paper with emphasis on pictures and sport. *Illustrations:* line and
half-tone.

Middle East Construction, A. Davis, Surrey House, 1 Throwley Way, Sutton,
Surrey, SM1 4QQ T. 01-643 8040. *Telex:* 944546 BOJG.
12 issues p.a.—Articles dealing with the design, execution and use of
equipment and materials for building, civil engineering and municipal projects of interest to the Middle East market (i.e. not necessarily about work in
the Middle East, although such articles would be considered). *Length:*
maximum 1500 words plus illustrations. *Payment:* by agreement. *Illustrations:* colour, half-tone and line. Some two-colour line illustrations can
be used.

Midland History (formerly **University of Birmingham Historical Journal**), Dr. R. C. Simmons, School of History, The University, Birmingham, B15 2TT   *T.* 021-472 1301.
£3.   Twice yearly.—Articles of historical research on Midland history. *Length:* up to 8000 words.

Millennium—Journal of International Studies (1971), John E. Barrett and A. P. Smith, London School of Economics and Political Science, Houghton Street, London, WC2A 2AE   *T.* 01-405 7686 ext. 558 or 487.
£1.25.   3 times a year.—Serious articles on International Studies; original research work published, as well as topical articles on all aspects of international affairs. *Length:* 2000–6000 words (in triplicate with abstract). *Payment:* by arrangement. *No illustrations.*

Mind (1876), Professor D. Hamlyn, Birkbeck College, Malet Street, London, WC1E 7HX
£2.25.   Q.—A quarterly review of philosophy intended for those who have studied and thought on this subject. Articles from about 5000 words. Shorter discussion notes. Critical notices and reviews. *No payment.*

Misty (1978), Malcolm Shaw, King's Reach Tower, Stamford Street, London, SE1 9LS   *T.* 01-261 5712.
8p.   W.—Scripts for picture strip stories. *Payment:* £40.50 per 3 page set.

Model Engineer (1898), L. Porter (Model & Allied Publications Limited), P.O. Box 35, Hemel Hempstead, Herts, HP1 1EE   *T.* Hemel Hempstead 42501.
40p.   Detailed description of the construction of models, small workshop equipment, machine tools and small electrical and mechanical devices; articles on small power engineering, mechanics, electricity, workshop methods and experiments. *Payment:* by arrangement. *Illustrations:* half-tone and line drawings.

Model Railway Constructor (1934), S. W. Stevens-Stratten, F.R.S.A., Terminal House, Shepperton, Middlesex.   *T.* Walton-on-Thames 28950.
35p.   M.—Short or medium length feature articles on relevant subjects; photo features. *Payment:* £4 per 1000 words. *Illustrations:* line and half-tone.

Model Railways (1971), C. J. Freezer (Model & Allied Publications Ltd.), P.O. Box 35, Hemel Hempstead, Herts, HP1 1EE   *T.* Hemel Hempstead 2501–2–3.
40p.   M—Descriptive articles on model railways and prototype railways suitable for modelling. Articles covering all aspects of construction, planning, electrical wiring, experimental model railway engineering, and operation of model layouts. *Length:* 1000–2000 words. *Payment:* by arrangement. *Illustrations:* photographs and line drawings.

Modern Churchman (1911), The Modern Churchmen's Union, The School House, Leysters, Leominster, Hereford
70p.   Q. (£2.50 p.a.).—To maintain the cause of truth, freedom and comprehensiveness in the Church of England. *Length:* 1500 to 3500 words. Most contributions voluntary.

Modern Language Review (1905), Professor C. C. Smith, St. Catharine's College, Cambridge, CB2 1RL.
£15 p.a. (U.K.), £17 overseas; $40 (USA).   Q.—Contains articles and reviews of a scholarly or specialist character, on English, Romance, Germanic, and Slavonic languages and literatures. No payment is made, but offprints are given.

Modern Languages (Journal of the Modern Language Association) (1905), General Editor: E. M. Batley, B.A., M.LITT., 24A Highbury Grove, London, N5 2EA   *T.* 01-359 7445.   Reviews Editor: Dr. I. Hilton, Penarbronydd Cottage, Tregarth, Nr. Bangor, North Wales, LL57 4AE.
£1.50 (£6.00 p.a.).   Four times yearly.—All aspects of modern language study, linguistic, pedagogic, and literary.   Articles to General Editor.   *No payment.*

Monographs of the Sociological Review, Managing Editors: W. M. Williams and Ronald Frankenberg, University of Keele, Staffs., ST5 5BG   *T.* Newcastle under Lyme 621111.
At least once a year, prices variable.—Articles of up to 10,000 words treating social subjects in a scientific way.   *No payment* is made.

Month, The (1864), Hugh Kay, 114 Mount Street, London, W1Y 6AH   *T.* 01-491 7596.
50p.   M.—A Catholic review of theology, literature and world affairs, edited by the Jesuit Fathers.   *Length:* 3000 to 3500 words.   *Payment:* by arrangement.

More (1975), Carol Burns, Morley College, 61 Westminster Bridge Road, London, SE1   *T.* 01-928 8501.
30p.   Twice a year.—Experimental fiction, poetry, interviews, documentary articles.   *Payment:* by arrangement.   *Illustrations:* line and half-tone.

Morning Star (formerly **Daily Worker,** 1930), Tony Chater (The Morning Star Co-operative Society Ltd.), 75 Farringdon Road, London, EC1M 3JX   *T.A.* Morsta Telex, London.   *T.* 01-405 9242.
12p.   D.—Articles of general interest.   *Illustrations:* photos, cartoons and drawings.

Morning Telegraph, J. D. Michael Hides, York Street, Sheffield, S1 1PU   *T.* 0742 78585.   London Office: 23–27 Tudor Street, EC4.   *T.* 01-583 9199.
8p.   D. (includes weekly Angling Telegraph).—Articles of regional interest on angling, education and business topics considered.   No short stories.   *Payment:* by arrangement.   *Illustrations:* picture news features.

Mother (1936), Catherine Munnion, King's Reach Tower, Stamford Street, London, SE1 9LS   *T.* 01-261 5164.
35p.   M.—Articles on subjects of interest to parents of young children.   *Length:* 1500 words.   Short stories of up to 3500 words.   *Payment:* by arrangement.   *Illustrations:* photographs and sketches.

Mother & Baby (1956), Else Powell, 12–18 Paul Street, London, EC2A 4JS   *T.* 01-247 8233.
40p.   M.—Personal experience articles about pregnancy, birth and the care of young children.   *Length:* 600–2000 words.   *Payment:* by arrangement.   *Illustrations:* line and half-tone; colour for cover.

Motor (1902), Anthony Curtis (IPC Specialist and Professional Press Ltd.), Surrey House, 1 Throwley Way, Sutton, Surrey, SM1 4QQ   *T.* 01-643 8040.
25p.   W.—Offers scope for topical and technical motoring articles and photographs.   Colour photographs considered.   *Payment:* varies.

Motor Boat and Yachting (1904), Dick Hewitt (IPC Transport Press Ltd.), Dorset House, Stamford Street, London, SE1 9LU *T*. 01-261 8733.
50p. M.—General interest as well as specialist motor boating material welcomed. Features up to 2000 words considered on all aspects sea-going and inland waterways. *Payment:* varies. *Illustrations:* photographs and line. Colour photographs considered.

Motor Cycle (1903), Mick Woollett, Surrey House, 1 Throwley Way, Sutton, Surrey. *T*. 01-643 8040.
15p. W.—Anything of general interest to motor cyclists. Articles up to 1200 words. *Payment:* minimum £20.00 per 1000 words. Press days, Friday and Sunday. *Illustrations:* photographs, colour, and black and white.

Motor Cycle News (1955), Bob Berry, Dryland Street, Kettering. *T*. Kettering 81651–6. *T.A.* Emap 34557, Telex.
18p. W.—Features (up to 1000 words), photographs and news stories of interest to motor cyclists.

Motorcycle Racing (1975), Ian Beacham, EMAP National Publications Ltd., Bretton Court, Bretton, Peterborough, PE3 8DZ *T*. 0733 264666.
60p. M.—Features, technical articles, profiles, etc., all on motor cycle road racing. *Payment:* £22 per 1000 words. *Illustrations:* half-tone.

Motorcycling Monthly (1975), John Thorpe, Westover House, West Quay Road, Poole, Dorset, BH15 1JG *T*. Poole 71191.
35p. M.—In-depth articles on general motorcycling themes. *Payment:* by arrangement. *Illustrations:* colour and half-tone.

Movie Maker (1967), Alan Cleave, Model & Allied Publications Ltd., P.O. Box 35, Hemel Hempstead, Herts.
45p. M.—Articles on narrow-gauge cinematography (silent and sound)—technical, constructional, cultural and educational. *Length:* 1000–2000 words. *Illustrations:* half-tone and line. Articles should preferably be illustrated.

Municipal Review (1930), a journal of urban affairs published by the Association of Metropolitan Authorities. David Peschek, 36 Old Queen Street, London, SW1H 9JE *T*. 01-930 9861.
£4.50 p.a. including postage. M. (11 issues p.a.)—Articles on the current urban local government scene *Length* and *payment* by arrangement with the editor who prefers to discuss topics and synopses with contributors before copy is submitted.

Museums Journal, The (1901), Pauline Maliphant, The Museums Association, 87 Charlotte Street, London, W1P 2BX *T*. 01-636 4600.
£2.50. Q. to non-members.—Articles on museum and art gallery policy, administration, research, architecture and display, notes on technical developments and conservation, book reviews. *Length:* 1000 to 4000 words. *Payment:* none; contributions voluntary. *Illustrations:* half-tone, line blocks.

Music and Letters (1920), Editorial: Professor Denis Arnold, Dr. Edward Olleson, c/o Faculty of Music, 32 Holywell, Oxford. For other matters: 44 Conduit Street, London, W1R 0DE.
£1.25. Q.—Scholarly articles, 2000–5000 words, on musical subjects, neither merely topical nor purely descriptive. Technical, historical, and research matter preferred. *Payment:* £1.00 per page. *Illustrations:* music quotations and plates.

Music and Musicians (1952), Michael Reynolds, Hansom Books, P.O. Box 294, 2 & 4 Old Pye Street, off Strutton Ground, Victoria Street, London, SW1P 2LR *T.* 01-222 5131.
60p. M.—Commissioned articles on composers, conductors, players and singers of serious music. *Length:* 1000 to 4000 words. *Payment:* by arrangement. *Illustrations:* line, photographs.

Music in Education, Paul Griffiths (Macmillan Journals Ltd), 4 Little Essex Street, London, WC2R 3LF *T.* 01-836 6633.
40p. M.—Articles and reviews. *Length:* 500–2000 words. *Payment:* £10 per 1000 words.

Music Review, The (1940), A. F. Leighton Thomas, Glyneithin, Burry Port, Dyfed, SA16 0TA. Other matters: Heffers Printers Ltd., King's Hedges Road, Cambridge, CB4 2PQ.
£4.20 (£14.00 p.a.). Q.—Articles from 1500 to 8000 words dealing with any aspect of standard or classical music (no jazz). *Payment:* small, by arrangement.

Music Teacher (1908), David Renouf (Evans Brothers, Ltd.), Montague House, Russell Square, London, WC1B 5BX *T.* 01-636 8521.
45p. M.—A magazine for the teacher and student of music. Deals fully with all examinations in music. Answers readers' technical questions. Page about 1000 words. Average rate of *payment:* by arrangement. Articles and illustrations must have a *teacher,* as well as a musical, interest.

Music Week (1959), Rodney Burbeck, Morgan-Grampian Publications, 40 Long Acre, Covent Garden, London, WC2E 9JT *T.* 01-836 1522.
65p. (£20.75 p.a.). W.—News and features on all aspects of the music industry. *Payment:* by arrangement. *Illustrations:* half-tone, black and white and colour.

Musical Opinion (1877), Bryan Hesford, 3–11 Spring Road, Bournemouth, Dorset, BH1 4QA *T.* 23397.
35p. M.—Musical articles, 500 to 2000 words of general musical interest, organ and church matters. *Payment:* (small) on publication. No verse. *Illustrations:* line and half-tone occasionally.

Musical Times (1844), Stanley Sadie, 1–3 Upper James Street, London, W1R 4BP *T.* 01-734 8080.
45p. M.—Musical articles, reviews, 150 to 2500 words. *Payment:* by arrangement. *Illustrations:* photographs and music. Intending contributors are advised to study recent numbers of the journal.

My Weekly (1910) (D. C. Thomson & Co., Ltd.), 80 Kingsway East, Dundee, DD4 8SL, and 185 Fleet Street, London, EC4A 2HS.
8p. W.—Serials, from 30,000 to 80,000 words, suitable for family reading. Short complete stories of 1500 to 5000 words with strong emotional theme. Articles on prominent people and on all subjects of feminine interest. All contributions should make their appeal to the modern woman. *No preliminary letter* required. *Payment:* on acceptance. *Illustrations:* colour and black-and-white.

My Weekly Story Library, D. C. Thomson & Co. Ltd., Courier Place, Dundee, DD1 9QJ *T.* Dundee 23131.
9p. M.—35,000 to 37,500-word stories. *Payment:* by arrangement; competitive for the market. No *illustrations.*

National Builder (1921), W. Sekules, 82 New Cavendish Street, London, W1M 8AD *T.* 01-580 4041. *T.A.* Natbuild, Westcent, London.
60p. M.—The official journal of the National Federation of Building Trades Employers. Articles on building and constructional methods, management techniques, materials and machinery used in building. Articles, 1000–3000 words, preferably with illustrations. *Preliminary letter* advisable. *Payment:* by arrangement. *Illustrations:* on subjects mentioned above.

Naturalist (1875), M. R. D. Seaward, M.SC., PH.D., F.L.S., The University, Bradford, BD1 1DP T. 33466, ext. 8540.
£6.00 p.a. Q.—Original papers on Natural History subjects of all kinds relating to this country to include various aspects of geology, archaeology and environmental science; length immaterial *No payment. Illustrations:* photographs and line drawings.

Nature (1869), Dr. David Davies (Macmillan Journals Ltd.), Little Essex Street, London, WC2R 3LF *T.* 01-836 6633. *T.A.* Phusis, London, WC2.
65p. W.—This journal is devoted to scientific matters and to their bearing upon public affairs. All contributors of articles have specialised knowledge of the subjects with which they deal. *Illustrations:* half-tone and line.

Nautical Magazine (1832), R. Ingram-Brown, F.R.A.S., M.R.I.N., M.N.I., 52 Darnley Street, Glasgow, G41 2SG *T.* 041-429 1234. *T.A.* Skipper, Glasgow.
£5.40 p.a. including postage; 3 years £15.50. M.—Articles relating to nautical and shipping profession, from 1500 to 2000 words, also translations. *Payment:* average rate £3.00 per 500 words. No *illustrations.*

Navy International, Anthony Preston, 13 Crondace Road, London, SW6 4BB *T.* 01-736 7021.
£6.50 p.a. M.—Philosophical and technical articles on current world maritime affairs. *Length:* 1500–3000 words. *Payment:* by arrangement. *Illustrations* used.

New Beacon (1930) (as **Beacon,** 1917), Donald Bell, R.N.I.B., 224–228 Great Portland Street, London, W1N 6AA *T.* 01-388 1266.
20p. M. (£2.25 p.a.).—Authoritative articles on all aspects of blind welfare. *Length:* from 800 words. Also original contributions in prose and verse by blind authors. *Payment:* £7.50 per 1000 words; verse by arrangement. *Illustrations:* half-tone. Also Braille edition.

New Blackfriars (1920), The English Dominicans (Rev. Herbert McCabe, O.P.), Blackfriars, Oxford. *T.* Oxford 57607.
50p. net. M.—A critical review, surveying the field of theology, philosophy, sociology and the arts, from the standpoint of Christian principles and their application to the problems of the modern world. Incorporates *Life of the Spirit. Length:* 3000 to 5000 words. *Payment:* by arrangement.

New Ecologist, The, Nicholas Hildyard, Ruth Lumley-Smith, 73 Molesworth Street, Wadebridge, Cornwall, PL27 7DS *T.* Wadebridge 2996–7.
60p. Alternate months.—Articles and news stories on economic, social and environmental affairs from an ecological standpoint. *Length:* 1000 to 3000 words. *Payment:* by arrangement. *Illustrations:* line and half-tone. Magazine should be studied for level and approach.

New Era (incorporating **World Studies Bulletin** and **Ideas**) (1920). Joint
Editors: C. Harris, R. Richardson, L. A. Smith, A. Weaver, 18 Campden
Grove, London, W8 4JG *T.* 01-937 3254.
50p. (6 issues a year) £3.00 p.a.—An international magazine devoted to
experiments in education and reflections upon results. Material is supplied
by practising teachers and educational specialists. *Length:* normally 3000
words. *No payment.*

New Humanist (1885), Nicolas Walter, 88 Islington High Street, London, N1 8EL
T. 01-226 7251.
50p. Bi-M.—Articles (1000–3000 words) with a humanist/rationalist outlook on current affairs, social problems, psychology, religion, philosophy,
ethics, science, social science, literature and art. *Payment:* by arrangement.
Illustrations: half-tone or line.

New Library World, 16 Pembridge Road, London, W11. *T.* 01-229 1825.
£11.00 p.a., personal subs. £6.00. M.—Professional and bibliographical
articles. *Illustrations. Payment:* £8.00 per 1000 words.

New Musical Express, Neil Spencer, 3rd Floor, 5–7 Carnaby Street, London,
W1V 1PG T. 01-439 8761.
18p. W.—Authoritative articles and news stories on British and American
rock personalities. *Length:* by arrangement. *Payment:* by arrangement.
Illustrations: action photos with strong news-angle of recording personalities.
Preliminary letter or phone call desirable.

New Outlook, 47 Clarence Avenue, Kingsthorpe, Northampton, NN2 6NX *T.*
0604 713850.
50p. M.—A liberal monthly. Political, general economic and sociological
articles of interest to liberals. A preliminary letter is advisable. *No payment.*

New Review, The (1974), Ian Hamilton, 11 Greek Street, London, W1V 5LE
T. 01-439 4594 and 437 4494.
75p. (£12.00 p.a.) M.—Short stories, poetry, criticism and reviews of literary
work and other areas of the arts; further details from the editor. *Payment:*
£10 per 1000 words. *Illustrations:* line and half-tone.

New Scientist, Bernard Dixon, IPC Magazines Ltd, King's Reach Tower, Stamford Street, London, SE1 9LS *T.* 01-261 5000. *T.A.* Newscient, London,
SE1.
35p. W.—Authoritative articles of topical importance on all aspects of
science and technology are considered. *Length:* 1000 to 3000 words. Preliminary letter or telephone call is desirable. Short items from specialists
also considered for *Monitor, Comment, This Week,* and *Technology.* Intending contributors should study recent copies of the magazine. *Payment:*
varies but average £3.00 per 100 words. *Illustrations:* line and half-tone.

New Society, Paul Barker, 30 Southampton Street, London, WC2E 7HE T. 01-
836 4736.
22p. W.—Social science, social policy, documentary reportage.

New Statesman (1913), Bruce Page, 10 Great Turnstile, London, WC1V 7HJ
T. 01-405 8471.
25p. W.—Political and economic articles are mainly written by the staff;
most welcome outside contributions are "middles", social reporting and
studies. This does not exclude expert contributions on scientific or other
topics or articles from foreign correspondents. *Length:* 1000 to 1500 words.
Usual *payment:* £25 to £35 per article.

New Universities Quarterly (1946), Boris Ford, Basil Blackwell & Mott Ltd., 5 Alfred Street, Oxford, OX1 4HB *T.* 722146.
£2.25 (£7.50 p.a.).—Articles on educational, cultural and general topics that will be of interest to those engaged in higher education. *Length:* 2000 to 5000 words *No payment:* 25 offprints.

New World, United Nations Association, 3 Whitehall Court, London, SW1A 2EL *T.* 01-930 2931.
20p. Q.

News Extra (1964), G. E. Duffield, Appleford, Abingdon, Oxfordshire, OX14 4PB *T.* 023-582 319. *Publishers:* Lyttelton Press Ltd., The Vyne, Sherborne St. John, Basingstoke, Hants. *T.* 0256-86 227.
From £1.80 per 100 (carriage free). M.—Monthly church magazine inset, evangelical, mainly Anglican but also nonconformist, religious and cultural articles of current popular interest. *Maximum length:* 900 words. *Payment:* honorarium. *Illustrations:* line.

News Plus (1972), Rev. Brian Brindley, M.A., Holy Trinity Presbytery, 32 Baker Street, Reading, RG1 7XY *T.* 0734 52650. *Publishers:* Lyttelton Press Ltd., The Vyne, Sherborne St. John, Basingstoke, Hants. *T.* 0256-86 227.
From £1.80 per 100 (carriage free). M.—Monthly church magazine inset, Anglican catholic, religious and cultural articles of current popular interest. *Maximum length:* 900 words. *Illustrations.*

News of the World (1843), B. Shrimsley, 30 Bouverie Street, London, EC4Y 8EX *T.* 01-353 3030.
11p. W.

19 (1968), Margaret Koumi, King's Reach Tower, Stamford Street, London SE1 9LS *T.* 01-261 6410.
35p. M.—A glossy, sophisticated fashion magazine for young women, including general features of strong contemporary interest.

Northern Scotland (Centre for Scottish Studies, University of Aberdeen), Donald J. Withrington. Distributed by Centre for Scottish Studies, King's College, University of Aberdeen, Old Aberdeen, AB9 2UB *T.* 40241 ext. 5551.
£1.75. Once yearly.—Contributions to the advancement of knowledge in all aspects of the history of the north and north-east of Scotland. *Length:* Up to 10,000 words. *Payment:* None. Contributors are given offprints. *Illustrations:* line and half-tone.

Nottingham Evening Post (1878), Forman Street, Nottingham, NG1 4AB *T.* Nottingham 45521. 8p. D.

Numismatic Chronicle (1839), Dr. D. M. Metcalf, Heberden Coin Room, Ashmolean Museum, Oxford, OX1 2PH.
£12 per annual volume:—The Journal of the Royal Numismatic Society. Articles on coins and medals. Memoirs relating to coins and medals are unpaid, and contributions should reach a high standard of quality.

Nursery World, Penny Kitchen, Cliffords Inn, Fetter Lane, London, EC4A 1PJ *T.* 01-242 0935 and 0912.
15p. W.—For mothers, all grades of nursery and child care staff, nannies, foster mothers and all concerned with the care of expectant mothers, babies and young children. Authoritative and informative articles, 750–1200 words, and photographs, on all aspects of child welfare, especially from 0–7 years, in the U.K. and abroad. Also personal family stories, light humorous articles, practical ideas and leisure crafts. Short stories for young children approx. 500–750 words. *Payment:* by arrangement. *Illustrations:* line and half-tone.

Nursing Mirror and Midwives Journal (1888), Patricia Young, Surrey House, 1 Throwley Way, Sutton, Surrey, SM1 4QQ   *T.* 01-643 8040.
18p. W.—Contains news, educational, technical, and descriptive articles and pictures of interest to all nurses and midwives. *Length:* 250 to 3000 words. *Payment:* by arrangement. *Illustrations:* line, half-tone and colour.

Nursing Times (1905), Alison Dunn, Macmillan Journals Ltd., 4 Little Essex Street, London, WC2R 3LF   *T.* 01-836 1776.
12p. W.—Articles of clinical interest, nursing education and nursing policy. Illustrated articles not longer than 1500 words. Contributions from other than nurses and doctors rarely accepted. Press day, Monday.

Observer, The (1791), Donald Trelford, 8 St. Andrew's Hill, London, EC4V 5JA   *T.* 01-236 0202. *T.A.* Observer, London, EC4.
20p. W.—Independent. Some articles and illustrations are commissioned.

Observer Colour Magazine, The (1964), P. Crookston, 8 St. Andrew's Hill, London, EC4V 5JA   *T.* 01-236 0202. *T.A.* Observer, London, EC4.
Free with newspaper. W.—Articles on all subjects. *Illustrations:* also accepted. *Payment:* by arrangement.

Opera, Harold Rosenthal, 6 Woodland Rise, London, N10 3UH   *T.* 01-883 4415; Seymour Press Ltd., 334 Brixton Road, London, SW9 7AG.
50p. 13 issues a year.—Articles on general subjects appertaining to opera; reviews; criticisms. *Length:* up to 2000 words. *Payment:* by arrangement. *Illustrations:* photographs and drawings.

Opinion (founded as **The Quill,** 1923), 124–130 Southwark Street, London, SE1 0TU   *T.* 01-928 9671.
20p. M.—Anything of interest to Civil Servants, articles on trade union problems and public administration. *Length:* up to 2000 words. *Payment:* £10 per page (about 1000 words) but higher payment by arrangement. *Illustrations:* line and photographs. Cartoons on Civil Service themes.

Organ, The (1921), Bryan Hesford, 3–11 Spring Road, Bournemouth, Dorset, BH1 4QA   *T.* 23397.
75p. Q.—Articles, 4000 to 5000 words, relating to the organ, historical, technical, and artistic. *Payment:* small. *Illustrations:* half-tone and line.

Outposts (1944), Howard Sergeant, M.B.E. (Outposts Publications), 72 Burwood Road, Walton-on-Thames, Surrey, KT12 4AL   *T.* 40712.
60p. Q.—Poems, essays and critical articles on poets and their work. *Payment:* by arrangement.

Over21 (1972), Audrey Slaughter, Wellington House, 6–9 Upper St. Martin's Lane, London, WC2. *T.* 01-836 0142.
30p. M.—Features of interest to independent women. *Length:* 800 to 2000 words. Fiction, strong, 4000 to 5000 words. *Payment:* by arrangement.

Paperback Buyer (1978), Brian Levy, 1–3 Worship Street, London, EC2A 2AB   *T.* 01-588 3091.
40p. M.—Articles on the book trade, author interviews.   *Payment:* £20 to £25 per 1000 words. *Illustrations:* line and half-tone.

Parents (1976), Anita Bevan, 98–104 Baylis Road, London, SE1 7AT *T.* 01-633 0030.
35p. M.—Articles on general family health, child upbringing and marital relations. Preliminary letter essential. *Payment:* £25 per 1000 words. *Illustrations:* Black and white half-tones or colour. Cartoons on family themes.

Parents Voice (1950), Janet Manning, National Society for Mentally Handicapped Children, 117–123 Golden Lane, London, EC1Y 0RT *T.* 01-253 9433.
£1.50 p.a. 4 issues per year.—Journal of the N.S.M.H.C. Contributions on the subject of mental retardation considered. *Illustrations:* photographs.

Parks & Sports Grounds (1935), 61 London Road, Staines, Middlesex, TW18 4BN *T.* Staines 61326.
£6.00 p.a. M.—Articles on the design, construction, maintenance and management of parks, sports grounds, golf courses, open spaces and amenity areas. Any aspect of outdoor recreation. *Length:* 750–2000 words. *Payment:* from £15.00 per 1000 words. *Illustrations:* line and half-tone. Cartoons.

Pax (1904), The Benedictines, Prinknash Abbey, Gloucester, GL4 8EX *T.* Painswick 812455.
Subscription £1.00. Bi-annual.—Chiefly articles connected with Monasticism and the Liturgy. No *payment.*

Peace News (1936), 8 Elm Avenue, Nottingham. *T.* 0602-53587 and 5 Caledonian Road, London, N1 9DX *T.* 01-837 9795.
15p. Fortnightly.—Political articles based on non-violence in every aspect of human life. *Payment:* none. *Illustrations:* line, half-tone.

People's Friend (1869) (D. C. Thomson & Co., Ltd.), 80 Kingsway East, Dundee, DD4 8SL, and 185 Fleet Street, London, EC4A 2HS.
8p. W.—An illustrated weekly appealing to women of all ages and devoted to their personal and home interests. Serial and complete stories of strong romantic and emotional appeal—serials of 60,000–70,000 words, completes of 1500–4000 words. Stories for children considered. Knitting, fashions and cookery are especially featured. *Illustrations:* colour and black and white. No *preliminary letter* is required. *Payment:* on acceptance.

People's Journal (1858) (D. C. Thomson & Co., Ltd.), 7 Bank Street, Dundee, DD1 9HU, and 185 Fleet Street, London, EC4A 2HS.
7p. W.—Short serials suitable for famiy reading. Must have a good plot and develop a strong love interest. Complete stories 2500 words, dealing with Scottish life and character, or having Scottish link. *No preliminary letter required. Payment:* on acceptance.

Personnel Management, Journal of the Institute of Personnel Management, Susanne Lawrence, Mercury House Publications Ltd., Mercury House, Waterloo Road, London, SE1 8UL *T.* 01-928 3388.
£1.10. M. (£12.50 p.a.),—Features and news items on employee selection, training and wage and salary administration; industrial psychology; industrial relations; welfare schemes, working practices and new practical ideas in personnel management in industry and commerce. *Length:* 3000 words. *Payment:* from £10.00 per 1000 words. *Illustrations:* Photographers and illustrators should contact Art Editor.

Petfish Practical Fishkeeping Monthly (1966), Anthony Evans, PF Publications, 554 Garratt Lane, London, SW17 0NY   *T.* 01-947 2805.
30p.   M.—Practical experiences in fishkeeping and informative interviews with people of special standing in this field.   *Payment:* by arrangement. *Illustrations:* line, half-tone, occasional colour.

Pharmaceutical Journal, The (1841), R. Blyth, F.P.S., 1 Lambeth High Street, London, SE1 7JN   *T.* 01-735 9141.   *T.A.* Pharmakon, London, SE1.
40p.   W.—The official organ of the Pharmaceutical Society of Great Britain. Articles of 1000 words on any aspects of pharmacy may be submitted. *Payment:* by arrangement.   *Illustrations:* litho.

Philatelic Magazine, Kenneth F. Chapman, 42 Maiden Lane, London, WC2E 7LW   *T.* 01-240 2286–8.
30p.   M.—Essentially a stamp collectors' journal.   Original information about stamps, their designs and artists, but not elementary.   Specialised features and articles on postal history.   Contributions by those without philatelic knowledge are unlikely to be suitable.   *Illustrations:* half-tone (100 screen) and line.

Philately (1964), Kenneth F. Chapman, 1 Whitehall Place, London, SW1A 2HE *T.* 01-930 5254.
10p.   Q.—Organ of the British Philatelic Federation Ltd.   Articles on all aspects of stamp collecting, especially dealing with the detection of forgeries and fakes.   *Length:* 500 to 1500 words.   *Illustrations:* half-tone and line.

Photography, John Wade, Model & Allied Publications Ltd., P.O. Box 35, Hemel Hempstead, Herts, HP1 3AH.
45p.   M.—Illustrated articles of 900 to 1400 words on all aspects of photography, pictorial and technical, and how-to-do-it articles, slanted towards the serious amateur and young professional.   *Payment:* approximately £10.00 per page black-and-white, £15.00 per page colour, £30.00 front cover (colour).   Special features by arrangement.   *Illustrations:* line, half-tone and colour.

Photoplay Film Monthly, Ken Ferguson, 12–18 Paul Street, London, EC2A 4JS *T.* 01-247 8233.
45p.   M.—Features on film personalities.   Stamped addressed envelope to be enclosed for return of MS. if not suitable.   *Payment:* by arrangement.

Physiotherapy, Journal of the Chartered Society of, Jill Whitehouse, 14 Bedford Row, London, WC1R 4ED   *T.* 01-242 1941.
60p.   M.—Articles on physiotherapy and related subjects, news and technical items regarding activities of members of the Society.   Contributions welcomed from the medical profession and from physiotherapists.   *Length:* 2000 words (average).   *Payment:* £8 per 1000 words for technical medical articles.   *Illustrations:* photographs and line drawings.

Pictorial Education (1927), Peter Aykroyd (Evans Brothers Ltd.), Montague House, Russell Square, London, WC1B 5BX   *T.* 01-636 8521.
55p.   M.—Large-scale reproductions in colour and black-and-white of pictures illustrating subjects of the school curricula.   First-class photographs of geographical and nature study subjects; historical drawings.   Must be sharp and clear.   Original drawings usually commissioned.   Extra quarterly numbers (45p. each) contain large pictures in full colour of historical literary and geographical subjects.   *Payment:* by arrangement.   Stamps should be enclosed for return of material.   No articles required.

Pig Farming, M. C. Looker, Farming Press Ltd., Wharfedale Road, Ipswich, IP1 4LG *T.* Ipswich 43011–5.
20p. M.—Practical, well-illustrated articles on all aspects of pig production required, particularly those dealing with new ideas in pig management, feeding and housing. *Length:* 1000 to 2000 words. *Payment:* £15.00 per 1000 words published. *Illustrations:* half-tone or line.

Pink (1960), King's Reach Tower, Stamford Street, London, SE1 9LS *T.* 01-261 6877.
14p. W.—For schoolgirls eleven to sixteen. Serials and complete stories told in pictures, also written series, *length* 1000 words. Short illustrated magazine features. Contributors should study paper before submitting ideas to the Editor. *Illustrations:* half-tone and line for web offset.

Pippin in Playland, G. S. Marler, Polly Perkins House, 382–386 Edgware Road, London, W2 1EP *T.* 01-723 3022.
10p. W.—Coloured picture weekly for the very young based on television series. *Payment:* variable. *Illustrations:* colour and half-tone.

Plays and Players (1953), Michael Coveney, Hansom Books, P.O. Box 294, 2 & 4 Old Pye Street, off Strutton Ground, Victoria Street, London, SW1P 2LR *T.* 01-222 5221.
60p. M.—Articles and photos on world theatre. Commissioned articles only accepted. *Payment:* by arrangement. *Illustrations:* line, photographs.

PN Review, formerly **Poetry Nation** (1973), Michael Schmidt, Department of English, University of Manchester, M13 9PL.
£1.50 (£4.90 p.a.) Q.—Poetry, essays, reviews, translations. *Payment:* by arrangement.

Pneu Journal now renamed **WES Journal,** *q.v.*

Poetry Review, Roger Garfitt, 21 Earls Court Square, London, SW5 9BY *T.* 01-373 7861–2.
90p. (£4.00 p.a.). Q.—Poems. Send no more than six, with s.a.e. *Very few unsolicited poems accepted.* Potential contributors are advised to read a copy of the magazine before submitting work. Enquire for details of poetry competitions (with prizes).

Poetry Wales (1965), J. P. Ward, Dept. of Education, University College, Swansea, SA1 8PP *T.* Swansea 21231. *Publisher:* Christopher Davies Ltd., 4/5 Thomas Row, Swansea, SA1 1NJ.
75p. Q. (£3.00 p.a.).—Poems mainly in English and mainly by Welshmen or Welsh residents: articles on Welsh, Anglo Welsh and other poetry; regular special features; reviews of new poetry. *Payment:* by arrangement. *Illustrations:* occasional photographs.

Police Journal (1926), H. V. D. Hallett, 20 Sportsfield, Maidstone, Kent, ME14 5LR *T.* Maidstone 65432, ext. 300.
£1.25. Q.—Articles of interest to the Police Force. *Payment:* by arrangement. *Illustrations:* half-tone.

Political Quarterly, The (1930), The Political Quarterly Publishing Company Ltd., Elm House, 10–16 Elm Street, London, WC1X 0BP   *T.* 01-278 2345   Editors: Bernard Crick and John Mackintosh, MP.   Literary editor: James Cornford.   Editorial Board B. Abel-Smith, Lord Ardwick, H. L. Beales, James Cornford, Bernard Crick, W. A. Robson, H. R. G.. Greaves, John P. Mackintosh, Janet Morgan, D. C. Watt, E. J. Mishan, Rudolf Klein, P. Self, D. Watt.   Books for review to be sent to: James Cornford, 4 Cambridge Terrace, London, NW1 4JL.
£2.10.   Q. £9.50 p.a. (Students £6.50).—A journal devoted to topical aspects of national and international politics and public administration; it takes a progressive, but not a party, point of view.   *Average payment:* £7.50 per 1000 words.   *Average length:* 4000 words.

Pony (1949) Michael Williams, 47 Moreton Street, London, SW1V 2NY   *T.* 01-821 0546.
35p.   M.—Articles and short stories with a horsy theme likely to be of interest to young readers between the ages of 8 and 18.   Technical accuracy and good writing essential.   *Length:* up to 1600 words.   *Payment:* by arrangement.   *Illustrations:* drawings (commissioned) and interesting photographs.

Popular Flying, Popular Flying Association, Chairman: D. F. Faulkner-Bryant, Terminal Building, Shoreham Airport, Shoreham-by-Sea, Sussex, BN4 5FF   *T.* Shoreham-by-Sea 61616.
50p.   Alt. M.—Topical articles and news paragraphs on ultra-light and light aviation; all aspects of private flying.   *Length:* up to 2000 words.   *No payment.*   *Illustrations:* photographs and line drawings.

Popular Gardening (1889), Fred Whitsey, King's Reach Tower, Stamford Street, London, SE1 9LS   *T.* 01-261 5787.
12p.   W.—A practical freely-illustrated magazine for the amateur gardener, the specialist and flower-arranger, printed in web offset with full colour covers and containing original and informative articles, photographs and diagrams.   *Length:* up to 800 words.   *Payment:* by arrangement.

Popular Hi-Fi (1971), Hugh Johnstone, Haymarket Publishing Ltd., Craven House, 34 Foubert's Place, London, W1V 1HF   *T.* 01-439 4242.
40p.   M.—Articles by professional contributors on audio equipment, related subjects and record reviews.   *Length:* up to 2000 words.   *Payment:* by arrangement.   *Illustrations:* line and half-tone.   *Preliminary letter* essential.

Popular Motoring (1962), Michael Twite, Aqua House, London Road, Peterborough, PE2 8AQ   *T.* 52271.
40p.   M.—Articles on motoring and car maintenance.   *Payment:* £25 per 1000 words.   *Illustrations:* half-tone.

Port of London, Port of London Authority, World Trade Centre, London, E1.   *T.* 01-476 6900.   *T.A.* Pola, London.   *Telex:* Polaldn 897477.
40p.   Q.—The magazine of the Port of London Authority.   Articles up to 2000 words considered, semi-technical, historical or having bearing on trade and commerce of London essential.   *Preliminary letter* essential.   *Payment:* by arrangement.   *Illustrations:* half-tone and line.

Post, The (1920), H. Burnett, UPW House, Crescent Lane, Clapham, London, SW4 9RN   *T.* 01-622 9977.   *T.A.* Postact, London, SW4.   *Telex:* 913585.   Free to members.   F.—The journal of the Union of Post Office Workers.   The Editor invites articles on postal, telephone and telegraph workers abroad and on other questions of interest to a Trade Union readership.   *Length:* 1000 words or less.   *Payment:* by arrangement.   *Illustrations:* line and half-tone occasionally.

Poultry World, John Farrant, Surrey House, 1 Throwley Way, Sutton, Surrey, SM1 4QQ *T.* 01-643 8040.
15p. W.—Articles on commercial poultry breeding, production, marketing and packaging. News of International poultry interest. *Payment:* by arrangement. Line and photographic illustrations.

Power Farming, Ted Fellows (Agricultural Press Ltd.), Surrey House, 1 Throwley Way, Sutton, Surrey, SM1 4QQ *T.* 01-643 8040, ext. 4116.
40p. M.—Articles concerning all aspects of farm equipment, its use and management. General engineering in its application to machinery maintenance, etc. *Length:* not exceeding 1500 words. Short practical workshop hints welcomed. *Payment:* by arrangement. *Illustrations:* photographs or drawings.

Practical Boat Owner (1967), Denny Desoutter, Westover House, West Quay Road, Poole, Dorset, BH15 1JG *T.* 02013-71191.
55p. M.—Articles of up to 2000 words in length, about practical matters concerning the boating enthusiast. *Payment:* by negotiation. *Illustrations:* photographs or drawings.

Practical Camper, John Lloyd, Haymarket Publishing Ltd., Regent House, Regent Street, London, W1A 4YJ *T.* 01-439 4242.
35p. M.—Practical articles based on picture strip information, subjects only by arrangement with editor. *Payment:* by arrangement. *Illustrations:* top quality bromides, some line. *Preliminary letter* essential in all cases.

Practical Electronics (1964), M. Kenward, Westover House, West Quay Road, Poole, Dorset, BH15 1JG *T.* 71191.
35p. M.—Constructional and theoretical articles. *Length:* 1000–2500 words. *Payment:* £15–£30 per 1000 words depending upon type of article. *Illustrations:* line and half-tone.

Practical Gardening (1959), Geoffrey Hamilton, Aqua House, London Road, Peterborough, PE2 8AQ *T.* 0733-63100.
35p. M.—500 to 1000 words on practical gardening subjects. *Payment:* £30 per 1000 words. *Illustrations:* line, half-tone, colour.

Practical Householder (1955), Alan Mitchell, Westover House, West Quay Road, Poole, Dorset, BH15 1JG *T.* 71191, ext. 218.
30p. M.—Articles about 1500 words in length, about practical matters concerning the home and its equipment. *Payment:* according to subject. *Illustrations:* line and half-tone.

Practical Motorist (1954), H. Heywood, Westover House, West Quay Road, Poole, Dorset, BH15 1JG *T.* 71191.
25p. M.—Practical articles on upkeep, overhaul and repair of all makes of cars, also practical hints and tips. *Payment:* according to merit. *Illustrations:* black and white, transparencies and line drawings.

Practical Photography (1959), Robert Scott, Park House, 117 Park Road, Peterborough, PE1 2TS *T.* (0733) 63100.
50p. M.—Features on any aspect of photography with practical bias. *Payment:* £20 per 1000 words. *Illustrations:* line, half-tone, colour. *Payment:* from £8 black-and-white or colour.

Practical Wireless (1933), IPC Magazines Ltd., Westover House, West Quay Road, Poole, Dorset, BH15 1JG *T.* 71191.
48p. M.—Articles on the practical aspects of domestic and amateur radio and communications, audio and popular applied electronics. Constructional projects. *Illustrations:* photographs, line drawings and wash half-tone for offset litho. *Payment:* according to subject and quality in the range of £15 to £25 per 1000 words, plus extra for illustrations.

Practical Woodworking, Derek Eddy, King's Reach Tower, Stamford Street, London, SE1 9LS *T.* 01-261 5000.
50p. M.—Articles of a practical nature covering any aspect of woodworking. *Not* articles on tools, joints or timber technology. *Illustrations.*

Practitioner, The (1868), Hugh L'Etang, B.M., D.I.H., Morgan-Grampian (Professional Press) Ltd., 30 Calderwood Street, London, SE18 6QH *T.* 01-855 7777.
£1.00. M. (£10.00 p.a., Overseas $36).

Prediction (1936), Jo Logan, Link House, Dingwall Avenue, Croydon, CR9 2TA *T.* 01-686 2599. *T.A.* Aviculture, Croydon.
40p. M.—Articles on all occult subjects. *Length:* 2000 words maximum. *Payment:* by arrangement. *Illustrations:* half-tone; full colour cover.

Preparatory Schools Review, W. L. V. Caldwell, 22 Millington Road, Cambridge, CB3 9HP *T.* 0223-67262.
£2.00 p.a. Three times yearly.—The organ of the Incorporated Association of Preparatory Schools. Articles dealing with the education and activities of children in the Association's schools, or of general educational interest. *Length:* 700 to 3000 words. Half-tone and line *illustrations* optional.

Printing World (1878), Roy Coxhead (Benn Publications Ltd.), 25 New Street Square, London, EC4A 3JA *T.* 01-353 3212.
30p. W.—Commercial, technical, financial and labour news covering all aspects of the printing industry in the UK and abroad. Outside contributions. *Payment:* by arrangement. *Illustrations:* half-tone and line.

Private Eye (1962), Richard Ingrams, 34 Greek Street, London, W1V 5LG *T.* 01-437 4017.
25p. F.—Satire. *Payment:* £5.00 cuttings; £28 per cartoon. *Illustrations:* black-and-white, line.

Professional Administration (incorporating **The Secretary,** 1892, **The Chartered Secretary,** 1961, etc.) (1971), C. Coulson-Thomas, 3–4 Lime Street, London, EC3M 7HA *T.* 01-623 7100 ext. 2679/2485. Lloyd's of London Press Ltd., in association with The Institute of Chartered Secretaries and Administrators.
35p. M. (£4.53 p.a. post free).—Practical and topical articles 750–1600 words (occasionally longer) on law, finance, and personnel-oriented problems and developments affecting company secretaries and other senior administrators in business, nationalised industries, local and central government and other institutions in Britain and overseas. Articles on management theory are generally *not* required: most articles commissioned from leading administrators with relevant experience. *Payment:* by arrangement. *Illustrations:* line and half-tone, only by special commission.

Progress (1881), Ann Lee, Royal National Institute for the Blind, 224–8 Great Portland Street, London, W1N 6AA *T.* 01-388 1266.
60p. M.—A magazine in braille type for the blind.

Psychologist Magazine (1933), The Psychologist Magazine Ltd., Denington Estate, Wellingborough, Northants, NN8 2RQ *T.* Wellingborough 76031.
20p. M.—Articles on popular practical psychology. Topics include self-knowledge, human relationships, self-improvement, coping with stress and tension, self-confidence, self-consciousness, nervousness, anxiety, worry, fears and phobias, overcoming bad habits, feelings of inadequacy and inferiority, psychosomatic disorders and nutrition. Articles must be practical and offer genuine guidance to the reader. *Length:* about 1500 words. *Payment:* minimum £7.50.

Pulse, John Stevenson, Morgan-Grampian (Professional Press) Ltd., Morgan-Grampian House, 30 Calderwood Street, Woolwich, London, SE18 6QH *T.* 01-855 7777.
£15.00 p.a. W.—Articles with a medical flavour or of direct interest to G.P.s. Purely clinical matter cannot be used. *Length:* 1200–2000 words, average 1500. *Payment:* £35 to £60 average. *Illustrations:* photographs. Cartoons.

Punch (1841), Alan Coren, 23–27 Tudor Street, London, EC4Y 0HR *T.* 01-583 9199.
25p. W.—Most articles are commissioned, but there is still a demand for outside material, particularly for short stories of up to 2500 words. Articles should not be more than 1000 words, must be humorous, and should preferably be topical or at least relevant to contemporary events. All submissions must be accompanied by a s.a.e. Cartoons welcomed. *Payment:* by arrangement, but not less than £50.00 per 1000 words. *Drawings:* line or half-tone; half-pages from £19.00 and small drawings from £12.00.

Quaker Monthly (1921), Enid Huws Jones, Friends House, Euston Road, London, NW1 2BJ *T.* 01-387 3601.
15p. M.—Mainly commissioned articles.

Quarterly Journal of Medicine (1907), Clarendon Press, Oxford. *Secretary to Editors:* Dr. J. M. Holt, Old Whitehill, Tackley, Oxford *T.* Tackley 241.
£5.50. Q. (£16.00 p.a.; Overseas £20.00 p.a.).—Devoted to the publication of original papers and critical reviews dealing with clinical medicine. *No payment.*

Question (1884), G. A. Wells, 88 Islington High Street, London, N1 8EN *T.* 01-226 7251.
£1.00 (paper), £2.25 (boards). Annual.—Articles on a wide range of subjects from a rationalistic standpoint (normally commissioned work only).

Radio & Record News (1976), G. Thain, 3rd Floor, 365 Euston Road, London, NW1. *T.* 01-388 3765 and 3887. *Telex:* 21697 N Time G.
60p. W.—Articles for radio, record and advertising industries. *Payment:* £25 per 1000 words.

Radio Times (The Journal of the BBC), Geoffrey Cannon, BBC, 35 Marylebone High Street, London, W1M 4AA *T.* 01-580 5577, Ext. 4555. David Driver (Deputy Editor), Ext. 2293.
12p. W.—Articles supporting and enlarging BBC Television and Radio programmes, which are, therefore, on every subject broadcast. *Length:* from 600 to 2500 words. *Payment:* by arrangement. *Illustrations:* in colour and black-and-white; photographs, graphic designs, or drawings.

Railway Gazette International, Dorset House, Stamford Street, London, SE1 9LU *T.* 01-261 8179.
£1.25. M.—Deals with the management, engineering, operation and finance of railways world wide. Articles of practical interest on these subjects are considered and paid for if accepted. Illustrated articles, of 1000 to 3000 words, are preferred. A *preliminary letter* is desirable.

Railway Magazine (1897), Dorset House, Stamford Street, London, SE1 9LU *T.* 01-261 8000.
35p. M.—An illustrated magazine dealing with all railway subjects; not fiction. Articles from 1500 to 2000 words accompanied by photographs. A *preliminary letter* is desirable. No verse. *Payment:* by arrangement. *Illustrations:* colour transparencies, half-tone and line.

Railway World (founded as **Railways** 1939), Michael Harris, Ian Allan Ltd., Terminal House, Shepperton, Middlesex, TW17 8AS *T.* Walton-on-Thames 28950.
40p. M.—Articles on railway and allied matters. *Length:* 500 to 3000 words. *Payment:* by arrangement. *Illustrations:* line, half-tone and colour.

Reader's Digest, Michael Randolph (The Reader's Digest Association, Ltd.), 25 Berkeley Square, London, W1X 6AB *T.* 01-629 8144.
50p. M.—British articles, up to 5000 words should conform in theme and style to the high Reader's Digest standard. Payment, for world rights, from £750 upwards. Original anecdotes—£75 for up to 300 words—are also required for humorous features.

Records and Recording (1957), Cis Amaral, Hansom Books, P.O. Box 294, 2 & 4 Old Pye Street, off Strutton Ground, Victoria Street, London, SW1P 2LR *T.* 01-222 4112.
50p. M.—Complete coverage of classical music with surveys of jazz, folk, drama, spoken word, film and theatre music. Reviews and articles on recording and equipment. Commissioned articles only accepted. *Payment:* by arrangement.

Red Letter (D. C. Thomson & Co., Ltd.), Courier Place, Dundee, DD1 9QJ, and 185 Fleet Street, London, EC4A 2HS.
7p. W.—Serials of strong emotion; romantic, with movement and incident. First instalment 5000 words. Short stories 1000 to 4000 words. Real-life series. Articles of interest to girls and women. *Payment:* on acceptance. *Illustrations:* line or wash.

Red Star Weekly (D. C. Thomson & Co., Ltd.), Courier Place, Dundee, DD1 9QJ, and 185 Fleet Street, London, EC4A 2HS.
7p. W.—Serials up to 40,000 words with strong emotional dramatic incident. First instalment 5000 words. Short stories 1000 to 4000 words. True life series with strong emotional appeal. Good romantic interest essential. *Payment:* on acceptance.

Red Tape (1911), C. J. Bush, Civil and Public Services Association, 215 Balham High Road, London, SW17 7BQ *T.* 01-672 1299.
3p. M.—Well-written articles on Civil Service, trade union and general subjects considered. *Length:* 750 to 1400 words. Also photographs and humorous drawings of interest to Civil Servants. *Illustrations:* line and half-tone.

Reform (1972), Norman Hart, 86 Tavistock Place, London, WC1H 9RT *T.* 01-837 7661.
15p. Monthly published by United Reformed Church (Congregational-Presbyterian).—Articles of religious or social comment. *Length:* 600–1200 words. *Illustrations:* full colour, half-tone and line subjects. *Payment:* by arrangement.

Reveille, Cyril Kersh, 80 Fetter Lane, London, EC4A 1EE *T.* 01-353 0246.
12p. W.—Human interest non-fiction stories, features, series and pictures.
Humorous off beat shorts. Dramatic/amusing/glamour photographs.
Humorous pocket cartoons. *Payment:* good.

Riding: The Horseman's Magazine (1936), E. Hartley Edwards, King's Reach
Tower, Stamford Street, London, SE1 9LS *T.* 01-261 5487.
40p. M.—Instructive and formative articles on breeding, care and schooling of horses and ponies, on riding in general, hunting, polo, shows,
on outstanding horses and riders and their history. *Length:* 500 to 1500
words. *Payment:* agreed NUJ rates. *Illustrations:* photographs and drawings.

Round Table (1910), Alexander MacLeod, 18 Northumberland Avenue, London,
WC2N 5BJ *T.* 01-930 9993.
£8 p.a. Q.—A non-party quarterly review of world affairs, especially of the
politics of the British Commonwealth. All articles commissioned.

Royal Air Forces Quarterly (incorporating **Air Power**) (1961). Founded in 1930.
Air Vice-Marshal A. D. Button, c.b., o.b.e., r.a.f.(Retd.), Dragons, 23 Upper
Icknield Way, Aston Clinton, Aylesbury, Bucks, HP22 5NF *T.* 0296-
631015.
75p. Q. (£2.95 p.a. post free).—Articles concerning defence philosophy and
military air power of all nations. *Length:* up to 4500 words. Lighter
articles, aviation reminiscences, etc, up to 2500 words. *Payment:* up to £15
per article, according to quality and interest rather than length. *Illustrations:* photographs, line maps and drawings.

Royal British Legion Journal, The (1921), R. L. Pennells, Pall Mall, London,
SW1Y 5JY *T.* 01-930 8131.
10p. M.—Authoritative articles preferably with ex-Service interest (Army,
Air or Naval), also vignettes, features concerning British Legion. *Length:*
not more than 1000 words. *Payment:* £3.00 to £10.00. *Illustrations:* occasional cartoons and half-tones.

RUSI Journal (Journal of the Royal United Services Institute for Defence
Studies), Rear Admiral E. F. Gueritz, c.b., o.b.e., d.s.c., Whitehall, London,
SW1A 2ET *T.* 01-930 5854.
£2.50. Q.—Articles from 2000 to 5000 words on strategy, tactics, logistics
and defence technology; military sociology and the economics of defence;
moral ethics, disarmament and the behavioural sciences; current affairs
affecting British defence, and military history. *Illustrations:* maps or
diagrams in each issue. *Payment:* £10 per printed page.

Safety Education (1966; founded 1840 as **Safety Training**; 1940 became **Child
Safety**), David Larder, Royal Society for the Prevention of Accidents, Cannon House, The Priory Queensway, Birmingham, B4 6BS *T.* 021-233 2461.
90p. p.a. 3 times a year.—Articles on every aspect of safety for children
and in particular articles on the teaching of road, home, water and leisure
safety by means of established subjects on the school curriculum. All
ages. *Illustrations:* line, half-tone and colour.

Samphire (1968), Kemble Williams, Michael Butler, Heronshaw, Holbrook,
Ipswich, Suffolk. *T.* Holbrook 369.
35p. (£1.25 p.a.). 3 times p.a.—Poetry, reviews, articles on poetry. *Payment:*
from £3.00 per poem/page.

Sandwell Evening Mail (1975), J. Holland, Shaftesbury House, 402 High Street, West Bromwich. *T.* 021-553 7221. London office: 23–27 Tudor Street, London, EC4Y 0LA *T.* 01-353 0811.
6p. D. Independent.—Features of topical West Midland interest considered. *Length:* 400–800 words.

School Librarian (1937), Walter Ovens, Victoria House, 29–31 George Street, Oxford, OX1 2AY *T.* 0865-722746.
£2.25. Four times a year (£9.00 p.a. post free).—Official journal of the School Library Assoc. (free to members). *Payment:* by arrangement.

Science Progress, Professor D. Lewis, F.R.S., Professor J. M. Ziman, F.R.S. (Blackwell Scientific Publications, Ltd.), Osney Mead, Oxford, OX2 0EL *T.* Oxford 40201.
£4.50. Q. (£17.50 p.a.).—Articles of 5000 to 10,000 words suitably illustrated on scientific subjects, written so as to be intelligible to workers in other branches of science. *Payment:* £1.50 per printed page. *Illustrations*: line and half-tone.

Scoop (D. C. Thomson & Co. Ltd.), Courier House, Dundee, DD1 9QJ, and 185 Fleet Street, London, EC4A 2HS.
15p. W.—For Sports fans. Picture stories on sport, mainly football. Instalments 3–4 pp. 8–10 frames per page. Also sports photo features in colour and black and white. *Payment:* on acceptance.

Scots Magazine (1739) (D. C. Thomson and Co., Ltd.), Bank Street, Dundee, DD1 9HU *T.* Dundee 23131.
25p. M.—Articles on all subjects of Scottish interest. *Payment:* varies according to quality. *Illustrations:* colour and black and white photographs, and drawings.

Scotsman (1817), Eric B. Mackay, 20 North Bridge, Edinburgh. *T.* 031-225 2468. London Office: Greater London House, Hampstead Road, London, NW1 7SH *T.* 01-387 2800.
10p. D.—Independent. Considers articles, 1000–1200 words on political and economic themes, which add substantially to current information. Prepared to commission topical and controversial series from proved authorities. *Illustrations:* outstanding news and scenic pictures.

Scottish Educational Journal, 46 Moray Place, Edinburgh, EH3 6BH *T.* 031-225 7443.
12p. 16–20 issues p.a.—Published by the Educational Institute of Scotland. Articles of 1000 to 1500 words in length on matters affecting education or the professional interests of teachers are considered.

Scottish Farmer, The (1893), Angus MacDonald, 39 York Street, Glasgow, G2 8JL *T.* 041-221 7911–4. *T.A.* Farming, Glasgow.
18p. W.—Articles on agricultural subjects. *Length:* 1000–1500 words. *Payment:* by arrangement. *Illustrations:* line and half-tone.

Scottish Field (1903), Roderick Martine (Holmes-McDougall Ltd.), 12 York Street, Glasgow, G2 8LJ *T.* 041-221 7000.
40p. M.—The Editor is prepared to consider articles on all Scottish subjects. These should be 1000–2000 words in *length*. Articles accompanied by first class photographs are preferred. Suitable suggestions by known authors will be commissioned. *Payment:* usually by arrangement, but where articles are submitted direct, payment is according to the merit of the matter. Payment is made after publication.

Scottish Historical Review (Company of Scottish History, Ltd.)—Joint Editors: D. J. Withrington, Prof. G. W. S. Barrow. Distributed by Aberdeen University Press, Farmers Hall, Aberdeen, AB9 2XT *T.* (0224) 630724. £6 (£7.60 through booksellers). Twice-yearly.—Contributions to the advancement of knowledge in any aspect of Scottish history. *Length:* up to 10,000 words. *Payment:* none; contributors are given offprints. *Illustrations:* line and half-tone.

Scottish Home and Country (1924), Mrs. Jean Stewart, 24 Castle Street, Edinburgh, EH2 3HT *T.* 031-225 1934. 15p. M.—Articles of a practical nature, crafts, tales of experience. Articles about village or country customs, pen portraits of vanishing country people. *Length:* 1000 to 2500 words. *Payment:* £7.00 per 1000 words.

Scottish Review, The (Arts and Environment) (1975), The Scottish Civic Trust, Glasgow and the Saltire Society, Edinburgh, in association with The National Trust for Scotland, with the support of the Scottish Arts Council, 24 George Square, Glasgow, G2 1EF *T.* 041-221 1466. 65p. Articles on all subjects relating to the arts and environment in Scotland. *Payment:* £5 per page.

Scottish Tatler, The, David M. Keddie, 28 North Bridge, Edinburgh, EH1 1QG *T.* 031-226 3791. 60p. M.—Articles preferably accompanied by photographs on all Scottish subjects, descriptive or written from personal experience. Plus contributions on contemporary Scottish life. *Payment:* by arrangement. *Illustrations:* line and colour.

Scouting, Ron Jeffries, M.A.I.E., The Scout Association, Baden Powell House, Queens Gate, London, SW7 5JS *T.* 01-584 7030. 40p. M.—The National Magazine of The Scout Association. Articles of interest to Leaders and supporters, Venture Scouts and Patrol Leaders; Training material, accounts of Scouting events and articles of general interest within the field of youth activity. *Illustrations:* photographs of Scouting today. *Payment:* Normal rates for illustrations only.

Screen International, Peter Noble, Film House, 142 Wardour Street, London, W1V 4BR *T.* 01-734 9452. Published by King Publications Ltd. 40p. W.

Sea Angler (1973), Peter Collins, East Midland Allied Press, Oundle Road, Peterborough, PE2 9QR *T.* 61471. 40p. M.—Topical articles on all aspects of sea-fishing around the British Isles. *Payment:* £12.00 and upwards per 1000 words. *Illustrations:* line, half-tone and colour.

Sea Breezes (1919), Craig J. M. Carter, 213 Tower Building, 22 Water Street, Liverpool, L3 1LN *T.* 051-236 4511. 40p. M.—Short factual articles, on the sea, seamen and merchant and naval ships, preferably illustrated. *Payment:* by arrangement. *Illustrations:* half-tone, line.

Secrets (D. C. Thomson & Co. Ltd.), Courier Place, Dundee, DD1 9QJ, and 185 Fleet Street, London, EC4A 2HS. 7p. W.—Complete stories of 1500 to 5000 words, with mainly romantic interest to appeal to women of most ages. Serials, 5000 words instalments. *No preliminary letter* required. *Payment:* on acceptance.

Secrets Story Library (D. C. Thomson & Co., Ltd.), Courier Place, Dundee, DD1 9QJ, and 185 Fleet Street, London, EC4A 2HS.
8p. M.—64 pages. Exciting and romantic stories in text.

Selling Today, the official journal of the United Commercial Travellers' Association Section of ASTMS. Magazine Services: M. Whitaker, Bexton Lane, Knutsford, Cheshire, WA16 9DA *T.* Knutsford 4136–7.
£3.50 p.a. M.—Professional and Trade Union guidance in selling and the various fields of salesmanship, e.g., staple goods, selling to industry, specialities, merchandising, export selling, etc.; allied subjects; educational on the techniques and practices of selling. Articles on cars, motoring, marketing, economics, packaging, public speaking. *Length:* average 1000 words. *Payment:* by arrangement.

She (1955), Pamela Carmichael, Chestergate House, Vauxhall Bridge Road, London, SW1V 1HF *T.* 01-828 5153; 01-834 2331.
25p. M.—Fiction, up to 3000 words, or 1000 word twist-ending stories; no romance. Articles 1000 to 2500 words on all subjects except fashion and beauty; controversial, factual, medical, general interest rather than "feminine." First person experiences. Picture features welcome. *Payment:* from £26.50 per 1000 words. *Illustrations:* photos; cartoons.

Ship & Boat International, Gordon Irons, Pax Marine Press AB, S-150 30 Mariefred, Sweden. *T.* 0159 106-15.
£13.00 p.a. M.—Technical articles on the design, construction and operation of all types of specialised small ships and workboats. *Length:* 500–1500 words. *Payment:* by arrangement. *Illustrations:* line and half-tone, photographs and diagrams.

Ships Monthly (1966), Robert Shopland, Waterway Productions Ltd., Kottingham House, Dale Street, Burton-on-Trent, DE14 3TD *T.* 0283-64290.
45p. M.—Illustrated articles of maritime interest—both mercantile and naval. Well researched, factual material only. No short stories or poetry. *Payment:* by arrangement. *Illustrations:* half-tone and line, colour on cover only.

Shooting Times and Country Magazine (1882), W. A. Jackson (Burlington Publishing Co. (1942), Ltd.), 10 Sheet Street, Windsor, Berkshire, SL4 1BG *T.* Windsor (075-35) 56061.
30p. W.—Articles on field sports, natural history and the countryside not exceeding 1400 words. *Payment:* by arrangement. *Illustrations:* photographs and drawings.

Shop Fitting and Display (1955), G. Carroll, Link House, Dingwall Avenue, Croydon, CR9 2TA *T.* 01-686 2599.
50p. M. (£6.50 p.a. post free).—Reviews, features and news, preferably illustrated, of shop, store, and commercial premises design, display, planning, construction and fitting, services and lighting. *Length:* 750–1250 words (or longer by arrangement), or short paragraphs; features by arrangement. *Payment:* by arrangement. *Illustrations:* photographs, plans and sketches; colour transparencies.

Short Wave Magazine, The (1937), Paul Essery, G3KFE, 34 High Street, Welwyn, Herts, AL6 9EQ *T.* 04-3871 5206–7.
40p. M. (£5.50 p.a.).—Technical and semi-technical articles, 2000 to 10,000 words, dealing with the design, construction and operation of radio amateur short wave receiving and transmitting equipment. *Payment:* £10.00 per page. *Illustrations:* line and half-tone.

Sight and Sound (1932), Penelope Houston (Published by the British Film Institute), 127 Charing Cross Road, London, WC2H 0EA   *T.* 01-437 4355.
70p.   Q.—Topical and critical articles on the cinema of any country. Highly specialised articles only occasionally.   1000 to 6000 words.   *Payment:* by arrangement.   *Illustrations:* relevant photographs.

Sign, The (1905), A. R. Mowbray & Co. Ltd., Saint Thomas House, Becket Street, Oxford, OX1 1SJ   *T.* Oxford 42507.
3p.   M.—Leading national inset for C. of E. parish magazines.   Unusual b. & w. photos, drawings considered.   *Payment:* by arrangement.   Items should bear the author's name and address, and sufficient stamps should accompany contributions for return where necessary.

Signature (1953), Morag Campbell, Diners Club Ltd., Diners Club House, Kingsmead, Farnborough, Hants.   *T.* (0252) 516261.
20p.   Bi-M.—Articles (not travel) on subjects likely to appeal to male readership director level.   Sophisticated humour particularly required but no cartoons.   No fiction.   *Length:* 1200–1800 words.   *Payment:* £20.00 per 1000 words.   *Illustrations:* colour and half-tone; *payment:* £15.00 for colour transparencies, £10.00 for black and white.

600 Magazine (1926), House Journal of The 600 Group Limited, Wood Lane, London, W12 7RL   *T.* 01-743 2070.
High quality satire and humour—informed and original articles in lively vein likely to interest intelligent business and professional readership. *Length:* 750–2000 words.   *Payment:* for full assignment of copyright dependent on quality and name.   Subtle cartoons and anecdotes always welcome for consideration; also brief filler paragraphs.

Slimmer Magazine (1972), Judith Wills, Spencer House, 23 Dartmouth Row, London, SE10 8AW   *T.* 01-691 2888.
30p.   Bi-M.—Articles of interest to people interested in health, nutrition, slimming.   *Length:* 500 to 1500 words.   *Payment:* £35–£50 per 1000 words (s.a.e. essential).

Social Service Quarterly (1947), National Council of Social Service, 26 Bedford Square, London, WC1B 3HU   *T.* 01-636 4066.
60p. plus postage.   Q.—Authoritative articles up to 2000 words on current social policy and community action.   Also book review section.   *Payment:* by arrangement.

Sociological Review, Managing Editors: W. M. Williams and Ronald Frankenberg University of Keele, Keele, Staffs., ST5 5BG   *T.* Newcastle under Lyme 621111.
£9.20; $23.00.   Q.—Articles of up to 6000 words treating social subjects in a scientific way.   No *payment* is made.   *Illustrations:* line.

Solicitors' Journal, The (1857), Norwich House, 11–13 Norwich Street, London, EC4A 1AB   *T.* 01-404 5721.
28p.   W.—Articles, preferably by practising solicitors on subjects of practical interest, are invited.   Articles should not generally exceed 2000 words.

Spaceflight (1956), K. W. Gatland, 10 Brook Mead, Ewell, Epsom, Surrey, KT19 0BD   *T.* 01-393 1030.   Published by The British Interplanetary Society. Free to members.   £1.00 to non-members.   M.—Articles up to 5000 words dealing with topics of astronomy, rocket engineering and astronautics.   *Illustrations:* line and half-tone.   *Payment:* none.

Spare Rib, 27 Clerkenwell Close, London, EC1R 0AT.
35p. M. (£5.00 p.a.).—Features, news, fiction, cartoons. *Illustrations:* black and white with second colour drawings; black and white photographs.

Special Education: Forward Trends, Official Journal of the National Council for Special Education. Margaret Peter, 12 Hollycroft Avenue, London, NW3 7QL *T.* 01-794 7109.
£4.00 p.a. (£8.00 institutions). Q.—Articles by specialists on the education of the physically, mentally and emotionally handicapped, including the medical, therapeutic and sociological aspects of special education. *Length:* about 2000 to 3000 words. *Payment:* by arrangement. *Illustrations:* half-tone and line.

Spectator (1828), Alexander Chancellor, 56 Doughty Street, London, WC1N 2LL *T.* 01-405 1706.
25p. W.—Articles of a suitable character will always be considered. The rate of *payment* depends upon the nature and length of the article.

Speech and Drama (1951), Kenneth Pickering, Society of Teachers of Speech and Drama, 211b Old Dover Road, Canterbury, Kent, CT1 3ER.
£2.50 p.a. Three issues yearly.—Specialist articles only. *Length:* from 3000 words. The publication covers the field of Speech and Drama in Education. Preliminary letter essential. *Payment:* none. No *illustrations.*

Spiritualist Gazette (1972), Tom Johanson, S.A.G.B. Ltd., 33 Belgrave Square, London, S.W.1. *T.* 01-235 3351.
£1.80 p.a. (£2.00 abroad; $8.50 USA) post free. M.—Spiritualism, Healing, Life after Death and allied subjects.

Spoken English (1968), Jocelyn Bell, English Speaking Board (International), 32 Roe Lane, Southport, Merseyside, PR9 9EA *T.* Southport 34587.
£3.25 p.a., 3 times a year.—Articles on all aspects of oral English and drama at all levels of education and of a serious nature. Overseas as well as United Kingdom. *Length:* from 1000 words. *Payment:* by arrangement.

Sport and Recreation (1949), Reginald Moore, The Sports Council, 70 Brompton Road, London, SW3 1EX *T.* 01-589 3411.
20p. Q.—Articles on various sports, physical education and outdoor activities. *Length:* 1000–2000 words. *Payment:* by arrangement. *Illustrated.* Sports photographers encouraged.

Sporting Life, The, O. W. Fletcher (Mirror Group Newspapers Ltd.), 9 New Fetter Lane, London, EC4A 1AR *T.* 01-353 0246. *T.A.* Sportinglife, London, EC4.
20p. D.

Stage and Television Today, The (1880), Peter Hepple (The Stage) and Edward Durham Taylor (Television Today), Stage House, 47 Bermondsey Street, London, SE1 3XT *T.* 01-403 1818.
10p. W.—Original and interesting articles on professional stage and television topics may be sent for the Editor's consideration, 500–800 words. *Illustrations:* line and half-tone.

Stamp Collecting, George C. Beal, Stamp Collecting Ltd., 42 Maiden Lane, Strand, London, WC2E 7LL *T.* 01-836 2684 and 01-240 2286.
20p. W.—Articles or notes of interest to stamp collectors, 500 to 2000 words. *Payment:* £10.00 per 1000 words or by arrangement for special commissions. *Illustrations:* half-tone up to 100 screen and line.

Stamp Lover (1908), Publisher: National Philatelic Society, 1 Whitehall Place, London, SW1A 2HE *T.* 01-839 1987. Editor: Philip Halward, F.R.P.S.L.
60p. Q.—Organ of the National Philatelic Society and material is mostly contributed by members. Technical articles only. *Length:* up to 4000 words. Rates average £2.10 per 1000. *Illustrations:* half-tone (100 screen) and line.

Stamp Magazine (1934) Richard West, Link House, Dingwall Avenue, Croydon, CR9 2TA *T.* 01-686 2599. *T.A.* Aviculture, Croydon.
45p. M.—Informative articles and exclusive news items on stamp collecting and postal history. *No preliminary letter.* *Payment:* by arrangement. *Illustrations:* photographs, half-tone and line.

Stamp Monthly, Russell Bennett, Drury House, Russell Street, London, WC2B 5HD *T.* 01-836 8444.
40p. M. (£6.70 p.a.).—Articles on philatelic topics. Previous reference to the editor advisable. *Length:* 500 to 2500 words. *Payment:* according to value of the contribution, £8.00 per 1000 words and up. *Illustrations:* photographs.

Stand (1952) Jon Silkin, Lorna Tracy, A. G. Jones, Ed Brunner, Robert Ober, Michael Wilding, Howard Fink, Ian Wedde, Neil Astley, 19 Haldane Terrace, Jesmond, Newcastle on Tyne, NE2 3AN *T.* Newcastle 812614.
67p. post free. Q. (£2.70 p.a.).—Short stories, literary criticism, art criticism, social criticism, poetry, theatre, cinema, and music. *Payment:* £7.00 per 1000 words of prose; £6.00 for poetry. S.A.E. for return.

Star, The (1887) (formerly **Yorkshire Telegraph and Star**), D. Flynn, York Street, Sheffield, S1 1PU T. 78585. London: 23–27 Tudor Street, EC4. *T.* 01-583 9199.
7p. D.—Well-written articles of local character. *Length:* about 800 words. *Payment:* according to values. *Illustrations:* topical photographs, and line drawings.

Star Love Stories (D. C. Thomson & Co., Ltd.), Albert Square, Dundee, DD1 9QJ, and 185 Fleet Street, London, EC4A 2HS.
9p. Four each month.—Romantic and emotional stories told in pictures. 63 pages, about 140 pictures, line illustrations. Script writers and promising artists encouraged. Synopsis required as an opener. *Payment:* on acceptance.

Stud & Stable (1961), Major Peter Towers-Clark, 59 High Street, Ascot, Berkshire, SL5 7HP *T.* Ascot 25925.
90p. M. (£13.00 p.a.).—Articles and illustrations of interest to the horse racing and breeding world. *Payment:* £20.00 per 1000 words.

Studies in Comparative Religion, F. Clive-Ross, Perennial Books Ltd., Pates Manor, Bedfont, Middlesex, TW14 8JP *T.* 01-890 2790.
90p. Q.—Articles on comparative religion, metaphysics, traditional studies, eastern religions, mysticism, holy places, etc. *Length:* 2000–4000 words.

Studio International (1893), Richard Cork, The Studio Trust, 25 Denmark Street, London, WC2H 8NJ *T.* 01-836 0767–8.
£2.00. M.—An international magazine dealing with the contemporary fine arts. *Remarks:* only *illustrated* articles and notes accepted. A *preliminary letter* is desirable. *Payment:* by arrangement. *Illustrations:* reproductions of paintings, sculpture, drawings, engravings, applied art, etc.

Studio Sound (1959), Angus Robertson, Link House, Dingwall Avenue, Croydon, CR9 2TA *T.* 01-686 2599. *Telex:* 947709 Linkho G. *T.A.* Aviculture, Croydon.
60p. M.—Articles on all aspects of professional sound recording. Technical and operational features on the functional aspects of studio equipment: general features on studio affairs. *Length:* widely variable. *Payment:* by arrangement. *Illustrations:* line and half-tone.

Sun, The (1969), Editorial Director and Editor: Larry Lamb; News Group Newspapers Ltd., 30 Bouverie Street, London, EC4Y 8DE *T.* 01-353 3030. *T.A.* Sunnews, London.
6p. D.

Sunday Express (1918), John Junor, Fleet Street, London, EC4. *T.* 01-353 8000.
15p. W.—Pays highest price in journalism for exclusive news, photographs, and articles by and about the leading thinkers and personalities of the world. Signed articles should be 900 to 1200 words.

Sunday Mail, Clive Sandground, Anderston Quay, Glasgow, G3 8DA T. 041-248 7000. London Office: 33 Holborn Circus, EC1P 1DQ.
12p. W.—Exclusive stories and pictures (in colour if possible) of national and Scottish interest. *Payment:* above average.

Sunday Mercury and **Weekly Post,** P. W. Slade, Colmore Circus, Birmingham, B4 6AZ *T.* 021-236 3366.
12p. W.—News specials or features of Midland interest. Any black-and-white *illustrations.* Special rates for special matter.

Sunday Mirror (1915) Robert Edwards, 33 Holborn, London, EC1P 1DQ *T.* 01-353 0246.
14p. W.—Concentrates on human interest news features, social documentaries, dramatic news and feature photographs. Ideas, as well as articles, bought. *Payment:* high, especially for exclusives.

Sunday News, Patrick J. Carville, 51–59 Donegall Street, Belfast, BT1 2GB *T.* Belfast 44441.
12p. W.—General topical articles of 500 words. *Payment:* £14.00 to £18.00 per 500 words approx. *Illustrations:* line and half-tone.

Sunday People, Geoffrey Pinnington (Odhams Newspapers Ltd.), Orbit House, 9 New Fetter Lane, London, EC4A 1AR *T.* 01-353 0246.
14p. W.—A Sunday paper for all classes of readers. Features, single articles and series, considered. Pictures should be supplied with contributions if possible. Features should be of deep human interest, whether the subject is serious or light-hearted. The first investigative newspaper, the People is particularly noted for its exposures of social evils, criminal activities, financial and other rackets and bureaucratic malpractices, in the public interest. Very strong sports following. Exclusive news and news-feature stories also considered. Rates of *payment* high, even for tips that lead to published news stories.

Sunday Post (D. C. Thomson & Co., Ltd.), 144 Port Dundas Road, Glasgow, G4 0HZ, Courier Place, Dundee, DD1 9QJ, and 185 Fleet Street, London, EC4A 2HS *T.* (Glasgow) 041-332 9933; (Dundee) 0382 23131; (London) 01-353 2586–8.
10p. W.—Human interest, topical, domestic, and humorous articles and exclusive news; and short stories up to 2000 words. *Illustrations:* humorous drawings. *Payment:* on acceptance.

Sunday Sun, The (1919), Malcolm Armstrong, Thomson House, Groat Market, Newcastle, NE99 1BO *T.* Newcastle 27500.
10p. W.—Immediate topicality and human sidelights on current problems are the keynote of the SUN's requirements. Particularly welcomed are special features of family appeal and news stories of special interest to the North of England. Photographs used to illustrate articles. *Length:* 500 to 1200 words. *Payment:* normal lineage rates, or by arrangement. *Illustrations:* photographs and line.

Sunday Telegraph, John Thompson, 135 Fleet Street, London, EC4P 4BL *T.* 01-353 4242.
16p. W.

Sunday Times, The (1822), Harold Evans, 200 Gray's Inn Road, London, WC1X 8EZ *T.* 01-837 1234.
22p. W.—Special articles by authoritative writers on politics, literature, art, drama, music, finance and science, and topical matters. Top payment for exclusive features. *Illustrations:* first-class photographs of topical interest and pictorial merit very welcome, especially sets in colour; also topical drawings.

Sunday Times Magazine, Ron Hall, 200 Gray's Inn Road, London, WC1X 8EZ *T.* 01-837 1234. *T.A.* Sunday Times, London, WC1.
Free with paper. W.—Articles and pictures. *Payment:* £65 per 1000 words. *Illustrations:* colour photographs; *payment* £65 per page.

Sussex Life (1965), F. J. Nixon, South Eastern Magazines Ltd, 109 Week Street, Maidstone.
40p. M.—Historical and other articles about Sussex. All MSS must have a Sussex connection. *Length:* normally 750–1250 words, but shorter items such as humorous anecdotes, sayings, etc., also considered. Sharp black and white pictures or good sketches preferred with articles. *Payment:* by arrangement. *Illustrations:* half-tone or line drawings, or full colour from transparencies or original artwork.

Swimming Pool (1960), M. Cope, Clarke & Hunter (London), Ltd., 61 London Road, Staines, Middlesex, TW18 4BN *T.* Staines 61326.
75p. Bi-M.—Articles on design, construction and maintenance of Swimming Pools for Municipal, School and Private Ownership. *Length:* 750 to 1500 words. *Payment:* from £15.00 per 1000 words. *Illustrations:* line and half-tone. Cartoons.

Tablet, The (1840), T. F. Burns, 48 Great Peter Street, London, SW1P 2HB *T.* 01-222 7462.
28p. W.—The oldest organ of the Roman Catholic Church in England, which contains news of the week, articles on topics of the day, notes, reviews, almost all written by experts. Freelance work welcomed. Articles should not exceed 1500 words. *Payment:* by arrangement.

Tammy, King's Reach Tower, Stamford Street, London, SE1 9LS *T.* 01-261 5000.
8p. W.—A picture-story paper for schoolgirls. Most of contents commissioned, but the Editor is always interested to see ideas and picture scripts by authors who have made a close study of the paper.

Target, merged into **TV Comic,** *q.v.*

TAVR Magazine, The (formerly **The Territorial Magazine**), Henry Howell, Centre Block, Duke of York's Headquarters, Chelsea, London, SW3 4SG *T.* 01-730 6122.
20p. M. (£2.40 p.a. post free).—Material required: brightly written articles on Reserve Forces subjects. *Length:* 400 to 1500 words. *Payment:* by arrangement. *Illustrations:* original photographs (black and white only), line drawings.

Teacher, The (1872), Peter Singer, Hamilton House, Hastings Street, London, WC1. *T.* 01-388 1952.
4p. W.—The official journal of the National Union of Teachers; News of current educational events. Features on teaching method and practice, preferably related to the teaching of a particular subject or age-range, and written from personal experience. *Length:* up to 1000 words. *Payment:* by arrangement. *Illustrations:* photographs and line drawings to accompany educational news items and articles. Cartoons.

Telegraph Sunday Magazine (formerly **The Daily Telegraph Magazine**) (1964), John Anstey, 135 Fleet Street, London, EC4P 4BL *T.* 01-353 4242. *T.A.* Teleweek London.
Free with the paper. W.—Articles of general interest, short stories, opinions. *Payment:* £80 per 1000 words. *Illustrations:* all types. *Payment for Illustrations:* dependent on the feature requirements. *Photographs* £100 colour page, £80 black and white minimum.

Television (1950), IPC Magazines Ltd., King's Reach Tower, Stamford Street, London, SE1 9LS *T.* 01-261 5752.
50p. M.—Articles on the technical aspects of domestic television sets; long distance television; constructional projects; video games; video recording, viewdata; test equipment. *Illustrations:* photographs and line drawings for litho. *Payment:* according to subject and quality, from £20 per 1000 words, plus extra for illustrations.

Tempo, Editor-in-Chief: David Drew, Managing Editor: Calum MacDonald (Boosey & Hawkes, Music Publishers, Ltd.), 295 Regent Street, London, W1R 8JH *T.* 01-580 2060.
50p. Q. (£2.59 p.a.).—Articles about 3000 to 5000 words invited which deal authoritatively with contemporary music. *Payment:* by arrangement. *Illustrations:* music type.

Tennis (1926 as **Lawn Tennis**), C. M. Jones, Golf World Associates Ltd., 41 Maltby Street, London, SE1 3PA *T.* 01-237 0043.
45p. M.—Unusual features about tennis, not about current events. *Payment:* N.U.J. Freelance rates. *Illustrations:* Half-tone and full colour transparencies.

Tennis World, Robin Davison-Lungley. Publisher: Mark H. McCormack, 183–185 Askew Road, London, W12 9AX *T.* 01-743 7501.
40p. 10 times p.a.—Tournament reports, topical features, personality profiles, instructional articles. *Length:* 600 to 1500 words. *Payment:* by arrangement. *Illustrations:* colour, black and white, line.

Thames Poetry (1976), A. A. Cleary, 160 High Road, Wealdstone, Harrow, Middlesex, HA3 7AX.
90p. Twice yearly.—Poetry and poetry criticism. *Payment:* by arrangement.

Theatre Quarterly (1971), Simon Trussler, 44 Earlham Street, London, WC2 9LA
  T. 01-836 1477.
  £2.50.   Q.—Articles, practical information and reference material covering
  all aspects of live theatre.   An informed, factual and serious—though not
  solemn—approach essential.   Submission of synopsis and preliminary discussion desirable. *Length:* 2000 to 10,000 words. *Payment:* by arrangement.   *Illustrations:* line and half-tone.   Also **British Theatrelog** and
  International Theatrelog. Both Q.—Classified diaries of British and International theatre events. **Theatre Checklist.** Q.—Full of biographical,
  bibliographical and performing information on major playwrights.

Theology (1920), John Drury, 26 The Close, Norwich, NR1 4DZ.
  90p.   Bi-M.—Articles and reviews on theology, ethics, Church and Society.
  Length: not exceeding 3500 words. *Payment:* only by arrangement.

Third Way (1977), Derek Williams, 19 Draycott Place, London, SW3 2SJ *T.*
  01-581 0051.
  30p.   Fortnightly.—Aims to present a biblical perspective on a wide range
  of current issues, e.g. sociology, politics, education, economics, industry,
  and the arts. *Payment:* on publication.

This England (1968), Roy Faiers, P.O. Box 52, Cheltenham, Gloucestershire,
  GL50 1HT *T.* 35185.
  90p.   Q.—Articles on towns, villages, traditions, customs, legends, crafts of
  England; stories of people. *Length:* 250 to 3000 words. *Payment:* £7 per
  page. *Illustrations:* line, half-tone, colour.

Thoroughbred & Classic Cars, Michael Bowler, Dorset House, Stamford Street,
  London, SE1 9LU *T.* 01-261 8288. *T.A.* Bisnespres, London 25137.
  50p.   M.—Specialist articles on older cars. *Length:* from 1000 to 4000
  words (subject to prior contract). *Payment:* £25 per page approx. *Illustrations:* half-tone and colour.

Tiger and Scorcher (1954), King's Reach Tower, Stamford Street, London, SE1
  9LS *T.* 01-261 5000.
  8p.   W.—Scripts for picture stories of sport, suitable for boys of 8 to 15
  years of age.

Time and Tide, Ian Lyon, 14 Bolton Street, London, W1Y 7PA *T.* 01-493 2283.
  30p.   M.—Independent. Has now been developed as a world news magazine. Welcomes exclusive, authentic news and photographs of people, and
  personal stories of business success.

Times, The (1785), William Rees-Mogg, P.O. Box 7, New Printing House Square,
  Gray's Inn Road, London, WC1X 8EZ *T.* 01-837 1234.
  15p.   D.—Independent. Outside contributions considered from (1) experts
  in subjects of current interest: (2) writers who can make first-hand experience
  or reflection come readably alive. Best *length:* up to 1200 words. *No preliminary letter* is required.

Times Educational Supplement, The, Stuart Maclure, P.O. Box 7, New Printing
  House Square, Gray's Inn Road, London, WC1X 8EZ *T.* 01-837 1234.
  18p.   W.—Articles on education (not exceeding 1200 words) written with
  special knowledge or experience. News items. *Illustrations:* suitable
  photographs and drawings of educational interest.

Times Educational Supplement Scotland (1965), Willis Pickard, 56 Hanover Street, Edinburgh, EH2 2DZ *T.* 031-225 6393.
18p. W.—Articles on education, preferably 1100 words, written with special knowledge or experience. News items about Scottish educational affairs. *Illustrations:* line and half-tone.

Times Higher Education Supplement (1971), Peter Scott, P.O. Box 7, New Printing House Square, Gray's Inn Road, London, WC1X 8EZ *T.* 01-837 1234.
20p. W.—Articles on higher education (not exceeding 1500 words) written with special knowledge or experience or articles dealing with academic topics. News items. *Illustrations:* suitable photographs and drawings of educational interest.

Times Literary Supplement, The, John Gross, P.O. Box 7, New Printing House Square, Gray's Inn Road, London WC1X 8EZ *T.* 01-837 1234.
25p. W.—General articles of literary interest are welcomed.

Today's Guide, Official Monthly of the Girl Guides Association, Mrs. J. V. Rush, 17–19 Buckingham Palace Road, London, SW1W 0PT *T.* 01-834 6242.
20p. M.—Articles of interest to Guides (aged 10–15) and general interest topics. Serials and short stories with Guiding background (800 words per instalments). Cartoons. *Payment:* £10.00 per 1000 words. *Illustrations:* line, and half-tone.

Together (1956), Church Information Office, Church House, Dean's Yard, London, SWIP 3NZ *T.* 01-222 9011. Editor: Mrs Pamela Egan, Church of England Board of Education, Church House, Dean's Yard, London SW1P 3NZ.
24p. 9 issues p.a.—Short, practical or topical articles dealing with all forms of children's religious education or concerned with the development and psychology of children. *Illustrations:* half-tone and line. *Length:* up to 1200 words. *Payment:* by arrangement.

Topper, The (D. C. Thomson & Co., Ltd.), Courier Place, Dundee, DD1 9QJ, and 185 Fleet Street, London, EC4A 2HS.
7p. W.—All-picture paper for children. Comic strip series, in sets of 6–18 pictures each. Picture stories of 10–20 pictures per instalment. Special encouragement to promising writers and artists. *Payment:* on acceptance.

Town and Country Planning (Journal of the Town and Country Planning Association), Derek Diamond, 17 Carlton House Terrace, London, SW1Y 5AH *T.* 01-930 8903–5.
80p. M. (£8.00 p.a.).—Informative articles on town and country planning, regional planning, land use, new towns, green belts, countryside preservation, homes and gardens, and industrial, business and social life in great and small towns, environment in general. *Length:* 250 to 1500 words. *Payment:* by arrangement. *Illustrations:* photographs and drawings.

Townswoman, Gwenllian Parrish, 2 Cromwell Place, London, SW7 2JG *T.* 01-589 8817/8/9.
10p. M.—Official journal of the National Union of Townswomen's Guilds. Lively, informative general articles and reports on work of Townswomen's Guilds. *Length:* 800–1200 words. Priority to T.G. members. *Illustrations:* half-tone and line.

Trefoil, The, Miss T. Scarffe, Official Journal of the Trefoil Guild, C.H.Q., The Girl Guides Association, 17–19 Buckingham Palace Road, London, SW1W 0PT *T.* 01-828 7610.
10p. Q.—Articles on careers for women, on the work of voluntary organisations and on subjects of topical interest. *Length:* not longer than 1400 words. Photographs. No fiction. No *Payment.*

Tribune, Richard Clements, 24 St John Street, London, EC1. *T.* 01-253 2094.
20p. W.—Political, literary, with Socialist outlook. Informative articles (about 800 words), short political notes (250–300 words). *Payment:* by arrangement. *Illustrations:* cartoons and photographs.

Trout and Salmon (1955), Roy Eaton, East Midland Allied Press, 21 Church Walk, Peterborough, PE1 2TW *T.* 63100. *Telex:* 32157.
45p. M.—Articles of good quality with strong trout or salmon angling interest. *Length:* 400 to 1500 words, accompanied if possible by photographs. *Payment:* good: minimum £15.00 per 1000 words. *Illustrations:* half-tone, four-colour cover.

True Magazine, Pamela Lyons, King's Reach Tower, Stamford Street, London, SE1 9LS *T.* 01-261 5692.
30p. M.—First person complete stories and serials reflecting human problems and situations of strong emotional interest; 2000–5500 words. Some verse. *Payment:* by arrangement.

True Romances, Mrs. M. Dean, 12–18 Paul Street, London, EC2A 4JS *T.* 01-247 8233.
35p. M.—First-person true stories with strong love interest. *Length:* 1500 to 5000 words. *Payment:* by arrangement, on acceptance.

True Story, Mrs. M. Dean, 12–18 Paul Street, London, EC2A 4JS *T.* 01-247 8233.
35p. M.—First-person true stories with strong love interest. *Length:* 1500 to 5000 words. *Payment:* by arrangement, on acceptance.

TV Comic, Robin Tucek, Polly Perkins House, 382–386 Edgware Road, London, W2 1EP *T.* 01-723 3022.
10p. W.—Mainly TV based picture strips. Commissioned work only (artwork and scripts). *Payment:* by arrangement.

TVTimes, Peter Jackson, 247 Tottenham Court Road, London, W1P 0AU *T.* 01-636 1599.
13p. W.—Features with an affinity to ITV programmes and personalities and television generally. *Length:* from 500 words or by arrangement. *Photographs:* only those of outstanding quality. *Payment:* by arrangement. Cartoons £10.

Twinkle (D. C. Thomson & Co., Ltd.), Courier Place, Dundee, DD1 9QJ, and 185 Fleet Street, London, EC4A 2HS.
8p. W.—Picture stories, features and comic strips, specially for little girls. Drawings in line or colour for gravure. *Payment:* on acceptance. Special encouragement to promising writers and artists.

Ulsterman (1975), Ken Lindsay, 10 Brown's Road, Newtownabbey, Co. Antrim, BT36 8RN *T.* Glengormley 2362.
10p. M.—Independent. News, features and cartoons on all aspects of contemporary Ulster. *Payment:* by arrangement. *Illustrations:* line, half-tone.

Un-Common Sense (1945) (incorporating **Progress** 1956) (formerly **Christian Party News Letter** 1943), Ronald S. Mallone, B.A., F.R.G.S., M.R.S.T., Woolacombe House, 141 Woolacombe Road, Blackheath, London, SE3. *T.* 01-856 6249.
12p. M.—Published by The Loverseed Press. Factual news articles (450 to 750 words) especially foreign affairs of international significance; cinema, books, art, politics, religion, drama, cricket, opera, poems, essays. New writers considered. *Payment:* £2.10 per 1000 words. *Illustrations:* photographs, line drawings.

Unesco Courier, The (1948), R. Caloz, Unesco, 7 Place de Fontenoy, Paris 75700. *T.* 577 16 10. *T.A.* Unesco, Paris.
£4.80 p.a. M.—Illustrated feature articles on scientific, cultural and educational subjects; promotion of international understanding; mass communication; human rights; first-hand accounts of ways of life—children and adults—in other lands. *Length:* 2000 words. *Payment:* £100.00 maximum. *Illustrations:* photographs, sometimes line drawings.

Universe, The (1860), Jack Walsh, Universe House, 21 Fleet Street, London, EC4Y 1AP *T.* 01-583 8383. *T.A.* Unicredo, London.
12p. W.—A newspaper and review for Catholics. News stories, features and photographs on all aspects of Catholic life required. MSS should not be submitted without stamped envelope. *Payment:* by arrangement.

Use of English, The, Christopher Parry (Hart Davis Educational), Frogmore, St. Albans, Hertfordshire, AL2 2NF *T.* St. Albans (0727) 72727.
£1.50. 3 issues p.a. (£3.75 p.a.).—For teachers in all fields of English in Great Britain and overseas. *Length:* usually up to 3000 words. *Payment:* £4.00 per 1000 words.

Victor (D. C. Thomson & Co., Ltd.), Courier Place, Dundee, DD1 9QJ, and 185 Fleet Street, London, EC4A 2HS.
7p. W.—Vigorous, well-drawn stories in pictures (line drawings) for boys and young men. War, adventure, Western, sport. Instalments 2, 3 or 4 pages; 8 to 10 frames per page. *Payment* on acceptance.

Video & Audio-Visual Review (1974), David Kirk, Link House, Dingwall Avenue, Croydon, CR9 2TA *T.* 01-686 2599. *Telex:* 947709 Linkho G.
50p. M.—Articles on all aspects of audio-visual aids. Features on practical applications and unusual uses of cctv and video tape equipment are particularly welcome. *Length:* 2000 to 3000 words. *Payment:* on acceptance; good rates. *Illustrations:* line and half-tone.

Visual Education (1950), Ros Hawkins, National Committee for Audio-Visual Aids in Education, 254 Belsize Road, London, NW6 4BY *T.* 01-624 8812.
50p. M (11 issues per year including Yearbook) (£5.80, U.K., £6.50 overseas).—Articles and news items on all aspects of audio-visual media and their use in schools, colleges and universities. Also monthly reviews of equipment, films, filmstrips, books and other teaching aids. *Length:* 1500 to 2000 words. *Payment:* by arrangement. *Illustrations:* line and half-tone.

Vogue, Beatrix Miller, Vogue House, Hanover Square, London, W1R 0AD *T.* 01-499 9080. *T.A.* Volon, London, W1.
75p. 16 issues yearly.—Fashion, beauty, decorating, art, theatre, films, literature, music, travel, cooking. Articles from 1000 words.

Vole (1977), Richard Boston, 20 Fitzroy Square, London, W1. T. 01-486 7718.
60p. M.—Well researched features on literary and environmental topics or
news. *Length:* up to 2000 words. *Payment:* £30 per 1000 words. *Illustrations:* line.

Voyager (1973), Ken Buggy, Trent Press (Nottingham) Ltd., 148 Gregory Boulevard, Nottingham, NG7 5JE T. 0602-708069. *Telex:* 377 837.
Distributed free to all passengers aboard British Midland Airways scheduled
and charter flights. Four times a year. High quality and upbeat material
for an intelligent readership. Articles about food and drink, sports, art,
industry, etc. Articles must be relevant to the area served by BMA, notably
France, Germany, Holland, Belgium, Ireland, Channel Islands, Great Britain
(particularly the Midlands) and European holiday areas. *Not* required are
poetry, jokes. *Payment:* by arrangement. *Illustrations:* colour, black-and-white.

War Cry (1879), Official Organ of The Salvation Army. Lieut.-Colonel Wesley
Harris, 101 Queen Victoria Street, London, EC4P 4EP T. 01-236 5222.
5p. W. (£5.98 p.a. UK and Overseas).—Voluntary contributions, mostly
by Salvationists. Photographs.

War Picture Library (1958), IPC Magazines Ltd., King's Reach Tower, Stamford
Street, London, SE1 9LS T. 01-261 5000.
12p. Twelve each month.—All picture war stories. Artists and authors
invited to submit sample work to the Editor.

Warlord (D. C. Thomson & Co. Ltd.) Courier Place, Dundee, DD1 9QJ and 185
Fleet Street, London, EC4 2HS.
8p. W.—Picture stories in line for boys. Subject: War. Instalments, 2–4
pages, 8–10 frames per page, also special war features. *Payment:* on
acceptance.

Warwickshire and Worcestershire Life (including **West Midlands**), D. J. N.
Green, 27 Waterloo Place, Leamington Spa, Warwickshire, CV32 5LF T.
Leamington Spa 22003 and 22372. A member of the Whitehorn Press
Group.
30p. M.—Articles of interest to the counties concerned based on first-hand
experience dealing with work, customs and matters affecting urban and rural
welfare. *Length:* 500 to 1500 words. *Payment:* by arrangement. Photographs also by arrangement. *Illustrations:* preference given to articles
accompanied by good photographs relating to subject.

Waterways World (1972), Robert Shopland, Kottingham House, Dale Street,
Burton-on-Trent, Staffordshire, DE14 3TD T. 0283 64290.
40p. M.—Feature articles on all aspects of inland waterways in Britain and
abroad, including historical material. Factual and technical articles preferred. No short stories or poetry. *Payment:* by arrangement. *Illustrations:* line and half-tone, colour cover.

Weekend, David Hill, Northcliffe House, London, EC4Y 0JA T. 01-353 6000.
13p. W.—Factual articles appealing to men and women, true-life dramas,
short stories (500 to 1000 words) with plenty of atmosphere. *Payment:* by
arrangement. *Illustrations:* mono and colour action photographs, glamour,
cartoons.

Weekly News, The (D. C. Thomson and Co., Ltd.), Courier Place, Dundee, DD1 9QJ *T*. 23131; 139 Chapel Street, Manchester, M3 6AA *T*. 061-834 2831– 7; 144 Port Dundas Road, Glasgow, G4 0HZ *T*. 041-332 9933; and 185 Fleet Street, London, EC4A 2HS *T*. 01-242 5086.
8p. W.—Real-life drama of around 2000 words and told in the first person. Short stories with domestic or emotional slant. Non-fiction series with lively themes or about interesting people. Keynote throughout is strong human interest. Joke sketches. *Payment:* on acceptance.

WES Journal formerly **Pneu Journal** (1890), Charles Smyth, O.B.E., Parents' National Education Union, Murray House, Vandon Street, London, SW1H 0AJ *T*. 01-222 7181.
65p. (£2.50 p.a.). Q.—Journal of the Parents' National Educational Union. Articles on education, psychology, teaching methods and children's activities within the age-range 3–16. Feature articles preferably related to children or parents of the PNEU movement. *Length:* 1000–2000 words. *Payment:* by arrangement.

West Africa, K. T. Mackenzie, Bath House, 53 Holborn Viaduct, London, EC1A 2FD *T*. 01-236 3381.
18p. W.—A weekly summary of West African news, with articles on political, economic and commercial matters, and on all matters of general interest affecting West Africa. Also book reviews. Covers Ghana, Nigeria, Sierra Leone, The Gambia, French-speaking African States, former Portuguese West Africa, Liberia and Zaire. Articles about 1200 words. *Payment:* as arranged. *Illustrations:* photographs, black-and-white.

Western Mail (1869), Duncan Gardiner, Thomson House, Cardiff, CF1 1WR *T*. 33022. London Office: Greater London House, Hampstead Road, London, NW1 7SH *T*. 01-387 2800.
9p. D.—Independent. Articles of political, industrial, literary or general interest are considered. *Payment:* according to value. Special fees for exclusive news. Topical general news and feature pictures.

Western Morning News, The (1860), John Carter, Leicester Harmsworth House, Plymouth, PL1 1RE *T*. 266626. London Office: 143–144 Fleet Street, EC4. *T*. 01-353 8641.
6p. D.—Articles up to 1500 words accepted on subjects of West Country interest, illustrated when necessary.

Whole Earth Magazine (1974), editorial collective, 11 George Street, Brighton, BN2 1RH *T*. Brighton 691318.
25p. (£1.40 p.a.). Q.—News and features on environmental issues, self-sufficiency, energy, alternative technology, worker co-operatives, wholefoods, land and food issues, communal living and working. *Length:* articles 500 to 1500 words. *No payment. Illustrations:* mainly line drawings.

Wildlife (formerly **Animals** 1963), Nigel Sitwell, 243 King's Road, London, SW3 5EA *T*. 01-352 9294.
50p. M.—Serious, scientifically-oriented articles about wildlife. *Length:* 1000–3000 words. *Payment:* £30.00 per 1000 words. *Illustrations:* top quality colour and black-and-white photographs used extensively; little art work.

(Wolverhampton) Express and Star (1874), Keith Parker, 50 Queen Street, Wolverhampton, WV1 3BU *T*. 22351. London: Chronicle House, 73–78 Fleet Street, London, EC4P 4BE.
7p. D.—Open to consider topical contributions up to 750 words with or without illustrations. *Payment:* by arrangement.

Woman (1937). Josephine Sandilands, King's Reach Tower, Stamford Street, London, SE1 9LS *T.* 01-261 5000.
13p. W.—Practical articles of varying length on all subjects of interest to women. Short stories of 2500 to 4000/5000 words, serials and serialisation of book material. *Payment:* by arrangement. *Illustrations:* colour transparencies, photographs, sketches.

Woman and Home (1926), Shirley Shelton, King's Reach Tower, Stamford Street, London, SE1 9LS *T.* 01-261 5423.
30p. M.—Centres on the personal and home interests of the home-making woman. Articles dealing with hobbies, gardening, dress ideas and accessories, needlework and knitting. Things to make for the home. Poems, personality features, and memoirs. Serial stories 3 to 6 instalments, and complete stories from 2000 to 7000 words in *length*, of strong romantic interest. *Illustrations:* photographs and sketches for full-colour and mono reproduction.

Woman Journalist, The, Organ of the Society of Women Writers and Journalists (1894). Pat Garrod, 45 Basildon Court, Devonshire Street, London, W1N 1RH *T.* 01-935 6948.
Free to members. Q.—Outside contributions accepted, but no *payment* is made. Articles of interest to professional writers. *Length:* 500–1500 words.

Womancraft with **Sewing and Knitting,** Mary K. Eddy, King's Reach Tower, Stamford Street, London, SE1 9LS *T.* 01-261 6776.
35p. M.—Specialised publication devoted to knitting, crochet, dressmaking, soft furnishings, embroidery and all aspects of handicrafts and home ideas. All things to make with instructions. *Payment:* by arrangement. *Illustrations:* Photographs in colour and monotone.

Woman's Journal (1927), Laurie Purdon, King's Reach Tower, Stamford Street, London, SE1 9LS *T.* 01-261 5000.
35p. M.—A magazine devoted to the interests of the intelligent woman. Contents include short stories of literary merit; serials; interviews and articles (1500–3000 words) dealing in depth with topical subjects and personalities; fashion, beauty and health, and a home section with special emphasis on cookery and entertaining. *Illustrations:* full colour, line and wash, first-rate photographs.

Woman's Own, Jane Reed, King's Reach Tower, Stamford Street, London, SE1 9LS *T.* 01-261 5000.
13p. W.—Appealing to modern women of all ages, all classes, predominantly in the 20–35 age group. There is a first-class opening for short stories of 2000–5000 words. Preference for stories with genuine emotional situations rather than complicated plots—stories with which the reader can identify. Crisp, modern technique essential. *Illustrations:* in full colour and mono. Original knitting, crochet, craft designs, interior decorating and furnishing ideas, fashion.

Woman's Realm (1958), Monica Tyson, King's Reach Tower, Stamford Street, London, SE1 9LS *T.* 01-261 6105.
11p. W.—Practical general interest magazine specialising in service to women with growing families. Articles on cooking, dressmaking, home making. Short stories of 1500 to 4000 words; serials of 40,000–60,000 words. *Payment:* by arrangement. *Illustrations:* four-colour and two-colour drawings; photographs in colour and monotone.

Woman's Story Magazine (1956), Mrs. M. Dean, 12–18 Paul Street, London, EC2A 4JS *T.* 01-247 8233.
35p. M.—Short stories with realistic characterisation and strong woman-interest plot. *Length:* 1500–5000 words. *Payment:* by arrangement, on acceptance.

Woman's Weekly (1911), Mary Dilnot, King's Reach Tower, Stamford Street, London, SE1 9LS *T.* 01-261 6131.
11p. W.—A lively, family-interest magazine. Two serials, averaging 6000 words each instalment, and one short story of 3000 to 5000 words of strong romantic interest. Important biographies, and memoirs of celebrities. Personality features with photographs. *Payment:* by arrangement. *Illustrations:* full colour and mono fiction illustrations, small line sketches and photographs.

Woman's Weekly Good Life (1977), Bill Williamson, IPC Magazines, King's Reach Tower, Stamford Street, London, SE1 9LS *T.* 01-261 6529.
20p. M.—Short stories, feature articles, short (350–500 words) newsy items for Town and Around. *Payment:* by arrangement. *Illustrations:* line, half-tone, colour.

Woman's Weekly Library (1962), King's Reach Tower, Stamford Street, London SE1 9LS *T.* 01-261 6130.
12p. Twelve issues each month.—Complete romantic novels of 42,000 words with accent on love interest, to appeal to women of all ages. *Payment:* by arrangement. *Cover:* four colour offset litho. Please submit specimen first chapter and synopsis to Mrs. B. Walker (Managing Editor).

Woman's Weekly Library Historical Romances, King's Reach Tower, Stamford Street, London, SE1 9LS *T.* 01- 261 5000.
Two issues each month. Complete romantic novels with period backgrounds, to appeal to women of all ages. *Payment:* by arrangement. *Cover:* four colour offset litho. Authors invited to submit specimen first chapter and synopsis to Mrs. B. Walker (Managing Editor).

Woman's Weekly Library Hospital Romances (1972), King's Reach Tower, Stamford Street, London, SE1 9LS *T.* 01-261 5000.
12p. Eight issues each month. Complete romantic novels with medical backgrounds and accent on love interest, to appeal to women of all ages. *Payment:* by arrangement. *Cover:* four colour offset litho. Authors invited to submit specimen first chapter and synopsis to Mrs. B. Walker (Managing Editor).

Woman's World (1977), Bridget Rowe, 27 Newman Street, London, W1P 3PE *T.* 01-637 9671.
35p. M.—A wide-ranging magazine for women, covering all aspects of a woman's world and her interests today. Personal profiles, viewpoints and opinions on topical and contemporary subjects, cartoons, humorous and thought-provoking articles on man-woman and family relationships; fashion, beauty, cookery, home, competitions; short stories. *Illustrations:* full colour, line and wash, photographs.

Woodworker, Antony Talbot, Model and Allied Publications Ltd., P.O. Box 35, 13–35 Bridge Street, Hemel Hempstead, Herts, HP1 1EE *T.* Hemel Hempstead 63841–3.
40p. M.—For the home and professional woodworker. *Payment:* by arrangement. Practical illustrated articles on cabinet work, carpentry, wood polishing, wood turning, wood carving, rural crafts, craft history, antique and period furniture. *Illustrations:* line drawings and photographs.

Work Study, F. Conyers (Sawell Publications, Ltd.), 127 Stanstead Road, London, SE23 1JE *T.* 01-699 6792. *T.A.* Sawells, London.
60p. including postage. M. (£4.00 p.a. post £2.00).—Authoritative articles about all aspects of Work Study, i.e. Motion and Time study, methods, engineering, process control, scientific managegment, incentive schemes, and business efficiency. *Length:* 1000 to 4000 words. *Payment:* by arrangement. *Illustrations:* half-tone and line.

World Bowls (1954), Donald Newby, Hooker House, Quay Street, Halesworth, Suffolk, IP19 8AP *T.* 09867 2368.
25p. M.—Unusual features and fiction about all codes of bowling. *Payment:* NUJ Freelance rates. *Illustrations:* half-tone.

World Development (incorporating **New Commonwealth**), Pergamon Press Ltd., Headington Hill Hall, Oxford, OX3 0BW *T.* Oxford (0865) 64881.
£41.66 p.a.; Overseas US $100.00.—The multi-disciplinary international journal devoted to the study and promotion of world development.

World Fishing (1952), Michael Wood, IPC Industrial Press Ltd., Dorset House, Stamford Street, London, SE1 9LU *T.* 01-261 8689.
£16 p.a. M.—A magazine for those who take their living from commercial fishing. Bright and informative views and articles on methods, design, construction and operation of fishing vessels and gear. *Length:* 500–1500 words. *Payment:* by arrangement. *Illustrations:* Photographs and diagrams for litho reproduction.

World Medicine (1965), Dr. Michael O'Donnell, Clareville House, 26–7 Oxendon Street, London, SW1Y 4EL *T.* 01-930 7244, 4667, 0073. *T.A.* Womed, London.
50p. Fortnightly—Articles on medical subjects. *Length:* 1000 to 1500 words. *Payment:* by arrangement. *Illustrations:* line, half-tone, colour.

World Outlook (formerly **The Layman**), B. W. Amey, 93 Gloucester Place, London, W1H 4AA *T.* 01-935 1482.
£1.20 p.a. Q.—Articles on world questions from a Christian standpoint. *Length:* from 1500 to 2000 words. *Payment:* £3.00 an article. No illustrations.

World Survey (incorporating **The British Survey** 1939), J. Eppstein, published by the Atlantic Education Trust, 37A High Street, London, SW19 5BY *T.* 01-947 4985.
£3.15 p.a. M.—The main subject of each number is devoted to a particular country or one subject of international importance. Contributions are considered only from writers with personal knowledge of the country or subject treated. *Illustrations:* maps. *Length*: 8000 words. *Payment:* average £75.

World Today, The (1945), Liliana Brisby, The Royal Institute of International Affairs, Chatham House, 10 St. James's Square, London, SW1Y 4LE *T.* 01-930 2233. *T.A.* Areopagus, London.
70p. M.—Objective and factual articles on current questions of international affairs. *Length:* about 3500 words. *Payment:* £20 each article.

World's Children, The (1920), the magazine of The Save the Children Fund, Gillian Wilson (Editorial Director), 157 Clapham Road, London, SW9 0PT *T.* 01-582 1414.
£2.00 p.a. Q.—Articles on child welfare in all its aspects throughout the world, 1000 words. *Payment:* none. Photographs for cover and article illustration.

Writers' Review (1963), Sydney Sheppard, Trevail Mill, Zennor, St. Ives, Cornwall, TR26 3BW *T*. St. Ives 6038.
50p. Bi-M.—Literary articles and market information of interest to the freelance writer. *Length:* 2000–6000 words. *Payment:* from £5.

Writing (1959), Sean Dorman, 4 Union Place, Fowey, Cornwall, PL23 1BY.
40p (£1.20 p.a.). Q.—Articles, 300 to 350 words, on all subjects of interest to authors and journalists. Verse of 8 to 20 lines. *Payment:* £2 per article or poem.

Y Faner (Banner and Times of Wales), (1843), Geraint Bowen, M.A., County Press, Bala, Gwynedd, LL23 7PG *T*. 067-82 262.
20p. W.—National weekly news review in Welsh; articles of economic, literary and political interest. Non-party. *Length:* 1500 words. *Payment:* Minimum £10 per article. *Illustrations:* line and photographs.

Yacht and Boat Owner (1978), Martin Green, Link House, Dingwall Avenue, Croydon, CR9 2TA *T*. 01-686 2599. *Telex:* 947709.
45p. M.—Features on boat buying. *Length:* 1500–3000 average. *Payment:* by arrangement. *Illustrations:* line and half-tone.

Yachting Monthly (1906), J. D. Sleightholme, King's Reach Tower, Stamford Street, London, SE1 9LS *T*. 01-261 6040.
55p. Technical articles, up to 1500 words, on construction, marine engines, sailing, and general handling of yachts. Well-written accounts, up to 3000 words, of cruises in yachts. *Payment:* quoted on acceptance. *Illustrations:* line and wash drawings, first-class marine photographs—black and white, colour.

Yachting World (1894), IPC Transport Press, Dorset House, Stamford Street, London, SE1 9LU *T*. 01-261 8539.
50p. M.—Practical articles of an original nature, dealing with sailing, 2000 to 3000 words. *Payment:* varies. *Illustrations:* black-and-white-photographs or drawings.

Yachts and Yachting (1947), Peter Cook, 196 Eastern Esplanade, Southend-on-Sea, Essex. *T*. Southend-on-Sea (0702) 582245.
35p. F.—Short articles which should be technically correct. *Payment:* by arrangement. *Illustrations:* line and half-tone; occasional colour.

Yorkshire Evening Press (1882), 7p. **Sports Press,** 7p. John White (York and County Press), 15 Coney Street, York, YO1 1YN *T*. York 53051. London Office: Newspaper House, 8–16 Great New Street, EC4. *T*. 01-353 1030.
Articles of Yorkshire or general interest, humour, personal experience of current affairs. *Length:* 500–1500 words. *Payment:* by arrangement. *Illustrations:* half-tone and line.

Yorkshire Gazette and Herald Series, N. Railton, 15 Coney Street, York, YO1 1YN *T*. York 53051.
5p. W.—Stories and pictures of local interest. *Payment:* varies. *Illustrations:* half-tone and line.

Yorkshire Life (1947), Maurice Colbeck, 33–35 Cross Green, Otley, LS21 1HD *T*. Otley 4901–2. A publication of the Whitethorn Press, Ltd., Thomson House, Withy Grove, Manchester M60 4BL *T*. 834 1234.
30p. M.—Topics of Yorkshire interest, with or without photographs. Humour and topical subjects treated from a Yorkshire angle especially required. *Payment:* varies. *Illustrations:* Colour, tone or line. Transparencies for colour.

Yorkshire Post (1754), John Edwards, Wellington Street, Leeds, LS1 1RF. *T.* 32701. London Office: 23–27 Tudor Street, EC4. *T.* 01-583 9199.

8p. D.—Conservative. Authoritative and well-written articles elucidating new topics or on topical subjects of general, literary or industrial interests are preferred. *Length:* 1000 words. *Payment:* by arrangement. Contributions to *People,* a column about personalities in the news, are welcomed. *Illustrations:* photographs and frequent pocket cartoons (single column width), topical whenever possible.

Yorkshire Riding Magazine (1964), Winston Halstead, 62 Town Gate, Heptonstall, Hebden Bridge, Yorkshire. *T.* 042-284 3633.

30p. Bi-M.—Articles exclusively about people, life and character of the three Ridings of Yorkshire. *Length:* up to 1500 words. *Payment:* £5.00 per 1000 words minimum. *Illustrations:* line and half-tone.

Young Soldier, The (1881), Maxwell Ryan, the official gazette of the young people of The Salvation Army; 101 Queen Victoria Street, London, EC4P 4EP *T.* 01-236 5222, Ext. 216.

5p. W.—Stories, pictures, and cartoon strips on Christian heroic themes. *Payment:* usual. *Illustrations:* half-tone and line.

UNITED KINGDOM MAGAZINE PUBLISHERS

The publishers included here are those who issue journals listed in the earlier pages of this *Yearbook.* For a complete list of all journal and magazine publishers, with the titles they publish, reference should be made to the *Directory of Publishers of British Journals* published by the Library Association.

Architectural Press Ltd., The (1902), 9 Queen Anne's Gate, London, SW1H 9BY *T.* 01-930 0611. *T.A.* Buildable, London, SW1. *The Architectural Review* (M.), *The Architects' Journal* (W.).

Baillière Tindall (1826), (a division of Cassell Ltd.), 35 Red Lion Square, London, WC1R 4SG *T.* 01-831 6100. *Telex:* 28648 Casmac G.

Benn Publications Ltd. (1977), 25 New Street Square, London, EC4A 3JA *T.* 01-353 3212. *T.A.* Benbrolish London Telex. *Telex:* 27844. *Directors:* James G. Benn, Peter Dark, Neil Hird, Iain Laughland, James Lear, Dennis Matthews, Arthur Wright.

Blackwell (Basil) & Mott, Ltd. (1922), 5 Alfred Street, Oxford, OX1 4HB *T.* Oxford 722146. *Directors:* Sir Basil Blackwell (President), Richard Blackwell (Chairman), D. Martin (Managing), J. Blackwell, J. E. Critchley, A. F. Doulton, A. T. Hale, P. Saugman, M. A. Holmes, *Secretary.*

Blackwell Scientific Publications, Ltd. (1939), Osney Mead, Oxford, OX2 0EL, 9 Forrest Road, Edinburgh, EH1 2QH, 8 John Street, London, WC1N 2ES, and P.O. Box 9, North Balwyn, Victoria 3104, Australia. *T.* (Oxford) 0865 40201, (Edinburgh) 031-225 4234 and (London), 01-405 9941. *Directors:* Sir Basil Blackwell, Richard Blackwell, J. E. Critchley, P. G. Saugman, Keith Bowker, Nigel Palmer, Oluf Møller, Peter Pleasance, John Robson.

Blandford Business Press, Pembroke House, Wellesley Road, Croydon, CR9 2BX *T.* 01-686 7181.

Cambridge University Press (1534), Cambridge: The Pitt Building, Trumpington Street, Cambridge, CB2 1RP *T.* 0223 58331. *T.A.* Unipress, Cambridge. *Chief Executive and Secretary to the Syndics:* G. A. Cass, M.A.; *Managing Director* (Publishing Division): P. E. V. Allin, M.A.; *Publisher:* M. H. Black, M.A. London Office: Bentley House, 200 Euston Road, London, NW1 2DB.

Cass (Frank) & Co., Ltd. (1958), 11 Gainsborough Road, London, E11 1RS *T.* 01-530 4226. *T.A.* Simfay, London. *Telex:* 897719 Cass G. *Directors:* Frank Cass (Managing), A. E. Cass, M. P. Zaidner.

Condé Nast Publications, Ltd., The (1916), Vogue House, Hanover Square, London, W1R 0AD *T.* 01-499 9080. *T.A.* Volon, London. *Directors:* Daniel Salem (Chairman), Bernard H. Leser (Aust.) (Managing Director), F. C. Beech, R. W. Brook-Jones, Beatrix Miller, R. S. Hill, W. G. Stanford.

EMAP National Publications Ltd., Bretton Court, Bretton, Peterborough, PE3 8DZ *T.* Peterborough 0733-264666.

Evans Brothers Ltd. (1905), Montague House, Russell Square, London WC1B 5BX *T.* 01-636 8521.

Hansom Books, P.O. Box 294, 2 & 4 Old Pye Street, off Strutton Ground, Victoria Street, London, SW1P 2LR *T.* 01-222 3325.

Harmsworth Press, Ltd., The, 8 Stratton Street, London, W1X 6AT *T.* 01-499 7881. *T.A.* Field Newspaper, London and Golfirst, Piccy, London, W1.

Haymarket Publishing, Regent House, 54–62 Regent Street, London, W1A 4YJ *T.* 01-439 4242.

I.P.C. Business Press, Ltd., Surrey House, 1 Throwley Way, Sutton, Surrey, SM1 4QQ *T.* 01-643 8040.

IPC Magazines Ltd., (International Publishing Corporation), King's Reach Tower, Stamford Street, London, SE1 9LS *T.* 01-261 5000.

Kark, Norman, Publications, 268–270 Vauxhall Bridge Road, London, SW1 1BB *T.* 01-834 8851.

Link House Publications, Ltd., Dingwall Avenue, Croydon, CR9 2TA *T.* 01-686 2599. *T.A.* Aviculture, Croydon. *Directors:* G. C. Burt (Chairman), R. J. Wenn (Managing), A. W. Isaac (Deputy Managing), A. H. Coy (Secretary), J. Morgan.

Macmillan Journals Ltd., 4 Little Essex Street, London, WC2R 3LF *T.* 01-836 6633. *Chairman:* F. H. Whitehead; *Directors:* R. Barker, M. Barnard, M. Hamilton, Jenny Hughes, N. G. Byam Shaw (Managing).

Mason (Kenneth) Publications Ltd. (1958), Homewell, Havant, Hampshire, PO9 1EF *T.* Havant 486262. *Directors:* Kenneth Mason, M. E. Mason, M. A. Mason, P. A. Mason.

Mirror Group Newspapers Ltd., Holborn Circus, London, EC1P 1DQ *T.* 01-353 0246.

Morgan-Grampian Ltd., 30 Calderwood Street, London, SE18 6QH *T.* 01-855 7777.

National Magazine Co., Ltd., The, Chestergate House, Vauxhall Bridge Road, London, SW1V 1HF *T.* 01-834 2331. *Telex:* 263879.

Pergamon Press Ltd. (1948), Headington Hill Hall, Oxford, OX3 0BW *T.* Oxford 64881. *T.A.* Pergapress, Oxford. *Telex:* 83177.

Royal National Institute for the Blind, The (1868), 224–6–8 Great Portland Street, London, W1N 6AA *T.* 01-388 1266. *T.A.* Pharnib, Wesdo, London. *Director of Publications:* Donald Bell.

Sawell Publications, Ltd., 127 Stanstead Road, London, SE23. *T.* 01-699 6792.

Scout Association, The, Baden-Powell House, Queen's Gate, London, SW7 5JS *T.* 01-584 7030. *T.A.* Scouting. *General Editor:* Ron Jeffries, M.A.I.E.

Scripture Union (1867), 47 Marylebone Lane, London, W1M 6AX *T.* 01-486 2561. Christian Publishers and Booksellers.

Stevens (Wm.), Ltd. (1842), 55 Conduit Street, London, W1R 0NY *T.* 01-434 1281.

Taylor & Francis, Ltd., 10–14 Macklin Street, London, WC2B 5NF *T.* 01-405 2237–9. *President:* Professor Sir Nevill Mott, F.R.S., *Directors:* S. A. Lewis (Managing), Professor K. W. Keohane, Dr. A. T. Fuller, G. R. Noakes, G. F. Lancaster (Secretary), Professor B. R. Coles, A. R. Selvey, M. I. Dawes.

Thomson-Leng Publications, Dundee, DD1 9QJ *T.* 23131. *T.A.* Courier, Dundee. *Telex:* DCThom 76380. London: 185 Fleet Street, London, EC4A 2HS *T.* 01-353 2586. *T.A.* Courier, London, EC4.

Times Newspapers, Ltd., P.O. Box 7, New Printing House Square, Gray's Inn Road, London, WC1X 8EZ *T.* 01-837 1234. *Telex:* 264971–80. *Directors:* Sir Denis Hamilton (Chairman and Editor-in-Chief), M. J. Hussey (Managing Director and Chief Executive), G. C. Brunton, J. Evans, T. D. P. Emblem, Sir Kenneth Keith, Lord Robens of Woldingham, Lord Roll of Ipsden, Lord Greene of Harrow Weald, Professor Hugh Trevor-Roper, J. A. Tory.

Whitaker (J.) & Sons, Ltd., 12 Dyott Street, London, WC1A 1DF *T.* 01-836 8911. *Directors:* Haddon Whitaker, O.B.E., M.A., A. C. E. Musk, C.V.O., David Whitaker, R. F. Baum, J. W. Coates F.L.A., Sally Whitaker.

Whitehall Press Ltd., 36 Ebury Street, London, SW1W 0LW *T.* 01-730 2136–9 and Earl House, Maidstone, Kent, ME14 1PE *T.* Maidstone 59841.

Wildings of Shrewsbury Ltd. (1874), Windsor Place, Shrewsbury, SY1 2DB *T.* Shrewsbury 51278.

Wright (John) & Sons, Ltd. (1825), 42–44 Triangle West, Bristol, BS8 1EX *T.* 23237. *Chairman:* C. N. Clarke. *Group Managing Director:* D. J. Kingham. *Directors:* P. R. Wilson, P. J. Wright, M. Weeks, A. V. Kennett. *Executive Sales Director:* Miss J. Eales. *Secretary:* A. Gay.

AFRICAN JOURNALS AND MAGAZINES

GHANA

Pleisure! (1973), Roland J. Moxon, M.A., O.B.E., P.O. Box M 160, Accra, Ghana. *T.* 66640. *T.A.* Moxon Accra.
40 pesewas. M.—Short stories, light hearted articles, book, theatre and cinema reviews, crosswords, poetry. *Payment:* by arrangement. *Illustrations:* line and half-tone.

KENYA

Busara, P.O. Box 30022, Nairobi; Editor: P.O. Box 30197, Nairobi.

Daily Nation, Managing Editor: J. Rodrigues, P.O. Box 49010, Nairobi, *T.* 337691. London: Overseas Publicity Ltd., 214 Oxford Street, London, W1N 0EA *T.* 01-636 8296.
1 (K) Sh. D.—News, features, etc. Pictures.

East Africa Journal, P.O. Box 30571, Nairobi.

East African Agricultural & Forestry Journal, P.O. Box 30148, Nairobi. *T.* Kikuyu 2121 ext. 259.
£1.50. Q. (£6.00 p.a.).—Papers on agriculture, forestry and applied Sciences. *Length:* 100 to 125 pages.

East African Medical Journal, Editor: N. W. Awori, M.B., F.R.C.S., D.R.C.O.G. Editorial Manager: Joan A. Greene, P.O. Box 41632, Nairobi.
£11.00 p.a. M.

East African Standard, Michael Peirson, P.O. Box 30080, Nairobi. *T.* 555633 and 32301.
90 cents daily. D.—News and topical articles of East African interest.

RHODESIA

Illustrated Life Rhodesia (1968), Heidi Holland, P.O. Box 2931, Salisbury. *T.* Salisbury 706207.
10c. F.—Articles concerning events and personalities relevant to Rhodesia. Average *length:* 2000 words. *Payment:* $35.00 per article including photographs. *Illustrations:* line, half-tone, colour.

Rhodesia Calls (1960), Clive Wilson, 4th Floor, Chamber of Mines Building, Gordon Avenue, Salisbury. *T.* 705911. *Postal Address:* P.O. Box 8045, Causeway, Salisbury.
40c Alt. months.—Non-political articles on various aspects of Rhodesia of world-wide interest. *Length:* 1000–1500 words. *Payment:* $20.00 per 1000 words. *Illustrations:* half-tone, colour.

Rhodesian Caravaner, Clive Wilson, P.O. Box 8045, Causeway, Salisbury.
12p. Alt. months.—Only articles dealing with caravanning or camping. *Payment:* $15.00 per 1000 words.

Rhodesian Farmer, The, published by Rhodesian Farmer Publications (1928), Bernard Miller, Agriculture House, Moffat Street, P.O. Box 1622, Salisbury. *T.* Salisbury 708245–6.
$10.20 (Rhodesian) p.a. Weekly Illustrated. Official journal of the Rhodesian National Farmers Union. Articles on all aspects of agriculture. *Payment:* by arrangement.

Rhodesia Herald, The (1891), R. J. Fothergill, P.O. Box 396, Salisbury. *T.* 704341. *T.A.* Manherald, Salisbury.
9c. D.—Topical articles of news value. *Payment:* varies, depends on length, content and news value. *Illustrations:* half-tone.

Rhodesian Hotel & Catering Gazette, Clive Wilson, P.O. Box 8045, Causeway, Salisbury. *T.* 705911.
Free—controlled circ. M.—Articles dealing with hotel and catering management. *Payment:* $20.00 per 1000 words.

Sunday Mail, The (1935), E. Richmond, P.O. Box 396, Salisbury. *T.* 704341. *T.A.* Manherald, Salisbury.
10c. W.—Topical articles of news value. *Payment:* varies, depends on length, content and news value. *Illustrations:* half-tone.

TANZANIA

Daily News, The, Ferdinand Ruhinda, P.O. Box 9033, Dar es Salaam. *T.* 29881. 2½p. D.

Sunday News, Ferdinand Ruhinda, P.O. Box 9033, Dar es Salaam. *T.* 29881. 4p. W.

UGANDA

Eastern Africa Journal of Rural Development, Makerere University, P.O. Box 7062, Kampala.

Voice of Uganda, P.O. Box 20081, Kampala. *T.* 34403.
40 cents D.—News, topical features, news pictures.

AUSTRALIAN JOURNALS AND MAGAZINES

NOTE.—*Newspapers are listed under the towns in which they are published.*

Adam (1945), W. Tuckey (The K. G. Murray Publishing Co., Pty., Ltd.), 142 Clarence Street, Sydney, 2000, N.S.W. *T.A.* Kenmurray.
75c. M.—Australian-based fiction and general articles. *Length:* 2500 to 4000 words. *Payment:* from $15.00 per 1000 words.

(Adelaide) Advertiser (1958), D. F. Colquhoun, Adelaide. London: 8–10 Cliffords Inn, Fetter Lane, London, EC4A 1BU *T.* 01-831 6041.
15c. D.—The only morning daily in S. Australia. Descriptive and news background material, 400–800 words, preferably with pictures.

(Adelaide) News, The (South Australia) (1923), Simon Galvin, 116 North Terrace, Adelaide. *T.* 51-0351.
12c. D.—One feature page open for topical articles. *Length:* preferably 600–750. *Payment:* by arrangement. Illustrated articles preferred.

(Adelaide) Sunday Mail (1912), G. Roach, 116 North Terrace, Adelaide, 5000. *T.* 51-0351.
25c. W.—Limited scope for free-lance writers.

Australasian Dirt Bike, G. Eldridge, Page Publications Pty. Ltd., 432–436 Elizabeth Street, Surry Hills, N.S.W. 2010. *T.* 699 7861. *Telex:* AA 21887.
$1.40. 6 times p.a.—Tests and reports of off-road bikes and equipment, news and features of interest to off-road enthusiasts. *Payment:* by arrangement.

Australian, The, L. Hollings, G.P.O. Box 4245, Sydney. *T.* 20924.
20c. Will consider topical articles from free-lance writers. *Length:* up to 1500 words. *Payment:* by arrangement.

Australian Angler, The, Ron Calcutt, Page Publications Pty. Ltd., 432–6 Elizabeth Street, Surry Hills, Sydney 2010. *T.* 699 7861. *Telex:* AA 21887.
$1.25. M.—All aspects of rock, surf, stream, deep sea and game fishing, with comprehensive sections on gear, equipment and boats. *Payment:* by arrangement.

Australian Cricket (1968), Leigh Emery, Phil Tresidder, 15 Boundary Street, Rushcutters Bay, New South Wales 2011. *T.* Sydney 33-4282. *T.A.* Modmags, Sydney.
$1.00. M. (October to March).—Articles on cricket. *Payment:* $50 per 1000 words. *Illustrations:* half-tone and colour.

Australian Financial Review, The, Maximilian Walsh, Sydney. London: 99 Aldwych, London, WC2B 4RJ *T.* 01-404 5812. New York: 1501 Broadway, N.Y. 10036. *T.* 536-6835.
15c. D. (except Saturday & Sunday).—Investment business and economic news and reviews; government and politics, production, banking, commercial, and Stock Exchange statistics; company analysis.

Australian Flying, Michelle Grahame, Page Publications Pty. Ltd., 432–6 Elizabeth Street, Surry Hills, Sydney 2010. *T.* 699 7861. *Telex:* AA 21887.
$1.00. 6 times p.a.—Appeals to light and medium aircraft owners, as well as those directly and indirectly associated with the aircraft industry. *Payment:* by arrangement.

Australian Home Beautiful, The (1913), A. J. Hitchin, 61 Flinders Lane, Melbourne. London: 8–10 Cliffords Inn, Fetter Lane, EC4A 1BU.
75c. M.—Deals with home building, interior decoration, furnishing, gardening, cookery, etc. Short articles with accompanying photographs with Australian slant accepted. *Preliminary* letter advisable. *Payment:* higher than Australian average, with special recognition for outstanding work.

Australian Home Journal (1894), Diana Wynne, The K. G. Murray Publishing Co. Pty. Ltd., 142 Clarence Street, Sydney, N.S.W. 2000. London: Ludgate House, 107 Fleet Street, London, EC4. *T.* 01-353 1040.
75c. M.—Homemaker magazine, with strong emphasis on home design, furniture, furnishing, room settings, materials, fabrics, etc. Also uses "how to makes", sewing ideas and handyman construction projects. A few light features on home topics but no fiction. Aims to appeal to the young homemaker and housewife. *Illustrations:* sketches and photographs (colour and mono). *Payment:* according to length and merit.

Australian Hot Rod, R. B. Hungerford, Page Publications Pty. Ltd., 432–6 Elizabeth Street, Surry Hills, Sydney 2010. *T.* 699 7861. *Telex:* AA 21887. $1.25. 4 times p.a.—News of hot rodding, custom cars and drag racing, with special articles on engine and car building and modifying. *Payment:* by arrangement.

Australian Hot-Rodding Review (1965), The K. G. Murray Publishing Co. Pty. Ltd., 142 Clarence Street, Sydney, 2000, N.S.W. *T.A.* Kenmurray. $1.25. M.—Articles up to 2500 words on hot-rodding subjects, including conversions, technical features. *Payment:* by arrangement. *Illustrations:* half-tone and line.

Australian House and Garden (1948), Maria Quinn, 142 Clarence Street, Sydney, New South Wales 2000. *T.A.* Kenmurray. $1.00. M.—Factual articles dealing with interior decorating, home design, homemaker themes and activities. *Payment:* by arrangement. *Illustrations:* line, half-tone, colour.

Australian Journal of Politics and History The, Prof. Gordon Greenwood, Department of History, University of Queensland Press, St. Lucia, Queensland 4067. *T.* 377 21264. $7.00; $18.00 p.a., UK £9.00 inc. postage. April, August, December.—Australian, Commonwealth, Asian, S.W. Pacific, and international articles. *Length:* 9000 words max. No *payment.* Necessary line *illustrations* only.

Australian Mining, Thomson Publications Australia Pty. Ltd., 47 Chippen Street, Chippendale 2008, N.S.W. *T.* 69-6731. $18 p.a. in Australia; $24 p.a. overseas.

Australian Outdoors (1947), Laurie Drake (The K. G. Murray Publishing Co. Pty. Ltd.), 142 Clarence Street, Sydney, 2000, N.S.W. *T.A.* Kenmurray. $1.00. M.—Articles of 1000–3000 words on hunting, shooting, fishing, bush-sciences and all non-competitive outdoor activities. *Payment:* from $10.00 per 1000 words. *Illustrations:* half-tone and line.

Australian Outlook, D. J. Goldsworthy, Department of Politics, Monash University, Clayton, Victoria 3168. $12.50 p.a. 3 times p.a.—Scholarly articles on international affairs. *Length:* 4000 to 8000 words. No *payment.*

Australian Quarterly, The (1929), Hugh Pritchard and Antoinette Wyllie, Australian Institute of Political Science, Room 9, 4th Floor, 181 Clarence Street, Sydney 2000. *T.* 27 2703. $2.00 ($8.00 p.a. in Australia and Territories; $10.00 overseas). Q.—Articles of high standard on politics, law, economics, social issues, etc. *Length:* 5000 words preferred. No *payment.*

Australian Sporting Shooter, R. B. Hungerford, Page Publications Pty. Ltd., 432–6 Elizabeth Street, Surry Hills, Sydney 2010. *T.* 699 7861. *Telex:* AA 21887. 80c.—All aspects of game shooting, collecting, antiques, archery (associated with hunting), pistol shooting, clay target shooting, reloading, ballistics and articles of a technical nature. *Payment:* by arrangement.

Australian Women's Weekly, The, Ita Buttrose (Australian Consolidated Press, Ltd.), 54 Park Street, Sydney, N.S.W. 2001. London: Australian Consolidated Press, Ltd., 107 Fleet Street, EC4. *T.* 01-353 1040.
40c. W.—Short stories, serials and features. *Length:* short stories, 1000 to 6000 words. Features 1000 to 2500 words plus colour or black-and-white photographs where available. *Payment:* according to length and merit. *Fiction illustrations:* sketches by own artists.

(Brisbane) Courier Mail, J. R. Atherton (Queensland Newspapers Pty., Ltd.), Campbell Street, Bowen Hills, Brisbane, 4000.
12c. D.—Occasional topical special articles required, 1000 words.

(Brisbane) Sunday Mail, H. G. Turner, G.P.O. Box No. 130, Brisbane, Queensland, 4001. London: 8–10 Clifford's Inn, Fetter Lane, EC4A 1BU.
15c. W.—Anything of general interest. Up to 1500 words. *Illustrations:* line, photographs, black-and-white, and colour. *Payment:* by arrangement. Rejected MSS. returned if postage enclosed.

(Brisbane) Telegraph (1872), L. K. S. Hogg, Campbell Street, Bowen Hills, Brisbane, 4006.
12c. D.

Bulletin, The (1880), Trevor Kennedy, 54 Park Street, Sydney 2001, N.S.W. *T.* 2–0666. *T.A.* Packpress, Sydney.
50c. W.—Short stories, current affairs commentary, arts, sport. *Payment:* $85 per 1000 words or by arrangement. *Illustrations:* line, half-tone and colour.

Catholic Weekly, R. J. Stapleton (Catholic Newspaper Co., Ltd.), V.I.P. House, 57–61 Foveaux Street, Surry Hills 2010, N.S.W. *T.* 2114499.
30c. W.—Christian news review magazine of general interest. *Length:* up to 1000 words. *Payment:* standard rates. *Illustrations:* half-tone.

Cleo (1972), Pat Dasey, 168 Castlereagh Street, Sydney 2000, N.S.W. *T.* 2-0666. *T.A.* Packpress, Sydney.
$1.20 M.—Short stories, articles up to 5000 words, longer fiction up to 15,000 words, some poetry, short quizzes. *Payment:* Articles $70–$100 per 1000 words; poetry, fiction by arrangement. *Illustrations:* colour, half-tone, cartoons.

Commercial Fishing & Marketing, Keith Bresch Pty. Ltd., 140 Phillip Street, Sydney, 2000; G.P.O. Box 268.
M.—Articles of general interest to the commercial fishing and marketing industries. Photographs of overseas fishing activities, etc. Articles on new developments, techniques, processes, by arrangement. *Payment:* according to length and informative interest to Australian and New Zealand fishing and marketing industries. Rejected MS. and photos returned if postage enclosed.

Countryman, The, George A. Boylen, Newspaper House, St. George's Terrace, Perth 6000. *T.* 321-0161. *T.A.* Westralian Perth. London: 8–10 Clifford's Inn, Fetter Lane, London, EC4A 1BU
10c. W.—Agriculture, farming or country interest features and service columns. *Payment:* standard rates. *Illustrations:* line and half-tone.

Current Affairs Bulletin (1942), Dr. D. W. Crowley, Department of Adult Education, University of Sydney, Sydney 2006, N.S.W.   *T.* Sydney 692-2583   *T.A.* Univsyd.
60c. $7.20   p.a.   M.—Authoritative well documented articles on all national and international affairs: politics, science, ecology, economics, literature, business and social questions. *Length:* 2000–6000 words. *Payment:* $30 per 1000 words, limit of $150 per article. *Illustrations:* line, half-tone.

Dolly (1970), Anne Goldie, 57 Regent Street, Chippendale, New South Wales 2008.   *T.* 699-3622.
80c.   M.—Features on fashion, make-up, etc. Fiction, including serials, mainly romantic boy-girl stories. *Length:* not less than 2000 words. *Payment:* by arrangement. *Illustrations:* line, half-tone, colour.

Electrical Engineer, Thomson Publications (Australia) Pty. Ltd., Box 65, P.O., Chippendale, N.S.W., 2008.
$18 p.a. Australia, New Zealand and New Guinea; $24 p.a. elsewhere.   M.

Electronics Australia (incorporating **Radio, Television and Hobbies** (1939), J. Rowe, Box 163, Beaconsfield, N.S.W. 2014.   London: 99 Aldwych, London, WC2B 4RJ   *T.* 01-404 5812.
$1.25.   M.—Illustrated magazine devoted to technical television and radio, hi-fi, popular electronics, microcomputers and avionics. *Length:* up to 3000 words. *Payment:* by arrangement. *Illustrations:* line, half-tone.

Hemisphere, P.O. Box 826, Woden, A.C.T. 2606.
75c.   M.—Asian-Australian magazine. Articles usually commissioned but contributions welcomed by experts on cultural, social, scientific or general interests. Ideas should first be submitted. *Payment:* $80.00 per 1000 words for first publication rights.

Historical Studies (formerly **Historical Studies—Australia and New Zealand),** J. B. Hirst, Melbourne University, Parkville, Melbourne 3052.
$6.00, plus postage, $10.50 p.a., $12.50 p.a. overseas. Twice yearly.— *Length:* 8000 words maximum. No *payment.* Tables and maps.

Labor News, Laurie Short, 188 George Street, Sydney, 2000, New South Wales.   *T.* 27-4021.
Bi-M.—Official Journal Federated Ironworkers' Association of Australia.

(Launceston) Examiner, Michael Courtney, Box 99A, P.O. Launceston, Tasmania, 7250.   *T.* 315111.   *T.A.* Examiner, Launceston, Tasmania.   *Telex:* 58511.   12c.   D.

(Launceston) Sunday Examiner-Express, Box 99A, P.O. Launceston, Tasmania, 7250.   *T.* 315111.
12c.   W.

Makar (1960), M. Duwell, P.O. Box 71, St. Lucia 4067.   T. 377 2570.
$1.00.   3 times a year.—Poetry and short stories. *Payment:* $7.50 per page of poetry, $7.50 per 500 words of prose. *Illustrations:* photographs.

Meanjin Quarterly (1940), J. H. Davidson, The University of Melbourne, Parkville, 3052, Victoria. T. 341 6950 and 345 1844.
Subscription: $14 p.a. post paid.—Authoritative articles and essays (not necessarily Australian) dealing with literature, art, drama, education, the humanities, national and international affairs, of permanent rather than temporary interest. Specialises in short stories and poetry of high quality; book reviews; illustrations. *Length:* 2000–5000 words. *Payment:* on acceptance according to quality and length.

(Melbourne) Age, G. J. Taylor (David Syme & Co., Ltd.), 250 Spencer Street, Melbourne, Victoria 3000. London: Room 223, New Printing House Square, Grays Inn Road, WC1X 8EZ T. 01-837 9978.
14c. D.—Independent liberal morning daily. Room occasionally for outside matter. There are features, background news and women's pages daily. An illustrated weekend magazine and literary review is published on Saturday. Accepts occasional freelance material.

(Melbourne) Australasian Post, Jack Hughes, Herald and Weekly Times, 44 Flinders Street, Melbourne. London: 8–10 Cliffords Inn, Fetter Lane, London, EC4A 1BU T. 01-831 6041.
25c. W.—Opening for casual contributions of topical factual illustrated articles. All contributions must have Australian interest. Male appeal. *Payment:* average $30 per 500 words plus $15 (minimum) per picture.

(Melbourne) Herald, John Fitzgerald, 44–74 Flinders Street, Melbourne. T. 63-0211. London: 8–10 Cliffords Inn, Fetter Lane, London, EC4A 1BU.
7c. D.—Evening boadsheet with greatest evening circulation in Australia. Articles with or without illustrations. *Length:* up to 750 words. *Payment:* on merit. *Illustrations:* half-tone and line.

(Melbourne) Sun News Pictorial (1922), J. A. T. Morgan, 44–74 Flinders Street, Melbourne, 3000.
10c. D.—Topical articles to 750 words. *Payment:* above standard rates. *Illustrations:* general interest, fashion, sport.

Modern Boating (1965), Barry Tranter, 15 Boundary Street, Rushcutters Bay, New South Wales, 2011. T. Sydney 33-4282. T.A. Modmags, Sydney. *Telex:* AA27243.
$1.00. M.—Articles on all types of boats and boating. *Payment:* $30 per 1000 words. *Illustrations:* half-tone and colour.

Modern Motor (1954), Matt Whelan, 15 Boundary Street, Rushcutters Bay, New South Wales, 2011. T. Sydney 33-4282. T.A. Modmags Sydney.
50c. M.—Articles on cars and all forms of motoring. *Payment:* $40 per 1000 words. *Illustrations:* half-tone and colour.

National Times, The, Max Suich, Sydney. London: 99 Aldwych, London, WC2B 4RJ T. 01-404 5812. New York: 1501 Broadway, N.Y. 10036. T. 536-6835.
45c. W.—Foreign affairs, government and politics, production, banking, commercial, entertainment, the arts, sport, good living.

New Idea, The (1902), Mrs. D. Boling, 32 Walsh, Melbourne, 3001. T. 3280241.
50c. W.—Woman's journal of knitting patterns, fashions, beauty service, short stories, and reading matter of general interest to women of all ages. Short stories and articles purchased: stories, 1500 to 4000 words: articles, 1200 to 2000 words. *Payment:* on acceptance. Minimum $50.00 per 1000 words. *Illustrations:* good pictures of general interest and fashion.

New Poetry, Cheryl Adamson, The Poetry Society of Australia, G.P.O. Box N110, Grosvenor Street P.O., Sydney 2000, N.S.W. *T.* 423861.
$16.00 p.a. Q.—Poetry, articles and reviews. *Payment:* minimum Poems $10.00, reviews $15.00, leading articles $50.00.

Newcastle Morning Herald and Miners' Advocate (1858), J. A. Allan, 28–30 Bolton Street, Newcastle, 2300, N.S.W. *T.* 2-0471.
14c. D. (Monday to Saturday).

Newcastle Sun, The (1918), K. Brock, 28–30 Bolton Street, Newcastle 2300. *T.* 2-0471.
12c. D. (Monday to Friday afternoons).

Overland, S. Murray-Smith, G.P.O. Box 98A, Melbourne, Victoria 3001.
$2.00. Q.—Literary and general. Australian material preferred. *Payment:* by arrangement. *Illustrations:* line blocks.

(Perth) Daily News (1840), I. L. Hummerston, Newspaper House, St. George's Terrace, Perth, 6000.
10c. D. (Evening).—Accepts special articles on subjects of outstanding interest. *Payment:* according to merit, on publication. *Illustrations:* photographs, cartoons, and comics.

(Perth) Sunday Times (1897), 34 Stirling Street, Perth, 6000, Western Australia. *T.* 28-1000.
15c. W.—Topical articles to 800 words. *Payment:* standard rates on acceptance.

(Perth) West Australian, The (1833) M. C. Uren, Newspaper House, 125 St George's Terrace, Perth, 6000. *T.* 21-0161. *T.A.* "Westralian", Perth. London: 8–10 Cliffords Inn, Fetter Lane, London, EC4 1BU *T.* 01-831 6041.
8c. D.—Articles and sketches about people and events in Australia and abroad. *Length:* 300–700 words *Payment:* Award rates or better. *Illustrations:* line or half-tone.

Pix People (National weekly news-pictorial), R. Wragg, Sungravure, 57 Regent Street, Sydney, N.S.W. *T.* 699-3622. London: 99 Aldwych, London, WC2B 4RJ *T.* 01-404 5812.
40c. W.—Mainly pictorial, but good documentary subjects needed. Photographs depicting exciting happenings, candid camera pictures of events affecting Australians, glamour and show business, modern-living features, and complete series of any subject such as unusual industries, rites, customs, etc. *Payment:* on highest Australian scale.

Poetry Australia (1964), Grace Perry, South Head Press, 350 Lyons Road, Fivedock, Sydney, 2046, N.S.W. *T.* 713-9754.
$2.50. Q.—Poetry and review articles concerned with new verse, or re-evaluations of verse, or verse criticism. *Payment:* $8 a new page (minimum).

Quadrant, Elwyn Lynn, Box C344, 181 Clarence Street, Sydney, 2000, New South Wales. *T.* 29-5899.
$2.00. M.—Articles, short stories, verse, etc. *Length:* 2000–5000 words. *Payment:* minimum $10 per 1000 words, verse $10 minimum.

Racing Car News (1961), C. Max Stahl, 177 Lawson Street, Redfern, New South Wales, 2016. *T.* 699-8504. *T.A.* Racecarnews, Sydney.
50c. M.—Short stories on racing cars or drivers up to 1000 words. *Payment:* from $20. *Illustrations:* half-tone, line.

Reader's Digest (Australian edition), Frank Devine, 26–32 Waterloo Street, Surry Hills, New South Wales, 2010. *T.* 699-0111 *T.A.* Readigest, Sydney.
75c. M.—Articles on Australian and New Zealand subjects of all kinds. *Length:* 3000 to 4000 words. *Payment:* $240–$1000 per article. Brief filler paragraphs, $25 to $75. *Illustrations:* half-tone, colour.

Revs (1968), Mac Douglas, 15 Boundary Street, Rushcutters Bay, N.S.W. 2011. *T.* Sydney 33-4282. *Telex:* AA27243 Modmags Sydney.
50c. (alt. Friday).—Features, photographs and news stories of interest to motorcyclists. *Payment:* minimum $30 per 1000 words.

Seacraft (1946), Paul Hopkins (The K. G. Murray Publishing Co. Pty., Ltd.), 142 Clarence Street, Sydney, 2000, N.S.W.
75c. M.—Articles up to 2000 words on yachting, seamanship, marine engines, naval design; technical data and high-quality illustrations. *Payment:* from $10 per 1000 words. *Illustrations:* colour and black and white (offset production).

Sports Car World (1956), Peter Robinson (The K. G. Murray Publishing Co. Pty. Ltd.), 142 Clarence Street, Sydney, 2000, N.S.W.
$1.50. Q.—Articles up to 2500 words on subjects allied to the high performance car, classic car, motor sport, etc. *Payment:* by arrangement. *Illustrations:* half-tone and line; colour.

Sunday Sun, R. M. Richards (Mirror Newspapers Limited), Brunswick and McLachlan Street, Fortitude Valley, Brisbane, 4006. *T.* 52 8050. London Office: 8 Bouverie Street, Fleet Street, London EC4Y 8HI.
20c. W.

Sun-Herald, The (Sunday edition of *The Sydney Morning Herald* and the *Sun*), L. Kepert, Sydney. London: 99 Aldwych, London, WC2B 4RJ *T.* 01-404 5812.
20c. W.—Topical articles to 1000 words; has sections on show business, finance, fashion and other articles of interest to women. Payment as for *The Sydney Morning Herald*.

(Sydney) Bulletin (1880), Trevor Kennedy, 54 Park Street, Sydney, N.S.W. *T.* 2-0666. London: Australian Consolidated Press, 107 Fleet Street, EC4A 2AL *T.* 01-353 1040. New York: Australian Consolidated Press, Room 2102, 444 Madison Avenue, New York, N.Y. 10022. *T.* 212-751-3383.
50c. W.—Concerned mainly with reporting Australia to Australians, or the world from an Australian aspect. *Payment:* by arrangement.

(Sydney) Daily Mirror (1941), Chairman of Directors: K. S. May, 2 Holt Street, Sydney, 2010, N.S.W. *T.* 2-0942.
10c. D.—Accept modernly written feature articles and series of Australian or world interest. *Length:* 1000 to 2000 words. *Payment:* according to merit and length.

(Sydney) Daily Telegraph (News Limited), J. Moses, 2 Holt Street, Surry Hills, 2010, N.S.W.   *T.* 20924.
14c.   D.

Sydney Morning Herald, The (1831), G. E. W. Harriott, Sydney.   London: 99 Aldwych, London, WC2B 4RJ   *T.* 01-404 5812.
14c.   D.—Saturday edition has pages of literary criticism and also magazine articles.   Topical articles not more than 1200 words.   *Payment:* varies, but minimum of $30.00 per 1000 words.   All types of illustrations acceptable.

(Sydney) Nation Review, Incorporated Newsagencies Pty. Ltd., 777b George Street, Sydney, 2000, New South Wales.
50c.

(Sydney) Sun (1910), G. R. Ford, Jones Street, Broadway, Sydney.   *T.* 20 944. London: 99 Aldwych, London, WC2B 4RJ   *T.* 01-404 5812.
12c.   D.—Topical articles, 900 to 1500 words, particularly on international subjects.   *Payment:* from $40 according to length and quality.   *Illustrations:* line or half-tone.

(Sydney) Sunday Mirror (1961), Chairman of Directors: K. S. May, Kippax Street, Sydney.   *T.* 2-0924.
10c.   Accept illustrated features and series, modernly written feature articles and series of Australian or world interest.   *Length:* 1000 to 2000 words.   *Payment:* according to merit and length.

TV Times (1958), C. N. Day, G.P.O. Box 3906, Sydney, 2001, N.S.W.
40c.   W.—Devoted exclusively to TV profiles, programmes and background.   *Length:* about 2000 words.   *Payment:* by arrangement.   *Illustrations:* colour and black-and-white.

Weekend News, J. R. Davies, Newspaper House, 125 St. George's Terrace, Perth 6000, Western Australia.   *T.* 321-0161.   *T.A.* Westralian, Perth.
12c.   W.—Articles, radio and television stories, non-fiction serials.   Highly technical articles not required.   *Payment:* standard rates.   *Illustrations:* line, half-tone.

Wheels (1953), Peter Robinson (The K. G. Murray Publishing Co. Pty., Ltd.), 142 Clarence Street, Sydney, 2000, N.S.W.
75c.   M.—Articles up to 2500 words on general interest motoring subjects, motor sport, history of motoring, technical developments; all strictly authentic, preferably by specialist writers.   *Payment:* by agreement.   *Illustrations:* half-tone and line.

Woman's Day, Mary Falloon, 57–59 Regent Street, Sydney 2008.   *T.* 699-3622.
50c.   W.—National women's magazine: news, fiction, fashion, general articles, cookery, home economy, TV.   Circulation in excess of 530,000. Printed in gravure.

CANADIAN JOURNALS AND MAGAZINES

NOTE.—*Newspapers are listed under the towns in which they are published.*

Atlantic Advocate, The, H. P. Wood, Gleaner Building, Phoenix Square, Fredericton, New Brunswick, E3B 5A2   *T.* 455 6671.
75c.   M.—Non-fiction and short stories, focus must be on Atlantic Provinces.   *Length:* up to 2000 words.   *Payment:* 5 cents per word.   *Illustrations:* line and half-tone.

Axiom Magazine (1974), D. T. Murphy, P.O. Box 1525, Halifax, Nova Scotia, B3J 3C6   *T.* 902-422 6797.
75c. $3.75 p.a.   M.—Feature articles on arts, science, business, etc., on Atlantic Canada.   Short stories.   *Length:* features 2000 words.   *Payment:* 10 cents a word approx.   *Illustrations:* half-tone, colour.

Beaver, Helen Burgess (Hudson's Bay Co.), Hudson Bay House, Winnipeg, Manitoba R3C 2R1.
$5.00 ($12.00 p.a.), foreign $6.00 ($15.00 p.a.).   Q.—Articles, historical and modern in the sphere of Hudson's Bay Company's activities and Canadian Arctic.   *Length:* 1500 to 3000 words, with illustrations.   *Payment:* on acceptance, about 7 cents a word.   *Illustrations:* photographs or drawings. Black-and-white and colour.

Broadcaster (1942), B. Byers, 77 River Street, Toronto, M5A 3P2   T. 416-363-6111.
$2.00 ($15.00 p.a.).   M.—Articles pertaining to broadcasting.   *Length:* 500 to 1500 words. *Payment:* minimum $100.

Canadian, The, Patrick Scott, 2180 Yonge Street, Suite 1701, Toronto, Ontario, M4S 2E7   *T.* 416-485-1552.
Distributed every Saturday by 11 newspapers across Canada.   W.—Topical articles of Canadian interest as: new developments in the political, industrial and medical fields; profiles of prominent persons in the news; trends and personalities in sport; entertainment scene; features about controversial subjects.   1500–4000 words.   *Payment:* $300 to $900, depending on length and subject matter—on acceptance.   Please send preliminary letter.

Canadian Author and Bookman, Duncan S. Pollock, 22 Yorkville Avenue, Toronto, Ontario, M4W 1L4.
$4.00 p.a.   Q.— Published by Canadian Authors Association.   Interviews, profiles, articles on the writer's craft and the marketing process.   *Query preferred.   Payment:* 1 cent per word or better.   Would be especially interested in reports on UK and Commonwealth writing scenes.

Canadian Aviation (1928), Hugh Whittington (Maclean-Hunter, Ltd), 481 University Avenue, Toronto, Ontario, M5W 1A7   *T.* 416-595 1811.   London: Maclean-Hunter, Ltd., 30 Old Burlington Street, W1X 2AE.
$13 (Gt. Britain) p.a.   M.—Stories with a Canadian angle, on civil or military aviation.   *Payment:* $200 per 1000 words minimum.   *Photographs:* $25 each minimum.

Canadian Forum, The, Denis Smith, 3 Church Street, Suite 401, Toronto, Ontario, M5E 1M2   *T.* 416-364-2431.
$1.00, $9.00 p.a.   10 issues p.a.—Articles on public affairs and the arts. *Length:* up to 2500 words.   *Payment:* $50 per article.   *Illustrations:* line and photographs.

Canadian Geographical Journal (1930), David Maclellan, 488 Wilbrod Street, Ottawa, Ontario, K1N 6M8   *T.* 613-236-7493.
subjects.   1500–4000 words.   *Payment:* $300 to $900, depending on length $12.50 p.a. to Soc. members in Canada, $14.50 elsewhere.   Non-members $13.50 in Canada. $15.50 elsewhere.   M.—Organ of Royal Can. Geog. Soc. Articles 2000 to 3000 words dealing authoritatively with Canadian subjects in a style for popular reading.   Must be amply illustrated with photographs (colour and black and white).   *Preliminary* letter advisable.   *Payment:* 5½ cents per word minimum.   Glossy prints.

Canadian Interiors, David Piper, 481 University Avenue, Toronto.   *T.* 416-595-1811.   *T.A.* Macpub.
$1.00 ($15.00 p.a.).   M.—Articles on all aspects of interior design.   *Payment:* $50 approx. for short articles to go with pictures.   *Illustrations:* half-tone and colour.

Canadian Literature (1959), W. H. New, University of British Columbia, Vancouver, B.C., V6T 1W5   *T.* 228 2780.
$3.00, $11.00 p.a.   Q.—Articles on Canadian writers and writing.   *Length:* up to 5000 words.   *Payment:* $12.50 per 1000 words.

Chatelaine, 481 University Avenue, Toronto, M5W 1A7   *T.* 416-595-1811.
50 cents.   M.—Articles with woman's slant used; Canadian angle preferred; interested in first short stories with serials, romance, marriage, adventure, children.   *Payment:* on acceptance; from $300 for non-fiction, $400 for fiction.   *Illustrations:* by leading artists in Canada and the U.S.

Dalhousie Review, The, Dr. Allan Bevan, Dalhousie University Press Ltd., Halifax, N.S., B3H 4H8   *T.* 902-424-2541.
$3.00.   Q. ($6.00 p.a. or $15.00 for 3 years).—Articles on literary, political, historical, educational and social topics; fiction; verse.   *Length:* prose, normally not more than 5000 words; verse, up to 300 words.   *Payment:* $1 per printed page; $3 per printed page for verse.   Contributors also receive one copy of issue and 25 offprints of their work.   Not more than one story and seven or eight poems in any one issue.

Fiddlehead, The (1945), Robert Gibbs, The Observatory, University of New Brunswick, P.O. Box 4400, Fredericton, N.B., E3B 5A3   *T.* 506-454-3591.
$2.00.   Q.—Reviews, poetry, short stories.   *Payment:* $5.00 per printed page.   *Illustrations:* line and half-tone.

Journal of Canadian Studies, Ralph Heintzman, Trent University, Peterborough, Ontario, K9J 7B8.
$8.00 p.a.   Q.—Major academic review of Canadian studies.   Articles of general as well as scholarly interest on history, politics, literature, society, arts.   *Length:* 2000–10,000 words.   No *illustrations.*

Maclean's Magazine, Peter Newman, 481 University Avenue, Toronto, M5W 1A7.   London: 30 Old Burlington Street, W1X 2AE.
60 cents.   M.—News magazine articles of interest to Canadian readers, 500 to 5000 words.   *Rates:* $800 up.   *Illustrations:* on assignment.

Malahat Review, The (1967), Robin Skelton, University of Victoria, P.O. Box 1700, Victoria, British Columbia, V8W 2Y2   *T.* 406-477 6911.
$10.00 p.a.; Overseas $12.00 p.a.   Q.—Short stories, poetry, short plays, critical essays, documents of literary and historical interest.   *Payment:* Prose: $25.00 per 1000 words; Poetry: $10.00 per page or per poem.   *Illustrations:* half-tone.

Makara Magazine (1975), Nora D. Randall, Saeko Usukawa, 1011 Commercial Drive, Vancouver, British Columbia, V5L 3X1.   *T.* 604-253-8931.
$1.50.   Q.—Articles, interviews, reviews, fiction, poetry, history, entertainment, work by and for children.   Material must be Canadian, reflecting alternatives in living, working, etc.   *Payment:* $10 to $100 depending on length.   *Illustrations:* line, half-tone.

Montreal Star, Limited, The, 241–5 rue St Jacques Ouest, Montreal, H2Y 1M6.
15 cents Mon.–Fri.; 40 cents Saturday.   D.

Outdoor Canada Magazine (1972), Sheila Kaighin, 953A Eglinton Avenue East, Toronto, Ontario, M4G 4B5   *T.* 416-429-5550.
$1.00, $4.97 p.a.   7 Times p.a.—Feature articles on Canadian outdoor subjects only.   *Length:* 1000 to 3500 words.   *Payment:* $75 to $150 and $250 for cover story (i.e. feature story and illustration, including appropriate cover shot to lead into story).   *Illustrations:* half-tone, colour.

Performing Arts in Canada Magazine (1961), Linda Kelley, 52 Avenue Road, Toronto, Ontario, M5R 2G3   *T.* 416-921-2601 and 5188.
$5.00 p.a., $6.50 p.a. outside Canada.   Q.—Feature articles on Canadian theatre, music and dance artists and organizations; technical articles on scenery, lighting, make-up, costumes, etc.   *Length:* 1500 to 2000 words.   *Payment:* $100.   *Illustrations:* black and white photographs, line.

Quebec Chronicle Telegraph (1764), Myles O'Farrell (Quebec Newspapers, Ltd.), 255 Avenue St. Sacrement, St. Malo, Quebec.   P.O. Box 100.   *T.* 418-527 2591.
10 cents.   D. (15 cents. Saturday).—Little or no freelance material published. Will cover Quebec assignments on request.

Quill & Quire (1935), Susan Walker, 59 Front Street East, Toronto, M5E 1B3   *T.* 416-364 3333.
$15.00 p.a.   17 p.a.—Articles of interest about the Canadian Book trade. *Payment:* From $75.   *Illustrations:* line, half-tone.

Reader's Digest (1922), Charles W. Magill, 215 Redfern Avenue, Montreal, Quebec, H3Z 2V9   *T.* 514-934-0751.
95 cents.   M.—Original articles on all subjects must be of broad general appeal, thoroughly researched and professionally written.   Outline or query recommended.   *Length:* 3000 words approx.   *Payment:* $1200 to $2000. Also previously published material.   *Illustrations:* colour, half-tone, line.

Saturday Night Magazine (1887), Robert Fulford, 69 Front Street East, Toronto, Ontario, M5E 1R3   *T.* 416-362 5907.
$1.00.   10 issues p.a.—Short stories, poetry, assigned articles.   *Payment:* $400 per column; $1000 feature articles and fiction; poetry $120.   *Illustrations:* line, half-tone, colour.

Spectator, The (1846), Executive Editor, John G. Doherty; Publisher, John D. Muir, 44 Frid Street, Hamilton, L8N 3G3 *T.* 416-526-3333.
15 cents. Monday to Friday; 30 cents Saturday.—Articles of general interest, political analysis and background; interviews, stories of Canadians abroad. *Length:* 800 maximum. *Payment:* rate varies; up to $75 per 800 words.

(Toronto) Globe and Mail, The (1844), Richard S. Malone, Publisher and Editor-in-Chief, 444 Front Street West, Toronto, Ontario, M5V 2S9. London: 164–167 Temple Chambers (2nd Floor), Temple Avenue, London, EC4Y 0EA *T.* 01-353-5795.
15 cents. D. (25 cents Saturday.)

Toronto Life (1967), Don Obe, 59 Front Street, Toronto, Ontario, M5E 1B3 *T.* 416-364-3333.
$1.25, $9.00 p.a. M.—Articles, profiles on Toronto and Torontonians. *Illustrations:* line, half-tone, colour.

Toronto Star (1892), One Yonge Street, Toronto, M5E 1E6 *T.* 367-2000. *L.A.:* London International Press Centre, Shoe Lane, London, EC4A 3JB *T.* 01-353 5909.
15 cents. D. (35 cents Saturday.)

(Vancouver) Province (1898), Paddy Sherman (Publisher), 2250 Granville Street, Vancouver, V6H 3G2. *T.* 732-2222.
20 cents. D.

Vancouver Sun, Stuart Keate, Publisher; Bruce Larsen, Managing Editor; David Ablett, Editor of Editorial Pages; Bruce Hutchison, Editorial Director, 2250 Granville Street, Vancouver, V6H 3G2, B.C. *T.* 732-2311. London: 164–167 Temple Chambers (2nd Floor), Temple Avenue, London, EC4Y 0EA *T.* 01-353 5796.
20 cents. D. Saturday 25 cents (not Sunday).—Rates depending on arrangements. Very little outside contribution. Photographs only.

Wascana Review (1966), William Howard, c/o English Department, University of Regina, Regina, Sask., S4S 0A2.
$2.00 per issue. Semi-annual ($3.50 p.a.; $9 for 3 years).—Criticism, short stories, poetry, reviews. *Length:* prose, not more than 6000 words; verse, up to 100 lines. *Payment:* $3 per page for prose; $10 per printed page for verse; $4.00 per page for reviews. Contributors also receive two free copies of the issue. Manuscripts from freelance writers welcome.

Windsor This Month (1974), Linda J. Steel, 27 Riverside Drive West, P.O. Box 1029, Station "A," Windsor, Ontario, N9A 6P4.
$1.00 ($9.00 p.a.). M.—General articles of interest to Windsor, including nostalgia, how-to, and humour. No fiction. *Illustrations:* line and half-tone.

Winnipeg Free Press (1872), Peter McLintock, 300 Carlton Street, Winnipeg, Manitoba, R3C 3C1 *T.* 943-9331.
15 cents, 25 cents Saturday. D.—Some freelance articles. *Payment:* $35 to $50.

Winnipeg Tribune (1890), E. H. Wheatley (Publisher), Gerry Haslam (Editor), 257 Smith Street, Winnipeg, Box 7000, Manitoba, R3C 3B2 *T.* 985-4512.
10 cents. D. (Friday and Saturday, 15 cents.)

INDIAN JOURNALS AND MAGAZINES

NOTE.—*Newspapers are listed under the towns in which they are published.*

American and British Book News (1977), Kunnuparampil P. Punnoose, 6/77 WEA Karol Bagh, New Delhi 110 005. *T.* 567749.
Rs. 2.50. Q.—Articles on books, authors, publishing, marketing of books. *Payment:* Rs. 100 per 1000 words. *Illustrations:* line, half-tone.

Aryan Path (1930), Sophia Wadia, Theosophy Hall, 40 New Marine Lines, Bombay, 400 020. London: 62 Queen's Gardens, Lancaster Gate, W2 3AH *T.* 01-273 0688.
20p. Alternate months (£1.05 p.a.).—An international review of philosophy, mysticism, comparative religion, psychical research, Indian culture and the brotherhood of humanity. Articles of 1500 to 2500 words. *Payment:* on acceptance and by arrangement.

(Bombay) Eve's Weekly, Mrs. Gulshan Ewing, Eve's Weekly, Ltd., Peraj Building, Samachar Marg, Bombay, 400 023. *T.* 271444.
Re. 1.50. W.—Articles and features on a wide variety of topics with special emphasis on women's issues, and reflecting a feminist point of view. Also social news, fashion, health, child development, handicrafts, etc. *Illustrations:* pictures, sketches, artwork.

(Bombay) Illustrated Weekly of India, The, Khushwant Singh, Bombay. U.K.: 26 Station Approach, Wembley, Middlesex, HA0 2LA *T.* 01-903 9696.
Re. 1.50. W.—First-class photo features and illustrated articles dealing with topical matters by authoritative writers only, for educated Indian public of modern outlook. *Length:* articles from 800–2000 words; fiction up to 2000 words; serials, 60,000 words. *Payment:* on publication. First reproduction rights India, Pakistan, Burma and Ceylon required.

(Bombay) The Indian Express (Daily) (Proprietors: Indian Express Newspapers (Bombay), Private, Ltd.), Express Towers, Nariman Point, Bombay 400 021. Editor-in-Chief: V. K. Narasimhan. Also Delhi, Madras, Madurai, Vijayawada, Ahmedabad, Bangalore and Cochin. London Office: 92 Hamilton Terrace, St. John's Wood, London, NW8 *T.* 01-289 3133.
35 paise. D.—For editorial page articles of current political interest. *Length:* from about 1000–2000. *Payment:* average £2 per 750 words.

(Calcutta) Capital (1888), A. K. Ganguly, 19 R.N. Mookerjee Road, Calcutta 700 001 *T.* 235825.
W. Subscriptions in advance. Rs. 125 p.a.—Dealing weekly with economic, industrial and public affairs in India.

(Calcutta) Statesman, S. Nihal Singh, Statesman House, Chowringhee Square, Calcutta. For Northern India a separate edition is published daily from Statesman House, New Delhi. London: Thanet House, 231 Strand, London, WC2R 1DA *T.* 01-353 5353.
40 paise. D.—Published simultaneously in Calcutta and Delhi. Circulates widely in India, and generally respected for its reliable news and independent policy. The magazine section has been temporarily suspended but there is room for occasional light pieces on the editorial page. *Rate of payment:* Rs. 250 per 1200 words. *Illustrations:* photographs or line drawings according to merit. **The Statesman Weekly** (Rs. 2.75). A digest of Indian news and views, market trends and quotations.

Commerce (1910), Vadilal Dagli, Post Box No. 11017, Bombay 400 020. *T.* 253505.

Rs. 2.50. W. (Rs. 125 p.a.).—Special articles from 1000 to 1500 words, on economic, commercial, financial, and industrial topics with special reference to India and the East generally; matters connected with Indian firms and companies domiciled in the United Kingdom. *Payment:* £2.00 per column (approximately 350 words).

Current Events Magazine (1955), Devdutt, 15 Rajpur Road, Dehra Dun. *T.* 3187 and 3792.

Rs. 2.50 M. (£5.00 or $10.00 p.a.).—Coverage: political, social and economic affairs of the world. Regular features on sports, medicines, terminology, business, law, literature, book reviews, etc. Articles of about 1500 words on the above subjects invited. Topical articles on current development in the international political scene. Asian perspective preferred. *Payment:* by arrangement. *Illustrations:* line and half-tone. Members: All-Indian Newspaper Editors Conference. *London Representative:* M/S Publishing & Distributing Co., Ltd., 177 Regent Street, London, W1R 7FB *T.* 01-734 6534.

Literary Market Review (1974), Kunnuparampil P. Punnoose, 6/77 WEA Karol Bagh, New Delhi, 110 005 *T.* 567749.

(Lucknow) National Herald (1938), M. Chalapathi Rau (Associated Journals, Ltd.), Bisheshwar Nath Road, Lucknow. *T.* Lucknow 22173 and 29832. 33 paise (35 paise on Sunday). D.—Articles and illustrations of all kinds, Rs. 30 per column. No fiction.

(Madras) Hindu, The, 201A Mount Road, Madras 600 002. Proprietors: Kasturi & Sons, Ltd. London: 26 Beaumont Avenue, Wembley, Middlesex. Washington: 6429, 31st Place, NW, Washington, D.C.20015. Tokyo: 9–15, 3–Chome Ebisu Hinami, Shibuya-Ku. Branches at Bombay, Calcutta, New Delhi, Bangladore, Hyderabad, Madurai, Tiruchirapalli, Coimbatore and Trivandrum.

45 paise. D.—Printed in English, having the widest and most influential circulation among the reading public in India. Accepts contributions on Indian affairs and international topics. *Payment:* by arrangement. *Illustrations:* photographs.

(Madras) Mail, V. P. V. Rajan, P.O. Box 1, 201 Mount Road, Madras. *T.* 83931. London: Wallace Cartwright & Co. Ltd., 55–56 St. James's Street, SW1A 1LQ *T.* 01-629 2476.

25 paise. D.—Short topical articles, illustrated preferred, principally dealing with some aspect of Indian affairs or India's relations and commerce with other countries. *Length:* about 800 words. Articles, sketches and photographs should be air-mailed direct to Madras. *Payment:* depends upon quality of articles. *Average rates:* Rs. 30 (£2.25) per 1000 words for non-syndicated material. *Illustrations:* topical sketches and photographs of Indian interest.

Minimax (1972), Durgadas Mukhopadhyay, K-5/8 Model Town, Delhi, 110009. *T.* 226390.

Rs. 3 (Rs. 10 p.a.), UK 50p. (£2.00 p.a.), USA $1.50 ($6.00 p.a.). Q.—Articles, poems, short stories, review articles, critical essays; also performing arts. *Payment:* by arrangement. *Illustrations:* half-tone.

(New Delhi) National Herald (1968), M. Chalapathi Rau (Associated Journals, Ltd.), Herald House, Bahadur Shah, Zafar Marg, New Delhi, 1. *T.* New Delhi 271547.
35 paise. D.—Articles and illustrations of all kinds, Rs. 20 per column. No fiction.

Onlooker, The (1939), S. Venkat Narayan, 21 Dalal Street, Bombay 400 023. *T.* 274143. *T.A.* Newsads.
Rs. 1.50. Fortnightly News Magazine.—Articles and photo features on travel and subjects of human interest with a news slant. *Length:* 1000–1500 words. *Payment:* £10 per article. *Illustrations:* photographs and drawings.

Thought (1949), Ram Singh, 35 Netaji Subhas Marg, Daryaganj, Delhi, 110006. *T.* 274648.
5p. W.—Deals with political, social and economic affairs from democratic standpoint. Publishes regular literary supplement, short stories, book reviews, etc. Articles of about 1300–1600 words on the above subjects and reviews of about 600–900 words are invited. *Payment:* by arrangement.

Times of India, The, Girilal Jain, Bombay, Delhi and Ahmedabad. U.K.: 26 Station Approach, Sudbury, Wembley, Middlesex, HA0 2LA *T.* 01-903 9696. *Telex:* 8951317.
40p. D.—Topical articles and photographs likely to be of particular interest in India and to Indian readers. *Length* preferred, 1000–1500 words. *Payment:* Rs. 150 to Rs. 400 per article. Action photographs and line drawings.

United Asia (1948), Editor-in-Chief: G. S. Pohekar, Editor: Dinkar Sakrikar, 12 Rampart Row, Bombay, 1. *T.* 252158.
Rs. 15 p.a.; $5 p.a. outside India. Bi-M.—Articles, short stories, poems of Asian interest. Insistence on an Asian perspective and mood. *Length:* 2000 to 3000 words. *Payment:* by arrangement. *Illustrations:* line, halftone, colour, photographs, drawings, cartoons of Asian interest.

IRISH JOURNALS AND MAGAZINES

Caritas (1934), Published by the Order of St. John of God in Ireland at Granada, Stillorgan, Co. Dublin. *T.* 880509, 880049.
15p. Q.—Magazine of Christian concern. Matter on mental and physical health concerning family and community well-being. Articles of 700 to 1200 words, and features on children and youth, personal case histories, biographies and articles of religious and topical interest. *Payment:* £2.10 to £26.25. *Illustrations:* Photographs and sketches in black and white only.

Catholic Standard, The incorporated in the **Catholic Herald**—see page 23.

Cross, The (1910), Rev. Columb O'Donnell, C.P., Mount Argus, Dublin, 6. *T.* Dublin 971469 and 971165.
15p. M. (£2.50 p.a. post free).—Illustrated magazine of Catholic and general interest. Articles, 900 to 1500 words on general topics of Catholic interest. Illustrated articles especially welcome. No Fiction. *Payment:* £10.00 to £15.00 on publication. *Illustrations:* half-tone from photos.

Hibernia (1936), John Mulcahy, 4 Beresford Place, Dublin 1. *T*. 788577.
25p. W.—Articles, features, comments on Irish politics, current affairs, and everything of interest to Irish people at home and abroad, including books, writers, theatre, the arts, etc. *Payment:* by arrangement. *Illustrations:* line and half-tone.

Ireland of the Welcomes, Baggot Street Bridge, Dublin, 2. *T*. Dublin 765871.
35p. Bi-M.—Irish items with cultural, sporting or topographical background designed to arouse interest in Irish holidays. No fiction. *Length:* 1200 to 1800 words. *Payment:* by arrangement. *Illustrations:* scenic and topical. Preliminary letter preferred. Mostly commissioned.

Ireland's Own (1902), John McDonnell, North Main Street, Wexford. *T*. 053-22155.
12p. W.—Short stories (1500 to 2000 words); romances in particular, but with an Irish background; articles of interest to Irish readers at home and abroad (1000 to 3000 words); general and literary articles (1000 to 2500 words). Special issues for Christmas and St. Patrick's Day. Cartoons, adventure strips for family reading. Suggestions for new features considered. *Payment:* varies according to quality, originality and length. Serials, of novel length, preliminary letter advisable, enclosing synopsis and S.A.E., payment by arrangement. *Illustrations:* half-tone and line.

Irish Independent, Aidan J. Pender, Independent House, 90 Middle Abbey Street, Dublin 1. *T*. 746841.
12p. D.—Special articles on topical or general subjects. *Length:* 700 to 1000 words. *Payment:* Editor's estimate of value.

Irish Journal of Medical Science (1st series 1832, 6th series January 1926, Volume 147, 1978), Royal Academy of Medicine, 6 Kildare Street, Dublin 2. *T*. 767650.
£1.50. M. (Subscription Great Britain and Ireland £10.00 post free; overseas £15.00 post free).—Official Organ of the Royal Academy of Medicine in Ireland. Original contributions in medicine, surgery, midwifery, public health, etc.; reviews of professional books, reports of medical societies, etc. Outside contributions not paid for. *Illustrations:* half-tone, line and colour.

Irish Press, The, T. P. Coogan, Burgh Quay, Dublin 2. *T*. 757931.
10p. D.—Topical articles about 1200 words. *Payment:* by arrangement. *Illustrations:* topical photographs.

Irish Tatler & Sketch, The (1972), John Kerry Keane, 34 Sydney Avenue, Blacknock, Co. Dublin. *T*. 01-889272.
35p. M. (£5.00 p.a.).—Pictorial review of the social round, with special features on the fine arts, wines, gardening, fashion, bridge, weddings, business round. *Length:* 1000 words. *Payment:* by arrangement. *Illustrations:* half-tones.

Irish Times, Douglas Gageby, 11–15 D'Olier Street, Dublin 2. *T*. Dublin 722022. *Telex:* 5167.
15p. D.—Mainly staff-written. Specialist contributions (800 to max. 2000 words) by commission on basis of ideas submitted, *payment* at editor's valuation. *Illustrations:* photographs and line drawings.

Reality (1966), Redemptorist Publications, Orwell Road, Dublin 6. *T*. Dublin 900840 and 903251.
15p. M.—Illustrated magazines for christian living. Articles on all aspects of modern life, including family, youth, religion, leisure. Illustrated articles especially welcome. Short stories. *Length* (articles or stories): 1000–1500 words. *Payment:* by arrangement; average £5.00 per 1000 words.

Studies An Irish quarterly review (1912). Rev. Patrick O'Connell, s.j., 35 Lower Leeson Street, Dublin 2. *T.* 766785.
£1.00 Q.—A general review of current affairs, literature, history, the arts, philosophy. Articles written by specialists for the general reader. Critical book reviews. *Length:* 5000 words. *Payment:* by arrangement. *Preliminary letter.*

Sunday Independent, Michael Hand, Independent House, 90 Middle Abbey Street, Dublin, 1. *T.* 746121.
15p. W.—Special articles. *Length:* according to subject. *Payment:* at Editor's valuation; good. *Illustrations:* topical or general interest.

Sunday Press, The, Vincent Jennings, Burgh Quay, Dublin, 2. *T.* Dublin 757931. *T.A.* Sceala, Dublin.
15p. W.—Articles of human interest. *Length:* 1000 words. *Illustrations:* line and half-tone.

Woman's Way (1963), Caroline Mitchell, J. S. Publications, 4 South Great George's Street, Dublin 2. *T.* 779321.
15p. W.—Short stories, light romance, career, holiday, 3500 to 4500 words. *Payment:* £20.00 to £30.00. Articles of interest to women. *Illustrations:* half-tone and colour.

Word, The (1936), Rev. Brother Paul Hurley, s.v.d. (The Word Press, Hadzor, Droitwich), Divine Word Hostel, Maynooth, Co. Kildare. *T.* Dublin 286391.
12p. M.—A Catholic illustrated magazine for the family. Illustrated articles of general interest up to 2000 words and good picture features. *Payment:* by arrangement. *Illustrations:* photographs and large colour transparencies.

NEW ZEALAND JOURNALS AND MAGAZINES

NOTE.—*Newspapers are listed under the towns in which they are published.*

(Auckland) New Zealand Herald (1863), J. F. W. Hardingham, P.O. Box 32, Auckland. *T.* 78-988. London: Ludgate House, 107 Fleet Street, EC4. *T.* 01-353 2686.
12c. D.—Literary and informative articles 800 to 1100 words. *Minimum payment:* $20–$100 according to length and nature. Half-tone blocks (65 screen).

Auckland Star (1870), Keith Aitken (New Zealand Newspapers, Ltd.), P.O. Box 3697, Auckland. *T.* 797-626. 12c. D.

(Christchurch) Press, The, N. L. Macbeth, P.O. Box 1005, Christchurch. London: 107 Fleet Street, EC4. *T.* 01-353 2686.
8c. D.—Articles of general interest not more than 1200 words. *Payment:* by arrangement. Extra payment for photographs and line drawings.

Christchurch Star (1868), M. B. Forbes (New Zealand Newspapers, Ltd.), Kilmore Street, Christchurch.
12c. D.—Topical articles.

(Dunedin) Otago Daily Times (1861), R. K. Eunson, P.O. Box 181, Dunedin. London: 107 Fleet Street, EC4. *T.* 01-353 2686.
12c. D.—Any articles of general interest of about 1000 words, but preference is given to New Zealand writers. Topical illustrations and personalities. *Payment:* Current New Zealand rates.

Gisborne Herald, The (1874), E. W. Dumbleton, P.O. Box 573, Gisborne. *T.* 82099. *T.A.* Herald, Gisborne.
10c. D.—Topical features of local interest. *Length:* 1000 to 1500 words. *Payment:* by arrangement. *Illustrations:* half-tone.

Hawke's Bay Herald Tribune (result of merger between Hawke's Bay Herald (1857), Hastings Standard (1896) and Hawke's Bay Tribune (1910), L. E. Anderson, Karamu Road, Hastings. *T.* 85-155.
12c. D.—Limited requirements. *Payment:* $6 to $30 for articles, $4 to $10 for photographs. *Illustrations:* Webb off-set.

(Invercargill) Southland Times, The (1862), P. M. Muller, P.O. Box 805, Invercargill. *T.* 82 079. *T.A.* Times, Invercargill. *Telex:* NZ 5254.
12c. D.—Articles of up to 1500 words on topics of Southland interest. *Payment:* 30c per inch (basic). *Illustrations:* line and half-tone.

Landfall (1947), Peter Smart, The Caxton Press, P.O. Box 25-088, Christchurch. *T.* 68516.
$2.00. ($2.25 overseas). Q.—All literary and general material by N.Z. writers considered, of any length. Illustrates the work of N.Z. painters, sculptors, architects, photographers, etc. *Payment:* by arrangement.

Management, S. C. Niblock (Modern Productions, Ltd.), Box 3159, Auckland. *T.* 768808. *T.A.* Amalmod.
75c. M.—Articles on management, efficiency, topics of general interest to the top businessman. A New Zealand angle or application preferred. *Length:* 500–1200 words. *Payment:* by arrangement. *Illustrations:* photographs, line drawings.

Motorman, Published by Fourman Holdings Ltd., P.O. Box 883, 44 Webb Street, Wellington. *T.* 850538.
$1.25. Q.—Circulation in New Zealand and Australia. New Zealand's only motoring monthly devoted to all aspects of motoring of interest to the family man and the sporting motorist. Road tests, new products, industry news, touring and general motoring. *Illustrations:* photographs, cartoons and line drawings. Contributions welcomed. *Payment:* on acceptance from $20 per 1000 words. Special rates for exclusive stories. $3.00 photos published.

NBR Marketplace, Ian F. Grant, Published by Fourth Estate Periodicals, P.O. Box 1449, Wellington. *T.* 736-876. *Cables:* Natbus.
Q.—Magazine on marketing and advertising developments in New Zealand. Each issue carries up to six carefully researched, brightly written 4000–8000-word articles. Staff written and commissioned, but contributor enquiries welcomed. *Payment:* up to $150 per article on publication.

(Napier) Daily Telegraph, The (1871), M. A. Berry, P.O. Box 343, Napier. *T.* 54488.
12c. D.—Mainly limited market for features on Hawke's Bay. *Payment:* up to $10. $2.50 upwards for pictures. *Illustrations:* line and half-tone.

Nelson Evening Mail, The, G. D. Spencer, P.O. Box 244, Nelson. *T.* 87-079.
6c. D.—Features, articles on New Zealand subjects. *Length:* 500–1000 words. *Payment:* up to $10 per 1000 words. *Illustrations:* half-tone, colour.

(New Plymouth) Daily News, The (1857), R. J. Avery, P.O. Box 444, New Plymouth. *T.* 80559.
10c. D.—Articles preferably with a Taranaki connection. *Payment:* by negotiation. *Illustrations:* half-tone.

New Zealand Bride, D. S. Lucas, Published by Lucas-Altman Publishing Co., Ltd., P.O. Box 1849. Auckland *T.* 362-933.
Published once a year in September.—Articles by arrangement—letter required.

New Zealand Farmer, Boyd Wilson, P.O. Box 1409, High Street, Auckland.
55c. F.—Authoritative, simply-written articles on new developments in livestock husbandry, grassland farming, cropping, farm machinery, marketing. *Length:* 1000 to 1800 words. *Payment:* according to merit.

New Zealand Gardener (Magazine of Outdoor Living), David F. Jones Ltd., P.O. Box 6117, Wellington.
40c. M.—Topical articles on gardening, new plants and methods of cultivation, new products of horticultural interest, home workshop project of all kinds for the home and garden. Authoritative articles by specialists only. *Payment:* $15.40 per 1000 words. *Illustrations:* photographs or line; payment $4.50 per print on publication; colour transparencies are used.

New Zealand Holiday, Wendy Pye, Box 1209, Auckland.
30c. Q.—Travel in New Zealand and subjects likely to interest tourists and intending travellers. *Payment:* $10 and upwards per 1000 words, on publication. *Illustrations:* photographs, colour transparencies on cover.

New Zealand Listener, The (1939), Tony Reid, P.O. Box 3140, Wellington. *T.* 721-777.
25c. W.—Topical features of New Zealand and international interest. Short stories, verse. *Length* for short stories and articles: up to 2500 words. *Illustrations:* mainly black and white; colour cover. *Payment:* from $50.00 per 1000 words, or by arrangement.

New Zealand Motorcycle News, published by Northrop-Bonner Publications Ltd., P.O. Box 1717, 44 Webb Street, Wellington. *T.* 850537.
50c. F.—Circulation New Zealand. New Zealand's only motorcycle publication. Contains reports, interviews, road tests, new products and developments, technical drawings. Contributions welcomed. *Payment:* minimum $12.00. Special rates for exclusive stories. $3.00 photos published.

New Zealand Outdoor (1937) (Associated Publications), V. V. Donald, P.O. Box 236, Masterton.
40c. M.—Stories or technical articles up to 2500 words on shooting, fishing, hunting, mountaineering, and other kindred outdoor sports. *Payment:* $5 per 1000 words: photographs $1.00, cover pictures $2.00. *Illustrations:* line or half-tone.

New Zealand Woman's Weekly (1932), Jean Wishart (New Zealand Newspapers, Ltd.), P.O. Box 1409, Auckland.
30c. W.—Pictorial features. Illustrated articles of general, family, world interest, particularly with a New Zealand slant. *Length:* articles 750–1750. *Payment:* on acceptance. *Illustrations:* photographs.

New Zealand Yachting and Power Boating, John Callen, P.O. Box 1034, Wellington. *T.* 676 068. *T.A.* Flashweek, Wellington. *Telex:* 3811.
75c. M.—Articles on all aspects of yachting. *Payment:* by arrangement but from $2.50 for full single column. *Illustrations:* line, half-tone, colour.

N.Z. Energy Journal (formerly **N.Z. Electrical Journal**) (1928), F. N. Stace, B.E., Technical Publications, Ltd., C.P.O. Box 3047, Wellington, 1.
70c. M.—Technical and trade news and articles. Preliminary letter essential. *Payment:* by arrangement.

N.Z. Engineering (1946), F. N. Stace, B.E., Technical Publications, Ltd., C.P.O. Box 3047, Wellington, 1.
$1.50. M.—Technical articles of interest to New Zealand engineers. Preliminary letter essential. *Payment:* by arrangement.

N.Z. Engineering News (1970), Alex G. Taylor, Baranduin Publishers Ltd., P.O. Box 41–033, Eastbourne.
Free. M. (not January).—Technical news items of interest to New Zealand engineers and technicians. Preliminary letter essential. *Payment:* by arrangement.

N.Z. Truth (Wellington Newspapers Ltd.), R. S. Gault, Press House, Willis Street, Wellington, P.O. Box 1122.
15c. W.—Bold investigative reporting, exposés. *Length:* 500–1000 words, preferably accompanied by photographs. *Payment:* about $20 per 500 words, extra for photographs.

Sea Spray (1945), David Pardon, 360 Dominion Road, Auckland (P.O. Box 793). *T.* 689-959.
75c. M.—Feature material and photographs on pleasure boating concerning New Zealanders, power or sail. Technical articles and how-to articles. *Payment:* $30 per 1000 words. *Illustrations:* line and half-tone.

Timaru Herald, The, G. J. Gaffaney, P.O. Box 46, 23 Sophia Street, Timaru. *T.* 5099 '
10c. D.—Topical articles of up to 800 words. *Payment:* by arrangement. *Illustrations:* half-tone.

(Wellington) Evening Post, The (1865), M. Robson, P.O. Box 1398, Willis Street, Wellington. *T.* 729-009. *London Office:* N.Z. Associated Press, 107 Fleet Street, EC4A 2AN *T.* 01-353 2686.
10c. D.—General topical articles, 600 words. *Payment:* N.Z. current rates or by arrangement. News illustrations.

SOUTH AFRICAN JOURNALS AND MAGAZINES

Argus South African Newspapers.
The Argus, Cape Town, 12c. D.; **Week-End Argus** (Sat.), 12c.; **The Star,** Johannesburg, 12c. D.; **The Daily News,** Durban, 12c. D.; **Sunday Tribune,** Durban, 25c.; **The Diamond Fields Advertiser, Kimberley,** 7c. D.; **The Chronicle,** Bulawayo, 8c. D.; **The Rhodesia Herald,** Salisbury, 9c. D.; **The Sunday Mail,** Salisbury, 10c.; **The Sunday News,** Bulawayo, 8c.; **Umtali Post,** Umtali, 7c. Accept articles of general, South African and Rhodesian interest. *Payment:* for contributions accepted for publication is made in accordance with an Editor's estimate of the value of the manuscript. Contributions should be addressed to the Managing Editor, Argus South African Newspapers Ltd., 85 Fleet Street, London, EC4Y 1ED (*T.* 01-353 3765), and not direct.

Bethlehem Express (1906), T. C. Roffe, 10 Muller Street, Bethlehem.
10c. W.—English and Afrikaans.

(Bloemfontein Friend, The, T. Ross-Thompson, P.O. Box 245, Bloemfontein 9300. London: Argus South African Newspapers Ltd., 85 Fleet Street, EC4Y 1ED   *T.* 01-353 3765.
10c.   D.

(Cape Town) Cape Times, The (1876), A. H. Heard, P.O. Box 11, or 77 Burg Street, Cape Town.   *T.* 41-3361.   London Editor: Stanley Uys, 135 Fleet Street, EC4.   *T.* 01-353 4473.
12c.   D.—Contributions must be suitable for daily newspaper and must not exceed a column (about 1000 words).   Articles of general, sporting, social or topical interest, also travel, and general articles.   *Payment:* approx. £10.00 per 1000 words.   *Illustrations:* photographs of outstanding South African interest.   Payment at minimum rate of £1.50 per picture.

Car (1957), Cedric Wright, P.O. Box 59, Cape Town.   *T.* 22-8561.   *T.A.* Confrere.
50c.   M.—New car announcements with pictures and full colour features of motoring interest.   *Payment:* by arrangement.   *Illustrations:* half-tone and colour.

Charmaine (1973), N. Willems, Republican Press (Pty.) Ltd., Box 32083, Mobeni 4060, Natal.   *T.* Durban 422041.   *T.A.* Keur, Durban.   London: London International Press Centre, Shoe Lane, London, EC4A 3JB   *T.* 01-353 3657.
30c.   M.—Show business articles, romantic fiction.   *Length:* 1500 words.
Payment: by arrangement.   *Illustrations:* half-tone, line, colour.

Darling, Marilyn Hattingh Republican Press (Pty.) Ltd., P.O. Box 2595, Johannesburg 2000.   *T.* 37-1300.   London: International Press Centre, Shoe Lane, EC4A 3JB   *T.* 01-353 3657.
40c.   F.—Articles of interest to women, contributions must be accompanied by colour or black and white photographs.   Modern fiction for women.   Average *length:* 3000 words for short story.   *Payment:* from R25 per 1000 words.   *Illustrations:* line, half-tone, colour.   *Payment:* by arrangement.

(Durban) Natal Mercury (1852), J. O. McMillan (Robinson & Co. Pty., Ltd.), Devonshire Place, Durban, 4001.   *T.* 319331.
12c.   D. (except Sunday).—Serious background news and inside details of world events.   *Length:* 700 to 900 words.   *Illustrations:* photographs of general interest.

Fair Lady, Jane Raphaely (National Magazine Company), P.O. Box 1802, Cape Town 8000.   *T.* 43 6886.   *T.A.* Ladyfair.   London: *T.* 01-353 3166.
40c.   F.—Articles and stories for women including showbiz, travel, humour.   *Length:* articles up to 5000 words, short stories approx. 3000 words; short novels and serialisation of book material.   *Payment:* on quality rather than length—by arrangement on acceptance.   *Illustrations:* Colour and black-and-white photographs for articles and features of general interest— celebrities, royalty, situation pictures.   Full colour and black-and-white art illustrations for stories and serials.

Family Radio and TV, L. Bennett, Republican Press (Pty.) Ltd., P.O. Box 32083, Mobeni 4060, Natal.   *T.* Durban 422041.   *T.A.* Keur, Durban.   London: International Press Centre, Shoe Lane, London, EC4A 3JB   *T.* 01-353 3657.
40c.   W.—Illustrated.   Primarily a television programme magazine but also a market for articles about people and places, preferably with South African angle.   Strong news features and/or photojournalism.   1000–4000 words.   Short stories 1500–5000 words.   *Illustrations:* usually commissioned.   *Payment:* by arrangement.

Farmer's Weekly (1911), E. C. Havinga, P.O. Box 32083, Mobeni 4060, Natal. *T.* Durban 425322. London: Republican Press (Pty.) Ltd., International Press Centre, Shoe Lane, EC4A 3JB   *T.* 01-353 3657 and 4484.
25c.   W. (R10.40 p.a. in South Africa, R31.20 p.a. overseas).—Articles, generally illustrated, up to 1000 words in length dealing with all aspects of practical farming and research with particular reference to conditions in Southern Africa. *Payment:* according to merit. *Illustrations:* continuous-tone, full colour and line. Includes women's section which accepts articles suitably illustrated, on subjects of interest to women. *Payment:* according to merit.

Garden and Home, Republican Press (Pty.) Ltd., P.O. Box 32083, Mobeni 4060, Natal.   *T.* Durban 422041.   *T.A.* Keur, Durban. London: International Press Centre, Shoe Lane, London, EC4A 3JB   *T.* 01-353 3657.
50c.   M.—Well illustrated articles on gardening, suitable for Southern Hemisphere. Articles for home section on furnishings, flower arrangement, food. *Payment:* by arrangement. *Illustrations:* half-tone and colour.

Huisgenoot (1916), Tobie Boshoff, 1 Leeuwen Street, Cape Town 8000.   *T.* 41-3181. London: National Magazines, 529 International Press Centre, Shoe Lane, London, EC4A 3JB.
30c.   W.—Serials, short stories, articles for a general interest magazine. *Length:* 1000 words. *Payment:* by arrangement. *Illustrations:* line, half-tone, colour.

(Johannesburg) Sunday Times, Tertius Myburgh, P.O. Box 1090, Johannesburg. *T.* 28-1700. London: South African Morning Newspapers Ltd., Daily Telegraph Building, 135 Fleet Street, EC4.   *T.* 01-353 4473.
30c.   Every Sunday.—Illustrated articles of human interest, from a South African angle if possible. Maximum 1000 words long and two or three photographs. Shorter essays, stories, and articles of a light nature from 500 to 750 words. *Payment:* average rate £20.00 a column. *Illustrations:* photographic (colour or black and white) and line.

Keur, Hannes Cilliers, Republican Press (Pty.) Ltd., P.O. Box 32083, Mobeni 4060, Natal. *T.* Durban 422041. *T.A.* Keur, Durban. London: International Press Centre, Shoe Lane, London, EC4A 3JB   *T.* 01-353 3657.
40c.   W.—Light romantic fiction and photo-stories, serials. Show business personalities. *Payment:* by arrangement. *Illustrations:* line, continuous tone, colour.

Living and Loving (1970), Jane Kinghorn, Republican Press (Pty.) Ltd., P.O. Box 32083, Mobeni 4060, Natal. *T.* Durban 422041. *T.A.* Keur Durban. London: International Press Centre, Shoe Lane, London, EC4A 3JB   *T.* 01-353 3657.
40c.   M.—Romantic fiction, 1500 to 4000 words. Articles dealing with first person experiences; baby, family and marriage, medical articles up to 3000 words. *Payment:* by merit. *Illustrations:* colour, line, half-tone. *Payment:* by arrangement.

Natal Witness (1846), R. S. Steyn, 244 Longmarket Street, Pietermaritzburg, Natal. *T.* Maritzburg 42011. London: 85 Fleet Street, EC4Y 1ED.
10c.   D.—Accepts topical articles. *Length:* 500 to 1000 words. *Payment:* Average of R20 per 1000 words. *Illustrations:* press photos R5.00 each. All material should be submitted direct to the Editor in Pietermaritzburg.

(Port Elizabeth) Eastern Province Herald, P.O. Box 1117, Port Elizabeth. *T.* 523470. London: 135 Fleet Street, London, EC4.   *T.* 01-353 4473.
10c.   D.—Contributions from 700 to 1500 words considered. *Payment:* £6.00 per 700 words minium. *Illustrations:* topical photographs.

Radio & TV Dagboek, Republican Press (Pty.) Ltd., P.O. Box 32083, Mobeni 4060, Natal. *T.* Durban 422041. *T.A.* Keur, Durban. London: International Press Centre, Shoe Lane, London, EC4A 3JB *T.* 01-353 3657.
40c. W.—Strong news features, well illustrated; preferably with radio or TV angle. Short stories, serials. *Payment:* by arrangement. *Illustrations:* continuous tone, colour and line.

Rand Daily Mail (1902), Allister Sparks, 171 Main Street, Johannesburg, South Africa. *T.* 28-1500. *T.A.* News, Johannesburg. *Telex:* 43-7044/7045 JH. *L.A.* South African Morning Newspapers, 135 Fleet Street, EC4. *T.* 01-353 4473. *Telex:* 261455.
10c. D. (except Sundays). Women's supplement, **Eve,** Thursdays.—Articles of general and women's interest, current affairs, fiction. *Length:* 1000 words. Special articles 1800 words (discussion beforehand). *Payment:* R15 to R50. *Illustrations:* Colour transparencies R10 upwards.

Rooi Rose, Republican Press (Pty.) Ltd., P.O. Box 32083, Mobeni 4060, Natal. *T.* Durban 422041. *T.A.* Keur, Durban. London: International Press Centre, Shoe Lane, London, EC4A 3JB *T.* 01-353 3657.
40c. F.—Features about people and places, ideally with women's interest. *Length:* 1000 to 3000 words. Short stories and serials. *Payment:* by arrangement. *Illustrations:* line, continuous tone, colour.

Scope, David Mullany, Republican Press (Pty.) Ltd., P.O. Box 32083, Mobeni 4060, Natal. *T.* Durban 422041. *T.A.* Keur, Durban. London: International Press Centre, Shoe Lane, London, EC4A 3JB *T.* 01-353 3657.
40c. W.—Strong news features, well illustrated, about people and places in all parts of the world. *Length:* up to 4000 words. Short stories 1500 to 5000 words, serials from 20,000 words. *Illustrations:* half-tone, colour.

South African Yachting, Power Waterski & Sail (1957), Brian Lello, P.O. Box 3473, Cape Town 8000. *T.* 43-6625. *T.A.* Fairlead. *Telex:* 57-7826 SA.
R1.00. M.—Articles on yachting, boating or allied subjects. *Payment:* R1.50 per 100 words. *Illustrations:* half-tone and line. Colour covers.

Southern Cross, P.O. Box 2372, 8000 Cape Town. *T.* 455007. *T.A.* Catholic.
20c. M.—The national English language Catholic weekly. Catholic news reports, world and South African. 1000-word articles, 1500-word short stories, cartoons of Catholic interest acceptable from free-lance contributors. *Payment:* 12c. per column cm. for all copy used. *Illustrations:* photographs, R1.00 per column width.

Top Sport, Louis Wessels, 1 Leeuwen Street, Cape Town 8001. *T.* 41 3181.
52c. M.—Sports articles up to 2000 words. *Payment:* £50 to £150. *Illustrations:* half-tone and colour.

Vleis/Meat, P.O. Box 6692, Johannesburg 2000. *T.* 8381351.
25c (R3.00 per annum in South Africa, R4.00 Africa and R6.00 elsewhere). M.—Bilingual magazine covering Southern Africa and abroad in the Livestock and Meat Industry, Dairy and Poultry and their Allied Trades. Articles generally illustrated up to 2000 words in *length* dealing with the above. *Illustrations:* Photographs of outstanding interest. *Payment:* according to merit.

Wings Over Africa, Walter Waldeck, P.O. Box 68585, Bryanston, Transvaal 2021. *T.* 48-2024.
45c. M.—Aviation news and features with an African angle. *Payment:* £20 per 1000 words. *Illustrations:* photographs, £2 each.

Your Family, Angela Waller-Paton, Republican Press (Pty.) Ltd., P.O. Box 32083, Mobeni 4060, Natal. *T.* Durban 422041. *T.A.* Keur, Durban. London International Press Centre, Shoe Lane, London, EC4A 3JB *T.* 01-353 3657.
45c. M.—Cookery, knitting, crochet and homecrafts. *Payment:* by arrangement. *Illustrations:* continuous tone, colour and line.

UNITED STATES JOURNALS AND MAGAZINES

Because of the difficulties in providing an up-to-date list of US journals, the Year Book does not contain a detailed list; instead we refer readers who are particularly interested in the US market to *The Writer's Handbook*, a substantial volume published by The Writer Inc. It contains 100 chapters, each written by an authority in his field, giving practical instruction on many aspects of freelance writing and including details of 2500 markets, payment rates and addresses. Copies of the book may be obtained from the UK sole agent: Freelance Press Services, Forestry Chambers, 67 Bridge Street, Manchester, M3 3BQ, price £9.45, or in America direct from The Writer Inc., 8 Arlington Street, Boston, Mass. 02116 ($14.95 post free).

Also helpful in finding US markets is the monthly magazine, *The Writer*, which contains articles of instruction, lists of markets for manuscripts, and special features of interest to writers everywhere. Available from Freelance Press Services, £8.75 per year, or direct from The Writer Inc., $14 per year.

Freelance Press Services is also agent for The Writer's Digest of Cincinnati, which publishes the monthly magazine *Writer's Digest* (£8.75 per year) and *Writer's Market* (£9.45). The book gives details of over 5000 US markets.

SUBMISSION OF MSS.

When submitting MSS. to US journals send your covering letter with the MS. together with any illustrations, stamped return envelope or international postage coupon. Make clear what rights are being offered for sale for some editors like to purchase MSS. outright, thus securing world copyright, i.e. the traditional British market as well as the US market. MSS. should be sent direct to the US office of the journal and not to any London office.

SYNDICATES, NEWS AND PRESS AGENCIES

In their own interests writers and others are strongly advised to make preliminary enquiries before submitting MSS., and to ascertain terms of work. Commission varies. The details given in the following entries should be noted carefully in respect of syndication, as many news and press agencies do not syndicate articles.

Advance Features, Kerry House, 34a High Street, East Grinstead, Sussex, RH19 3AS *T.* 0342-28562. *Managing Editor:* Peter Norman. Supplies text and visual services to the regional press in Britain and newspapers overseas. Editorial for advertising supplements on consumer, commercial and industrial themes. Instructional graphic panels on a variety of subjects. Daily and weekly cartoons.

African Press Features (1947), P.O. Box 165, Goodwood 7460, South Africa. *Manager:* A. C. Immelman. South African agent for many British, French and American syndicates and Press Agencies. Considers the syndicating of feature articles, short stories, book serialisations, photos and colour transparencies of general interest for the South African market.

Ameuropress, Lafinur 3060, 1425 Buenos Aires, Argentina. *T.* 71-7081. *Cables:* Ameuropress. *Director:* José Gregorio Rîos. Illustrated features to newspapers and magazines world-wide. Specialising in Latin American subjects including travel, human interest stories, hobbies, science, animal features. Regularly supplying women's material including cookery, beauty, fashion, interior decorating, glamour. Also stock colour library for advertising, calendars and illustrations. Undertakes assignments for Latin American subjects.

Associated News Service, 30 Fleet Street, London, EC4. *T.* 01-353 6280. *T.A.* Ansnews, London. General news and photographic agency. Serving U.K. national, provincial, suburban and British Commonwealth and foreign newspapers and periodicals. Feature department supplies London letters, political, sport, fashion, entertainment and general features.

Associated Press (The), Ltd. (News Department), 83–86 Farringdon Street, London, EC4A 4BR. *T.* 01-353 1515. *T.A.* Associated Londonpsy.

Associated Press, The (of America), London Office: 83–86 Farringdon Street, London, EC4A 4BR. *T.* 01-353 1515.

Australasian News & Press Services (D. J. Varney & Associates 1964), Box T 1834, G.P.O., Perth, W. Australia, 6001. *T.* 322-5434, 293-1455. Australian correspondents for international trade, technical and specialist publications. Airmailed trade news summaries prepared on a weekly, monthly or quarterly basis, generally at normal news rates. Special articles, features or research carried out only when commissioned. Commercial intelligence and special news letters prepared. Full range of professional public relations and market research services available.

Australian Associated Press (1935), R. Harbour (*Chief London Correspondent*), 85 Fleet Street, London, EC4Y 1EH *T.* 01-353 0153–4. *T.A.* Austpress, London. *Telex:* 24661. News service to the Australian and New Zealand press, radio and television.

Australian Press Bureau, James M. Dobbie, 129 Molloy Road, Morningside, Brisbane, Queensland, 4170, Australia. *T.* 07-399 6029. Australian correspondent for overseas publications. News, humorous topical columns, feature articles every kind although specialising rural, local authority affairs, strong "people's" interest and movie nostalgia articles (member N.F.T.A.). Outside contributions seldom accepted. No syndicated material.

Ayrshire Press Agency (1956), Gordon Snead, 30 Brodick Avenue, Kilwinning, Ayrshire, KA13 6RL *T.* 0294 52530. Supplies photo news features to daily and weekly papers. Assignments undertaken by own staff photographers. Representatives of the national and provincial press. Photo news articles of particular interest to Scottish readers invited also glamour, fashion and sport.

Barnett, Roger, Associates (1970), *Proprietor:* Roger Barnett, 4 Shaftesbury, Loughton, Essex, 1G10 1HN *T.* 01-508 8856. London Office: 143 Holborn, London, EC1. *Rates:* 30% home, 40% overseas. Books 10%.

Barrow, Ivo, P.O. Box 49, Carnegie, Victoria 3163, Australia. Supplies features for newspapers, periodicals, syndicates and press agencies, world wide. Special interests: Migrants' status, cricket, trade. Research assignments welcomed.

BIPS—Bernsen's International Press Service, Ltd., 2 Barbon Close, Great Ormond Street, London, WC1N 3JS *T.* 01-405 2723. Theo. C. Bernsen, Managing Director-Editor; M. E. De Vries, Managing Editor. Specialise in photo-features, both black-and-white and colour. Want human interest, oddity, gimmicky, popular mechanical, scientific, medical, etc., material suitable for marketing through own branches (London, New York, Paris, Hamburg, Milan, Stockholm, Amsterdam (for Benelux), Helsinki) in many countries. Give full information, well researched. Willing to syndicate, but prefer to assign free-lancers either on BIPS' ideas or photographer's ideas. Buy outright and pay on acceptance. Query with picture story ideas.

BP Singer Features, Inc. *Chairman:* Kurt Singer, 3164 Tyler Avenue, Anaheim, California, 92801. *T.* 714-527 5650. Use 15 features every week which are distributed to publications in 35 countries. Current needs for foreign reprint rights (no originals) are the following: Profiles of famous people— 1–3 parts; Men's fiction; Women's fiction (high standard only); Adventure features (which are not blood-dripping or over-sexed); Colour transparencies; Westerns—short stories and books; books published by reputable publishers. "We accept only previously published material." Interested in British books for North and Latin America, serial and book rights.

Bulls Presstjänst AB, Birger Jarlsgatan 58, Box 5603, 114, 86 Stockholm, Sweden. *T.* 23 40 20. *Telex:* 19 482. *Cables:* Prebull. **Bulls Pressedienst GmbH,** Eysseneckstrasse 50, 6000 Frankfurt am Main 1, Western Germany. *T.* 59 04 18. *Telex:* 0412117. *Cables:* Pressbull. **Bulls Pressetjeneste A/S,** Rådhusgaten 28, Oslo, Norway. *T.* 42 03 63, 42 55 95. *Telex:* 11439. *Cables:* Bullpress. *Market:* Newspapers, magazines and weeklies in Sweden, Denmark, Norway, Finland, Iceland, Germany, Austria and German-speaking Switzerland. *Syndicates:* dramatic and human interest picture stories; topical and well illustrated background articles and series; photographic features dealing with science, people, personalities, glamour; condensations and serialisations of best-selling fiction and non-fiction, cartoons, comic strips.

Camera Press, Ltd., Russell Court, Coram Street, London, WC1 *T.* 01-837 4488, 0606 and 9393. *Telex:* 21654. Syndicates picture stories, portraits, illustrated short stories, and cartoons to the press of 42 countries. *Terms:* 50-50 per cent commission.

Canadian Press, The (1919), Bruce Levett (Chief Correspondent), 83–86 Farringdon Street, London, EC4A 4BS *T.* 01-353 6355. *T.A.* Canapress. London Bureau of the national news agency of Canada.

Capital Press Service, 13 Esher Avenue, Walton-on-Thames, Surrey. *T.* 982-0812. *Cables:* Emespiar. *Directors:* M. Stone, E. W. Stone. *News Editor:* Nicholas Miller. Stories of trade, commerce and industry for trade papers in this country and abroad, and diary paragraphs for the National and provincial press. Interested in tobacco, medicine, air-cargo affairs and business travel for U.K. and U.S. journals.

Caters News Agency, Ltd., 184 Corporation Street, Birmingham, B4 6QE *T.* 021-236 9001. *T.A.* Copy, Birmingham. *Joint Managing Directors:* J. Barnwell and T. A. Stone. Collection of news and pictures throughout Midlands. Representatives of Overseas, National and Provincial Press.

Central Press Features, 80 Fleet Street, London, EC4Y 1ES *T.* 01-353 7792. *T.A.* Features, London, EC4. Supplies every type of feature to newspapers and other publications in 50 countries. Included in over 100 daily and weekly services are columns on international affairs, politics, sports, medicine, law, finance, motoring, science, women's and children's features, strips, crosswords, cartoons and regular 6–12 article illustrated series of international human interest; also editorial material for advertising features.

Children's International News Agency, 2nd Floor, 53 High Street, Belfast, BT1 2AB, Northern Ireland. Children's features/articles affecting in international affairs, politics, sports, medicine, law, finance, science, education, parent children relationship in the modern world, children's topical features in strips, cartoons, art drawings or illustrated photographic feature stories of high quality of international appeal in colour or B/W invited from freelance and professional people for Books, Magazines, Daily and Sunday Newspapers/Weeklies. Short stories, serial novels, non-fiction stories and subject with strong human interest, of true incidents or adventures of children in their daily life, also photographs are in demand every time.

Colwell, Morris A., & Associates, 282 Hatfield Road, St. Albans, Herts, AL1 4UN *T.* 56535. News and feature articles for trade and technical press covering all aspects of industrial and consumer electronics, radio, television, video. Press releases prepared for distribution. Welcome overseas sources requiring British and European coverage. No syndication. Moderate fees negotiable according to assignment. Commissions undertaken: technical press features, special articles and reports.

Crabtree (J. W.) and Sons (1919), 36 Sunbridge Road, Bradford, BD1 2AA *T.* 32937 (Office); 637312 (Home). News, general, trade and sport; information and research for features undertaken.

Daily Telegraph Syndication, 135 Fleet Street, London, EC4P 4BL *T.* 01-353 4242, exts. 139/529. *Telex:* London 22874 Telesyndic. *Cables:* Telesyndic London. News, features, cartoon-strips, photography, book serialisation. World-wide distribution and representation. (See also Daily Telegraph Colour Library and Peterborough Literary Agency.)

Editoriale Aurora Televisione, Viale delle Belle Arti, 7, 00196 Rome. *T.* 3600748/3600790. *Director:* Jacopo Rizza, *General Manager:* Vinicio Congiu. TV films, documentaries, educational, industrial and publicity films.

Elkins, Ted, News and Features Agency, 61 Park Lea, East Herrington, Sunderland, Co. Tyne and Wear. *T.* 0783-280855, and c/o Denham Garden Village, Denham, Bucks. *T.* Denham 2567. News and features on the licensed trade and liquor industry. Commissioned books and magazines.

Europa-Press, Hälsingegatan, 5, Box 6410, S-113 82, Stockholm, Sweden. *T.* 34 94 35. *Cables:* Europress. *Managing Director:* Sven Berlin. Market: Newspapers, magazines and weeklies in Sweden, Denmark, Norway and Finland. Syndicates: High quality features of international appeal such as topical articles, photo-features, black-and-white and colour, women's features, short stories, serial novels, non-fiction stories and serials with strong human interest, cartoons, comic strips.

Exchange Telegraph Co., Ltd., The, Extel House, East Harding Street, London, EC4P 4HB. *T.* 01-353 1080. Alan B. Brooker (*Chairman and Managing Director*), Ernest W. H. Bond (*Secretary*).

Features Illustrated News Agency, 2nd Floor, 53 High Street, Belfast, BT1 2AB Syndicates features and pictorial material to magazines throughout the world. Interviews, first person series, true life adventures. Tells EEC and Commonwealth export story overseas. Supplies newsworthy photographs and articles of latest industrial, commercial and chemical development to world press on request, on reciprocal, exchange, or straightout basis. Fast air mail—telephone service for all copy and photos. Material from freelance sources considered. Articles are commissioned from statesmen, politicians, overseas editors and prominent writers with an international reputation.

Features International, Spencer House, 23 Dartmouth Row, London, SE10 8AW *T.* 01-691 2888. *Cables:* Deadline, London. *Editorial Director:* Anthony Sharrock. Syndicates features and picture stories to magazines and newspapers throughout the world. The agency produces a wide range of material —mainly from freelance sources—including topical articles, women's features, strips, weekly columns, popular photo-features, series by international celebrities, glamour and pin-up photographs. Distributes directly to all English-language countries, and to major European magazines. Agents throughout the Common Market countries, Scandinavia, Japan, the Americas and Eastern Europe. Buys copy outright and welcomes story ideas. Average commission rate for picture material: 40–50%.

Gemini News Service, 21 John Street, London, WC1N 2BS *T.* 01-353 2567/8. *Cables:* Gemininews. Derek Ingram (*Managing Editor*). Network of correspondents and specialist writers all over the world. Some opening for freelance. Specialists in news-features of international and topical interest. Preferred *length* 1000–1200 words.

Geopress, 51 Cleveland Street, London, W1P 5PQ *T.* 01-637 1977–8. *Directors:* E. G. Templeton, F. C. Schmidt. Current affairs and personality features. Also photographs. Outright purchase preferable.

Gibson's, J. F., Literary Agency (1950), P.O. Box 173, London, SW3. *T.* 01-242 9637 and 70 Windsor Road, Bexhill-on-Sea, Sussex, TN39 3PE *T.* 21-4400. *Proprietor:* J. F. Gibson. *Secretary:* Bernard Ross, F.C.A. *Editor:* Mrs. Freda Stock. Welcomes fiction and non-fiction published in this country or English-speaking countries for translation and publication abroad. Terms: 15%. No reading fee.

Globe Photos, 404 Park Avenue South, New York, N.Y., 10016. *T.* 212-689 1340. *Cables:* Globe-photos New York. Require magazine stories with text, black-and-white, and colour photos on all subjects. Single stock photos transparencies only. Send International Reply Coupons for return of material.

Hampton Press (1939), Features Syndicate, P.O. Box 114, Drummoyne, N.S.W., 2047, Australia. *T.* 81-3083. Original or reprint rights of romance stories (2000–4000 words). Photo stories with dramatic impact. Cartoons. Features with photographs. Nothing of a topical nature. Must have universal appeal. All MSS, etc., must be accompanied by a s.a.e.

India-International News Service, *Head Office:* Jute House, 12 India Exchange Place, Calcutta, 700001. *T.* 22-9563, 22-6572, 45-0009. *T.A.* Zeitgeist. *Proprietor:* Ing. H. Kothari, B.SC., D.W.P.(Lond.), M.I.Mech.E., M.I.E., A.M.B.I.M. "Calcutta Letters" and Air Mail news service from Calcutta. Specialists in Industrial and Technical news. Also acts as public relations and publicity consultants. (Controlled by Kothari Organisation.)

Inter-Prensa, Florida 229, 1005 Capital Federal, Argentina. *Cables:* Interprensa Baires. Picture stories, fashion photos, comics. 40% commission.

Inter-Press Features, 69 Fleet Street, London, EC4Y 1HB. *T.* 01-659 0099. Specialists in news-features for newspapers and magazines in Britain and abroad. The main outlet is for top-level series of articles on all subjects of popular interest, especially those whose subject matter makes them of interest to women. Serial rights acquired in biographies, human stories, in fact all stories of a top-level nature.

International Feature Service, 99, Bd. Em. Jacqmain, 1000 Brussels, Belgium. *T.* 217-03-42. *Managing Director:* Max S. Kleiter. Feature articles, serial rights, tests, cartoons, comic strips and illustrations. Handles English TV-features and books; also production of articles for merchandising.

International Press Agency (Pty) Ltd., The (1934), P.O. Box 682, Cape Town 8000. *Managing Editor:* Mrs. U. A. Barnett, Ph.D. *London Office:* Mrs. S. Power, 411 London Press Centre, 76 Shoe Lane, London, EC4A 3JB *T.* 01-353 0186. South African agent for many leading British, American and Continental Press firms. Considers the syndicating and merchandising of comic strips, cartoons, jokes, feature articles, short stories, serials, press photos for the South African market. South African feature material, illustrated articles, news stories, etc., supplied to world press.

International Press Bureau, 30 Fleet Street, London, EC4. *T.* 01-353 7940. *T.A.* Newswire London. International news and features for home and overseas press. London columns about news in Britain.

Irish International News Service. *Editor:* Barry J. Hardy, P.C., Ashling, 12 Greenlea Park, Terenure, Dublin 6. *T.* 906183. News, sport, TV, radio, photographic department; also equipment for TV films, etc.

Jewish Telegraphic Agency, Ltd., 150 Fleet Street, London, EC4A 2HH. *T.* 01-353 7107–8. *T.A.* Jewcorrau, London. *Editor:* Michael Almaz. *London Manager:* D. H. Blackman. Gathering and distributing news of Israel and Jews everywhere. Network of own correspondents in five continents.

Keystone Press Agency, Ltd. (1920). Bertram Garai, Bath House, Holborn Viaduct, London, EC1A 2FE *T.* 01-236 3331. *T.A.* Pressillu, London, EC1. *Telex:* 888258. News and feature pictures. *Commission:* 50% to 60%.

London Express News and Feature Services, 41–42 Shoe Lane, London, EC4A 3BS *T.* 01-353 8000. Strips, features, cartoons, photographs, book serialisations and rights, merchandising, etc.

London Syndication (1977), The Old Forge, Redhill, nr Buntingford, Herts, SG9 0TH *T.* Broadfield (076 388) 348. *Partners:* Carole Blake, Carol Smith, Abner Stein. Short stories, serials, features of all kinds. Represents journalists expert in a wide range of subjects, novelists and short story writers. Material must have international appeal to magazines and newspapers. All correspondence to Carole Blake. *Commission:* 25%.

Maharaja Features Private Ltd., 5/226 Sion Road East, Bombay, 22, India. *Cables:* Mahrajfeat, Bombay 022. *T.* 484776. *Managing Editor:* K. R. Padmanabhan. Syndicates feature and pictorial material to newspapers and magazines in India and abroad. Specialists in well researched articles on India by eminent authorities for publication in prestige journals throughout the world. Also topical features 1000–1500 words. *Illustrations:* Monochrome prints and colour transparencies.

Monitor International, 17–27 Old Street, London, EC1V 9HL *T.* 01-253 7071 and 01-253 6281. *Telex:* 24718. *Managing Director:* S. R. White. *Picture Editor:* Mark McCaffrey. International picture agency. General subjects, features and large library of portraits and action photos of world personalities from sport, politics, entertainment and commerce, in colour and black-and-white. Own studio and aerial photography facilities.

National Press Agency, Ltd. (1873), Newspaper House, 8–16 Great New Street, London, EC4P 4ER *T.* 01-353 1030. *T.A.* Typo, Fleet, London. *Telex:* Westprov 27202. Caters for daily and weekly papers: supplies leading articles, leader-page articles, topical articles, industrial, motoring, home affairs and political correspondent's features and news stories, crossword puzzles, special matter for women's pages and advertising supplements.

New Zealand Associated Press, 107 Fleet Street, London, EC4A 2AN *T.* 01-353 2686.

New Zealand Press Association, 85 Fleet Street, London, EC4. *T.* 01-353 7040.

News Blitz International, Via Cimabue 5, 00196 Rome. *T.* 36.00.620–36.03.087–36.01.489. *President:* Vinicio Congiu. *Sales Manager:* Gianni Piccione. *Graphic Dept.:* Giovanni A. Congiu. *Literary Dept.:* Giovanni A. Congiu. *Television Dept.:* Paola F. Congiu. Syndicates cartoons, comic strips, humorous books with drawings, general books, feature and pictorial material, especially high quality nudes, throughout the world and Italy. Material from freelance sources required. Averages rate of commission 60–40%—monthly report of sales, payments every 3 months.

North West News & Sports Agency, Ltd. (1956), 54 Hamilton Square, Birkenhead, Merseyside, L41 5AS *T.* 051-647 7691 and 632 5261. News and sports coverage, Birkenhead, Bebington, Wallasey and Wirral.

Orion Press, 55 1-Chome, Kanda-Jimbocho, Chiyoda-ku, Tokyo, 101. *T.A.* Orionserv, Tokyo. *Telex:* J24447 Orionprs. International press service.

Owen & Baker Press Agency, Delta House, Cornet Street, St. Peter Port, Guernsey, Channel Islands. *T.* 0481-23019. News, features and picture coverage of the Channel Islands.

P. A. Features (the Feature Service of the Press Association, Ltd.), 85 Fleet Street, London, EC4P 4BE *T.* 01-353 7440. Terry Timblick (*Editor*). World-wide syndication to newspapers, magazines and trade journals of regular text, graphic and strip services.

Pixfeatures (Mr. P. G. Wickman), 5 Latimer Road, Barnet, Hertfordshire. *T.* 01-449 9946 and 01-440 3663, *Telex:* 27538. Specialises in London representation of South African, German, Dutch, Scandinavian, Belgian and American magazines.

Press Alliances, Ltd., 63 Fleet Street, London, EC4Y 1HU. *T.* 01-353 6991. *T.A.* Pressallia, Fleet, London. Specialises in London representation (advertising) of provincial newspapers.

Press Association Ltd., The (1868), I. H. N. Yates (General Manager), D. A. Chipp (*Editor-in-Chief*), J. Purdham (*Financial Controller and Secretary*), 85 Fleet Street, London, EC4P 4BE *T.* 01-353 7440. *T.A.* Press Association, London. Home News Agency: News, photographs, features. Also distributes world agencies' news in British Isles outside London.

Rann, Christopher and Associates (1977), *Proprietor:* Christopher Rann, Box 303, P.O., Unley, Adelaide, South Australia 5061. *T.* 08-717505. *Cables:* Ausnews Adelaide. Representing radio stations, newspapers and magazines in Australia, New Zealand, Britain and South Africa. Speciality: radio news voice reports and actuality about Australian events for broadcasting media in Australia and overseas. Occasionally commissions outside work; welcomes exclusive news information.

Reportage Bureau Laszlo, Fredrikinkatu, 63 A 7, 00100 Helsinki-10, Finland. *T.* 640 522. *Cables:* Reportage Helsinki.

Reuters Limited, 85 Fleet Street, London, EC4P 4AJ *T.* 01-353 6060.

Sandesa News Agency, 23 Canal Row, Colombo—1, Sri Lanka. *Director:* Gamini Navaratne, B.SC.(ECON.) LOND. Supplies—news, features, photographs and press cuttings to local and overseas newspapers and agencies.

Skye Agencies, Calum Mackenzie Neish, Portnalong, Isle of Skye. *T.* Portnalong (047 872) 272. *Telex:* 75317 Skpres G. News, features and picture agency for the Inner Hebrides and adjacent mainland (Skye and Lochalsh District).

South Bedfordshire and St. Albans Crown Court News Agency, 134 Marsh Road, Luton, LU3 2NL *T.* 52222. *Telex:* 826634. Night: Luton 27131, 51789, 32039, and Bedford 852799.

Space Syndications, Ltd., Graham Payne, Newspaper House, P.O. Box 17, Shenley Avenue, Ruislip Manor, Middlesex, HA4 6DQ *T.* Ruislip 76123. Cartoons from new and established artists wanted. No strips, just singles. No card, but on bond-type 10ins. × 8ins. paper. Nothing on reverse sides, not even your own name or address. Send sample selection and s.a.e. for criticism, commission rates, etc.

Sporting Pictures (UK) Ltd., 7A Lambs Conduit Passage, Holborn, London, WC1. *T.* 01-405 4500. *Directors:* Frank Baron, Crispin J. Thruston. Specialising in sports, sporting events, sportsmen. Black and white and colour library.

Sunderland News Agency (1948), Ted Elkins, 19 The Broadway, Grindon, Sunderland. *T.* 284268. Press, radio and television news and feature writers. Supply general news and features of shipping, industrial and human interest.

Syndication International, Ltd., 40 Northampton Road, London, EC1R 0JU *T.* 01-837 2800. Strips, features, cartoons, photography, book serialisations, merchandising, etc.

Tauber, Peter, Press Agency (1950), 94 East End Road, London, N3 2SX *T.* 01-346 4165. *T.A.* Tauberpres. Regular syndication of exclusive interviews and human interest features to national newspapers and magazines in the U.K., U.S.A., Canada, Australia, South Africa, Japan and all countries of Western Europe. *Commission* 25%

Tass Agency, Room 205 (2nd Floor), Communications House, 12–16 Gough Square, London, EC4A 3JH. General news service to USSR. *T*. 01-353 9831: economic and commercial news service to USSR. *T*. 01-353 2661; wire room 01-353 2606; Telex: 24201.

TransAtlantic News Service, 7100 Hillside Avenue, Suite 304, Hollywood, California 90046. *T*. 213-874-1284. News and photo agency serving the British and Foreign press. Staffed by former Fleet Street reporters, TANS supplies entertainment news, features and columns from Hollywood, and topical news in general from California. Covers all Hollywood events and undertakes commissions and assignments in all fields. Candid photos of stars at major Hollywood events a speciality.

Trans World Press Agency, 44 Seaview Drive, Great Wakering, Southend-on-Sea, Essex, SS3 0BE *T*. Southend-on-Sea 219770. Supplies news features statistics, photographs, colour photographs, provides reporters and photographers for special purposes. Cover all International Motor Rallies, Grand Prix's, Yachting and Power Boat Races.

Transworld Feature Syndicate (UK) Ltd., Tubs Hill House, Sevenoaks, Kent. *T*. 0732-58204–7.

United Press International (UK), Ltd., News Division, 8 Bouverie Street, London, EC4Y 8BB *T*. 01-353 2282.

Universal News Services, Ltd., Communications House, Gough Square, Fleet Street, London, EC4P 4DP *T*. 01-353 5200. *Managing Director:* Alfred Geiringer.

Van Hallan Photo Features, 57 South Street, Isleworth, Middlesex, TW7 7AA. *T*. 01-568 0792. See also entry in **Photographic Agencies and Picture Libraries.**

World-Wide News Bureau, 309 Varick Street, Jersey City, N.J. 07302. *T*. 201-333 4660. *Editor/Manager:* Arejas Vitkauskas. Authors' news of forthcoming or published books on any subjects. Reviewing any books. English resumés of non-English books requested.

Yaffa Newspaper Service of New Zealand, P.O. Box 509, 31–35 Dixon Street, Wellington, 1, New Zealand. *T*. 845-505. *T.A.* and *Cables:* Yaffaz, Wellington.

Yaffa Syndicate Pty, Ltd., 432–6 Elizabeth Street, Surry Hills, Sydney, N.S.W. 2010. *T*. 699 7861. *Telex:* AA 21887.
Largest and oldest established Australian syndicate and literary agency.

MARKETS FOR VERSE

DOUGLAS GIBSON

Nobody can be taught to be a poet; but those with a love of words and a sense of rhythm may learn to write verse. Most of them will then want to see it in print, and preferably paid for. Neither of these will be easy.

Since in my experience more men, women and schoolchildren are attempting to write verse, the competition is greater than for many years, and only the most gifted and determined are likely to succeed.

The most obvious medium is the periodicals. Though those which accept verse has shrunk, there are still a few literary magazines of high standard such as *Encounter, Listener, London Magazine, News Statesman,* and *Stand,* which regularly publish poetry.

Country magazines which publish verse include *Countryman, Country Life, Field,* and some County periodicals.

Women's magazines, worth trying with domestic or light verse, are *Woman, Woman & Home, Woman's Realm.*

The best hope is in periodicals devoted mainly to poetry, including *Agenda, Ambit, Anglo-Welsh Review, Outposts, Poetry Review, Poetry Wales.* There are also masses of "little" poetry magazines, only a few of which I have included in my list, since many of them are here today and gone tomorrow!

Payment for poetry varies widely, depending on the resources of the periodical and the reputation of the poet. Some "little" magazines can afford only a free copy to contributors, while most fees range from £1 to £10 and upwards. A fair average is £5. A fee is normally for one use only, leaving copyright with the author and the option to offer the poem for publication elsewhere.

Though most Editors are overstocked with poetry, today there are more encouraging prospects for poets in other directions.

More anthologies, especially for children and school use, are being published. There are an increasing number of national poetry competitions, some in conjunction with Arts Festivals. Verse readings, often with music, in clubs and pubs and poetry groups, remain popular, and the young poet with a good voice may gain his or her first audience this way.

Poets should keep in touch with their Regional Arts Association (see under **Societies**), some of which will sponsor new talent. For those who live in or near London, the Arts Council and the Poetry Society are useful contacts. For others, the local library, especially if it is a large one; will enable them to study many of the periodicals I have listed.

I should mention radio and television, both of which use a limited amount of poetry. Several radio School programmes include verse, though usually by established poets and/or from published work.

Finally, to the dream which most poets have: the eventual publication of a collection of their work by a reputable firm. This has never been easy, and few publishers will risk almost certain loss on a new volume except for the most promising or unusual work. Yet it is still possible. First collections, often by poets who have already made a reputation through periodicals or with other more profitable books, continue to appear.

BRITISH MARKET FOR VERSE

(For full details of these journals see Newspapers and Magazines)

Agenda
Ambit
Anglo-Welsh Review
Blackwood's Magazine
Country Life
Countryman
Encounter
Field
Lady
Listener

London Magazine
New Review
New Statesman
Observer
Outposts
PN Review
Poetry Review
Poetry Wales
Samphire
Stand

Sunday Times
Thames Poetry
Times Literary
   Supplement
Un-Common Sense
Woman and Home
Woman's Realm
Writing

Other specialist Poetry Journals

Bananas, 2 Blenheim Crescent, London, W11.
Gallery, 17 Pandora Road, London, NW6.
Meridian, Rondo Publications Ltd., 123 The Albany, Old Hall Street, Liverpool, L3 9EG.
New Poetry (formerly Workshop New Poetry), 99 Pole Barn Lane, Frinton-on-Sea, Essex.

book
publishers

WRITING BOOKS

Care should be taken when submitting manuscripts to book publishers. A suitable publisher should be chosen, by a study of his list of publications or an examination in the bookshops of the type of books in which he specialises. It is a waste of time and money to send the typescript of a novel to a publisher who publishes no fiction, or poetry to one who publishes no verse, though all too often this is done. A preliminary letter is appreciated by most publishers, and this should outline the nature and extent of the typescript and enquire whether the publisher would be prepared to read it (writers have been known to send out such letters of enquiry in duplicated form, an approach not calculated to stimulate a publisher's interest). Finally, it is desirable to enclose the cost of return postage when submitting the typescript.

Authors are strongly advised not to pay for the publication of their work. If a MS. is worth publishing, a reputable publisher will undertake its publication at his own expense, except possibly for works of an academic nature. In this connection attention is called to the paragraphs on Vanity Publishing on page 216 and to the articles on Publishers' Agreements on page 405.

UNITED KINGDOM PUBLISHERS

*—Membership of the Publishers' Association.

*Abelard-Schuman, Ltd., 450 Edgware Road, London, W2 1EG *T.* 01-723 8412-5. A member of **The Blackie Group.** *Directors:* M. Miller (Managing), A. D. Mitchell.
Children's Books (Picture, Fiction, Non-Fiction, Information).

*Academic Press Inc. (London), Ltd., 24–28 Oval Road, London, NW1 7DX *T.* 01-267 4466. *Managing Director:* Roger Farrand.

*Academy Editions (1967), 7 Holland Street, Kensington, London, W8 4NA *T.* 01-937 6996. *T.A.* Acaded, London, W8. *Director:* Dr. A. C. Papadakis.
Art, Architecture, Crafts, Design, Typography, Photography.

Actinic Press, Ltd., 129 St. John's Hill, London, SW11 1TD *T.* 01-228 8091.
Medical Science.

*Addison-Wesley Publishers Ltd. (1970), West End House, 11 Hills Place, London, W1R 2LR *T.* 01-439 2541. *T.A.* Adiwes, London. *Telex:* 8811948.
Directors: D. Hammonds, P. H. Neumann, P. R. Chapman.
Educational, Pure and Applied Sciences, Children's Books.

*Adlard Coles, Ltd. (1933), Granada Publishing, 29 Frogmore, St. Albans, Herts, AL2 2NF *T.* Park Street 72727. *Directors:* W. R. Carr, A. R. H. Birch.
Nautical, Yachting, Motor Sailing and other maritime subjects.

Albyn Press, 2 & 3 Abbeymount, Edinburgh, EH8 8EJ *T.* 031-661 9339.
General literature, books on Scottish subjects and Guide Books.

* Aldus Books Ltd (1960), 17 Conway Street, Fitzroy Square, London, W1P 6BS *T.* 01-387 2811. *T.A.* Alday, London W1. *Directors:* John T. Sargent (Chairman) (USA), Nelson Doubleday (USA), Wolfgang Foges (Managing), I. W. Frame-Smith, D. H. Bekhor.
Illustrated non-fiction, including atlases, on the Supernatural, Discovery and Exploration, Natural History.

Alison Press, The, 5 Harley Gardens, London, SW10 9SW *T.* 01-373 1924 or 437 2075. *T.A.* Psophidian, London, W1. *Director:* Barley Alison. An associate of **Secker & Warburg, Ltd.**
Fiction, Belles Lettres, Biography, Humour.

*Allan (Ian), Ltd., Terminal House, Shepperton, Middlesex, TW17 8AS *T.* Walton-on-Thames (WT) 28950.
Transport—Railways, Aircraft, Shipping, Road, Naval and Military History and reference books, Travel; no fiction.

*Allan (Philip) Publishers Ltd. (1973), Market Place, Deddington, Oxford, OX5 4SE *T.* Deddington (08693) 652. *Directors:* I. P. G. Allan, J. F. Allan, S. M. E. Allan, Professor D. E. W. Laidler, Professor M. H. Peston.
Economics and Business Studies.

*Allen (George) & Unwin, Ltd., Ruskin House, 40 Museum Street, London, WC1A 1LU *T.* 01-405 8577. *Telex:* 826261. Sales, Distribution, Production and Accounts: P.O. Box 18, Park Lane, Hemel Hempstead, Herts, HP2 4TE *T.* Hemel Hempstead 3244. *Directors:* Rayner Unwin, C.B.E. (Chairman), Jim Hodgson (Managing Director), John Churchill, Charles Furth, Bryan Fuller, John Bright-Holmes, Adrian Stephenson, Robert Gellman. Publish: Series for *The Royal Institute of Public Administration, Political and Economic Planning, The National Institute for Social Work, The School of Oriental and African Studies, The Royal Economic Society,* etc. Owners of **Thomas Murby & Co.** *q.v.*
Popular and Academic, Secondary School and University level. Philosophy, Psychology, History, Anthropology, Sociology, Economics, Management, Political Theory, Government and Administration, Current Affairs, Natural Sciences and Geology, Oriental Religions, Transport, Travel, Biography, The Arts, Children's Books.

*Allen (J. A.) & Co., Ltd. (1926), 1 Lower Grosvenor Place, Buckingham Palace Road, London, SW1W 0EL. *T.* 01-834 5606–7 and 01-828 8855. *T.A.* Allenbooks, Sowest, London. *Managing Director:* Joseph A. Allen.
Veterinary and Bloodstock Publications, especially those dealing with the Thoroughbred Horse and the Art of Riding, Hunting and Polo, etc.

*Allen (W. H.) & Co., Ltd., 44 Hill Street, London, W1X 8LB   *T.* 01-493 6777, 01-629 7335.   *Telex:* 28117.   *Chairman:* Jeffrey Simmons; *Managing Director:* Francis Bennett.
Art, Belles-Lettres, Biography and Memoirs, Current Affairs, Children's, Educational (Primary, Secondary, Technical), Fiction, Films, General, History, Humour, Practical Handbooks, Reference, Sociology, Television, Theatre and Ballet, Travel, Made Simple Books.

Allison & Busby, Ltd. (1968), 6A Noel Street, London, W1V 3RB   *T.* 01-734 1498.
Directors: Clive Allison, Margaret Busby.
Art, Belles-Lettres, Biography and Memoirs, Current Affairs, Economics, Fiction, General, History, Politics, Sociology, Translations.

Allman & Son (Publishers), Ltd. (1800), 17–19 Foley Street, London, W1A 1DR *T.* 01-580 9074/0   *T.A.* Millsator, London.   *Chairman:* J. T. Boon, C.B.E.; *Managing Director:* Paul Scherer; *Directors:* A. W. Boon, Mrs. E. J. Bryant, A. T. McKay; *Financial Director and Secretary:* B. C. J. Rogers.
Educational books of all types.

Andersen Press Ltd. (1976), 3 Fitzroy Square, London, W1P 6JD   *T.* 01-387 2888 (Trade) 0621 816362.   *Telex:* 261212.   *T.A.* Literarius, London.
Directors: Klaus Flugge, J. Flugge, P. Durrance.
Children's Picture Books and Fiction.   International coproductions.

*Angus and Robertson (U.K.), Ltd., 16 Ship Street, Brighton, East Sussex, BN1 1AD   *T.* 23631.   *Telex:* 877419.   *T.A.* Ausboko Brighton.
Biography and Memoirs, Children's Books (Fiction, Non-Fiction), Cinema, Sports, Crafts, Travel, Humour.

Appletree Press Ltd (1974), 6 Dublin Road, Belfast, BT2 7HL   *T.* 0232 43074.
Director: John Murphy.
Photographic, Social History, Art Books, Academic and Educational Music, Literature, Guide Books, Ornithology, History.

*Applied Science Publishers Ltd. (1963), 22 Rippleside Commercial Estate, Ripple Road, Barking, Essex, 1G11 0SA   *T.* 01-595 2121.   *T.A.* Elsbark, Barking.   *Managing Director:* Leslie E. Rayner.
Architectural Science, Building and Civil Engineering, Chemistry, Ceramics, Food Technology, Materials Science, Petroleum Technology, Pollution, Plastics Technology.

Aquarian Publishing Company (London) Ltd., The (1952), The Denington Estate, London Road, Wellingborough, Northants, NN8 2RQ   *T.* Wellingborough 76031–4.   *Directors:* J. A. Young, M. E. Young.
Astrology, Comparative Religion, Magic, Metaphysics, Mysticism, Occultism, Parapsychology, Philosophy, Psychic Research.

*Architectural Press Ltd. (1902), 9 Queen Anne's Gate, London, SW1H 9BY *T.* 01-930 0611.   *T.A.* Buildable, London, SW1.
Architecture, the Environment, Planning, Townscape, Building Technology; General.

Argus Books Ltd., Fountain Press, Model & Allied Publications, Harleyford Publications, Bellona Publications, Argus House, 14 St. James Road, Watford, WD1 8EA   *T.* Watford 47281.
Photography, Cinematography, Radio/TV, Audio, Electronics, Modelling, Railway and Traction Engines, Military, Wargaming and Aviation.

Armada paperbacks—see William Collins.

Armada Lions—see William Collins.

*****Arms and Armour Press** (1966), 2–6 Hampstead High Street, London, NW3. *T.* 01-794 0246. *Directors:* L. Leventhal, A. Leventhal, D. A. Gibbons. Books for Collectors on Arms, Armour, Uniforms, etc.

*****Arnold (E. J.) & Son, Ltd.** (1863), Butterley Street, Leeds, LS10 1AX: also Edinburgh. *T.* Leeds 442944; Edinburgh, Caledonian 7134. *T.A.* Arnold, Phone, Leeds. *Book Depot:* Ring Road, Seacroft, Leeds, LS14 2AW *T.* Leeds 643171. *Directors:* E. M. Arnold, J. O. Arnold, M. Wayte, P. D. Brown, D. G. Howe, F. Furniss, N. J. Williams. Educational (Primary, Secondary).

*****Arnold (Edward) (Publishers), Ltd.,** 41–42 Bedford Square, London, WC1B 3DP *T.* 01-637 7161. *T.A.* Scholarly, London. *Founded* by Edward Arnold in 1890. *Directors:* E. A. Hamilton, B. W. Bennett, P. J. Price, M. Husk, J. G. Martyn, C. N. E. McDowall, J. E. Peck, W. R. Smeeton, G. N. Davies. Educational books in all subjects (Secondary, Technical, University): advanced works in Humanities, Social Sciences, Pure and Applied Science, and Medicine; Journals.

*****Arrow Books, Ltd.** (1948), 3 Fitzroy Square, London, W1P 6JD. *T.* 01-387 2888. *Telex:* 261212. (Trade) 0621-81 6362. *Telex:* 99487. *Directors:* R. A. A. Holt (*Chairman*), Roger Lloyd-Taylor (Managing), Charles Clark, David Harsent, Richard Tucker, Terence Blacker, Paul Walton. An imprint of the **Hutchinson Publishing Group.** Paperback publications, Fiction and Non-Fiction.

 Art Trade Press, Ltd., 9 Brockhampton Road, Havant, Hampshire, PO9 1NU *T.* Havant 484943. Publishers of *Who's Who in Art.*

 Aslib (1924), 3 Belgrave Square, London, SW1X 8PL. *T.* 01-235 5050. (For further details see entry under Societies and Clubs.)

*****Associated Book Publishers, Ltd.,** 11 New Fetter Lane, London, EC4P 4EE *T.* 01-583 9855, the parent company of a group which includes the following firms: Chapman & Hall Ltd., Eyre Methuen Ltd., Eyre & Spottiswoode (Publishers) Ltd., W. Green & Son Ltd., Methuen & Co. Ltd., Methuen Children's Books Ltd., Methuen Educational Ltd., Methuen Paperbacks Ltd., Police Review Publishing Co. Ltd., E. & F. N. Spon Ltd., Stevens & Sons Ltd., Sweet & Maxwell Ltd., Tavistock Publications Ltd., Associated Book Publishers (Aust.) Ltd., The Law Book Co. Ltd., Australia, Methuen of Australia Ltd., The Carswell Co. Ltd., Canada, Methuen Publications, Canada, Methuen Inc., New York, Associated Book Publishers (NZ) Ltd., Methuen of New Zealand Ltd., Sweet & Maxwell (NZ) Ltd. *Directors:* M. W. Maxwell (President), P. H. B. Allsop (Chairman), A. F. J. Crosthwaite Eyre (Vice-Chairman), M. R. Turner (Managing Director), B. M. Cardy, Sir J. Eden Bt., C. D. O. Evans, D. L. T. Oppé, D. W. Potter, C. H. Shirley, D. G. Sampson (Secretary).

Astragal Books—see The Architectural Press Ltd.

*Athlone Press of the University of London, The (1949), 4 Gower Street, London, WC1E 6DR   *T.* 01-580 9535–6.
Archaeology, Architecture, Art, Belles-Lettres, Biography and Memoirs, Economics, Educational (Secondary, Technical, University), History, Law, Medical, Music, Oriental, Philosophy, Political Economy, Science, Sociology, Theology and Religion.

BBC Publications, 35 Marylebone High Street, London, W1M 4AA   *T.* 01-580 5577.   *T.A* Broadcasts, London.   *Telex:* 265781.
Television and Radio.

B.P.C. Publishing, Ltd. (British Printing Corporation), Print House, 44 Great Queen Street, London, WC2B 5AS   *T.* 01-242 3974.   *Directors:* A. M. Alfred (Chairman), P. G. Morrison (Director and Secretary), V. Broadribb. Divisions of the Group in the U.K.: Phoebus Publishing Company, Macdonald Educational Ltd., Macdonald & Jane's Publishers Ltd., Futura Publications Ltd., *q.v.*

Babani, Bernard (Publishing) Ltd., The Grampians, Shepherds Bush Road, London, W6 7NF   *T.* 01-603 2581 and 7296.   *Directors:* S. Babani, M. H. Babani, BSc.(Eng).
Practical Handbooks on Radio and Electronics.

Bachman & Turner (1972), 4th Floor. 5 Plough Place. Fetter Lane, London, EC4A 1LD   *T.* 01-353 1145.   *Telex:* 27950.   *Directors:* Marta Bachman (Swedish), C. N. Turner.
Fiction, Biography, Autobiography, Parapsychology, Health, Reference.

Bagster (Samuel) & Sons, Ltd. (1794), 1 Bath Street, London, EC1V 9LB   *T.* 01-251 2925.   *Directors:* M. Raeburn, P. J. Lardi, S. W. Grant.
Theology and Religion.

*Bailey Bros. & Swinfen, Ltd., Warner House, Folkestone, Kent CT19 6PH   *T.* Folkestone 56501–8   *T.A.* Forenbuks, Folkestone.   *Telex:* 96328.
General, Humour, Reference, Science, Sports, Games and Hobbies.

*Baillière Tindall (1826) (a Division of Cassell Limited), 35 Red Lion Square, London, WC1R 4SG   *T.* 01-831 6100.   *Divisional Directors:* S. A. Reynolds, D. H. Tindall, N. Mendelson.   Exclusive agents for the Veterinary books of Lea & Febiger, The Williams & Wilkins Company and the Iowa State University Press.
Medical, Veterinary, Nursing, Pharmaceutical books and journals. *Age and Ageing, Animal Behaviour, Animal Behaviour Monographs, Rheumatology and Rehabilitation,* the *British Journal of Diseases of the Chest,* the *British Veterinary Journal,* the *International Journal of Psycho-Analysis* and *International Review of Psycho-Analysis, Occupational Health.*   Exclusive agents for Williams & Wilkins, Baltimore, medical and scientific journals.

Baker (Howard) Press, Ltd., 27A Arterberry Road, Wimbledon, London, SW20 8AF   *T.* 01-947 5482.   *Cables:* Bakerbook, London.   *Directors:* W. Howard Baker, I. T. Baker, H. C. I. D. Baker, J. K. Montgomerie.   *Company Secretary:* D. R. Ridgwell, A.C.I.S.
General Fiction and Non-Fiction.   Library reprints.   Omnibus volumes of pre-war juvenile fiction (*Magnet,* etc.).   Political Science, Biography, Poetry.   Preliminary letter and synopsis required.

Baker (John) Publishers, Ltd., 35 Bedford Row, London, WC1R 4JH *T.* 01-242 0946. *T.A.* Biblos, London, WC1. *Telex:* 21792, ref. 2546. *Directors:* Charles Black (Chairman), David Gadsby. An imprint of **A. & C. Black, Ltd.**
Art, Archaeology, Crafts, Natural History, Social History, Topography and Country Life.

Bantam paperbacks—see **Transworld.**

*****Barker (Arthur), Ltd.,** 11 St. John's Hill, London, SW11 1XA   *T.* 01-228 8888. *Directors:* Lord Weidenfeld (Chairman), S. Dally (Managing), J. Curtis, A. Miles, B. MacLennan, E. Henderson, D. Livermore, Ray Compton, A. Wells.
Fiction, Biography, History, Military History, Criminology, Sport, Handbooks, Games and Pastimes.

Barrie & Jenkins, Ltd., 24 Highbury Crescent, London, N5 1RX   *T.* 01-359 3711. *Telex:* 21373. *Directors:* A. M. Palmer, J. B. R. Dare, F. R. F. Singer, M. Hodson.
Antiques and Collecting, Angling, Archaeology, Architecture, Art, Belles-Lettres, Biography, Fiction, History, Music, Reference, Shooting and Rural subjects, Theatre, Travel, Books for the Hotel and Catering Industry, General.

*****Bartholomew (John) & Son, Ltd.** (1826), Duncan Street, Edinburgh, EH9 1TA *T.* 031-667 6981. Book Division: 216 High Street, Bromley, Kent, BR1 1PW *T.* 01-460 3239.   Cartographic printers and publishers.
Maps, Atlases and Non-Fiction Leisure Books.

*****Batsford (B. T.), Ltd.** (1843), 4 Fitzhardinge Street, Portman Square, London, W1H 0AH   *T.* 01-486 8484.   *Directors:* Samuel Carr, Alex Cox, Peter Kemmis Betty, John Faulder, John Beevor, Roger Huggins, William Waller.
Architecture, Chess. Children's Books (Non-Fiction), Education (Secondary, Technical, University), Fine Arts, Crafts and Needlecraft, History, Social Sciences, Travel, General.

Bayard Books—see **Barrie & Jenkins, Ltd.**

Bedford Square Press, National Council of Social Service, 26 Bedford Square, London, WC1B 3HU   *T.* 01-636 4066.
Social planning and policy, community action, counselling, training, environment. Standard reference books and practical guides relevant to these areas.

*****Bell & Hyman Ltd.** (1838), Denmark House, 37–39 Queen Elizabeth Street, London, SE1 2QB   *T.* 01-407 0709 and 5237.   *T.A.* Bellhyman London. *Telex:* 24224.   *Directors:* R. P. Hyman (Chairman and Managing), N. C. Britten, R. J. B. Glanville, E. E. A. Melbourne, C. H. Sporborg, A. D. Stark, L. F. Wise.
Educational Books, particularly mathematics, secondary school books, chess, collecting, crafts, dictionaries, dolls, geography, music, reference. Publishers of Pepy's Diary.

*Benn (Ernest), Ltd. (1923), Sovereign Way, Tonbridge, Kent, TN9 1RW *T.* Tonbridge (0732) 364422. *T.A.* Bentitle, Tonbridge, Kent. *Telex:* 27844 and 25 New Street Square, London, EC4A 3JA *T.* 01-353 3212. *T.A.* Benbrolish London. *Telex:* 27844. *Directors:* Timothy Benn, Keon Hughes, Kenneth Day, o.b.e., Michael Jourdier, John V. Wilson, f.c.a., John Beer.
Archaeology, Children's Books (Fiction, Non-Fiction, Remedial, Picture), Directories and Guide Books, Drama, General, History, Music, Fishing, Local Government, Printing, Science, Technology.

*Bingley (Clive), Ltd. (1965), 16 Pembridge Road, London, W11. *T.* 01-229 1825 and 7451.
Librarianship, information work, Education, Music, Reference Books.

*Black (A. & C.), Ltd. (1807), 35 Bedford Row, London, WC1R 4JH *T.* 01-242 0946. *T.A.* Biblos, London, WC1. *Telex:* 21792 Ref. 2546. *Directors:* A. A. G. Black (President, great-grandson of founder), Charles Black (Chairman and Joint Managing Director), David Gadsby (Joint Managing Director), Leonard Brown. *Associate Director and Secretary:* William Still. Proprietors of A. & C. Black (Publishers) Ltd., John Baker (Publishers), Ltd., The Dacre Press, F. Lewis (Publishers) Ltd., *q.v.*

*Black (A. & C.) (Publishers) Ltd. (1978), 35 Bedford Row, London, WC1R 4JH *T.* 01-242 0946. *T.A.* Biblos, London, WC1. *Telex:* 21792, Ref. 2546. *Directors:* A. A. G. Black, Charles Black, David Gadsby, Leonard Brown, Paul White.
Children's and Educational Books for 3–15 years, Collectors, Costume, Dictionaries, Fishing, History, Natural History, Railways, Reference, Sport. Publishers of *Who's Who* since 1897.

*Blackie & Son, Ltd. (1809), Bishopbriggs, Glasgow, G64 2NZ *T.* 041-772 2311. *T.A.* Blackie, Glasgow.
Directors: John Tannahill (Chairman), George Ogg (Vice-Chairman), R. M. Miller (Managing), J. W. G. Blackie, Euan Cooper-Willis, Alexander D. Mitchell, Dr. A. Graeme Mackintosh.
Educational (Infant, Primary, Secondary), Children's Books (Fiction and Non-Fiction for all ages), Scientific and Technical (Biological Sciences, Chemistry, Engineering, Mathematics and Physics), General Books.

*Blackwell (Basil) & Mott, Ltd. (1922), 5 Alfred Street, Oxford, OX1 4HB. *T.* Oxford 722146. *Directors:* Sir Basil Blackwell, R. Blackwell (Chairman), David Martin (Managing), M. A. Holmes, J. Blackwell, J. E. Critchley, P. Saugman, A. T. Hale, Angus Doulton.
Classical Studies, Economics, Education (Infants, Primary, Secondary, Technical, University), History, Literature and Criticism, Modern Languages and Philology, Philosophy, Politics and Sociology, Theology.

*Blackwell Scientific Publications, Ltd. (1939), Osney Mead, Oxford, OX2 0EL, 8 John Street, London, WC1N 2ES, and 9 Forrest Road, Edinburgh, EH1 2QH *T.* Oxford 40201, London, 01-405 9941–2, Edinburgh 031-225 4234. *Directors:* Sir Basil Blackwell, Per Saugman, Richard Blackwell, John Critchley, Keith Bowker, Nigel Palmer, Oluf Møller, Peter Pleasance, John Robson. Branch in Australia, *q.v.*
Medicine and Biology.

*Blackwood (William) & Sons, Ltd. (1804), 32 Thistle Street, Edinburgh, EH2 1HA
T. Edinburgh 031-225 3411–3. *Directors:* G. Douglas Blackwood (Chairman), J. M. D. Blackwood, J. R. Snowball, D. J. Fletcher.
Blackwood's Magazine (1817).
Publishers of the Scottish Connection series of monographs; occasional general books.

*Blandford Press, Ltd., Link House, West Street, Poole, Dorset, BH15 1LL *T.*
Poole 02013-71171. *Directors:* G. C. Burt, R. J. Wenn, R. G. Dingwall, T. C. A. Goldsmith, J. E. Morgan.
Art, Educational (Infants, Primary, Secondary, Technical), Gardening, History, Hobbies, Militaria, Music, Natural History, Practical Handbooks, Religion.

Bles, Geoffrey (Publishers), Ltd. (1923), P.O. Box 233, London, SW3 *T.* 01-589
5578. *T.A.* Balfbooks, London, SW3. *Directors:* Michael D. Balfour (Managing), D. J. Balfour.
Biography, Autobiography, History, Travel, Adventure, Criticism, Philosophy, Stage, Countryside, Animals.

Blond & Briggs, Ltd (1971), 44–45 Museum Street, London, WC1A 1LY *T.*
01-405 2766. *T.A.* Literary, London, WC1. *Directors:* Anthony Blond, Desmond Briggs, Anthony B. J. S. Rubinstein, Sheila Thompson.
Fiction, Biography, General Non-Fiction, Topical Commentaries.

Blond Educational—see Hart-Davis Educational Ltd.

*Bodley Head, Ltd., The (founded by John Lane in 1887), 9 Bow Street, London, WC2E 7AL *T.* 01-836 9081. *T.A.* Bodleian, Westcent, London. *Directors:* Sir Hugh Greene, K.C.M.G., O.B.E. (Chairman), Max Reinhardt (Managing), J. R. Hews, F.C.A. and Judy Taylor, M.B.E. (Joint Deputy Managing), J. B. Blackley, L. A. Hart, James Michie, Sir Ralph Richardson, John Ryder, Quentin Hockliffe, Margaret Clark, Euan Cameron, Peter Sullivan, Jill Black, Maureen Rissik.
Proprietors of Hollis and Carter, Putnam & Co., Ltd., Bowes & Bowes (Publishers), The Nonesuch Library, T. Werner Laurie, Ltd., Nattali & Maurice.
Distributors for **The Nonesuch Press,** *q.v.*
Belles-Lettres, Biography and Memoirs, Children's Books (Fiction, Non-Fiction, Picture), Current Affairs, Economics, Essays, Fiction, Films, General, History, Practical Handbooks, Sociology, Travel.

Bowes & Bowes (Publishers), Ltd. (1850), 9 Bow Street, London, WC2E 7AL *T.*
01-836 9081. *T.A.* Bodleian, Westcent, London. An imprint of **The Bodley Head, Ltd.**

Bowker Publishing Company, Ltd., Erasmus House, Epping, Essex, CM16 4BU
T. Epping 77333. *Telex:* 81410. *Directors:* N. E. A. Farrow, R. D. Collischon, R. Asleson (USA).
Bibliographies and Reference Directories, mainly for the book trade and library world.

Boyars, Marion, Publishers Ltd., 18 Brewer Street, London, W1R 4AS *T.* 01-439 7827–8. *Cables:* Bookdom, London, W1. *Directors:* Marion Boyars, Arthur Boyars.
Belles Lettres and Criticism, Fiction, Sociology, Open Forum, Ideas in Progress, Poetry, Music, Travel, Drama, Cinema.

Boydell Press, The (1969), P.O. Box 24, Ipswich, Suffolk, IP1 1JJ *T.* 039-441 320. *Directors:* R. W. Barber, H. R. Barber, S. R. M. Wilson, M. J. Wilson, H. R. Tempest Radford, J. F. Platt.
Local History and Topography (especially East Anglia), Field Sports, History, Literature.

*British and Foreign Bible Society, 146 Queen Victoria Street, London, EC4V 4BX *T.* 01-248 4751. Bibles, Testaments, portions and selections. The sole object of the B.F.B.S. is to encourage the wider circulation of the Holy Scriptures. *General Director:* Rev. Neville B. Cryer, M.A.

Brockhampton Press, Ltd.—see Hodder & Stoughton Children's Books.

Brodie (James), Ltd. (1926), 15 Queen Square, Bath, BA1 2HW *T.* 22110. *Directors:* Frank E. Sandy (Chairman and Managing Director), Corinne Wimpress (Secretary), John K. Wimpress.
Educational (Primary and Secondary), Film Strips and Tape Recordings.

Brown, Son & Ferguson, Ltd. (1860), 52 Darnley Street, Glasgow, G41 2SG *T.* 041-429 1234. *T.A.* Skipper, Glasgow, G41.
Nautical books; Scottish books and Scottish plays. Boy Scout, Cub Scout, Brownie story Books.

Brown Watson, Ltd., Warner House, 135–141 Wardour Street, London, W1V 4QA. *T.* 01-734 3493. *T.A.* Bookstocks, London. *Telex:* 21996. A Howard & Wyndham Company.

*Burke Publishing Co., Ltd., Pegasus House, 116–120 Golden Lane, London, EC1Y 0UD *T.* 01-253 2145. *Trade:* The Barn, Northgate, Beccles, Suffolk, NR34 9AX *T.* 0502-713 239 and 714473. *Directors:* Harold K. Starke (Chairman and Managing Director), Peter Stuart-Heaton, Naomi Galinski, Anthony Rubinstein.
Children's Books (Fiction, Non-Fiction), Educational (Pre-school and Nursery, Primary, Secondary).

Burke's Peerage Ltd., 56 Walton Street, London, SW3 1RB *T.* 01-584 1106. *Managing Director:* J. G. Norman.
Scholarly and popular works in the fields of Genealogy, Heraldry, Architectural History, Social History, etc. Suggestions for new projects, books, essays, etc., should be made to Felicity Mortimer.

Burns & Oates Ltd. (1847), Publishers to the Holy See, 2–10 Jerdan Place, London, SW6 5PT *T.* 01-385 6261–2. *Directors:* Charlotte de la Bedoyere, Alfred Zimmermann.
Theology, Philosophy, Spirituality, History, Biography, Literary Criticism, Education and books of Catholic interest.

Burrow (Ed. J.) & Co., Ltd. (1900), Publicity House, Streatham Hill, London, SW2 4TR *T.* 01-674 1222. *Chairman:* Bernard Lewis. *Directors:* Paul Lewis (Managing), P. J. Molland.
Guide Books, Street Plans and Maps, Travel, Year Books, etc.

Business Books, Ltd. (1921), 24 Highbury Crescent, London, N5 1RX *T.* 01-359 3711. *Directors:* J. B. R. Dare, F. R. F. Singer.
Business, Advertising, Marketing, Scientific, Technical and Industrial, Reference, Directories, Paperbacks.

*Butterworths (1818), 88 Kingsway, London, WC2B 6AB *T.* 01-405 6900 and Borough Green, Sevenoaks, Kent, TN15 8PH *T.* Borough Green (0732) 884567. *T.A.* Butterwort, London. *Directors:* W. G. Graham (Chairman and Chief Executive), S. M. Carey, P. Cheeseman, T. Kelley, E. Hunter, A. McAdam, E. R. Norton, S. H. W. Partridge, D. E. Saville, A. K. L. Stephenson. *Branches overseas:* Australia, Canada, New Zealand, South Africa, USA.
Law, Medicine, Science, Technology.

Butterworth & Co. (Publishers), Ltd., see **Butterworths.**

C.B.D. Research Ltd. (1961), 154 High Street, Beckenham, Kent, BR3 1EA *T.* 01-650 7745. *Directors:* G. P. Henderson, S. P. A. Henderson, A. F. Christlieb.
Directories, Reference Books, Bibliographies, Guides to Business and Statistical Information.

*Calder and Boyars, Ltd., 18 Brewer Street, London, W1R 4AS *T.* 01-734 1985, and 6900. *Directors:* John Calder, Marion Boyars, Michael Hayes.
International and British Fiction, Plays and Creative Literature. Criticism, especially Literature, Music, Opera, Art, Cinema, Politics, Current Affairs, Humanities, Social Sciences. Some general books, classics and poetry. Many translations.

Calder, John (Publishers) Ltd., 18 Brewer Street, London, W1R 4AS *T.* 01-734 3786–7. *Directors:* John Calder, Christopher Davidson.
European, International and British fiction and plays, Art, Literary, Music and Social Criticism, Biography and Autobiography, Essays, Humanities and Social Sciences, European Classics. Series include: Scottish Library, New Writing and Writers, Platform Books. Publishers of *Gambit*, the quarterly drama magazine, and the *Journal of Becket Studies*. British publishers in the new *International Publishers' Prize* (*Prix des Septs*).

*Cambridge University Press (1534), Cambridge: The Pitt Building, Trumpington Street, Cambridge, CB2 1RP *T.* Cambridge (0223) 58331. *T.A.* Unipress, Cambridge. London: Bentley House, 200 Euston Road, London, NW1 2DB *T.* 01-387 5030. *T.A.* Cantabrigia, London, NW1. U.S.A.: 32 East 57 Street, New York, N.Y., 10022. Australia, 296 Beaconsfield Parade, Middle Park, Melbourne, 3206. *Chief Executive:* Geoffrey A. Cass, M.A. *Managing Director (Publishing Division):* Philip E. V. Allin, M.A. *Publsiher:* Michael H. Black, M.A. *Director:* American Branch: Euan H. Phillips, M.A. *Managing Director,* Australian Branch: Brian W. Harris.
Archaeology, Educational (Secondary, Tertiary), History, Language and Literature, Law, Oriental, Philosophy, Science (Physical and Biological), Social Sciences, Theology and Religion. The Bible and Prayer Book.

Canongate Publishing Ltd. (1973), 17 Jeffrey Street, Edinburgh, EH1 1DR *T.* 031-556 0023. *Directors:* Charles Wild, J. J. Douglas, Stephanie Wolfe Murray. Associated company Southside (Publishers) Ltd.
General.

*Cape (Jonathan), Ltd. (1921), 30 Bedford Square, London, WC1B 3EL *T.* 01-636 5764 (five lines), 01-636 9395 (three lines). *T.A.* and *Cables:* Capajon, London, WC1. General Publisher. *Directors:* Tom Maschler (Chairman), Graham C. Greene (Managing), W. Robert Carr, David Machin (Deputy Managing), Anthony Colwell, J. Robinson. *Special Director:* Norman Askew.
Archaeology, Biography and Memoirs, Children's Books, Current Affairs, Drama, Economics, Fiction, History, Philosophy, Poetry, Sociology, Travel.

Carruthers (Robt.) & Sons (1817), P.O. Box 13, Bank Lane, Inverness, IV1 1QW *T.* Inverness (0463) 33059. *T.A.* Courier, Inverness. *Present Proprietor and Editor:* Miss Eveline Barron, O.B.E., M.A. Publishers of *Inverness Courier* and of books concerning the Highlands.

Cass (Frank) & Co., Ltd. (1958), Gainsborough House, 11 Gainsborough Road, London, E11 1RS *T.* 01-530 4226. *T.A.* Simfay, London. *Telex:* 897719. *Directors:* Frank Cass (Managing), A. E. Cass, M. P. Zaidner.
Economics, History, Social Sciences, Politics, African Studies, Literary Criticism, Art, International Affairs, Development Studies. Also *The Journal of Development Studies, Middle Eastern Studies, Business History, Journal of Peasant Studies, Journal of Commonwealth and Comparative Politics, Journal of Imperial and Commonwealth History, West European Politics, Journal of Strategic Studies.*

*Cassell Ltd. (1848), 35 Red Lion Square, London, WC1R 4SG *T.* 01-831 6100. *T.A.* Caspeg, London, WC1. *Telex:* 28648 Casmac-G. Melbourne, Sydney, Auckland, N.Z., Johannesburg and Toronto. *Directors:* Marshall D.Mascott (USA), (Managing), Frederick Kobrak (Germany), Eric Magness, Harry R. Most (USA), Dennis Napier, Aidan Reynolds. *Publishing Divisions:* Cassell, Bailliere Tindall, Studio Vista. Geoffrey Chapman, Johnston & Bacon.
General Books of all classes: Biographies, Fiction, Music, Dictionaries and Reference Books, Educational (Primary, Secondary, Technical), Further Education.

Catholic Truth Society (1868), P.O. Box 422, 38–40 Eccleston Square, London, SW1V 1PD *T.* 01-834 4392. *T.A.* Apostolic, London, SW1. *Telex:* 922369. *Chairman:* Rt. Rev. Bishop Alan C. Clark, D.D. *Hon. Treasurer:* Brian Godfrey, O.B.E., C.A. *General Secretary:* David Murphy, M.A.
Bibles, Prayer Books and pamphlets of Doctrinal, Historical, Devotional, or Social Interest are published. MSS. of about 2500 to 3000 words with up to six illustrations are suitable.

Centaur Press, Ltd., Fontwell, Arundel, Sussex, BN18 0TA *T.* 024-368 (Easter-gate) 3302. *Directors:* Jon Wynne-Tyson, Jennifer M. Wynne-Tyson. A preliminary letter should be sent before submitting MS.
Philosophy, Biography, the Arts, Dictionaries, Reference, Guides, *Centaur Classics, The Regency Library, Travellers' Classics, Centaur Monographs.*

*Chambers (W. and R.), Ltd. (1820), 11 Thistle Street, Edinburgh, EH2 1DG *T.* 031-225 4463–4. *T.A.* Chambers, Edinburgh. *Chairman:* A. S. Chambers. *Managing Director:* I. Gould. *Directors:* Dr. David Dickson, W. Gordon Graham, I. C. Inglis, J. Ramage.
Educational (Infants, Junior, Secondary) especially Modern Mathematics and Computer Studies; Dictionaries and Reference Books; Mathematical Tables; Children's Books, especially Picture Books; General Books, fiction and non-fiction.

*Chapman & Hall, Ltd. (1830), 11 New Fetter Lane, London, EC4P 4EE *T.* 01-583 9855. *T.A.* Pickwick, London, EC4. Agents outside USA and Canada for American Society of Metals, Ohio. *Directors:* Richard Stileman (Managing Director), John von Knorring (Assistant), Richard Green, B. West, P. Read, B. Shurlock.
Science, Technology, Medical.

*Chapman, Geoffrey, Publishers (1957) (a Division of Cassell Ltd.), 35 Red Lion Square, London, WC1R 4SG *T.* 01-831 6100. *Telex:* 28648 Casmac-G. Catholic books. Books for religious education. Religious books for Africa.

*Chatto & Windus, Ltd. (1855), 40–42 William IV Street, London, WC2N 4DF *T.* 01-836 0127. *Directors:* Norah Smallwood, O.B.E., J. F. Charlton, D. J. Enright, Christopher MacLehose, Sebastian Walker.
Archaeology, Art, Biography and Memoirs, Children's Books (Fiction, Non-Fiction), Current Affairs, Drama, Economics, Educational (Technical, University), Essays, Fiction, History, Poetry, Political Economy, Sociology, Travel.

Church of Scotland Department of Publicity and Publication, 121 George Street, Edinburgh, EH2 4YN *T.* 031-225 5722.

Churchill (J. & A.) now **Churchill Livingstone.**

*Churchill Livingstone (a division of **Longman Group Ltd.**), 23 Ravelston Terrace, Edinburgh, EH4 3TL *T.* 031-343 1991. *T.A.* Churchliv, Edinburgh. *Telex:* 727511. *Divisional Managing Director:* R. G. B. Duncan.
Medical, Nursing, Dental, Veterinary, Scientific, Dictionaries.

Clarendon Press—see **Oxford University Press.**

*Clark (T. & T.), Ltd. (1821), 36 George Street, Edinburgh, EH2 2LQ *T.* 031-225 4703. *T.A.* Dictionary, Edinburgh. *Directors:* P. H. Bartholomew, M.C., C.A. (Chairman), T. G. Clark, T. G. R. Clark, C.A. (Managing), Geoffrey F. Green, M.A., PH.D., D. A. Ross Stewart, B.A.
Dictionaries, Philosophy, Theology and Religion.

Clarke (James) & Co., Ltd. (1859), 7 All Saints' Passage, Cambridge, CB2 3LS *T.* 0223 50865. *Telex:* 817570. *Managing Director:* Adrian Brink.
Theology, Religion, Educational, Technical, Reference Books.

Cleaver-Hume Press, Ltd., now **Collier Macmillan Schools, Ltd.,** *q.v.*

*Collet's (Publishers), Ltd., *Registered Address and Head Office:* Denington Estate, Wellingborough, Northampton, NN8 2QT T. (0933) 224351. *Directors:* Mrs. J. Birch, Thomas A. Russell.
Politics, Art, Music Studies, Technical and Scientific, Travel Guides, Language Study materials, specialising in Russian.

*Collier Macmillan Ltd., Stockley Close, Stockley Road, West Drayton, Middlesex, UB7 9BE *T.* (81) 40651. *Cables:* Pachamac West Drayton. *Directors:* Brian J. Collins (Managing), Robert A. Barton (USA), Harry R. Most (USA), Jack I. Mills (USA), G. Eric Magness. *Imprints:* Macmillan, The Free Press, Collier Books, Crowell-Collier Press, Hafner Press, P. J. Kennedy & Sons, Benziger Bruce & Glenco, Inc., Schirmer Books, Collier Macmillan International, Macmillan Information.

Collier Macmillan Schools Ltd., Aldermaston Court, Aldermaston, Reading, Berks, RG7 4PF *T.* Woolhampton 2241. *Managing Director:* R. P. Wellsman.

Collingridge (W. H. & L.), Ltd., books—see **The Hamlyn Publishing Group, Ltd.**

Collings (Rex), Ltd. (1969), 69 Marylebone High Street, London, W1M 3AQ *T.* 01-487 4201 *T.A.* Hujambo, London. *Telex:* 337340 Bookps G. *Directors:* Ian Coltart, Rex Collings.
Children's Books, Africana, Poetry, Reference Books.

*Collins (William), Sons & Co., Ltd. (1819), General and Children's Book Publishing Offices, and Fontana and Armada Paperback Publishing Offices, 14 St. James's Place, London, SW1A 1PS *T.* 01-493 7070. Printing Offices and Editorial Offices for Bibles, Educational, Children's and Reference Books, Westerhill Road, Bishopbriggs, Glasgow, G64 2QT *T.* 041-772 3200. *Overseas Companies:* Cleveland, Toronto, Sydney, Auckland, Johannesburg. *Holding Company Directors:* W. J. Collins (Chairman), F. I. Chapman (Deputy Chairman), D. W. Nickson (Vice-Chairman), C. E. Allen, S. A. M. Collins, G. Craig, K. W. Wilder.
Archaeology, Architecture, Art, Belles-Lettres, Bibles, Biography and Memoirs, Children's Books (Fiction, Non-Fiction, Rewards, Toy and Picture, Annuals), Current Affairs, Dictionaries, Directories or Guide Books, Educational (Infants, Primary, Secondary), Essays, Fiction, General History, Humour, Liturgical Books, Maps and Atlases, Natural History, Naval and Military, Philosophy, Practical Handbooks, Reference, Science (history of), Sports, Games and Hobbies, Travel, Theology and Religion; Crime Club, Fontana, Fontana Library, Fount Religious paperbacks and Armada Children's paperbacks.

Common Ground Filmstrips, Longman Group, Ltd., Longman House, Burnt Mill, Harlow, Essex, CM20 2JE *T.* Harlow 26721. *Telex:* 81259.

*Connoisseur, The, Chestergate House, Vauxhall Bridge Road, London, SW1V 1HF *T.* 01-834 2331.
Authoritative features on Art and Antiques.

*Conservative Political Centre (1945), 32 Smith Square, London, SW1P 3HH *T.* 01-222 9000. *Director:* David Knapp.
Political Economy, Current Affairs, Sociology.

*Constable & Co., Ltd. (1890), 10 Orange Street, London, WC2H 7EG *T.* 01-930 0801-7. *Trade:* 062-181 6362. *T.A.* Dhagoba, London. *Directors:* Benjamin Glazebrook (Chairman and Managing Director), Noel Holland, R. A. A. Holt, Miles Huddleston, P. N. Marks, Richard Tomkins.
Fiction: general, thrillers, historical. General non-fiction: Literature, Biography, Memoirs, History, Politics, Current Affairs, Food, Travel and Guide Books, Social Sciences, Psychology and Psychiatry, Counselling, Social Work, Sociology, Mass Media.

Cooper (Leo), Ltd. (1968), 196 Shaftesbury Avenue, London, WC2H 8JL *T.* 01-836 6225. *Directors:* Leo Cooper, J. Cooper, T. R. Hartman, J. M. Carew, M.C., Alastair Service, Alison Harvey.
Military History, Memoirs and Biography.

Corgi paperbacks—see **Transworld.**

Coronet—see **Hodder & Stoughton, Ltd.**

Council for British Archaeology (1944), 112 Kennington Road, London, SE11 6RE *T.* 01-582 0494. *Director:* Henry Cleere.
British Archaeology—academic; no general books.

Country Life, books—see **The Hamlyn Publishing Group, Ltd.**

*Croom Helm Ltd., 2–10 St. John's Road, London, SW11 5BR *T.* 01-228 9343. *Directors:* C. Helm, D. Croom, J. Foyle, B. Ackerman, M. Helm.
Humanities, Social Sciences and Life Sciences.

*Crosby Lockwood Staples Ltd., P.O. Box 9, 29 Frogmore, St. Albans, Herts, AL2 2NF *T.* Park Street 72727. *T.A.* Granada, St. Albans. *Telex:* 262802. *Directors:* W. R. Carr, A. R. T. Birch, D. M. Fulton, J. R. R. Yglesias.
Agriculture, Architecture, Building & Construction, Civil Aviation, Civil & Structural Engineering, Electrical and Electronic Engineering, Fashion, Mechanical Engineering Psychology, Special Education, Surveying and Quantity Surveying, Town and Country Planning.

Dacre Press, The (1939).   An imprint of **A. & C. Black, Ltd.**

Dalton (Terence), Ltd. (1966), Water Street, Lavenham, Sudbury, Suffolk, CO10 9RN *T.* Lavenham (0787-24) 572. *Directors:* T. R. Dalton (Managing), J. M. Dalton, T. A. J. Dalton.
Biographies, Geography, History, Maritime Subjects, Rivers, Aviation. Non-Fiction generally.

Daniel (The C. W.) Company, Ltd. (1902), 60 Muswell Road, London, N10 2BE *T.* 01-444 8650.   *Directors:* Ian Miller, Jane Miller.
Natural Healing, Homeopathy, Diet.

*Darton, Longman & Todd, Ltd. (1959), 89 Lillie Road, London, SW6 1UD *T.* 01-385 2341. *T.A.* Librabook, London, SW6. *Directors:* T. M. Longman, J. M. Todd, E. A. C. Russell, R. J. Baird-Smith, D. W. Crutcher.
Bibles, Directories or Guide Books, History, Hobbies, Music, Theology and Religion, Travel.

Darwen Finlayson, Ltd.—see Phillimore & Co., Ltd.

*David & Charles (Holdings), Ltd. (1960), Brunel House, Forde Road, Newton Abbot, Devon. TQ12 2DW *T.* Newton Abbot 61121. *Telex:* 42904 Books Nabbot. *Directors:* J. Angell, C. Carr, K. G. Davis, R. Dexter, L. Springfield, Mrs. P. M. Thomas, D. St. John Thomas.
Agriculture, Antiques and Collecting, Archaeology, Architecture, Art, Astronomy, Aviation, Boating, Business, Canals and Waterways, Economics, Fishing, Gardening, Genealogy and Heraldry, General, Geography, Geology, Health, History, Industrial History and Archaeology, Maritime, Music and Films, Natural History, Practical and Crafts, Railway, Regional, Road Transport, Sports, Topography, Wine and Food.   Ideas welcome but no Fiction.   Author's guide supplied on request.

Davies, Christopher, Publishers, Ltd. (1949), 4–5 Thomas Row, Swansea, West Glamorgan, SA1 1NJ *T.* 0792 41933. *Directors:* Christopher Talfan Davies, John Mark Phillips.
Biography, Children's Books (fiction and non-fiction), Economics, Politics, Educational Books, Fiction, History, Poetry, Sport, Welsh Dictionaries, *Triskel Books.*

*Davies, Peter, Ltd. (1925), 15–16 Queen Street, Mayfair, London, W1X 8BE *T.* 01-493 4141 and The Windmill Press, Kingswood. Tadworth, Surrey. *T.* Mogador 3511. *Directors:* C. S. Pick (Chairman), D. E. Priestley (Managing Director), J. W. Dettmer, N. Hollis, Michael House (Secretary).
Fiction and General, Biography and Memoirs, Village and country crafts, Seafaring, Naval and Military, Theatre.

*Davis & Moughton, Ltd. (1883), Ludgate House, 23 Waterloo Place, Leamington Spa, Warwickshire, CV32 5LA *T.* 092-6 24003.
Educational (Primary, Secondary).

Davis-Poynter, Ltd. (1971), 20 Garrick Street, London, WC2E 9BJ *T*. 01-240 3144. *T.A.* Deepeebook, London, WC2. *Directors:* Lord Goodman (Chairman), R. G. Davis-Poynter (Managing Director), Susan M. Herbert (Secretary), Alan U. Schwartz (USA).
Fiction, Modern History, Biography, Playscripts, Theatre, Popular Medicine and Ecology.

*Dawson, Wm., & Sons, Ltd. (1809), Cannon House, Folkestone, Kent, CT19 5EE *T*. 0303-57421. *T.A.* Dawbooks, Folkestone. *Telex:* 96392. *Directors:* A. A. Smith (Chairman), G. P. C. Krayenbrink (Managing), R. W. Hall, D. A. Brewer, J. A. Beech, W. F. Hammond, L. Johnson, R. K. McCrow, A. R. MacDonald-Bell, A. Roche, H. S. Swallow, I. R. C. Williams.
Literature, Geography, History, Asian Studies, Cartography, Science and Medicine, Politics.

Dean & Son, Ltd. (The Hamlyn Publishing Group, Ltd.), 2nd Floor, 52–54 Southwark Street, London, SE1 1UA *T*. 01-407 6682.
Children's Books. (Unsolicited manuscripts not accepted.)

*Dent (J. M.) & Sons, Ltd. (1888), Aldine House, 26 Albemarle Street, London, W1X 4QY *T*. 01-491 2970. *T.A.* Malaby, London, W1. *Telex:* J. M. Dent G 825751. *Directors:* Piers Raymond (Chairman and Managing), F. J. Martin Dent, J. J. Nelson, V. F. Chamberlain, Peter Collins, Malcolm Gerratt, Vanessa Hamilton, Peter Shellard, John Sundell.
Everyman's Library, Everyman's Encyclopaedia, Everyman's Reference Library, Everyman's University Library, Dent Dolphins, Everyman Paperbacks. Proprietors of the Malaby Press and the Phoenix House imprints.
Archaeology, Biography and Memoirs, Children's Books (Fiction, Non-Fiction), Gardening, Guide Books, Drama, General History, Humour, Military History, Music, Natural History, Popular Psychology, Science Fact, Travel.

*Deutsch, André, Ltd. (1950), 105 Great Russell Street, London, WC1B 3LJ *T*. 01-580 2746–9. *T.A.* Adlib, London, WC1. *Cables:* Adlib, London, WC1. *Telex:* 21792, mono ref. 1818. *Directors:* André Deutsch, Diana Athill, Nicolas Bentley, Piers Burnett, David Heimann, F. P. Kendall, Bill McCreadie, June Bird, Faith Evans, Pamela Royds, Michael Salinger. *Secretary:* Philip Tammer.
Art, Belles-Lettres, Biography and Memoirs, Children's Books, Fiction, General, History, Humour, Politics, Travel, Grafton Books on Library Science, The Language Library. Also handling **Rapp & Whiting, Ltd.** *Directors:* Georg Rapp, B. M. Igra, Miriam Rapp.

*Dinosaur Publications Ltd. (1967), Beechcroft House, Over, Cambridge CB4 5NE *T*. Swavesey (0954) 30324. *Directors:* Althea Braithwaite, Bruce Graham-Cameron.
Children's Books (Fiction, Non-Fiction, Picture).

*Dobson (Dennis) (1944), 80 Kensington Church Street, London, W8 4BZ *T*. 01-229 0225, and 6022. *Directors:* Dennis Dobson, Margaret Dobson.
Belles-Lettres, Biography and Memoirs, Children's Books (Fiction, Non-Fiction), Current Affairs, Drama, Films, Economics, Educational, Fiction, Science-Fiction, General, History, Humour, Music, Philosophy, Political Economy, Science, Sociology, Theatre, Travel.

Dolphin Book Co., Ltd., The (1935), 58 Hurst Lane, Cumnor, Oxford, OX2 9PR *T.* Cumnor 2175. *T.A.* Dolphin, Oxford. *Directors:* J. L. Gili, E. H. Gili, M. L. Gili.
Spanish Literature and Scholarship.

*Dragon Books—see Mayflower Books Ltd.

Drummond Press, The, 64 Murray Place, Stirling, FK8 2BX *T.* Stirling 3384. *Director:* Rev. John Birkbeck, M.C. (see also **Stirling Tract Enterprise**).
Religious and Theological.

Dryad Press, Northgates, Leicester, LE1 9BU *T.* 50405. *T.A.* Dryad, Leicester. *Directors:* D. C. Pool, M. Waddington.
Art, Educational (Infants, Primary, Secondary, Technical (Craft)), Practical Handbooks.

Duckworth (Gerald), & Co., Ltd. (1898), The Old Piano Factory, 43 Gloucester Crescent, London, NW1 7DY *T.* 01-485 3484. *T.A.* Platypus, London, NW1. *Directors:* Ray Davies, Anna Haycraft, Colin Haycraft (Chairman and Managing Director), C. C. de Pass.
General, Fiction, and Academic.

*E P Publishing Ltd. (1946), Head Office: Bradford Road, East Ardsley, Wakefield, West Yorkshire, WF3 2JN *T.* 823971. *T.A.* Edpro, Wakefield; 10 Snow Hill, London, EC1A 2EB *T.* 01-834 1067. *Directors:* B. Lewis, J. S. Lofthouse, J. S. Gummer, J. A. Oldham, N. D. J. Freeman.
Sport and leisure, Facsimile reprints, Academic Books.

*Ebury Press, Chestergate House, Vauxhall Bridge Road, London, SW1V 1HF *T.* 01-834 2331.
Food and Wine, Travel, Gardens, General and Practical subjects, Art and Antiques. Publishers of *Good Housekeeping* illustrated books on cookery and household management and Connoisseur books on art and antiques.

Edinburgh House Press. All enquiries to: **Lutterworth Press,** *q.v.*

Edinburgh University Press, 22 George Square, Edinburgh, EH8 9LF. *T.* 031-667 1011. *T.A.* Edinpress.

*Educational Explorers Ltd. (1962), 40 Silver Street, Reading, RG1 2SU. *T.* 0734 83103–4. *Directors:* C. Gattegno, D. M. Gattegno.
Educational, Mathematics: *Numbers in colour with Cuisenaire Rods,* Languages: *The Silent Way,* Literacy, Reading: *Words in Colour,* Science, Careers: *My Life & My Work Series.* Educational films.

*Elek (Paul) Ltd., 54–58 Caledonian Road, London, N1 9RN *T.* 01-278 6552. *Directors:* Elizabeth Elek (Chairman), David Herbert (Managing), Moira Johnston (Joint Managing), Mary Butler, Ann Douglas, Peter Phillips, Antony Wood, Prof. D. A. Bullough.
Academic, Archaeology, Architecture, Art, Biography and Memoirs, Current Affairs, Drama, Fiction, General History, Humour, Philosophy, Psychology, Scientific, Travel, *Plays of the Year* series.

Elliot Right Way Books, Kingswood Buildings, Brighton Road, Lower Kingswood, Tadworth, Surrey, KT20 6TD *T.* Mogador 2202–3. Specialist in instructional and motor books, and publishers of the series *Paperfronts.* Careful consideration for all new ideas, and editorial help can be provided. Popular Technical, Popular Educational, Popular Medical, Pets, Self-help, Sport, Commerce, General, Humour, Paperbacks.

*Encyclopaedia Britannica International, Ltd. Mappin House, 156–162 Oxford Street, London, W1N 9DL *T.* 01-637 3371. *Managing Director:* Joe D. Adams.

English Universities Press, Ltd., The—see **Hodder & Stoughton Educational.**

Epworth Press—see **Methodist Publishing House.**

Europa Publications Ltd., 18 Bedford Square, London, WC1B 3JN. *T.* 01-580 8236. *Directors:* Percy F. Hughes (Chairman), W. Simon (Managing), P. G. C. Jackson, H. J. Wombill, P. A. McGinley, C. H. Martin.
Directories, Economics, International Relations, Reference, Year Books, History.

*Evans Brothers Ltd. (1905), Montague House, Russell Square, London, WC1B 5BX *T.* 01-636 8521. *T.A.* Byronitic, London, WC1. *Directors:* L. J. Browning (Chairman), F. S. J. Austin, J. Bentley, H. Buckingham, R. C. Chesher (Deputy Managing), D. S. Dyerson, the Hon. Mrs. A. M. Evans, Miss A. F. White, R. R. S. White. *Secretary:* R. C. Chesher.
Educational books and periodicals, particularly Infant, Primary, Secondary and E.L.T., Children's Books, Plays (acting editions), Dictionaries, Practical Books.

Evelyn (Hugh) Ltd. (1958), 53 Charlbert Street, London, NW8 6JN *T.* 01-586 5108. *Directors:* Hugh Evelyn Street (Managing), M. O. C. Street.
Illustrated books on Architecture and Nautical Subjects.

*Everest Books Ltd. (1973), 4 Valentine Place, London, SE1 8QH *T.* 01-261 1536. *Directors:* Robin McGibbon (Managing), Clive Mattock, A.C.A.
Showbusiness autobiographies.

Exley Publications Ltd. (1976), 63 Kingsfield Road, Watford, Herts, WD1 4PP *T.* Watford 43892 and 36961. *Directors:* Richard Exley, Helen Exley.
Humour, Gift Books, Political, Books by Children.

*Eyre Methuen Ltd., 11 New Fetter Lane, London, EC4P 4EE *T.* 01-583 9855. *T.A.* Elegiacs, London, EC4. *Directors:* Charles Shirley (Chairman), Geoffrey Strachan (Managing), Charles Hammick, Christopher Holgate, Jan Hopcraft, Nicholas Hern, David Ross, Bob Woodings.
General, Fiction, Biography and Memoirs, History, Current Affairs, Topography, Humour, Performing Arts. Please write with synopsis before submitting MSS.

*Eyre & Spottiswoode (Publishers), Ltd., 11 New Fetter Lane, London, EC4P 4EE *T.* 01-583 9855. *T.A.* Exaltedly, London, EC4. *Telex:* 263398.
Directors: F. C. Friend (Chairman), A. J. Holder, C. Shirley, D. Ross.
Publishers of the Bible and Book of Common Prayer, Religious Books.

*Faber & Faber Ltd. (1929), 3 Queen Square, London, WC1N 3AU *T.* 01-278 6881. *T.A.* Fabbaf, London, WC1. *Directors:* Charles Monteith (Chairman), Matthew Evans (Managing), T. E. Faber, A. T. G. Pocock, O.B.E., Rosemary Goad, Giles de la Mare, George Taylor.
Aeronautics, Agriculture, Archaeology, Architecture, Art, Biography and Memoirs, Children's Books (Fiction, Non-Fiction, Picture), Cookery Books, Current Affairs, Drama, Economics, Educational Books, Fiction, Films, Gardening. History, Humour, Linguistics, Medical and Nursing, Music, Naval and Military, Oriental, Philosophy, Poetry, Politics, Science, Sociology, Sports, Games and Hobbies, Television, Theatre and Ballet, Theology and Religion, Travel. *Faber Paperbacks* cover many of the subjects shown above. *Art Books* include the following series: Faber Monographs on Pottery and Porcelain, Glass, Furniture and Silver, Faber Collectors Library.

Faber & Faber (Publishers) Ltd. (1969), 3 Queen Square, London, WC1N 3AU *T.* 01-278 6881. *T.A.* Fabbaf, London, WC1. *President:* Richard de la Mare. *Directors:* T. E. Faber (Chairman), Matthew Evans (Vice-Chairman), Charles Monteith, P. W. G. Du Buisson, Donald Mitchell, A. T. G. Pocock, O.B.E. Holding company of **Faber & Faber Ltd.,** *q.v.*

Fabian Society (1884), 11 Dartmouth Street, London, SW1H 9BN *T.* 01-930 3077 (from Spring 1979: 01-222 8877) (also controls **NCLC Publishing Society Ltd.).**
Current Affairs, Economics, Educational, Political Economy, Sociology.

Faith Press Ltd. (1905), Wing Road, Leighton Buzzard, LU7 7NQ *T.* Leighton Buzzard 3365. Religious Books (Anglican).

Fieldhouse, Arthur, Ltd. (1895), Advertiser Press Ltd., Premier Works, Paddock Head, Huddersfield, HD3 4ES. *T.* Huddersfield 20444.
Commerce, Educational (Technical).

*Focal Press, Ltd. (1938), 31 Fitzroy Square, London, W1P 6BH *T.* 01-387 4294 and 387 7261. *T.A.* Focalpress, London, W1, and New York. *Directors:* Colin Ancliffe (Managing), A. Kraszna-Krausz, L. S. Temple, R. W. Dear, Nicolas Thompson.
Illustrated Technical and Scientific books on Photography, Cinematography, Television, Sound and Image Recording, Printing and Graphic Art. Practical Handbooks, Textbooks, Reference.

Fontana paperbacks—see **William Collins.**

*Foulsham (W.) & Co., Ltd. (1819), Yeovil Road, Slough, Berks, SL1 4JH *T.* 75-38637.
Art Dictionaries, General Manuals, Educational, School Library, Do-It-Yourself, Hobbies and Games, Sport, Travel.
Foulsham-Tab Technical Books—electronics and allied subjects. *Foulsham-Technical*—radio. electronics.

*Foundational Book Company, Ltd., The, Trade: 29 Pinfold Road, Streatham, London, SW16 2SL *T.* 01-584 1053.
Philosophy, Theology and Religion.

Fountain Press, Model & Allied Publications Ltd.—see **Argus Books, Ltd.**

Fowler (L. N.) & Co. Ltd. (1880), 1201–3 High Road, Chadwell Heath, Romford, Essex, RM6 4DH T. 01-597 2491.
Astrology, Health and Healing, Mental Science, Yoga, Occult, Psychology, Religious.

Foyle, W. & G., Ltd., 119–125 Charing Cross Road, London, WC2H 0EB *T.* 01-437 5660. For book clubs handled by this firm see p. 214.

*Fraser (Gordon) Gallery Ltd., The (1936). Editorial: Fitzroy Road, London, NW1 8TP *T.* 01-722 0077. *T.A.* Frasercard London. *Telex:* Fraser London 25848. *Distribution:* Eastcotts Road, Bedford. *Director:* Gordon Fraser.
Fine Arts, Graphic Art, Architecture, Film, Photography, Buddhism.

Freeman (W. H.) & Co., Ltd. (1959), 58 Kings Road, Reading. RG1 3AA *T.* Reading 583250. *Directors:* Sir Jonathan Backhouse, A. Kudlacik, S. Schaefer, R. Warrington.
Science, Technical, Medicine, Politics, Economics, Psychology, Sociology, Archaeology.

*French (Samuel), Ltd. (1830), 26 Southampton Street, Strand, London, WC2E
7JE *T.* 01-836 7513. *Branches:* New York, Hollywood, Toronto, Sydney
q.v. *Directors:* Abbott Van Nostrand (Chairman), John Laurence Hughes
(Managing), Lionel Noel Woolf (Editorial), John William Bedding, Harold
Lesley Pumfrett (Sceretary). Publishers of plays and agents for the collection of royalties.
Drama.

Friedmann, Julian, Publisher, Ltd. (1974), 4 Perrins Lane, Hampstead, London,
NW3 1QY *T.* 01-794 0061. Directors: J. Friedmann, C. V. King, I. M.
Stoller.
Social Science, Current Affairs, History, African Studies, Gardening, Fiction.

*Futura Publications Ltd. (1973), 110 Warner Road, Camberwell, London, SE5
9HQ *T.* 01-737 2431. *T.A.* Futurapub, London, SE5. *Telex:* 916042.
Directors: A. M. Alfred, B. R. Cannon, A. J. V. Cheetham, P. G. Morrison,
P. M. Mortemore, D. Richardson, P. C. K. Roche.
Mass market paperbacks: fiction, non-fiction, reference, large format illus-
trated (biography, history, archaeology.)

Gairm Publications, incorporating Alex MacLaren & Sons, (1875), 29 Waterloo
Street, Glasgow, G2 6BZ *T.* 041-221 1971.
Dictionaries, Language Books, Novels, Poetry, Music, Quarterly Magazine
(Gaelic only).

*Gall & Inglis Ltd. (1810), 12 Newington Road, Edinburgh, EH9 1RB *T.* 031-
667 2791. *T.A.* Reckoners, Edinburgh. *Directors:* J. Horsburgh, V. E. M.
Inglis, E. G. Horsburgh.
Reference, Science.

Garnstone Press Ltd., The (1965), P.O. Box 233, London, SW3 *T.* 01-589 5578.
Cables: Balfbooks, London, SW3. *Directors:* Michael D. Balfour (Manag-
ing), D. J. Balfour.
Non-Fiction, Biography, Literature, Criticism, Prehistory, Guide, Travel,
Antiques, Hobbies, Health, Reference, Anthropology, Aviation and Mili-
tary.

Gee & Co. (Publishers), Ltd. (1874), Head Office and City Library, 151 Strand,
London, WC2R 1JJ *T.* 01-836 0832. *Directors:* Percy F. Hughes (Chair-
man and Managing Director), R. J. Gee, P. Gee-Heaton, Harold P. Kennett,
Geoffrey K. Browne (Secretary).
Accountancy, Business Management and Taxation.

*Geographia Ltd., 93 St. Peter's Street, St. Albans, Herts., AL1 3EH *T.* St. Albans
30121. *Telex:* 923578. *Directors:* R. A. A. Holt (Chairman), Charles
Clark, J. D. Stevenson (Managing), A. W. Ross, C. C. Tagg.
Maps, Atlases, Plans, Guides, Travel, Educational.

Geographical Publications Ltd. (1933), *E.A.:* The Keep, Berkhamsted Place,
Berkhamsted, Herts, HP4 1HQ *T.* Berkhamsted 2981. *Directors:* A. N.
Clark, G. N. Clark, G. N. Blake, D. R. Denman. *Secretary:* G. N. Clark.
Maps, atlases, books on land affairs, and photographs, both on own account
and jointly with other publishers. Publishers and general agents to World
Land Use Survey and International Geographical Union.

*Gibbons (Stanley) International, Ltd. (1856), 391 Strand, London, WC2R 0LX
T. 01-836 8444. *T.A.* Philatelic, London, WC2. *Directors:* A. L. Michael
(Chairman), R. A. Hamilton-Smith, H. O. Fraser (Deputy Chairman), D. V.
Whatley, S. Zimmerman, B. Kelly, J. N. Farthing, C. C. Narbeth.

Gibson, Robert & Sons Glasgow, Ltd. (1885), 17 Fitzroy Place, Glasgow, G3 7SF *T.* 041-248 5674. *Directors:* R. D. C. Gibson, R. G. C. Gibson, Dr. J. S. McEwan, M. Pinkerton, H. C. Crawford.
Educational.

Gifford (John) Ltd. (1937), 125 Charing Cross Road, London, WC2H 0EB. *T.* 01-437 0216. *Telex:* 261107. *Directors:* R. Batty, C. Batty. *Manager:* Alistair MacQueen.
Gardening, Sport, Natural History, Travel and Practical Books, Art, Collecting Antiques, Marine Aquaria.

Gill (George) & Sons Ltd. (1862), 59–61 Norman Road, St. Leonards-on-Sea, East Sussex, TN38 0EG *T.* 0424 428561. *T.A.* Gillerva, Hastings. *Directors:* H. J. Lavington, M. E. Forrest (Mrs.), P. Hall (Mrs.), H. D. Milroy, D. F. Saw.
Educational (Infants, Primary, Secondary, Technical).

*Ginn & Company, Ltd. (1926), Elsinore House, Buckingham Street, Aylesbury, Bucks, HP20 2NQ *T.* Aylesbury (STD 0296) 88411. *T.A.* Ginnbooks Aylesbury. *Telex:* 83535. *Directors:* N. A. E. Farrow, G. D. S. Blunt, E. F. Keartland.
Educational (Infants, Primary, Secondary).

*Glasgow, Mary, Publications Ltd. (1956), 140 Kensington Church Street, London, W8 4BN *T.* 01-229 9531. *T.A.* Emgeebee, London, W8.
Directors: M. J. Calmann, B. J. Clifton, A. E. J. Bedale, L. K. Upton, D. Raggett, C. A. Bayne.
Modern languages: French, Spanish, German, and English; language magazines and readers, courses, films, filmstrips, tapes.

Globe Education, Houndmills, Basingstoke, Hampshire, RG21 2XS *T.* Basingstoke 29242.
Educational (Infants, Primary, Special).

*Godwin (George), Ltd. (1962), 1–3 Pemberton Row, London, EC4A 3HA *T.* 01-353 2300. *Telex:* 25212. *Directors:* W. G. Askew, M.C., K.S.G., M.I.M., F.I.E.E. (Chairman), J. L. Brooks (Managing), Sir Herbert Ashworth, A. E. L. Cox, W. B. Griffin, F.C.A., A. H. Phebey.
Technical books with particular reference to the construction industry, Architecture and planning, Chemical and Process Engineering, Manufacturing Chemistry.

Golden Eagle Press Ltd. (1973), 55 Vaughan Way, Leicester, LE1 4NT *T.* 50899. *Directors:* Grace Hart (Managing), Alison Bowcock.
Personality Publishers—interested in autobiographies by stage, screen, television or public-life personalities. Biographies, non-fiction, fiction. Also Company histories and memoirs of business personalities.

*Gollancz (Victor), Ltd. (1927), 14 Henrietta Street, London, WC2E 8QJ *T.* 01-836 2006. *T.A.* Vigollan, London, WC2. *Directors:* Livia Gollancz, John Bush, David Burnett, Liz Calder, Joanna Goldsworthy, Kenneth Kemp, Ian Smith.
Biography and Memoirs, Children's Books (Fiction, Non-Fiction), Current Affairs, Fiction, Crime Fiction, Science Fiction, Fantasy & Macabre, General, History, Music, Philosophy, Sociology, Travel.

Gomer Press (1892), J. D. Lewis & Sons, Ltd., Gomer Press, Llandysul, Dyfed, SA44 4BQ *T.* 2371. *T.A.* Gomerian, Llandysul. *Directors:* J. Huw Lewis, John H. Lewis.
School Books in Welsh; Biography, Fiction.

Gower Press (1968), Teakfield Ltd., 1 Westmead, Farnborough, Hampshire, GU14 7RU *T.* Farnborough (0252) 41196. *Directors:* G. R. Cyriax, N. A. E. Farrow, M. J. Hanrahan.
Practical management and business reference.

Grafton Books. All books published by Grafton Books have been taken over by **André Deutsch, Ltd.**

*****Granada Publishing Ltd.,** 29 Frogmore, St. Albans, Herts, AL2 2NF *T.* Park Street (0727) 72727. *T.A.* Granada St. Albans. *Telex:* 262802. *Directors:* W. R. Carr, A. R. H. Birch (Managing), Lord Bernstein, Alex Bernstein, K. A. Hills, T. J. Kitson, M. Barty-King. Controlling—*General Division:* Hart-Davis MacGibbon Ltd. *Paperback Division:* Dragon Books, Mayflower Books, Paladin Books, Panther Books. *Technical Division:* Crosby Lockwood Staples Ltd, Adlard Coles Ltd—Sailing and Nautical. Hart-Davis Educational Ltd., comprising Chatto & Windus (Educational) Ltd., Blond Educational Ltd.

Griffin (Charles) & Co., Ltd. (1820), Charles Griffin House, Crendon Street, High Wycombe, Bucks, HP13 6LE *T.* 0494-36341. *T.A.* Explanatus, High Wycombe.
Scientific and Technical, notably Statistics.

Grisewood & Dempsey Ltd. (1973), Elsley House, 24–30 Great Titchfield Street, London, W1. *T.* 01-580 6236. *T.A.* Greatbooks, London. *Telex:* 27725. *Directors:* A. M. Alfred, M. W. C. Dempsey, D. Grisewood (Managing), J. Grisewood, J. Richards, A. Sheehan.
Children's Books, Educational (Primary and Secondary).

*****Guinness Superlatives, Ltd.** (1954), 2 Cecil Court, London Road, Enfield Middlesex, EN2 6DJ *T.* 01-367 4567. *Telex:* 23573.
Reference.

Gwasg Gee (1809), Denbigh, LL16 3SW *T.* Denbigh 2020. *Partners:* Charles Charman, M.B.E., Morfydd Charman, Edgar Rees, LL.B., Erina M. Rees, J.P.
Oldest Welsh publishers. Books of interest to Wales, in Welsh.

*****H. F. L. (Publishers), Ltd.,** (1884), 9 Bow Street, London, WC2E 7AL *T.* 01-836 9081. *Directors:* Max Reinhardt (Chairman), J. R. Hews, F.C.A. (Managing Director), D. J. Reinhardt, M. E. Wraith, Quentin Hockliffe.
Accountancy, Taxation, Commercial Law.

*****HM&M Publishers Ltd.,** Milton Road, Aylesbury, Bucks, HP21 7TH *T.* 0296 3211. *Directors:* Peter Medcalf, John Medcalf, L. Sinclair. *Editor:* Patrick West.
Medicine, Scientific, Nursing.

Hale (Robert) Ltd. (1936), Clerkenwell House, 45–47 Clerkenwell Green, London, EC1R 0HT *T.* 01-251 2661. *T.A.* Barabbas, London, EC1.
Archaeology, Architecture, Biography and Memoirs, Cinema, Cookery, Crafts, Current Affairs, Fiction, General History, Humour, Military, Music, Practical Handbooks, Sports, Games and Hobbies, Theatre and Ballet, Topography, Travel, War.

*Hamilton (Hamish), Ltd. (1931), 90 Great Russell Street, London, WC1B 3PT. *T.* 01-580 4621. *T.A.* Hamisham, Westcent, London. *Cable Address:* Hamisham, London. *Directors:* Hamish Hamilton, M.A., LL.B. (Chairman), Christopher Sinclair-Stevenson, M.A. (Managing), Nigel Sisson, Julia Mac-Rae, Michael Brown, Peter Kilborn, Jane Turnbull, Caroline Gueritz, Teresa King, Douglas McCreath, Iain Harvey.
Belles-Lettres, Biography and Memoirs, Children's Books (Fiction, Non-Fiction), Current Affairs, Drama, Fiction, General, History, Humour, Music, Political, Theatre and Ballet, Travel.

*Elm Tree Books (1969), a subsidiary of **Hamish Hamilton, Ltd.,** 90 Great Russell Street, London, WC1B 3PT *T.* 01-580 4621. *T.A.* Hamisham, Westcent, London. *Directors:* Roger Machell (Chairman), Christopher Sinclair-Stevenson, Peter Kilborn (Managing), Hamish Hamilton, Nigel Sisson, Jane Turnbull, Teresa King, Iain Harvey.
Entertainment, Cookery, Crafts, Sport, Hobbies, Literary Reference.

*Hamilton (Hamish) Children's Books, Ltd. (1970) (formerly the Children's Book Department of Hamish Hamilton), 90 Great Russell Street, London, WC1B 3PT *T.* 01-405 5148. *T.A.* Hamisham, Westcent, London. *Telex:* 298265. *Directors:* Hamish Hamilton (Chairman), Julia MacRae (Managing) Caroline Gueritz (Deputy Managing), Michael Brown, Rosemary Lister, S. J. Sambels (Secretary), Christopher Sinclair-Stevenson, Nigel Sisson.
Children's Books (Fiction, Non-Fiction and Picture Books, no annuals).

*Hamlyn Publishing Group, Ltd., The (1947), Astronaut House, Hounslow Road, Feltham, Middlesex, TW14 9AR *T.* 01-890 1480. *T.A.* Pleasbooks, Feltham. *Directors:* Hugh Campbell (Chairman and Chief Executive), Barry Rowland (Deputy Chief Executive), Bill Dancer (Marketing), Terry Higham (Financial), Douglas Dring (Company Secretary), Brian Busteed, Ron Chopping (Managing Director, Children's books), Ken Stephenson (Non-Executive), Dick Morris (Non-Executive), Jim Matthews (Non-Executive), Christopher Dolly (Non-Executive). *Associate companies overseas:* A. & W. Publishers Inc., USA.

Hammond, Hammond & Co., Ltd. Incorporated with **Barrie & Jenkins,** *q.v.*

*Harper & Row, Ltd., 28 Tavistock Street, London, WC2E 7PN *T.* 01-836 4635. *T.A.* Harprow, London, WC2. *Directors:* M. Dubois, B. Thomas, T. Razzall, Cass Canfield, Jr., R. E. Baensch, Paul Kuipers (Managing).
Textbooks, Medical, Juveniles, Religious, General, Paperbacks.

*Harrap (George G.) & Co., Ltd. (1901), P.O. Box 70, 182–4 High Holborn, London, WC1V 7AX *T.* 01-405 9935 and 01-405 0941. *T.A.* Harrapbook, London, WC1. *Hon. President:* R. Olaf Anderson. *Directors:* Paull Harrap (Chairman and Joint Managing Director), Nicholas W. Berry (Joint Managing Director), David L. Bangs, C. Richard Butterworth, Peter H. Collin, Michael P. Hills, Rene P. L. Ledesert.
Educational, Bi-Lingual Dictionaries, Reference, General and Children's Books.

Harris, Paul, Publishing (1975), 25 London Street, Edinburgh, EH3 6LY *T.* 031-556 9696. *Directors:* Paul A. Harris (Managing), Robert Wishart, J. Geddes Wood.
Scottish Art, Architecture, Maritime. General non-fiction.

*Hart-Davis Educational Ltd., incorportating **Chatto & Windus (Educational) Ltd.** and **Blond Educational Ltd.** (1972), 29 Frogmore, St. Albans, Herts, AL2 2NF *T.* Park Street (0727) 72727. *T.A.* Granada, St. Albans. *Telex:* 262802. *Directors:* W. R. Carr, K. A. Hills, A. R. H. Birch, Lord Bernstein, A. M. Thompson, Mrs. P. D. Green.
Educational (Primary and Secondary), School Text and Library Books.

*Hart-Davis MacGibbon Ltd., 29 Frogmore, St. Albans, Herts, AL2 2NF *T.* Park Street (0727) 72727. *Directors:* W. R. Carr, A. R. H. Birch, R. Schlesinger.
Biography and Memoirs, Cookery, Fiction, General, History, Popular Science, Sport, Travel and Adventure.

Harvester Press Ltd., The (1969), 2 Stanford Terrace, Hassocks, Sussex. *T.* Hassocks 4378 and 5532. *T.A.* Harvester Hassocks. *Telex:* 24224. *Directors:* John Spiers (Chairman and Managing), Dr. Margaret A. Boden (Secretary), Alastair Everitt.
History, Politics, English Literature, Economics, Philosophy, Psychology, Literary Fiction.

*Harvey Miller Publishers (1968), 20 Marryat Road, London, SW19 5BD *T.* 01-946 4426. *Directors:* H. I. Miller, E. Miller.
Art History, Medical Atlases.

*Harvill Press, Ltd., 30A Pavilion Road, London, SW1X 0HJ *T.* 01-589 1631, 1096. (Trade) Wm. Collins, P.O. Box, Glasgow, G4 0NB *T.* 041-552 4488. *Directors:* F. I. Chapman, Lady Collins, M. Villiers, R. Knittel.
Art, Belles-Lettres, Biography and Memoirs, Current Affairs, Fiction, Humour, Philosophy, Travel.

Haynes Publishing Group, Sparkford, Yeovil, Somerset, BA22 7JJ *T.* North Cadbury 635–7. *Directors:* J. H. Haynes (Chairman), F. Day (Managing), T. Egan, M. Yorke.
Motoring (History, Technical, Sport and Touring), Motor Cycling, Road Tests, Histories.

Health for All Publishing Company—see Thorsons Publishers Ltd.

*Heinemann Group of Publishers, Ltd., 48 Charles Street, London, W1X 8AH *T.* 01-493 9103. *T.A.* Hebooks, London, and The Windmill Press, Kingswood, Tadworth, Surrey, KT20 6TG *T.* 073 783 3511. *T.A.* Sunlocks, Tadworth. *Directors:* D. J. Manser (Chairman), Alan Hill, C.B.E. (Managing Director), A. R. Beal, C. S. Pick, Peter Range, T. G. Rosenthal, Mark Houlton (Secretary).

*Heinemann (William), Ltd., 15–16 Queen Street, London, W1X 8BE *T.* 01-493 4141. *T.A.* Sunlocks, London, W1 and The Windmill Press, Kingswood, Tadworth, Surrey. *T.* 073783 3511. *T.A.* Sunlocks, Tadworth. *Directors:* C. S. Pick (Chairman and Managing Director), T. R. Manderson and N. M. Viney (Joint Managing Directors), Roland Grant (Editorial), J. W. Dettmer, Judith Elliott, Christopher Forster, A. J. W. Hill, C.B.E., Nigel Hollis, Peter Ireland, John St. John, W. Roger Smith, Susanna Yager, Michael House (Secretary).
Art, Biography and Memoirs, Belles-Lettres, Children's Books, Drama, Fiction, General, Poetry, Sports, Games and Hobbies, Technical, Travel.

*Heinemann Educational Books, Ltd., 48 Charles Street, London, W1X 8AH
T. 01-493 9103. *T.A.* Hebooks, London. *Telex:* 261888. *Directors:*
A. J. W. Hill, C.B.E. (Chairman), A. R. Beal (Managing Director), H. Mac-
Gibbon (Deputy Managing Director), E. D. Thompson, K. Nettle, H. K.
Sambrook, P. Richardson, C. S. Pick, R. Gale, J. Currey, M. Houlton
(Secretary).
African Studies, African Writers, Biology, Chemistry, Physics, Mathematics,
English, Drama, History, Geography, Economics, Business Studies, Home
Economics, Modern Languages, Education, Primary, Social Science, Tech-
nical, English as a Foreign Language.

*Heinemann, William, Medical Books, Ltd., 23 Bedford Square, London,
WC1B 3HT *T.* 01-580 0641. *T.A.* Heinemed, London, and Kings-
wood, Tadworth, Surrey. *T.* 073 783 3511. *Directors:* R. Greene, D.M.,
F.R.C.P., Owen R. Evans, Alan Hill, C.B.E., R. S. Emery (Managing), Selwyn
Taylor, D.M., F.R.C.S. (Chairman), Andrew Barrett, A.C.A.
Medical, Surgical, Dental, Science, Veterinary.

*World's Work, Ltd., The Windmill Press, Kingswood, Tadworth, Surrey.
T. Mogador 3511. *T.A.* Sunlocks, Tadworth. *Directors:* Alan Hill, C.B.E.
(Chairman), D. A. Elliot (Managing Director), R. A. Aspinall, C. Forster,
D. E. Priestley, M. J. House, A.C.C.A. (Secretary).
General, Religion, Practical Psychology, Business Management, Children's
Books.

Heinemann and Zsolnay, Ltd., The Windmill Press, Kingswood, Tadworth,
Surrey. *T.* 073783 3511. *T.A.* Sunlocks, Tadworth. *Directors:* D. L.
Range, F.C.A. (Chairman), J. Beer, M.B.E. (Managing Director), A. J. W. Hill,
C.B.E., C. S. Pick, H. W. Polak, T. G. Rosenthal, M. J. House, A.C.C.A.
(Secretary).
Editions in German of general books of topical and lasting interest and of
novels of literary value.

Her Majesty's Stationery Office, *Head Office,* Sovereign House, Botolph Street,
Norwich, NR3 1DN *T.* 0603 22211. *T.A.* Hemstonery, Norwich.
Atlantic House, Holborn Viaduct, London, EC1P 1BN. *T.* 01-538 9876.
T.A. Hemstonery, London, EC1. *Government Bookshops* (retail) 49 High
Holborn, WC1V 6HB *T.* 01-928 6977; London Post Orders: P.O. Box 569,
London, SE1 9NH *T.* 01-928 1321; Brazenose Street, Manchester, M60
8AS *T.* 061-832 7583; 13A Castle Street, Edinburgh EH2 3AR (wholesale
and retail). *T.* 031-225 6333–6; 258 Broad Street, Birmingham, B1 2HE
T. 021-643 3740; 41 The Hayes, Cardiff, CF1 1JW *T.* 0222 23654–5;
Southey House, Wine Street, Bristol, BS1 2BQ *T.* 0272 24306–7; 80
Chichester Street, Belfast, BT1 4JY *T.* 0232–34488. Publications Sale
Office (wholesale): Cornwall House, Stamford Street, London, SE1 9NY
T. 01-928 6977, Ext. 334.
Archaeology, Architecture, Art, Current Affairs, Directories or Guide Books,
Educational (Infants, Primary, Secondary, Technical, University), General,
History, Naval and Military, Practical Handbooks, Reference, Science,
Sociology, Year Books.
Authorised to publish only official material sponsored by Parliament or a
Department of State and cannot consider original work by private citizens.

Hestair Kiddicraft Publishing Limited (formerly **Three Four Five Publishing Limited**)—see Macdonald Educational Ltd.

Hestair Hope Ltd. (1947), St. Philip's Drive, Royton, Oldham, Lancashire, OL2 6AG *T.* 061-633 3935–9.
Educational Books (Infant and Primary).

*****Hilger (Adam) Ltd.,** Techno House, Redcliffe Way, Bristol, BS1 6NX *T.* 0272-297481. *Telex:* 449149.
Science (Chemistry, Physics, Optics, Spectroscopy, Astronomy, Earth Sciences).

*****Hodder & Stoughton Ltd.,** Mill Road, Dunton Green, Sevenoaks, Kent, TN13 2YA *T.* Sevenoaks (0732) 50111. *Telex:* 95122. *T.A.:* Expositor, Sevenoaks, and 47 Bedford Square, London WC1B 3DP. *T.* 01-636 9851 *Telex:* 885887. *Directors:* Philip Attenborough (Chairman), Michael Attenborough, R. S. Fowles, Mark Hodder-Williams, J. R. McKenzie, Ronald Read, L. M. H. Timmermans. *Joint Secretaries:* R. S. Fowles, H. J. Jones.
General, Fiction, Religious and Theology, Educational, Children's, Medical, Dictionaries, Guide Books, Travel, Sports and Games.

Hodder & Stoughton. *Directors:* Eric Major (Managing), Philip Attenborough, Michael Attenborough, David Dick, Edward England, J. R. McKenzie, Maureen Rissik, Haydon Stead.

*****Hodder & Stoughton Educational.** *Directors:* L. M. H. Timmermans (Managing), Philip Attenborough, C. W. Davies, H. S. Foster, Brian Steven, J. C. Williams.

*****Hodder & Stoughton Paperbacks.** *Directors:* Michael Attenborough (Managing), Philip Attenborough, Philip Evans, Ronald Read, E. Bell, A. Gordon Walker, J. A. G. Wilson.

*****Hodder & Stoughton Children's Books.** *Directors:* Ronald Read (Managing), Philip Attenborough, J. R. McKenzie, Jane Osborn (Editorial), Michael Attenborough.

Hodgson (Francis) (F. H. Books Ltd.) (1884), P.O. Box 74, Guernsey, C1. *T.* 0481-24332.
Scientific and technical reference books.

*****Hogarth Press, Ltd., The,** 40–42 William IV Street, London, WC2N 4DG *T.* 01-836 5549. *Directors:* Norah Smallwood, O.B.E., J. F. Charlton, D. J. Enright.
Biography and Memoirs, Essays, Fiction, History, Psycho-Analysis, Psychology, Poetry, Sociology.

Holland Press, The, 37 Connaught Street, London, W2 2AZ *T.* 01- 262 6184. *Director:* Stephanie Hoppen.
Bibliography, Arms and Armour, Music, Travel, Reference works of all kinds in limited editions, books of interest to collectors, specialising in reprinting in de-luxe editions, original MSS. also considered.

Hollis & Carter, 9 Bow Street, London, WC2E 7AL *T.* 01-836 9081. *T.A.* Bodleian, Westcent, London. An imprint of **The Bodley Head Ltd.** Nautical, Travel.

*Holmes McDougall Ltd., Allander House, 137–141 Leith Walk, Edinburgh, EH6 8NS *T.* 031-554 9444. *Cables:* Educational Edinburgh. *Telex:* 727508. Educational (Infant, Primary and Secondary).

Holt, Rinehart & Winston, 1 St. Anne's Road, Eastbourne, East Sussex, BN21 3UN *T.* (0323) 638221. *Telex:* 877503 Volmists, Eastbourne. See **Holt-Sanders Ltd.** Educational Books (School, College, University) in all subjects.

*Holt-Saunders Ltd., 1 St. Anne's Road, Eastbourne, East Sussex, BN21 3UN *T.* (0323) 638221. *Telex:* 877503 Volmist. *T.A.* Volumists, Eastbourne. *Directors:* R. Kiernan, C. J. Sehmer, E. Auer, J. L. Hayes, R. H. Malthouse, Ian G. McIntyre. Educational, Scientific, Technical, School, General.

Hughes & Son, Publishers Ltd. (1820), 4–5 Thomas Row, Swansea, SA1 1NJ *T.* 0792 52168. *Directors:* J. M. Phillips, C. H. T. Davies. Educational Publications, Fiction (adult and children's).

*Hulton Educational Publications Ltd., Raans Road, Amersham, Bucks, HP6 6JJ *T.* Amersham 4196–7–8. *Directors:* Sir Edward Hulton (Chairman), L. G. Marsh (Managing), Nika Hulton, E. J. Lowman. Educational (Infants, Primary, Secondary, Grammar, Technical).

Hurst & Blackett, Ltd. (1812), 3 Fitzroy Square, London, W1P 6JD *T.* 01-387 2888 (Trade) 0621 816362. *Telex:* 261212. *T.A.* Literarius, London, *Chairman:* R. A. A. Holt. *Director:* Charles Clark. *Editorial Manager:* Theresa Carlson. An imprint of the **Hutchinson Publishing Group.** Fiction.

*Hutchinson & Co. (Publishers) Ltd. 3 Fitzroy Square, London, W1P 6JD *T.* 01-387 2888. *Telex:* 261212. (Trade) 062-181 6362. *Telex:* 99487. *T.A.* Literarius, London, W1. General Publishers. *Chairman:* R. A. A. Holt. *Managing Director:* Charles Clark. *Directors:* Harold Harris, David Roy, Gerald Austin, Philippa Fraser Harrison, Tony Whittome. Belles-Lettres, Biography and Memoirs, Children's Books (Fiction, Non-Fiction, Toy and Picture Books), Current Affairs, Essays, Fiction, General, History, Humour, Music, Poetry, Reference, Travel. An imprint of the **Hutchinson Publishing Group.**

*Hutchinson Publishing Group, Ltd. (1887), 3 Fitzroy Square, London, W1P 6JD *T.* 01-387 2888. *Telex:* 261212. (Trade) 062-181 6362. *Telex:* 99487. *T.A.* Literarius, London, W1. General Publishers. *Chairman:* R. A. A. Holt. *Managing Director:* Charles Clark. *Directors:* Harold Harris (Deputy Managing), Brian Perman, David Roy, Mark Cohen, Geoffrey Pearce, Grahame Griffiths, Philippa Fraser Harrison, Roger Lloyd Taylor. Controls Hutchinson & Co. (Publishers) Ltd., Hutchinson General Books Ltd., Hurst & Blackett, Ltd.; also Hutchinson Junior Books Ltd., Rider & Co., John Long Ltd., Stanley Paul & Co. Ltd., Arrow Books Ltd., Hutchinson Educational Ltd., Hutchinson University Library, Popular Dogs Publishing Co. Ltd.

*Hutchinson Educational Ltd. (1958), 3 Fitzroy Square, London, W1P 6JD *T.* 01-387 2888. *Telex:* 261212. (Trade) 062-181 6362. *Telex:* 261212. *T.A.* Literarius, London, W1. *Directors:* R. A. A. Holt (Chairman), Charles Clark, Mark Cohen, Bob Osborne, John Fulford, Douglas Fox. An imprint of the **Hutchinson Publishing Group.**
Educational (Secondary, Technical, University).

Hutchinson General Books Ltd., 3 Fitzroy Square, London, W1P 6JD *T.* 01-387 2888. *Telex:* 261212. (Trade) 0621 816362). *T.A.* Literarius, London, W1. *Chairman:* R. A. A. Holt. *Managing Director:* Brian Perman. *Directors:* Charles Clarke, Harold Harris, David Roy, Mark Cohen, Grahame Griffiths, Jeremy Cox, Roderick Bloomfield, Philippa Harrison, Anne Sworder, Kathleen Nathan, Robert Hyde. An imprint of the **Hutchinson Publishing Group.**

I.P.C. Business Press Information Services Ltd. (1970). Incorporating **Kelly's Directories, Ltd., Thomas Skinner Directories, Kompass Publishers Ltd.** Neville House, Eden Street, Kingston upon Thames, Surrey, KT1 1BY *T.* 01-546 7722. *T.A.* Directory Kingston. *Directors:* R. Haddrell (Managing), S. Brown, R. Dangerfield, T. J. Ulrick, A. M. Tillin, D. W. Lee.
Reference Books and Directories.

*Institute of Physics, Techno House, Redcliffe Way, Bristol, BS1 6NX *T.* 0272 297481. *Telex:* 449149.
Science (Physics and related topics).

*International Textbook Co. Ltd., a member of **The Blackie Group,** Bishopbriggs, Glasgow, G64 2NZ *T.* 041-772 2311. Imprints: Intertext Books; Leonard Hill; Surrey University Press. *Director:* Dr. Graeme Mackintosh. Reference and text books in Engineering; Hotel Catering and Food Science; Planning ad Architecture; Business ad Administration; Chemistry; Physics. Biology; Agriculture; Mathematics and Computing.

*Inter-Varsity Press, 38 De Montfort Street, Leicester, LE1 7GP *T.* 0533-536 771. Theology and Religion.

Jack (T. C. and E. C.), Ltd. Incorporated with **Thomas Nelson & Sons, Ltd.,** *q.v.*

*Jackdaw Publications Ltd., 30 Bedford Square, London, WC1B 3EL *T.* 01-636 5764. *T.A.* Capajon, London, WC1. *Directors:* Graham C. Greene, Tom Maschler.
Folders of facsimile historical documents. Publishers of Rainbow and Magpie Series.

James (Arthur) Ltd. (1935), The Drift, Evesham, Worcestershire, WR11 4NW *T.* Evesham (0386) 6566. *Directors:* F. A. Russell, M. Macqueen.
Religion, Sociology, Psychology, Autobiography.

Jenkins (Herbert), Ltd. Incorporated with **Barrie & Jenkins,** *q.v.*

Jewish Chronicle Publications, 25 Furnival Street, London, EC4A 1JT *T.* 01-405 9252 *Manager:* M. Weinberg. Agents for Jewish Publications Society of America.
Theology and Religion, Reference, Year Book, Jewish Travel Guide.

*Johnson Publications Ltd. (1946), 11/14 Stanhope Mews West, London, SW7. *T.* 01-373 8543. *Directors:* Donald McI. Johnson, Ivor R. M. Davies, Norman McI. Johnson, Betty M. Johnson, Carol E. Johnson.
Belles-Lettres, Biography and Memoirs, Current Affairs, Economics, General, History, Law, Political Economy, Sociology, Travel, Medical, Philosophy. Return postage should be sent with unsolicited manuscripts.

Johnsons (1846), 10 Stafford Street, Edinburgh, EH3 7AZ *T.* 031-225 4410. *T.A.* Designs, Edinburgh 3. *Principal:* Christopher Yate Johnson, F.R.S.A. Past President, Royal Scottish Society of Arts.
Industrial Designs and Trade Marks.

*Johnston and Bacon Publishers, 35 Red Lion Square, London, WC1R 4SG and Tanfield House, Tanfield Lane, Edinburgh, EH3 5LL *T.* 01-831 6100 and (Edinburgh) 031-556 0298. *T.A.* Caspeg, London, WC1. *Telex:* 28648 Casmac-G. A division of Cassell Ltd.
Tourist Maps and Guides, Books on Scottish subjects.

Jones (John) Cardiff Ltd. (1968), 41 Lochaber Street, Cardiff, CF2 3LS *T.* 0222-41267. *Directors:* John Idris Jones, M.A., G. Idris Jones, Gwen P. Jones.
Books about Wales for the visitor. Incorporating Welsh Book Distributors and West Country Book Distributors.

*Jordan & Sons Ltd. (1836), Jordan House, Brunswick Place, London, N1 6EE *T.* 01-253 3030. *Telex:* 261010. *Directors:* Dennis Lloyd, David Clark, Archie Broomsgrove, Andrew Kampe, Ralph Leake, James Thomas, Michael Whitwell, Charles Smith.
Accountancy, Commerce, Educational and Law.

*Joseph (Michael), Ltd. (1935), 52 Bedford Square, London, WC1B 3EF. *T.* 01-637 0941. *T.A.* Emjaybuks, London, WC1. *Telex:* 21322. *Warehouse:* Book Centre, Rufford Road, Crossens, Southport, Lancashire. *T.* 0704 26881. *Directors:* The Hon. Mrs. Michael Joseph (Chairman), Victor Morrison (Managing Director), G. C. Brunton, Richard Douglas-Boyd, Eric Marriott, Alan Brooke, Malcolm Seymour, Jenny Dereham, Keith Ireland. Belles Lettres, Biography and Memoirs, Current Affairs, Fiction, General, History, Humour.

Justice of the Peace Ltd. (1837), Little London, Chichester, Sussex, PO19 1PG *T.* Chichester (0234) 83637. *T.A.* Juslocgov, Chichester. *Directors:* Barry Rose, P. D. Madge, B. H. Lewis, D. J. C. Rose, N. M. Marsch.
Law, Police, Local Government, Criminology, Penology.

Kahn & Averill—see Stanmore Press Ltd.

*Kaye & Ward Ltd., 21 New Street, London, EC2M 4NT *T.* 01-283 7495–6–7. *Cables:* Kayebooks, London, EC2. *Directors:* D. E. Webb, F.C.A., Stanley Pickard, Austen T. Smith, I. F. L. Straker, John A. Smith.
Sports, Travel, Children's Books, Cookery, Bibliography, Practical Handbooks, Recreations, Physical Education, Hobbies.

Kaye, Nicholas Ltd.—see Kaye & Ward Ltd.

Kelly's Directories Ltd.—see I.P.C. Business Press Information Services Ltd.

Kenyon-Deane Ltd., 129 St. John's Hill, London, SW11 1TD *T.* 01-223 3472.
Directors: P. St. C. Assinder (Managing), F. R. St. C. Assinder, N. St. C. Assinder.
Plays and drama textbooks. Specialists in plays for women and classroom playscripts for schools.

Kestrel Books—see Penguin Young Books Ltd.

*****Kimber (William) & Co. Ltd.** (1950), Godolphin House, 22a Queen Anne's Gate, London, SW1H 9AE *T.* 01-839 7684. Trade Counter: 72–74 Paul Street, London, EC2. *T.* 01-739 4755. *Directors:* W. T. Kimber, O. J. Colman, Audrey Kimber, F. M. de Salis, Amy Howlett.
Biography and Memoirs, Current Affairs, Fiction, General, History, Travel, Sport, Naval, Military and Aviation.

*****Kimpton (Henry) Ltd.** (1854), 7 Leighton Place, Leighton Road, London, NW5 2QL *T.* 01-267 5483.
Medical, Nursing, Dental, Physical Education.

*****Kingsway Publications Ltd.,** Lottbridge Drove, Eastbourne, East Sussex, BN23 6NT *T.* 0323 27454. *T.A.* Livletters, Eastbourne. *Telex:* 877415.
Directors: Dr. K. N. Taylor (International President), USA, Dr. J. Hywel-Davies (Chairman), H. D. Fuller (Managing), C. Henshall (Sales), F. B. Phillips, Harold Shaw (USA), Mark D. Taylor (USA).
Religious books.

*****Knight (Charles) & Co. Ltd.,** 25 New Street Square, London, EC4A 3JA *T.* 01-353 3212. *Directors:* H. W. Bailey-King, O.B.E. (Chairman), T. J. Benn, M. S. Gale, A. D. A. Balfour. *Managing Editor:* S. C. Cotter.
Local Government, Local Government Law, Planning and the Environment.

Kogan Page Ltd. (1967), 120 Pentonville Road, London, N1 9JN *T.* 01-837 7851–4. *Directors:* P. Kogan, B. Kogan, M. Gabb, P. Jackson, P. Newman.
Transport, Personnel Management, Educational Technology, Offshore Oil and Gas, Reference works in Careers.

LSP Books Ltd., 8 Farncombe Street, Farncombe, Godalming, Surrey, GU7 3AY *T.* Godalming 28622–3. *Telex:* 919101, Video Teknik, London. *Cables:* Litserve, Godalming. *Directors:* C. P. de Laszlo and B. R. Lincoln.
Cinema, Travel, Science Fiction.

*****Ladybird Books Ltd.** (1924) P.O. Box 12, Beeches Road, Loughborough, Leicestershire, LE11 2NQ *T.* Loughborough 68021. *T.A.* Ladybird, Loughborough. *Telex:* 341347. *Directors:* Lord Allan of Kilmahew, D.S.O., O.B.E. (Chairman), M. P. Kelley (Managing), Hon. C. P. Gibson, C. W. Hall, V. Mills, G. H. Towers, A. T. Warren, R. P. West.
Children's Books, General and Educational (Infants, Primary, Junior and Secondary).

Lakeland Paperbacks—see **Marshall Morgan & Scott Publications Ltd.**

Lane, Allen, the hardcover imprint of **Penguin Books,** *q.v. Editorial Office:* 17 Grosvenor Gardens, London, SW1W 0BD *T.* 01-828 7090. *Chief Editor:* Peter Carson.
Fiction, General Non-Fiction, Illustrated Books; History, Literature, Art, Archaeology, Architecture and Social Sciences.

Latimer New Dimensions (1971), 19 Westbourne Road, London, N7 8AN *T.* 01-607 4074. *Directors:* Nicola H. St. J. Smith, John L. Smith.
Art, Architecture, Music, Occult, Games and Puzzles, Crafts, Collectors' Books, and other non-fiction.

Laurie (T. Werner) Ltd. (1904). An imprint of **The Bodley Head Ltd.,** *q.v.*

*Lawrence & Wishart, Ltd., 39 Museum Street, London, WC1A 1LQ *T.* 01-405 0103. *T.A.* Interbook, London, WC1. *Directors:* S. Seifert, R. Simon, J. Skelley (Managing Director), N. Jacobs, M. Cornforth, M. Costello, A. Michaelides, M. Jacques, P. Goodwin, D. Wynn.
Current Affairs, Economics, History, Literary Criticism, Philosophy, Political Economy, Sociology.

*Leicester University Press (1951), 2 University Road, Leicester, LE1 7RB *T.* Leicester 20185. *Secretary:* Peter L. Boulton, M.A.
Academic books, especially in History (including English Local History and Urban History), Archaeology, International Relations, Transport Studies, Victorian Studies, Mass Media Research, and English and Foreign Literature.

Letts (Charles) (Holdings) Ltd. (1796), Diary House, Borough Road, London, SE1 1DW *T.* 01-407 8891. *Directors:* A. A. Letts (Chairman and Managing), L. C. Letts, D. N. Letts, R. H. Letts, J. M. Letts, T. R. Letts, H. M. Bates, D. F. Myers, J. M. Tennent, F.C.A.
Diary and book publishers and manufacturers.

Leventhal, Lionel, Ltd.—see under **Arms and Armour Press.**

*Lewis (A) (Masonic Publishers), Ltd. (1870), Terminal House, Shepperton, TW17 8AS *T.* Walton-on-Thames 28950. *Managing Director:* Ian Allan.
Masonic books.

Lewis (F.), Publishers, Ltd., The Tithe House, 1461 London Road, Leigh-on-Sea, Essex SS9 2SD *T.* 0702 78163. *Directors:* Frank Lewis, Elsie F. Lewis (Governing).
Art, Dictionaries (Art), Reference, Ceramics, Textiles, Illustrated Gift Books.

*Lewis (H. K.) & Co. Ltd. (1844), 136 Gower Street, London, WC1E 6BS *T.* 01-387 4282. *T.A.* Publicavit, London, WC1. *Directors:* G. W. Edwards, R. D. Spence, R. Salter, J. L. Haynes.
Science, Medical.

Linden Press, Fontwell, Arundel, Sussex, BN18 0TA *T.* 024-368 3302. *Directors:* Jon Wynne-Tyson, Jennifer M. Wynne-Tyson. A preliminary letter should be sent before submitting MS. Publishers of theses and sociological works, etc. Subsidiary imprint of **Centaur Press, Ltd.,** *q.v.*

Lindsey Press, Essex Hall Bookshop, 1–6 Essex Street, Strand, London, WC2R 3HY *T.* 01-836 0525.
Theology and Religion.

*****Liverpool University Press** (1901), J. G. O'Kane (Secretary and Publisher), 123 Grove Street, Liverpool, L7 7AF *T.* 051-709 3630. *T.A.* Cormorant, Liverpool.
Academic and Scholarly books and journals for scholars and University-level students; special interest: English Literature, Social Sciences, Economic and Political History, Archaeology and Oriental Studies, Philosophy and the Natural Sciences, particularly Ecology, Marine Biology, and Environmental Problems, Town and Country Planning.

Livingstone (E. & S.). Now **Churchill Livingstone.**

London Editions Ltd. (1973), 30 Uxbridge Road, London, W12 8ND *T.* 01-749 3926–9. *Telex:* 933855. *T.A.* Lonedit, London, W12. *Directors:* Ulrik Sort (Managing), Roger Multon, John Turner, Robin Wright, David Kirkness (Financial).
International co-edition publishers specialising in Sports, Wildlife, Encyclopaedia and Reference Works, Art, Anthropology.

Long (John), Ltd., 3 Fitzroy Square, London, W1P 6JD *T.* 01-387 2888. *Telex:* 261212. Trade Department: 0621 816362. *Telex:* 99487. *T.A.* Literarius, London, W1. *Chairman:* R. A. A. Holt. *Directors:* Charles Clark, Gerald Austin. An imprint of the **Hutchinson Publishing Group.**
General books on Criminology and Law. Detective Novels and Thrillers.

*****Longman Group Limited** (1724), 5 Bentinck Street, London, W1M 5RN *T.* 01-935 0121. *T.A.* Longman, London, W1. Longman House, Burnt Mill, Harlow, Essex, CM20 2JE *T.* Harlow 26721. *Telex:* 81259. *T.A.* and *Cables:* Longman, Harlow. C. R. E. Brooke (Chairman), W. A. H. Beckett (Joint Vice-Chairman), T. J. Rix (Chief Executive and Joint Vice-Chairman). *Directors:* R. P. West, Hon. C. P. Gibson, R. G. B. Duncan, R. D. Welham, R. A. Hobbs, W. P. Kerr, D. J. Mortimer, P. J. Munday, C. J. Rea, R. P. Watson, M. G. P. Wymer, J. D. Williamson (Finance). Associated Companies (*q.v.*) in Canada, India, Australia, New Zealand, Uganda, Kenya, Tanzania, Malawi, Rhodesia, Zambia, Hong Kong, Malaysia, Nigeria, The Caribbean, South Africa, U.S.A., Singapore.
Aeronautics, Architecture, Art, Atlases, Belles-Lettres, Biography and Memoirs, Commerce, Current Affairs, Dictionaries, Drama, Economics, Educational (Infants, Primary, Secondary, Technical, University), Essays, Fiction, General, History, Humour, Law, Medical, Naval and Military, Oriental, Philosophy, Poetry, Political Economy, Reference, Science, Sociology, Sports, Theatre and Ballet, Theology and Religion, Travel, Year Books.

Longman Young Books, Ltd.—now **Penguin Young Books, Ltd.,** *q.v.*

Low, Sampson, Berkshire House, Queen Street, Maidenhead, Berkshire, SL6 1NF *T.* 37171. A division of **Purnell & Sons Ltd.** *General Manager:* Charles Harvey.

*Lund Humphries Publishers Ltd., 26 Litchfield Street, London, WC2H 9NJ *T.* 01-836 4243. *T.A.* Lundhumpub, London, WC2. *Directors:* D. Zwemmer, J. A. Taylor, H. Spencer.
Art, Architecture, Graphic Art and Design, Languages, Oriental.

*Lutterworth Press (1799), Luke House, Farnham Road, Guildford, Surrey, GU1 4XD *T.* Guildford 77536. *T.A.* Lutteric, Guildford. *General Manager:* M. E. Foxell.
Archaeology, Biography and Memoirs, Children's Books (Fiction, Non-Fiction, Rewards), Educational, General, Science, Sociology, Theology and Religion, Travel.

Luzac & Company, Ltd., Specialist Booksellers & Publishers since 1740, P.O. Box 157, 46 Great Russell Street, London, WC1B 3PE *T.* 01-636 1462. *T.A.* Obfirmate, Westcent, London. *Managing Director:* J. B. Knight-Smith. *Chairman:* F. H. Cornelius.
Africa, Middle East & Islam, Far East, Eastern Religions.

*Macdonald Educational Ltd., Holywell House, 72–90 Worship Street, London, EC2A 2EN *T.* 01-247 5499. A division of **BPC Publishing Ltd.**

Macdonald & Evans, Ltd. (1907), Estover Road, Estover, Plymouth, PL6 7PZ *T.* 0752 705251. *T.A.* Macevans, Plymouth. *Directors:* G. B. Davis, R. B. North, M. W. Beevers, W. D. Argent.
Accountancy and Book-keeping, Banking, Commerce, Economics, Educational (Secondary, Technical, University), Geography, Law, Chemistry and Physics, Dance and Movement Notation.

*Macdonald & Jane's Publishers Ltd., 8 Shepherdess Walk, London, N1 7LB *T.* 01-251 1666. *Directors:* A. M. Alfred (Chairman), R. Whiting (Managing), P. Hoare, S. Jackson, A. Smith, D. Rivers, John Stoddant (Financial), P. G. Morrison. An operating company within The British Printing Corporation.

MacGibbon & Kee, Ltd., now **Hart-Davis, MacGibbon Ltd.,** *q.v.*

*McGraw-Hill Book Company (UK), Ltd., McGraw-Hill House, Shoppenhangers Road, Maidenhead, Berkshire, SL6 2QL *T.* Maidenhead 23432. *T.A.* McGraw-Hill, Maidenhead. *Telex:* 848484. *Directors:* Derek Speake (Managing), Neil Chambers (Book Services), Margaret Tilling (Publishing). *Company Secretary:* Richard Billing.
Technical, Scientific, Professional Reference, Medical, Art and General.

MacLaren (Alex.) & Sons. Incorporated with **Gairm Publications,** *q.v.*

*Macmillan Publishers, Ltd. (book holding company), 4 Little Essex Street, London, WC2R 3LF *T.* 01-836 6633. *T.A.* Publish, London, WC2. Houndmills, Basingstoke, Hants. *T.* Basingstoke 29242. *Foreign Cables:* Publish, London. *Chairman:* F. H. Whitehead; *Directors:* A. D. A. Macmillan (Deputy Chairman), N. G. Byam Shaw (Managing), M. Hamilton, A. D. Maclean.

Operating Subsidiaries:
*Macmillan Education, Ltd. *Chairman:* N. G. Byam Shaw; *Directors:* S. A. Josephs (Managing), D. Fothergill, W. S. D. Jollands, M. J. Thorrowgood, M. G. Wace.
Educational Books and Visual Aids of all grades from Infant to Teachers Training level.

*Macmillan Press, Ltd., The. *Chairman:* N. G. Byam Shaw; *Directors:* A. Soar (Managing), T. S. Creed, T. M. Farmiloe, J. Jackman, B. Turner. College, Academic, Scientific and Technical Works, publishers of Grove's Dictionary of Music and Musicians, and The Statesman's Year-Book, and other Reference Works.

*Macmillan London, Ltd. *Chairman:* N. G. Byam Shaw; *Directors:* A. D. Maclean (Managing), C. Paterson (Deputy Managing), J. F. K. Ashby, R. D. Garnett, Lord Hardinge, J. Hadfield, Miss T. Sacco, P. Sampson. General literature, Biography, Fiction and Juvenile literature. *Allied and Subsidiary Companies:* Macmillan Journals, Ltd., Macmillan Administration (Basingstoke) Ltd., Gill & Macmillan, Ltd., The Macmillan Company of India, Ltd., St. Martin's Press Inc., Macmillan Nigeria Publishers, The Macmillan Co. of Australia Pty., Ltd., Macmillan South Africa (Publishers) (Pty.), Ltd., Macmillan Publishers (H.K.), Ltd., Macmillan Southeast Asia Pte. Ltd., Macmillan Shuppan K.K., Japan.

Magnet and Magnum—see Methuen Paperbacks Ltd.

*Manchester University Press (1912), Oxford Road, Manchester, M13 9PL *T.* 061-273 5539–30. *Publisher:* J. M. N. Spencer, M.A. Books of value for higher education in all branches. Anthropology, Archaeology, Architecture, Autobiography, Belles-Lettres, Current Affairs, Drama, Economics, Education (Secondary and University), English Language and Literature, Essays, History, Law, Medicine, Modern Languages (including texts), Music, Oriental, Philosophy, Political Economy, Science (all branches), Sociology and Theology and Religion.

*Mansell Information/Publishing Ltd. (1966), 3 Bloomsbury Place, London, WC1A 2QA *T.* 01-580 6784. *T.A.* Infoman London. *Telex:* 28604 ref. 1647. *Director:* J. E. Duncan (Managing). Bibliographies, catalogues and reference works of special interest to libraries and academic research institutions.

*Map Productions, Ltd. (1964), 27A Floral Street, London, WC2E 9LP *T.* 01-836 7869. *Directors:* R. F. A. Edwards (Managing), R. J. Shattock, D. Reeves (Secretary). A Member Company of the **George Philip Group.**

*Marshall, Morgan & Scott Publications, Ltd. (1928), 1 Bath Street, London, EC1V 9LB *T.* 01-251 2925. *Directors:* P. J. Lardi (Managing), S. W. Grant, D. Payne, N. Halsey, C. Lock (Secretary). Evangelical Books, Theology and Music.

Martin Brian & O'Keeffe, Ltd. (1971), 37 Museum Street, London, WC1A 1LP *T.* 01-405 8302. *Directors:* Timothy O'Keeffe, Catharine Carver. General Literature including Biography, Fiction, History, Travel, Science, Economics and Poetry.

*Martin Robertson & Co. Ltd. (1969), 108 Cowley Road, Oxford, OX4 1JF *T.* 0865–49109. *T.A.* Marcobooks London N1. *Directors:* Rachel Douglas, Norman Drake, Edward Elgar, Michael Holmes, David Martin. Economics and Management, Sociology, Social Policy, Sociology of Law and Criminology, Politics, International Politics and Public Administration, Geography, Education.

*Mason (Kenneth) Publications, Ltd. (1958), 13 and 14 Homewell, Havant, Hampshire, PO9 1EF *T.* Havant 486262. *Directors:* Kenneth Mason, M. E. Mason, M. A. Mason, P. A. Mason. General and Academic, Directories and Guide Books, Reference. Publishers of the *With BP Series.* Technical Journals, High Court Law Reports.

*Mayflower Books Ltd., 29 Frogmore, St. Albans, Herts, AL2 2NF   *T.* Park Street (0727) 72727.   *Directors:* W. R. Carr, A. R. H. Birch, J. Wharton, R. W. Chester.
Paperbacks—Originals and Reprints.   Dragon Books.

Meadowfield Press Ltd. (1976), I.S.A. Building, Dale Road Industrial Estate, Shildon, Co. Durham, DL4 2QZ   *T.* Ponteland 71719.   *Directors:* Dr. J. G. Cook, M. Cook.
Microbiology, Zoology, Archaeology, Botany, Biology.

Medici Society Ltd., 34–42 Pentonville Road, London, N1 9HG.   *T.* 01-837 7099.   Publishers of the Medici Prints, greeting cards and other colour reproductions of Old Masters and Modern Artists.
Art, Children's Books, General.

Melrose Press Ltd. (1969), Market Hill, Cambridge, CB2 3QP   *T.* 0223 66631. *T.A.* Melrospres Cambridge.   *Telex:* 81584.   *Directors:* Ernest Kay, D. B. Law, D. G. C. Mockridge, R. A. Kay, N. Lashmar.
International biographical reference works, including *International Authors & Writers Who's Who.*

Merlin Press, Ltd., 3 Manchester Road, London, E14 9BD   *T.* 01-987 7959. *Directors:* D. Musson, A. Weitzel, M. W. Eve.
Politics, Economics, History, Philosophy.   Publishers of *The Socialist Register.*   Distributors for Augustus M. Kelley (USA).

*Merrow Publishing Company Limited (1951), Meadowfield House, Ponteland, Newcastle-upon-Tyne, NE20 9SD   *T.* Ponteland 71719.   *Directors:* J. G. Cook, M. Cook.
Textiles, Plastics, Popular Science, Scientific.

Methodist Church, Division of Education and Youth, 2 Chester House, Pages Lane, Muswell Hill, London, N10 1PR   *T.* 01-444 9845.
Theology and Religion.

*Methodist Publishing House (Epworth Press) (1773), Wellington Road, London, SW19 8EU   *T.* 01-947 5256.
Theology and Religion.

*Methuen & Co., Ltd. (1889), 11 New Fetter Lane, London, EC4P 4EE.   *T.* 01-583 9855.   *T.A.* Elegiacs, London.   *Directors:* John Naylor (Managing Director), Janice Price, Carol Somerset, John Spragg, John von Knorring. Books in the Humanities and Social Sciences for Universities and Colleges of Education.

*Methuen Children's Books, Ltd., 11 New Fetter Lane, London, EC4P 4EE   *T.* 01-583 9855.   *Directors:* Charles Shirley (Chairman), Marilyn Malin (Managing), Joy Backhouse, Charles Hammick, Christopher Holgate, David Ross, Jan Hopcraft.
Children's Books (Picture, Fiction, Non-Fiction, for Young Children to early teens).

*Methuen Educational, Ltd. (1967), 11 New Fetter Lane, London, EC4P 4EE   *T.* 01-583 9855.   *T.A.* Elegiacs, London.   *Directors:* Marilyn Malin (Chairman), Ian McKee (Vice-Chairman), Nick Hern, Peter Bennett, John Naylor. Educational (Primary, Secondary), Education and Teaching Methods, Educational Materials.

*Methuen Paperbacks Ltd., 11 New Fetter Lane, London, EC4P 4EE *T.* 01-583 9855. *T.A.* Elegiacs, London. *Directors:* Charles Shirley (Chairman and Managing), Chris Holifield, Peter Bennett, Chris Holgate, Graham Lane, Marilyn Malin, Geoffrey Strachan.
Methuen Paperbacks consists of *Magnum*, a general paperback imprint publishing originals and reprints; *Magnet*, a children's paperback imprint publishing originals and reprints; *Methuen Notes*, a study aid series.

Michael Joseph Limited—see Joseph (Michael) Limited.

Midas Books (1968), 12 Dene Way, Speldhurst, Tunbridge Wells, Kent, TN3 0NX *T.* Langton 2860. *Directors:* Ian Wentworth Morley-Clarke, Kathleen Joyce Morley-Clarke.
Militaria, Art, Leisure and Sport, Social History, Biographies, Guide Books.

Miller (J. Garnet), Ltd. (1951), 129 St. John's Hill, London, SW11 1TD *T.* 01-228 8091. *Directors:* John G. F. Miller, Mrs. M. J. Miller.
Antiques, Children's Books, Drama, Science, Theatre.

Millington Books Ltd. (1973), 109 Southampton Row, London, WC1B 4HH *T.* 01-580 5656. *Directors:* A. K. Davison, N. Hayward, T. Tessier.
Literature, History, Biography, Memoirs, Art, Politics, Current Events, Nature, Science Fiction, General Fiction.

*Mills & Boon, Ltd. (1909), 17–19 Foley Street, London, W1A 1DR *T.* 01-580 9074-0. *T.A.* Millsator, London. *Chairman:* J. T. Boon, C.B.E. *Managing Director:* Paul Scherer. *Directors:* Richard A. N. Bonnycastle, A. W. Boon, W. Lawrence Heisey, John Rendall, W. F. Willson. *Executive Directors:* Mrs. E. J. Bryant, A. T. McKay. *Financial Director and Secretary:* B. C. J. Rogers.
Fiction; Library Novels and Paperbacks. Most types of Educational Books but specialities are Home Economics, Crafts, "Doing" books, Technical books, Chemistry and Applied Art.

Mitchell Beazley Ltd. (1969), Artists House, 14–15 Manette Street, London, W1V 5LB. *T.* 01-434 1694. *Telex:* MB Book 24892. *Directors:* James Mitchell, Peter Mead, Christopher Parker, Ken Banerji. Controls Mitchell Beazley Publishers Ltd., Mitchell Beazley Encyclopaedias Ltd, Mitchell Beazley Marketing Ltd.

Mitchell Beazley Encyclopaedias Ltd. (1972), Artists House, 14–15 Manette Street, London, W1V 5LB *T.* 01-434 1694. *Telex:* MB Book, 24892. *Directors:* James Mitchell, Christopher Parker, Harold Bull, Peter Mead, Ed Day, Frank Wallis, Adrian Webster, Tony Cobb, Mike Powell.
International Reference Books and Encyclopaedias.

Mitchell Beazley Marketing Ltd., Artists House, 14–15 Manette Street, London, W1V 5LB *T.* 01-434 1694. *Telex:* MB Book 24892 London. *Directors:* Kenneth Banerji (Managing), David Hight, Peter Mead, James Mitchell.
Non-fiction generally, Hobbies, Crafts, Encyclopaedias, Reference.

Mitchell Beazley Publishers Ltd (1969), Mill House, 87–89 Shaftesbury Avenue, London, W1V 7AD *T.* 01-439 3711. *Telex:* Millho G 261401. *Directors:* James Mitchell, Christopher Parker, Peter Mead, Harold Bull, Michael Powell, Adrian Webster, Ed Day, Tony Cobb, Jan van Gulden.
Atlases of the Universe, Earth and Wine; Astronomy, Astrology, Family Reference Books.

Moonraker Press (1975), 26 St. Margaret's Street, Bradford-on-Avon, Wiltshire. *T.* Bradford-on-Avon 3469. *Directors:* M. A. Ash, Anthony Adams. Archaeology, Biography, Industrial History, Topography and Local History of Wessex, Wildlife.

Mothers' Union, The (1876), 24 Tufton Street, London, SW1P 3RB *T.* 01-222 5533. *T.A.* Marisumner, London, SW1. Religious, Educational and Social Problems concerned with marriage and the family.

*Mowbray (A. R.) & Co., Ltd., Saint Thomas House, Becket Street, Oxford, OX1 1SJ *T.* 0865 42507. Theology and Religion, Biography, History, Humour, Philosophy, Sociology, Children's Books.

*Muller (Frederick) Ltd., Victoria Works, Edgware Road, London, NW2 6LE *T.* 01-450 2566. *Telex:* 267163. *Directors:* V. Andrews, M. A. A. Baig, A. Williams. Children's, Cinema, Collecting, Creative Hobbies, Educational, History, Occult, Science and Technology, Sociology, Biography, Natural History, Sports and Pastimes, Fiction.

Murby (Thomas) & Co. (1866), 40 Museum Street, London, WC1A 1LU *T.* 01-405 8577. *T.A.* Deucalion, London, WC1. *Telex:* 826261. *Proprietors:* George Allen & Unwin (Publishers) Ltd. *Chairman:* Rayner Unwin. Science (Geology, Soil Science).

*Murray, John (Publishers), Ltd. (1768), 50 Albemarle Street, London, W1X 4BD *T.* 01-493 4361. *T.A.* Guidebook, London, W1. *Directors:* John G. Murray, C.B.E., B.A.(Oxon), Kenneth J. Foster, Leslie A. Miller, Simon B. Young, Kenneth J. Pinnock, John R. Murray, C. J. Bray, N. Perren. Aeronautics, Architecture, Art, Biography and Memoirs, Children's Books (Fiction, Non-Fiction), Crafts, Current Affairs, Dictionaries, Educational (Primary, Secondary, Technical, University), Success Studybooks, Essays, Fiction, General, History, Humour, Sports, Games and Hobbies, Theology and Religion, Travel, Oriental, Philosophy, Nautical, Nutrition, Catering and Cookery.

National Adult School Organisation (1899), Drayton House, Gordon Street, London, WC1H 0BE *T.* 01-387 5920. Adult Educational Handbooks for Study Groups.

*National Christian Education Council (incorporating **Denholm House Press** and **International Bible Reading Association),** Robert Denholm House, Nutfield, Redhill, RH1 4HW *T.* Nutfield Ridge, 2411. Books on all aspects of Christian Education. Material for Children's Work in the Church, also R.E. and M.E. material for Day Schools. Activity, Visual and Resource Material.

Nautical Publishing Company Ltd (1967), Nautical House, Lymington, Hants, SO4 9BA *T.* Lymington 72578. *Hon. President:* K. Adlard Coles. *Directors:* Commander Erroll Bruce, R.N.Rtd., Richard Creagh-Osborne, Sir Peter Johnson, Bt. *Associates:* George G. Harrap & Co., Ltd., United Nautical Publishers, S.A. Basel.

*Nelson (Thomas) & Sons, UK Ltd. (1798), Lincoln Way, Windmill Road, Sunbury-on-Thames, TW16 7HP *T.* Sunbury-on-Thames 85681. *T.A.* Thonelson, Sunbury-on-Thames. Sister Companies in Ikeja (Nigeria), Los Angeles, Melbourne, Don Mills, Ontario. *Directors:* J. C. Fleming (Chairman), M. Givans, J. Jermine (Managing), M. Thompson, D. Worlock, G. Wright.
Atlases, Bibles, Children's Dictionaries, Educational (Infant, Primary, Secondary, Technical, University), English language teaching, Reference.

*New English Library, Ltd. (1957), Barnards Inn, Holborn, London, EC1N 2JR *T.* 01-242 0767. *T.A.* Nelpublish, London. *Telex:* 21924. *Directors:* H. P. Tanner (Managing), T. R. D'Cruz, Martin P. Levin (USA), N. G. Chantiles (USA), J. O'Leary, D. F. Morse. *Associate Directors:* R. G. Gray, D. J. Rennie, C. C. Smith, G. H. Vincent.
Fiction and Non-Fiction.

New Left Books, Ltd. (1969), 7 Carlisle Street, London, W1V 5RG *T.* 01-437 3546. *Directors:* Anthony Barnett, Robin Blackburn, Quintin Hoare.
Politics, Biography, Sociology, Economics, History, Aesthetics, Philosophy.

Newman Neame Ltd., see **Pergamon Press Ltd.**

Newnes-Butterworths, Borough Green, Sevenoaks, Kent, TN15 8PH *T.* Borough Green (0732) 884567. *T.A.* Butterwort, Sevenoaks, Kent. *Managing Director:* W. G. Graham. *Publisher:* K. G. Jackson. Technical Division of **Butterworths.**
Agriculture, Architecture and Building, Catering and Food Technology, Computers, Electronics, Engineering: Automobile, Chemical, Civil, Control and Systems, Electrical, Electronic, Marine, Mechanical and Production; Gemmology, Horology and Jewellery Trades, Packaging, Plastics and Rubber Technology, Public Health, Radio/TV/Audio, Textiles, Industrial Management.

Nisbet (James) & Co., Ltd. (1810), Digswell Place, Welwyn Garden City, Herts, AL8 7SX *T.* Welwyn Garden 25491–2–3. *T.A.* Stebsin, Welwyn Garden City. *Directors:* G. H. B. McLean, Miss E. M. Mackenzie-Wood, Mrs. R. M. Mackenzie-Wood, A. D. M. Hill, Mrs. A. A. C. Bierrum.
Dictionaries, Economics, Educational (Infants, Primary, Secondary, University), Theology and Religion.

Nonesuch Library, The (1951), 9 Bow Street, London, WC2E 7AL *T.* 01-836 9081. An imprint of **The Bodley Head Ltd.** New editions of the English classics.

Nonesuch Press, Ltd., The, *Directors:* Dame Alix Meynell, D.B.E., Max Reinhardt, Benedict Meynell, Pamela Zander. Special editions designed by the late Sir Francis Meynell. Distributors: The Bodley Head, Ltd, 9 Bow Street, London, WC2E 7AL *T.* 01-836 9081.

Normal Press, The (1889), 25 Vicarage Lane, Upper Hale, Farnham, Surrey, GU9 0PG. *Director:* L. W. Cradwick.
Educational.

Octopus Books Ltd. (1971), 59 Grosvenor Street, London, W1X 9DA *T.* 01-493 5841. *T.A.* Octobooks, London. *Telex:* 27278. *Directors:* Paul Hamlyn (Chairman), Sue Thomson (Deputy Chairman), Timothy Clode (Managing), Ronald Setter, David Martin, Robert Gavron, Gordon Cartwright.
Cookery, Handicrafts, Arts and Antiques, Children's, Gardening, Natural History, Mythology, Entertainment, War Histories and Military Books, Fiction.

Odhams Books—see **The Hamlyn Publishing Group, Ltd.**

Oleander Press, The (1965), 17 Stansgate Avenue, Cambridge, CB2 2QZ *T.* 44688. *T.A.* Oleander. *Managing Director:* P. Ward.
Poetry, Drama, Law, Language, Literature, Libya, Arabia and Middle East, Indonesia and Far East, Cambridgeshire, Travel, Reference Works. Preliminary letter required before submitting MSS; please send s.a.e. for reply.

Oliphants—see **Marshall, Morgan & Scott Publications, Ltd.**

*****Oliver & Boyd** (1778), A Division of **Longman Group. Ltd.,** Croythorn House, 23 Ravelston Terrace, Edinburgh, EH4 3TJ *T.* 031-343 1991. *T.A.* Almanac, Edinburgh. *Director:* R. P. Watson (Divisional Managing).
School Books.

*****Open Books Publishing Ltd.** (1974), 11 Goodwins Court, London, WC2N 4LB *T.* 01-240 2107. *T.A.* Openings, London. *Directors:* P. Taylor (Managing), H. Fryer.
Social and Behavioural Sciences, Education, English Literature.

*****Open University Press, The** (1977), 12 Cofferidge Close, Stony Stratford, Milton Keynes, MK11 1BY *T.* 566744. *Directors:* Sir Charles Troughton, H. Saunders, John Cox, Sir Walter Perry, John Boon, W. Morrison, Dr. C. Wilson, Miss L. Lonsdale-Cooper, A. Marwick, Dr. K. Attenborough.
Education, Environmental and Earth Sciences, Psychology, Sociology, Social and Community Studies, Systems.

*****Oriel Press, Ltd.** (1962), Stocksfield Studio, Branch End, Stocksfield, Northumberland, NE43 7NA *T.* Stocksfield 3065. *Directors:* Bruce Allsopp (Chairman and Managing), Malcolm Crocker, Alan Goodwin (Secretary).
A subsidiary company of **Routledge and Kegan Paul Ltd.**
Architecture, Art, Archaeology, Landscape, Town Planning, History, Librarianship, Science, Oriel Guides Séries, Conferences.

*****Osprey Publishing, Ltd.** (1968), 12–14 Long Acre, Covent Garden, London, WC2E 9LP *T.* 01-836 7863. *Directors:* R. J. Shattock (Chairman), Tony Bovill (Managing), John Bennett, David Reeves, Roger Bonnett.
Aircraft, Automotive, History, Military, Reference Books, General.

Outposts Publications (1956), 72 Burwood Road, Walton-on-Thames, Surrey, KT12 4AL *T.* Walton-on-Thames 40712. *Directors:* Howard Sergeant, Jean Sergeant.
Poetry.

*****Owen, Peter, Ltd.,** 73 Kenway Road, London, SW5 0RE *T.* 01-373 5628. *Directors:* Peter L. Owen (Managing), Beatrice Musgrave, Robin J. Gurland.
Art, Belles-Lettres, Biography and Memoirs, Fiction, General, Theatre.

Oxford Illustrated Press Ltd. (1975), Shelley Close, Headington, Oxford, OX3 8HB *T.* Oxford 63739. *Directors:* Per Saugman, John Webb, I. W. Goodgame, F.C.A., Jane Marshall.
Well-illustrated Non-Fiction Books, Leisure Interests: Sports, Hobbies; Local History, Transport.

*Oxford University Press (1478). *Secretary to the Delegates:* G. B. Richardson, Oxford University Press, Walton Street, Oxford, OX2 6DP *T.* 0865 56767. *Telex:* Clarpress, Oxford, 837330. *Publishers:* R. A. Denniston (Academic), Sir John Brown, C.B.E. (General), R. E. Brammah (Educational). *London Office:* Ely House, 37 Dover Street, London, W1X 4AH *T.* 01-629 8494. *T.A.* Frowde, London, W1. Trade Dept.: Press Road, Neasden Lane, NW10 0DD *T.* 01-450 8080. *T.A.* Oxonian, London, NW10. *Telex:* Oxonian, London 262749. Branches or offices *q.v.* in New York, Toronto, Mexico City, Melbourne, Wellington, Delhi, Bombay, Calcutta, Madras, Karachi, Cape Town, Johannesburg, Durban, Salisbury, Nairobi, Dar es Salaam, Lusaka, Ibadan, Zaria, Accra, Cairo, Kuala Lumpur, Singapore, Hong Kong, Tokyo, Jakarta.
Aeronautics, Archaeology, Architecture, Art, Belles-Lettres, Bibles, Biography and Memoirs, Cartography, Children's Books (Fiction, Non-Fiction, Picture), Commerce, Current Affairs, Dictionaries, Drama, Economics, Educational (Infants, Primary, Secondary, Technical, University), English Language Teaching, Essays, General, History, Hymn and Service Books, Law, Maps and Atlases, Medical, Music, Naval and Military, Oriental, Philosophy, Poetry, Political Economy, Prayer Books, Reference, Science, Sociology, Sports, Games and Hobbies, Theatre and Ballet, Theology and Religion, Travel, Year Books.
Academic Books published under the imprint **Clarendon Press.**

Oyez Publishing Ltd. (1888), Norwich House, 11–13 Norwich Street, London, EC4A 1AB *T.* 01-404 5721. *T.A.* Oyez, London, EC4. *Telex:* 888870. *Directors* J. F. Platt (Managing), M. W. Bacon, O. N. Freeman, R. A. Hodges, P. M. Luff, C. S. Johnson.
Associated Company in Belgium.
Law, Business, Local Government and Social Welfare books.

*P.S.I. Policy Studies Institute (formerly **P.E.P. Political and Economic Planning**) (1931), 12 Upper Belgrave Street, London, SW1X 8BB *T.* 01-235 5271. *Directors:* John Pinder, O.B.E., Richard Davies (Admin.). *Deputy Director:* Dr. Michael Fogarty.
Contemporary Affairs, Economics, Industry, Political Economy, Social Sciences.

*Paddington Press Ltd. (1971), 21 Bentinck Street, London, W1M 5RL *T.* 01-935 3738. *Telex:* London 27604. *Director:* J. Marqusee.
Art, Biography, Cooking, Sport, Photography, History, General Non-Fiction.

Paladin Books—see Panther Books, Ltd.

*Pan Books, Ltd. (1944), Cavaye Place, London, SW10 9PG *T.* 01-373 6070. *Directors:* R. Vernon-Hunt (Managing), F. I. Chapman, W. J. Collins, A. D. Maclean, S. H. Master, C. S. Pick, D. L. Range, F. H. Whitehead, T. W. V. McMullan, S. Mehta.
Paperback reprints of notable fiction and non-fiction including novels, detective fiction, travel, adventure, war books, biography, memoirs, current affairs, humour, reference, crafts, practical handbooks, etc. Also *Piccolo*, a children's fiction and non-fiction series, *Picador*, an imprint for outstanding international fiction and non-fiction and *Brodie's Notes*, Literature Study notes for secondary level and college students.

*Panther Books Ltd, 29 Frogmore, St. Albans, Herts, AL2 2NF *T.* Park Street (0727) 72727. *Directors:* W. R. Carr, A. R. H. Birch, T. Kitson, J. Warton. Paperback Publishers—Originals and Reprints. Paladin Books.

*Paternoster Press, Ltd., The, Paternoster House, 3 Mount Radford Crescent, Exeter, Devon, EX2 4JW *T.* 0392–50631.
Children's Books (Non-Fiction, Rewards), Educational (University), Theology and Religion.

Paul (Stanley) & Co., Ltd. (1908), 3 Fitzroy Square, London, W1P 6JD *T.* 01-387 2888. *Telex:* 261212. Trade Dept.: 062-181 6362. *Telex:* 99487. *T.A.* Literarius, London, W1. *Directors:* R. A. A. Holt (Chairman), Charles Clark, R. Bloomfield. An imprint of the **Hutchinson Publishing Group.** Sports, Games, Hobbies and Handicrafts.

Pearson (C. Arthur); books—see The Hamlyn Publishing Group, Ltd.

Pelham Books, Ltd. (1959), 52 Bedford Square, London, WC1B 3EF *T.* 01-637 0941. *T.A.* Emjaybuks, Westcent, London. *Directors:* Victor Morrison (Chairman), Eric T. L. Marriott (Managing), Richard Douglas-Boyd, Muriel Gascoin, Keith Ireland.
Pears Cyclopaedia, Junior Pears Encyclopaedia, full colour Encyclopaedias. Autobiographies of men and women in Sport, Sports Handbooks, Hobbies, Crafts and Pastimes, Practical Handbooks on Dogs and other Pets, and Children's fiction and non-fiction.

Pemberton Publishing Co., Ltd. (1954), 88 Islington High Street, London, N1 8EN *T.* 01-226 7251. Dr. David Stewart (Chairman), Antony M. Chapman, Dr. Roger Manvell, Nicolas Walter (Managing Editor), F. Cooke (Secretary).
Archaeology, Biography and Memoirs, Education, History, Science, Sociology, Humanism, Ethics, Philosophy.

*Penguin Books Limited, Bath Road, Harmondsworth, Middlesex, UB7 0DA *T.* 01-759 1984 and 5722. *T.A.* Penguinook, West Drayton. *London Office:* 17 Grosvenor Gardens, London, SW1. *T.* 01-828 7090. *Founder:* Sir Allen Lane. *Chairman and Chief Executive:* E. J. B. Rose. *Vice-Chairman and Joint Managing Director:* R. J. E. Blass. *Joint Managing Director* R. Maskery, *Directors:* E. A. G. Mott, Kaye Webb, P. W. Hardy, J. W. Webster.
Penguin Books consist of reprints of Novels, Detective and Science Fiction, Travel, Adventure, and Biographical works. *Pelican Books* include more serious works on general aspects of the Sciences and Arts, including many entirely new works. *Peregrines* are books of more academic interest. *Puffin Books* are full-length children's stories, often illustrated. *Peacock Books* are for older children. *Kestrels* are hard-cover children's books. *Penguin Classics* are new translations of the world's greatest books. *Penguin Modern Classics* consist of reprints of twentieth-century classics. *Penguin Handbooks* are a series of Practical Handbooks on many subjects of fairly widespread interest. *Penguin Specials* are books on Topical Subjects, in particular Politics and Current Affairs. The *Penguin English Library* consists of some of the English literary masterpieces produced since the fifteenth century. *Allen Lane* are hard-cover editions. There are also the *Penguin African Library, Buildings of England, Penguin Poets, Penguin Plays, Penguin Reference Books, Penguin Shakespeare, Pelican History of Art.*

Penguin Young Books, a Division of Penguin Books Limited, Bath Road, Harmondsworth, Middlesex, UB7 0DA *T.* 01-759 5722. *T.A.* Penguinook, West Drayton. *Telex:* 263130. *Editorial Director Children's Publishing and Puffin:* Kaye Webb, *Deputy Editorial Director, Children's Publishing and Kestrel:* P. W. Hardy.
Children's Books: Puffin Books and Kestrel Books.

*Pergamon Press, Ltd. (1948), Headington Hill Hall, Oxford, OX3 0BW *T.* Oxford 64881. *T.A.* Pergapress, Oxford. *Telex:* 83177. *Directors:* Robert Maxwell, M.C. (Chairman), C. T. Clark (Deputy Chairman), G. F. Richards (Managing), Mrs. P. Ducker, M. Kermian (USA), B. J. Moss, A. J. Steel, H. A. Stephens, L. Straka (USA), R. E. Strange, A. J. Wheaton. *Overseas:* New York, Toronto, Sydney, Frankfurt.
Economics, Educational (Secondary, Technical, University), Medical, Research, Science, Technology, Engineering, Sociology.

Perpetua Press, Ltd. (1971), 32 Wellington Street, London, WC2E 7BD. *T.* 01-836 7342. *Directors:* Paul Minet (Chairman and Managing), Bryan Balls, Bryce Pickering.
Children's, Art, General Literature, History, Military.

*Phaidon Press, Ltd., Littlegate House, St. Ebbes Street, Oxford, OX1 1SQ *T.* 0865-46681–7 and 43557. *T.A.* Phaidon Oxford. *Telex:* 83308. *Managing Director:* George Riches.
Fine Arts, the History of Art and Civilization, Archaeology, History, Biography, Cooking, Gardening.

*Philip (George) Alexander, Ltd., Norfolk House, Smallbrook Queensway, Birmingham, B5 4LJ *T.* 021-643 8641. *Directors:* R. J. Shattock (Chairman), Alan Alexander (Managing), D. S. Reeves.
Educational (Nursery, Primary, Middle).

*Philip (George) & Son, Ltd. (1834), 12–14 Long Acre, London, WC2E 9LP *T.* 01-836 7863. *Directors:* R. J. Shattock (Managing), P. N. Godfrey, H. Fullard, J. A. Bennett, D. S. Reeves, A. J. Alexander.
Maps, Atlases, Globes, Guide Books, General, and Educational Books.

Philip, Son & Nephew, Ltd. (1834), 7 Whitechapel, Liverpool, L1 6HF *T.* Liverpool 051-236 0246–8. *T.A.* Philip, Liverpool. English and Foreign Booksellers. *Directors:* John Philip (Chairman and Managing Director), J. Mason Porter, J. S. Smith, J. Waters.

Phillimore & Co., Ltd. (incorporating **Darwen Finlayson Ltd.**), Shopwyke Hall, Chichester, Sussex, PO20 6BQ *T.* Chichester 87636. *Hon. Pres.:* Lord Darwen. *Directors:* Philip Harris, J.P. (Chairman and Managing), Noel Osborne, M.A.(Cantab.) (Editorial), Ian Macfarlane, F.C.A.
Publishers of local and family history; architectural history, archaeology, genealogy and heraldry; also publishers of the Darwen County History Series and of Delta Paperbacks.

Phoebus Publishing Co., 169 Wardour Street, London, W1A 2JX *T.* 01-437 0686. A division of **BPC Publishing Ltd.,** publishing partworks, continuity sets and one-shot magazines.

Picador—see **Pan Books, Ltd.**

Piccolo—see **Pan Books, Ltd.**

*Pickering & Inglis, Ltd., 26 Bothwell Street, Glasgow, G2 6PA *T.* 041-552 5044. 1 Creed Lane, London, EC4V 5BR. Editorial Department at Glasgow. Children's Books, Theology and Religion.

Pitkin Pictorials, Ltd. (1941), 11 Wyfold Road, London, SW6 6SG *T.* 01-385 4351. *Directors:* Norman Garrod, R. E. Willson, Dennis Potts, Julian Shuckburgh.

*Pitman Publishing Ltd. (1845), 39 Parker Street, Kingsway, London, WC2B 5PB *T.* 01-242 1655. *T.A.* Ipandsons, London, WC2. *Chief Executive:* Navin Sullivan.
Art and Craft, Performing Arts, Cookery and Gardening, Hobbies, Shorthand, Elementary Commercial and Technical Texts, University and College Technical and Professional Texts, Advanced Monographs and Reference Works.

*Pitman Medical Publishing Co., Ltd. (1973), P.O. Box 7, Tunbridge Wells, Kent, TN1 1XH *T.* Tunbridge Wells (0892) 38488-9. *T.A.* Pitmed, Tunbridge Wells, Kent. *Chief Executive:* David Dickens.
Medical and Nursing.

Planned Action Ltd—see Midas Books.

Popular Dogs Publishing Co., Ltd., 3 Fitzroy Square, London, W1P 6JD. *T.* 01-387 2888. (Trade) Tiptree 816362. *Telex:* 99487. *T.A.* Literarius, London, W1. *Telex:* 261212. *Chairman:* R. A. A. Holt. *Directors:* Charles Clark, Gerald Austin. An imprint of the **Hutchinson Publishing Group.**
Practical Books on Breeding, Care, Training, and General Management of Dogs.

Priory Press (1969), 49 Lansdowne Place, Hove, East Sussex, BN3 1HF *T.* 0273 722561. *T.A.* Bookwright, Hove. *Directors:* R. Diprè, R. E. Ferneyhough, J. W. Lewis, D. M. Middleton, R. F. J. Stafford. An imprint of **Wayland Publishers Ltd.**
Educational: Science and Natural History, Medical, General.

Profile Publications, Ltd. (1965), Dial House, 6 Park Street, Windsor, Berks, SL4 1UU *T.* Windsor 69777. *Directors:* B. A. Cracknell, H. B. Jones.
Aircraft, AFV's, Warships, Locomotives, Small Arms, Cars and Related Subjects, Semi-technical part publications—these require 5,000–10,000 words, 30–50 pictures, plans for colour; case-bound books.

Puffin Books—see Penguin Young Books Ltd.

Purnell Books, Berkshire House, Queen Street, Maidenhead, Berkshire, SL6 1NF *T.* 37171. *General Manager:* Charles Harvey. A division of **Purnell & Sons, Ltd.**

*Putnam & Company, Ltd. (1840), 9 Bow Street, London, WC2E 7AL *T.* 01-836 9081. *T.A.* Bodleian, Westcent, London. An imprint of **The Bodley Head Ltd.**
Aeronautics, Music, Naval and Military.

Quaritch (Bernard), Ltd. (1847), 5 Lower John Street, London, W1R 4AU *T.* 01-734 2983. *T.A.* Quaritch, London, W1. *Directors:* E. M. Dring, G. S. Warburg, P. N. Poole-Wilson, H. E. Radclyffe, Lord Parmoor, S. D. Sainsbury.

Quartet Books, Ltd. (1972), 27–29 Goodge Street, London, W1P 1FD *T.* 01-636 3992–5. *Directors:* N. I. Attallah (Chairman, J. Boothe, W. Miller, H. Nagourney (USA), B. Thompson, S. J. Cockburn, D. Elliott. Member of the **Namara Group.**
General Fiction and Non-Fiction, Sociology, Politics, Topical Issues, Jazz, Biography, original and reprint paperbacks.

Queen Anne Press, Ltd., The, Paulton House, 8 Shepherdess Walk, London, N1 7LW. *T.* 01-251 1666, the sponsored book division of **Macdonald & Jane's publishers.** *Directors:* A. M. Alfred (Chairman), Ronald Whiting (Managing Director), A. Smith, Penelope Hoare, S. W. Jackson, P. G. Morrison, D. Rivers.
Sporting publications.

*Rainbird (George) Ltd., 36 Park Street, London, W1Y 4DE *T.* 01-491 4777. *Cables and Telex:* Rainmac, London, 261472. *Directors:* Michael Rainbird (Managing), Peter Phillips (Deputy Managing), Ib Bellew, James Fairweather, John Hadfield, Michael O'Mara (USA), Valerie Reuben.
Archaeology, Architecture, Biography, Fine Art, Antiques, History, Natural History, Travel, Reference Books and Encyclopaedias on all subjects.

Raleigh Press. An imprint of **David & Charles (Publishers), Ltd.,** *q.v.*

Rapp & Whiting, Ltd.—see **André Deutsch Ltd.**

Rationalist Press Association, Ltd.—see **The Pemberton Publishing Co., Ltd.**

*Reader's Digest Association, Ltd., The, 25 Berkeley Square, London, W1X 6AB. *T.* 01-629 8144. *T.A.* Readigest, London, W1. *Directors:* V. Ross (Managing), G. A. G. Selby-Lowndes, S. N. McRae, A. R. P. Fairlie, P. A. A. Glemser, B. C. Gray, R. W. Hewett, M. Randolph, J. O'Hara, M. Tourrenc (France).

Reinhardt, Max, Ltd., 9 Bow Street, London, WC2E 7AL *T.* 01-836 9081. *Directors:* Max Reinhardt (Chairman and Managing Director), L. A. Hart, J. R. Hews, F.C.A., Mrs. J. Reinhardt. Proprietors of **The Bodley Head, Ltd.**
Drama, Fiction, Films, Theatre and Ballet.

*Religious Education Press, Hennock Road, Exeter, EX2 8RP *T.* Exeter 74121. A member of the Pergamon Group. *Managing Director:* John Halsall.
Religious and moral education and works on current social problems.

Renwick of Otley, Printerdom, Otley, Yorkshire, LS21 1QH *T.* 2376, and 151 Fleet Street, London, EC4.

Rider & Co. (1892), 3 Fitzroy Square, London, W1P 6JD. *T.* 01-387 2888. *Telex:* 261212. (Trade 062-181 6362. *Telex:* 18130. *Chairman:* R. A. A. Holt, *Director:* Charles Clark. *Editorial Manager:* Kevin McDermott.
An imprint of the **Hutchinson Publishing Group.**
Oriental Religion and Philosophy, Mysticism and Meditation.

*Rivingtons (Publishers) Ltd., Montague House, Russell Square, London, WC1B 5BX *T.* 01-636 8521. *Directors:* L. J. Browning, Hon. Mrs. A. M. Evans. Subsidiary of **Evans Brothers Ltd.**
Educational (Secondary).

*Robinson & Watkins Books Ltd.—see **Watkins Publishing.**

*Robson Books (1973), 28 Poland Street, London, W1V 3DB *T.* 01-734 1052–3.
T.A. Robsobook, London, W1. *Directors:* Jeremy Robson (Managing),
J. R. Morris, M.A., A.C.A.
General, biography, music, humour.

Rodale Press Inc., Chestnut Close, Potten End, Berkhamsted, Herts, HP4 2QL
T. Berkhamsted 71471–2. *Director of UK Book Operation:* Josie A.
Holtom.
Self-sufficiency, Organic Gardening, Farming, Environment, Health, Natural
Living.

*Ronald (George) (1939), 46 High Street, Kidlington, Oxford, OX5 2DN *T.*
08675-5273. *Telex:* 837646. *T.A.* Talisman, Oxford. *Partners:* David
Hofman, Marion Hofman. *Manager:* M. W. Hofman.
Religion and Philosophy.

*Rose (Barry) (Publishers), Ltd. (1971, Little London, Chichester, Sussex, PO19
1PG *T.* Chichester (0243) 83637. *T.A.* Juslocgov, Chichester. *Directors:*
Barry Rose, D. J. C. Rose, N. M. Marsch, B. H. Lewis, R. C. Childs, P. J.
Madge.
Law, Local Government, Police, Criminology, Penology.

Roundwood Press, The, The Roundwood Press (1978) Ltd., Kineton, Warwick,
CV35 0JA *T.* Kineton (0926) 640400. *Directors:* Gordon Norwood,
A. A. F. Macpherson, Peter Guy.
Architecture, Art, Biography, History, Social History.

*Routledge & Kegan Paul, Ltd. (1834), 39 Store Street, London, WC1E 7DD *T.*
01-637 7651. *T.A.* Columnae, London, WC1, and Broadway House,
Newtown Road, Henley-on-Thames, RG9 1EN *T.* Henley 78321. 9
Park Street, Boston, Mass. 02108. *Chairman:* Norman Franklin. *Direc-
tors:* R. Locke, R. Bailey, Malcolm Crocker, David Bacon, Alan Godwin.
Terence Lucas, Peter Hopkins, Rosemary Sprigg.
Archaeology, Art, Belles-Lettres, Dictionaries, Economics, Educational
(Secondary, Technical, University), Fiction, General, History, Political
Economy, Reference, Science, Sociology, Music, Occult, Oriental, Philo-
sophy, Psychology, Literary Criticism.

Rowland Ward, Ltd., Taxidermists, Publishers, Booksellers, Crawley Road,
Wood Green, London, N22 6AG *T.* 01-889 6433. *T.A.* Jungle, London,
N22.
Big Game, Natural History, Ornithology, Antiquarian.

Royal National Institute for the Blind, The (1868), 224–6–8 Great Portland Street,
London, W1N 6AA *T.* 01-388 1266. *T.A.* Pharnib, Wesdo, London.
Director of Publications: Donald Bell.
Magazines and books for the blind, in Braille and Moon embossed types.
Also tape-recorded books (Talking Books). For complete list of magazines
see Classified Index.

Sackett & Marshall Ltd. (1977), 2 Great Marlborough Street, London, W1 *T.*
01-437 6006. *Directors:* Per Saugman, Peter Sackett, Jane Marshall.
Children's Books, General, Non-Fiction.

*Saint Andrew Press, The, 121 George Street, Edinburgh, EH2 4YN. *T.* 031-
225 5722. *T.A.* Free, Edinburgh, 2.
Theology and Religion.

*SCM Press Ltd. (1896), 56–58 Bloomsbury Street, London, WC1B 3QX *T.*
01-636 3841. *T.A.* Torchpres, Westcent, London. *Directors:* John Bowden (Managing Director), Mark Hammer (Production Director and Company Secretary), Margaret Lydamore (Editorial).
Educational, Philosophy, Sociology and Current Affairs, Theology and
Religion.

St. George's Press (1969), 37 Manchester Street, London, W1M 5PE *T.* 01-486
5481. *Directors:* C. M. Ardito (Chairman), R. A. Duparc, The Hon. Julian
Fane, J. M. Hatwell, J. McClafferty.
General (fiction and non-fiction), Belles Lettres, Educational (English as a
Foreign Language).

Salvationist Publishing and Supplies, Ltd., 117 Judd Street, London, WC1H 9NN
T. 01-387 1656.
Devotional books, Theology, Biography, world-wide Christian and Social
Service, Children's Books, Music.

*Saunders (W. B.) Co. Ltd., 1 St. Anne's Road, Eastbourne, East Sussex, BN21
3UN *T.* (0323) 638221. *Telex:* 877503 Volmists Eastbourne. See **Holt-
Saunders Ltd.**
Medical and Scientific.

Saville (J.) & Co., Ltd. (1912), Audley House, North Audley Street, London, W1Y
2EU *T.* 01-629 6506.
Educational (Infants), Music.

*Schofield & Sims, Ltd. (1902), 35 St. John's Road, Huddersfield, HD1 5DT
T. Huddersfield (0484) 30684. *T.A.* Schosims, Huddersfield. *Directors:*
Frank R. Lockwood (Chairman), John S. Nesbitt (Deputy Chairman and
Managing Director), J. Stephen Platts (Secretary), C. Bygott, E. J. C.
Bygott, C. Nesbitt, L. M. C. Payne, E. P. C. Platts.
Educational (Infants, Primary, Secondary, Technical, Music for Schools).

Scientific Publishing Co., The, 40 Dalton Street, Manchester, M4 4JP *T.* 061-
205 1514.
Engineering textbooks.

*Scolar Press (1967), 39 Great Russell Street, London, WC1B 3PH *T.* 01-636
1865. *T.A.* Catchword London. *Directors:* J. Commander (Chairman),
J. Price (Managing).
Facsimile Reprints, Mediaeval Studies, Bibliography and Manuscript
Studies, History, Literature, Horticulture, Natural History, Architecture,
Art, Design, Social Science, Fine Editions.

Scottish Academic Press Ltd. (1969), 33 Montgomery Street, Edinburgh, EH7
5JX T. 031-556 2796. *Directors:* Principal J. Steven Watson, Douglas
Grant, Principal Matthew Black, Professor Christopher Blake, Professor
W. N. Everitt, Professor P. McL. D. Duff.
All types of academic books and books of Scottish interest.

Scout Association, The, Baden-Powell House, Queen's Gate, London, SW7 5JS
T. 01-584 7030. *T.A.* Scouting. *General Editor:* Ron Jeffries, M.A.I.E.
Technical books dealing with all subjects relevant to Scouting and monthly
journal *Scouting.*

*Scripture Union (1867), 47 Marylebone Lane, London, W1M 6AX *T.* 01-486
2561. Christian Publishers and Booksellers.
Music, Bible reading aids, Sunday School materials and Christian books
especially for children and young people.

Search Press, Ltd. (1962), 2–10 Jerdan Place, London, SW6 5PT *T.* 01-385 6261-2. *Directors:* Charlotte de la Bedoyère, John M. Todd, John Cumming.
Philosophy, Social Sciences, Literature, History, Theology, Exegesis, Spirituality, Educational and Children's Books, Crafts, Travel and Leisure.

*****Secker (Martin) & Warburg, Ltd.** (Founded 1910. Reconstructed and enlarged, 1936), 54 Poland Street, London, W1V 3DF *T.* 01-437 2075. *T.A.* Psophidian, London. *Directors:* T. G. Rosenthal (Managing), Barley Alison, John Blackwell, David Farrer, Peter Ireland, T. R. Manderson, Professor Peter Murray, PH.D., F.S.A., Charles Pick, Gillian Vale.
Art, Belles-Lettres, Biography and Memoirs, Economics, Fiction, History, Political Economy, Science, Sociology, Theatre and Ballet, Travel.

Seeley, Service & Co., Ltd. (1744), 196 Shaftesbury Avenue, London, WC2H 8JL *T.* 01-836 6225. Alastair Service, Leo Cooper, T. R. Hartman, M. Rodenburg, G. N. Thompson, D. B. D'Eath, John Hemming, Alison Harvey.
Biography and Memoirs, General History, Naval and Military, Sports.

Shakespeare Head Press (1904), Basil Blackwell & Mott, Ltd., 5 Alfred Street, Oxford, OX1 4HB.
Finely printed books; Scholarly works.

Sheed & Ward Ltd. (1926), 6 Blenheim Street, London, W1Y 0SA *T.* 01-629 0306. *T.A.* Stanza, London, W1. *Directors:* M. T. Redfern, K. G. Darke.
Publishers of books, mostly by Catholics.
History, Philosophy, Theology, Catechetics, Scripture and Religion.

*****Sheldon Press,** SPCK Building, Marylebone Road, London, NW1 4DU *T.* 01-387 5282. *T.A.* Futurity, London. *Editor-in-Chief:* Darley Anderson.
Biography and Memoirs, Current Affairs, General, Mysticism, Parapsychology, Philosophy, Politics, Psychiatry, Psychology, Religion, Social Studies and Occasional Fiction.

Shepheard-Walwyn (Publishers), Ltd (1971), 60 Fleet Street, London, EC4Y 1JU *T.* 01-353 6741 *T.A.* Shepwyn, London, EC4. *Directors:* C. Shepheard-Walwyn, A. R. A. Werner, P. M. Shepheard-Walwyn.
General non-fiction.

Sheppard Press, Ltd. (1944), P.O. Box 42, Russell Chambers, Covent Garden, London, WC2E 8AX *T.* 01-240 0406. *T.A.* Iffcass, London, WC2 *Directors:* B. N. Rendall Davies and TreforRendall Davies.
Directories and Guide Books, General, Practical Handbooks, Reference, Year Books.

Sherratt, John & Son, Ltd., 78 Park Road, Altrincham, Cheshire, WA14 5QQ *T.* 061-973 5711.
Educational (Primary, Secondary, Technical, University), Medical, Practical Handbooks, Collector's Books.

Shire Publications Ltd. (1966), Cromwell House, Church Street, Princes Risborough, Aylesbury, Bucks, HP17 9AJ *T.* 08444-4301. *Directors:* J. P. Rotheroe, J. W. Rotheroe.
"Discovering" Paperbacks, "Lifelines" Illustrated Biographies, Shire Albums, History in Camera Series, Family Care Books, and Shire Archaeology.

*Sidgwick & Jackson, Ltd. (1908), 1 Tavistock Chambers, Bloomsbury Way, London, WC1A 2SG *T.* 01-242 6081. *T.A.* Watergate, London. *Directors:* The Earl of Longford, P.C. (Chairman), W. Armstrong (Managing), W. D. Procter, Stephen du Sautoy, R. A. Shadbolt, Rocco Forte.
Archaeology, Belles-Lettres, Current Affairs, Fiction, General, History, Military History, Music, Philosophy, Poetry, Political Economy, Science (Biology), Sociology, Theology and Religion, Travel.

Skilton (Charles), Ltd., 2 & 3 Abbeymount, Edinburgh, EH8 8EJ *T.* 031-661 9339. A preliminary letter is desirable.
Art, Biographies, Histories, Reference, de Luxe Editions.

Smythe (Colin), Ltd. (1966), P.O. Box 6, Gerrards Cross, Bucks, SL9 7AE *T.* Gerrards Cross 86000. *T.A.* Smythebooks, Gerrards Cross, Bucks. *Directors:* Colin Smythe (Managing), Peter Bander.
Education, Religion, Biography, Current Affairs, Histories, Parapsychology and Anglo-Irish Literature.

*Society for Promoting Christian Knowledge (1698), Holy Trinity Church, Marylebone Road, London, NW1 4DU *T.* 01-387 5282. *T.A.* Futurity, London. *General Secretary:* P. N. G. Gilbert. *Editors:* Robin Brookes, David Craig.
Theology and Religion. See also **Sheldon Press.**

Soncino Press, Ltd. (1929), Audley House, 9 North Audley Street, London, W1Y 2EU *T.* 01-629 6506. *Cables:* Soncino, London, W1. *Directors:* P. Bloch, S. M. Bloch, A. Wix. Translations with Commentaries of Hebrew Classics.
Theology and Religion.

Southside (Publishers), Ltd. (1968)—see **Canongate Publishing Ltd.**

*Souvenir Press, Ltd., 43 Great Russell Street, London, WC1B 3PA *T.* 01-580 9307–8. *T.A.* Publisher, London. *Telex:* 24710. *Directors:* Ernest Hecht, B.SC.(Econ.), B. Com (Managing), T. E. Wiseman, A. Hecht. *Executive Directors:* Rodney King, Jane Greenhalgh, Mrs Jeanne Manchee.
Archaeology, Biography and Memoirs, Children's Books (Non-Fiction, Rewards), Educational (Secondary, Technical), Fiction, General, Humour, Practical Handbooks, Psychiatry, Psychology, Sociology, Sports, Games and Hobbies, Travel.

Spearman (Neville), Ltd., The Priory Gate, 57 Friars Street, Sudbury, Suffolk. *T.* 078-73 71818. *Directors:* Neville Armstrong, M. J. Armstrong.
Fiction, Reminiscences, Biography, Autobiography; particularly interested in original, topical and controversial themes on all subjects, especially Mysticism and the Occult.

*Sphere Books, Ltd., 30–32 Gray's Inn Road, London, WC1X 8JL *T.* 01-405 2087. *T.A.* Spherbooks, London, WC1. *Directors:* Edmund Fisher (Managing), N. R. Austin, Susan Beavan, D. Jewell, C. F. J. Vine, T. N. Wilton Steer.
Paperbacks: original works and reprints.

*Spon (E. & F. N.), Ltd. (1830), 11 New Fetter Lane, London, EC4P 4EE *T.* 01-583 9855.
Architecture, Building, Engineering, Science, Mathematical Tables, Building Price Books.

*Sporting Handbooks, Ltd. (1926), 12 Dyott Street, London, WC1A 1DF *T.* 01-836 8911. *Directors:* Haddon Whitaker, o.b.e., m.a., F. H. C. Tatham, m.a., David Whitaker, A. C. E. Musk, c.v.o., R. F. Baum, Sally Whitaker. Sports, Games and Hobbies.

Spring Books—see **The Hamlyn Publishing Group, Ltd.**

*Stainer & Bell, Ltd. (1906), 82 High Road, London, N2 9PW *T.* 01-444 9135. *Directors:* A. D. Percival, m.b.e. (Executive Chairman and Editorial), K. Robinson (Marketing), W. J. Oxenbury, G. Thompson (USA), B. A. Braley (Managing), Mrs. G. Allen (Secretary). Non-Fiction and Children's Books.

Stanford (Edward), Ltd. (1852), 12, 13 and 14 Long Acre, London, WC2E 9LP. *T.* 01-836 1321. *T.A.* Estonfomap, Rand, London. *Directors:* R. J. Shattock (Chairman), D. P. Woods (Managing), P. N. Godfrey, D. S. Reeves (Secretary). Maps and Atlases.

Stanmore Press, Ltd. (1947), 25 Thurloe Street, London, SW7. *T.* 01-589 6807, and 01-743 3278. *Directors:* G. A. Averill, M. Kahn, C. Kahn, O. M. Averill. Associated imprint: **Kahn & Averill.** General Non-Fiction, Music, Educational.

Staples Press, Ltd. now **Crosby Lockwood Staples Ltd,** *q.v.*

Star Books—see **Wyndham Publications Ltd.**

*Starke (Harold), Ltd., Pegasus House, 116–120 Golden Lane, London, EC1Y 0TL *T.* 01-253 2145–6. *Trade:* The Barn, Northgate, Beccles, Suffolk. *T.* Beccles (0502) 713239 and 714473. *Directors:* Harold K. Starke (Chairman/Managing), Peter Stuart-Heaton, Naomi Galinski, Anthony Rubinstein. Biography and Memoirs, Medical and Reference.

*Stephens (Patrick), Ltd. (1967), Bar Hill, Cambridge, CB3 8EL *T.* Crafts Hill 80010. *Telex:* 817677. *Directors:* Patrick J. Stephens, Darryl Reach, E. F. Heaton, A. Guichard, W. J. Germing, f.c.a., Colin Webb (Secretary). Motoring, Militia, Modelling, Aviation, Ships and the Sea, Transport History, Motor Cycling, Fine Art, Photography, Crafts, Wargaming, and Commercial Vehicles.

*Stevens and Sons, Ltd. (1889), 11 New Fetter Lane, London, EC4P 4EE *T.* 01-583 9855. *Directors:* P. H. B. Allsop (Chairman and Managing Director), C. D. O. Evans, A. Prideaux, Mrs. E. Bramwell, H. Jones, R. McKay, Miss S. Nicholas, Miss A. Toovey, D. Sampson (Company Secretary). Law.

*Stillit Books, Ltd., 72 New Bond Street, London, W1Y 0QY *T.* 01-493 1177. *Telex:* 23475. *Directors:* Gerald B. Stillit, Randolph Vigne. Stillitron language-learning systems consisting of programmed books, cassettes, the Stillitron teaching aid and cassette recorder.

Stirling Tract Enterprise (1848), (The Drummond Press), 64 Murray Place, Stirling, FK8 2BX *T.* Stirling 3384. *Director:* Rev. John Birkbeck, m.c. Religious books for Adults and Children.

*Studio Vista Publishers (a division of Cassell Ltd.), 35 Red Lion Square, London, WC1R 4SG   *T.* 01-831 6100.   *Telex:* 28648 Casmac-G.
Art, Applied Art, Design, Crafts, Architecture, Interior Design, General, Non-Fiction, *Decorative Art in Modern Interiors* (1906), *Modern Publicity* (1924), *Association of Illustrators* (1976), Cinema, Theatre, Ballet.

Sumner Press, The (1962), 24 Tufton Street, London, SW1P 3RB   *T.* 01-222 5533.   *T.A.* Marisumner, London, SW1.
Religious: emphasis on marriage and Christian family life.

Sussex University Press (1971), Sussex House, Falmer, Brighton, BN1 9QZ   *T.* 0273 606755.   *Publications Committee:* Professor R. J. Blin-Stoyle, Professor A. K. Thorlby, Professor D. F. Pocock, Professor G. F. A. Best.
Publications distributed by **Scottish Academic Press Ltd,** *q.v.*
All types of academic books.

Swedenborg Society, 20–21 Bloomsbury Way, London, WC1A 2TH   *T.* 01-405 7986.
Theology and Religion.

*Sweet & Maxwell, Ltd. (1889), 11 New Fetter Lane, London, EC4P 4EE   *T.* 01-583 9855.   *Directors:* P. H. B. Allsop (Chairman), C. D. O. Evans (Managing Director), B. M. Cardy, H. Simpson, A. Prideaux, D. Sampson (Company Secretary).
Law.

Systems Publications Ltd., Gatehouse Industrial Estate, Gatehouse Road, Aylesbury, Bucks.   *T.* Aylesbury 24596.   *Editorial and Sales:* 72–90 Worship Street, Holywell House, London, EC2.   *T.* 01-247 8492.   *Telex:* 886048.
Encyclopaedias and allied reference works.

TQ Publications (the theatre publishing division of **IRAT Services Ltd.)** (1971), 44 Earlham Street, London, WC2H 9LA   *T.* 01-836 1477.   *Directors:* Michel Julian (Managing), Simon Trussler (Editorial).
Theatre, plays, reference, bibliography, publications for the British Centre of the International Theatre Institute.

Talmy, Franklin, Ltd. (1970), 29 Rupert House, Nevern Square, London, SW5 9PL   *T.* 01-584 7545.   *T.A.* Franklit, London.   *Director:* Mike Franklin, M.A. (Managing).
Fiction, Sociology, Psychology, Biography, General Non-Fiction, Travel, Adventure.

Tandem Publishing Ltd—see Wyndham Publications Ltd.

*Tavistock Publications Ltd., 11 New Fetter Lane, London, EC4P 4EE   *T.* 01-583 9855.   *Directors:* Gill Davies, John Naylor, Carol Somerset.
Sociology, Anthropology, Psychology, Psychiatry, Social Administration, Management Studies, Women's Studies.

*Taylor & Francis, Ltd., 10–14 Macklin Street, London, WC2B 5NF   *T.* 01-405 2237-9.   *President:* Professor Sir Neville Mott, F.R.S.   *Directors:* S. A. Lewis (Managing Director), Dr. A. T. Fuller, G. R. Noakes, G. F. Lancaster (Secretary), Professor B. R. Coles, Professor K. W. Keohane, A. R. Selvey, M. I. Dawes.   Publishers of scientific journals and books.
Educational (University), Science (Physics, Electronics, Natural History, Optical, History of Science, Ergonomics).

*Technical Press, Ltd. (1933), Freeland, Oxford, OX7 2AP   *T.* Freeland (0993) 881788. *Directors:* P. Stobart, B.A., A. G. Down. Publishers of the *Common-Core* series of technical training manuals in electricity/electronics. Aerospace, Building and Decorating, Civil Engineering and Surveying, Educational (Secondary, Technical, Vocational and Industrial), Electrical/ Electronics and TV, Handicrafts and Hobbies, Mechanical and Automobile Engineering, Reference (Legal, Professional, Chemical), Valuation.

Temple Smith, (Maurice) Ltd., (1969), 37 Great Russell Street, London, WC1B 3PP   *T.* 01-636 9810. *Directors:* Maurice Temple Smith, Jean Temple Smith, W. F. Hayles.
Non-Fiction.

Teredo Books, Ltd., P.O. Box 430, Brighton, BN1 6GT   *T.* Brighton 505432. *Directors:* Frank G. C. Carr, C.B., C.B.E., F.R.Inst.Nav., Richard M. Cookson, Alex A. Hurst (Managing).
Maritime Publications and Marine Art.

*Thames and Hudson Ltd., 30–34 Bloomsbury Street, London, WC1B 3QP   *T.* 01-636 5488. *T.A.* Thameshuds, London, WC1. *Telex:* 25992. *Directors:* E. Neurath, T. M. Neurath, H. J. Jarrold, C.B.E., T. Craker, W. Guttmann, S. Baron, E. Bates, I. Carriline, S. Huntley, C. M. Kaine, I. H. B. Middleton. Archaeology, Architecture, Art, Travel, History, Science.

Thomas (A.) and Co., Denington Estate, Wellingborough, Northants, NN8 2RQ   *T.* Wellingborough 76031–4.
General, Practical Handbooks, Inspiration and Self-Improvement, Yoga.

Thomson-Leng Publications, Dundee, DD1 9QJ   *T.* 23131. *T.A.* Courier, Dundee. *Telex:* DC Thom 76380. London: 185 Fleet Street, London, EC4A 2HS   *T.* 01-353 2586. *T.A.* Courier, London, EC4. Publishers of newspapers and periodicals.
Children's Books (Annuals), Fiction.

*Thorsons Publishers Ltd. (1930), Denington Estate, Wellingborough, Northants, NN8 2RQ   *T.* Wellingborough 76031–4. *Directors:* J. A. Young (Managing), M. E. Young, D. J. Young, D. C. J. Palmer, J. R. Hardaker, J. A. Winslow.
Health and Healing embracing Nature Cure and Diet Reform, Natural Foods and Cookery, Vegetarianism, Herbalism, Acupuncture, Homoeopathy, Biochemistry, Yoga, Occultism, Self-Improvement, Self Sufficiency and Guides to Practical Management Techniques.

Thurman Publishing Ltd. (1974), The Mill Trading Estate, Acton Lane, Harlesden, London, NW10.   *T.* 01-961 4477. *Directors:* R. C. Williams, S. J. T. Marshall, A. D. Stirling, D. Z. Williams, M. J. Marshall.
Children's Books (picture), Model Books.

Tiranti (Alec), Ltd. taken over by **Academy Editions,** *q.v.*

*Transworld Publishers Ltd., Century House, 61–63 Uxbridge Road, London, W5 5SA   *T.* 01-579 2652.
Corgi, Bantam, Storychair and Carousel Books. How and Why Books, Wonder Why Books.

Triton Publishing Company Ltd. (1964), 1A Montagu Mews North, London, W1H 1AJ   *T.* 01-935 8090. *T.A.* Trifem, London, W.1. *Directors:* Sydney Box, D. G. Trustcott, F.C.A., Carolyn Whitaker.
Fiction and General Non-Fiction.

Tuck (Raphael) & Sons, Ltd., Raphael House, Selbourne Road, Blackpool, Lancashire, FY1 3PW *T.* 36201. *Directors:* F. R. Kerry (Chairman, D. T. Barnes, G. B. Barnes, R. F. Kerry, W. N. Rigby, D. Sneath (Managing). Fine art and greeting card publishers.

*t*Turnstone Books (1971), 37 Upper Addison Gardens, London, W14 8AJ. *T.* 01-602 6885. *Directors:* Alick Bartholomew (Managing), Geoffrey M. Watkins, Robin Campbell.
Alternative Lifestyles and Therapies, Mysticism, Mythology, Fantasy, Practical Philosophy, Parapsychology, Prehistory.

United Society for Christian Literature, Luke House, Farnham Road, Guildford, Surrey, GU1 4XD *T.* Guildford 77536. *T.A.* Lutteric, Guildford. Has for over 150 years acted for the British missionary societies to assist book production in all languages by subsidy grants. *General Secretary:* Rev. Alec Gilmore, M.A., B.D.
Theology and Religion.

United Society for the Propagation of the Gospel, 15 Tufton Street, London, SW1P 3QQ *T.* 01-222 4222. *T.A.* Gospelize, London, SW1.
Publish: *Network, Adventurer,* pamphlets, posters, visual aids, lesson material for Schools and Sunday Schools and publications dealing with the work of the Church Overseas.

United Trade Press Ltd. (1927), 33–35 Bowling Green Lane, London, EC1. *T.* 01-837 1212. *T.A.* Markeba. *Telex:* 299049 Utpres G. *Directors:* B. Gilbert, J. Baars, J. Hopes, K. Hollingdale, J. Birks.
Electronics, Technology, Science, Fashion, Reference.

University of London Press, Ltd.—see Hodder & Stoughton Educational.

University of Wales Press (1922), 6 Gwennyth Street, Cathays, Cardiff, CF2 4YD *T.* Cardiff (0222) 31919.
Educational (Welsh and English). Publishers of *Bulletin of the Board of Celtic Studies, Welsh History Review, Studia Celtica, Llên Cymru, Y Gwyddonydd, Efrydiau Athronyddol.*

*****University Tutorial Press, Ltd.** (1901), 842 Yeovil Road, Slough, SL1 4JQ *T.* 0753-29844. *T.A.* Tutorial Slough. Editorial offices: Bateman Street, Cambridge, CB2 1NG.
Economics, Government, Psychology, Education, Commerce, Mathematics, Sciences, Languages, Literature, History, Geography (Secondary, Technical, University).

Unwin Brothers Ltd. (1971), The Gresham Press, Old Woking, Surrey, GU22 9LH *T.* 04862 61971. *Directors:* L. H. Green (Managing), M. E. Gaff. *Publishing Administrator:* C. Ellis.
History, Music, Reference, Antiques, Current Affairs, Education, Biography, Science, Printing Technology, Conference Proceedings.

Usborne Publishing (1973), 20 Garrick Street, London, WC2. *T.* 01-836 1806 and 1470. *Directors:* T. P. Usborne, M. Alfred.
Children's books.

Vallentine, Mitchell & Co. Ltd. (1950), Gainsborough House, 11 Gainsborough Road, London, E11 1RS   *T.* 01-530 4226.   *T.A.* Valmico, London. *Telex:* 897719.   *Directors:* F. Cass (Managing), M. P. Zaidner, Viscount Samuel, C.M.G.
Mainly books of Jewish interest, educational, historical, Middle East problems.

*Van Nostrand Reinhold Co. Ltd., Molly Millars Lane, Wokingham, Berkshire. *T.* Wokingham (0734) 789456.   *Directors:* R. S. R. Hutchison, A. J. Davis. Aeronautics, Current Affairs, Dictionaries, Economics, Educational (Secondary, Technical and University), General, History, Mathematics, Medicine, Philosophy, Political Economy, Psychology, Reference, Pure and Applied Science, Sociology, Technology, Insights, Momentums, Anvil Books and Searchlights (original works in paper binding), Art and Craft, Sport and Leisure.

Vegetarian Society (UK), Ltd., The, Parkdale, Dunham Road, Altrincham, Cheshire, WA14 4QG   *T.* 061-928 0793.
Food Reform, Vegetarianism, Dietetics, Recipes.

Vernon & Yates Ltd. 1963), 8 Farncombe Street, Farncombe, Godalming, Surrey, GU7 3AY   *T.* 04868-28622-3.   *Directors:* George Hammer, David Rendel, S. M. H. Vernon, Erica Watson.
Aviation, Medical Biography, Bird Photography.

Vine Books Ltd., 7 Wine Office Court, Fleet Street, London, EC4A 3DA   *T.* 01-583 1484.

Virago Ltd. (1974), Fourth Floor, 5 Wardour Street, London, W1V 3HE   *T.* 01-734 4608.   *T.A.* Caterwaul London W1.   *Directors:* Carmen Callil, Ursula Owen, Harriet Spicer.
Books about women, non-fiction, fiction, educational, reference.

Virtue & Co., Ltd. (1819), 25 Breakfield, Coulsdon, Surrey, CR3 2UE   *T.* 01-668 4632.   *Directors:* Guy Virtue, M. F. Virtue, E. M. Ottaway, Michael Virtue, L. J. Vincent, R. S. Cook.
Books for the Catering Trade and the home.

Vision Press Ltd. (1946), 11–14 Stanhope Mews West, London, SW7 5RD   *T.* 01-589 7456.   *Directors:* Alan Moore, B.A. (Managing), Amber G. Moore. Art, Education, Film, History, Literary Criticism, Music, Philosophy, Politics, Psychology, Religion, Science, Sociology, Theatre.

Walker (Wm.) & Sons (Otley), Ltd. (1811), Otley, Yorkshire, LS21 1QH   *T.* Otley 2375.
Newspapers, Children's Picture Books.

*Walter (Henry E.), Ltd., 26 Grafton Road, Worthing, Sussex, BN11 1QU   *T.* Worthing 204567.
Religious publishers.

*Warburg Institute, University of London, Woburn Square, London, WC1H 0AB *T.* 01-580 9663.
Archaeology, Art, History, Philosophy.

Ward, Edmund (Publishers) Ltd.—see Kaye & Ward Ltd.

*Ward Lock Limited (1854), 116 Baker Street, London, W1M 2BB *T.* 01-486 3271. *T.A.* Warlock, London, W1. *Telex:* 262364 Warlock G. *Directors:* T. Maher (Chairman), M. Raeburn, P. Lock, C. Lock, Peter Lardi, R. Royce, Robin Woolf, S. White, J. Harris, G. Charters. Free-lance artists' and designers' work used. Member of the **Pentos Group.**
Cookery, Gardening, Antiques and Collecting, Crafts, Equitation, General Reference, Sports, Bridge, Children's illustrated story books, General Knowledge and Encyclopaedias. No fiction.

*Ward Lock Educational Ltd. (1946), 116 Baker Street, London, W1M 2BB *T.* 01-486 3271 *Directors:* M. Raeburn (Chairman), R. Royce (Managing), C. Lock, J. Rivers.
Secondary and primary pupil materials, reading workshops, staff-room library and teacher training books.

*Warne (Frederick) (Publishers) Ltd. (1865), 40 Bedford Square, London, WC1B 3HE. *T.* 01-580 9622. *Telex:* 25963. *T.A.* Warne, London, WC1; and New York City. *Directors:* C. W. Stephens (Chairman and Managing Director, D. W. Bisacre, R. D. Traube. *Secretary:* F. R. White.
Children's Books, Reference Books including Natural History and Dictionaries, Observer's Pocket Series, Transport, General Interest.

Watkins Publishing, 24 Greville Road, London, NW6 5JA *T.* 01-624 1321. *Trade:* Bridge Street, Dulverton, Somerset, TA22 9HJ *T.* (0398) 23395. Science, Religion, Philosophy, Psychology, Ecology, General.

Watts (C. A.) & Co., Ltd. (1885)—see **Pitman Publishing Ltd.**

*Watts, Franklin, Limited (1969 in London, 1942 in New York), Aldine House, 26 Albemarle Street, London, W1X 4BN *T.* 01-493 8557. *T.A.* Frawatts, London, W1. *Telex:* 299575 Frawat G. *Directors:* David Howgrave-Graham (Managing), Howard B. Graham (USA) (Chairman), Margaret Crush (Deputy Managing), William E. Bloodworth, Gordon W. McKean (USA), Alan Hills, A.C.A, Richard H. Walker (USA).
Non-Fiction, Education (Primary), Juvenile, Reference Books.

Wayland (Publishers) Ltd. (1969), 49 Lansdowne Place, Hove, Sussex, BN3 1HS *T.* Brighton (0273) 722561. *Directors:* R. Diprè, R. E. Ferneyhough, J. W. Lewis, D. M. Middleton, R. F. J. Stafford.
General, History, Biography, Art, Military History, Educational and Popular Illustrated Books.

*Weidenfeld, George, & Nicolson Ltd., 11 St. John's Hill, London, SW11 1XA *T.* 01-228 8888. *Directors:* Lord Weidenfeld (Chairman), Christopher Falkus (Deputy Chairman), A. R. Miles (Managing and Secretary), H. H. Coudenhove, Gila Falkus, John Curtis, Richard Hussey, B. J. MacLennan, David Livermore, R. J. Compton, E. R. Henderson, Nigel Nicolson, Simon Dally, Behram Kapadia, Alexandra Wells, Colin Webb.
Anthropology, Architecture, Art, Belles-Lettres, Biography and Memoirs, Current Affairs, Economics, Fiction, General, History, Philosophy, Politics, Naval and Military, Science, Sociology, Sport, Travel.

*Wheaton (A.) & Co. Ltd. (1780), Hennock Road, Exeter, EX2 8RP *T.* Exeter (0392) 74121. A member of the Pergamon Group. *Managing Director:* John Halsall.
Educational (Infant, Junior and Secondary), Dictionaries, Reference Books, Picture and Story Books for young children.

Wheldon & Wesley, Ltd., Lytton Lodge, Codicote, Hitchin, Herts, SG4 8TE   *T.*
Stevenage (0438) 820370.
Natural history booksellers and publishers.   Agency of the British Museum
(Natural History) and Hunt Botanical Library.

*Whitaker (J.) & Sons, Ltd., 12 Dyott Street, London, WC1A 1DF   *T.* 01-836
8911.   *Directors:* Haddon Whitaker, O.B.E., M.A., A. C. E. Musk, C.V.O.,
David Whitaker, R. F. Baum, James Coates, Sally Whitaker.   *Whitaker's
Almanack* (1868), *The Bookseller* (1858), Whitaker's *Books of the Month &
Books to Come, British Books in Print* (*The Reference Catalogue of Current
Literature*) (1874), *Whitaker's Cumulative Book List* (1924), *Paperbacks in
Print,* etc.
Reference.

Whizzard (G.) Publications, Ltd., 11A Camden High Street, London, NW1 7JE
T. 01-388 7411–2.   *T.A.* Whizzkids, London, NW1.   *Telex:* Whizzard
896691.   *Joint Managing Directors:* Douglas Maxwell, Graham Tarrant.
Children's Books (fiction and non-fiction).   Adult Books (Whizzard Press).

Wildings of Shrewsbury, Ltd. (1874), Windsor Place, Shrewsbury, SY1 2DB   *T.*
Shrewsbury 51278.
Histories and Guide Books, Medical, Educational (Magazines, Year Books,
Prospectuses), Periodicals (National and Private).

Wildwood House Ltd. (1972), 1 Prince of Wales Passage, 117 Hampstead Road,
London, NW1 3EE   *T.* 01-388 5389.   *Directors:* Dieter Pevsner, Oliver
Caldecott, David Harrison.
General Non-Fiction, Illustrated Books, Politics, Sociology, Psychology,
Philosophy, Biology & Ecology, Social History, Guide Books, Fiction.

Wiley (John) & Sons Ltd. (incorporating **Interscience Publishers**), Baffins Lane,
Chichester, Sussex, PO19 1UD   *T.* 84531.   *T.A. and Cables:* Wilebook,
Chichester.   *Telex:* 86290.   *Directors:* W. B. Wiley (Chairman), J. A. E.
Higham (Managing), R. A. Watson, A. H. Neilly, Jr. (USA), P. Marriage,
C. B. Stoll (USA), H. G. Newman, F.C.A. (Financial), Mrs. M. Orlando
(USA), M. B. Foyle (Marketing).
Scientific, Engineering, Business, Social Science, Mathematics, Medical.

Winsor & Newton Ltd. (1832), Wealdstone, Harrow, Middlesex, HA3 5RH   *T.*
01-427 4343.   *T.A.* Sepia, Harrow. Retail Dept.: 51–52 Rathbone Place,
London, W1P 1AB   *T.* 01-636 4231.
Painting (Oil and Water Colour), etc.

*Witherby (H. F. & G.), Ltd., 5 Plantain Place, London, SE1 1YN   *T.* 01-407
1801.   *Directors:* A. Witherby, R. C. F. Witherby, T. F. Witherby, T. A. F.
Witherby, D. F. Witherby.
Science (Natural), Sports, Games and Hobbies, Travel.

Woburn Press, The (1968), Gainsborough House, 11 Gainsborough Road,
London, E11 1RS   *T.* 01-530 4226.   *T.A.* Simfay, London.   *Telex:* 897719.
Directors: Frank Cass (Managing), A. E. Cass, M. P. Zaidner.
Woburn Educational Series, History, Literary Criticism, Biography, Psychi-
atric Topics for Community Workers series, Current Social and Political
Issues.

Wolfe Medical Publications Ltd., 10 Earlham Street, London, WC2H 9LP *T.* 01-240 2935. *T.A.* Wolfebooks London. *Directors:* Peter Wolfe (Managing), G. Hayward, W. J. S. Clutterbuck, P. Heilbrunn, K. C. Briscoe, K. R. Wolfe.
Specially commissioned medical titles dealing with diagnostic medicine, most in colour.

*****Wolff, Oswald (Publishers), Ltd.,** 52 Manchester Street, London, W1M 6DR *T.* 01-935 3441 and 3481. *T.A.* Bookwolff, London. *Directors:* I. R. Wolff, H. S. Wolff.
Modern European History, Economics, Sociology, Biography, German Studies and Literary Criticism.
Distributed by Interbook, Ltd., at the same address.

Woodhead-Faulkner (Publishers), Ltd. (1972), 8 Market Passage, Cambridge, CB2 3PF *T.* Cambridge (0223) 66733. *Directors:* A. Jessup (Chairman) M. J. Woodhead (Managing), I. C. Faulkner, P. J. S. Andersen, R. S. Dawes.
Finance and Investment, Management, Social and Welfare Topics, Cookery, Gardening and other popular subjects.

World Distributors (Manchester) Ltd., 12 Lever Street Manchester, M60 1TS *T.* 061-228 3841. *T.A.* Sydpem, Manchester. *Directors:* Michael Thomas (Managing Director), Clive Gregory, John Pemberton, Gordon Wood, Campbell Goldsmid, Lionel Cordell, Barry McKenzie, Jerimy Reynolds.
Children's activity, gift and information books, and Annuals.

*****World's Work, Ltd.**—see under **Heinemann Group of Publishers, Ltd.**

*****Wright (John) & Sons, Ltd.** (1825), 42–44 Triangle West, Bristol, BS8 1EX *T.* Bristol 23237. *Chairman:* C. N. Clarke. *Group Managing Director:* D. J. Kingham. *Directors:* P. R. Wilson, P. J. Wright, M. Weeks, A. V. Kennett. *Executive Sales Director:* Miss J. Eales. *Secretary:* A. Gay. Subsidiary Company: **Wright's Scientechnica.** Publishers of *The British Journal of Surgery, Injury, Community Health, The Medical Annual* and *The Veterinary Annual, Burns: including Thermal Injury, International Dental Journal, Journal of Dentistry incorporating Quarterly Dental Review, Medicine, Science and The Law.*
Medical, Dental, Veterinary, Nursing, Science, Technology.

Writers and Readers Publishing Co-operative, The (1974), 9–19 Rupert Street, London, W1V 7FS *T.* 01-437 8917 and 8942. *Directors:* Siân Williams, Glenn Joseph Thompson, Lisa Appignanesi.
Education, Children, Politics, Fiction, Poetry.

Wyndham Publications, Ltd. (incorporating **Star, Tandem, Target),** 44 Hill Street, London, W1X 8LB *T.* 01-493 6777. *Directors:* Ralph A. Fields (USA) (Chairman), Donald Morrison (Deputy Chairman), Henry Kitchen (Managing Director), Piers Dudgeon (Editorial Director), Ralph Copping, F.C.A., Jeffrey Simmons.
Adult and Juvenile (paperback).

*****Zwemmer (A.), Ltd.** (1951), 26 Litchfield Street, London, WC2H 9NJ *T.* 01-836 1749.
Architecture, Art.

AUSTRALIAN PUBLISHERS

Angus & Robertson Publishers (1884), 102 Glover Street, Cremorne Junction, N.S.W. 2090. *T.* 909-1166. *Telex:* 26452. U.K.: 16 Ship Street, Brighton, East Sussex, BN1 1AD *T.* 0273 23631. *Telex:* 877419. *Chief Executive:* Richard Walsh. *Management:* Richard Walsh, David Harris, Norm Lurie, Judith Clegg, Barry Watts. General Fiction and Non-Fiction Australiana Poetry, Pictorial, Practice, Veterinary, Agricultural, Medical, Technical, Children's, Paperbacks.

*Arnold, Edward **(Australia) Pty. Ltd.,** 373 Bay Street, Port Melbourne, Victoria 3207. *T.* 64-1346. Publishers and Agents.

*Australasian **Publishing Co., Pty., Ltd.,** Corner Bridge Road and Jersey Street, Hornsby, N.S.W. 2077. *T.* 476-2000. *Directors:* A. S. M. Harrap, G. A. Rutherford, G. P. M. Harrap, G. C. Greene, R. S. Unwin. General, Fiction, Juvenile, Education, Art and Technical.

*Australian **Council for Educational Research, Ltd., The,** Frederick Street, Hawthorn, Victoria, 3122. *T.* 818 1271. Educational Books.

*Bacon **(S. John), Pty., Ltd.,** 13 Windsor Avenue, Mt. Waverley, Victoria 3149. *T.* 03-277 3944. *Directors:* John Ferguson Bacon, Joan Diemar. Religious and Educational Material. Children's Books and illustrated Gift Books. Religious art, Greetings Cards.

Blackwell Scientific Publications (Australia) Pty., Ltd., P.O. Box 9, North Balwyn, Victoria 3104. *T.* 859-4880 and 347-6272.

*Butterworths **Pty. Limited,** 586 Pacific Highway, Chatswood, N.S.W. 2067. *T.* 412-3444.

*Cambridge **University Press (Australia) Pty. Ltd.,** 296 Beaconsfield Parade, Middle Park, Melbourne, 3206. *Managing Director:* B. W. Harris.

*Cassell **Australia Ltd.,** P.O. Box 52, Camperdown, N.S.W., 2050, 31 Bridge Road, Stanmore, N.S.W., 2048. *T.* 516-2155. *Cables:* Pachamac, Sydney. *Directors:* E. Magness, W. J. Mackarell. Fiction, Travel, Biography, Educational.

*Collins **(Wm.) Sons & Co., Ltd.,** represented by William Collins Publishers Pty. Ltd, 36 Clarence Street, Sydney, N.S.W., 2000. *T.* 29-1388. *Directors:* K. W. Wilder, A. S. Rein, S. Dearnley, I. L. Morton, G. D. Stewart. Publishers of General Literature, Fiction, Children's Books, Bibles and School Textbooks. Head Office: 14 St. James's Place, London, SW1.

*Currawong **Publishing Co., Pty. Ltd.,** 4–5 Kareela Road, Cremorne Point, N.S.W., 2090. *T.* 90-5638. Books of general appeal by Australian authors, mainly Non-Fiction.

French, Samuel (Australia) Pty. Ltd., represented by Dominie Pty. Ltd., Drama Department, 8 Cross Street, Brookvale, N.S.W. 2100. *T.* 930201. Publishers of plays and agents for the collection of royalties for Samuel French Ltd. & Samuel French Inc., The Society of Authors, and A.C.T.A.C.

*Georgian House Pty. Ltd., 296 Beaconsfield Parade, Middle Park, Victoria, 3206. *T.* 94-0457. *Directors:* Brian W. Harris, G. K. Scambler, Mrs. J. Jaboor. All types of books published.

*Hamlyn, Paul, Pty. Ltd., 176 South Creek Road, Dee Why West, N.S.W. 2099. *T.* (02)982 2344. *Telex:* AA21546. *Cables:* Pleasbooks Sydney. Incorporates the publishing imprints of **Summit Books, Ure Smith, Lansdowne Press, Lansdowne Editions.** *Chief Exec. Books Division:* Max Henry. *Publishing Manager:* Bill Templeman. *Chief Editor:* Sue Wagner. Fiction, Humour, General, Art, Australiana, Practical, Children's, Historical, Sociological, cased and paperbacks.

*Heinemann, William, Australia Pty. Ltd., 60 Inkerman Street, St. Kilda 3182. *T.* 940-383. *T.A.* Sunlocks, Melbourne. *Manager:* John Burchall. Fiction, Travel, Biography, History, Drama, Children's Books, Technical, Medical, Educational.

*Hill of Content Publishing Co. Pty., Ltd. (1965), 86 Bourke Street, Melbourne, 3000. *T.* 662-2711. *T.A.* Colbook, Melbourne. *Directors:* S. R. Lewis, M. Slamen, M. G. Zifcak, B. Meyers, P. Shaw. Australiana, History, Educational, General.

*Hodder and Stoughton (Australia) Pty. Ltd., 2 Apollo Place, Lane Cove, N.S.W. 2066. *T.* 428 1022. *Directors:* Philip Attenborough, Edward Coffey (Managing), John Carroll, Margaret Hamilton. Fiction, General, Educational, Children's, Religious, Hardback and Paperback.

*Holt-Saunders Pty. Limited, 9 Waltham Street, Artarmon 2064, New South Wales. *T.* Sydney 439-3633.

Horwitz Group Books Pty. Ltd., including **Horwitz Publications, Martin Educational,** 506 Miller Street, Cammeray, 2062. *T.* 929-6144. *Cables:* Horbooks, Sydney. *Directors:* S. D. L. Horwitz (Chairman), L. J. Moore (Managing Director), M. C. Phillips (Deputy Managing Director), Fiction (Paperback and Hardbound), Educational (Primary, Secondary and Tertiary), Reference Books, Non-Fiction, Technical, Cookery.

*Jacaranda Wiley Ltd., 65 Park Road, Milton, Queensland, 4064. *T.* 36-2755; 83 Palmerston Crescent, South Melbourne, Victoria, 3205. *T.* 699-4355; 151 Victoria Road, Gladesville, N.S.W., 2111. *T.* 888-2766; 303 Wright Street, Adelaide, S.A., 5000. *T.* 51-6827; 136 Victoria Avenue, Dalkeith, W.A., 6009. *T.* 86-3463; 32 Nikau Street, Mount Eden, Auckland 3, New Zealand. *T.* 73016; P.O. Box 3395, Port Moresby, Papua New Guinea. *Managing Director:* J. Collins; *Editor-in-Chief:* D. Moore; *Controller:* Q. Smith; *Marketing Director (College):* P. Searle; *Marketing Manager (School and General):* J. Braithwaite. Educational, Technical, Atlases.

Lansdowne Books (an imprint of **Paul Hamlyn Pty. Ltd.),** 176 South Creek Road, Dee Why West, N.S.W., 2099. *T.* (02)982 2344. *Telex:* AA21546. *Cables:* Pleasbooks Sydney. *Chief Executive:* Max Henry. *Publishing Manager:* Bill Templeman. *Managing Editor:* Sue Wagner. Australiana, Art, Historical Books.

*Lansdowne Editions (a division of **Paul Hamlyn Pty. Ltd.),** 14 Lansdowne Street, East Melbourne, Victoria, 3002. *T.* (03) 419 7493. *Cables:* Pleasbooks Melbourne. *Publisher:* Terry Greenwood. Limited Editions, Natural History, Fine Art and Australiana.

*Law Book Company Ltd., The, 301–305 Kent Street, Sydney, 2000. *T.* 29-1611.

*Longman Cheshire Pty. Ltd., Longman Cheshire House, 346 St. Kilda Road, Melbourne, Victoria, 3004. *T.* 699-1522. *Telex:* AA33501. *Managing Director:* W. P. Kerr. Educational and general publishers.

*Lothian Publishing Co. Pty. Ltd., 4–12 Tattersalls Lane, Melbourne, Victoria, 3000. *T.* 663-4976. *Directors:* Louis A. Lothian (Managing), L. N. Jupp, P. H. Lothian, K. A. Lothian. Juveniles, Practical Books, Educational, General Literature.

*Macmillan Company of Australia Pty. Ltd., The, 107 Moray Street, South Melbourne, 3205. *T.* 699 8922. *T.A.* Scriniaire, Melbourne. *Telex:* AA34454. 12 Berry Street, North Sydney, 2060, N.S.W. *T.* 92 1275. *Managing Director:* K. B. Stonier. Head Office: Melbourne. All types of books.

*Melbourne University Press, 932 Swanston Street, Carlton, Victoria, 3053. *T.* 3473455. *Postal Address:* P.O. Box 278, Carlton South, Victoria 3053. Prepared to consider works of Academic, Scholastic or Cultural Interest, Educational Textbooks and books of reference. Terms of publication are royalty, commission or profit-sharing agreements, according to the nature of the work. Representatives: Britain and Europe, International Book Distributors Ltd., 66 Wood Lane End, Hemel Hempstead, Herts; North America, International Scholarly Book Services Inc.; Tokyo, Hong Kong and Singapore, United Publishers Services Ltd. *Chairman:* Professor, J. R. Poynter. *Director:* P. A. Ryan, M.M., B.A.

*Nelson (Thomas) Australia Pty. Ltd., 19–39 Jeffcott Street, West Melbourne, Victoria, 3000. *T.* 329 2261. *Telex:* 33088.

Octopus Books, Ltd., 55 Lavender Street, Milsons Point, N.S.W. 2061. *T.* 922 4888. *Australasian Manager:* Shirley McEwin.

*Oxford University Press, Australia, David Cunningham, *Manager,* 7 Bowen Crescent, Melbourne. *Postal address:* G.P.O. Box 2784Y, Melbourne, 3001, Victoria. *Cables:* Oxonian, Melbourne. *T.* 26-3748. Australian History, Biography, Literary Criticism, Travel and General, including Children's Books, but excluding Fiction. School Books in all subjects.

*Pacific Publications (Aust.) Pty. Ltd., 76 Clarence Street, Sydney, N.S.W., 2000. *Postal address:* G.P.O. Box 3408, Sydney, N.S.W., 2001. General and Reference for Pacific Islands market and agricultural/technical.

*Penguin Books Australia Ltd. (1946), (P.O. Box 257), 487 Maroondah Highway, Ringwood, Victoria, 3134. *T.* 870 3444. *T.A.* Penguinook, Melbourne. *Directors:* R. N. Walford (Chairman), R. J. E. Blass, Sir Roger Darvall, R. A. Davis (Deputy Managing), T. D. Glover (Managing), J. Hooker (Publishing), R. Maskery, T. J. Rix. Paperbacks: Fiction, General Non-Fiction, Current Affairs, Sociology, Economics, Environmental, Anthropology, Politics, Children's.

*Pitman Publishing Pty., Ltd., 158 Bouverie Street, Carlton, Victoria 3053. *T.* 347-3055. Sydney office: 449-6774. Brisbane office: 358-2819. *Cables:* Fono, Melbourne. *Chairman:* Sir George Paton; Managing *Director:* Philip Harris; *Deputy Managing Director:* Jack McCartney; *Associate Deputy Managing and Publishing Director:* Tudor Day; *Finance Director:* Roger Ford; *Sales Manager:* Ken Pryse. Technical, Educational, General, Commercial, Medical, Legal, Photography and Art and crafts.

*Reed (A. H. & A. W.) Pty. Ltd. (1964), 53 Myoora Road, Terrey Hills, N.S.W., 2084. *T.* 450-2555. Also at Wellington, Auckland and Christchurch, New Zealand. *Directors:* J. M. Reed (Chairman and Managing), M. J. Mason, Mrs. E. J. Reed, A. W. Reed, F. A. Davey, B. E. Robson. General and Educational.

*Rigby Ltd. (1859), 30 North Terrace, Kent Town, South Australia, 5067. *T.* 23-5566. *Cables:* Rigbylim, Adelaide. *Telex:* 88090. *Directors:* R. L. Mead (Chief Executive), W. H. Hayes (Chairman), Sir James Irwin, R. D. E. Bakewell, E. H. Burgess, A. R. Grabrovaz, V. P. Kean. Educational, General Literature, Fiction and Paperbacks.

Shakespeare Head Press, 2–12 Tennyson Road, Gladesville, Sydney 2111. *T.* 890421. Educational and General, Fiction, Classics, Children's Books.

Summit Books (an imprint of **Paul Hamlyn Pty. Ltd.**), 176 South Creek Road, Dee Why West, N.S.W., 2099. *T.* (02)982 2344. *Telex:* AA21546. *Cables:* Pleasbooks, Sydney. *Chief Executive:* Max Henry. *Publishing Manager:* Bill Templeman. General interest books, Children's, Practical.

Sun Books Pty. Ltd. (1965), 107 Moray Street, South Melbourne, Victoria 3205. *T.* 699 8922. *T.A.* Sunbooks. *Directors:* K. B. Stonier, G. P. H. Dutton, G. T. Bills, N. G. Byam Shaw. Paperbacks—fiction, non-fiction, educational, especially Australian titles. Subsidiary of **The Macmillan Company of Australia Pty. Ltd.**

*Sydney University Press, (1964), Press Building, University of Sydney, N.S.W., 2006. *T.* 660-4997. *T.A.* Sydpress. *Director:* Malcolm Titt. Social Sciences and the Humanities.

*University of Queensland Press (1948), P.O. Box 42, St. Lucia, Queensland, 4067. *T.* 377 2127. *Manager:* F. W. Thompson. Scholarly works, Australian history, Australian poetry and prose, Asian and Pacific writing; general interest books.

*Ure Smith (an imprint of **Paul Hamlyn Pty. Ltd.**), 176 South Creek Road, Dee Why West, N.S.W., 2099. *T.* (02)982 2344. *Telex:* AA21546. *Cables:* Pleasbooks, Sydney. *Chief Executive:* Max Henry. *Publishing Manager:* Bill Templeman. *Managing Editor:* Sue Wagner. General Interest Books, Fiction, Humour, Art, Australiana, Practical, Children's, Historical, Sociological.

Whitcombe & Tombs Pty., Ltd., 159–163 Victoria Road, Marrickville, 2204, N.S.W., and at Melbourne and Perth. *T.* 560-9888. *T.A.* Whitcombes, Sydney. *Directors:* P. E. Bourne, D. H. J. Gillies, J. Smytheman, E. M. Rogers. Educational, General and Fiction.

Wild & Woolley (1974), P.O. Box 41, Glebe, New South Wales 2037 *T.* 02-699 9819. *Directors:* Pat Woolley, Michael Wilding. Fiction, Literary Criticism, Political Cartoons, Drug information.

*Wren Publishing Pty. Ltd. (1971), Shoreham Road, Red Hill South, Victoria, 3937. *T.* (059) 892-152. *Directors:* Dennis Wren (Managing), H. Markby, Mrs. D. Wren.
General, Fiction and Non-Fiction, Historical, Travel, Education, Juveniles.

CANADIAN PUBLISHERS

NOTE.—The paragraph prefixing "US Publishers" applies to this section also.

*Members of Canadian Book Publishers' Council

Anansi Press, Ltd., House of (1967), 35 Britain Street, Toronto, M5A 1R7 *T.* 416-363-5444. *Directors:* Ann Wall (President), Harald Bohne, B. D. Sandwell, Norma Goodger. Poetry, Fiction, Non-Fiction. Only Canadian writers.

Book Society of Canada, Limited, The (1946), 4386 Sheppard Avenue East, Box 200, Agincourt, Ontario, M1S 3B6 *T.* 416-293-4175. *President:* J. W. Irwin. *Comptroller:* C. J. Walker. Textbooks for primary, high schools and colleges. Represent in Canada Heinemann Educational Books Limited; William Heinemann Medical Books Limited; Hulton Educational Publications Ltd.; Continental Press; McDougal, Littell & Company; Hammond Inc. (educational), Basil Blackwell, Martin Robertson & Co., RJM Exports, Verlag Fur Sprochmethodik (Germany), Open Court Publishing Co.

Burns & MacEachern Limited, 62 Railside Road, Don Mills, Ontario, M3A 1A6 *T.* 447-5131. *President:* B. D. Sandwell. *Vice-Presidents:* Helen M. Sandwell and Douglas Sandwell. Publishers of Canadian Educational Books and Non-Fiction Trade Books. Agents for a number of British and American publishing companies.

*Butterworth & Co. (Canada), Ltd., 2265 Midland Avenue, Scarborough, Ontario, M1P 4S1 *T.* 416-292 1421.

Canadian Stage and Arts Publications, George Hencz, 52 Avenue Road, Toronto, Ontario, M5R 2G3 *T.* 416-921-2601, 921-5188. Primarily interested in children's books of an educational nature.

Clarke, Irwin & Company Limited, 791 St. Clair Avenue West, Toronto, M6C 1B8 *T.* 654-3211. *Telex:* 06-23132. General Trade and Educational publishers.

*Collier Macmillan Canada, Ltd. (1958), 1125B Leslie Street, Don Mills, Ontario, M3C 2K2 *T.* 449-6030. *Directors:* L. L. Hammer (President). Academic, Technical, Medical, Educational, Trade.

*Collins (Wm.) Sons & Co. (Canada), Ltd., 100 Lesmill Road, Don Mills, Ontario, M3B 2T5. *T.* 416-445-8221. Publishers of General Literature, Fiction, Children's Books, Bibles and paperbacks. Publishers in Canada for Wm. Collins, Sons & Co., Ltd., Totem Books, Pan Books Ltd., André Deutsch, Ltd., Harvill Press, Ltd., William Heinemann, Ltd., Martin Secker and Warburg, Ltd., Peter Davies Ltd., Ladybird Books, Corgi Books, Rapp & Whiting, World's Work (1913) Ltd.

*Copp Clark Ltd. (1841), 517 Wellington Street West, Toronto, M5V 1G1 *T.* 416-366 4911. *T.A.* Noblecop, Toronto. *President:* M. I. Pitman. *Vice-President Publishing:* Hugh R. Furneaux. Educational Textbooks for Elementary, Secondary and College use. Preliminary letter required before submitting manuscript.

*Dent (J. M.) & Sons (Canada), Ltd., 100 Scarsdale Road, Don Mills, Ontario, M3B 2R8. Textbooks and General publishers. Most textbooks commissioned.

Dodd, Mead & Company (Canada), Ltd., 25 Hollinger Road, Toronto, M4B 3G2 *T.* 416-751-4520. General publishers.

*Doubleday Canada Ltd. (1937), 105 Bond Street, Toronto, Ontario, M5B 1Y3 *T.* 416-366 7891. *President:* William Havercroft. *Senior Vice President:* Peter Maik; *Vice-Presidents:* J. L. Dickson, H. Ford.
General Trade Fiction and Non Fiction, School Textbooks.

Douglas & McIntyre Ltd. (1963), 1875 Welch Street, North Vancouver, B.C., V7P 1B7 *T.* 604-986-4311. *Directors:* J. J. Douglas, Scott McIntyre. General non-fiction, Canadian fiction. Children's books and high quality graphic books.

Fitzhenry & Whiteside Ltd. (1966), 150 Lesmill Road, Don Mills, Ontario, M3B 2T5 *T.* 416-449-0030. *T.A.* Godwit. *Telex:* 06-966523. *Directors:* R. I. Fitzhenry, Cecil L. Whiteside. Trade, Educational, College Books.

*Gage Educational Publishing Ltd. (1884), 164 Commander Boulevard, Agincourt, Ontario, M1S 3C7 *T.* 416-293-8141. *T.A.* Gagepub, Toronto. Publishers of Primary, Elementary, Secondary, Post-Secondary and University Textbooks and Trade publications.

General Publishing Co., Ltd., 30 Lesmill Road, Don Mills, Ontario, M3B 2T6 *T.* 416-445-3333.

*Harlequin Enterprises Ltd. (1949), 5th Floor, 220 Duncan Mill Road, Don Mills, Ontario, M3B 3J5 *T.* 416-445-5860. *Telex:* 06-966697. *Directors:* Richard A. N. Bonnycastle (Chairman). Romance.

Hodder & Stoughton, Ltd., 30 Lesmill Road, Don Mills, Ontario, M3B 2T6 *T.* 416-445-3333.

*Holt, Rinehart & Winston of Canada, Ltd., 55 Horner Avenue, Toronto, Ontario, M8Z 4X6 *T.* 416-255-4491.

House of Grant Canada Ltd., 98 Scarsdale Road, Don Mills, Ontario, M3B 2R8. Textbooks and General publishers.

Hurtig Publishers (1967), 10560 105 Street, Edmonton, Alberta, T5H 2W7 *T.* 403-426-2359. *President:* M. G. Hurtig. Reference, Humour, Biography, Political Science, Canadiana, Energy, Environment, Juvenile.

Lippincott (J. B.) Company of Canada, Ltd., 75 Horner Avenue, Toronto, Ontario, M8Z 4X7 *T.* 416-252-5277. Medical, Nursing, College and Allied Health publications.

*Longman Canada Limited, *Executive Offices:* 55 Barber Greene Road, Don Mills, Ontario, M3C 2A1 *T.* 444-7331. General, Educational and Medical.

*McClelland & Stewart, Limited (1908), 25 Hollinger Road, Toronto, M4B 3G2
T. 416-751-4520. *Directors:* J. G. McClelland, L. H. Ritchie, Pierre Berton,
F. Newfeld, Mrs. E. Franklin, Farley Mowat, R. I. Martin, Q.C., D. C.
Early, D. W. Casey, S. L. Orenstein, P. Taylor, Mrs. A. Porter. General
and Educational publishers.

*McGill-Queen's University Press, 1020 Pine Avenue West, Montreal, Quebec,
H3A 1A2 *T.* 514-392-4421. London Agents: Canada Books International,
Bedford Road, London, N2. *T.* 01-444 5237. Academic.

*McGraw-Hill Ryerson Ltd., 330 Progress Avenue, Scarborough, Ontario, M1P
2Z5 *T.* 416-293-1911. Educational and Trade Books.

Maclean-Hunter Ltd. (1887), 481 University Avenue, Toronto, M5W 1A7.
Magazines, Financial, Business and Industrial Newspapers, Books and
Educational Materials. London Office: Maclean-Hunter Ltd., 30 Old Burl-
ington Street, London, W1X 2AE.

Macmillan Company of Canada Limited (1905), 70 Bond Street, Toronto, M5B
1X3. General publishers who pay special attention to what is worth while
of Canadian authorship. Unsolicited MSS not accepted. Agents for:
Academy Editions, London; Edward Arnold & Co., London; Lea & Febiger,
Philadelphia; Macmillan Publishers Ltd., London; St. Martin's Press Inc.,
New York; Gambit, Boston; Gill & Macmillan Ltd., Dublin; J. P. Tarcher
Inc., California; Oresko Books Ltd., London; Smithsonian Institution Press,
Washington, D.C.

Musson Book Company, 30 Lesmill Road, Don Mills, Ontario, M3B 2T6 *T.*
416-445-3333.

*Nelson (Thomas) & Sons (Canada), Ltd. (1914), 81 Curlew Drive, Don Mills,
Ontario, M3A 2R1 *T.* 416-444-7315. *T.A.* Thonelson, Don Mills, Ontario.
Telex: 06-966606. *Directors:* Jack Fleming (Chairman), Alan G. Cobham
(President), James A. Connolly, Barry G. Jones, Gerald Hamill, Kevin
Nolan, Paul T. Piper. Educational—Readers, Mathematics, French,
Science, Atlases. Some trade titles.

Oberon Press, 401A The Inn of the Provinces, Ottawa, K1R 7S8 *T.* 613-238-
3275. General.

*Oxford University Press (Canada), 70 Wynford Drive, Don Mills, Ontario, M3C
1J9 *T.* 441-2941. *Cables:* Frowde, Toronto. *Telex:* Frowde-Tor-
06-966518. *Manager:* L. M. Wilkinson. General, Educational, Medicine,
Religious, Juvenile and Canadiana.

PaperJacks, 330 Steelcase Road East, Markham, Ontario, L3R 2M1 *T.* 416-
495-1261.

*Prentice-Hall of Canada, Ltd. (1960), 1870 Birchmount Road, Scarborough,
Ontario, M1P 2J7 *T.* 293-3621. *Telex:* 065-25184. *Directors:* F. Dunni-
gan, W. A. Matheson, H. M. Warrington, G. B. Halpin and E. E. Campbell. Educational (Elementary, Secondary, Post-Secondary), General
History, Natural History, Politics, Sports.

University of Toronto Press, University of Toronto, Toronto, M5S 1A6 *T.*
978-2231 (Editorial); 978-2239 (Administration).

*Van Nostrand Reinhold, Ltd. (1970) (Canadian subsidiary).   This firm is wholly owned subsidiary of Litton Education Publishers, New York, and is affiliated with Van Nostrand Reinhold, Ltd., London.   1410 Birchmount Road, Scarborough, Ontario, M1P 2E7   *T.* 416-751-2800.   *Director:* Campbell B. Hughes (President). Science, Arts and Crafts, School Textbooks, College Texts, Non-Fiction Trade Books.

INDIAN PUBLISHERS

Allied Publishers Private, Ltd., 15 J. N. Heredia Marg, Ballard Estate, Bombay, 400 038; 17 Chittaranjan Avenue, Calcutta, 700 072; 13/14 Asaf Ali Road, New Delhi, 110 002; 150/B-6 Mount Road, Madras, 600 002; Jayadeva Hostel Building, 5th Main Road, Gandhi Nagar, Bangalore, 560 009. Distribution for A. & C. Black, Ltd., W. & R. Chambers, Ltd., John Murray (Publishers), Ltd., etc.

Asia Publishing House, Calicut Street, Ballard Estate, Bombay, 400 038; 67 Ganesh Chandra Avenue, Calcutta, 700 013; East View, 199 Mount Road, Madras, 600 002; Indra Palace, Connaught Circus, New Delhi, 110 001; Ananda Press, 18 Purana Quila, Lucknow, 226 001; 621–22 Avenue Road, Bangalore, 560 002. *London Office:* 10 Laystall Street, London, E.C.1. *T.* 01-278 2135. *New York Office:* 440 Park Avenue South, New York, N.Y., 10016. *T.* (212) 684-6246. Literature, General, including Art, Biography, Economics, Politics, World Affairs, Education, History, Library Science, Philosophy and Psychology, Science and Technology.

Atma Ram & Sons (1909), Post Box 1429, Kashmere Gate, Delhi, 110 006. *T.* 228159, 223092, 226137. *Cables:* Books Delhi. *Managing Proprietor:* Ram Lal Pury; *Senior Director:* Dr. V. S. Puri; *General Manager:* I. K. Puri. *Branches:* Chaura Rasta, Jaipur; University Enclave, Chandigarh; 17 Ashok Marg, Lucknow. Art, Literature, Reference, Biography, Fiction, Economics, Politics, Education, History, Philosophy, Psychology, Science, Technology. Books published in English and Hindi languages. Translations and reprints of foreign books undertaken. Bookseller and importers of foreign books on a large scale.

B.I. Publications, *Proprietor:* British Institute of Engineering Technology (India) Private, Ltd., 54 Janpath, New Delhi, 110001. *T.* 320973. *Chairman:* R. D. Bhagat. *General Sales Manager:* K. P. Churamani. Scientific, Technical, Medical, Business and Industrial Management, Eductional, Children's, Reference and General.

Blackie & Son (India), Ltd., Blackie House, 103–5 Walchand Hirachand Marg, Post Box 21, Bombay 400 001; 285-J Bepin Behari Ganguly Street, Calcutta, 700 012; 4/16-B Asaf Ali Road, New Delhi, 110 001; 2/18 Mount Road, Madras, 600 002.

English Book Depot (1923), 15 Rajpur Road, Dehra Dun (U.P.). *T.* 3792 and 3187. *Directors:* Sukhdev Arora, Dev Dutt Arora. Military Science and allied subjects.

Hind Pocket Books Orient Paperbacks, 36-c Connaught Place, New Delhi, 110 001. *T.* 40115–6. *T.A.* Pocketbook Delhi. Paperbacks in Indian languages and English. *Managing Director:* D. N. Malhotra.

Indian Press (Publications) Private, Limited, 36 Pannalal Road, Allahabad (U.P.) *T.* 53190. *T.A.* Publikason. Branches and agencies in all principal towns of India. *Overseas Stockists:* Luzac & Co., Ltd., 46 Great Russell Street, London, WC1. Stecher Hafner Inc., 31 East 10th Street, New York, 10003, N.Y. Publishers of *Saraswati Hindi Monthly Magazine,* and School, College, University and General books in Hindi, Bengali, English; Gurumukhi, Urdu, Marathi, Nepali ltnguages. *Directors:* M. D. D. P. Ghosh, S. P. Ghosh, P. K. Mukherjee and P. K. Ghosh.

Kothari Publications, Jute House, 12 India Exchange Place, Calcutta, 700001, G.P.O. Box 382. *T.* 22-9563, 22-6572, 45-0009. *Proprietor:* Ing H. Kothari of Sujangarh, Rajasthan. Publishers of Technical, General and Reference books. Publishers of *Who's Who* series in India. (Controlled by Kothari Organisation.) Agents for many foreign publishers.

Little Flower Co., The (1929), Bhurangam Buildings, 8 Ranganathan Street, Thyagarayanagar, Madras, 600017. *T.* 441538. *T.A.* LIFCO, Madras. LIFCO books. General, Fiction, Technical, Dictionaries, Astrology, Medicine, Legal, Commercial, Educational and Religious.

Macmillan Co. of India Ltd., The, *Head Office:* 2/10 Ansari Road, Daryaganj, New Delhi, 110 002. *Branches:* Bombay: Mercantile House, Magazine Street, Reay Road (East), Bombay, 400010; Calcutta 294 Bepin Behari Ganguly Street, Calcutta, 700012; Delhi: 2/10, 4252 Ansari Road, Daryaganj, New Delhi, 110002; Madras: 6 Patullo Road, Madras, 600002. Associate Company of Macmillan Publishers Ltd., London. Publishers of Educational, Scientific, Technical, Medical, Fiction and General Books. Agents in India, Burma, Ceylon, Nepal and Bangladesh for: Dean & Son Ltd., London, J. M. Dent & Sons, Ltd., London (including Phoenix House and Galley Press), Gill & Macmillan Ltd., Dublin, The Macmillan Co. of Canada Ltd., Toronto, St. Martins Press, Inc., New York, The Hamlyn Publishing Group Ltd., Middlesex, England, Wm. Collins Sons & Co., Ltd., Glasgow (Educational Books and Fontana Paperbacks), Pan Books Ltd., London, Holt, Rinehart & Winston Inc., New York, W. B. Saunders Company, Philadelphia and London.

Natraj Publishers, 17 Rajpur Road, Dehra Dun, U.P., 248001. *T.* 3382. *Proprietor:* Sohan Lall. Specialists books on Military Science, Forestry, Agriculture and Geology.

New Book Company, Private, Ltd., The (1936), Kitab Mahal, 188–90 Dr. Dadabhai Naoroji Road, Bombay. *T.* 263544–5. Art, Technical, General.

Orient Longman Ltd., Regd. Office: 3/5 Asaf Ali Road, New Delhi, 110 002, and regional offices at 17 Chittaranjan Avenue, Calcutta, 700 072; Kamani Marg, Ballard Estate, Bombay, 400 038; 36A Anna Salai, Mount Road, Madras, 600 002; 1/24 Asaf Ali Road, New Delhi, 110 002. Educational, Scientific, Technical, Medical, General and Children's. Associated with the Longman Group Ltd. Agents and Distributors in India for Longman Group Ltd.; Macdonald & Co., Ltd., U.N.E.S.C.O., Paris; Penguin Books, Ltd., Macdonald & Evans, Ltd.

Oxford University Press (Indian Branch). *General Manager:* R. Dayal, Post Box 7035, 2/11 Ansari Road, Daryaganj, New Delhi, 110002; Post Box 31, Oxford House, Apollo Bunder, Bombay, 400 039; G.P.O. Box 530, Faraday House, P17 Mission Row Extension, Calcutta, 700 013; Post Box 1079, Oxford House, Mount Road, Madras, 600 006. *Cables:* Oxonian, Delhi, Oxonian, Bombay, Oxonian, Calcutta, Oxonian Madras. *T.* Delhi 27-3841–2 and 27-7812; Bombay 23-1029, 23-1198; Calcutta 23-3533, 23-3534; Madras 81-2267. Publishers in all lines. Agents in India, Burma, Sri Lanka and Nepal for Faber & Faber Ltd., and in India, Burma and Sri Lanka for Geo. G. Harrap & Co., Ltd. (educational books), Ginn & Co., Ltd. (selected titles), and Monthly Review Press, New York. It distributes books for the following university presses: Harvard, Princeton and Stanford.

Pustak-Bhandar, Govind Mittra Road, Patna, PIN 800 004 *T.* 50341. *Founder:* Acharya Ramlochan Saran. *Partners:* M. S. Singh, Dr. S. S. Singh, S. R. Saran, J. B. Saran. Literary, Scientific, and Educational books in English, Hindi, Nepali, Bengali, Urdu, Mathili, Sanskrit, Santhali, Oriya. Comic books for Children; publishes Children's Monthly Magazine in Hindi *Balak.*

R & K Publishing House now **H & K Publishing House**—see page 195.

Rajkamal Prakashan Private Ltd., 8 Netaji Subhash Marg, Delhi 110006. *T.* 274463. *T.A.* Prakashak. *Branch:* Opp. Science College, Patna, 6 *Publishers* of original and translated Literary and Educational books in Hindi and English, magazines (*Alochana, Prakashan Samachar*). Children's books.

Rajpal & Sons, Kashmere Gate, Delhi, 110006. *T.* 226201 and 223904. *T.A.* Rajpalsons, Delhi. Publishers of General and Textbooks in Hindi and English and also reprints and translations. *Managing Partner:* V. N. Malhotra.

Ranjan Gupta (1969), 22/3-C Galiff Street, Calcutta 700004. *T.* 55-4387. Specialising in rare books of Indology, Indian Philosophy, Religion, Art, Literature, History, Linguistics, Periodicals.

Rupa & Co., P.O. Box 12333, 15 Bankim Chatterjee Street, Calcutta, 700073. *T.* 34-4821. *T.A.* Rupanco, Calcutta-73.

Shiksha Bharati, Madarsa Road, Kashmere Gate, Delhi 110006. *T.* 229174. Publishers and printers of Textbooks in Hindi and English: also Juvenile Literature. *Partners:* V. Malhotra, S. Malhotra, K. Malhotra, M. Malhotra.

Taraporevala (D. B.) Sons & Co., Private, Ltd. (Original firm established 1864), 210 Dr. Dadabhai Naoroji Road, Bombay *T.* 261433. *Directors:* Mrs. Manekbai J. Taraporevala and Miss Sooni J. Taraporevala. *Chief Executive:* Prof. Russi J. Taraporevala. Books on India and on Indian Interest, Fine Arts, Handicrafts, Pictorial Albums, Business, Economics, Education, Electronics, Psychology, Cookery, Domestic Economy, Pets, Hobbies, Reference, Languages, Religion, Philosophy, Mysticism, Occult Sciences, Law, History, Culture, Mythology, Sociology, Health, Medical, Sex, Science, Technology, Self-Improvement, Self-Instruction, Sports, Indian Classics.

Thacker, Spink & Co, (1933), **Private, Ltd.,** P.O. Box 54, 3 Esplanade East, Calcutta, 1. *T.* 23-4214-5. Publishers of books on Indian Law, Engineering, Medicine, Anthropology, Gardening, Agriculture, Fiction, Domestic Economy, Sport, Shikar, Botany, Zoology, Science, Autobiography, Religion, History, Criminology, Philosophy and other subjects relating to India.

Thacker & Co., Ltd., P.O. Box 19, Rampart Row, Bombay 400 023. *T.* 252613, 252722 and 297466. *T.A.* Booknotes, Bombay. *Chairman:* Arvind N. Kilachand; *Chief Executive:* V. H. Khote. Publishers of books on all subjects of special Indian and Asiatic interest, also Economics, Sociology, History, Politics, Law, etc.

Theosophical Publishing House, The, Adyar, Madras, 600020. *T.* 412904.. *T.A.* Theotheca, Madras. Theosophical, Mystical and Occult literature. Publishers of *The Theosophist*, official organ of the President, Thesophical Society. *Editor:* International President of The Theosophical Society, John B. S. Coats. *Manager:* K. N. Ramanathan.

Theosophy Co. (India), Private, Ltd., Theosophy Hall, 40 New Marine Lines, Bombay, 400 020. *T.* 299024. *T.A.* Aryahata, Bombay. *Publishers Theosophical Movement, Aryan Path*, and other Theosophical publications.

United Asia Publications Pvt., Ltd. (1948), 12 Rampart Row, Bombay-1. *T.* 252158. Publishers of books and periodicals.

Vision Books Pvt. Ltd. (1975), 36-c Connaught Place, New Delhi, 110 001. *T.* 42062, 40116. *T.A.* Visionbook New Delhi. *Directors:* Sudhir Malhotra (Managing), Kapil Malhotra, Vishwanath. Fiction (including Indo-Anglian, translation from Indian languages and other languages), Indian Culture, Politics, Biography, Travel, Poetry, Drama, Management, Military, Religion.

Wiley Eastern Ltd. (1966), AB 8 Safdarjang Enclave, New Delhi, 110 016. *T.* 663972, 663806. *T.A.* Wileyeast. *Directors:* W. Bradford Wiley, Mrs. M. Orlando, E. B. Desai, A. R. Kundaji, F. N. Mulla, K. K. Lalkaka, B. D. Bharucha. Biology, Physics, Chemistry, Mathematics, Engineering Sciences.

H & K Publishing House, 5 Scindia House, New Delhi-1. *T.* 46118. Books on and about Indian Art, History, Cookery, Economics, Politics and Travel.

IRISH PUBLISHERS

Blackwater Press, The, an imprint of **Folens & Co. Ltd.,** *q.v.*
General Non-Fiction, Irish interest.

Catholic Communications Institute of Ireland, Inc.—see **Veritas Publications.**

*Dolmen Press, Nth. Richmond Street, Dublin 1. *T.* 01-740324. *Directors:* Liam Miller, Josephine P. Miller, Thomas Kinsella, William C. Browne, Alec Reid, Brendan Marnell.
Irish Literature and books of Irish interest.

Duffy (James) & Co., Ltd. (1830), 21 Shaw Street, Dublin, 2. *T.* 778115. Works of a Catholic, Irish, historical or educational nature, and plays.

Educational Company of Ireland, Ltd., The, Ballymount Road, Walkinstown, Dublin 12. *T.* Dublin 500611. *Directors:* M. W. Smurfit (Chairman), J. J. Smurfit, W. J. Connolly, J. Harrison, G. F. Carroll, F. Maguire, D. F. T. Austin, M. O'Sullivan.
Educational MSS. on all subjects in English or Gaelic.

Fallon (C. J.) Ltd. (1927), Lucan Road, Palmerstown, Dublin 29. *T.* 365777. *Directors:* C. Gore-Grimes (Chairman), E. J. White, H. J. McNicholas, A. Gore-Grimes.
Educational and Religious text books.

Figgis (Allen) & Co., Ltd., The Mall, Donnybrook, Dublin 4. *T.* 760461. *Directors:* S. E. Allen Figgis (Managing), Jonathan Goodbody.
Books by Irish authors, or of Irish interest: Archaeology, Art, Belles-Lettres, Biography and Memoirs, Fiction, General, History, Law, Travel.

Folens & Co., Ltd., Airton Road, Tallaght, Co. Dublin. *T.* 502932.
Educational (Primary, Secondary, Comprehensive, Technical, in English and Irish). Educational Children's Magazines.

*Gill & Macmillan, Ltd. (1968), 15–17 Eden Quay, Dublin 1. *T.* 788455.
Biography or Memoirs, Educational (Primary, Secondary, University), History, Philosophy, Sociology, Theology and Religion, Literature.

Irish Academic Press (1974), 3 Serpentine Avenue, Ballsbridge, Dublin, 4. *T.* 01-688236. Publishes under the imprints **Irish University Press, Irish Academic Press** and **Ecclesia Press.** *Directors:* Michael Adams, Frank Cass, Leonard Maxwell Harvey, John Mladinich, Gilbert Raff, Michael Richard Sefi, Michael Philip Zaidner.
Scholarly, Technical, Scientific, Religious and Bibliographical Books.

Longman, Browne & Nolan, Ltd., now incorporated in **Educational Company of Ireland, Ltd.,** *q.v.*

*Mercier Press, Ltd., The (1945), 4 Bridge Street, Cork, Ireland.   *T.* Cork 54022.
Directors: Capt. J. M. Feehan, J. C. O'Connor, P. W. McGrath, D. J. Keily, C. U. O. Marcaigh, M. Feehan, L. McNamara, J. F. Spillane.
Irish Literature, Folklore, History, Education, Theology.

National Press, The (1935), 2 Wellington Road, Dublin, 4.   *T.* Dublin 689105.
Director: P. Cannon.   *Secretary:* M. A. Fortune.
Educational.

O'Brien Educational (1976), 11 Clare Street, Dublin 2.   *T.* 979598 and 452162.
Directors: Michael O'Brien, Seamus Cashman.
Humanities, Science.

O'Brien Press Ltd., The (1974), 11 Clare Street, Dublin 2.   *T.* 979598.   *Directors:* Michael O'Brien, Valerie O'Brien.
Folklore, Nature, Fiction, Architecture, Topography.

*Runa Press, The (1942), 2 Belgrave Terrace, Monkstown, Dublin.   *T.* 801869 and 805000.
Belles-Lettres, Educational (University), Essays, Poetry, Science, Philosophy.

School and College Services Ltd. (1968), 16 Pembroke Road, Dublin, 4   *T.* 600187, 600493, 681254.   *Directors:* Patrick M. O'Brien, Geraldine O'Brien, J. Dooley, S. McGowan.
Educational Books for Primary and Secondary Schools.

*Talbot Press, Ltd., Ballymount Road, Walkinstown, Dublin, 12.   *T.* 500611.
T.A. Publish Dublin.
Publishers of books which reflect the Irish way of life in History, Sociology, Folklore, Poetry and Fiction.   Religious and Liturgical work also published.

*Veritas Publications, a division of the **Catholic Communications Institute of Ireland, Inc.,** Veritas House, Lower Abbey Street, Dublin, 1   *T.* 788177.
Religion, including Social and Educational Works, and material relating to the Media of Communication.

NEW ZEALAND PUBLISHERS

* Membership of the New Zealand Book Publishers' Association

*Auckland University Press (1966), University of Auckland, Private Bag, Auckland. *T.* 74740, ext. 354. *Chairman of University Press Committee:* M. P. K. Sorrenson. *Managing Editor:* R. D. McEldowney. Represented by Oxford University Press. New Zealand Studies—especially history and literature. Works of scholarship in general.

Butterworths of New Zealand, Ltd., 77–85 Customhouse Quay, Wellington. *T_e* 722-021.

*Cassell Limited, Box 36-013, Northcote Central, Auckland, 9. *T.* 484-371, and 484-055.

*Caxton Press, The, Ltd., 119 Victoria Street, Christchurch, N.Z., P.O. Box 25–088. *T.A.* Imprint, Christchurch. *Directors:* L. V. Bensemann, D. L. Donovan. Fine printers, and publishers since 1935 of New Zealand books of many kinds, including Verse, Fiction, Biography, History, Natural History, Travel, and Children's books. Publishers of the literary quarterly *Landfall* (*q.v.*).

*Collins (William) Publishers Ltd., P.O. Box 1, Auckland. *T.* 447-299. *Cables:* Folio Auckland. (Parent Company **William Collins, Sons & Co., Ltd.,** 14 St. James's Place, London). *Managing Director:* D. L. Bateman. *Managing Editor:* Ian MacArthur. *Publishing Editor:* David Elworthy. Publishers of General Literature, Fiction, Bibles, Children's Books, Reference Books, Educational, Technical, Paperbacks.

*Heinemann, William (N.Z.), Ltd., 16–18 College Road, P.O. Box 36020, Northcote, Auckland, 9 *T.* 487 193. William Heinemann, Ltd.; Wm. Heinemann Medical Books, Ltd.; Peter Davies, Ltd.; Secker & Warburg, Ltd.; World's Work, Ltd.; representing also Epworth Press, John Murray (Publishers), Ltd., Student Christian Movement Press, Daily Express, Lutterworth Press, Sotheby Parke Bernet, Stemmer House, Springwood Books Ltd.

*Heinemann Educational Books (N.Z.). Ltd. (1969), 26 Kilham Avenue, P.O. Box 36064, Auckland, 9. *T.* 489153–4. *T.A.* Hebooks, Auckland. *Telex:* NZ2244 Alptrav. *Directors:* A. Hill (Chairman), D. J. Heap (Managing), A. R. Beal, K. Nettle, A. G. Wernham. Secondary and Tertiary Textbooks, specialist and technical titles, New Zealand literature.

*Hodder & Stoughton Ltd., P.O. Box 39038 Auckland West. *Showroom:* 52 Cook Street, Auckland. *T.* 799-865. *T.A.* Expositor, Auckland. *Telex:* NZ21422.

*Hutchinson Group (NZ) Ltd. (1977), P.O. Box 40086, 32–34 View Road, Glenfield, Auckland, 10. *T.* 447-197 and 524. *Directors:* R. A. A. Holt (Chairman), K. C. Pounder (Managing), N. G. Sturt (General Manager). Fiction, Junior Books, Educational and University; Sports and Pastimes, Religion, Non-Fiction.

*Jacaranda Wiley Ltd., 32 Nikau Street, Mt. Eden, Auckland 3. *T.* 773016. *Head Office:* Milton, Queensland, 4064, Australia, *q.v.*

*Longman Paul Limited, P.O. Box 4019, Auckland. *T.* 446-183 and 446-089. *Cable and T.A.* Freegrove, Auckland. Publishers of New Zealand books both Educational and General.

*McIndoe, John, Ltd. (1968), 51 Crawford Street, P.O. Box 694, Dunedin. *T.* 70-355. *Directors:* J. McIndoe, M. M. McIndoe. All categories.

Methuen New Zealand Ltd., 238 Wakefield Street, Wellington, 1. *T.* 847 629. *Directors:* A. D. Mackie (Managing), Miss E. A. Mallinson. Educational, Tertiary, General.

*Minerva Bookshop, Ltd. (1946), C.P.O. Box 2597, 13 Commerce Street, Auckland, 1. *T.* 30-863. *T.A.* Minerva. *Managing Director:* Esther Porsolt, *Director:* Nigel Faigan. Books of New Zealand interest, Educational.

*New Zealand Council for Educational Research (1933), Box 3237, Education House, 178–182 Willis Street, Wellington, 1. *T.* 847 939. *T.A.* Edsearch. *Director:* John E. Watson. Education including educational administration and planning, rural education, early childhood education, higher education, Maori schooling, educational achievement tests, etc.

New Zealand University Press, Suite 4, Book House, Boulcott Street, Wellington. *Postal Address:* P.O. Box 2919, Wellington. *T.* 727 533. *T.A.* MICE. Scholarly and Educational books. A division of **Price Milburn & Co., Ltd.**

*Oxford University Press (New Zealand Branch), Walton House, 66 Ghuznee Street, Wellington, C.1. *Manager:* John Griffin. *Postal Address:* G.P.O. Box 11344. *Cables:* Oxonian, Wellington. *T.* 847 413 and 844 945.

*Pegasus Press, Ltd. (1948), 14 Oxford Terrace, Christchurch. *T.* 64-509. *Directors:* Albion Wright (Managing), M. R. Muir (Editorial), P. J. Skellerup, P. J. Low, D. H. Wallace. Publishers of high quality Fiction and Poetry, Historical works, Biographies, Art, and other illustrated books on Sport and Travel in New Zealand. Proprietors of the Pegasus Press.

*Pitman Publishing New Zealand Ltd., 58 Fitzherbert Street, Petone, Wellington, New Zealand. *T.* 684 568. *Chairman:* Philip Harris; *Managing Director:* Gil McGahey; *Sales Manager:* Murray Grigg. Technical, Educational, General, Commercial, Medical, Legal, Photography and Art and Crafts.

*Price Milburn & Co., Ltd., *Editorial and Trade:* Suite 2, Book House, Boulcott Street, Wellington. *Postal Address:* P.O. Box 2919, Wellington. *T.* 727 533. *Warehouse:* 39 Whiteman's Road, Silverstream. *T.* UH-85254. *Cables:* MICE Wellington. *Directors:* James Milburn, Helen Anderson, Lex Familton, Hugh Price, *Secretary*, Syd Heppleston. New Zealand books, particularly Cookery, University Textbooks, Literature, quality Children's Fiction, Primary School Texts especially School Readers and Social Studies. *Allied Activities:* New Zealand University Press. Distributors for Kea Press, Limited, Bowmar Publishing Corp., PM Records. Publishers to N.Z. Institute of International Affairs, the New Zealand Council of Civil Liberties, and Victoria University Press. Distributors of Records and Cassettes.

*Reed (A. H. & A. W.), Ltd. (1907), 65–67 Taranaki Street, Wellington.   Also at Auckland, Christchurch, Sydney and London.   *T.* Wellington 858849. *T.A.* Reedkiwi, Wellington.   *Directors:* M. J. Mason (Chairman), A. W. Reed, F. A. Davey, J. M. Reed.   General books in all categories, Primary and Secondary School books, Polytechnic and University Textbooks.

Sweet & Maxwell (N.Z.), Ltd., 238 Wakefield Street, Wellington, C1.   *T.* 859 777. *T.A.* Comlaw.   *Directors:* A. D. Mackie (Managing), Miss E. A. Mallinson.   Law and Accounting.

*Taylor (Alister), Publishing Ltd. (1971), Waiura, Martinborough, Wairarapa. *T.* Featherston 69847.   *T.A.* Taylor.   *Directors:* Alister Taylor, G. D. McGregor.   Publishers of New Zealand books: General, Educational (Secondary and Tertiary), Limited Edition Art Books, Contemporary N.Z. Art, Poetry, Fiction, N.Z. Social and Political History.

Victoria University Press (1974), Victoria University of Wellington, Private Bag, Wellington.   *T.* 721-000.   *Chairman of the Publications Committee:* Professor D. F. McKenzie.   *Publisher:* Hugh Price of Price Milburn.   Academic, scholarly books.

*Viking Sevenseas Ltd., 5–7 Tory Street, P.O. Box 1431, Wellington.   *T.* 859-759.   *T.A.* Viking.   *Managing Director:* M. B. Riley.   Music, Craft books, Polynesian, General.

*Whitcoulls Ltd.   *Head Office and Editorial:* Whitcoulls Ltd., Private Bag, Christchurch, 1.   *T.A.* Whitcoulls, Christchurch.   Publishers of New Zealand books of all descriptions, General and Educational.

OTHER COMMONWEALTH PUBLISHERS

GHANA

Sedco Publishing Ltd., 16 South Liberia Road, Liberty Avenue, Accra. *T.* 21332. *Postal address:* P.O. Box 2051, Accra.

Moxon Paperbacks, Ltd. (1967), P.O. Box M. 160, Accra. *T.* 66640. *T.A.* Moxon, Accra. *Directors:* R. J. Moxon, M.A., O.B.E., Mark Gilbey, M.A., Oliver Carruthers, M.A., M.B.E. Biographies, Current Affairs, Travel, Short Novels, Short Stories, Cookery books and Cookery cards, Magazines and Journals.

Oxford University Press (Ghana Office), E. K. Nsiah (Representative), P.O.B. 5282, 9 Odoi Kwao Crescent, Nima Residential Area, Accra. *Cables:* Oxonian, Accra. *T.* Accra 25238.

HONG KONG

Heinemann Educational Books (Asia), Ltd. (1963), Yik Yin Building, 1st Floor, 321–3 To Kwa Wan Road, Kowloon, Hong Kong. *Postal Address:* K.P.O., Box 6086, Tsim Sha Tsui P.O., Kowloon, Hong Kong. *T.* 3-649221–4. *T.A.* Heinebooks, Hong Kong. *Telex:* HK 84463. *Directors:* Alan Hill, C.B.E. (Chairman), Leon Comber (Managing), K. Sambrook, A. R. Chettle, Tan Sri Professor Hamzah Sendut. Mathematics, Science, English Language, Asian Literature (in English), Geography, Social Studies, History, Medical, Dentistry, Management.

Longman Group (Far East) Ltd., G.P.O. Box 223, Hong Kong. *T.* 5-618171–5.

Macmillan Publishers (HK) Limited, Watson's Estate, Block A, 13/F, Causeway Bay, Hong Kong. *T.* 5-711373-4. *Cables:* Macpublish Hong Kong. *Telex:* HX5688. *Directors:* N. Carr (Managing), N. Byam Shaw, J. Ashby. Rupert Li. Educational (all subjects) and General.

Oxford University Press (East Asian Branch), News Building, 5th Floor, 633 King's Road, North Point, Hong Kong. *T.* 5-610138. *Cables:* Oxonian, Hong Kong.

KENYA

Longman Kenya Ltd., P.O. Box 45925, Nairobi. T. 555477, 555574.

Nelson, Thomas, & Sons Ltd., P.O. Box 73146, Nairobi. *T.* 26628.

Oxford University Press (East African Branch), A. Nassir (General Manager), P.O.B. 72532, 1st Floor, Science House, Monrovia Street, Nairobi, Kenya. *Cables:* Oxonian Nairobi. *T.* Nairobi 336377.

MALAYSIA

Heinemann Educational Books (Asia), Ltd. (1963), Suite 4012–4013, The Regent of Kuala Lumpur, Jalan Imbi, Kuala Lumpur 06-23. *T.* 420440 and 420451—see under Hong Kong.

Longman Malaysia Sdn. Berhad, 2nd Floor, Wisma Damansara, Jalan Semantan, Damansara Heights, Kuala Lumpur. *T.* 941461. *T.A.* Freegrove, Kualalumpur.

Oxford University Press (East Asia Branch), J. A. Nicholson (Regional Manager, East Asia), 3 Jalan 13/3, P.O. Box 1050, Jalan Semangat, Petaling Jaya, Selangor, Malaysia; Enshu Building, 3–3 Otsuka, 3-chome Bunkyo-Ku, Tokyo. *Cables:* Oxonian, Petaling Jaya, Oxonian Tokyo. *T.* Petaling Jaya 563111, Tokyo (942)-0101-3.

NIGERIA

African Universities Press, Pilgrim Books Ltd., 305 Herbert Macaulay Street, Yaba, P.O. Box 3560, Lagos. *T.* Lagos 45939. *Cables:* Pilgrim, Lagos. UK: Elsinore House, Buckingham Street, Aylesbury. *Directors:* L. N. Namme, J. E. Leigh. Educational, Law, Africana.

Evans Brothers (Nigeria Publishers), Ltd., Jericho Road, P.M.B. 5164, Ibadan. *T.* 62970–1–2. *Telex:* 31104 Edbook NG.

Longman Nigeria, Ltd., Private Mail Bag, 1036, Ikeja. *T.* Lagos 33007, 33176.

Macmillan Nigeria Publishers, Ltd., Molete Roundabout, P.O. Box 1463, Ibadan, Oyo State, Nigeria. *T.* 24316. *T.A.* Macbooks Ibadan. *Warehouse and Accounts:* Ilupeju Industrial Estate, Mushin, P.O. Box 264, Yaba. *T.* 31188. *Directors:* N. G. Byam Shaw, Olu Anulopo, Dr. A. Babs Fafunwa, C. R. Harrison. A branch of **Macmillan Education, Ltd.,** London.

Oxford University Press (Nigerian Branch), M. O. Akinleye, General Manager. Oxford House, Iddo Gate, Ibadan. *Postal address:* Private Mail Bag 5095, Ibadan. *T.* Ibadan 23066–7. *T.A.* and *Cable:* Oxonian Ibadan. *Trade Department:* OUP Reservation, Ibadan. *Postal Address:* P.M.B. 5142, Ibadan. *T.* 24117. *T.A.* and *Cable:* Frowde, Ibadan. *Telex:* 31121.

RHODESIA

Collins, William, (Africa) (Pty) Ltd., P.O. Box 2800, Salisbury.

Longman Rhodesia (Pvt.) Ltd., P.O. Box ST 125, Southerton, Salisbury. *T.* Salisbury 62711–4. *T.A.* Freegrove, Salisbury.

SINGAPORE

Chopmen Enterprises (1966), 428 Katong Shopping Centre, Singapore, 15. *T.* 401495. *Proprietor:* N. T. S. Chopra. Scholarly, Educational, Reference, Literary.

Federal Publications (S) Pte Ltd. (1957), 1A New Industrial Road, off Upper Paya Lebar Road, Singapore, 19. *T.* 2827545. *T.A.* Fedpubs, Singapore. *Telex:* Timesse RS 21239. *General Manager:* H. H. Chiam. Educational, Children's Books and General.

Heinemann Educational Books (Asia) Ltd. (1963), 41 Jalan Pemimpin, Singapore, 20. *T.* 252 1255—see under Hong Kong.

Oxford University Press (East Asian Branch), 41 Jalan Pemimpin (2nd Floor), Singapore, 20. *T.* 2523604/05. *Cables:* Oxonian, Singapore.

Soviet Gallery (1971), Shop 117, Shaw Centre, Scotts Road, Singapore, 9. *T.* 376673. *Proprietor:* Cho Jock Yong. Children's Books, General.

TANZANIA

Longman Tanzania Ltd., P.O. Box 3164, Dar es Salaam. *T.* Dar es Salaam 29748. *T.A.* and *Cables:* Longman, Dar es Salaam.

Oxford University Press (East African Branch), P.O.B. 5299, Maktaba Road, Dar es Salaam. *T.* Dar es Salaam 29209. *Cables:* Oxonian, Dar es Salaam.

UGANDA

Longman Uganda Ltd., P.O. Box 3409, Kampala. *T.* Kampala 42940.

ZAMBIA

Longman Zambia Ltd., P.O. Box 886, Lusaka. *T.* 73746.

Oxford University Press (Eastern African Branch), P.O. Box 2335, Lusaka. *T.* Lusaka 74583. *Cables:* Oxonian, Lusaka.

SOUTH AFRICAN PUBLISHERS

*Members of South African Publishers' Association

*Balkema (A. A.) Pty Ltd. (1931), P.O. Box 3117, 93 Keerom Street, Cape Town, 8000. *T.* 229009. *Director:* A. A. Balkema. Africana Series, Fine Art, Architecture, Nature. Balkema Academic and Technical Publications. South African historical and biographical studies. Learned journals and annuals. Distribution outside South Africa: A. A. Balkema, P.O. Box 1675, Rotterdam, Netherlands; and for USA and Canada: ISBS P.O. Box 555, Forest Grove, Oregon 97116.

Books of Africa (Pty) Ltd. (1961), 1004 Cape of Good Hope Savings Bank Building, St. George's Street, P.O. Box 1516, Cape Town, 8000. *T.* 22-7921. *Directors:* T. V. Bulpin, H. C. Ingle, G. Mackenzie. Books on any subject about Africa.

Butterworth & Co. (S.A.) (Pty) Ltd., 152–154 Gale Street, Durban, 4001. *T.* 66516. *T.A.* and *Cables:* Butterlaw, Durban.

Collins (William), (Africa) (Pty) Ltd., 602 CNA Building, 110 Commissioner Street, Johannesburg, 2001 (P.O. Box 8879, Johannesburg 2000). *T.* 838 2147–9. *Cables:* Fontana, Johannesburg. General Publications, Fiction, Reference Books, Bibles, Juveniles, School Textbooks and Paperbacks.

Hodder & Stoughton Southern Africa, P.O. Box 94, 45 Shortmarket Street, Cape Town, 8000. *T.* 41-1228.

*Juta & Company Ltd., P.O. Box 30, Cape Town, 8000. *T.* 71-1181 and P.O. Box 1010, Johannesburg, 2000. *T.* 833-6113. Educational and legal publishers. General and Educational Booksellers and Importers. Established 1853.

*Longman Penguin Southern Africa (Pty) Ltd., P.O. Box 1616, Vrystaat Street, Paarden Eiland, Cape Town. *T.* 51 7324.

*Lovedale Press, Lovedale, 5702, Cape Province. *T.* Alice 278, 167. Educational Religious and General book publications for African market.

*Macmillan South Africa (Publishers) (Pty) Ltd., Braamfontein Centre, Jorissen Street, Braamfontein, Johannesburg. (P.O. Box 31487, Braamfontein, 2017). *T.* 724-3364. Publishers of Academic Educational and General Books, as well as those of South African interest.

*Maskew Miller Ltd., 7–11 Burg Street, Cape Town, 8001. *T.* 22-4151. *Postal address:* P.O. Box 396, Cape Town, 8000. Educational and general publishers and booksellers; dealers in prints, artists' materials and stationery.

*Oxford University Press (Southern African Branch), Neville Gracie, *General Manager.* Oxford House, 11 Buitencingle Street, Cape Town, 8001. *Postal address:* Box 1141, Cape Town, 8000. 69 Walter Wise Building, 50 Joubert Street, Johannesburg, 2001. *Postal address:* P.O. Box 10413, Johannesburg, 2000. P.O. Box 37166, Overport 4067. Rms. 57–58, Roslin House, Baker Avenue, Salisbury. *Postal address:* Box 3892, Salisbury. *Cables:* Oxonian, Cape Town, Oxonian, Johannesburg, or Oxonian, Salisbury. *T.* Cape Town 41-0171; Johannesburg 22-2621; Salisbury 27848.

*Philip (David) Publisher (Pty) Ltd. (1971), P.O. Box 408, Claremont, 7735, Cape Province. *T*. 65-4968. *Directors:* David Philip, Marie Philip. Academic, History, Social Sciences, Biography, Belles Lettres, Africana, Reference Books, Food and Wine, Fiction.

Purnell & Sons (S.A.) (Pty) Ltd., Head Office: 97 Keerom Street, Cape Town. Branch Office: 505 C.N.A. Building, 110 Commissioner Street, Johannesburg. *T.A.* "Purprint". *Chairman:* D. A. da Cunha. *Managing Director:* J. St. C. Whittall. Publishers of Books of South African interest and stockists of General and Juvenile books for the B.P.C. Group, England, and other United Kingdom publishers.

*Shuter and Shooter (Pty) Ltd. (1925), Church Street, Pietermaritzburg, Natal. *T*. 28121. *T.A.* Shushoo. *Directors:* M. N. Prozesky (Managing), F. B. Oscroft, D. M. Craib, H. Lanzer, C. L. S. Nyembezi, C. A. Roy, W. N. Vorster, R. J. Watkinson, L. van Heerden.

*Struik (C.) Publishers (Pty) Ltd. (1957), Corner Wale & Loop Streets, P.O. Box 1144, Cape Town, 8000. *T*. 224204, 227456. *T.A.* Dekena. *Directors:* Mrs. J. W. Struik, G. Struik, P. Struik, W. F. Struik. Specialise in Non-Fiction Books dealing with Southern Africa.

Timmins (Howard B.) (Pty) Ltd. (1937), 45 Shortmarket Street, Cape Town, 8001. P.O.Box 94, Cape Town, 8000. *T*. 411228, 431485. *T.A.* Composite, Cape Town. General South African interest, Travel, Biography, Gardening, History. Represented by Robert Hale & Co.

*Van Schaik (J. L.) (1914), Pretoria, P.O. Box 724. Publishers of books in English, Afrikaans and African languages. Specialists in Afrikaans books.

Winchester Press (Pty) Ltd. (1967), P.O. Box 41490, Craighall, Transvaal, 2024. *T*. 42-8789. *Directors:* G. A. Winchester-Gould, Pamela Hadfield. Travel, Natural History, Africana.

Witwatersrand University Press, Jan Smuts Avenue, Johannesburg, 2001. *T*. 39-4011.

UNITED STATES PUBLISHERS

The following is a selected list; it includes few of the very many smaller firms, and few of the specialist publishers.

The introductory note "Writing Books" applies also to US Publishers.

*Members of the Association of American Publishers Inc.

L.H.: London house.

Abelard-Schuman, Limited, 666 Fifth Avenue, New York, N.Y., 10019. *T.* 212-489 2200. Biography, Science, History, Travel, Belles-Lettres, Children's Books. L.H.: Abelard-Schuman, Ltd., 450 Edgware Road, W2 1EG.

Abingdon Press, Editorial and Business Offices: 201 Eighth Avenue S., Nashville, Tennessee, 37202. *T.* 615-749 6403. *Editorial Director:* Ronald P. Patterson. Religious, General, College and Children's Books.

*Addison-Wesley Publishing Company, Inc., Reading, Massachusetts 01867. *T.* 617 944-3700. University and School Books in Pure and Applied Science, Business and Economics, Education, Social Science; Children's Books.

*Atheneum Publishers (1960), 122 East 42nd Street, New York, 10017. *T.* 212-661-4500. General, Fiction, Poetry, Drama, Juveniles.

*Atlantic Monthly Press, 8 Arlington Street, Boston, Massachusetts, 02116. *Director:* Peter Davison. *Editor of Children's Books:* Melanie Kroupa. (Books are published in association with Little Brown & Co., and appear under joint imprint "Atlantic-Little, Brown".)

MSS. of permanent interest, Fiction, Biography, Autobiography, History, Current Affairs, Social Science, Poetry, Belles Lettres, Natural History, Children's books. The opportunity of serialising our books in whole or in part in *The Atlantic* is frequently of assistance in advancing the interests of the author.

Baker (Walter H.) Company (1845), 100 Chauncy Street, Boston, Mass., 02111. *President:* M. Abbott Van Nostrand. *Editor:* John B. Welch. *Treasurer:* Louis Cooper. Plays and Books on the Theatre. Also agents for plays. *London agents:* Samuel French, Ltd., 26 Southampton Street, London, WC2E 7JE.

Barnes (A. S.) & Co., Forsgate Drive, Cranbury, New Jersey, 08512. *T.* 609-655 0190. General publishers.

Beacon Press, 25 Beacon Street, Boston, Mass., 02108. *T.* 617-742 2110. Non-Fiction only in fields of Religion, Ethics, Philosophy, Current Affairs, History, Literary Criticism, Psychology and Sociology.

Better Homes and Gardens Books (Publishing Group, Meredith Corporation), 1716 Locust Street at 17th Des Moines, Iowa, 50336. *T.* 515-284-9011. *Editorial Director:* Don Dooley. Publishes Non-Fiction in all family and home service categories including Decorating, Gardening, and Do-It-Yourself How to do it books. Publisher suggests outline be submitted first. Address manuscripts and/or material to the above address.

Bobbs-Merrill Company, Inc., The, 4300 West 62nd Street, Indianapolis, Indiana, 46268, and 4 West 58th Street, New York, N.Y., 10019. *T.* 212-688 6350 (trade editorial office). Biographies, History, Travel, Current Affairs, Novels and Children's Books.

*Bowker (R. R.) Co.,** 1180 Avenue of the Americas, New York City, N.Y., 10036. *T.* 212-764-5100. Bibliographies and reference tools for the book trade and literary and library worlds.

*Braziller, George, Inc.** (1954), 1 Park Avenue, New York, N.Y., 10016. *T.* 212-889-0909. Philosophy, Science, Art, Architecture, History, Fiction, Environment, Ecology.

Breakthrough Press Inc. (1971), 27 Washington Square North, New York, N.Y. 10011. *T.* 212-228 1440. *Directors:* Anthony De Vito, Stewart H. Benedict. Contemporary Playwrights, full length and one-act plays both American and foreign authors represented.

*Cambridge University Press (American branch),** 32 East 57th Street, New York, N.Y., 10022. *T.* 212-688-8885.

Collier Macmillan International, 866 Third Avenue, New York, N.Y., 10022. *Cable address:* Pachamac, N.Y. *London:* Cassell and Collier Macmillan Publishers Ltd., 35 Red Lion Square, WC1R 4SG; *Australia:* Collier Macmillan Australia, P.O. Box 52, Camperdown, N.S.W., 2050; *New Zealand:* Cassell and Company Ltd., P.O. Box 36013, 48 Lake Road, Northcote, Auckland, 9; *Canada:* Collier Macmillan Canada Ltd, 1125 B Leslie Street, Don Mills, Ontario; *South Africa:* Collier Macmillan South Africa (Pty) Ltd., P.O. Box 17, Kempton Park, Transvaal. Publishers of Encyclopaedias, Text and Reference Books, Paperbacks, General Trade and Juvenile Books.

Collins+World (Wm. Collins+World Publishing Co., Inc.), 2080 West 117th Street, Cleveland, Ohio, 44111. *T.* 216-941-6930. Bibles, Webster's New World Dictionaries, Children's Books, Religious and Inspirational, Fount Religious Paperbacks, General Books.

*Columbia University Press,** 562 West 113th Street, New York, N.Y., 10025. *T.* 212-678-6777. England: 15A Epsom Road, Guildford, Surrey, GU1 1JT. Scholarly work in all fields and serious Non-Fiction of more general interest.

Concordia Publishing House (1869), 3558 S. Jefferson Avenue, St. Louis, Mo., 63118. *T.* 314-664-7000. Religious Books, Prayer Books, etc.

Contemporary Books Inc (formerly **Henry Regnery Co.**) 180 North Michigan Avenue, Chicago, Illinois, 60601. *T.* 312-782-9181. *President:* Harvey Plotnick. Fiction, Non-Fiction.

*Cornell University Press** (including **Comstock Publishing Associates**) (1869), 124 Roberts Place, Ithaca, New York, 14850. *T.* 607-257-7000. *University Publisher:* Roger Howley. Scholarly Books. *Agents Overseas:* Cornell University Press, Ltd., 2–4 Brook Street, London, W1Y 1AA.

Coward, McCann & Geoghegan, Inc., 200 Madison Avenue, New York, N.Y., 10016. *T.* 212-576-8900. *Cables:* Cowmagan, N.Y. *President:* John J. Geoghegan. *Vice-President & Editor-in-Chief:* Patricia B. Soliman. *Executive Editor:* Joseph Kanon. *Managing Editor:* Catherine Rossbach. *V.P. Juvenile Dept. & Editorial Director:* Ferdinand N. Monjo. General publishers. Fiction, Juveniles, Religion, Biography, Mystery, History.

Criterion Books, 666 Fifth Avenue, New York, N.Y., 10019. *T.* 212-489-2200. General Fiction and Juveniles.

*Crowell, Thomas Y., Co.** (1834), 10 East 53rd Street, New York, 10022. *T.* 212-593-7000. Non-Fiction, Juvenile, Reference, College and Secondary School Texts and Audio-Visual Materials.

*Crown Publishers, Inc.,** One Park Avenue, New York, N.Y., 10016. *T.* 532-9200. *President:* Nat Wartels. *Editor-in-Chief:* Herbert Michelman. General Fiction, Non-Fiction, Illustrated Books and Children's Books.

Devin-Adair Co., The** (1911), 143 Sound Beach Avenue, Old Greenwich, Connecticut, 06870. *T.* 203-637 4531. *Directors:* Devin A. Garrity (President). General Non-Fiction.

*Dial Press, The,** a division of **Dell Publishing Co., Inc.,** 1 Dag Hammarskjold Plaza. New York, N.Y. 10017. *T.* 212-832-7300 General Fiction, Non-Fiction and Juveniles.

*Dodd, Mead & Co., Inc.,** 79 Madison Avenue, New York, N.Y., 10016. *T.* 685-6464. Fiction, Children's Books, History, Biography, Art, Belles-Lettres, Sports, College Textbooks, etc. A leaning toward Biography, Travel, Fiction of a permanent kind, Mystery Stories, and Juveniles.

*Doubleday & Company, Inc.,** 245 Park Avenue, New York, 10017. *T.* 212-953 4561. *T.A.* Doubday, New York. L.H.: 100 Wigmore Street, W1H 9DR. *T.* 01-935 1269. Trade, Crime, Science Fiction and Westerns. Anchor Press—Books for young readers.

*Dutton (E.P.) & Co., Inc.,** 2 Park Avenue, New York, N.Y., 10016. *T.* 212-725-1818. General publishers. General Non-Fiction of all kinds, including Biographies, Adventure, History, Travel; Fiction, Mysteries, Juveniles, Paperbacks.

*Farrar, Straus & Giroux, Inc.** (incorporating **Octagon Books, Hill and Wang** and **The Noonday Press**—paperbacks), 19 Union Square West, New York City, N.Y., 10003. General publishers.

Fearon/Pitman Publishers, Inc.,** 6 Davis Drive, Belmont, California 94002. *T.* 415-592-7810. Elementary/High School special education materials, Textbooks, Reading Materials, Teacher-Aids, High School business education materials.

French (Samuel), Inc.,** 25 West 45th Street, New York, N.Y. 10036. *T.* 212-582-4700, and 7623 Sunset Boulevard, Hollywood, California, 90046. Play publishers and author's representatives (dramatic).

*Greene (Stephen) Press** (1957), Fessenden Road, Indian Flat, Brattleboro, Vermont, 05301. *T.* 802-257-7757. *Directors:* Janet C. Greene, Stephen Greene, Robert T. Gannett, Ralph Nading Hill, Stephanie N. F. Greene. Americana, Conservation and Nature, Country Living, Cook Books, Sports: Skiing, Snowshoeing, Kayaking, Riding, Orienteering, Crafts, Shortline Railroad (books), General adult non-fiction, etc.

*Grosset & Dunlap, Inc.,** 51 Madison Avenue, New York, N.Y. 10010. *T.* 212 MU9-9200. Adult Non-Fiction, Juveniles, Popular Reference Books, Children's Picture Books, Series Books, Activity Books, and Religious Books.

Hale, E. M. & Company** (1934), 20 Waterside Plaza, New York, N.Y., 10010. *T.* 212-889-9520. Distributes books under the **Harvey House** imprint.

Harcourt Brace Jovanovich, Inc. (1919), 757 Third Avenue, New York, N.Y., 10017. *T.* 212-888-4444. *Chairman and President:* William Jovanovich. U.K. office: 24–28 Ovan Road, London, NW1 7DX. General, Textbook and Educational Tests publishers. Fiction, Biography, Travel, Juveniles, Poetry, Current Events, History.

*Harper & Row, Publishers (1817), 10 East 53rd Street, New York, N.Y., 10022. *T.* 593-7000. *Cable Address:* Harpsam, N.Y. London Office: 28 Tavistock Street, London, WC2E 7PN. Fiction, History, Biography, Poetry, Science, Travel, Juvenile, Educational, Business, Technical, Medical, and Religious.

*Harvard University Press, 79 Garden Street, Cambridge, Mass., 02138. *T.* 617-495-2600. *London:* 126 Buckingham Palace Road, London, SW1. *T.* 01-730 9208.

Harvey House (a division of **E. M. Hale & Co.**) (1956), 20 Waterside Plaza, New York, N.Y. 10010. *T.* 212-889-9520. *President:* Lawrence F. Reeves; *Vice-President:* Paul D. Rust. *Managing Editor:* L. J. Bognod. Original children's books.

Hastings House Publishers Inc. (1936), 10 East 40th Street, New York, N.Y. 10016. *T.* 689-5400. *Cables:* Hastinpub New York. *Directors:* Walter W. Frese, Russell F. Neale, Margaret P. Frese.
General, Architecture, Decoration, Design, History, Travel, Americana, Photography, Graphic Arts, Sports, Cookery and Wines, Children's Books, Communication Arts (Television, Film, Radio).

*Hawthorn Books, Inc. (1952), 260 Madison Avenue, New York, N.Y., 10016. *T.* 212-725 7740. General Non-Fiction. *European Representative:* Feffer and Simmons, Inc.

*Heath (D. C.) and Co., a division of **Raytheon Co.,** 125 Spring Street, Lexington, Mass., 02173. *T.* 617–862-6650.

*Holt, Rinehart and Winston, Inc. (1866), 383 Madison Avenue, New York, N.Y., 10017. *T.* MU8-9100. A subsidiary of **C.B.S.** General publishers. Fiction, History, Biography, etc.; College and School Textbooks of all kinds; Children's; Technical; Reference; Religious; Dictionaries. Publishes books formerly published by **Dryden Press, Henry Holt & Co., Rinehart & Co.,** and **The John C. Winston Co.**

*Houghton Mifflin Company (1832), 2 Park Street, Boston, Mass., 02107. *T.* 617-725-5000. Fiction, Biography, History, works of General Interest of all kinds, both adult and juvenile, also School and College Textbooks in all departments, and Standardised tests. Best *length:* 75,000–180,000 words; juveniles, any reasonable length.

John Day Company, Inc., The, 666 Fifth Avenue, New York, N.Y., 10019. *T.* 212-489-4695. *Cable address:* Daypublish, N.Y. Fiction, Non-Fiction, Juveniles.

Keats Publishing Inc. (1971), 36 Grove Street, P.O. Box 876, New Canaan, Connecticut, 06840. *T.* (203) 966-8721. *Directors:* Nathan Keats (President), An Keats (Editor-in-Chief), Gilbert Raff, John Weiboldt. Natural Health, Medical, Regional and Religious Books.

*Knopf (Alfred A.), Inc. (1915), a division of **Random House, Inc.,** 201 East 50th Street, New York, N.Y., 10022. *T.* 212-572-2131. *T.A.* Knopf, New York. General Literature, Fiction, Belles-Lettres, Sociology, Politics, History, Nature, Science, etc.

*Lippincott (J. B.) Co. (1792), East Washington Square, Philadelphia, Pa., 19105. *T.* 215-574-4200. *Cable:* Lippcot, Phila., and New York office (Adult and Juvenile Trade Editorial Depts.), 521 Fifth Avenue, New York, 10017. *T.* 212-MU7-3980. All classes of literature. Full-Length Fiction of all descriptions, also Biography, Juveniles, and other forms of General Literature. Educational Textbooks and Medical and Nursing Books and Journals. Religious books and Bibles published by **A. J. Holman Company** division (1801), East Washington Square, Philadelphia, Pa., 19105. *T.* 215-574-4200.

*Little, Brown and Company, 34 Beacon Street, Boston, Mass., 02106. *T.* 617-227-0730. *Cable:* Brownlit, Boston. General Literature, especially Fiction, Non-Fiction, Biography, History, Trade Paperbacks, Books for Boys and Girls as well as College, Law and Medical Books. Also publish *Atlantic Monthly Press Books* in association with **The Atlantic Monthly Company.**

Lothrop, Lee & Shephard Co., Inc. (1859), a division of **William Morrow & Co., Inc.,** 105 Madison Avenue, New York, N.Y., 10016. *T.* 212-889-3050. *Vice President / Editor-in-Chief:* Mrs. Edna Barth. Children's Books only.

*McGraw-Hill Book Co., 1221 Avenue of the Americas, New York, N.Y., 10020. *T.* 212-997-1221. Professional and Reference: Engineering, Scientific, Business, Architecture, Encyclopaedias. College Textbooks. High School and Vocational Textbooks: business, secretarial, career. Trade Books. See also McGraw-Hill Publishing Co., Ltd., McGraw-Hill House, Maidenhead, England, and McGraw-Hill Ryerson Ltd. of Canada.

McKay, David, Co., Inc., 750 Third Avenue, New York, N.Y., 10017. *T.* 949-1500. *T.A.* Davmacay. *President and Editor-in-Chief:* James Louttit. General Fiction, Non-Fiction, Juveniles, Reference Books, Foreign Language Manuals and Dictionaries.

Macrae Smith Co., 225 South 15th Street, Philadelphia, Pa., 19102. *T.* K15-4270. Adult and Juvenile ages 6 and up. Fiction and general Non-Fiction. No poetry or textbooks. Send manuscript.

*Messner, Julian (a **Simon & Schuster Division of Gulf & Western Corporation),** 1230 Avenue of the Americas, New York, N.Y., 10020. General Non-Fiction for ages 8 through high school.

Morehouse-Barlow Co., Inc., 14 East 41st Street, New York, N.Y., 10017. *T.* 212-532-4350. *President:* Ronald C. Barlow. *Vice-President:* Stanley Kleiman. *Editor-in-Chief* and *Production Manager:* Margaret L. Sheriff. Religious Books, Juveniles, Secondary Level Texts.

*Morrow (William) & Co., Inc., 105 Madison Avenue, New York, N.Y., 10016. *T.* 212-889-3050. J. Lawrence Hughes (President), Hillel Black (Editor-in-Chief), Constance Epstein (Juvenile Editor). General Literature, Fiction, and Juveniles. Interested in works dealing with American and Non-Fiction Foreign Life and History. Royalty.

Nelson (Thomas), Inc. (1854), 407 Seventh Avenue S., Nashville, Tennessee 37203. *T.* 615-244-3733. *New York Office (Juvenile editorial and Promotion):* 30 East 42nd Street, Room 1403, New York, N.Y., 10017. *T.* 212-697-5573. Publishers of Bibles, Juveniles, Religious, Non-Fiction.

Norton (W. W.) & Company, Inc., 500 Fifth Avenue, New York, 10036. *T.* 212-354-5500. General Fiction and Non-Fiction, Music, Boating, Psychiatry, reprints, College Texts, Science.

*Oxford University Press, Inc., 200 Madison Avenue, New York, N.Y., 10016. *T.*
212-679-7300. *Cables:* Frowde, New York. *President:* Byron S. Hollins-
head. All Non-Fiction, Bibles, College Textbooks, Religion, Medicals,
Technicals, Music.

Pantheon Books, a division of **Random House, Inc.,** 201 East 50th Street, New
York, N.Y., 10022. *T.* PL-1-2600. Fiction, Belles-Lettres, Translations,
Philosophy, History and Art, Sociology, Psychology, and Juvenile Books.

Pitman Publishing Corporation—see **Fearon/Pitman Publishers Inc.**

*Praeger Publishers (a Division of **Holt, Rinehart and Winston Inc.),** 383 Madi-
son Avenue, New York, N.Y., 10017. *T.A.* Prabooks, New York. Non-
Fiction on International Relations, History, Social Sciences, Economics,
Architecture, Design, Archaeology, Reference, Contemporary Issues, Urban
Affairs, Education.

*Prentice-Hall, Inc. (1913), Englewood Cliffs, New Jersey, 07632. *Overseas repre-
sentative:* Prentice-Hall International, Inc., 66 Wood Lane End, Hemel
Hempstead, Hertfordshire, HP2 4RG *T.* 0442-58531. *Cables:* Prenhall,
Hemel, England. *Telex:* 82445. Text, Technical and General Non-Fiction,
Business Selling and Management Books, Juveniles; Biographies and Auto-
biographies. Free-lance artists' and designers' work used.

Putnam's (G. P.) Sons, 200 Madison Avenue, New York, N.Y., 10016. *T.* 212-
883-5500. *President:* Walter J. Minton, *Secretary and Comptroller:* Robert
Copp. *Vice-President* and *Managing Director:* Peter Israel. *Vice-President, Sales:* William Thomas. *Editor-in-Chief:* Phyllis Grann. Publications of books in all divisions of literature. History, Economics, Political
Science, Natural Science, and Standard Literature. Also an important
group of Fiction. One of the largest publishers of books for children of all
ages.

*Rand McNally & Company, P.O. Box 7600, Chicago, Illinois, 60680. *T.* 312-
OR3-9100. Trade, School and College Publications including Juvenile
and Adult Non-Fiction, Textbooks, Maps, Guides, Atlases, Globes; Banking
Publications. *Chairman:* Andrew McNally III. *President:* Andrew
McNally IV.

*Random House, Inc., 201 East 50th Street, New York, N.Y., 10022. *T.* 212-PL
1-2600. General publishers.

Revell (Fleming H.) Co., Old Tappan, New Jersey, 07675. *T.* 201-768-8060.
Religious Books.

Rinehart & Company, Inc.—see **Holt, Rinehart and Winston, Inc.**

Roy Publishers, Inc. (1942), 30 East 74th Street, New York, 10021. *T.* 212-TR9-
5935. Well known before 1939 as the Warsaw publishing house Rój.
General publishers.

*St. Martin's Press, Inc., 175 Fifth Avenue, New York, N.Y., 10010. *T.* 674-5151.
T.A. Saintmart, New York. General.

*Scribner's (Charles) Sons (1846), Scribner Building, 597 Fifth Avenue, New York,
N.Y., 10017. *T.* 212-486 2700. General publishers of standard books in
Education, Biography, History, Science, Fiction, Belles-Lettres, Juveniles,
etc.

*Seabury Press (1951), 815 2nd Avenue, New York, N.Y., 10017. *T.* 557-0500. *President:* Werner Mark Linz. *Continuum Books Editor:* J. George Lawler. *Crossroad Books Editor:* Theodore McConnell. *Children's Books Editor:* James C. Giblin.   General Non-Fiction, Education, Literature, Psychology, Religious, Juveniles, Paperbacks.

Sheed Andrews and McMeel, Inc. (1933), 6700 Squibb Road, Mission, Kansas, 66202. *T.* 913-362-1523. *Editor-in-Chief:* James F. Andrews. General trade publishing, with emphasis on how-to-do-it and cartoon books.   Also books from a Catholic viewpoint.

*Simon & Schuster, 1230 Avenue of the Americas, New York, N.Y., 10020. *T.* 212-245-6400. *President:* Richard Snyder. *Editor-in-Chief:* Michael V. Korda. *Chairman Editorial Board:* Peter Schwed. General Non-Fiction, Fiction, Biography, Detective, Humour, Occasional Novelty Books.   Manuscripts not addressed to an editor by name will be returned unread.

*Stanford University Press, Stanford, California, 94305.   Scholarly Non-Fiction.

Theatre Arts Books, 333 Avenue of the Americas, New York, N.Y., 100144. *T.* 212-OR5-1815. *Director:* George Zournas. *Consultant:* Rosamond Gilder. Successor to the book publishing department of Theatre Arts (1921–1948), and controls all books formerly published by the magazine. Theatre, Dance and Allied Books—Costume, Materials, Tailoring, etc, a few Plays.

Tuttle (Charles E.), Co., Inc. (1949), Rutland, Vermont, 05701. *T.* 802-773-8930 and Suido I-chome, 2–6 Bunkyo-ku, Tokyo, Japan. *T.* 811-7106-9. *T.A.* Tuttbooks, Tokyo. *President:* Charles E. Tuttle. Oriental Art, Culture, History, Manners and Customs, Americana.

*University of California Press, 2223 Fulton Street, Berkeley, California, 94720. Publishes scholarly books, books of general interest, series of scholarly monographs, and scholarly journals. *British Office:* IBEG, Ltd., 2–4 Brook Street, London, W1Y 1AA.

University of Chicago Press, 5801 South Ellis Avenue, Chicago, Ill., 60637. *T.* 312-753-3344. *London Office:* 126 Buckingham Palace Road, SW1W 9SD *T.* 01-730 9208. The Press publishes Scholarly Books and Monographs, College Textbooks, Religious, Medical and Scientific Books, General Trade Books, Text/Fiche pictorial publications and a number of scholarly journals.

*Vanguard Press, Inc., 424 Madison Avenue, New York, N.Y., 10017. *T.* 753-3906. *Cable:* Vangpress, N.Y. *Director:* Miss Evelyn Shrifte. General trade publishers, Fiction, Non-Fiction and Juveniles.

*Viking Penguin, The (1925), 625 Madison Avenue, New York, N.Y., 10022. *T.* Plaza 5-4330. *President:* Thomas H. Guinzburg. *Executive Vice-President:* Morton Levin. *Editorial Director of Senior Trade Division:* Alan D. Williams. *Senior Consulting Editors:* Marshall Best and Malcolm Cowley. *Senior Editor:* Elizabeth N. Sifton. *Executive Editor:* William B. Decker, *Junior Books:* George Nicholson. *Studio Books:* David Bell. *Grossman Publishers:* Dan Okrent. General books, Fiction, Non-Fiction, Juveniles, Biography, Sociology, Poetry, Art, Travel, Studio Books, Viking Portable Library, Viking Compass Books, Viking Junior Books, Seafarer.

Walck (Henry Z.), Inc. (1958), a division of **David McKay & Co, Inc.,** 750 Third Avenue, New York, N.Y., 10017. *T.* 212-949-1500.   Juvenile Books. *Agents Overseas:* Feffer & Simons Inc., and Oxford University Press, Toronto.

Walker & Co. (1960), 720 Fifth Avenue, New York, N.Y., 10019. *T.* 265-3632. Samuel S. Walker Jr. (President). General publishers. Biography, History, Religion, Philosophy, Natural History, Travel and Adventure, World Affairs, Criticism, Fiction, Detective Fiction, Science Fiction, Juveniles.

*****Warne (Frederick) & Co., Inc.,** 101 Fifth Avenue, New York, N.Y., 10003. *T.* 212-675 1151. L.H.: 40 Bedford Square, London, WC1B 3HE. Juvenile and Young Adult Books.

*****Watts (Franklin), Inc.,** a subsidiary of **Grolier Inc.,** 730 Fifth Avenue, New York, N.Y., 10019. *T.* 212-757-4050. K-12, Jane's USA and New Viewpoints.

*****Westminster Press,** Witherspoon Building, Philadelphia, 19107. *T.* 215-893-4400. Fiction, Non-Fiction, Juveniles, and Religious.

*****Wiley (John) & Sons, Inc.** (1807), *now incorporates* **Interscience Publishers Inc.,** 605 Third Avenue, New York City, N.Y., 10016. *T.* 212-867-9800. *Directors:* W. Bradford Wiley, Charles B. Stoll, Eric S. Proskauer, Francis Lobdell, Andrew H. Neilly, Jr., William C. Eiseman, Marianne Orlando, Michael Harrris, Robert L. Sproull, Charles H. Lieb, Antonie T. Knoppers, Robert C. Douglas, Nils A. Kindwall. Scientific, Engineering, Agricultural, Business, Social Science, and Chemical Books. Royalty Basis. *Illustrations:* half-tones and line cuts. L.H.: John Wiley & Sons Ltd., Baffins Lane, Chichester, Sussex.

Winchester Press, 205 E. 42nd Street, New York, N.Y., 10017. *T.* 212-661-7210. *Cables:* Winchpress, N.Y. Outdoor, Sport, Nature, Conservation, Natural History, Games, Collecting, College textbooks.

Winston (The John C.) Company—see **Holt, Rinehart and Winston, Inc.**

World Publishing Company—see **Collins + World.**

BOOK CLUBS

A book club supplies its subscribing members, usually monthly, with its chosen book at less than the bookshop price of the publisher's original edition, and gives the opportunity for this to be exchanged for an alternate choice. Members undertake to purchase a minimum number of books in a club's programme of publication over the period covered by their subscription. The bargain appeal of the clubs is made possible by the guaranteed circulation of their choices, which in the case of a successful club can be very large indeed.

There are two kinds of Book Club, namely simultaneous and reprint. Simultaneous clubs, as their name suggests, issue their choices at approximately the same time as the trade editions of those titles are published.

The majority of book clubs are still *reprint clubs*, producing for their members reprinted club editions of books which have been published for nine months or more and offering these usually at appreciably lower prices than the simultaneous club prices.

The author's remuneration is normally in one payment on a royalty basis in respect of the number of copies sold of the club edition, and in some cases the author can obtain before publication a guarantee of a minimum figure.

Book Club Associates, 16 Mortimer Street, London, W1N 8QX   *T.* 01-637 0341.

Monthly Book Clubs
  *Ancient History Book Club
  *Biography Book Club
  *Book of the Month Club
  *Family Book Club
  *History Book Club
  *History Guild
  *The Literary Guild
   Master Storytellers
  *Military Book Society
  *Mystery Guild
   Skylark Children's Book Club
   World Books

Quarterly Book Clubs
  *Arts Guild
  *British Heritage Guild
  *Home and Garden Guild
  *Military Guild
  *Readers Choice
  *World of Nature
Series
   Cordon Bleu
   Kings and Queens
   20th Century Classics

Bookmark Ltd., Royal Mills, Esher, Surrey, KT10 8AT   *T.* 0372 67861.
   Bookmark

Fernstyle Limited, Premier House, 150 Southampton Row, London, WC1B 5AL   *T.* 01-278 2817.
   Books for Children.

W. & G. Foyle Ltd., 121 Charing Cross Road, London, WC2H 0EB   *T.* 01-437 5660.

   The Book Club
   Catholic Book Club
   Children's Book Club
   Garden Book Club
   Quality Book Club

   Romance Book Club
   Scientific Book Club
   Thriller Book Club
   Travel Book Club
   Western Book Club

   * Publishes the Club Edition simultaneously with the Trade Edition.

Hamlyn Group Mail Order Division, Astronaut House, Hounslow Road, Feltham, Middlesex, TW14 9AR *T.* 01-890 1480.

Alison Burt's Super Saving	Illustrated Wildlife Treasury
Cookery Cards	Marguerite Patten's
Companion Book Club	Cookery Card Club
Creative Learning Programme	Silver Needles
Home Medical Guide	Stag Club

IS Books Ltd., 265 Seven Sisters Road, London, N4 2DE *T.* 01-802 6145.
Bookmarx Club

The Leisure Circle Ltd., York House, Empire Way, P.O. Box 61, Wembley, Middlesex, HA9 0PF *T.* 01-903 3161.
The Leisure Circle

Merlin Press Ltd, Sufferance Wharf, 2–4 West Ferry Road, London, E14. *T.* 01-987 7959.
Merlin Book Club

New Fiction Society, The, in association with **The Arts Council of Great Britain** and the **National Book League,** 196 Shaftesbury Avenue, London, WC2H 8JL *T.* 01-240 2967. *Editor:* Sebastian Faulks; *Manager:* Felicity Morgan.

Purnell Book Services Ltd.—see Book Club Associates.

Reader's Union Ltd., Brunel House, Newton Abbot, Devon, TQ12 2DW *T.* 61121.

*The Arts Book Society	*Maritime Book Society
Country Book Club	Readers Union Book Club
*Country Book Society	Science Fiction Book Club
*Craft Book Society	Sportsman Book Club
*Gardeners Book Society	

SCM Press Ltd., 56–58 Bloomsbury Street, London, WC1B 3QX *T.* 01-636 3841.
*SCM Book Club

*Publishes the Club Edition simultaneously with the Trade Edition.

VANITY PUBLISHING

A reputable publisher very rarely asks an author to pay for the production of his work, or to contribute to its cost, or to undertake to purchase copies. The only exception is in the case of a book of an extremely specialised nature, with a very limited market or perhaps the first book of poems by a new writer of some talent. In such instances, especially if the book is a good one making a contribution to its subject, an established and reliable publisher will be prepared to accept a subvention from the author to make publication possible, and such financial grants often come from scientific or other academic foundations or funds. This is a very different procedure from that of the *vanity publisher* who claims to perform, for a fee to be paid by the author, all the many functions involved in publishing a book.

In his efforts to secure business the vanity publisher will usually give exaggerated praise to an author's work and arouse equally unrealistic hopes of its commercial success. The distressing reports we have received from embittered victims of vanity publishers underline the importance of reading extremely carefully the contracts offered by such publishers. Often these will provide for the printing of, say, two thousand copies of the book, usually at a quite exorbitant cost to the author, but will leave the "publisher" under no obligation to bind more than a very limited number. Frequently, too, the author will be expected to pay the cost of any effective advertising, while the "publisher" makes little or no effort to promote the distribution and sale of his book. Again, the names and imprints of vanity publishers are well-known to literary editors, and their productions therefore are rarely, if ever, reviewed or even noticed in any important periodical. Similarly, such books are hardly ever stocked by the booksellers.

We repeat, therefore, except in rare instances never pay for publication, whether for a book, an article, a lyric or a piece of music. If a work is worth publishing, sooner or later a publisher will be prepared to publish it at his own expense. But if a writer cannot resist the temptation of seeing his work in print, in book form, or in an anthology, even though he has to pay a substantial sum, he should first discover just how much or how little the publisher will provide and will do in return for the payment he demands.

theatre, tv radio, agents

MARKETING A PLAY

JULIA JONES
Society of Authors

As soon as a play is written, it is protected under the Copyright laws of this country (see p. 353). No formalities are necessary here to secure copyright protection but it is a good plan to deposit a copy with the bank and take a dated receipt for it, so as to be able to prove the date of its completion, if this should be necessary at some time either, for example, to enforce a claim for infringement of copyright or to rebut such a claim. The copyright belongs to the author unless and until he parts with it and this he should never do, since the copyright is in effect the sum total of all his rights in his work. He should, so far as possible, deal separately with the component rights which go to make up the copyright and grant limited licences for the principal rights with, where customary or necessary, limited interests in the ancillary rights. A West End production agreement (see below) illustrates this principle.

The author can try to market the play himself, but once a play is accepted, it is wise to have professional assistance. There is no standard author's contract in this country; all points are, therefore, open for negotiation and the contractual complications are best handled by a reputable literary agent.

Although most ambitious young playwrights visualise a West End opening for their plays, the first step, except for the established dramatist, is usually to try to place the play with a repertory company known to be interested in presenting new plays. It is wise to write to the company first, giving salient details, such as type of play, size of cast, number of sets, etc., and ask if the management would be willing to read it. This saves the frustration and expense of copies of the play being kept for long periods by managements who have no interest in it. (Do not send your only copy of the play away—this seems obvious, but many authors have suffered the torment of having to rewrite from memory when the only copy has been lost.) It is also possible to get a first production by entering the play for the various competitions which appear from time to time, but in this case great care should be taken to study the rules and ensure that the organisers of the competition do not acquire unreasonably wide rights and interests in the entries.

Many repertory companies will give a new play a try-out production in the hope that it will be seen by London managements and transfer to the West End. For the run at the repertory company's own theatre the company will receive a licence for a given period from a fixed date and pay the author a royalty of between 6 per cent and 10 per cent calculated on the gross box office receipts. In return for the risk involved in presenting a new play, the repertory company will expect a share in the author's earnings from subsequent professional stage productions of the play during a limited period (usually two years). Sometimes on transfer the West End management will agree to take over responsibility for part or all of this payment.

The contract, for repertory or West End production, or for the use of any other rights in the play, should specify precisely the rights to which it refers, the territory covered, the period of time covered, the payments involved and make it clear that all other rights remain the property of the author.

For a first-class production in the West End of London, usually preceded by a short provincial tour, the author's contract will include clauses dealing with the following main heads of agreement. The substance, as well as the phrasing of these clauses will vary considerably, but those given below probably represent the average, as do the figures in brackets, which must not be assumed to be standard:

1. *U.K. Option.* In consideration of a specified minimum sum (between £200 and £400) as a non-returnable advance against royalties, the Manager shall have the exclusive option for a specified period (usually six months) to produce the play in a first-class theatre in the West End of London (preceded possibly by a tour of specified number of weeks) with an extension for a further period upon payment of a further similar sum.

2. *U.K. Licence.* When the Manager exercises his option he shall have the U.K. Licence for a specified period (three or five years) from the date of the first performance under the licence such licence to terminate before the expiry of the specified period if
   (*a*) the play is not produced before a specified date;
   (*b*) (i) less than a specified number (between 50 and 75) of consecutive professional performances are given and paid for in any year; or
   (ii) the Manager has not paid at the beginning of any year a non-returnable advance against royalties. This variant on clause (*b*) (i) prevents the rights being tied up for a year while waiting to check if the qualifying performances have been given and is thus desirable from the author's point of view.

3. *U.S. Option.* If the Manager gives a specified number (usually 24) of consecutive performances in the West End he shall have an option exercisable within a specified period of the first West End performance (six weeks) to produce the play on Broadway on payment of a specified non-returnable advance royalties (between £300 and £500).

4. *U.S. Licence.* When the Manager exercises his option the Broadway licence shall be for a specified period (3 years) on terms not less favourable than those specified in the Minimum Basic Agreement of the Dramatists' Guild of America.

5. *Other Rights.* Provided the play has run for the qualifying period (usually 24 performances) the Manager acquires interests in some of the other rights as follows:
   (i) *Repertory.* The author should reserve these rights paying the Manager a share (one-third) of his royalties for a specified period (two years after the end of the West End run or the expiry of the West End licence whichever is the shorter.) The author agrees not to release these rights until after the end of the West End run without the Manager's consent, this consent not to be unreasonably withheld. It is recommended that a play should be released to theatres on the A* list immediately after the end of the West End run, and to theatres on the B* list within three months from the end of the West End run, if an option for a tour has not been taken up by then, otherwise at the end of the tour.
   (ii) *Amateur.* The author should reserve these rights and pay the Manager no share in his royalties, but should undertake not to release these rights for an agreed period, to allow the repertory theatres to have maximum clear run.

*These are the theatres recommended by the Theatres' National Committee for immediate and early release of plays to repertory.

(iii) *Radio and Television*.   The author should reserve these rights but it may well be in his interest not to release them until some time after the end of the West End run.   During the run of the play in the West End, however, the Manager may arrange for an extract from the play to be broadcast or televised for publicity purposes, the author's fee for such broadcast or television performances being paid to him in full without any part of it going to the Manager.

(iv) *Film*.   If the Manager has produced the play for the qualifying period it is expected that the author will pay him a percentage (often 20 per cent) of the author's net receipts from the disposal of the film rights, if these rights are disposed of within a specified period (one year) from the last West End performance.   If the Manager has also produced the play on Broadway for the qualifying period the author is expected to allow him a further percentage (20 per cent) of the author's net receipts from the disposal of the film rights if the rights are disposed of within a specified time (one year) of the last Broadway performance.   This is a field where the established dramatist can, not unnaturally, strike a much better bargain than the beginner.   In no case, however, should the total percentage payable to the Manager exceed 40 per cent.

(v) *Foreign Language*.   These rights should be reserved to the author, the Manager receiving no share of the proceeds.

(vi) *Cassette*.   These rights should be specifically reserved to the author.

Other clauses which should appear include:

(a) *A royalty clause* setting out the royalties which the author shall receive from West End and touring performances of the play—usually a scale rising from 5 per cent through $7\frac{1}{2}$ per cent to 10 per cent.   If the author is registered for VAT, provision for VAT payment should be included here.

(b) *Cast approval, etc.*   The author should be consulted about the casting and the director of the play, and in some cases may be able to insist on approval of the casting of a particular part.

(c) *Rehearsals, scripts, etc.*   The author should be entitled to attend all rehearsals of the play and no alteration in the title or script should be made without the author's consent.   All approved alterations in or suggestions for the script should become the author's property.   In this clause also should appear details about supply of tickets for the author for opening performances and any arrangements for tickets throughout the West End run.

(d) *Credits*.   Details of billing of the author's name on posters, programmes and advertising matter should be included.

(e) *Lord Chamberlain's Licence*.   The Theatres Act 1968 abolishes the power of the Lord Chamberlain to censor stage plays and play licences are no longer required.   However, it is obligatory for managers to deposit a copy of the script on which the public performance of any new play is based with the Keeper of Manuscripts, British Museum, London, WC1. within one month of the performance.

(f) The author will normally warrant that the play contains nothing that is obscene or defamatory or that infringes copyright.

There must also be:

(g) An accounting clause giving details of payment and requiring a certified statement of box office receipts.

(h) A clause giving the conditions under which the agreement may be assigned or sub-leased.

(i) A termination clause, stating the conditions under which the agreement shall terminate.

ARRANGEMENTS FOR OTHER RIGHTS
AFTER THE FIRST-CLASS RUN OF THE PLAY

Repertory. The author or his representative will license repertory perform-ances for a fixed royalty on the gross box office receipts—usually 10 per cent for a new play immediately after its West End run, dropping perhaps to 7½ per cent in later years.

Amateur. The author or his representative will license amateur performances of the play for a flat fee (normally between £7–£12).

Publication. A firm specialising in acting editions of plays may offer to pub-lish the play in which case it will expect to license amateur performances and collect the fees on a commission basis (20 per cent to 50 per cent). The publica-tion contract will also usually provide for the author to receive a royalty of 10 per cent of the published price of every copy sold.

Radio and Television. Careful negotiation is required and care should be taken that repeat fees for repeat performances are included in the contract in addition to the initial fee for the first broadcast.

Film Rights. Professional advice is absolutely necessary when dealing with a film contract as there are many complications. The rights may be sold outright or licensed for a number of years—usually not less than 7 or 10 or more than 15. The film company normally acquires the right of distribution throughout the world in all languges and expects a completely free hand in making the adapta-tion of the play into a film.

Foreign Rights. It is usual to grant exclusive foreign language rights for the professional stage to an agent or translator who will arrange for a translation to be prepared and produced—it is wise to ask for evidence of the quality of the translator's work unless the translator is very well known. The financial arrangement is usually an advance against royalties for a given period to enable a translation to be prepared and then a licence to exploit the translation for a further period after production (usually five years).

MARKETS FOR PLAYS

It is not easy for a new or comparatively unknown writer to find a management willing to present his play. The Royal Court Theatre and one or two similarly enterprising organisations present a number of plays by new authors. The new and inexperienced writer may find it easier to persuade amateur drama groups or provincial repertory theatres to present his work. A further possible market may be found in the smaller fringe theatre companies.

The Stage reports productions of most new plays first produced by repertory theatres and a study of this journal may reveal other potential new markets for plays.

The Arts Council of Great Britain publishes a leaflet *New Writing in the Theatre*, which gives details of various forms of assistance available to theatres and playwrights. The help given by the Arts Council includes Bursaries (including the John Whiting Award), help to writers who are being commissioned or encouraged by a theatre company, and Supplements to authors' royalties. There is also a Writing Project Scheme to encourage initiation of such activities as writers' workshops, and there is a limited number of Resident Dramatists' Attachments available as well Copies of the leaflet and further information may be obtained from The Drama Director, The Arts Council of Great Britain, 105 Piccadilly, London, W1V 0AU.

It is probable that competitions for full-length and one-act plays and other special opportunities for new plays will be announced after the *Yearbook* has gone to press, and writers with plays on the stocks would do well to watch carefully for announcements in the Press. *The Observer, The Author, Plays and Players, Drama, Amateur Stage*, and *The Stage*, are the journals in which announcements are most likely to appear.

Sketches for revues, concert parties, and broadcasting, and plays for youth organisations are in demand. Sketches are usually bought outright, but in any case authors should make quite certain of what rights they will be disposing before accepting any offer.

In every case it is advisable to send a preliminary letter before submitting a manuscript. Suggestions for the preparation of manuscripts will be found on page 431 of the *Yearbook*.

Writers of plays are also referred to Marketing a Play on page 217, and to the section on Television on pages 235, 237 and 244, a medium which provides a very big market for the writers of plays.

Writers of plays are also referred to Marketing a Play on page 217, and to the section on Television on pages 235, 237 and 244

LONDON

Arnold, Tom, Presentations Ltd., London Pavilion Chambers, Great Windmill Street, London, W1V 7FB   *T.* 01-437 2702 and 9384.

Banbury, Frith, Ltd., 4 St. James's Terrace, Prince Albert Road, London, NW8 7LE   *T.* 01-722 8481.

Bridge, Peter, 16 Red Lion Square, London, WC1R 4QB   *T.* 01-242 3988.

Codron, Michael, Ltd., 117–119 Regent Street, London, W1R 8JY   *T.* 01-437 3577.

Cooney, Ray, Ltd., Suite 35, 26 Charing Cross Road, London, WC2H 0DH *T.* 01-836 9831.

Dolphin Theatre Company, Shaw Theatre, 100 Euston Road, London, NW1 2AJ *T.* 01-388 0031.

English Stage Company Ltd., Royal Court Theatre, Sloane Square, London, SW1W 8AS *T.* 01-730 5174.

Freedman, Bill, Ltd., 3 Goodwin's Court, St. Martin's Lane, London, WC2N 4LL *T.* 01-240 3086.

Gale, John, Strand Theatre, Aldwych, London, WC2B 5LD *T.* 01-240 1656.

Gordon, David, Productions, 405 Strand, London, WC2R 0NE *T.* 01-836 2613 and 3793.

Grosvenor Entertainments, 32 Curzon Street, London, W1Y 7AE *T.* 01-499 1392.

Hampstead Theatre, Swiss Cottage Centre, London, NW3 3EX *T.* 01-722 9224.

Knightsbridge Theatrical Productions Ltd., 2 Goodwin's Court, St. Martin's Lane, London, WC2N 4LL *T.* 01-836 7517.

Lister, Laurier, Productions, Ltd., Crouch House, 34 High Street, Rickmansworth, Herts, WD3 1ER.

Littler, Sir Emile, Palace Theatre, London, W1V 8AY *T.* 01-734 9691.

Macdonald, Murray and John Stevens Ltd., 5 Paultons House, Paultons Square, London, SW3 5DU.

Mermaid Theatre (Sir Bernard Miles), Puddle Dock, Blackfriars, London, EC4V 3DB *T.* 01-236 9521.

Mitchell, Stephen, London Pavilion Chambers, Great Windmill Street, London, W1V 7FB *T.* 01-437 2702.

National Theatre, South Bank, London, SE1 9PX *T.* 01-928 2033.

Open Space Theatre, 303–7 Euston Road, London, NW1 3AD *T.* 01-387 5175–6.

Questors Theatre, Mattock Lane, Ealing, London, W5 5BQ *T.* 01-567 0011.

Rix, Brian, Enterprises, c/o Duke of York's Theatre, St. Martin's Lane, London, WC2N 4BG *T.* 01-836 9831.

Ross, Charles, Productions, 17A Mercer Street, London, WC2H 9QJ *T.* 01-240 3232 and 836 3144.

Rowland, Toby, Ltd., Cranbourn Mansions, Cranbourn Street, London, WC2H 7AG *T.* 01-437 2274.

Saunders, Peter, Ltd., Vaudeville Theatre Offices, 10 Maiden Lane, London, WC2E 7NA *T.* 01-240 3177.

Tennent, H. M., Ltd., Globe Theatre, Shaftesbury Avenue, London, W1.   *T.* 01-437 3647.

Theatre Projects Associates Ltd., 10 Long Acre, London, WC2E 9LN   *T.* 01-240 5411.

Theatre Workshop, Theatre Royal, Stratford, London, E15 1BN   *T.* 01-534 7374.

Triumph Theatre Productions Ltd., Suite 4, Waldorf Chambers, 11 Aldwych, London, WC2.   *T.* 01-836 0186–7.

Unicorn Theatre for Young People, Arts Theatre, 6–7 Gt. Newport Street, London, WC2H 7JA   *T.* 01-240 2076.   (Plays for children only.)

White, Michael, 13 Duke Street, St. James's, London, SW1Y 6DB   *T.* 01-839 3971.

Young Vic Company, 66 The Cut, London, SE1 8LP   *T.* 01-633 0133.

PROVINCIAL

Abbey Theatre, Lower Abbey Street, Dublin, 1.   *T.* 748741.   The Abbey Theatre is mainly restricted to the production of plays in Irish or English written by Irish authors or on Irish subjects.   Foreign plays are however regularly produced.

Belgrade Theatre, Corporation Street, Coventry, CV1 1GS   *T.* 56431/7.

Birmingham Repertory Theatre, Ltd., Broad Street, Birmingham, B1 2EP   *T.* 021-236 6771.

Bristol Old Vic Company, Theatre Royal, Bristol, BS1 4ED   *T.* 27466.

Cambridge Theatre Company Ltd., 8 Market Passage, Cambridge.   *T.* 0223-57134.

Canterbury Theatre Trust, Ltd., Marlowe Theatre, Canterbury, Kent, CT1 2TP   *T.* 0227-64748.

Chesterfield Civic Theatre, Ltd., Civic Theatre, Corporation Street, Chesterfield, S41 7TX   *T.* 0246-34633.

Chester Gateway Theatre Trust, Ltd., Gateway Theatre, Chester.   *T.* 0244–40392.

Chichester Festival Theatre Productions Company Ltd., Chichester Festival Theatre, Oaklands Park, Chichester, Sussex, PO19 4AP   *T.* 0243 84437.

Coliseum Theatre, The, Oldham.   *T.* 061-624 2829.

Contact Theatre Company, University Theatre, Devas Street, Manchester, M15 6JA   *T.* 061-273 6952.

Crewe Theatre Trust Ltd., Crewe Theatre, Heath Street, Crewe, CW1 2DA   *T.* 0270-56397.

Crucible Theatre Trust, The Crucible Theatre, Norfolk Street, Sheffield, S1 1DA *T.* 0742 70621.

Derby Playhouse, Ltd., Theatre Walk, Eagle Centre, Derby, DE1 2NF *T.* 363271.

Duke's Playhouse, Moor Lane, Lancaster, LA1 1QE *T.* 67461.

Dundee Repertory Theatre, Lochee Road, Dundee, DD1 5RD *T.* 23514

Everyman Theatre, Regent Street, Cheltenham, GL50 1HQ *T.* 52515.

Everyman Theatre, Hope Street, Liverpool, L1 9BH *T.* 051-709 4776.

Farnham Repertory Company, Ltd., The Redgrave Theatre, Brightwell, Farnham, Surrey, GU9 7SB *T.* Farnham 721810.

Glasgow Citizens' Theatre, Ltd., Gorbals, Glasgow, G5 9DS *T.* 041-429 5561.

Grand Theatre, Singleton Street, Swansea, SA1 3QJ *T.* 55141.

Grand Theatre, Lichfield Street, Wolverhampton, WV1 1DE *T.* 21914.

Harrogate Theatre, Oxford Street, Harrogate, HG1 1QF *T.* 502710.

Haymarket Theatre, Belgrave Gate, Leicester, LE1 3YQ *T.* 0533-52021.

The Hornchurch Theatre Trust, Ltd., The Queen's Theatre, Hornchurch, Essex, RM11 1QT *T.* Hornchurch 56118.

Key Theatre, Embankment Road, Peterborough, PE1 1EG *T.* 52437.

Leeds Playhouse, Calverley Street, Leeds, LS2 3AJ *T.* 0532-42141.

Library Theatre Company, Manchester, M2 5PD *T.* 061-236 9422 (Manchester Library Theatre & Wythenshawe Forum Theatre).

Liverpool Repertory Theatre, Ltd., The Playhouse, Williamson Square, Liverpool, L1 1EL *T.* 051-709 8478.

Lyceum Little Theatre—see **Royal Lyceum Theatre Company Ltd.**

Mercury Theatre, Balkerne Gate, Colchester, Essex, CO1 1PT *T.* 0206 77006.

Northampton Repertory Players, Ltd., Royal Theatre and Opera House, Guildhall Road, Northampton, NN1 1EA *T.* Northampton 38343.

Northcott Theatre, Stocker Road, Exeter, EX4 4QB *T.* 56182.

Nottingham Playhouse, Nottingham Theatre Trust Ltd., Wellington Circus, Nottingham, NG1 5AF *T.* 0602-44361.

Octagon Theatre, Howell Croft South, Bolton, BL1 1SB   *T*. 29407.

Oxford Playhouse Company, Anvil Productions Ltd., The Playhouse, 12 Beaumont Street, Oxford, OX1 2LW   *T*. 0865-723238/9.

Palace Theatre, Clarendon Road, Watford, WD1 1JZ   *T*. 35455/6/7.

Peacock Theatre, The Abbey Theatre, Lower Abbey Street, Dublin, 1.   *T*. 748741. The experimental theatre associated with the Abbey Theatre and presents mostly new writing as well as exploring the entire canon of world drama.

Perth Repertory Theatre, Ltd., Perth Theatre, Perth, PH1 5UW   *T*. 21996.

Phoenix Theatre, Upper Brown Street, Leicester.   *T*. 57589.   Young Peoples & Community Theatre of the Leicester Theatre Trust.

Plymouth Theatre Company, St. John's Road, Plymouth, Devon.   *T*. 0752-23227 and 25615.

Regional Theatre of Suffolk, Ipswich Theatre, Tower Street, Ipswich, IP1 3BE   *T*. 0473-52717.   Suffolk plays only.

Royal Exchange Theatre Company Ltd., The Royal Exchange, St. Ann's Square, Manchester, M2 7DH   *T*. 061-833 9333.

Royal Lyceum Theatre Company Ltd., Royal Lyceum Theatre, Grindlay Street, Edinburgh, EH3 9AX   *T*. 031-229 7404; and Lyceum Little Theatre, Cambridge Street, Edinburgh, EH1 2ED.

St. Andrews Byre Theatre, Abbey Street, St. Andrews, KY16 9QP   *T*. 2544 and 4493.   (Small cast plays only.)

Salisbury Playhouse, Malthouse Lane, Salisbury, SP2 7RA   *T*. 20117.

Scarborough Theatre Trust Ltd., The Stephen Joseph Theatre-in-the-Round, Valley Bridge Parade, Scarborough, YO11 2PL   *T*. (0723) 70540/1/2.

Swan Theatre, The Moors, Worcester, WR1 3EF   *T*. 27463.

Thorndike Theatre, Church Street, Leatherhead, Surrey.   *T*. 76211.

Vance, Charles, Productions, Leas Pavilion Theatre, Folkestone, CT20 2DP   *T*. 59097.

Victoria Theatre, Hartshill Road, Stoke-on-Trent, ST4 6AE   *T*. 0782-613954. Theatre in the round.

Watermill Theatre Ltd., Bagnor, Newbury, Berkshire, RG16 8AE   *T*. 0635-45834.

Welsh National Opera and Drama Company, Ltd., John Street, Cardiff, CF1 4SP   *T*. 40541.

Windsor Theatre Company (Capoco Ltd.), Theatre Royal, Windsor, SL4 1PS.

Worthing and District Connaught Theatre Trust, Ltd., Connaught Theatre, Union Place, Worthing, Sussex, BN11 1LG   *T.* 0903-39770.

York Citizens' Theatre Trust, Ltd., Theatre Royal, York, YO1 2HD   *T.* 58162.

Yvonne Arnaud Theatre Management Ltd., Yvonne Arnaud Theatre, Millbrook, Guildford, Surrey, GU1 3UX   *T.* 0483-64571.

Touring Companies and Theatre Clubs

The following is a list of some touring companies in the regions which use writers.

EMMA Theatre Company, Mountfields House, Forest Road, Loughborough, Leicestershire, LE11 3HU *T.* 0509 67136.

Humberside Theatre Trust Ltd., Humberside Theatre, Spring Street, Hull, HU2 8RW *T.* 0482-20925.

M6 Theatre Company, Gracie Fields Theatre, Oulder Hill, Rochdale, Lancashire.

Orchard Theatre Company, 108 Newport Road, Barnstaple, N. Devon, EX32 9BA *T.* 0271-71475.

Pentabus, c/o The Old Schools Arts and Recreation Centre, Exchange Street, Kidderminster, Worcestershire, DY10 1BT *T.* 0562-2176.

Theatre Mobile, c/o Mid-Pennine Arts Association, 20 Hammerton Street, Burnley, Lancashire. *T.* 0282-29513 and 21986.

Wearabout Theatre Co., T.I.E. & Community Theatre, 27 Stockton Road, Sunderland, SR2 7AQ *T.* 0783-74046.

The following is a list of smaller organisations, including lunch-time theatre clubs and touring groups, who are interested in producing new plays. Further details are available from the Drama Director at The Arts Council.

Almost Free Theatre, Inter-Action Centre, Talacre Open Space, 53–90 Prince of Wales Road, London, NW5 3NG *T.* 01-485 6224.

Bubble Theatre Company, 9 Kingsford Street, London, NW5. *T.* 01-485 3420.

Bush Theatre, Shepherd's Bush Green, London, W12. *T.* 01-743 3388. *Offices:* 38 Shepherd's Bush Road, London, W6 7PJ *T.* 01-602 3703.

Common Stock Theatre Company, (Community Theatre), 31 Fulham Palace Road, London, W6. *T.* 01-741 3086.

Foco Novo, 2 Nugent Terrace, London, NW8. *T.* 01-289 3226.

Greenwich Theatre Ltd., Greenwich Theatre, Crooms Hill, London, SE10 8ES *T.* 01-858 4447.

Half Moon Theatre, 27 Alie Street, London, E1 8DA *T.* 01-480 6465 and 6727.

Joint Stock Theatre Group, 16 St. John's Wood Road, London, NW8. *T.* 01-289 2556/7.

King's Head Theatre, 115 Upper Street, London, N1 1QN   *T.* 01-226 1916.

Overground Theatre Company, 19 Ashdown Road, Kingston-upon-Thames, Surrey, KT1 2PH   *T.* 01-549 5893.

Pentameters, Three Horseshoes, Heath Street, London, NW3.   *T.* 01-435 6757.

Richmond Fringe, Orange Tree Theatre, 45 Kew Road, Richmond, Surrey.   *T.* 01-940 3633.

Soho Poly Theatre, 16 Riding House Street, London, W1.   *T.* 01-636 9050.   One act plays only.

Wakefield Tricycle Company, 7 Acklam Road, London, W10.   *T.* 01-960 3094, 960 5257.

PUBLISHERS SPECIALISING IN THE PUBLICATION OF PLAYS

(For other particulars regarding Publishers, see under "UK Publishers," page 129, and "US Publishers," page 206.)

Atheneum Publishers, 122 East 42nd Street, New York, N.Y. 10017.

Baker (Walter H.) Company, 100 Chauncy Street, Boston, Mass., 02111.

Breakthrough Press Inc., 27 Washington Square North, New York, N.Y. 10011.

Cagney, Peter, Script Service (1952), 2nd Floor, 17 Second Avenue, Hove, Sussex, BN3 2LL *T.* 0273-778007.   Considers scripts for all kinds of Light Entertainment—Music Hall, Variety, Cabaret Scripts, Comedy routines, formats for visual comedy (but not plays).

Calder, John, Publishers, Ltd., 18 Brewer Street, London, W1R 4AS.

Cape (Jonathan), Ltd., 30 Bedford Square, London, WC1B 3EL.

Davis-Poynter Ltd., 20 Garrick Street, London, WC2E 9BJ.

English Theatre Guild, Ltd., 5A South Side, Clapham Common, London, SW4 7AA *T.* 01-720 6410 and 6296.

Evans Brothers Ltd. (Evans Plays), Montague House, Russell Square, London, WC1B 5BX.

Eyre Methuen Ltd., 11 New Fetter Lane, London, EC4P 4EE.

Faber & Faber Ltd., 3 Queen Square, London, WC1N 3AU.

French (Samuel), Ltd., 26 Southampton Street, Strand, London, WC2E 7JE.

French (Samuel) Inc., 25 West 45th Street, New York, N.Y. 10036.

Kenyon-Deane Ltd., 129 St. John's Hill, London, SW11 1TD.

Miller (J. Garnet), Ltd., 129 St. John's Hill, London, SW11 1TD.

New Playwrights' Network, 35 Sandringham Road, Macclesfield, Cheshire, SK10 1QB *T.* 0625-25312.

Theatre Arts Books, 333 Avenue of the Americas, New York, N.Y. 10014.

(For a list of periodicals dealing with the Theatre see the Classified Index.)

MARKETS FOR SCREENPLAYS

JEAN McCONNELL

Despite the slightly healthier scene as far as writers are concerned following the setting up of the Script Development Fund, this is still a highly specialised and very difficult market to break into. The recommended approach is through a recognised literary agent, but most film companies have a Story Department and are usually willing to consider material sent direct to them. It is naturally wise to check with the company first to make sure it is worth your while submitting your work. Drop them a letter.

It is a fact that the majority of feature films these days are based on already best-selling books, but there are some companies making documentaries and children's films, particularly those with a television outlet, which will sometimes accept unsolicited material if it seems to be exceptionally original. It is obviously sensible to try to sell your work to a company which is currently in active production, such as those listed below. But again remember the best way to achieve success is through the knowledge and efforts of a literary agent.

American International Productions (England) Ltd., 25 Newman Street, London, W1P 3HA *T.* 01-637 4038.

Angel, Daniel, Films Ltd., 21 Sospel Court, Farnham Royal, Bucks.

Ariel Productions, 2 Lower James Street, Golden Square, London, W1R 3PN *T.* 01-437 7015.

Avco Embassy Pictures (UK) Ltd., 113–117 Wardour Street, London, W1V 3TD *T.* 01-734 9561 (will pass on material for consideration by their Los Angeles office).

Bowden Productions Ltd., EMI Elstree Studios, Boreham Wood, Herts, WD6 1JG *T.* 01-953 1600.

Children's Film Foundation Ltd., 6–10A Great Portland Street, London, W1N 6JN *T.* 01-580 4796.

Columbia Pictures Corporation Ltd., St. Margarets House, 19 Wells Street, London, W1P 3FP *T.* 01-580 2090 (prefer material to be submitted through an agent).

Walt Disney Productions, Ltd., 68 Pall Mall, London, SW1Y 5EX *T.* 01-839 8010. *Telex:* 21532 (will only consider material submitted through an agent).

EMI Films Ltd., 142 Wardour Street, London, W1V 4AE *T.* 01-437 0444 (prefers material to be submitted through an agent).

Fetter Productions Ltd., P. Fetterman, 193 Sussex Gardens, London, W2. *T.* 01-402 1815.

Hammer Film Productions, Ltd., Hammer House, Pinewood Studios, Iver, Bucks, SL0 0NH *T.* Iver (0753) 651700.

ITC Entertainment Ltd., ATV House, 17 Great Cumberland Place, London, W1A 1AG *T.* 01-262 8040. *Telex:* 261807.

Klinger, Michael, Ltd., 9 Clifford Street, London, W1X 1RB *T.* 01-439 7321. *Telex:* 261828.

Memorial Films, Ltd., 74 Campden Hill Court, Campden Hill Road, London, W8 7HN *T.* 01-937 1879.

Paramount Pictures (UK), Ltd., 162 Wardour Street, London, W1V 4AB *T.* 01-437 7700.

Parker, Alan, Film Company, 11 Great Marlborough Street, London, W1.

Romulus Films Ltd., 36 Park Lane, London, W1Y 3LE *T.* 01-493 7741.

Tyburn Film Productions Ltd., Pinewood Studios, Iver Heath, Bucks. *T.* Iver 651700 (prefers material submitted through an agent—in the case of "traditional" Gothic Horror subjects will not even read material not so submitted or not carrying a W.G. or A.C.T.T. copyright registration).

United Artists Corporation, Ltd., Mortimer House, 37/41 Mortimer Street, London, W1A 2JL *T.* 01-636 1655.

Universal Pictures Ltd. (MCA), 139 Piccadilly, London, W1V 9FH *T.* 01-629 7211 (will pass on material for consideration by their U.S. office, and prefer submissions through an agent).

Warner Brothers Productions Ltd., Warner House, Pinewood Studios, Iver Heath, Bucks. *T.* Iver 654545 (will only consider material submitted through an agent).

Welbeck Film Distributors Ltd., 52 Queen Anne Street, London, W1M 9LA.

13   (continued)

She moves across the barn to the door, where she turns.

                    ELIZABETH
          I still think the police ought to know.

She goes out. ALAN stands immobile until her
footsteps retreat, and then he sighs with relief.
He darts quickly to the large wine vat, climbs
up and begins heaving at the lid.

                                                    CUT TO:

14   EXT. FARMYARD DAY

DONALD intercepts ELIZABETH as she crosses yard.

                    DONALD
          What does he say?

                    ELIZABETH
          Nothing.

                    DONALD
                   (frowning)

          Right! Now it's my turn.

He starts for the barn. ELIZABETH watches him
anxiously.

                                                    CUT TO:

15   INT. BARN DAY

Donald's shadow falls across the threshold.
He hesitates while his eyes get used to the gloom.

                    DONALD
          Alan?

ALAN lets the lid of the vat fall and jumps down.
He stands quite still as DONALD crosses the barn
and stands staring at him. The two men are silent
a moment.

                    DONALD
                (then, with realisation)
          You knew it was there, didn't you?

CLOSE SHOT — DONALD'S POINT OF VIEW
ALAN'S face is haggard.

                    ALAN
          I hoped to God it wouldn't be.

SCREENPLAYS FOR FILMS

JEAN McCONNELL

Despite the old saying that the plot of the best movie can be written on a post-card, film companies do not actually welcome a plot on a postcard. Nor is it enough simply to send a story in narrative form. You should be prepared to write your idea into a full screenplay. In consequence, it is advisable to check as far as possible in case a company is already working on a similar idea and your efforts likely to be wasted.

LAY-OUT

1. Use A4 size typing paper.
2. It is not necessary to put in elaborate camera directions. A shooting script will be made later. Your job is to write the master scenes, clearly broken down into each incident and location.
3. Your screenplay will tell your story in terms of visual action and dialogue spoken by your characters. If you intend it to be a full-length feature film, running about 1½ hours, your script will be about 100–130 pages long.
4. The general lay-out of a page of screenplay can be seen from the specimen page opposite. The following points should be noted.

(a) Each scene should be numbered on the left, and given a title which indicates whether the scene is an interior or an exterior, where it takes place, and a rough indication of the lighting conditions, i.e. Day or Night. The situation of each scene should be standardised; don't call your "sitting room" a "lounge" the next time you come to it, or people will think you mean a different place.

(b) Note that the dialogue is spaced out, with the qualifying directions such as "(frowning)" on a separate line, slightly inset from the dialogue. Double space each speech from the previous one.

(c) Always put the names of the characters in CAPITALS, except when they occur in the actual dialogue. Double space the stage directions from the dialogue, but single space the lines of the stage directions themselves.

(d) Leave at least a 1½ inch margin on the left hand and a reasonably wide right-hand margin. It is false economy to cram the page. You will, of course, type on one side of the page only.

(e) If you have to make a correction, cross it out neatly and type the whole section out again. But don't irritate your reader with too many corrections. Better to re-type the page.

(f) Only give camera directions when you feel it to be essential. For instance, if you want to show something from a particular character's point of view, or if you think you need it to make a point, i.e. "HARRY approaches the cliff edge and looks down. LONG SHOT — HARRY'S POINT OF VIEW. ALICE fully-clad is walking into the sea. CUT TO: CLOSE UP OF HARRY'S HORRIFIED FACE." Note the camera directions are put in capital letters on a separate line, as in the specimen page opposite.

PREPARATION OF MANUSCRIPT

1. Make at least two copies, and never send your very last copy out to anyone. It will invariably be lost.

2. The length of your manuscript will depend on whether you are submitting a feature film, a short film for children, say, or a documentary. But it is better to present a version which is too short rather than too long.

3. Prepare the title page in the same way as for a story or article to an editor, except that it is not necessary to state the number of words.

4. If you give a list of characters, do not suggest the actor or actress you would like to play it. This is a decision to be made elsewhere and relies on many factors about which you cannot know. Don't attach character sketches, as these should appear in the body of the screenplay.

5. Bind your screenplay, giving it a front and back cover, and securing the pages firmly.

SUBMISSION

Attach a stamped, addressed envelope to your manuscript, whether sending it through an agent or direct. But do remember that if film companies state that they will only consider material sent through an agent, they definitely mean it.

Most companies have Story Departments to which you should address your material. As Story Editors are very busy people, you can make their life easier by complying with the following rules.

1. If you have based your screenplay on someone else's published work you should make the fact clear in a covering letter, stating (*a*) that the material is no longer in copyright, or (*b*) that you yourself own the copyright, or at least an option on it, or (*c*) that you have not obtained the copyright, but have reason to believe that there would be no difficulty in doing so.

2. Apart from a note of any relevant credits you may already possess, do not regale the Editor with your personal details, unless they bear a direct relation to the material submitted. For instance, if your story concerns a brain surgeon, then it would be relevant for the Editor to know that you actually are one. Otherwise, trust your work to stand on its own merit.

3. There is no need to mention if your work has been turned down by other companies, however regretfully. The comments of others will not influence a Story Editor one way or the other.

4. Don't pester the company if you don't get a reply, or even an acknowledgement, for some weeks. Most companies will formally acknowledge receipt and then leave you in limbo for at least six weeks. However, after a passage of three months or more, a brief letter asking politely what has happened is in order. A telephone call is unlikely to be helpful. It is possible the company may have liked your work enough to have sent it to America, or to be getting further readers' opinions on it. This all takes time. If they don't like it, you will certainly get it back in due course.

5. Be prepared, this is really a tough market, for which there are at least three reasons. One, films cost so much to make these days that the decision to go ahead is only taken after a great many important factors have been satisfied and an even greater number of important people are happy about it. Two, the number of films made is small in relation to, say, books published or T.V. plays produced. Three, writing a screenplay calls for knowledge and appreciation of the technicalities of film-making, as well as the ability to combine dialogue, action and pictures, visualising the story throughout in the language of the cinema.

6. Try to get an agent. A good agent will give you a fair opinion of your work. If he thinks it worthwhile, then he is the one who will know the particular film company to whom he can sell it.

(Agents who handle film material see page 270.)

WRITING FOR TELEVISION
MALCOLM HULKE

A favoured myth of our times is that to write for television You Have To Know Someone. No one imagines you have to know anyone to write a book. You write it, have it rejected by five publishers, taken up by the sixth, and you're a world bestseller (*The Naked and the Dead* and *The Day of the Jackal* spring to mind). To extend the argument, you don't have to know anyone to knit a pair of socks for sale at the church bazaar, nor to build an ocean-going oil tanker. Only two considerations count—(*a*) that the person you try to sell it to wants it at that time, and (*b*) your product meets their demands. Fulfil those conditions in television writing and your success will be instant. The appalling fact that you don't know a cameraman at Pebble Mill, that the tea lady at Anglia House isn't your aunty, and that your father has never met Lord Grade, will be decently overlooked.

Is there, though, some basis in the myth? Yes, in TV series writing you have to be invited. Someone must know your work is good for television; and, most important, that you are a reliable person who will write to format and deliver on time. Mounting a series costs money. The indecision of programme planners often results in producers and script editors having impossibly tight deadlines to meet. No one in conveyor-belt drama has the time or patience for beginners.

All is different in plays. Despite the enormous popularity of series, both the BBC and ITV are thankfully pledged to a steady output of one off (or single shot) plays, and nowadays one off serials, which provides an open door for everyone to write for television. All unsolicited scripts, provided they're not in Greek on round pieces of cardboard, are duly read and considered. No script department is going to pass up the chance of finding a Jack Rosenthal or a Colin Welland.

The doors are wide open for new names and fresh ideas. It does help, though, if before writing your prize-winning television play you find out how to do it.

Modesty not being one of my vices, I must recommend to you *Writing for Television in the Seventies*, which is by me, and is published by Adam and Charles Black, price £4.75. With the help of 70 experts, all duly thanked right after the contents page, I try to take the reader through the intricacies of television production, both electronic and film, explaining how these technicalities affect the writer. How to lay out a script, and why we do it in such a peculiar way, is dealt with. Pages of badly written script, with numbers and a key to explain the errors, are followed by pages of the same story properly written for television. A group of eight eminent TV writers contribute excerpts from their favourite scripts in the chapter on contents, *What to write about*. Having studied the book all you will need is talent, staying power, and the salesmanship to submit the right kind of play to the right people at the right time.

Having sold your first play, you are on the threshold of the chosen few, the series writers whose names appear so frequently on our screens. Your agent can put your name forward when new series are coming up. With luck a series producer who saw your one off play may seek you to write for him. If you feel that format writing is somehow impure, you may turn your back on your new found position. But series writing can provide a regular income, plus a lot of creative opportunities, whereas your original ideas for further one off plays may be few and far between.

Many would-be TV playwrights make these four fundamental errors:

1. They give up on the first rejection.
2. They think only of the BBC in London as a market, not only overlooking

the ITV drama buyers but also the BBC's regions.
3. They don't always watch enough TV output, and they don't watch it analytically, e.g. they submit plays with stories like old B-movies, whereas this year it's all slices-of-life with open-ended plots, or whatever is the fashion.
4. (Dare I say it?) They don't read my book; or, having read it, they fail to grasp what I and 70 other people try to explain to them.

Always address unsolicited scripts to the Script Department, never to individual producers or script editors. The most active ITV buyers of drama and light entertainment are ATV, Anglia, Granada, HTV, London Weekend, Scottish, Thames and Yorkshire. The addresses of these ITV Contractors will be found on pages 244–6, BBC addresses are on pages 239–41. Other organisations exist that produce independently or in association with the BBC or ITV Contractors, e.g. Talbot Television, Screen Gems, Time-Life, etc. You will find them, and much other useful information, in a booklet called *Contacts* (to get a copy write to *The Spotlight*, 42–43 Cranbourn Street, London, WC2H 7AP and send £1.00). Jaguar Books of 3 Carlisle Place, London, SW1 (*T*. 01-834 1174), provide a useful information service. For £5.00 you get their weekly *Production & Casting Report* for five weeks, from which you may glean what anthologies and series are being mounted; during the period you have paid for you can also phone them every day if you wish.

With situation comedy series, a big payer if you can do it, the rule used to be that everything was written around a pre-selected star—rather awkward if you happened to live on a remote Scottish island and were not on close chatty terms with Britain's top comedians. In both the BBC and most ITV companies that's all changed. The new trend is that situation comedy shows are written first, cast later, which favours writers enormously. Some situation shows start as one off plays; non-comedy actors have been cast, it's all worked out funny, and a series has emerged.

Contracts for TV writers are standardised through The Writers' Guild of Great Britain (430 Edgware Road, London, W2 1EH, *T*. 01-723 8074), which is the appropriate trade union (see page 411). With the BBC payment is usually in two parts, half on commission, half on delivery and acceptance. The ITV Contractors generally have a three stage system, a third on commission, a third on delivery, and a final third on acceptance (i.e. after any necessary rewrites). Everybody in the business is remarkably honest, no one will forget to pay up and no one will deliberately steal your ideas.

While the writer untried on television cannot hope to make a sale on a synopsis and must write a whole play to break in, even a non-writer stands a chance of selling an idea for a series. You should submit a detailed description of the background, the main continuing characters, and the story-making potential. If it's a thumping good idea you may make a sale. You will receive a royalty for every episode produced, plus a creator's credit, even though as a non-television writer you aren't invited to write a line of dialogue.

Never write complete scripts on spec for series already on the screen. What you're seeing may have been recorded a year ago. Don't send novels to the BBC, or anyone else, seeking a commission to adapt them unless you already have some track record as a TV playwright. Whatever unsolicited material you submit, do please include a big stamped addressed envelope or postage stamps.

Most important of all, don't give up trying. What Harlech doesn't buy Granada may. The script turned down this year by the BBC may be acceptable to them two or three years hence. If anyone explains why they didn't buy—and television script departments are full of helpful people—never argue. Take their golden advice and try again.

(My thanks to Colin Rogers, Head of Script Department, ATV Network Ltd., and to Keith Williams, Head of BBC Television Script Unit, for their help in the preparation of this article.—MH.)

BROADCASTING: RADIO AND TV

BRITISH BROADCASTING CORPORATION

For fuller information see *Writing for the BBC*—a guide for writers on possible markets for their work within the B.B.C. Published by the B.B.C., price 75p (by post £1.09) obtainable through booksellers or from B.B.C. Publications, P.O. Box 234, London, SE1 3TH.

TELEVISION

Drama.—Original plays dealing with contemporary problems are most wanted. Plays needing only a few sets and characters start at an advantage. Specially-shot film sequences should only be written into a script if essential for the story. No standardised layout is expected in unsolicited scripts. Dialogue should be set out in a way that makes it clearly distinguishable from "stage directions" and sound/visual effects. Further details about length and type of plays currently required are available from Script Unit.

All scripts should be clearly typed and sent to Head of Script Unit, BBC Television Centre, London, W12 7RJ.

RADIO

Short Stories.—Short stories specially written for broadcasting will be considered. A short story written for a fifteen-minute broadcasting space should be between 2150 and 2250 words in length.

Plays.—Approximately five hundred new plays are broadcast each year on the basic services, and several hundreds more in the Regions. Many of these are written specially for radio, some are stage plays, and there is a wide field for adaptations of short stories and novels. *Before starting on an adaptation*, it is essential to find out from the BBC Drama Department if such an adaptation would be acceptable. (There might, for example, be copyright difficulties, or the book might have been previously adapted.)

If an adaptation is agreed in principle, a short synopsis, accompanied by a few pages of dialogue, enables the BBC to judge whether it is worthwhile to encourage the writer to proceed. This also applies in the case of original radio plays although the BBC will assess completed manuscripts which have not been preceded by a synopsis. It should be remembered that the standard of writing required is a high one and demands real distinction in dramatic writing and also considerable concentrated study of the radio medium. A preliminary letter should be addressed to the Script Editor, Drama (Radio) BBC, Broadcasting House, London, W1A 1AA. A free leaflet, *Notes on Radio Drama*, giving guidance on radio writing and the market for plays, is available from the Script Editor. *Manuscripts must be clearly typed.*

Music.—The music policy of the BBC, dedicated to the encouragement of the best music old and new, continues to enlarge its range. Audition sessions for professional soloists and ensembles are held every week, except in July and August, with an outside professional assessor on the listening panel.

A Music Panel of distinguished musicians meets regularly to advise on the suitability for performance of the large number of MSS. constantly submitted. The BBC also commissions from British composers works of various kinds. These have included opera and works for special occasions. Incidental music is also commissioned for features and drama. In the case of music commissioned by the BBC the original score is now returned to the composer at his request and not as in the past automatically retained by the BBC.

Light Entertainment.— Careful consideration is given to new ideas for Light Entertainment programmes by the Script Editor and senior members of the Light Entertainment Department. The chief requirement is originality; the vast majority of scripts sent in are merely variations of existing programmes. A particular need exists for topical sketches and "one-liners" for programmes such as *Weekending*. In general it is inadvisable to write scripts for a particular star artist unless the writer has a really intimate knowledge of the artist's work; and even then material for "solo" performances (as distinct from scripts for comedy series) is almost invariably provided by the artists themselves. No real decision can be reached on a new proposition until the completed script is seen: but the Script Editor is prepared to look at detailed synopses and specimen dialogue and offer opinions if requested. Fees are a matter for negotiation with the Corporation's Copyright Department. Typewritten scripts should be addressed to the Script Editor (Light Entertainment), BBC Broadcasting House, London, W1A 1AA.

BROADCASTING RIGHTS AND TERMS

Specially written material for television: Fees for one performance of a 60-minute original television play in 1978 were a minimum of £1325 for a play written by a beginner and a 'going rate' of £1750 for an established writer, or *pro rata* for shorter or longer timings. Half the fee is paid on a work being commissioned and half on its acceptance as being suitable for television. If the work is submitted it is paid for on acceptance. Fees for a 50-minute episode in a series in 1978 were a minimum of £1000 for a beginner and a 'going rate' of £1350 for an established writer. Fees for a 50-minute dramatisation were a minimum of £750 for a beginner and a £1000 'going rate' for an established writer. All fees are subject to negotiation above the minima. Additional fees are paid for repeats.

Specially written material for radio: Fees are assessed on the basis of the type of material, its length, the author's status and experience in writing for radio. Minimum fees for one performance of specially written radio dramas in English (other than educational programmes) are £7.00 a minute for beginners and a 'going rate' of £11.00 a minute for established writers. Higher rates are paid to very well-known contributors or to those with very great experience of writing for radio programmes. For Light Entertainment programmes rates are a little higher. Fees for submitted material are paid on acceptance, and for commissioned material half on commissioning and half on acceptance as being suitable for broadcasting.

Short stories specially written for radio: Fees range from £36.50 for 15 minutes.

*Stage plays for television: Fees for stage plays are negotiable.

Stage plays and published material for radio (domestic services): Dramatic works: £3.70 per minute up to 60 minutes; thereafter £2.85 per minute. Prose works: £3.45 per minute.

Prose works required for adaptation into dramatic form: £2.85 per minute up to 60 minutes; thereafter £2.55 per minute.

Poems: £3.70 per half minute up to 2 minutes; thereafter £2.85 per half minute. For the External Services, 50% of the above rates is paid for up to four broadcasts in English or 10% for one foreign language broadcast.

Prose and poems for television: prose works, £5.50 per minute; poems, £6.60 per half minute up to two minutes and £4.60 thereafter.

    * At time of going to press, the fees shown in this paragraph were in process of re-registration.

Repeats in BBC programmes: Further proportionate fees are payable for repeats.

Use abroad of recordings of BBC programmes: If the BBC sends abroad recordings of its programmes for use by overseas broadcasting organisations on their own networks or stations, further payments accrue to the author, usually in the form of additional percentages of the basic fee paid for the initial performance. This can apply to both sound and television programmes.

Value Added Tax: A self-billing system for V.A.T. was introduced in January 1978 for programmes made in London for radio and external services and for Television Equity type EC1 and Television Talks type G contracts. The system is being extended to cover other areas as soon as possible including programmes sold abroad which are now subject to V.A.T.

TALKS FOR TELEVISION

Contributors to talks will be offered the standard Television talks contract which provides the BBC certain rights to broadcast the material in a complete, abridged and/or translated manner, and which provides for the payment of further fees for additional usage of the material whether by television, domestic radio and external broadcasting. The contract also covers the assignment of material and limited publication rights. Fees are arranged by the contract authorities in London and the Regions.

TALKS FOR RADIO

Contributors to talks for domestic Radio and External Broadcasting may be offered either the standard talks contract which takes rights and provides for residual payments as does the Television standard contract above or be offered an ARR (All Rights) Contract which takes all broadcasting and non-paying audience rights where the contribution is of a short, ephemeral nature, not exceeding an air-time of five minutes and which has set fees or disturbance money payable, or an ARC contract where no payment is made which provides an acknowledgement that a contribution may be used by the BBC.

ADDRESSES

Letters addressed to speakers c/o the BBC will be forwarded, but may be opened before being forwarded. Letters marked "Personal" are forwarded unopened.

LONDON

Head Office: Broadcasting House, London, W1A 1AA
Telegrams Broadcasts, London.
Telex 265781
Cables Broadcasts, London, W.1.
Telephone 01-580 4468

Television: Television Centre, Wood Lane London, W12 7RJ
Telegrams Telecasts, London
Telex 265781
Telephone 01-743 8000

Publications: 35 Marylebone High Street, London, W1M 4AA
Telegrams Broadcasts, London
Telephone 01-580 5577

External Broadcasting: P.O. Box 76, Bush House, Strand, London, WC2B 4PH
Telephone 01-240 3456
Telegrams & Cables Broadbrit, London
Telex 265781

NETWORK PRODUCTION CENTRES

BIRMINGHAM

Broadcasting Centre, Pebble Mill Road, Birmingham, B5 7QQ
Telephone 021-472 5353

MANCHESTER

New Broadcasting House, Oxford Road, Manchester, M60 1SJ
Telephone 061-236 8444

BRISTOL

Broadcasting House, 21–33b Whiteladies Road, Clifton, Bristol, BS8 2LR
Telephone 0272-32211

REGIONAL TELEVISION STATIONS

EAST

St. Catherine's Close, All Saints Green, Norwich, NR1 3ND
Telephone 0603-28841

MIDLANDS

Broadcasting Centre, Pebble Mill Road, Birmingham, B5 7QQ
Telephone 021-472 5353

NORTH

Broadcasting Centre, Woodhouse Lane, Leeds, LS2 9PX
Telephone 0532-41188

NORTH-EAST

Broadcasting House, 54 New Bridge Street, Newcastle-upon-Tyne, NE1 8AA
Telephone 0632-20961

NORTH-WEST

New Broadcasting House, Oxford Road, Manchester, M60 1SJ
Telephone 061-236 8444

SOUTH

South Western House, Canute Road, Southampton, SO9 1PF
Telephone 0703-26201

SOUTH-WEST

Broadcasting House, Seymour Road, Mannamead, Plymouth, PL3 5BD
Telephone 0752-62283 and 29201

WEST

Broadcasting House, 21–33b Whiteladies Road, Clifton, Bristol, BS8 2LR
Telephone 0272-32211

BBC NATIONAL REGIONS

NORTHERN IRELAND

Broadcasting House, 25–27 Ormeau Avenue, Belfast, BT2 8HQ
Telephone 0232 44400

SCOTLAND

Broadcasting House, Queen Margaret Drive, Glasgow, G12 8DG
Telephone 041-339 8844
Edinburgh Office
Broadcasting House, 5 Queen Street, Edinburgh, EH2 1JF
Telephone 031-225 3131

Aberdeen Representative
Broadcasting House, Beechgrove Terrace, Aberdeen, AB9 2ZT
Telephone 0224 25233

WALES

Llantrisant Road, Llandaff, Cardiff, CF5 2YQ
Telephone 0222 564888
North Wales Representative
Bryn Meirion, Bangor, LL57 1YU
Telephone 0248 2214

OVERSEAS OFFICES

U.S.A.

630 Fifth Avenue, New York, N.Y., 10020, U.S.A.
Cables   Broadcasts, New York City
Telephone 212-581–7100
Telex   4200-93

CANADA

Postal Address: P.O. Box 500, Terminal A, Toronto, Ontario, Canada
Cables   Loncalling, Toronto
Telephone (416) 925 3311
Telex   06-23577

MIDDLE EAST

P.O.Box 2642, Cairo, Egypt
Telephone Cairo 706098
Telex   2635 BBCMed UN

SOUTH EAST ASIA

B.B.C. Representative, L2, 11th Floor International Building, 360 Orchard Road, Singapore, 9
Cables   Loncalling, Singapore
Telephone Singapore 372937

AUSTRALIA AND NEW ZEALAND

Westfield Towers, 100 William Street, Sydney, N.S.W. 2011, Australia
Cables   Loncalling, Sydney
Telephone Sydney, 3586411
Telex   BBCorp 20705

FRANCE

155 rue du Faubourg Saint-Honoré, BP 487 08, 75366 Paris, Cedex 08
Cables   Broadbrit, Paris
Telephone 225, 3900/3901/3902
Telex   650341

GERMANY

B.B.C. German Service Representative, 1 Berlin, 12 Savignyplatz, 6, W. Germany
Telephone West Berlin 316773, 3133063
Telex   Berlin 184469

LATIN AMERICA

Officina 67, Edificio Safico Corrientes 456, Buenos Aires, 1366 Argentina
Telephone Buenos Aires 49-3112

BELGIUM

International Press Centre, 1 Boulevard
Charlemagne, Brussels 1040
Telephone Brussels 736 8015
Telex 25912

INDIA

1 Nizamuddin East, New Delhi 110013
Cables Loncalling, Newdelhi
Telephone Delhi 624192

BBC LOCAL RADIO STATIONS

Material should be submitted to the Programme Organiser.

Birmingham, BBC Radio Birmingham, Pebble Mill Road, Birmingham, B5 7SA
T. 021 472 5141. *Telex:* 33921.

Blackburn, BBC Radio Blackburn, King Street, Blackburn, Lancashire, BB2 2EA
T. 0254 62411. *Telex:* 63491.

Brighton, BBC Radio Brighton, Marlborough Place, Brighton, BN1 1TU *T.*
0273 680231. *Telex:* 87313.

Bristol, BBC Radio Bristol, 3 Tyndalls Park Road, Bristol, BS8 1PP *T.* 0272
311111. *Telex:* 449170.

Carlisle BBC Radio Carlisle, Hilltop Heights, London Road, Carlisle, CA1 2NA
T. 0228 31661.

Cleveland, BBC Radio Cleveland, 91/93 Linthorpe Road, Middlesbrough,
Teeside, Cleveland, TS1 5DG *T.* 0642 48491. *Telex:* 58203.

Derby, BBC Radio Derby, 56 St. Helen's Street, Derby, DE1 3HY *T.* 0332
361111. *Telex:* 37257.

Humberside, BBC Radio Humberside, 9 Chapel Street, Hull, HU1 3NU *T.*
0482 23232. *Telex:* 527031.

Leeds, BBC Radio Leeds, Merrion Centre, Leeds, LS2 8NJ *T.* 0532 42131.
Telex: 57230.

Leicester, BBC Radio Leicester, Epic House, Charles Street, Leicester, LE1 3SH
T. 0533 27113. *Telex:* 34401.

London, BBC Radio London, 35A Marylebone High Street. London, W1A 4LG
T. 01-486 7611. *Telex:* 267223.

Manchester, BBC Radio Manchester, P.O. Box 90, New Broadcasting House,
Oxford Road, Manchester, M60 1ST *T.* 061-228 3434. *Telex:* 668708.

Medway, BBC Radio Medway, 30 High Street, Chatham, Kent. *T.* 0634 46284.
Telex: 965011.

Merseyside, BBC Radio Merseyside, Commerce House, 13–17 Sir Thomas Street,
Liverpool, L1 5BS *T.* 051-236 3355. *Telex:* 62364.

Newcastle, BBC Radio Newcastle, Crestina House, Archbold Terrace, Newcastle-
upon-Tyne, NE2 1DZ *T.* 0632 814243. *Telex:* 537007.

Nottingham, BBC Radio Nottingham, York House, York Street, Nottingham,
NG1 3JB *T.* 0602 47643. *Telex:* 37464.

Oxford, BBC Radio Oxford, 242–254 Banbury Road, Oxford, OX2 7DW *T.*
0865 53411. *Telex:* 83571.

Sheffield, BBC Radio Sheffield, Ashdell Grove, 60 Westbourne Road, Sheffield,
S10 2QU *T.* 0742 686185. *Telex:* 54400.

Solent, BBC Radio Solent, South Western House, Canute Road, Southampton,
SO9 4PJ. *T.* 0703 31311. *Telex:* 47420.

Stoke-on-Trent, BBC Radio Stoke-on-Trent, Conway House, Cheapside, Hanley,
Stoke-on-Trent, Staffordshire, ST1 1JJ *T.* 0782 24827. *Telex:* 36104.

INDEPENDENT LOCAL RADIO

Independent Broadcasting Authority, 70 Brompton Road, London, SW3 1EY
T. 01-584 7011.

The Independent Television Authority became the Independent Broadcasting
Authority on 12 July 1972 and is now responsible for Independent Local
Radio as well as Independent Television. Nineteen companies have currently
been appointed.

ILR Belfast: Downtown Radio, Kiltonga Radio Centre, P.O. Box 230, New-
townards, C. Down. *T.* 0247-815555.

ILR Birmingham: BRMB Radio, Radio House, P.O. Box 555, Birmingham,
B6 4BX *T.* 021-359 4481-9.

ILR Bradford: Pennine Radio, P.O. Box 235, Pennine House, Forster Square,
Bradford, BD1 5NP. *T.* 0274-31521.

ILR Edinburgh: Radio Forth, Forth House, Forth Street, Edinburgh, EH1 3LF
T. 031-556 9255.

ILR Glasgow: Radio Clyde, Ranken House, Blythswood Court, Anderston
Cross Centre, Glasgow, G2 7LB *T.* 041-204 2555.

ILR Ipswich: Radio Orwell, Electric House, Lloyds Avenue, Ipswich, IP1 3HU
T. 0473-216971.

ILR Liverpool: Radio City, P.O. Box 194, 8-10 Stanley Street, Liverpool, L69
1LD *T.* 051-227 5100.

ILR London (General Entertainment Service): Capital Radio, Euston Tower,
London, NW1 3DR *T.* 01-388 1288.

ILR London (News & Information Service): London Broadcasting Company
(LBC), Communications House, Gough Square, London, EC4P 4LP *T.* 01-
353 1010.

ILR Manchester: Piccadilly Radio, 127-131 The Piazza, Piccadilly Plaza, Manchester, M1 4AW *T.* 061-236 9913.

ILR Nottingham: Radio Trent, 29-31 Castle Gate, Nottingham, NG1 7AP *T.*
0602-581731.

ILR Plymouth: Plymouth Sound, Earl's Acre, Alma Road, Plymouth, PL3
4HX *T.* 0752-27272.

ILR Portsmouth: Radio Victory, P.O. Box 257, Portsmouth, PO1 5RT *T.*
0705-27799.

ILR Reading: Radio 210 Thames Valley, P.O. Box 210, Reading, RG3 5RZ
T. 0734 413131.

ILR Sheffield & Rotherham: Radio Hallam, P.O. Box 194, Hartshead, Sheffield,
S1 1GP *T.* 0742-71188.

ILR Swansea: Swansea Sound, Victoria Road, Gowerton, Swansea, SA4 3AB
  T. (Gorseinon) 0792-893751.

ILR Teesside: Radio Tees, 74 Dovecot Street, Stockton-on-Tees, Cleveland
  TS18 1LL *T.* 0642-615111.

ILR Tyne/Wear: Metro Radio, Newcastle upon Tyne, NE99 1BB *T.* 0632-
  884121.

ILR Wolverhampton: Beacon Radio, P.O. Box 303, 267 Tettenhall Road, Wolverhampton, WV6 0DQ *T.* 0902-757211.

Independent Radio News (IRN). A subsidiary of LBC which acts as a news
  agency for all other ILR Companies by providing spoken and other live
  material and a teleprinter service.

INDEPENDENT TELEVISION

Independent Broadcasting Authority, 70 Brompton Road, London, SW3 1EY *T.* 01-584 7011. The Authority does not produce programmes, and material intended for broadcasting on the Authority's service should be addressed to the programme contractors, who are responsible for supplying programmes for transmission.

Material required by the Programme Contractors as listed below depends upon the contract held by the Company, i.e. London mid-week programmes will obviously differ from those for the Midlands. In all cases scripts are preferred to synopses. Programmes should be planned with natural breaks for the insertion of advertisements.

Contracts are held by the following companies:

Anglia Television Ltd., Anglia House, Norwich, NR1 3JG *T.* 0603-28366. Brook House, 113 Park Lane, London, W1Y 4DX *T.* 01-408 2288. Provides programmes in the East of England during the whole week and drama and natural history programmes. 60-minute original dramas are welcomed. Writers should contact the Head of Anglia Drama Dept.

ATV Network, Ltd., ATV Centre, Birmingham, B1 2JP *T.* 021-643 9898, and ATV Elstree Studios, Eldon Avenue, Boreham Wood, Herts, WD6 1JF *T.* 01-953 6100. Provides programmes for the Midlands area during the whole week.—ATV Network's requirements are constantly changing, and interested professional writers are asked to contact the Script Department at the Elstree Studios for information.

Border Television, Ltd., The Television Centre, Carlisle, CA1 3NT *T.* 0228-25101. 33 Margaret Street, London, W1N 7LA *T.* 01-323 4711. Provides programmes for Southern Scotland, Cumbria, the Isle of Man and North Northumberland, including Berwick-upon-Tweed, during the whole week. Occasionally scripts are commissioned from outside sources. Suggestions should be sent to the Assistant Controller of Programmes (Production) in Carlisle.

Channel Television, The Television Centre, St. Helier, Jersey, C.I. *T.* 0534 23451. Provides programmes in the Channel Islands during the whole week —relating mainly to Channel Islands news and current affairs.

Grampian Television Limited, Queens Cross, Aberdeen, AB9 2XJ *T.* 0224 53553. 103–105 Marketgait, Dundee, DD1 1QT *T.* 0382 21777. Provides programmes in North and East Scotland during the whole week.

Granada Television Limited, TV Centre, Manchester, M60 9EA *T.* 061-832 7211 and 36 Golden Square, London, W1R 4AH *T.* 01-734 8080. Provides programmes for Lancashire throughout the week. Granada has for some time largely pursued a policy of initiating its own dramatic material, e.g. *Family at War, Sam* and *This Year Next Year* or adaptations of established works like the stories of D. H. Lawrence, *The Sinners* and *Country Matters.* It is, therefore, advisable for writers to make their approach through agents who would have some knowledge of Granada's current requirements.

HTV Ltd., HTV Wales, The Television Centre, Cardiff, CF1 9XL *T.* 0222 21021. HTV West, The Television Centre, Bath Road, Bristol, BS4 3HG *T.* 0272 770271. 99 Baker Street, London, W1M 2AJ *T.* 01-486 4311. Provides programmes for Wales and West of England during the whole week.

London Weekend Television, Ltd., South Bank Television Centre, Kent House, Upper Ground, London, SE1 9LT *T.* 01-261 3434. Provides programmes for London area from Friday 7 p.m. to Sunday Close Down. Professional writers please get in touch first with Pat Sandys (Drama Script Consultant) for latest information.

Scottish Television, Ltd., Cowcaddens, Glasgow, G2 3PR *T.* 041-332 9999. The Gateway, Edinburgh, EH7 4AH *T.* 031-556 5372. Provides programmes for Central Scotland during the whole week. *Material:* Scripts for contemporary plays and ideas and formats for programmes with a European or international flavour. Approach in the first instance to Director of Programme's Office.

Southern Television, Ltd., Southern Television Centre, Northam, Southampton, SO9 4YQ *T.* 0703-28582. Glen House, Stag Place, London, SW1E 5AX *T.* 01-834 4404. Dover Studios, Russell Street, Dover, CT16 1PY *T.* 0304-202303. Provides programmes for the South of England during whole week.
Material required: Most scripts are specially commissioned, but professional writers wishing to submit material should get in touch with the Drama Scripts Organiser at Southampton.

Thames Television, Ltd., Thames Television Ltd., Thames Television House, 306 Euston Road, London, NW1 3BB *T.* 01-387 9494 (Features). Teddington Lock, Teddington, Middlesex, TW11 9NT *T.* 01-977 3252 (Drama / Light Entertainment). Provides programmes for the London area from Monday to Friday 7 p.m.
Material required: Drama Department: Most of the material produced by the Drama Department is specially commissioned, and it is advisable that a preliminary letter should be sent before submitting any unsolicited scripts. Correspondence should be addressed to Joan Rodker, Script Executive, Drama Department.
Light Entertainment Department: Material is generally specially commissioned but the Light Entertainment Department invites ideas and scripts for 30-minute situation comedies, also material for sketch shows. Submissions to Light Entertainment, Thames Television Ltd.

Tyne Tees Television, Ltd., The Television Centre, City Road, Newcastle upon Tyne, NE1 2AL *T.* 0632 610181. Trident House, 15–16 Brooks Mews, London, W1Y 2PN *T.* 01-493 1237. Brazennose House, Brazennose Street, Manchester, M2 5BP *T.* 061-834 4228–9. Provides programmes in North-East England during the whole week.

Ulster Television, Ltd., Havelock House, Ormeau Road, Belfast, BT7 1EB. *T.* 0232-28122. 19 Marylebone Road, London, NW1 5JJ *T.* 01-486 5211. Provides programmes in Northern Ireland during the whole week. Company staff provide majority of scripts, but occasionally they are commissioned from other sources.

Westward Television, Ltd., Derry's Cross, Plymouth, PL1 2SP *T.* 0752-69311. Sloane Square House, Holbein Place, Sloane Square, London, SW1W 8NT *T.* 01-730 5101. Dominions House, 23–25 St. Augustine's Parade, The Centre, Bristol, BS1 4UG *T.* 0272 211321. 3 Frederick Place, St. Thomas Street, Weymouth. *T.* 75050. Provides programmes for South-West England during the whole week.

Yorkshire Television, Ltd., The Television Centre, Leeds, LS3 1JS   *T.* 0532 38283.   *Telex:* 557232.   Trident House, 15–16 Brooks Mews, London, W1Y 2PN   *T.* 01-493 1237.   *Telex:* 25202.   29–30 Old Burlington Street, London, W1X 1LB   *T.* 01-493 1237.   *Telex:* 25202.   Provides programmes for the Yorkshire area during the whole week.

Independent Television News, Ltd., ITN House, 48 Wells Street, London, W1P 4DE   *T.* 01-637 2424.   Provides the national and international news programmes for all ITV areas.

NATIONAL AND INDEPENDENT RADIO AND TELEVISION COMPANIES

Australian Broadcasting Commission, Box 487, GPO, Sydney, NSW 2001. Manager for Europe: Australian Broadcasting Commission, 54 Portland Place, London, W1N 4DY. The Australian Broadcasting Commission is a statutory authority established by Act of Parliament and responsible to Parliament. It provides television and radio programmes in the national broadcasting service and operates Radio Australia.
ABC television restricts its production resources to work closely related to the Australian environment. For this reason scripts submitted from outside Australia in the field of television drama and short stories have little chance of success. ABC radio also looks principally to Australian writers for the basis of its drama output. However, ABC radio is interested in auditioning new creative material of a high quality from overseas sources and this may be submitted in script or taped form. No journalistic material is required. Talks on international affairs are commissioned.

Federation of Australian Broadcasters, 47 York Street, Sydney, NSW 2000 —from whom information should be obtainable on the numerous commercial radio stations in Australia.

Federation of Australian Commercial Television Stations, Suite 401, 4th Floor, Caltex House, Sydney, 2000. *T.* 27 5741. *T.A.* Telefed, Sydney. There are at present 49 commercial television stations in Australia which are members of FACTS.

Our enquiries thus far show that the following six stations accept freelance material:

ATN Channel 7, Amalgamated Television Services Pty. Ltd., Television Centre, Epping, NSW 2121. *T.* 85 0111. *T.A.* Telecentre, Sydney. *Telex:* AA 20250. Willing to consider original television material of all types, especially 90 minute "one-off" plays, 60 minute drama series, 30 minute situation-comedy series and 30 minute children's drama series. All material should have an Australian background and deal with Australian characters. For series submit sample script with some future story-lines. Writers should preferably be Australian-based.

BTQ Channel 7, Brisbane TV Limited, Sir Samuel Griffith Drive, Mt. Coot-Tha, GPO Box 604, Brisbane 4001. *T.* 36 0111. *T.A.* Beeteeque. Writers should be Australian-based. Children's Educational-type series, children's entertainment programmes and local drama (Queensland writers only).

HSV Channel 7, Herald-Sun Television Pty. Ltd., GPO Box 215d, Melbourne, Vic. 3001. For requirements see entry for ATN Channel 7.

NWS Channel 9, Southern Television Corporation Ltd., 202 Tynte Street, PO Box 9, North Adelaide, South Australia 5006. *T.* 267 0111. *T.A.* Newsnine, Adelaide. *Telex:* 82238.

Publishing & Broadcasting Ltd. (TCN Channel 9), Television Corporation Limited, 24 Artarmon Road, Box 27, PO Willoughby, NSW 2068. *T.* 43 0444. *T.A.* Diffusion, Sydney. *Telex:* AA 20689. Interested in receiving material from freelance writers strictly on the basis of payment for material or ideas used. No necessity for writers to be Australian-based, but membership of the Australian Writers' Guild is helpful.

STW Channel 9, Swan Television & Radio Broadcasters Limited, PO Box 99, Tuart Hill, Western Australia 6060. *T.* 349 9999. *T.A.* Swantel, Perth. *Telex:* AA92142. Writers should be Australian-based.

CANADA

Canadian Broadcasting Corporation, Script Services, PO Box 500, Station "A", Toronto, M5W 1E6. The CBC's interest in plays for television and radio has a natural emphasis on Canadian writers and Canadian themes. There is also a smaller market for plays from abroad which should be submitted in complete script form. Submission through an agent is not required.
The right to a single broadcast on each station of the network within a three-year period is usually bought, and the fees refer to these terms. Fees are by individual negotiation and are according to ACTRA rates.

Television:
One Hour.—These scripts are mainly commissioned for both series and anthology productions. Ideas are considered also. The series traditionally are based on Canadian themes, contemporary and historical.
Half Hour.—Series and anthology programmes in this length are similar in concept to the one-hours.

Radio: Very small market for superior ninety-minute scripts.
One Hour.—Originals preferred but adaptations considered. All types of drama used.
Half Hour.—Small market. Every type of story considered.
Requirements for scripts other than drama, such as children's, schools, documentary, etc., are mainly met locally on commission, after discussion. Ideas can be forwarded, however, on speculation.

Canadian Radio-Television and Telecommunications Commission, Ottawa, Ontario, K1A 0N2 *T.* (613) 997-0313—the federal authority which regulates telecommunications and the broadcasting system in Canada.

INDIA

All India Radio, Broadcasting House, Parliament Street, New Delhi, 110 001, is the department of the Government of India which operates the broadcasting network in the country. There are 82 centres covering all the important cultural and linguistic regions of the country. These centres are under five zones: North, East, West, South and Kashmir. In addition there are auxiliary studio centres at Baroda, Mysore and Shantiniketan; there are also two Vividh Bharati/Commercial centres at Chandigarh and Kanpur. Programmes are planned by Station Directors and are drawn up well in advance of their scheduled dates. Programmes are arranged and produced locally and consist of music, talks, plays; special programmes for women and children, school broadcasts and rural broadcasts for community listening. Programmes are broadcast in nineteen languages: English, Sanskrit, Hindi, Bengali, Tamil, Telugu, Marathi, Sindhi, Gujarati, Kannada, Malayalam, Oriya, Kashmiri, Punjabi, Assamese, Dogri, Gorkhali, Nefa-Assamese and

Urdu. In its broadcasts, AIR emphasise the instructional, cultural and entertainment items. It avoids politics of a controversial nature and does not accept sponsored broadcasts or any matter that would amount to commercial advertising. It does not include in its programmes any appeal for funds or contributions. It strives to maintain and uphold canons of good taste.

The External Services of All India Radio broadcast programmes in 25 languages for a duration of 53 hours every day. Programme for listeners abroad consist of news, daily commentary and press review, talks, discussions and music, mainly light classical, light, film and folk. These are broadcast in two major services: General Overseas Service and the Urdu Service. The West Asian service broadcasts programmes in Arabic, Dari, Persian, Pushtu and Baluchi. East African countries are served by the Swahili service, while the French service is directed to South East Asia and North and West Africa. Other area-oriented services are in Burmese, Chinese, Indonesian, Nepali, Russian, Sinhala, Thai and Tibetah languages. Composite programmes comprising news, press reviews, commentaries, talks, music and features are broadcast in Indian languages, Bengali, Gujarati, Hindi, Konkani, Punjabi, Sindhi, Tamil and Urdu. The object of these programmes is to entertain Indians abroad and keep them in touch with the events and developments in India.

Programmes for the youth or "Yuv Vani" are broadcast from Delhi, Calcutta, Hyderabad, Jammu, Srinagar and Patna Stations of All India Radio. In addition, 50 stations of All India Radio broadcast programmes of varying duration and frequency in different languages for the youth. Yuv Vani provides a forum to the young between the ages of fifteen plus and twenty-five, who present their viewpoint by participating in a wide range of programmes—talks, discussions, interviews, plays, features and music. A youth news bulletin is also broadcast by the youth themselves.

The Commercial Service from AIR was started from Bombay-Poona-Nagpur on November 1, 1967. Encouraged by advertisers and the listeners it was extended to Calcutta (1968); Delhi and Madras-Tiruchirapalli (1969); Chandigarh-Jullundur, Bangalore-Dharwar, Ahmedabad-Rajkot, Kanpur-Lucknow-Allahabad (1970) and Hyderabad-Vijayawada (1971). In 1975 10 more stations came into operation. Sponsored programmes were first introduced in the Bombay-Poona-Nagpur beam in May, 1970. Later on the programmes were extended to all the Commercial Centres.

Television

There are five television centres: at Amritsar, Bombay, Delhi, Poona TV Relay Centre and Srinagar, providing entertainment, information and education. Details from the Director General, Door Darshan, Mandi House, New Delhi.

IRELAND

Radio Telefis Eireann, Donnybrook, Dublin 4. *T.* 693111. *Telex:* 5268.
The Irish national broadcasting service operating radio and television.
Television: script requirements: original television plays, minimum length 52 minutes, preferably set in Ireland or of strong Irish interest. Plays should be sent to the Head of Drama. Before submitting material to Public Affairs, Features or Children's programmes, authors are advised to write to the department in question.
Radio: talks and short stories (length 14 minutes) in Irish or English suitable for broadcasting: features, dramatic or narrative and plays are welcomed and paid for according to merit. Plays should run 30, 45, 60, 75 or 90 minutes. MSS. should be addressed as follows: R.T.E. (Sound programmes), Donnybrook, Dublin 4.
At present there is no independent local radio or commercial television in the Republic of Ireland.

NEW ZEALAND

Broadcasting Corporation of New Zealand, The Secretary, PO Box 98, Wellington, C1. The Corporation lays down radio and television standards, and supplies certain common services to the three operating services listed below. Writers should write to the following addresses:

Radio New Zealand, The Director-General, PO Box 2092, Wellington, C1. *T.* 721-777. This Corporation controls three public radio networks (one commercial), and also a shortwave service directed primarily to the Southwest Pacific Islands and Southeastern Australia.

South Pacific Television (TV2). The Director-General, P.O. Box 3819, Auckland. This commercial network is a Service of the Broadcasting Corporation of New Zealand. There are seven main transmitters covering 85% of the population: Waiatarua (Auckland), Te Aroha (Waikato/Bay of Plenty), Wharite (Manawatu), Kaukau (Wellington), Sugarloaf (Canterbury), Cargill (Dunedin), Hedgehope (Southland). Programmes normally run from 3 p.m. to midnight, daily, and are broadly divided into 30% N.Z., 30% U.K., 30% U.S.A. and 10% from other sources, mostly Australia. Most are in colour. Local studio production is centred in Auckland, Christchurch and Hamilton although news is injected from all main centres. The network carries national and local advertising every day except Friday and Sunday.

Television Service One (TV1), The Director-General, PO Box 30–355, Lower Hutt. TV-1, a Service of the Broadcasting Corporation of New Zealand, operates a semi-commercial nationwide colour television network originating from Wellington and with additional production studios in Dunedin and Auckland. *Controller of Programmes:* D. J. Monaghan; *Head of Drama:* M. Scott-Smith.

SOUTH AFRICA

South African Broadcasting Corporation, PO Box 8606, Johannesburg 2000. *T.* 714-0111. The South African Broadcasting Corporation, established in terms of the Broadcasting Act No. 22 of 1936 as amended, operates three national networks: the English, Afrikaans, and Springbok Radio and three regional services, Radio High Veld, Radio Port Natal and Radio Good Hope. The Bantu Service operates seven regional services in seven languages, viz. Zulu, Xhosa, Southern Sotho, Northern Sotho, Tswana and Venda/Tsonga. Services in four languages are broadcast to the native people of South-west Africa. The SABC introduced an External Service on May 1st 1966 known as Radio RSA, *The Voice of South Africa* which transmits programmes to all corners of the world. This service echoes around the world in nine languages to carry a positive and objective message about South Africa, its peoples and their achievements, their culture, tradition and ideals. The languages used are English, Afrikaans, Portuguese, French, German, Dutch, ChiChewa, Swahili and Lozi.

Plays.—Most types are produced—classical and modern dramas, comedies and thrillers, original radio plays and adaptations of stories, etc. Contributions are welcomed in all sections. The most convenient lengths are 30, 60 and 90 minutes. The Afrikaans network also accepts high quality material for translation. Programmes on the Commercial Service (Springbok Radio) are typical of modern commercial radio, and serials of 15-minute episodes are widely used. Series of self-contained episodes of 15, 30 or 60 minutes are also acceptable. Variety programmes of 30 minutes' duration are always in demand.

Feature Programmes.—Material of topical, scientific and historical interest of 30 to 60 minutes' duration is welcomed.

Talks.—Most are commissioned locally, but outstanding material of particular interest may be submitted. Most suitable length is 5, 10 and 15 minutes.

Short Stories.—There are occasional openings for short stories of 1500–1800 words.

Light entertainment.—Variety material, light entertainment scripts, and light plays with music may be submitted. The SABC particularly needs first-class variety material.

Youth and Children's Programmes.—Plays, talks, stories, and serials may be submitted. Lengths: plays, up to 15 minutes, and 30 minutes for youth; stories, from 5 to 10 minutes.

It should be stressed that all outside contributors should take into consideration the fact that Radio South Africa caters for a South African public, a public, that is to say, with its own needs, ideas, and tastes.

Television: Full colour television came into operation in January 1976.

There are no independent commercial radio or TV Stations in South Africa.

UNITED STATES

American Broadcasting Company, ABC News, 8 Carburton Street, London, W1P 7DT *T.* 01-580 0531.

CBS News, 100 Brompton Road, London, SW3. *T.* 01-584 3366.

IBC Sound Recording Studios Ltd., 35 Portland Place, London, W1N 3AG *T.* 01-637 2111.

NBC News Worldwide, Inc., 8 Bedford Avenue, London, WC1B 3NQ *T.* 01-637 8655.

LITERARY AGENTS

In the absence of an established code of practice, a questionnaire was circulated to agents in the British Isles with a view to providing the following list, more selective and more informative than hitherto.

It should be noted that most agents do not charge a fee for marketing or placing manuscripts. Some firms charge a reading fee which is refunded on acceptance of the material. All the agents in this list will suggest revision of worthwhile manuscripts where necessary, suggesting in the first instance that revision should be done by the author. In certain cases, an agency is prepared to recommend a qualified person not connected with their agency to undertake revision. In a few cases where agencies themselves are prepared to undertake revision, this fact is clearly stated. In their own interests writers are strongly recommended to think twice before agreeing to pay for revision. Some agents are prepared to give an author a report and advice on a MS. and they make an appropriate charge for this. The reference to "Short MSS." in many of the following entries is almost invariably to short stories and not to journalistic articles.

Literary agents exist to sell saleable material. It must be remembered that, while they are always looking for new writers and are often prepared to take immense pains with a writer whose work, in their opinion, shows potential quality or distinctive promise, agents do not exist to teach people how to write. Short manuscripts, unless they are of an exceptional nature, are unlikely to be profitable or even to pay an agent for the work involved. Writers must not expect agents, publishers or editors to comment at length on unsuitable work submitted to them, although often they are asked to do so. Every writer must expect disappointments, especially at the outset of his career, but if he has something to say and knows how to say it, then eventually (if he is patient) he will learn how to satisfy an editor's requirements, or alternatively he will learn that he should give up attempting to write and turn to some other form of activity. He must not expect other people to tell him his mistakes, although not infrequently a new writer is helped in this way by an agent, editor or publisher who has detected a spark of promise in a manuscript submitted to him.

If a writer of some proven ability is contemplating using an agent, he is advised in his own interests to write a preliminary letter to ascertain whether the agent will consider him as a potential client. He should also enquire the agent's terms if they are not given in the entry in the following pages. Reputable agents do not accept work unless they consider it to be of a marketable standard and an author submitting work to an agent for the first time should therefore enclose return postage.

This list of literary agents does not purport to be exhaustive. If any who are not included would like to receive a copy of the questionnaire and to be considered for inclusion, application should be made to the publishers.

* Members of The Association of Authors' Agents.

Adamastor Agency (1961). *Directors:* Sydney Clouts, Marjorie Clouts. 6 Somerton Road, London, NW2. *T.* 01-452 8101. *T.A.* Storsta, London, NW2.
Full-length non-fiction for book publication. Preliminary letter essential. S.A.E. appreciated. Terms on application. No reading fee.

Alpha Book Agency (1967). *Director:* P. H. Hargreaves, Boydon End, 260 Hayes Lane, Kenley, Surrey, CR2 5EG *T.* 01-668 2907.
Educational MSS only (home 10%, overseas 19%). No reading fee.

Aquarius Literary Agency (1977, 1955 in South Africa). *Directors:* Gilbert Gibson (Managing), Borek Nemecek. *Postal address:* P.O. Box 78, London, SE19. *Registered address:* 1st Floor, 44A Westow Street, Upper Norwood, London, SE19. *T.* 01-653 8457. *T.A.* Treblig, London, SE19.
Full-length and short MSS. (home 10%, overseas 20%). Theatre, films, television (10%), radio (15%). Office in Johannesburg. Markets direct everywhere. Aquarius is a literary division of Sun Pacific Music (London) Ltd., music publishers. No reading fee.

Authors' Alliance (1911). Mrs. Deborah Greenep, 64 The Dean, Alresford, Hants.
Full-length MSS. (home and overseas 10%). Theatre (10%), Films (10%), Television and sound broadcasting (10%). Represented in Europe and U.S.A. Does not accept MSS. for children's books, articles or short stories. No reading fee. S.A.E. please, and/or return postage.

Barnett, Roger, Associates (1970). *Proprietor:* Roger Barnett, 4 Shaftesbury, Loughton, Essex, IG10 1HN *T.* 01-508 8856. *London Office:* 143 Holborn, London, EC1N 2NJ.
Full-length MSS. (home 10%, overseas 20%), short MSS. (home 30%, overseas 40%).

Benson, Dorothea, Literary Agency (1968). *Director:* Dorothea Benson, Beckington, Doyle Road, St. Peter Port, Guernsey. *T.* Guernsey 24336.
Full-length and short MSS. (home 10%; overseas 20%). Theatre, films, television, radio (10%). Will suggest revision if promising, by author or competent outsider. Represented in London. English stamps not accepted in Guernsey; International Reply Coupons or Postal Orders only for returning MSS. No reading fee.

Blake, Carole (1977). *Proprietor:* Carole Blake, The Old Forge, Redhill, nr. Buntingford, Herts, SG9 0TH *T.* Broadfield (076 388) 270.
Full-length MSS. fiction and non-fiction, no juvenile (home 10%, overseas 20%), short MSS. (home 25%, overseas 25%). Theatre, films, television, sound broadcasting (10%). Preliminary letter preferred. No reading fee.

Bolt & Watson Ltd. (1971). *Directors:* David Bolt, Sheila Watson. 8-12 Old Queen Street, Storey's Gate, London, SW1H 9HP *T.* 01-930 5378. *T.A.* Bandwag, London, SW1. Full length and short MSS (home 10%, U.S.A. 15%, translations 19%). Theatre, films, television, sound broadcasting (10%). Will sometimes suggest revision. *U.S.A. Representative:* Georges Borchardt Inc., 136 East 57th Street, New York, N.Y., 10022, and works in association with many foreign agencies. No reading fee.

Byrne, Myles. *Directors:* Myles Byrne, Keith Byrne and T. Byrne. Embassy Theatre, Western Road, Hove, BN3 1AE, Sussex. *T.* Brighton 735124.
Full-length MSS. (home 20%, U.S.A. & other countries 25%, translations 19% of amount received). Theatre, film, television and sound broadcasting, novels (home 10%, abroad 20%). No poetry. Represented in most European countries, U.S.A., South America, Israel, etc. No reading fee but return S.A.E. essential.

C and B (Theatre), a wholly-owned subsidiary of **Calder & Boyars, Ltd.,** 18 Brewer Street, London, W1R 4AS *T.* 01-734 1985, 6900, 3786, 3787. *Directors:* J. M. Calder, Marion Boyars, Michael Hayes.
An agency handling the sale of dramatic rights to professional and amateur theatre companies, radio, television and film.

Cadell, John, Ltd. (1963). *Directors:* John Cadell, Mrs. Gillian Cadell, Ann Thomas. 2 Southwood Lane, London, N6 5EE *T.* 01-348 1914.
Only theatre, films, television, sound broadcasting (10%). Will suggest revision. Works in conjunction with Harold Freedman, Brandt & Brandt, Dramatic Dept. Inc., New York. No reading fee.

*Campbell Thomson & McLaughlin, Ltd. *Directors:* Christine Campbell Thomson, John McLaughlin, Kenneth Thomson, John Parker, Stephanie Townsend, Hal Cheetham. 31 Newington Green, London, N16 9PU *T.* 01-249 2971. *T.A.* Peterlaine, London, N16.
Full-length book MSS. (home 10%, overseas up to 20% including commission to foreign agent). No poetry. U.S.A. agents represented: Raines & Raines, 475 Fifth Avenue, N.Y., 10017; The Fox Chase Agency, Inc., 419 East 57th Street, N.Y., 10022. Representatives in most European countries. No reading fee. Subsidiary company: **Peter Janson-Smith Ltd.**

*Carnell, E. J., Literary Agency (1951). *Proprietor:* Leslie Flood, Rowneybury Bungalow, Sawbridgeworth, Nr. Old Harlow, Essex, CM20 2EX *T.* 0279 29408.
Science fiction specialists. All MSS (home 10%, overseas 15%). Direct representation abroad including U.S.A., also works in conjunction with some agencies. No reading fee.

Christy and Moore—see **Sheil, Anthony, Associates, Ltd.**

Clowes, Jonathan, Ltd. (1960). *Directors:* Jonathan Clowes, Ann Evans, Donald Carroll, Enyd Clowes. 19 Jeffrey's Place, London, NW1 9PP *T.* 01-267 4885. *T.A.* Agenclow, London, NW1.
Full-length MSS. (home and overseas 10%). Theatre, films, television and sound broadcasting (10%). Works in association with agents in France, Italy, Germany and Scandinavia. No reading fee.

Cochrane, Elspeth, Agency (1967). *Director:* Miss Elspeth Cochrane, 1 The Pavement, London, SW4 0HY *T.* 01-622 0314.
Full-length MSS. (home and overseas 10%). Theatre, films, television, sound broadcasting (10%). No reading fee.

Colin, Rosica, Limited (1949). *Directors:* Rosica Colin, Sylvie Marston, M.A., Joanna Marston. 4 Hereford Square, London, SW7 4TU *T.* 01-373 7678. *T.A.* Colrep, London, SW7 4TU.
All full-length MSS. (home 10%: overseas 20%). Theatre, films, television and sound broadcasting (10%). Works in U.S.A., European countries and overseas. No reading fee.

Copeman, Donald, Ltd. *Directors:* Donald Copeman, M. J. Copeman, John Pawsey. 52 Bloomsbury Street, London, WC1B 3QT *T.* 01-637 4909.
Full-length non-fiction and fiction MSS. (home 10%, overseas 20%). Will suggest revision if MSS. sufficiently promising. No poetry or short stories. Preliminary letter, and return postage with submitted MSS. Works in conjunction with agencies in Europe and U.S.A. No reading fee.

Crawford, Diana, Ltd.—see **Curtis Brown Group Ltd.** (Diana Baring).

*Crew, Rupert, Limited (1927). *Directors:* F. R. Crew, K. A. Crew, D. Montgomery, S. Russell. King's Mews, London, WC1N 2JA *T.* 01-242 8586–7. *T.A.* Authorship, Holb., London.
International business management for authors and feature writers desiring world representation by a highly geared, personal service, available only to a limited clientele. Preliminary letter. Commission 10%–25% by arrangement, no reading fees except in certain circumstances where optional criticism is offered. Also acts independently as publishers' consultants.

Crouch, Peter, Plays Ltd.—see **Spokesmen.**

Curtis Brown Group Ltd. (1899). *Directors:* Graham Watson (Chairman), Richard Odgers (Deputy Chairman), Peter Grose (Managing), Diana Baring, Andrew Best, James Brown (U.S.A.), John Johnston, Peter Murphy, Michael Shaw, George M. Webster (Secretary). 1 Craven Hill, London, W2 3EP *T.* 01-262 1011. *Telex:* 261536. Wholly owned subsidiary companies in the Group: Curtis Brown Ltd., Curtis Brown Academic Ltd., D. D. Spokesmen Ltd. (Spokesmen). James Brown Associates Inc.. 25 West 43rd Street, New York, N.Y. 10036. *T.* 736- 3777; Curtis Brown (Australia Pty. Ltd., P.O. Box 19, Paddington, Sydney, N.S.W. 2021, Australia. *T.* 31-8301. See separate entries for **Curtis Brown Ltd., Curtis Brown Academic Ltd., Spokesmen.**

Curtis Brown Ltd. (1899). *Directors:* Graham Watson (Chairman), Peter Grose (Managing), Diana Baring, Andrew Best, Felicity Bryan, Richard Odgers, Michael Shaw, Mollie Waters, George M. Webster (Secretary). 1 Craven Hill, London, W2 3EP *T.* 01-262 1011. *Telex:* 261536.
Agents for the negotiation in all markets of novels, general non-fiction, children's books and associated rights. (Home 10%, U.S.A. 15%, Foreign 19%.) Works in conjunction with other companies in Curtis Brown Group, Ltd. Unsolicited MSS are not accepted without a previous letter discussing the nature of the work and the professional or publishing record of the author. No reading fee.

Curtis Brown Academic Ltd. (1974). Incorporating **Shaw Maclean.** *Directors:* Graham Watson (Chairman), Andrew Best (Managing), Diana Baring, Peter Grose, Richard Odgers, Michael Shaw, George Webster (Secretary). 1 Craven Hill, London, W2 3EP *T.* 01-262 1011. *Telex:* 261536.
Agents in all academic and professional disciplines for academic and specialist writers. Textbooks at all levels, learned works, reference, scholarly biography, professional, technical and specialist books. (Home 10%, U.S.A. 15%, Foreign 19%.) Works in conjunction with other companies in Curtis Brown Group, Ltd: Curtis Brown, Ltd. for foreign rights; Spokesmen for radio and television; James Brown Associates for American rights; Curtis Brown Australia. No reading fee.

Cutten, John H., Associates. Literary Agency transferred to **Radala & Associates,** *q.v.*

Dalzell Durbridge Authors Limited (1970). *Directors:* Larry Dalzell, Stephen Durbridge—see **Harvey Unna & Stephen Durbridge, Ltd.**

De Wolfe, Felix (1946). *Principal:* Felix de Wolfe. 1 Robert Street, Adelphi, London, WC2N 6BH *T.* 01-930 7514. *T.A.* Hayhill, London, WC2.
Theatre, films, television, sound broadcasting, fiction and non-fiction. Works in conjunction with many foreign agencies.

English Theatre Guild, Ltd., The. *Directors:* Judith Truman, John E. Hunter, Leslie Collins, Laurence Fitch, Joan Ling. 5A Clapham Common Side South, London, SW4 7AA *T.* 01-720 6410 and 6296. Full-length and short MSS. (home 15%, overseas 20% to 30% according to circumstances). Theatre, radio (15%). No musicals. No reading fee. Preliminary letter requested.

*Farquharson, John, Ltd. (1919). *Directors:* Innes Rose, George Greefield, Vivienne Schuster, Vanessa Holt. Bell House, 8 Bell Yard, London, WC2A 2JU *T.* 01-242 2445–50. *T.A.* Jofachad, London, WC2.
Full-length MSS. (home 10%; overseas 19%, including commission to foreign agents). Films, television, sound broadcasting. U.S.A. Associate: Julian S. Bach Inc., 3 East 48th Street, New York, N.Y. 10017. Works in conjunction with agents in all European capitals. No reading fee.

Film Rights Ltd. (1932). *Directors:* John E. Hunter, D. M. Sims, Maurice Lambert, Laurence Fitch. 113–117 Wardour Street, London, W1V 4EH *T.* 01-437 7151.
Theatre, films, television and sound broadcasting (10%). Represented in U.S.A. and abroad.

Fitch, Laurence, Ltd. (1952) (incorporating The London Play Company) (1922). *Directors:* F. H. L. Fitch, L. Ruscombe-King, John Hunter, Joan Potts, William Corlett. 113–117 Wardour Street, London, W1. *T.* 01-437 7151.
Theatre, films, television and sound broadcasting. Also works with several agencies in New York and in Europe.

Foster, Jill, Ltd. (1976). *Director:* Jill Foster. 35 Brompton Road, London, SW3 1DE *T.* 01-581 0084/5.
Full-length and short MSS. (10%). Theatre, films, television, sound broadcasting (10%). No reading fee.

Fraser & Dunlop Scripts, Ltd. (1959)—in association with Robin Dalton and Fraser & Dunlop, Ltd. (1949). Kenneth Ewing, Richard Wakeley, Tim Corrie. 91 Regent Street, London, W1R 8RU *T.* 01-734 7311 *T.A.* Frasanlop, London.
Full-length MSS. (home 10%, overseas 10–20%, including any overseas agent's commission). Theatre, films, television and sound broadcasting (10%). Negotiates with several U.S. agencies. No reading fee.

French (John) Artists Agency, Ltd. *Directors:* John French, Lynne Jarrett. 26–28 Binney Street, London, W1Y 1YN *T.* 01-629 4159.
All MSS. home and overseas (10%). Theatre, films, television, radio (10%). No reading fee. S.A.E. should be enclosed with all MSS.

Gibson's J. F., Literary Agent (1950). *Proprietor:* J. F. Gibson, *Secretary:* Bernard Ross, F.C.A. *Editor:* Mrs. Freda Stock. *Personal Secretary:* Mrs. E. D. Keats, M.A., P.O. Box 173, London, SW3 *T.* 01-242 9637. *Accounts only:* 70 Windsor Road, Bexhill-on-Sea, Sussex, TN39 3PE *T.* 21-4400. *Terms:* full-length MSS. (home 10%, overseas 15%). No reading fee. Please send preliminary letter describing subject matter, etc.

Glass, Eric, Ltd. (1932). *Directors:* Eric Glass, Blanche Glass, Janet Crowley, Barry J. Glass. 28 Berkeley Square, London, W1X 6HD *T.* 01-629 7162. *T.A.* Blancheric, London, W1.
Full-length MSS. only (home 10%, overseas 20%). Theatre, films, television, and sound broadcasting (10%). Will occasionally recommend someone for revision of promising material if the author is unable to undertake it. No reading fee. Sole representatives of the French Society of Authors (Societé des Auteurs et Compositeurs Dramatiques).

Goodwin Associates (1977), 12 Upper Addison Gardens, London, W14 8AP *T.* 01-602 6381.
Dramatic works only—theatre, films, radio, TV.

*Greene, Elaine, Ltd. (1962). *Directors:* Elaine Green (U.S.A.), Kenneth Thomson, Ilsa Yardley. 31 Newington Green, Islington, London, N16 9PU *T.* 01-249 2971. *T.A.* Peterlaine, London, N16.
Full-length MSS. (home 10%; U.S.A. 12½%; translation rights 20%); film television, sound broadcasting (10%). *U.S.A. Associate:* International Creative Management, 40 West 57th Street, New York, N.Y., 10019. Works in conjunction with agencies in most European countries. No reading fees. Preliminary letter preferred.

Harben, Robert, Literary Agency, 3 Church Vale, London, N2 9PD *T.* 01-883 0141. Specialising in translation arrangements of English works into European languages (particularly German and Dutch), and vice versa.

*Harrison, Alec, and Associates (1954). *Senior Partner:* Alec Harrison. International Press Centre, Shoe Lane, London, EC4A 3JB *T.* 01-353 4484–5. *T.A.* Litalic, London, EC4. *Telex:* 264461.
Full-length MSS. (home 10%, overseas 19% where another agent is concerned). Short MSS. (home 15%, overseas 15%–25%). Films (10%), television and sound broadcasting (10% for series, 15% for single items). "In the main, all the people we handle are professional writers who come to us on recommendation. The great bulk of the material we handle is non-fiction, such as educational books and autobiographies, which often have to be ghosted. Most of our work is commissioned. For syndication we work with literary agents in almost every country in the world". No reading fee.

*Heath, A. M. & Co., Ltd. (1919. *Directors:* Mark Hamilton (Chairman and Managing Director), Michael Thomas (Secretary), Hester Green, Jacintha Alexander. 40–42 William IV Street, London, WC2N 4DD *T.* 01-836 4271. *T.A.* Script, London, WC2. *Cables:* Script, London.
Full-length and short MSS. (home 10%, U.S.A. 15%, translations 20%). Theatre, films, television and sound broadcasting (10%). Interested in work of both new and established writers. *U.S. Associate:* Brandt & Brandt Inc., New York. Agents in all European countries and Japan. No reading fee.

Higham, David, Associates Ltd. (1935). *Directors:* Bruce Hunter, Jacqueline Korn, Anthony Crouch, John Rush. 5–8 Lower John Street, Golden Square, London, W1R 4HA *T.* 01-437 7888. *Cables:* Highlit, London, W1. *Telex:* 28910.
U.S.A. Associate Agency: Harold Ober Associates Inc., 40 East 49th Street, New York, 10017. Works in conjunction with many foreign agencies in all parts of the world. Terms on application. No reading fee.

*Hughes Massie Ltd. (1912). *Directors:* Edmund Cork, Patricia Cork, J. E. Lunn, N. E. Cork. 31 Southampton Row, London, WC1B 5HL *T.* 01-405 8137. *T.A.* Litaribus, London, WC1.
Full-length MSS. (home 10%, U.S.A. 15%, translations 20%, including 10% to local agents). Short MSS. (home 10%, or 15%, translations 20%, including 10% to local agents). Theatre, films, television, sound broadcasting (10%). U.S.A. Associates: Harold Ober Associates Inc., 40 East 49th Street, New York 10017; L. David Otte, The Otte Company, 9 Park Street, Boston, Mass. 02108. Works in conjunction with agents in most European countries, Israel and Japan. No reading fee.

Intercontinental Literary Agency (1965). *Director:* Anthony Gornall. 10 Buckingham Street, London, WC2N 4HX *T.* 01-839 1612. *T.A.* Interlitag. Concerned only with translation rights exclusively for all authors of A.D. Peters & Co., London, Harold Matson Co. Inc. New York and The Sterling Lord Agency, New York.

Janson-Smith, Peter, Ltd.—see **Campbell Thomson & McLaughlin Ltd.**

*Johnson, John (1956). Clerkenwell House, 45–47 Clerkenwell Green, London, EC1R 0HT   T. 01-251 0125.   T.A. Litjohn London.
Full-length and short MSS. (home 10%, overseas 10%, if foreign agent is concerned maximum of 19%), theatre, films, television, sound broadcasting (10%).   U.S.A. associate agency: Sterling Lord, 660 Madison Avenue, New York, N.Y. 10021. Works in conjunction with agents in many European countries. No reading fee, but send SAE please.

Jones Blakey, 14 Monteith Crescent, Boston, Lincolnshire, PE21 9AX T. Boston (0205) 63437.
Book length MSS. only—non-fiction and fiction (10%–15%). Theatre, television and sound broadcasting scripts (10%–15%). No reading fee, but return postage with all MSS. essential.

Josephy, Irene. 35 Craven Street, Strand, London, WC2N 5NG   T. 01-930 6936.
Full service for professional writers. Basic commission 10%. Connections in U.S.A. and Europe. Preliminary letter preferred. No reading fee.

Juvenilia (1973). Proprietor: Mrs. Rosemary Bromley, Colden Common, near Winchester, Hants, SO21 1TE   T. 0962 712383.
Full-length MSS. for the children's market, fiction and non-fiction (home 10%, overseas 15%). No verse or short stories unless specifically for picture books, radio or TV. Theatre, films, television, radio (10%). No unsolicited MSS; preliminary letter with full details essential. No reading fee. Postage for acknowledgement and return of material essential.

Lavell, Charles, Limited (1927). Directors: Carl Routledge, Kay Routledge. 176 Wardour Street, London, W1V 3AA   T. 01-437 5807.   T.A. Lavnews, London, W1.
Full-length MSS. (home 10%; where overseas agent employed additional 10%). Short MSS. (home and overseas 15%). No unsolicited manuscripts. New clients by personal recommendation only. Preliminary letter essential and S.A.E. No reading fees.

Le Dain Management. Director: Yvonne Le Dain. 92 North Road, Highgate, London, N6 4AA.
Plays only. Theatre, films, television, sound broadcasting. Terms on application. Preliminary letter essential.

*Leresche Hope & Sayle (1960), successor to Richard Steele & Son, est. 1942; successor to J. B. Pinker est. 1900). Tessa Sayle. Drama Assistant: Dawn Arnall.   11 Jubilee Place, Chelsea, London, SW3 3TE   T. 01-352 4311, 01-352 2182.   T.A. Bookishly, London, SW3.
Full-length MSS. (home 10%, overseas 20%). Plays, films, television, sound broadcasting (10%). U.S.A. Associates: Georges Borchardt, 136 East 57th Street, New York, N.Y. 10022. Represented in all foreign countries. No reading fee.

Lloyd-George & Coward (1959). Directors: W. Lloyd-George, B. G. Coward, Nicolette Milnes Walker, M.B.E., 31 Theberton Street, London, N1 0QY T. 01-226 3622.
Full-length MSS. (10%). No reading fee.

London Independent Books, Ltd. (1971). Directors: Sydney Box, Carolyn Whitaker, Patrick Whitaker.   1A Montagu Mews North, London, W1H 1AJ.   T. 01-935 8090.   T.A. Trifem, London, W1.
Full-length MSS. (home 15%, overseas 20%). Films, television and sound broadcasting (10%). Will suggest revision of promising MSS. No reading fee.

*London Management, Jackie Baldick, Marc Berlin.   235 Regent Street, London,
W1A 2JT   *T.* 01-734 4192.
   Full-length and short manuscripts (home 10%, overseas 19%).   Theatre,
films, television and sound broadcasting (10%).   *U.S.A. Associates:* Robert
Lantz, 114 East 55th Street, New York, N.Y., 10022.   Paul Kohner/
Michael Levy Agency, 9169 Sunset Boulevard, Hollywood, California,
90069.   Pat Feeley, 52 Vanderbilt Avenue, N.Y., 10017.   No reading fee.

Marvin, Blanche, 21A St. John's Wood High Street, London, NW8.   *T.* 01-722
2313.
   Full-length MSS. (home and overseas 10%).   Theatre, films, television,
sound broadcasting (10%).   No reading fee.

Michael, Maurice, (1953).   *Partners:* M. A. Michael, P. K. Michael.   Partridge
Green, Horsham, Sussex, RH13 8EJ   *T.* 040-371 0412.   *T.A.* Bartolo,
Horsham.
   Specializes in books from and for Scandinavia and the Continent.   Full-
length and short MSS. (home and overseas 10%).   Works direct, and in conjunction with several agents, in U.S.A.   Negotiates directly with Continental
publishers.   No reading fee.

Milne, Richard, Limited (1956)   *Directors:* R. M. Sharples, K. N. Sharples.   28
Makepeace Avenue, Highgate, London, N6.   *T.* 01-340 7007.
   Specialising in scripts for films, television, sound broadcasting (10%).   Un-
able to represent any additional authors at present.

Motley, Michael, Ltd. (1973).   *Directors:* M. J. Motley, C. O. Motley.   78
Gloucester Terrace, London, W2 3HH   *T.* 01-723 2973.   *T.A.* Bookplate,
London, W2.
   Full-length MSS. only (home 10%, U.S.A. 15%, translations 20%).   Theatre,
films, television and radio (10%).   Will suggest revision if MSS. sufficiently
promising.   Represented in all publishing centres of the world.   No reading fee.   Preliminary letter essential.

*Nurnberg, Andrew, Associates Ltd., Clerkenwell House, 45–47 Clerkenwell
Green, London, EC1R 0HT   *T.* 01-251 0321.   *Cables:* Nurnbooks, Lon-
don.   *Telex:* 23353.
   Specialising in translation arrangements of English-language works into
European languages (particularly German, Dutch, Soviet, Spanish and
Portuguese).

Paterson, Mark & Associates (1955).   *Proprietor:* Mark Paterson.   11 & 12
West Stockwell Street, Colchester, CO1 1HN.   *T.* Colchester (0206) 65151.
T.A. Paterson, Colchester.   *Telex:* 896616MP G.
   Full-length MSS. including psychology and psychiatry (20% including sub-
agent's commission).   No short stories or articles.   No reading fee.

Penman Literary Agency (1950).   *Director:* Leonard G. Stubbs, F.R.S.A., 175
Pall Mall, Leigh-on-Sea, Essex, SS9 1RE   *T.* Southend 74438.
   Full-length MSS. (home 10%, overseas 15%).   Theatre, films, television,
sound broadcasting (10%).   Revision undertaken by agency at author's
request; fees depending upon amount of revision required.   No reading fee.

Peterborough Literary Agency (1973).   *Executive Manager:* Ewan MacNaugh-
ton.   135 Fleet Street, London, EC4P 4BL   *T.* 01-353 4242, ext. 529/139.
T.A. Telesyndic, London.   *Telex:* London 22874 Telesyndic.
   Rates (home 10%, overseas 17%).   New and established authors.   Fiction,
non-fiction.   No reading fee but return postage essential.

*Peters, A. D., & Company, Ltd (1924). *Directors:* Michael Sissons (Managing), Anthony Jones, Pat Kavanagh. 10 Buckingham Street, London, WC2N 6BU   *T.* 01-839 2556.

Associated agencies: Harold Matson, 22 East 40th Street, New York, N.Y., 10016. Sterling Lord, 660 Madison Avenue, New York, N.Y., 10021. Intercontinental Literary Agency (foreign language rights), 10 Buckingham Street, London, WC2N 6BU. Specialists in the negotiation of all rights in general fiction and non-fiction, film and television scripts, plays, and certain technical, specialist and academic works. No unsolicited manuscripts accepted without an introductory letter from the author describing the work and unless return postage included. *Rates of commission:* 10% on all work negotiated except 15% in U.S.A. and 20% on foreign language rights. No reading fee.

Pollinger, Laurence, Limited. *Directors:* Gerald J. Pollinger, Rosemary Gould. *Secretary:* Denzil De Silva. 18 Maddox Street, London, W1R 0EU *T.* 01-629 9761. *T.A.* Laupoll, London, W1.

Authors' agents for all material with the exception of original film stories, poetry and free-lance journalistic articles. Dramatic associate, Margery Vosper, *q.v.* Terms for book rights are a commission of 10% of the amounts obtained, except on translation and American sales, where the total commission of 20% and 15% respectively may include the commission to the associate in the territory concerned. On original magazine, newspaper, and serial rights the commission is 15%. No reading fee.

*Pollinger, Murray (1969), 4 Garrick Street, London, WC2 9BH *T.* 01-836 6781. *T.A.* and *Cables:* Chopper, London, WC2.

Agents for the negotiation in all markets of novels for both adults and children and general non-fiction, including film, television and broadcasting rights in book material. (Home 10%, U.S.A. 15%, translations 20%). Preliminary letter preferred. No reading fee.

Radala & Associates (1970). *Directors:* Richard Gollner, István Siklós. 17 Avenue Mansions, Finchley Road, London NW3 7AX *T.* 01-794 4495.

Full length MSS. (10%). Theatre, films, television, sound broadcasting (10%). *U.S.A. Associate:* Alyss Dorese, 41 West 82nd Street, New York, N.Y., 10024. Special representation in South America, Eastern Europe, Middle East.

Ramsay, Margaret, Ltd. (1953). *Directors:* M. Ramsay, Tom Erhardt. 14A Goodwin's Court, London, WC2N 4LL *T.* 01-836 7403, 01-240 0691 and 01-836 6807. *T.A.* Ramsyplay, London.

MSS. Theatre, films, television, sound broadcasting only (commission 10%). Works in conjunction with agents in U.S.A. and in all foreign countries. Preliminary letter essential. No reading fee.

Reddage Editorial Ltd. *Directors:* G. R. Schrager, E. R. Sorell, H. J. Schrager, 3 The Park, London, N6 4EU *T.* 01-348 3314.

Full-length MSS. (home 10%, overseas maximum 20%). Handle only material with scientific background, up to and including University level. No reading fee.

*Rogers, Deborah, Ltd. (1967). *Directors:* Deborah Rogers, Ann Warnford Davis, Patricia White, Brenda Leys, 5–11 Mortimer Street, London, W1N 7RH *T.* 01-580 0604. *T.A.* Debrogers, London, W1.

Full-length MSS. (home 10%, overseas 15%, translations 20%). Theatre, films, television, sound broadcasting (10%). *U.S.A. Associate:* International Creative Management, 40 West 57th Street, New York, N.Y. 10019. No reading fee. Preliminary letter requested.

Routledge, Kay, Associates (1967). *Principal:* Mrs. Kay Routledge. 176 Wardour Street, London, W1V 3AA *T*. 01-437 5807.
For the professional woman writer of good fiction (book and magazine).
Specialises in serials. Full-length MSS. 10%, shorter material 15% (where
overseas agent employed additional 10%). Represented overseas. No
unsolicited manuscripts. New clients by personal recommendation only.
Preliminary letter essential and S.A.E. No reading fees.

*****Seale, Patrick, Books Ltd.** (formerly **Observer Books & Features, Ltd.**) (1969).
2 Motcomb Street, Belgrave Square, London, SW1X 8JU *T*. 01-235 0934.
T.A. Obseale, London, SW1. *Management:* Patrick Seale, Jane Blackstock,
Maureen McConville, Mary Bruton. *Terms:* Home 10%, Overseas 15%–
20%, including commission to foreign agents. No reading fee.

Shaw Maclean—see **Curtis Brown Academic, Ltd.**

*****Sheil, Anthony, Associates, Ltd.** (1962), incorporating Christy & Moore, Ltd.
(1912). 2–3 Morwell Street, London, WC1B 3AR *T*. 01-636 2901. *T.A.*
Novelist. Anthony Sheil, Giles Gordon, Gill Coleridge, Lois Wallace
(U.S.A.).
Full-length MSS. (home 10%, U.S.A. 15%, overseas up to 20%); theatre,
films, television, sound broadcasting (10%). *U.S.A. associates:* Wallace &
Sheil Agency, Inc., 118 East 61st Street, New York, N.Y. 10021. Repre-
sented in all European capitals.

*****Smith, Carol, Literary Agency** (1976). *Partners:* Carol Smith, the Hon. A. G.
Samuel. 2 John Street, London, WC1N 2HJ *T*. 01-405 4072.
Full-length and short MSS (home 10%). Will suggest revision of promising
MSS. Works in conjunction with many foreign agencies. No reading fee.

Spokesmen (D. D. Spokesmen Ltd.) (1973). Directors: Graham Watson (Chair-
man), Richard Odgers (Managing), Diana Baring, Peter Grose, Sheila
Lemon, Peter Murphy, George M. Webster (Secretary). 1 Craven Hill,
London, W2 3EP *T*. 01-262 1011. *Telex:* 261536.
MSS for films, theatre, television and radio. Also agents for directors and
designers. (Home 10%, Foreign 19%.) Works in conjunction with other
companies in the Curtis Brown Group Ltd. Preliminary letter essential.
No reading fee.

*****Stein, Abner.** *Director:* Abner Stein. 43 Albany Mansions, Albert Bridge
Road, London, SW11 4PQ *T*. 01-223 5408.
Full-length and short MSS. (home 10%, U.S.A. 15%, foreign 19%).
Theatre, films, television, sound broadcasting (10%). No reading fee.

Strathmore Literary Agency, The (1973). *Directors:* Diana, Lady Avebury,
William Holden (Canadian), Douglas Gardner (Canadian). 145 Park Road,
London, NW8. *T*. 01-722 6166 and 01-352 1171.
Full-length and short MSS (home 10%, overseas 20%). Will suggest re-
vision of promising MSS. Works in conjunction with many overseas
agents. No reading fee.

Tauber, Peter, Press Agency—see page 263.

Towndrow, Jenny, Associates Ltd. (1977). *Directors:* J. Towndrow, W. Dolle-
man. 49 Hornton Street, London, W8 7NT *T*. 01-937 1931 and 8230.
Full-length MSS (home 10%; overseas 15%). Films, television, radio
(10%). Will suggest revision of promising MS. No reading fee.

*Unna, Harvey, & Stephen Durbridge, Ltd. (1975). *Director:* Harvey Unna, Stephen Durbridge, Nina Froud. 14 Beaumont Mews, Marylebone High Street, London, W1N 4HE *T.* 01-935 8589. *Cables:* Undur, London, W1. Specialise in dramatic works for all media; handle also book MSS. Widely represented in most European and Overseas countries. Commission charged by agency 10% in all instances: where sub-agents are employed overseas, additional commission by arrangement, but not exceeding 9%. No reading fee.

Unna, Harvey, Limited (1950). *Directors:* Harvey Unna, Elizabeth Unna, Nina Froud—see **Harvey Unna & Stephen Durbridge, Limited.**

Van Loewen, Dr. Jan, Ltd. (1944). *Directors:* Jan Van Loewen, LL.D., Michael Imison, M.A., Elisabeth Van Loewen, Katherine Gould, 81–83 Shaftesbury Avenue, London, W1V 8BX *T.* 01-437 5546–7. *T.A.* Van Loewen, London, W1.
Fiction and general MSS. (full length *only*) (home 10%, overseas 12½% except when working with a regional sub-agent—20%). Theatre, films, television, sound broadcasting. Represented in all major countries. No reading fee, but send S.A.E.

Vestey, Lorna (1971). *Principal:* Mrs. Lorna Vestey. 33 Dryburgh, London, SW15. *T.* 01-788 6740.
Full-length MSS. (home 10%, U.S.A. 15%, other overseas 20%). Theatre, films, television, sound broadcasting (10%). Will occasionally suggest revision. Works in conjunction with agencies in Germany, Italy, Japan, Scandinavia, Spain and U.S.A. No reading fee, but return postage must be sent with all MSS.

*Victor, Ed, Ltd. (1976). *Directors:* Ed Victor (U.S.A.), Carol Ryan (U.S.A.), Leon Morgan. 27 Soho Square, London, W1V 6AY *T.* 01-734 4795. *T.A.* Victorious, London, W1.
Full-length and short MSS. (home 10%, U.S.A. 15%, translation 20%). Theatre, films, television, sound broadcasting (10%). Preliminary letter preferred. Represented in major foreign markets. U.K. representatives of William Morris Inc., Paul Reynolds Inc., Knox Burger Associates, Peter Lampack Literary Agency. No reading fee.

Vosper, Margery, Ltd. (1932). Suite 8, 26 Charing Cross Road, London, WC2H 0DG *T.* 01-836 5912. *T.A.* Margevos, London, WC2.
Full-length and short MSS. (home and overseas 10%). Theatre, films, television and sound broadcasting (10%). Will suggest revision and sometimes suggest suitable person to do it. Works in conjunction with agents in New York, and in all foreign countries.

Walker, S., Literary Agency (1939). *Directors:* S. Walker, E. K. Walker. 199 Hampermill Lane, Oxhey, Watford, WD1 4PJ *T.* Watford 28498.
Full-length novels only (home 10%, overseas 20% including 10% to overseas agent). Do not handle short topical articles, poetry or stories for juveniles. Works in conjunction with agencies in most European countries, and also negotiates directly with foreign publishers. No reading fee.

Walls, J. C. (1936). 37 Henley Grove, Henleaze, Bristol, BS9 4EQ *T.* (0272) 627075 and 621912.
Full-length and short MSS. (home and overseas 10%). Provides criticism, revision and typing services, from 75p per 1000 words. No reading fee.

*Watt, A. P. Ltd. (1978). *Directors:* Michael Horniman, Hilary Rubinstein, James Hayes, Maggie Noach, Caradoc King. 26/28 Bedford Row, London, WC1R 4HL   *T.* 01-405 1057. *T.A.* Longevity, London, WC1.
Full-length MSS. (home 10%, U.S. 15%, foreign 19% including commission to U.S. or foreign agent). *U.S.A. associate agency:* Curtis Brown Ltd., 575 Madison Avenue, New York, N.Y. 10022. Works in conjunction with agents in most European countries, Japan and South America. No reading fee.

*Winant, Towers Ltd. (1965). *Managing Director:* Ursula R. Winant. 14 Clifford's Inn, London, EC4A 1DA   *T.* 01-405 2362. *T.A.* Towben, London. *Cables:* Towben, London.
Full-length MSS (home 10%, translation 20%). Will suggest revision if MS. promising; sometimes suggests outside help. Representatives overseas. Preliminary letter essential. No reading fee.

Tauber, Peter, Press Agency (1950). *Directors:* Peter Tauber, Martha Tauber, Robert Tauber. 94 East End Road, London, N3 2SX   *T.* 01-346 4165. *T.A.* Tauberpres.
Full-length and short MSS (home 12½% to 20%; overseas 25%). Theatre, films, television, broadcasting (10%). No reading fee.

UNITED STATES LITERARY AGENTS

*Membership of the Society of Authors' Representatives.

It has long been customary among literary agencies that the agent retains a 10% commission on domestic sales and up to 20% on foreign sales, subject to various exceptions and special policies established by each agent individually. Some agencies charge a reading fee for unsolicited MSS. and for the work of beginners and new writers, such fees sometimes being refunded on the acceptance of the material.

In all cases, and in their own interests, writers are advised to send a preliminary letter and to ascertain terms before submitting MSS.

*American Play Company Inc., 52 Vanderbilt Avenue, New York, N.Y., 10017. T. 212-697-9763.

*Bach, Julian, Literary Agency Inc., 3 East 48th Street, New York, N.Y., 10017. T. PL3-2605. *Cables:* Turtles, New York.

*Berger, Bill, Associates Inc., 444 East 58th Street, New York, N.Y. 10022. T. 212-486-9588.

*Blassingame, Lurton, 60 East 42nd Street, New York, N.Y., 10017. T. 212-687-7491.

*Borchardt, Georges, Inc., 136 East 57th Street, New York, N.Y. 10022. T. 212-753-5785. *Cables:* Literary, New York.

*Brandt & Brandt, Literary Agents Inc., 101 Park Avenue, New York, N.Y., 10017. *British representative:* A. M. Heath & Co., Ltd.

*Brown, James, Associates Inc., 25 West 43rd Street, New York, N.Y., 10036. T. 212-736-3777.

Collier Associates, 280 Madison Avenue, New York, N.Y., 10016.

*Cushman, John, Associates Inc., 25 West 43rd Street, New York, N.Y., 10036. *T.A.* Cushcurt, New York. T. 212-MU 5-2052. Affiliate and U.S.A. representative of Curtis Brown, Ltd. of London.

*Daves, Joan, 515 Madison Avenue, New York, N.Y., 10022. T. 212-PL9-6250.

*Donadio, Candida & Associates, Inc., 111 West 57th Street, New York, N.Y., 10019. T. PL 7-5076.

*Elmo, Ann, Agency Inc. (1936), 52 Vanderbilt Avenue, New York, N.Y., 10017. T. 661-2880.

Feeley, Patricia Falk, 52 Vanderbilt Avenue, New York, N.Y., 10017. T. 697-1322. *T.A.* Authellmer Newyork. General fiction and non-fiction. West Coast representation.

Fischer, Hanns, Literary Agency, 2332 West Farwell Avenue, Chicago, Illinois, 60645. T. 312-465-1216.

Fishbein, Frieda, 353 West 57th Street, New York, N.Y., 10019. *T.* 212-247-4398.

Fles, Barthold, 507 Fifth Avenue, New York, N.Y., 10017. *T.* MU 7-7248.

*French, Samuel, Inc., 25 West 45th Street, New York, N.Y., 10036. *T.* 212-582-4700.

Garon-Brooke, Jay, Associates Inc., 415 Central Park West, New York, N.Y., 10025. Writer must be referred by an editor or a client. Will not read unsolicited MSS. *London representative:* Abner Stein, *T.* 01-223 5408.

Greenburger, Sanford, J., Associates, Inc., 825 Third Avenue, New York. N.Y., 10022. *T.* PL 3-8581–2.

*Harold Freedman Brandt & Brandt Dramatic Dept., Inc., 101 Park Avenue, New York, N.Y., 10017. *T.* MU3-5890.

*Harvey & Hutto Inc., 110 West 57th Street, New York, N.Y., 10019.

*International Creative Management, 40 West 57th Street, New York, N.Y., 10019. *T.* 212-556 5732.

King, Daniel P. (1974), 5125 North Cumberland Blvd., Whitefish Bay, Wisconsin, 53217. *T.* 414-964 2903.

*Kroll, Lucy, Agency, 390 West End Avenue, New York, N.Y., 10024. *T.* 212-877-0627. *T.A.* Lucykroll, New York.

*Lescher, Robert, Literary Agent, 155 East 71st Street, New York, N.Y., 10021.

MacCampbell, Donald, Inc., 12 East 41st Street, New York, N.Y., 10017. *T.* Murray Hill 3-5580.

*McIntosh, McKee & Dodds Inc., 22 East 40th Street, New York, N.Y., 10016. *T.* 212-679-4490. *Cables:* Halmatson. See A. D. Peters & Co., London.

*McIntosh & Otis Inc. (1928), 475 5th Avenue, New York, N.Y., 10017.

*Marton, Elisabeth, 96 Fifth Avenue, New York, N.Y., 10011. *T.* (212) 255-1908.

*Matson, Harold, Company Inc. (1937), 22 East 40th Street, New York, N.Y., 10016. *T.* 212-679-4490. *Cables:* Halmatson. See A. D. Peters & Co., London.

Moorepark, Howard, 444 East 82nd Street, New York, N.Y., 10028. *T.* 212-737 3961. *T.A.* Homopark, New York.

*Ober, Harold, Associates Inc., 40 East 49th Street, New York, N.Y., 10017. *T.* Plaza 9-8600.

Porter, Gould, & Dierks, Authors' Agents, 215 W. Ohio Street, Chicago, Illinois 60610. *T.* 312-644-5457.

*Raines & Raines, 475 Fifth Avenue, New York, N.Y., 10017. *T.* 684-5160. *Cables:* Rainesbuck, New York.

*Reynolds, Paul R., Inc. (1893), 12 East 41st Street, New York, N.Y., 10017. *T.* 212-689-8711. *Cable address:* Carbonato, New York.

*Roberts, Flora, Inc., 65 East 55th Street, New York, N.Y., 10022. *T.* 355-4165.

*Rodell, Marie—Frances Collin Literary Agency, 141 East 55th Street, New York. N.Y., 10022. *T.* PL2-2046. *Cables:* Rodellitag, New York. *Associate:* John Meyer.

*Russell & Volkening Inc., 551 Fifth Avenue, New York, N.Y., 10017.

*Safier, Gloria, Inc., 667 Madison Avenue, New York, N.Y., 10021. *T.* 212-838-4868.

Salisbury, Leah, Inc., c/o Flora Roberts, Inc, 65 East 55th Street, New York, N.Y., 10022. *T.* 355-4165.

*Schaffner, John, Suite 6D, 425 East 51st Street, New York, N.Y., 10022. *T.* Murray Hill 8-4763.

Schulberg-Dorese Agency, Alyss Barlow Dorese, 41 West 82nd Street, New York, N.Y., 10024. *T.* 580-2855.

Scott Meredith Literary Agency Inc., 845 Third Avenue, New York, N.Y., 10022. *T.* (212) Circle 5-5500. *T.A.* Scottmere. *Cables:* Esemela 224705. *London:* Mark Hamilton, A. M. Heath & Co., Ltd., *q.v.*

Seligmann, James, Agency, 280 Madison Avenue, New York, N.Y., 10016. *T.* 212-679-3383.

*Sterling Lord Agency Inc., 660 Madison Avenue, New York, N.Y., 10021. *T.* 212-PL 1-2533. *T.A.* Lordage. *British representative:* A. D. Peters, *q.v.*

Swanson, H. N., Inc. (1934), 8523 Sunset Boulevard, Los Angeles, California, 90069. *T.* 213-652-5385. *T.A.* Swanie.

*Tams-Witmark Music Library, Inc., 757 Third Avenue, New York, N.Y., 10017.

*Targ, Roslyn, Literary Agency Inc. (formerly Franz J. Horch Associates Inc.), 250 West 57th Street, New York, N.Y., 10019. *T.* 582-4210.

Wahl, Austin, Agency, 332 South Michigan Avenue, Chicago, Illinois, 60604. *T.* 922-3329. Normally requires an author to sign a contract.

*Wallace & Sheil Agency, Inc., 118 East 61st Street, New York, N.Y., 10021. *T.* 212-751 1944. *T.A.* Aswaslit, New York.

Watkins, A., Inc., 77 Park Avenue, New York, N.Y., 10016. *T.* 212–LE2–0080. *Cables:* Anwat, Newyork. *London:* A. P. Watt & Son.

~Wilkinson, Max, Associates, Shelter Island, N.Y., 11964. *T.* 516-749-0716.

Williams, Wesley, Winant (1976), 30 Sutton Place, New York, N.Y., 10022. *T.* 212-MU8-0768 *T.A.* Willwynant, New York.

*Yost, Mary, Associates, 141 East 55th Street, New York, N.Y. 10022. *T.* 212-755-4682.

OTHER LITERARY AGENTS

Most of the agents whose names and addresses are given below work in association with an agent in London.

In all cases, and in their own interests, writers are advised to send a preliminary letter and to ascertain terms before submitting MSS. or books.

ARGENTINA

Lawrence Smith B.A. (1938), Avenida de los Incas 3110. Buenos Aires. 1426. *T.* 784-5012. *Cables:* Litagent, Baires.

AUSTRALIA

Curtis Brown (Australia) Pty., Ltd., 86 William Street, Paddington, N.S.W., 2021, *T.* 31-8301 and 31-9161. *Cables:* Browncurt.

Harrison, Alec, and Associates (1954). *Senior Partner:* Alec Harrison. International Press Centre, Shoe Lane, London, EC4A 3JB *T.* 01-353 4484–5. *T.A.* Litalic, London, EC4. *Telex:* 264461.

Yaffa Syndicate Pty., Ltd., 432–6 Elizabeth Street, Surry Hills, N.S.W., 2010. *T.* 699-7861. *Telex:* AA21887.

BRAZIL

Dr. J. E. Bloch (Associate: Mrs. Karin Schindler), Rua Oscar Freire 416, Ap. 83, 01426 São Paulo. *T.* 282-3053. *Cables:* Copyright Sãopaulo.

Miss Carmen Barcells, Agencia Literaria Carmen Barcells, Rua Joaõ Lira 97-203-204, Leblon, 20.000 Rio de Janeiro. *T.* 294-32-48. *Cables:* Copyright Rio.

CZECHOSLOVAKIA

Dilia Theatrical and Literary Agency Vyšehradská 28, 128 24 Prague 2. *T.* 296651–5.

Lita Slovak Literary Agency, ul.Čs. armády 37, 894 20 Bratislava. *T.* 550-07, 550-25, 591-79, 543-54, 541-60, 587-68. *T.A.* Lita Bratislava.

DENMARK

A/S Bookman, Fiolstraede 12, DK-1171, Copenhagen K. *T.* 01-14-57-20.

Edith Kiilerich, Fiolstraede 12, DK-1171, Copenhagen K.

Albrecht, Leonhardt ApS, Studiestraede 35, DK-1455, Copenhagen K. *T.* 01-132523.

Michaels & Licht, Østerbrogade 84, DK-2100 Copenhagen Ø, *T.* (01) 42-46-08.

FINLAND

A/S Bookman, 12 Fiolstraede, DK-1171, Copenhagen K. *T.* 01-14-57-20.

FRANCE

Mrs. W. A. Bradley, 18 Quai de Bethune, 75004 Paris. *T.* 033-75-14.
Bureau Litteraire International Marguerite Scialtiel, Geneviève Ulmann, 14 rue Chanoinesse, 75004 Paris. *T.* 033-71-16.
Agence Hoffman, 77 Boulevard Saint-Michel, 75005 Paris. *T.* 033-71-15, 033-23-27.
Mme. Michelle Lapautre, 6 rue Jean Carriès, 75007 Paris. *T.* 734-82-41 and 734-64-50.
McKee & Mouche, 16 rue du Regard, 75006 Paris. *T.* 548-45-03 and 222-42-33.
Mme. Janine Quet, Bureau Littéraire, 20 rue de la Michodière, 75002 Paris. *T.* 033-38-50.
Maurice Renault, 2 rue de Florence, 75008 Paris. *T.* 387-44-58.
Mme. Helena Strassova, 4 rue Git-Le-Coeur, 75006 Paris. *T.* 633-34-57.

GERMANY

Geisenheyner & Crone, Gymnasiumstrasse 31B, 7000 Stuttgart. *T.* 293738.
Agence Hoffman, Seestrasse 6, Munich 40.
Dr. Ruth Liepman, Maienburgweg 23, 8044 Zürich, Switzerland. *T.* (01) 47 76 60. *Cables:* Litagent. *Telex:* Litag 56739.
Linder AG, Jupiterstrasse 1, 8007 Zürich, Switzerland. *Postal Address:* Postfach 8032 Zürich. *T.* (01) 53 41 40.
Mohrbooks Literary Agency, Rainer Heumann, Klosbachstrasse 110, Postfach, CH-8030 Zürich, Switzerland. *T.* (01) 32-16-10.
Niedieck Linder AG, Holzgasse 6, 8002 Zürich, Switzerland. *Postal Address:* Postfach, 8039 Zürich. *T.* (01) 202-1450.
Thomas Schlück, Literary Agency, Hinter der Worth 12, 3008 Garbsen 9. *T.* 05131-93053.

HUNGARY

Artisjus. Agency for Literature, Theatre and Music of the Hungarian Bureau for Copyright Protection, Vörösmarty tér 1, Budapest V. *Post address:* H-1364 Budapest PB 67. *T.* 328-790. *Cables:* Artisjus. *Telex:* 226527 Arjus H.

ICELAND

Sveinbjorn Jonsson Literary and Dramatic Agent (1960), P.O. Box 438, Gardastraeti 21, Reykjavik. *T.* 13206 and 28110.

ISRAEL

Bar-David Literary Agency, 41 Montefiore Street, P.O. Box 1104, Tel-Aviv. *T.* 294239, 294240–1. *Cables:* Davidbarco. *Telex:* 032470–1 BarDavid.
Moadim, Play Publishers and Literary Agents, 144 Hayarkon Street, 63 451 Tel-Aviv. *T.* 228 449.

ITALY

Agenzia Letteraria Internazionale, 3 Corso Matteotti, 20121 Milan. *T.* 79-36-09.
Dais Literary Agency, Via Nicotera 7, Rome. *T.* 353126.
ILA—International Literary Agency (1969), 1-18015 Terzorio Im. *T.* 184-44 111. *T.A.* Friedmann 1-18015 Terzorio.
News Blitz International (1949), Via Cimabue 5, 00196 Rome. *T.* 36 01 489. 36 00 620, 36 03 087. *T.A.* Blitz, Rome.
Transafrica Books, Via Trieste 34, 25100 Bresica. *T.* 55080. Only for African subjects.

JAPAN

Orion Press, 55, 1-Chome, Kanda-Jimbocho, Chiyoda-ku, Tokyo, 101. *T.A.* Orionserv, Tokyo. *Telex,* J 24447 Orionprs.
Charles E. Tuttle Co., Inc., 1-2-6 Suido, Bunkyo-ku, Tokyo 112. *T.* 811-7106. *Cables:* Tuttbooks, Tokyo. *Telex:* 02723170.

NETHERLANDS

Alexander Gans, Literair Agent, Witte de Withstraat 20, Noordwijk aan Zee, The Netherlands. *T.* 01719-13133.
Hans Keuls, International Bureau Voor Auteursrecht B.V., Flat 21, Burg, Van Alphenstraat 61, Zandvoort.
Internationaal Literatuur Bureau B.V., Hein & Menno Kohn, Koninginneweg 2A, 1217 KW, Hilversum. *T.* 035-13500.
Prins & Prins Literary Agents (Henk Prins), de Lairessestraat 6, P.O. Box 5400, 1007 AK Amsterdam. *T.* 76 10 01.

NEW ZEALAND

Alec Harrison, International Press Centre, Shoe Lane, London, EC4A 3JB. *T.* 01-353 4484.

NORWAY

A/S Bookman, 12 Fiolstraede, DK-1171, Copenhagen K. *T.* 01-14-57-20.
Carlota Frahm Literary Agent. *Owners:* Carlota Frahm and Suzanne Palme. Valkyriegaten 17, Oslo 3. *Mail address:* P.O. Box 5385, Majorstua, Oslo 3. *T.* 46-30-02. *Cables:* Frahmbook.
Hanna-Kirsti Koch, P.O.B. 3043, Oslo 2.

PORTUGAL

Ilidio da Fonseca Matos, Rua de S. Bernardo, 68-3, Lisbon 2. *T.* 66 97 80. *Cables:* Ilphoto.

SOUTH AFRICA

International Press Agency (Pty) Ltd., P.O. Box 682, Cape Town 8000. *T.* 53-1926. *London Office:* Mrs. S. Power, 411 London Press Centre, 76 Shoe Lane, London, EC4A 3JB *T.* 01-353 0186.

SPAIN

Miss Carmen Balcells, Agencia Literaria Carmen Balcells, Diagonal 580, Barce- lona 21. *T.* 217 17 40 and 217 99 95. *Cables:* Copyright, Barcelona.
International Editors Co., S.A., Rambla Cataluña, 39, Barcelona 7. *T.* 318 89 80.
Julio F. Yañez, Agencia Literaria (Universitas), Marco Aurelio, 5 5°, 3ª, Barce- lona 6. *T.* 247 93 60.

SWEDEN

A/S Bookman, 12 Fiolstraede, DK-1171, Copenhagen K. *T.* 01-14-57-20.
Gösta Dahl & Son, AB, Aladdinsvägen 14, S-161 38 Bromma. *T.* 08-25 62 35.
Mrs. Lena I. Gedin, Linnégatan 38, 114 47 Stockholm.
Arlecchino Teaterförlag, Gränsvägen 14, S-131 00 Nacka. *T.* 08-718 17 18.

AGENTS SPECIALISING IN PLAYS, FILMS, TELEVISION AND RADIO

Further particulars about Agents and a Note to which special attention is called will be found on page 252.

Aquarius Literary Agency
Authors' Alliance
Benson, Dorothea
Blake, Carole
Bolt & Watson, Ltd.
Byrne, Myles
Cadell, John, Ltd.
Clowes, Jonathan
Cochrane, Elspeth, Agency
Colin, Rosica, Ltd.
Copeman, Donald, Ltd.
De Wolfe, Felix
English Theatre Guild, Ltd.
Farquharson, John, Ltd.
Film Rights, Ltd.
Fitch, Laurence, Ltd.
Foster Jill, Ltd.
Fraser & Dunlop Scripts, Ltd.
French, John, Artists Agency Ltd.
Gibson's, J. F. Literary Agency
Glass, Eric
Goodwin, Clive, Associates
Harrison, Alec, and Associates
Higham, David, Associates, Ltd.
Hughes Massie, Ltd.
Johnson, John
Jones Blakey

Juvenilia
Le Dain Management, Ltd.
Leresche Hope & Sayle
London Independent Books, Ltd.
London Management
Marvin, Blanche
Milne, Richard
Motley, Michael, Ltd.
Paterson, Mark & Associates
Penman Literary Agency
Peters, A. D., & Company, Ltd.
Pollinger, Laurence, Ltd.
Pollinger, Murray
Radala & Associates
Ramsay, Margaret, Ltd.
Rogers, Deborah, Ltd.
Sheil, Anthony, Associates, Ltd.
Spokesmen
Stein, Abner
Tauber, Peter, Press Agency
Towndrow, Jenny, Associates Ltd.
Unna, Harvey and Stephen Durbridge, Ltd.
Van Loewen, Dr. Jan, Ltd.
Vestey, Lorna
Vosper, Margery, Ltd.
Winant, Towers, Ltd.

art, music prizes, clubs

OPPORTUNITIES FOR FREELANCE ARTISTS

CAMILLA BRYDEN-BROWN

FINE ART

Opportunities for freelance artists are more numerous than is generally supposed. For fine art such as painting, it is best to contact galleries, of which there are many in this country, particularly in London. It is worth remembering, though, that they have the choice of a large market and usually specialise in a fairly limited field. If you want to exhibit at these galleries, perhaps to have a one-man show, it is advisable to find out about the type of exhibitions they usually hold. This you can do by visiting each gallery yourself and assessing the current work. It is best to visit likely galleries frequently in order to get to know their work and how they function. (*The Arts Review Yearbook and Directory* (£2.95), published by Eaton House Publishers Ltd., 1 Whitehall Place, London, SW1A 2HE, contains a guide to London Galleries—including a description of the type of work in which they specialise—together with a list of Regional Galleries.) If you decide to approach a gallery, it is usual to write to the director with a short description, and photographs of some of your work, with a stamped addressed envelope for their return. The photographs should be clear, but not necessarily up to reproduction quality. It is possible to take the photographs yourself, but most towns have commercial photographers who work freelance for industry. Ask for an estimate first. Printmakers can take their work to galleries, which produce excellently printed runs of limited editions of high quality work, which are sold both by themselves and by other galleries under an agreement. Some of the greetings-card manufacturers already listed in this book are interested in paintings for reproduction. It would be wiser to write to them, if possible enclosing good colour transparencies of your work, before becoming involved in the expense of packing and sending paintings by post or carrier. Another useful reference book and directory for the fine and commercial artist is *The Artist Guide* (published by *The Artist*, 7 Carnaby Street, London, W1V 1PG).

One of the best methods of displaying and selling paintings is at the annual Summer Exhibition at the Royal Academy in London. Anyone can submit work which is put up for selection to the Council. Sending in days are usually in March and these dates must be strictly adhered to. A small handling fee (at the moment £7.50) allows artists to enter up to three pieces of work. Should any subsequently be hung and sold the Royal Academy charges commission at 15%. Full details will be found in the leaflet entitled 'Notice to artists' which is obtainable from mid-February each year from the Royal Academy of Arts, Piccadilly, London, W1V 0DS. This leaflet refers to the exhibition of the coming summer of that year. If requests for it are sent at other times of the year the Royal Academy can only send the leaflet from the previous February.

ILLUSTRATION AND DESIGN

For a career in the field of illustration and design it is advisable to have a training in illustration, and also in typography if possible. Although the latter is not absolutely essential, it is helpful to the artist and to the publisher. Artists who launch into freelance work often do so gradually from the security of full-time employment, probably in an allied field. It is useful to have the experience of working with a publisher or in an advertising agency or a studio first, as this gives the artist valuable background knowledge of suppliers and sources of work. Training in illustration can be obtained through a recognised course at art school, or through employment in a studio. Either method is an advantage, for even the most brilliantly gifted illustrator should know how to think in terms of printed work and to realise how work will reduce and reproduce.

Once an artist feels competent to accept commissions it is important to be available and reliable. Both these attributes are essential, and busy clients will not be bothered with artists who say vaguely that they had to go away or that the children were ill. Freelance work is a business, and will stand or fall by the competence or otherwise of the staff—you.

THE FOLIO

Artists who have already been in full-time employment in an advertising agency or publishing house will know of clients who are prepared to give them commissions, or they probably would not have started on the freelance venture, and if one commission is a success it will very often lead to another. For all artists, but particularly those with no connections, it is essential to make up a professional folio of work, spending some time and money on it, and showing as versatile a range of work as possible. For instance, it should include work in line, pencil, ink, line and tone, two or more colour line and full colour, and be on a variety of subjects. There are excellent folders, plastic envelopes or elaborate specimen books or cases containing plastic folders, for sale at most shops which stock equipment for designers. Work should be neatly trimmed and mounted on coloured cover paper (try black if in doubt) of a size to fit the folder or envelope. Paste the specimens of work on the cover paper, but do not use petroleum-based rubber solution if the sample of work is to be enclosed in a plastic envelope. Rubber solution is suitable for almost every other glueing purpose, and is usually used to mount for presentation all finished drawings that are not enclosed permanently in plastic.

Gradually you will collect together printed specimens as the commissions increase, and your folio of work should be brought up to date all the time. Always get as many samples as you can beg, although if it is a book you will probably only get one copy. In this case, see if you can get some extra dust-jackets so that if the first one becomes worn you can replace it, and if necessary buy more copies of the book if that should also become worn. The publisher may well give you a discount on books on which you have worked. Any book specimens should be kept separately in plastic bags, but it would be expedient to ask for spare block pulls of your illustrations early on in the proceedings, and they should be mounted up in your specimen book. Try to keep your specimens immaculate.

PUBLISHERS

When the specimen folder is complete it is time to write letters, typed on headed paper, if possible, to the production manager of as many publishing houses as practicable, asking for an interview in order to show your work, whether for illustrations or for book-jackets, or both. Space these letters out, or you may find yourself with too many appointments in one week. The production managers will usually grant you interviews (be on time), since they are interested in seeing new work, and they will probably be helpful about prices too, if you have no experience in this field. Book-publishing houses as a rule are not able to pay as highly as advertising agencies or popular magazines but they are usually fair. Do not overlook educational departments of publishing houses for there is considerable scope for illustrating modern school books. You may have to accept low fees to begin with until you know your market and your worth, but you will be gaining valuable knowledge and experience.

At each interview it would be a good idea to ask if there is anyone else in the firm who would be interested in seeing your work, such as the advertising manager or in some firms the editors, who occasionally commission artists. Do not expect to be seen by other people in the firm at the same time as your first interview, but be prepared to come back another time. It would be better not to leave your samples to be seen by other people, particularly if you have only one folio. You will be needing your folio for other interviews, and there is a very real danger that it will go astray or that specimens will be damaged beyond use, with no redress. If your work is liked and your first commission is satisfactory, you will often find that your work has been recommended to other people in similar fields.

ARTISTS' AGENTS

Advertising agencies frequently use the services of artists' agents, who can be good or bad, but if you are accepted on the books of a good one life will be much easier for you. Agents generally work very hard on behalf of both clients and artists: they take the brief, negotiate the price and commission you to do the work, usually taking 25 per cent of the fee. Although this percentage may seem high, you should remember that they do a lot of work on your behalf and invariably manage to get a more professional fee for you than you can obtain for yourself, even after the 25 per cent has been deducted.

ADVERTISING AGENCIES

Advertising agencies employ art buyers who are very skilled and capable people and should be approached by a letter similar to that previously described, giving details of the type of work at which you are best. Here again, once you have obtained the interview and have shown your work, you might ask if there is anyone else who would be interested, not necessarily at that moment.

STUDIOS

Studios exist in most cities, and the type of their work varies; some specialise in purely commercial work in finished lettering and finished artwork, and they employ highly skilled and extremely able artists. Often their work involves the use of airbrushes and photographic skills, but they do sometimes employ freelance artists for specific commissions, and may well like to have photocopies of your work on file in case they need drawings or diagrams for catalogues or similar uses. Technical drawing is called technical drawing with good reason and requires specific training. If you feel your work would be of interest to a studio, write to the studio manager and ask for an interview. Should they ask for photocopies of your work, a commercial photographic studio will prepare these for you, but it is likely that the studio will have facilities for taking copies for themselves. If you wish to have photocopies made, the photographic studio will help you with the details and give you prices before they take on the work.

GRAPHIC DESIGNERS

A graphic designer, who may be running a one-man studio of his own and doing freelance design and typography (designing for printing), may also use illustrators from time to time. Graphic designers are difficult to track down, but once you have found one you are likely to be on the trail of many others.

They will not be able to use your work all the time, even if they like it, as not all their commissions require drawings. The more versatile you are the more opportunities are available to you, and artists skilled only in very specialised fields, such as lettering and illumination, usually know where to offer their work.

IMPORTANCE OF RELIABILITY

Remember also that once you have started to get commissions, you must be accurate and reliable, as well as available. If you are given a date for the work, it must be presented on time, even if this means sitting up half the night before. Do not, for example, fall back on the excuse of mild illness or you will lose sympathy and understanding should you have the misfortune to be more seriously ill. Once you have received the commission you are part of a team, even though you may not know the other members of it. There are often unforeseen events which hold up production anyway, and it is as well to see that you do not come to be considered one. It is wise to take trouble over the presentation, and you have only yourself to blame if you have not protected your finished work adequately. It is distressing to have one's precious work destroyed or damaged, the more so if it means doing it all again.

You will discover that once you have started freelance work your commissions will build up gradually, although most artists have some periods when there is little work available. Use these 'rests' advantageously to prepare more specimen drawings and to experiment with new techniques and equipment, and to make sure your folio is ready to show again. At such times you should be looking for new outlets, visiting more agencies and publishers, or checking with the ones you have visited in the past.

Above all decide whether or not you really want to do this work: are you sure it is not just a pleasant day-dream with the appeal of being called an artist? It is hard work, but if you have ability and are consistent, reliable, enthusiastic and optimistic, even at those times when there is a lull, then you will be happy and successful.

ARTISTS AND DESIGNERS

CODE OF PROFESSIONAL CONDUCT

Issued by the Society of Industrial Artists and Designers (see page 335)

Introduction

1. This Code issued by the Society of Industrial Artists and Designers establishes a workable pattern of professional conduct for the benefit of its members and of those who employ their services.

2. All members of the Society undertake as a condition of membership that they will abide by this Code.

3. The Council of the Society has empowered its Conduct Committee to question any member thought to be behaving in a manner contrary to this Code and may as a result of the Committee's report reprimand, suspend or expel that member.

4. When members are working or seeking work abroad they will observe the rules of professional conduct currently in use in that country.

The designer's professional responsibilities

5. Designers work primarily for the benefit of their clients or their employers. Like everyone engaged in professional activities, designers have responsibilities not only to their clients or employers but also to their fellow practitioners and to society at large. It follows therefore that designers who are members of the Society accept certain obligations specifically in regard to these responsibilities.

The designer's responsibility to his client or employer

6. Good professional relations between a designer and his employer or client depend on the designer's acceptance of the need to be professionally and technically competent and on his ability to provide honourable and efficient advice and performance.

7. They will also depend on the reliance which the employer or client can place on a designer's integrity in all confidential matters relating to his business.

8. No member may work simultaneously for more than one employer or known to be in competition, without their knowledge and approval. Similarly no member, or his associates or staff, may divulge information confidential to his client or employer without their consent, subject to any requirement under law.

9. The Society believes that it is in the interest of the design profession and of industry that the employment of qualified designers should be increased. Members may therefore promote their own services and those of their profession in a manner appropriate to the various fields of practice in which

they work. It is essential however, that any claims made by them, or by those acting for them, are factually correct, honourable and clear as to their origin, and that the effect shall not be at variance with this Code nor cause harm to their fellow members.

10. It is normal for designers to be paid for their professional services, whether executive or advisory. But whether members work for a fee, a salary, or an honorarium must ultimately depend upon the circumstances, providing always that member shall not use the offer of reduced charges to gain an advantage over their fellow members to obtain work or some other professional benefit.

11. The Society recommends methods of charging which it considers appropriate for various types of work, but members will use their own judgement in agreeing fees with their clients.

12. The Society recommends conditions of engagement to enable proper working relationships to be established between members and their clients.

13. Whereas a member will make for his client the best possible trading arrangements with contractors, manufacturers and suppliers, his responsibility to contractors or suppliers is as professionally important as is his responsibility to his client. He must therefore be prepared to act as impartial arbitrator, if need be, to ensure fair dealing on both sides.

14. Whilst acting for his client, a member may not divert to his own advantage any discounts, reductions or other financial benefits offered as inducement by contractors, manufacturers or suppliers. Similarly a member must disclose any financial involvement which he may have with contractors or suppliers he may recommend.

15. On the other hand, if a member is also a manufacturer, retailer or agent in his own right, he may accept those financial terms which are normally honourably offered within the trade, provided they accrue to his company or his organisation and not to himself privately.

16. Although the relationship between a staff designer and his employer may well differ from that between consultant and client, the employed designer, who is a member of the Society, shall accept a responsibility to his employer on the same terms of professional integrity and confidentiality.

The designer's responsibility to his fellow practitioners

17. From time to time members may find themselves called upon to comment on other designers' work and in a consultative capacity may reasonably be expected to do so. Personal opinion must play a significant part in any criticism, but members should be aware of the fine dividing line between objective and destructive criticism. Personal denigration amongst members is regarded as intolerable and the Society will support any member who is shown to have been so affronted.

18. Similarly the Society regards copying or plagiarism with intent as wholly unprofessional.

19. There are occasions when more than one designer may be engaged on the same project. Where, however, a member suspects that his engagement may supplant rather than augment the service of another, he shall seek an assurance from the client that any previous association with another designer has been terminated. Similarly no member shall knowingly seek to supplant another designer currently working on a project whether satisfactorily or not.

20. Neither shall a member charge nor receive a fee, neither make nor receive a gift or other benefit, from a fellow member, in recognition of a recommendation to a post or an assignment.

21. Members should assure themselves that competitions they may be invited to assess or may wish to enter are in accordance with the Society's regulations for holding of design competitions.

The designer's responsibility to society

22. Since design is properly regarded as being a professional activity, a designer's work may be expected to contain a degree of social benefit in addition to client satisfaction. It follows therefore that the Society expects from its members an acceptance of their social responsibility and an understanding that this responsibility accords with the concept of professionalism expressed in this Code.

MARKETS FOR ARTISTS

ART AGENTS AND COMMERCIAL ART STUDIOS

In their own interests Artists are advised to make preliminary enquiries before submitting work, and to ascertain terms of work. Commission varies but averages 25 per cent.

A.L.I. Press Agency, Ltd., Boulevard Anspach 111–115, B9—1000 Brussels, Belgium. *T.* 02 512.73.94. *Director:* G. Lans. Cartoons, comics, strips, washwork, illustrations for covers, posters on order or in syndication. All feature material for newspapers and magazines. The biggest choice in picture stories for children and adults. Art studio with 90 Continental artists. Market for transparencies.

Artists Partners Ltd., 14–18 Ham Yard, London, W1V 8DE *T.* 01-734 7991. *Chairman:* John Barker. *Managing Director:* Christopher Candler. Represent large number of artists; work sold to advertising agencies, publishers in Europe, America, South Africa.

Associated Freelance Artists Limited, 19 Russell Street, London, WC2B 5HP *T.* 01-836 2507–8. *Directors:* Eva Morris, Doug FitzMaurice. General illustrators, graphic designers, lettering artists, strip illustrators, technical illustrators, a few writers, and a stock colour photographic library.

Bardon Press Features, Ltd, (1957), 17 Farringdon Street, London, EC4A 4AB *T.* 01-236 8200. Also Barcelona and Copenhagen. International Artists' and Publishers' Agents. Commission by arrangement. Sole interests: newspaper and juvenile picture strips. *No spot cartoons. Preliminary letter essential.*

Clement Dane Studio, Ltd., 49 Wellington Street, Covent Garden, London, WC2E 7BN *T.* 01-836 9222–5.

Coulthurst Day, 1A Ferney, Dursley, Gloucestershire, GL11 5AB *T.* 0453 3159. Christmas and fancy box and wrapping paper designs, greeting cards, etc. Specialising in design for the manufacturing Stationers.

Gossop (R. P.) Ltd. (1923), 106 Great Russell Street, London, WC1B 3NA *T.* 01-636 8563. *Directors:* Bronson Gossop, Kathleen Wheston. Illustration, book decoration, educational drawings and diagrams, maps, graphic design for publicity, and jackets. *Rate of commission:* 20 to 25 per cent.

Grestock & Marsh, Ltd., 15 Heddon Street, Regent Street, London, W1R 7LF *T.* 01-437 5788–9. *Directors:* J. L. Marsh, W. Marsh, K. Berry. Specialising in magazine illustration, features and many other types of artwork.

Juvenilia. *Proprietor:* Mrs. Rosemary Bromley, Colden Common, nr. Winchester, Hants. *T.* 0962 712383. Professional artwork for the children's market considered. Picture books—particularly author illustrated. No games or play books. Preliminary letter. Terms: 20%. Return postage for artwork and S.A.E. for acknowledgement essential.

Link Studios, 106 Great Arthur House, Golden Lane, London, EC1Y R0H *T.* 01-253 5824.

London Art Services Ltd., 5–11 Lavington Street, London, SE1. *T.* 01-928 3523. Artists, designers, illustrators and photographers. (Art Studio.)

Martin, John & Artists, Ltd., 5 Wardour Street, London, W1V 3HE *T.* 01-734 9000. *Directors:* W. Bowen-Davies, C. M. Bowen-Davies, L. L. Kemp, L. A. Richardson. *Production Manager:* W. Bowen-Davies. Illustrations for children (educational and fictional), dust jackets, paperbacks, magazines, encyclopaedias, advertising.

Middleton (N. E.), Ltd., 15 Half Moon Street, London, W1Y 7RB *T.* 01-491 7592. General.

Rogers & Co., Artists' Agents (1906), 61 Carey Street, London, WC2A 2JG *T.* 01-405 1821 (3 lines). *Directors:* J. W. A. Wall, K. M. Woolley.

Schlück, Thomas, Hinter der Worth 12, 3008 Garbsen 9, Germany. *T.* 05131-93053. Art agency. *Commission for artwork:* 25%–33%.

Temple Art Agency (1939), 93–94 Chancery Lane, London, WC2A 1DT *T.* 01-405 8295 and 01-242 9301. Magazine and book illustration; picture strips; book wrapper designs; historical art.

Towndrow, Jenny, Associates Ltd. (1977), 49 Hornton Street, London, W8 7NT *T.* 01-937 1931 and 8230.

Wake, Geoffrey, 37 Ashley Road, Thames Ditton, Surrey, KT7 0NH *T.* 01-398 1087. Illustrators, designers. *Average commission:* 25%.

DRAWINGS, DESIGNS AND VERSES FOR CARDS, ETC.

* Membership of the Greeting Card and Calendar Association.

Arnold (Joseph) & Co. Ltd., Church Bridge Works, Accrington, Lancashire, BB5 4EL *T.* Accrington 382121. Designs and paintings suitable for reproduction as greetings cards from experienced artists only.

Athena International, P.O. Box 13, Bishops Stortford, Herts. *T.* 0279-56627. *Publishing Manager:* B. M. Everitt. Designs for greetings cards, note cards, writing paper, gift tags, gift wrap, and general stationery. Paintings and illustrations of a professional standard for reproduction as prints and posters.

C.C.A. Stationery Ltd., Maitland Street, Preston, PR1 4AP. *T.* (0772) 794508. Publishers of personalised wedding stationery and Christmas cards. Pleased to consider any original artwork but verses not required.

Chelsea Studios, Ltd. (1921), 10–12 Emerald Street, London, WC1N 3QA *T.* 01-242 0139. General and illustration.

*Delgado Mansell, Ltd., 224–236 Walworth Road, London, SE17 1JE *T.* 01-701 4261. Publishers of Christmas cards, calendars, and all other kinds of greeting cards. Pleased to receive and consider original paintings, drawings and designs, suitable for the purpose. *Verses* not required. Enclose S.A.E. for return.

Evershed Ltd., Alma Road, St. Albans, Herts. *T.* 0727 54652.

Fairservice (Geo. C.), Ltd., 42 Bain Street, Glasgow, G40 2LB *T.* 041-552 1649. Designs suitable for reproduction by line for high class personal wedding stationery.

Felix Rosentiel's Widow & Son, Ltd., Fine Art Publishers, 33–35 Markham Street, London, SW3 3NR *T.* 01-352 3551. Invite offers of Originals of a professional standard for reproduction as Picture Prints for the Picture Framing trade.   Oil paintings and strong Water-colours.   Any type of subject considered.   Verse or cards are not required.

Hallmark Cards Inc., European Art Department, 22–24 Market Place, Henley on Thames, Oxon, RG9 2AH *T.* 4106. Designs from professional freelance artists only for high quality reproduction in greeting cards. Verses not required.

Hanson White Publishing Company Ltd. (1958), 2 High Street, Redhill, Surrey, RH1 1RH *T.* Redhill 69128. Humorous contemporary designs for greeting cards.

*****Kardonia Ltd.,** Alric Avenue, Stonebridge Park, London, NW10 8RA *T.* 01-459 2116–7.

*****Mason (A.) & Co., Ltd.,** Arrol Road, Wester Gourdie Industrial Estate, Dundee, DD2 4UJ *T.* 0382-644111. *Publishing Manager:* T. Webster. Colour rough designs of freelance professional artists for greeting cards suitable for the general market.

Medici Society, Ltd., The, 34–42 Pentonville Road, London, N1 9HG *T.* 01-837 7099. Requirements: paintings suitable for reproduction as large prints or greeting cards.

*****Royle Publications, Ltd.,** Royle House, Wenlock Road, London, N1 7ST *T.* 01-253 7654. Greeting cards, postcards, calendars, prints and gift wrap.

*****Rust Craft Greeting Cards (U.K.) Ltd.,** Mill Street East, Dewsbury, West Yorkshire. *T.* Dewsbury 465200.

Solomon & Whitehead (Guild Prints) Ltd., Lynn Lane, Shenstone, Staffs. WS14 0DX Fine Art prints framed and unframed, Calendar prints. London Showrooms: 5 Ave Maria Lane, Ludgate Hill, London, EC4M 7DB.

Thomas Leach Limited, Ock Street, Abingdon-on-Thames, Oxfordshire, OX14 5DE *T.* Abingdon (0235) 20444. (Address to Edward Jones.) Sketches of religious subjects suitable for reproduction as Christmas or Easter Cards.

*****Valentines of Dundee, Ltd.,** P.O. Box 74, Kingsway West, Dundee, DD3 8QB *T.* 814711. Everyday greeting cards, Christmas cards, gift wraps, social stationery, St. Valentine's Day, Easter, Mother's Day, Father's Day. Address to *The Publishing Manager.*

*****Waldorf Stationery & Greeting Cards Ltd.,** Newton Mill, P.O. Box No. 2, Hyde, SK14 4BG *T.* 061-386 2601. Greeting cards, informal notes, stationery, party invitations.

Webb Ivory Limited, Queensbridge Works, Queen Street, Burton upon Trent, Staffs, DE14 3LP *T.* 0283-66311. Everyday and Christmas greetings cards.

*****Wilson Bros. Greeting Cards, Ltd.,** Academy House, 45 Uxbridge Road, Hayes, Middlesex, UB4 0JY *T.* 01-573 3877.

MARKETS FOR PHOTOGRAPHERS

Photographers are advised to study carefully the detailed requirements of journals at the beginning of the *Yearbook*. Book publishers, especially those issuing technical books and school books, will be glad to know the range of subjects covered by a photographer.

GREETINGS, VIEWCARD, CALENDAR AND COLOUR SLIDES

* Membership of the Greeting Card and Calendar Association

A preliminary letter to ascertain requirements is advisable.

So far as colour is concerned, and most of the firms mentioned below are concerned with colour, usually colour transparencies are required. Very few firms will consider 35 mm. frames; 5 in. × 4 in. is preferred, and 3¼ × 2¼ is acceptable. 2¼ in. square is the minimum size acceptable to film libraries and agencies. Only top quality transparencies should be submitted; inferior work is never accepted. Postage for return of photographs should be enclosed.

Athena International, P.O. Box 13, Bishops Stortford, Herts *T.* 0279 56627. *Publishing Manager:* B. M. Everitt. Professional quality transparencies for posters and greetings cards, preferably not 35 mm.

*Delgado Mansell, Ltd., 224–236 Walworth Road, London, SE17 1JE *T.* 01-701 4261. 35 mm. not acceptable.

Dennis (E. T. W.) & Sons, Ltd., Printing House Square, Melrose Street, Scarborough, Yorkshire, YO12 7SJ *T.* Scarborough 0723-61317. Especially interested in first class transparencies for reproduction as calendar views and local view cards. 5 in.×4 in., 3¼×2¼ in. or 35 mm transparencies ideal for postcard reproduction.

Dixon (J. Arthur), Forest Side, Newport, Isle of Wight, PO 30 5QW *T.* Newport 3381. Greeting cards, postcards, gift wrap, colour slides and booklets.

Evershed Ltd., Alma Road, St. Albans, Herts. *T.* 0727 54652.

Hallmark Cards Inc., European Art Department, 22–24 Market Place, Henley-on-Thames, Oxfordshire, RG9 2AH *T.* 4106. Transparencies suitable for greeting cards and associated products.

*Kardonia, Ltd., Alric Avenue, Stonebridge Park, London, NW10 8RA *T.* 01-459 2116–7.

Keystone Press Agency, Ltd., Bath House, 52–62 Holborn Viaduct, London, EC1A 2FE *T.* 01-236 3331–4. *T.A.* Pressillu, London, EC1. *Telex:* 888258.

Lowe Aston Calendars, Ltd., Saltash, Cornwall, PL12 4HL *T.* Saltash 2233. Calendar printers.

*Mason (A.) & Co., Ltd., Arrol Road, Wester Gourdie Industrial Estate, Dundee, DD2 4UJ *T.* 0382-644111. *Publishing Manager:* T. Webster. Colour transparencies, mainly upright, for greeting cards. Minimum 2¼×2¼ in.

Medici Society, Ltd., The, 34–42 Pentonville Road, London, N1 9HG *T.* 01-837 7099. Photographs suitable for reproduction as greeting cards.

Mowbray (A. R.), & Co., Ltd., Saint Thomas House, Becket Street, Oxford, OX1 1SJ. 2¼ in. square colour transparencies for parish magazine covers. Seasonal scenes, human interest subjects. Also unusual black and white photographs for editorial articles.

Philmar, Ltd., 47–53 Dace Road, London, E3 2NG *T.* 01-986 5522. Popular children's toys, games, cardboard and wooden jigsaws. Ideas for toys and novelties considered; also colour transparencies from size 5 in. × 4 in.

Photo Precision, Ltd., Caxton Road, St. Ives, Huntingdon, Cambridgeshire, PE17 4LS *T.* St. Ives (Hunts.) (0480) 64364.

Pictorial Press, Ltd., Woodbridge House, 1 Woodbridge Street, London, EC1R 0BL *T.* 01-253 4023.

Pillans & Wilson, Ltd., 20 Bernard Terrace, Edinburgh, EH8 9NY *T.* 031-667 2036.

*Royle Publications, Ltd., Royle House, Wenlock Road, London, N1 7ST *T.* 01-253 7654. Greeting cards, postcards, calendars, prints and gift wrap.

*Salmon (J.), Ltd., 100 London Road, Sevenoaks, Kent. *T.* Sevenoaks 52381. Picture postcards, calendars and greeting cards.

Scott, Walter (Bradford), Ltd., Ivanhoe Works, 280 Canal Road, Bradford, BD2 1AR *T.* Bradford 24671. Local view postcards, greeting cards and calendars.

*Waldorf Stationery & Greeting Cards Ltd., Newton Mill, P.O. Box No. 2, Hyde, SK14 4BG *T.* 061-368 2601. Greeting cards, stationery, informal notes, party invitations.

Walton Sound and Film Services Ltd., 87 Richford Street, London, W6 7HN *T.* 01-743 9421.

Webb Ivory Limited, Queensbridge Works, Queen Street, Burton on Trent, Staffs, DE14 3LP *T.* 66311–8. Everyday and Christmas greeting cards.

Whitehorn Press, Ltd., The, P.O. Box 237, Thomson House, Withy Grove, Manchester, M60 4BL *T.* 061-834 1234. Transparencies not smaller than 2¼ in. × 2¼ in. Pictures required relevant to Cheshire, Lancashire, Yorkshire, Warwickshire, Worcestershire, Gloucestershire and Avon only.

*Wilson Bros. Greeting Cards, Ltd., Academy House, 45 Uxbridge Road, Hayes, Middlesex, UB4 0JY *T.* 01-573 3877.

PHOTOGRAPHIC AGENCIES AND PICTURE LIBRARIES

THE FREELANCE PHOTOGRAPHER AND THE AGENT
Bruce Coleman

Photographic agencies and libraries have a dual role in the service they provide. They meet the needs and demands of Picture Editors, Picture Researchers and Art Buyers and, at the same time, provide a service to the freelance photographer. The enterprising photographer, wishing to penetrate the publishing market, would do well to consider employing the services of an agent whose knowledge of current trends and client contact will gear the photographer's output to the requirements of the markets. The complexities of reproduction rights are best left to an agent—that's if the photographer wishes to protect the copyright of his work!

Selecting the right agent very much depends on the type of work the photographer is producing and he should, therefore, take a look at several agencies before choosing the one he thinks will be of advantage to him. Some agents, for example, work in the syndication area, selling news and topical pictures to the world's press; others are in the stock business maintaining a library of photographers' work orientated to the editorial market. Agents normally do not sell pictures outright but lease them for a specific use and fee from which they deduct a commission. A good photograph in the hands of a good agent can be published several times over and bring in royalties for many years.

Before submitting your work to an agent, a preliminary letter is recommended enquiring if (1) he is accepting new photographers and (2) details of his specific needs.

The agent will wish to see an initial presentation of at least two hundred photographs and the photographer should indicate the number of photographs he plans to submit in the course of a year. Agents are keen to encourage the active photographer who can supply a regular stream of good quality work. Serious attention should be given to the caption of every picture as this can often mean the difference between a sale or a rejection. A caption should be brief and legible and an example of a good nature caption would be:

> Spotted Hyena (C. crocuta)
> Serengeti
> Aggressive behaviour

or, a geographical caption:
> Canada: Northwest Territories
> Eskimo fur trappers and dogsled

Some time spent on the presentation of your work, editing for composition, content, sharpness and in the case of transparencies, colour saturation, will create a favourable impression. When submitting original colour transparencies, to ensure they are protected from damage and also to facilitate easy examination place them in clear plastic sleeves, never between glass. Do not submit transparencies which you may require for personal use as it is quite impossible for an agent to recall pictures at short notice from his client.

One final point, never supply similar photographs to more than one agent as the problems created by almost identical pictures appearing, say, on a calendar or a greeting card can be embarrassing and costly to rectify. Indeed, for this reason, many agents insist on an exclusive arrangement between themselves and their photographers.

A-Z Botanical Collection, Ltd., Holmwood House, Mid Holmwood, Dorking, Surrey, RH5 4HE   *T.* Dorking (0306) 6130.   Colour transparencies, minimum size 2¼ in. square, of all subjects of a botanical nature.

Aarons, Leo, 14 rue Rougemont, 75009 Paris   *T.* 246-1205.   General photo libraries: Paris, London, Milan.   Genuine international sales network for top quality transparencies.

Aerofilms Limited (1919), Elstree Way, Boreham Wood, Herts, WD6 1SW   *T.* 01-207 0666.   *Telex:* 23517.   Library of Aerial and Ground Photographs. The most comprehensive collection of its kind in the United Kingdom, including many historical aviation photographs.

American History Picture Library, 86 Park Road, Brentwood, Essex, CM14 4TT   *T.* 0277 217643.   Photographs, engravings, colour transparencies covering the exploration, social, political and military history of North America from 15th to 20th century.   Conquistadores, Civil War, Gangsters, Moon landings, etc.   Prints and photos purchased.

Aquila Photographics, P.O. Box 1, Studley, Warwickshire, B80 7JG   *T.* Studley 2357.   Specialists in ornithological subjects, but covering all aspects of natural history in both colour and black and white.

Ardea London Ltd., 35 Brodrick Road, London,, SW17 7DX   *T.* 10-672 2067 and 8787.   *T.A.* Ardeaphotos.   *Telex:* 896691 TLXIR G.   Su Gooders, John Gooders.   Agents for photographs of animals, all aspects of natural history and anthropological and travel subjects.   Representing Ron and Valerie Taylor, Clem Haagner, Ken Fink, Eric Lindgren and 70 others. Library of wildlife colour transparencies and black and white prints covering whole world.

Asian Affairs, Royal Society for, 42 Devonshire Street, London, W1N 1LN   *T.* 01-580 5728.   Archive Library of original 19th and 20th century black-and-white photographs, glass slides, etc., of Asia.   Publishes *Asian Affairs* 3 times p.a.

Associated Freelance Artists Limited, 19 Russell Street, London, WC2B 5HP   *T.* 01-836 2507–8.   Stock colour photographic library, mainly natural history and geography.

Associated News Photos, 30 Fleet Street, London, EC4Y 1AA   *T.* 01-353 6280. *T.A.* Ansfotos, London.   News photos and feature pictures; animal and human interest.   Good rates for exclusive material.   Pin-ups (black-and-white) and colour transparencies must be exclusive.

Associated Press (The), Ltd., (News Photo Department), 83–86 Farringdon Street, London, EC4A 4BR   *T.* 01-353 1515.   *T.A.* Appho, Telex, London. News and feature pictures.   Negatives preferred.   Terms by agreement.

Band, Alan, Associates, 25 Longdown Road, Farnham, Surrey, GU10 3JL   *T.* 0252 713022.   *T.A.* Alband, Farnham, Surrey.   Specialists in international news and feature pictures for British and overseas publishers.

Barnaby's Picture Library, 19 Rathbone Street, London, W1P 1AF   *T.* 01-636 6128–9.   Requires photographs for advertising and editorial publication and always interested to see new work of outstanding quality in black-and-white and colour, of all subjects, British and foreign.

Bassano Studios (1850), 35 Moreton Street, London, SW1.   *T.* 01-821 9182. Incorporating **Elliott & Fry and Vandyk Studios.**   Specialists in historical portraits, royals, composers, politicians, academic, actors, writers, etc.

Biofotos, Highways, Vicarage Hill, Farnham, Surrey, GU9 8HJ *T.* Farnham (025 13) 6700 or (0252) 716700. Heather Angel, M.SC., F.I.I.P., F.R.P.S. Colour transparencies (35 mm. and 2¼ in. square) and monochrome prints of wide range of natural history and biological subjects, with world-wide coverage. Detailed catalogues on request.

BIPS-Bernsen's International Press Service, Ltd., 2 Barbon Close, Great Ormond Street, London, WC1N 3JS *T.* 01-405 2723. (For full details see under **Syndicates, News and Press Agencies.**)

Bord, Janet and Colin, Melangell House, Princes Street, Montgomery, Powys, SY15 6PY *T.* Montgomery 405. Library of black and white photographs and colour transparencies, specialising in the prehistoric and Roman sites of Britain, but also covering rural and scenic Britain in general, e.g. landscapes, wild flowers, villages, churches. Do not act as agents for other photographers.

Boxing Picture Library, 86 Park Road, Brentwood, Essex, CM14 4TT *T.* 0277 217643. Prints, engravings and photos of famous boxers, boxing personalities and famous fights from 18th century to recent years. Reproduction fees on application. Interested in purchasing illustrations on boxing.

British Tourist Authority Photo Library, 239 Old Marylebone Road, London, NW1 5QT *T.* 01-262 0141. General UK travel including many special subjects. Colour, black and white. Mon. to Fri. 11 a.m.–4 p.m.

Brown, Hamish, 21 Carlin Craig, Kinghorn, Fife, KY3 9RX *T.* Kinghorn 422. Photographs and 35 mm. transparencies of Scottish Highlands, Scottish "gazeteer," Mountain Ranges of Europe, Africa, India and South America.

Cash, J. Allan, Ltd., 23 Martaban Road, London, N16 5SJ *T.* 01-802 0254. Worldwide photographic library; travel, landscape, natural history, wild life. Full details available for photographers interested in contributing.

Central Press Photos, Ltd., The, 6 & 7 Gough Square, Fleet Street, London, EC4A 3DJ *T.* 01-353 2266–7. *T.A.* Exposure, London, EC4. Independent coverage of news events at home and abroad, with special emphasis on sport including cricket. Supporting features give all-round picture service, and the particular requirements of overseas newspapers are carefully watched. Extensive Picture Library dates from 1914.

Coleman, Bruce, Inc., 381 Fifth Avenue, New York, N.Y., 10016. *T.* 212-683–5227. *President:* Bruce Coleman. *Vice-President:* Norman Owen Tomalin. Specialising exclusively in colour transparencies of natural history, geographical and science subjects. Welcome and encourage new photographers who can produce material that meets the exacting standards set by our customers. All formats from 35 mm. are acceptable.

Coleman, Bruce, Ltd., 16A–17A Windsor Street, Uxbridge, Middlesex, UB8 1AB *T.* Uxbridge 32333 and 36398. *Telex:* 932439. Colour transparencies on all aspects of natural history, ecology, environment, geographical, archaeology, anthropology, horticulture, agriculture, science subjects and social documentary.

Colorific Photo Library, Garden Offices, Gilray House, Gloucester Terrace, London, W2 3DF *T.* 01-723 5031 and 01-402 9595. Handling photographs of top international photographers, most subjects currently on file, upwards of 150,000 images. Also representing Life Picture Collection, People Magazine, Time-Life Books, Time Magazine (including text), Camera Tres, Rio de Janeiro, Contact Press Images Inc., New York, David Moore Library, Sydney.

Cooper-Bridgeman Picture Library, 51 Sloane Gardens, London, SW1W 8ED
T. 01-730 1345, 730 0938. Paintings, silver, glass, porcelain, jewellery, pottery, furniture, militaria, social history, etc. Colour transparencies and
black and white prints.

Cross Sections, James Cross, 52 Crockford Park Road, Addlestone, Weybridge,
Surrey, KT15 2LX *T.* Weybridge (0932) 47554. Library of high quality
transparencies and monochromes, specialising in natural history. Also
travel. Other photographers' work not accepted.

Cutten, John H., Associates, 22 Belsize Park, London, NW3 4DU *T.* 01-794
3972. Photographs and colour transparencies relating to Psychical Research. Library includes many portraits of notable personalities from the
19th century to present day. Also historical.

Daily Telegraph Colour Library, 75–79 Farringdon Street, London, EC4P 4BL
T. 01-353 4242 ext. 152. Over 500,000 transparencies (mainly 35 mm.)
covering a diverse range of subjects from Telegraph Magazine and freelance photographers. See also **Daily Telegraph Syndication.**

Dixon, C. M., 13 Danes Court, Dover, Kent, CT16 2QE *T.* 0304-208056. Colour
library covering most countries of Europe and Ethiopia, Iceland, Sri Lanka,
Tunisia, Turkey, USSR. Main subjects include agriculture, archaeology,
architecture, clouds, geography, geology, horses, industry, meteorology,
mosaics, mountains, occupations, people.

Elisabeth Photo Library, London, Ltd., 51 Cleveland Street, London, W1P 5PQ
T. 01-580 7285–6. Agriculture, archaeology, architecture, art, commerce
and markets, environment, geography, industry, natural history, people,
religion, space, travel.

Evans, Mary, Picture Library, 1 Tranquil Vale, Blackheath, London, SE3 0BU
T. 01-318 0034. Library containing more than a million historical illustrations from antiquity to the recent past. Also runs of British and foreign
illustrated periodicals. Special collections: *Sigmund Freud Copyrights* and
Society for Psychical Research.

Feature-Pix Colour Library (Travel Photographic Services Ltd.), 20 Great Chapel
Street, London, W1V 3AQ *T.* 01-437 2121. *Directors:* Gerry Brenes, Ken
Hackett. Colour transparencies (2¼ in. sq. or larger), and black-and-
white, on travel and allied subjects. Undertake photography on assignment
for tour operators, National Tourist Offices. *Terms:* 50% to photographer.

Features International, Spencer House, 23 Dartmouth Row, London, SE10 8AW
T. 01-691 2888. International syndication of pictures and photo-features.

Fotolink Picture Library, Lynwood House, 24–32 Kilburn High Road, London, NW6 5XW *T.* 01-624 6805. A World travel and documentary picture
library with specialist section on industrial subjects. Require colour transparencies (6×6 or 6×7 cm.) of tourist locations of the world, and industrial
subjects. Preliminary enquiry for details. Commission to the photographer, 50 per cent.

Gadsby, Brian (Visual Life), 8 Fairhaven Road, Southport, Merseyside. *T.*
29180. Library of colour transparencies (2¼ sq. and 35 mm.) and black
and white prints. Wide range of subjects but emphasis on children, natural
history, travel.

Geoscience Features, 6 Orchard Drive, Wye, Nr. Ashford, Kent, TN25 5AU
T. Wye (0233) 812707. *Director:* Dr. Basil Booth. Specialising in colour
transparencies and black and white prints of geological, geographical, geo-
physical, travel and environmental subjects. Peru, Mexico, Caribbean,
Atlantic Isles, Asia. Most comprehensive collection in the United Kingdom of volcanic eruptions. Photographs must be of outstanding quality.
Terms: 50 per cent to photographer.

Geoslides, 4 Christian Fields, London, SW16 3JZ *T.* 01-764 6292. *Director:*
John Douglas. Library of 35 mm. colour transparencies of geographical
and general interest of subjects from Africa, Asia, Antarctic, Arctic and sub-
Arctic areas. Interested only in large recent collections of relevant colour
transparencies, regionally based. *Terms:* 50 per cent to photographer on
UK sales; 40 per cent on overseas. Photographs for all types of publications, television, advertising, etc.

Glo Syndicate, The, 20 Honor Oak Road, London, SE23 3SB *T.* 01-699 5324.
Photographs and colour transparencies of transport subjects, topography,
countryside, contemporary maritime, canal, land transport, speciality railways and steam trains, world wide coverage.

Greater London Council Photographic Library, Room B66, County Hall, London, SE1 7PB *T.* 01-633 3255. Over 250,000 photographs of London and
the London area from *c.* 1860 to present day. Especially strong on Council
projects—schools, housing, open spaces, etc.

Griggs, Susan, Agency (1968), 17 Victoria Grove, London, W8 5RW *T.* 01-584
6738. *T.A.* Susanpix, London, W8. Stock library of 100,000 35 mm
colour transparencies.

Harding, Robert, Associates, 5 Botts Mews, Chepstow Road, London, W2 5AG
T. 01-229 2234. *T.A.* Rohard. Photographic Library. Require photographs for editorial publications which must be of outstanding quality and
geographically oriented basis. Telephone or write for details.

Hardwick, Iris, Library of Photographs, The, 13 Duck Street, Cerne Abbas,
Dorset, DT2 7LA *T.* Cerne Abbas 502. *Administrator:* K. Sanecki.
Photographs and colour transparencies of gardens, garden features, plant
portraits, trees, herbs, vegetable gardening, cottage gardens, landscape and
countryside of England and Wales, rural activities.

Harper Horticultural Slide Library, 219 Robanna Drive, Seaford, Virginia
23696, U.S.A. 35 mm. slides of plants and gardens.

Historical Picture Service, 86 Park Road, Brentwood, Essex, CM14 4TT *T.*
Brentwood (0277) 217643. Engravings, prints and photographs on all
aspects of history from ancient times to 1920. Special collection Old London: buildings, inns, theatres, many of which no longer exist.

Horticultural Photo Supply Service, The International Horticultural Advisory
Bureau, Arkley, Barnet, Herts, EN5 3HS *T.* 01-449 3031 and 2177.

Hosking Eric, O.B.E., Hon.F.R.P.S., F.I.I.P., and **David Hosking,** A.R.P.S., 20
Crouch Hall Road, London, N8 8HX *T.* 01-340 7703. Library of 60,000
colour transparencies and 250,000 black and white prints of most natural
history subjects, especially birds, covering whole world.

Hutchison, Alan, Library, 2 Logan Mews, London, W8 6QP *T.* 01-373 4830
and 6153. Over 100,000 transparencies on Third World subjects, especially
strong on Africa and the Middle East. All subjects covered including environment, culture, calendar type pictures and personalities.

India Foto News Features, 44 East Avenue Road, Punjabi Bagh, Delhi 110 026, India. *T.* 564545. Undertake news and feature assignments, in colour and black and white. Do not buy photographs.

International News Service, Ltd., Tokyo Central P.O. Box 1651, Tokyo, Japan. *T.* 571–0245 and 572–3598. *Cables:* Newsinter, Tokyo. News items, features, black and white photographs, colour transparencies, cartoons. *Terms:* 30–70.

International Press Bureau, 30 Fleet Street, London, EC4Y 1AA *T.* 01-353 7940 *T.A.* Newswire London. International news features and pictures.

Inter-Prensa Features, Florida 229, 1005 Capital Federal, Argentina. *T.A.* Interprensa Baires. Picture-stories, fashion photographs, hair styles, men's fashions, etc. Good market for colour transparencies. Terms 40 per cent.

Irish International News Service, Barry J. Hardy, **P.C.,** 12 Greenlea Park, Terenure, Dublin 6. *T.* 906183.

Kemp, Roger Clive, Bellair Cottage, Bellair Terrace, St. Ives, Cornwall. Black and white photographs and colour transparencies of Devon, Cornwall and the Isles of Scilly; candid studies of Pop Stars since 1960, and portraits of Westcountry writers and artists. Also represents a number of Westcountry photographers, specialising in regional and general subjects. Terms 50%. Photographs not purchased; sender retains negative and copyright.

Kershaw, Peter, Associates, 3 Sandringham Road, Birkdale, Southport, Merseyside, PR8 2JZ *T.* Southport 60814.

Kevin Court Universal now incorporated in **Spectrum Colour Library** *q.v.*

Keystone Press Agency, Ltd. (1920), Bath House, Holborn Viaduct, London, EC1A 2FE. *T.* 01-236 3331. *T.A.* Pressillu, London, EC1. *Telex:* 888258. Mainly "hot" news pictures; feature pictures; colour, studio for creative photography; publicity; industrial. Colour and mono library. Global service. Terms: When negatives are supplied, 60–40 per cent. When prints are supplied, 50–50 per cent. Payment and reports of sales, 15th–20th of month.

Lane, Frank W., Drummoyne, Southill Lane, Pinner, Middlesex, HA5 2EQ *T.* 01-866 2336. Natural history.

Lensmen Ltd., Press P.R. Photo Agency, Lensmen House, Essex Street, E., Dublin 2. *T.* Dublin 773447.

Les & Joyce (L.J.B. Features), 133 Barton Hill Road, Torquay, Devon, TQ2 8HY *T.* 0803 37254. 35 mm. and 2¼ in. sq.–4 in. × 5 in. colour; comprehensive international; towns and cities; general scenics; geography; farming; factories; folk lore and folk dancing; national costume. Own production only.

MacQuitty International Collection, The, Mote Mount, Mill Hill, London, NW7 4HH *T.* 01-959 5311. Over 200,000 photographs used by leading publishers throughout the world, on a wide variety of subjects and countries; extensive coverage of China, Egypt and oriental subjects.

Mander (Raymond) and Joe Mitchenson Theatre Collection (a Registered Charity), 5 Venner Road, Sydenham, London, SE26 5EQ *T.* 01-778 6730. Prints, drawings, photographs, programmes, etc., theatre, opera, ballet, music hall, and other allied subjects including composers, playrights, etc. All periods. Available for books, magazine, T.V. Reproduction by arrangement.

Mansell Collection, Ltd., 42 Linden Gardens, London, W2 4ER   *T.* 01-229 5475.

Massey Stewart, John, 27 John Adam Street, Strand, London, WC2N 6HX   *T.* 01-839 2456.   Library of colour and black and white covering many countries, particularly Europe and Asia, with major collection of Russia past and present.

Mathews Sheila and Oliver, West Lodge, Rook's Nest, Godstone, Surrey, RH9 8BY   *T.* Godstone (0883) 842648.   Specialist library of fine colour transparencies concentrating on the landscape, topography, buildings, flora and country activities of the British Isles, in all seasons.   No agency work.

May, Robin, Collection, 23 Malcolm Road, London, SW19 4AS   *T.* 01-946 8965.   Library specialises in Western Americana and the theatrical arts.

Merrill, John N., Yew Cottage, West Bank, Winster, Matlock, Derbyshire, DE4 2DQ   *T.* Winster 454 (STD 062 988).   Picture library of 35 mm. colour transparencies and black and white photographs covering English and Welsh National Parks, Derbyshire and the Peak District, N.W. Scotland, Hebridean islands, St. Kilda, Fair Isle, Orkneys, Shetland, west coast of Ireland and islands, long distance footpaths and English cathedrals, also the whole of the British coastline.

Monitor International, 17–27 Old Street, London, EC1V 9HL   *T.* 01-253 7071 and 6281.   *Telex:* 24718.   *Picture Editor:* Mark McCaffrey.   International picture agency.   Large library of personality portraits in colour, black and white from sport, politics, entertainment, business, general subjects.   Large geographical colour library and aerial photography facility.

Mustograph Agency, The, 19 Rathbone Street, London, W1P 1AF   *T.* 01-636 6128–9.   Photographs and colour transparencies of Britain only.   General subjects of countryside life, work, history and scenery.   Terms: 50 per cent, payable on receipt of client's cheque.   Applicants *must* first write for particulars.

National Motor Museum, Beaulieu, Photographic Library, Beaulieu, Hampshire, SO4 7ZN   *T.* Beaulieu 612345 (STD0590).   Over 60,000 black-and-white photographs of all aspects of motoring, cars, commercial vehicles, motor cycles, traction engines, etc.   Period covers from the dawn of motoring up to the present day, including many illustrations of period scenes and motor sport.   Also large library of 5 in. × 4 in. and smaller colour transparencies of veteran, vintage and modern cars, commercial vehicles and motor cycles.

News Blitz International, 5 Via Cimabue, 00196 Rome, Italy.   *T.* 36 00 620, 36 03 087, 36 01 489.   (For full details see under **Syndicates, News and Press Agencies.**)

Newman, M., Natural History Photographic Agency, Moray Lodge, Sandling Road, Saltwood, Nr. Hythe, Kent, CT21 4QN   *T.* 0303-66676.   Representing 50 of the leading natural history photographers specialising in colour transparencies.

Orion Press, 55, 1-Chome, Kanda Jimbocho, Chiyoda-ku, Tokyo, 101.   *Cable:* Orionserv, Tokyo.   *Telex:* J2 4447 Orionprs.

P.F.B. Photo Library, 11A Hyde Park Crescent, Leeds, LS6 2NW *T.* 789869. Extensive library of colour transparencies 35 mm. to 5 in.–4 in. covering a wide range of subjects with emphasis on glamour, sport, advertising, fashion and calendar material, etc. World-wide syndication. Terms 50% to photographer.

Peerless, Ann & Bury, 22 King's Avenue, Minnis Bay, Birchington-on-Sea, Kent, CT7 9QL *T.* Thanet (0843) 41428. Picture library of 35 mm. colour transparencies covering art, architecture, geography, history, social and cultural aspects in India, Pakistan, Bangla Desh, Sri Lanka and parts of the Middle East and Africa. Specialist material on World Religions.

Photo Library International, St. Michael's Hall, Bennett Road, Leeds, LS6 3HN *T.* (0532) 789321. High quality stock colour transparencies 35 mm. to 10×8. Most subjects. New material always welcome. Terms on application, 50% to photographer.

Photo Precision, Ltd., Caxton Road, St. Ives, Huntingdon, Cambridgeshire, PE17 4LS *T.* St. Ives (Hunts) (0480) 64364.

Photographic Society, The Royal (1853), 14 South Audley Street, London, W1Y 5DP *T.* 01-493 3967. Library of books and photographs.

Photolog Picture Library, Dr. W. H. Findlay, 9 Rosemount Place, Perth, PH2 7EH *T.* 0738 24157. Specialises in Scotland, Russia, Yugoslavia, Italy.

Photoresources, 21 Ashley Road, London, N19 3AG *T.* 01-272 5062 and (0304) 208056. Library of colour transparencies covering ancient civilizations, art, archaeology, world religions, myth, and museum objects covering the period from 8000 B.C. to A.D. 1200.

Pictor International, Ltd., Lynwood House, 24–32 Kilburn High Road, London, NW6 5XW *T.* 01-328 1581. *Telex:* 21497. General photo libraries: London, Paris, Milan. International sales network for top quality transparencies.

Pictor International, Piazza Bertarelli 1, 20122 Milan. *T.* 02-890710. General photo libraries: Milan, London, Paris.

Pictorial Press, Ltd., Woodbridge House, 1 Woodbridge Street, London, EC1R 0BL *T.* 01-253 4023 and 4024. *Directors:* L. W. Gale, A. F. Gale, K. V. Gale. Established in Fleet Street in 1938, handles photographic features dealing with show business, personalities, animals, children, woman subjects, medical and scientific stories and glamour. Handles freelance work but prefers to commission. Sells direct to media in every part of the world.

Picturepoint, Ltd., 770 Fulham Road, London, SW6 5SJ *T.* 01-736 5865. Have ready world-wide markets for high quality colour transparencies 6×6 cm. or larger. Any subject other than *news.* Only accepts work of exceptional merit. Minimum of 250 pictures in first submission. Send by Registered Mail enclosing stamps or I.R.C. for returns. *Terms:* 5 year contract, 50% commission.

Pixfeatures (Mr. P. G. Wickman), 5 Latimer Road, Barnet, Herts. *T.* 01-449 9946. *Telex:* 27538. Picture-features, preferably topical. Especially for sale to German, Scandinavian, South African, Belgian and American magazines. 35 per cent of all sales, unless otherwise arranged.

Popperfoto (Paul Popper, Ltd.), 24 Bride Lane, London, EC4Y 8DR *T.* 01-353 9665-6. Offer and require documentary photos (black and white and colour) from all countries of the world. The existing general collection includes Exclusive News Agency, Odhams Periodicals Photo Library, Conway Picture Library, United Press International (UPI) Library and Planet, with more than 12 million illustrations on file.

Press Association Photos (the news picture service of The Press Association), 85 Fleet Street, London, EC4P 4BE *T.* 01-353 7440.

Radio Times Hulton Picture Library, 35 Marylebone High Street, London, W1M 4AA *T.* 01-580 5577.

Ronan, Ann, Picture Library, 37 Church Lane, Loughton, Essex, IG10 1PD *T.* 01-508 1705. Woodcuts, engravings, photographs of history of science and technology.

Rudeni Photography, 161 Preston New Road, Blackburn, Lancashire, BB2 6BN *T.* Blackburn 59368. Consider exclusive feature series, photographs with copy, or copy which requires illustrating, devoted to women's interests. Outright purchase or on percentage sale basis by arrangement. No "hot" news.

S & G Press Agency, Ltd., 68 Exmouth Market, London, EC1R 4RA *T.* 01-278 1223. Send photographs, but negatives preferred. Press photographs and vast photo library.

Sheridan's Photo Library, Ronald, 6 Kenton Road, Harrow-on-the-Hill, Middlesex, HA1 2BL *T.* 01-422 1214. Specialising in the civilisations of the Middle East, Mediterranean countries and Europe, from ancient times to recent past, their arts, architecture, landscapes, beliefs, peoples past and present. 70,000 pictures currently stocked. Interested in outstanding quality material, fully and accurately documented, particularly from East Europe, Middle East. 50% to photographer.

Showbiz Photo Collection, 12 Waldemar Avenue, Ealing, London, W13 9PY *T.* 01-567 2796. Contains some 30,000 colour transparencies and black and white negatives covering mainly the world of entertainment between 1950 and 1970.

Skye Agencies, Calum Mackenzie Neish, Portnalong, Isle of Skye. *T.* Portnalong (047-872) 272. *Telex:* 75317. News, features and picture agency for the Inner Hebrides and adjacent mainland (Skye and Lochalsh District).

Source Photographic Archives (1974), 5 Henrietta Street, Dublin, 1. *T.* 01-740983. *Director:* Thomas Kennedy. Mostly recent photographs by living photographers on many different subjects. Photographers retain copyright. Monthly photographic exhibitions in our gallery. Agency service provided, Ireland and Britain.

Spectrum Colour Library, 44 Berners Street, London, W1P 3AB *T.* 01-637 2108. Require high quality black and white prints and colour transparencies (35 mm. or larger) for advertising and editorial publication. Now handling the work of **Kevin Court International Library** and **Wildlife Photolibrary.** Need all subjects except topical or "hot" news pictures—list of requirements available on request. *Terms:* 50 per cent to photographer. Also purchase transparencies outright occasionally.

Sporting Pictures (UK) Ltd., 7A Lambs Conduit Passage, Holborn, London, WC1. *T.* 01-405 4500. *Directors:* Frank Baron, Crispin J. Thruston. Specialising in sports, sporting events, sportsmen. Black and white and colour library.

Stiles, Peter, Picture Library, 14 Tregothnan Road, Stockwell, London, SW9 9JX *T.* 01-733 0212. Most subjects covered, but specialises in natural history and horticulture. *Terms:* 50% to photographer.

Stone, Tony, Associates Ltd., 28 Finchley Road, St. John's Wood, London, NW8 6ES *T.* 01-586 3322. Internationally oriented colour transparency library. Subjects required: travel, girls, children, industrial, historic transport, etc. Information leaflet on request. *Terms* 50–50.

Sutcliffe Gallery, 1 Flowergate, Whitby, Yorkshire YO21 3BA *T.* Whitby 2239. Collection of 19th-century photography all by Frank M. Sutcliffe, HON. F.R.P.S. (1853–1941). Especially inshore fishing boats and fishing community, also farming interests. Period covered 1872 to 1910.

Syndication International, Ltd., 40 Northampton Road, London, EC1R 0JU *T.* 01-837 2800.

Theatre Museum, Victoria & Albert Museum, South Kensington, London, SW7 2RL *T.* 01-589 6371, ex. 428. Prints, drawings, playbills, programmes, press cuttings, photographs, theatre documents including the Enthoven Collection, the Guy Little Photographic Collection, the London Archives of the Dance, the Dame Marie Rambert-Ashley Dukes Ballet Collection, the M. W. Stone Toy Theatre Collection, the Gerald Morice Puppetry Collection, the Harry R. Beard Theatre Collection and the collections of the British Theatre Museum Association and the Friends of the Museum of Performing Arts.

Topham, J. P. L./John Topham Ltd. (1928), Edells, Markbeech, Edenbridge, Kent. *T.* Cowden (034-286) 313. Large general picture library, colour and monotone, historical and modern. *Specialities:* World topography and travel, personalities, wild life, agriculture, France, social history. *Represents:* Farmer's Weekly, Geographical Magazine, Bruce Coleman Limited (Monotone Wildlife), C.P.R.E., John Markham collection, Kenneth Scowen monotone collection, Fotogram of Paris, and Phoebus/BPC Picture Library of War, Crime, Occult, English History, Cinema, etc.

Topix, The Picture Service of The Thomson Organization, Ltd., Greater London House, Hampstead Road, London, NW1 7SH *T.* 01-387 2800. Produces topical news and feature pictures covering the British Isles and Europe, and has a Photographic Library of over one million pictures covering news and sporting events, royal activities, people and places over the last seventy years.

Tourist Photo Library, Ltd., 12 Waldemar Avenue, Ealing, London, W13 9PY *T.* 01-579 6449. Colour transparencies (minimum 6 cm. sq.) of tourist attractions and places abroad. Also of domestic pets, fish, insects, and animals in their natural environment. *Terms:* 50 per cent, payable on receipt of our client's cheque. Please write first.

Trans World Press Agency, 44 Seaview Drive, Great Wakering, Southend-on-Sea, Essex. *T.* Southend-on-Sea 219770. Features black and white and colour transparencies. Only outstanding quality required. Yachting, power boats and other sports. World-wide service. *Terms:* 50 per cent.

Transafrica Pix, via Trieste 34, 25100 Brescia, Italy. *T.* 55080–54844. *T.A.* Transafrica-Brescia. Picture library of African subjects. Geography, geology, tribes, arts, folklore, zoology, botany, industry and agriculture of Africa and its islands. Seek skilled contributors from all parts of the world. Act as agents on commission basis.

Travel Trade Photography, Colour Library, 18 Princedale Road, London, W11 4NJ T. 01-727 5471. *Principal:* Teddy Schwarz. Considers colour transparencies ($2\frac{1}{4}$ sq. i.e. 6×6 cm. only) of landscapes, townscapes, ancient monuments and buildings of historical interest in England and foreign countries, peoples and their customs. Terms 50% to the photographer.

United Press International (U.K.) Limited, 8 Bouverie Street, Fleet Street, London, EC4Y 8BB *T.* 01-353 2282. *T.A.* Unipix London. Any pictures suitable for press generally on spot news and features, both black and white and colour. Terms on application.

Universal Pictorial Press & Agency, Ltd. (1929), New Bridge Street House, 30–34 New Bridge Street, London, EC4V 6BN *T.* 01-236 6730 (Library) and 01-236 5840 (News Desk). Suppliers of a daily press and library service of black and white photographs and colour transparencies to the national and provincial press, periodicals and television companies throughout the British Isles and overseas. The library contains over 350,000 black and white photographs and 85,000 colour transparencies of notable Political, Company, Academic, Legal, Diplomatic, Church, Military, Pop, Arts, Entertaining and Sports personalities and well-known views and buildings.

Van Hallan Photo Features, 57 South Street, Isleworth, Middlesex, TW7 7AA *T.* 01-568 0792. Agency issues a regular photographic service of news, society and current events to the world's press, magazines and television organisations. The commercial division specialises in P.R. and industrial photography. Picture reference library section contains over 100,000 negatives of prominent personalities including business, company, diplomatic, political, sporting executives and the aristocracy.

Vickers, John, 27 Shorrolds Road, London, SW6 7TR *T.* 01-385 5774. Archives of British Theatre and portraits of actors, writers and musicians from 1939–1960.

Warner, Simon, 7 Main Street, Stanbury, Keighley, West Yorkshire, BD22 0HA *T.* Haworth (0535) 44644. Expanding collection of own landscape/ countryside pictures in colour transparency and black and white, featuring especially Yorkshire and English nature reserves. Commissions accepted.

Western Americana Picture Library, 86 Park Road, Brentwood, Essex, CM14 4TT *T.* Brentwood (0277) 217643. Prints, engravings, photographs and colour transparencies on all aspects of the American West, cowboys, gunfighters, Indians, including pictures by Frederic Remington and Charles Russell, etc. Interested in buying pictures on American West.

Wildlife Photolibrary now incorporated in **Spectrum Colour Library,** *q.v.*

Woodmansterne Ltd., Holywell Industrial Estate, Watford, WD1 8RD *T.* Watford 28236 and 45788. Picture library of 10,000 subjects, all available as 35 mm. transparencies, many also as $2\frac{1}{4}$ in.$\times3\frac{1}{4}$ in. (sometimes 4 in.$\times$ 5 in.) Ektachromes. Town and countryside in Britain, British cathedrals, churches and abbeys, Europe, the Holy Land, space travel, transport, natural history and historic portraits (incl. 500 from the National Portrait Gallery). No new photographs required.

Woodward, Zenka, Picture Library, 19 Gallows Hill, King's Langley, Hertfordshire, WD4 8PG *T.* King's Langley 63242 (STD 40). International pictorial documentation of the ancient and recent past—engravings, woodcuts, paintings, photographs, etc. Colour and black-and-white. Also comprehensive newspaper cuttings library specialising in music, opera and ballet.

PICTURE RESEARCH

JUDITH BYRNE

Picture research is the term given to the selection and collection of illustrations suitable for reproduction. Publishers either employ a researcher full-time, or submit their requests to freelance researchers, and some commercial picture libraries offer their own research facilities.

A picture researcher is responsible, to a large extent, for the publisher's end product. The publisher's needs may be highly specialised, but there is nearly always a choice of pictures. The researcher makes this initial choice, whether it be between different views of a subject or between pictures of a different quality. For example, when asked for a picture of the Eiffel Tower the researcher would be quite correct in either presenting a worm's eye view, an aerial view, or both. In this case quality would really mean different techniques, i.e., a picture illustrating the architectural structure of the tower or a picture indicating the splendid view it gives of Paris. The only indication an editor may give in his request may be whether he requires a portrait or a landscape shaped picture. The researcher is also responsible for copyright permission, correct acknowledgement and providing the editor with all the information about the photograph as a basis for caption copy. A picture researcher fully employed by a group of publishers, or one publisher, is expected to attend to everything. This includes the payment of all reproduction fees (new editions to be remembered) and the safe return of any material from the printer to the source. If not directly involved in these final stages the freelance researcher can at least check their completion. Costs must be kept down at all times (in the case of a freelance researcher this will ensure that she never lacks work).

Publishers who employ a permanent researcher will always be appreciative of any material which does not have to be returned, being formed into a picture library of their own, or a reference "bank".

Picture research can cover a tremendous variety of topics but there is a fundamental core to the actual research. For me, the process from beginning to end, forms the following pattern.

BOOKING IN OF PROJECTS

Each separate request is booked-in, just as a production department books in a manuscript. The title, author, date of publication, number of copies going into print, the sales market, and the budget allocation for pictures are noted. General information is wanted by anyone who may supply a picture, certain facts may influence their decision. For example, publication date may be far ahead, and the picture wanted elsewhere (you then offer to have a copy made at your expense), or sometimes in the case of a syndication department, or a foreign source, the number of copies going into print affects the permission fee. Remember to set some of your budget aside for extras, which will probably include any photocopying you want done, and print fees. (Some agencies keep their stock in negative form only.)

Colour transparencies are very valuable and require special attention. They are usually signed for and the indemnity for loss or damage varies enormously. It may be £50 or £500 for each transparency. The loan period is usually one month and if a transparency is not returned on the requested date the borrower is asked to pay a holding fee. This fee, for each transparency for every week it is held, varies with each library or agency.

TYPE OF RESEARCH

The line of research depends entirely on the type of picture one is looking for. It is not logical to go to a photograph library dealing in news pictures for an engraving, nor is it ideal to go to the same library for a photograph of a bar of chocolate when you can approach the maker of that particular bar and be given a picture with no reproduction fee. So, content and design dictate the direction of one's research. Many professional authors (scientists, doctors, engineers, architects, etc.) submit illustrations with their manuscripts, or their needs are highly specialised, and the research clear-cut. The author may have an idea of the illustrations he wants, but not every picture asked for will be available, and the researcher involved should have access to the manuscript so that substitutes can be found. *Most important*, at this stage, is the checking of any information necessary to obtain the picture required. "Wants" may be expressed loosely, e.g. "Royalty visiting the Empire and Colonies in 1907." In this case one would need to know which of the royal family was referred to and which country, before approaching a source. It is much more efficient to do the fact finding before contacting any would-be source, as it just slows up the process having your list queried by an agency, or a picture library.

Reference libraries are of great service to a picture researcher for information. When there is no obvious source for a particular picture one can work backwards from printed material. This applies when a "want" is expressed in general terms, e.g. "a twentieth-century woodcut". One can go straight to books on the subject, select a number of artists and examples of their work from which a choice can be made. The source is then traceable from the library book. Useful libraries in London are:

British Museum Reading Room
London Library
United States Reference Library, US Embassy

Victoria and Albert Museum Library
Westminster Central Reference Library

CONTACTING SOURCES

It is a good idea to visit, at some time, picture agencies and libraries with whom you will be constantly dealing. It is necessary to be familiar with their stock, and *their* system. It is particularly helpful if you can single out one member of their staff, and deal with that person whenever possible. Personal relations may be vital when you need a certain picture in a hurry, but cannot leave your office. Many projects can be dealt with, as time goes on and you accumulate more information, over the telephone or by sending out want lists. A want list should be specific to each source, as it is a waste of time and effort to have a number of agencies and libraries duplicating the request. An agency's time is just as valuable as the researcher's, and where a wide choice is involved a visit can eliminate a research fee, but please telephone first. Many agencies operate an appointment system and they do so because they can deal more efficiently with the client's request.

Most important, at this stage, is to see that every picture is clearly marked with the agency's name. It is also a good idea to count the number of pictures, and write the figures down, even if the agency sends its own list. This will eliminate any disagreement about the number of pictures supplied. This is to be followed up by noting down the number of pictures you return (and the date) either as unsuitable for selection, or when a definite choice has been made.

COVER PICTURE AND CAPTIONS COPY

A researcher is not responsible for deciding on cover material but is often asked to provide suitable material for selection by the editor and the art department. If a picture reproduced inside a book is repeated on the cover the researcher may quite reasonably ask for a reduction on the cover-rate remembering that a cover rate is usually double that of an "inside" reproduction fee. At this point you make certain that all pictures have their correct captions, and that all relevant information has been passed on to the Publisher or Editor. It is a good idea to discuss any print fees or reproduction rates at the beginning of the assignment with each individual source. These rates can vary enormously.

LAST STAGES

A researcher employed by a publisher would now write to each source, confirming what pictures were being used. An acknowledgement list to be included in the book would also be prepared at this point.

A freelance researcher should retain a copy of the list of pictures supplied to the publisher. (This list will be of sources, and costings.) Reproduction fees are usually paid on publication day, although it is a good policy to pay freelance photographers on completion of their work. (Their work can be irregular, and this arrangement is advantageous to both.) After publication, the final task is to ensure the safe return of any material from the printer (and this includes the cover picture) back to you. A permanently employed researcher is usually responsible for the safe return of any material back to its source. If a picture is damaged, or lost, you must see that it is paid for. In the case of photographs worked on by the art department you are responsible for paying for a replacement print. A freelance researcher does not usually have these responsibilities.

FURTHER HINTS

Professional picture researchers jot down every useful source, and a card index system is a time-saving one. Useful addresses, ranging from collections and agencies to freelance photographers, and private individuals are filed in categories, e.g. Scientific, Geographical, Political, Transport, etc. Against each source one can note useful details such as: research fee (if required), willingness to send material through the post, how prompt their service is, and if one must make an appointment in advance of a visit. The card index provides quick reference, but a comprehensive file is necessary. This can be made by dividing a looseleaf file into three sections:

In the *first* section file any literature from public collections, museums, government offices, and other official bodies, such as permission conditions, reproduction details, and application forms;

in the *second* section, keep a complete record of the detailed fees of all sources;

the *last* section will be a comprehensive version of your quick-reference card index file, i.e. a complete subject list from each source (where available). It will include any up-to-date information on new subjects they cover. These lengthy subject lists cannot be accommodated on a simple card index.

SOURCES

These are endless and international. The obvious ones being: public collections, publishers, photographers, agencies, and commercial picture libraries. One is guided to these and others through books such as those listed below (and of course the pages immediately preceding this article!) Two of the books listed below are invaluable to all users of photographs and vital to every picture researcher's reference shelf. They are *The Picture Researcher's Handbook* and the *Directory of British Photographic Collections*.

The Picture Researcher's Handbook: An International Guide to Picture Sources —and How To Use Them (Hilary and Mary Evans, Andra Nelke), David & Charles.

THE SOCIETY OF AUTHORS

defends the rights and promotes the interests of *all* authors. If you have written a book, play or script, you would greatly benefit by membership. Why not ask for information?

Please send me a copy of your booklet:

Name ....
Block letters please

Address ....

....

☐ I have had work published in the United Kingdom

☐ I am having work published in the United Kingdom

Signature.. Date................

2

Do not affix Postage Stamps if posted in
Gt. Britain, Channel Islands or N. Ireland

Postage
will be
paid by
Licensee

BUSINESS REPLY CARD
Licence No. SW 893

THE SOCIETY OF AUTHORS

84 DRAYTON GARDENS

LONDON, SW10 9SD

Directory of British Photographic Collections, published by William Heinemann on behalf of The Royal Photographic Society. The Directory, as its title implies (and for the first time), comprehensively lists all the photographic collections in the British Isles. It gives a detailed description of each collection, including subject matter and all other relevant details specific to each collection: location; number of photographs; type and size; owner/custodian; historical data; photographer; further sources of information; accessibility; details of inspection, loan, sale and reproduction.

World of Learning Europa Publications, London (annually). Lists museums, learned societies, universities, galleries, etc.

International Directory of Arts Verlag Muller KG, of Frankfurt. A comprehensive 2-volume directory of museums, galleries, universities, academies, collections, associations, dealers, publishers, collectors, etc., throughout the world. Technical data appears in English, French, German, Italian and Spanish. Presently the two volumes of the 14th edition (79/80) are complete. The set may be ordered from the U.K. representatives, George Prior, Associated Publishers Ltd., 2 Rugby Street, London, WC1N 3QU.

The State Association of the Press Photographic Agencies and Archives in Western Germany. Bundesverband der Pressebild—Agenturen Bilderdierste und Bildarchive e.V. 8000 München 22-Maximilianstr. 17.

Official Museum Director of America and Canada (Latest edition 1970) Ed. U.S. association of museums. Crowell-Collier Education Corporation.

Guide to the Special Collections of Prints and Photographs in the Library of Congress Paul Vanderbilt. Government Printing Office, Washington.

Picture Sources Ed. Celestine Frankenburg. Special Libraries Association, New York (latest edition 1964). Should be available for consultation at most major libraries.

The Libraries, Museums and Art Galleries Year Book (new edition every three years). James Clarke, Cambridge, England.

Picture Source Book for Social History Allen & Unwin, London 1961. A 6-volume work with a wealth of pictures, indicating their sources.

Sources of Illustration 1500–1900 Adams & Dart, London 1971.

EXHIBITIONS

These are now becoming an excellent opportunity of seeing a wide variety of photography, both foreign and British, and include the work of many young photographers. Exhibitions are held in a number of places and, more and more, the daily newspapers are drawing attention to them, as well as reviewing the exhibitions. The weekly *British Journal of Photography* also lists current exhibitions. The Photographer's Gallery, besides giving us an opportunity to see some marvellous photography, has a very good bookstand where one may look at (and buy!) books on early and contemporary photography. There is also a study centre. A number of exhibitions of photography are sponsored by the Arts Council of Great Britain. Both the Photographer's Gallery and the Arts Council have advance mailing lists, and some specialist galleries in London are listed below.

Half Moon Gallery, 27 Alie Street, London, E1.
Kodak Photographic Gallery, The, 246 High Holborn, London, WC1.
Photographer's Gallery, 8 Great Newport Street, London, WC2.
Serpentine Gallery, Kensington Gardens, London, W2.
Victoria and Albert Museum, South Kensington, London, SW7.
Whitechapel Art Gallery, High Street, London, E1.

The galleries listed below are located outside London and exclusively show photography, both Victorian and Contemporary. The Gallery of Photography in Southampton, is particularly good about forwarding details of their exhibitions and lectures. It is always a good idea to be on as many mailing lists as possible.

Gallery of Photography, The University, Southampton.
Sutcliffe Gallery, 1 Flowergate, Whitby.
Impressions Gallery of Photography, 39A Shambles Market Place, York.

PICTURE RESEARCH COURSE

The Publishers Association do run a Picture Research Course, but like all their courses, it is open only to publishing employees from firms who are members of the P.A. The objectivity of the course is to give a professional approach to the search for and use of suitable sources; to make picture researchers aware of all the implications of their task: suitability for reproduction, legal and financial aspects, plus efficient administration.

Details of the course, with the outline of the programme may be obtained from Mary Perry, *Training and Development Officer*, Publishers Association, 19 Bedford Square, London, WC1 3HJ.

A central organisation of picture researchers has now been formed called S.P.R.Ed. (Society of Picture Researchers and Editors) and it has compiled a questionnaire to find out the needs of researchers. Those interested, or who would like a copy of the questionnaire, should write to the Society, c/o National Westminster Bank Ltd., 110 Wardour Street, London, W1V 3LD. Please enclose a S.A.E. Notices of meetings appear on the noticeboard of the Photographers' Gallery.

MUSIC PUBLISHERS

UNITED KINGDOM MUSIC PUBLISHERS

Note.—Copyright in musical compositions comprises (*a*) the right of publication in print and sale of printed copies; (*b*) the right of public performance, and (*c*) the right to use the work for the purpose of making gramophone records, sound films or other similar contrivances. The musical composer should bear that in mind when entering into an agreement for the publication of his work.

Mr. Rutland Boughton's warning to amateurs given many years ago, still stands. He said that amateurs, "like the more hardened professional composers, find pleasure in seeing their musical thoughts in print. Because of that human weakness they become the prey of tenth-rate publishers, who offer to issue their music for them (however poor and ineffective it may be) *if they will pay for the privilege. If a piece of music is worth publishing a publisher will be willing to pay for it in cash or royalty.*" Music publishers requiring work for issue on cash or royalty terms no more advertise in the public press for music and lyrics than a first-class publisher of books advertises for MSS. on that basis.

The Publishers in the following list are all members of the Performing Right Society except those marked †. The list does not include all publisher-members of the Performing Right Society.

Lyrics without a musical setting are not accepted unless stated by individual firms

Arcadia Music Publishing Co., Ltd., P.O. Box 1, Rickmansworth, Herts, WD3 3AZ *T.* 01-584 6671. Light orchestral.

Ashdown (Edwin), Ltd. (1860), 275–281 Cricklewood Broadway, London, NW2 6QR *T.* 01-450 5237. Educational, ballads, instrumental, pianoforte, organ, choral.

Background Music Publishers, Ltd. (1964), 10–16 Rathbone Street, London, W1P 2BJ *T.* 01-580 2827. *Cables:* Operetta, London, W1. *Directors:* R. M. Toeman, S. Buchman.

Banks Music Publications (Ramsay Silver), 139 Holgate Road, York, YO2 4DF *T.* 0904 21818. Publishers of choral and instrumental music.

Bayley & Ferguson, Ltd. (1884) 65 Berkeley Street, Glasgow, G3. *T.* 041-221 7240. Accept for publication music, anthems, part-songs, etc.

Belwin-Mills Music Ltd., 250 Purley Way, Croydon, CR9 4QD *T.* 01-681 0855. Orchestral, instrumental, choral and vocal works by classical and contemporary composers, educational music, light orchestral music, music for military and brass bands and popular music.

Benson Ltd., Fred (1954), 10–16 Rathbone Street, London, W1P 2BJ *T.* 01-580 2827. *Cables:* Operetta, London, W1. *Directors:* S. Buchman, R. M. Toeman.

Black (A & C) (Publishers) Ltd. (1978), 35 Bedford Row, London, WC1R 4JH *T.* 01-242 0946. *T.A.* Biblos, London, WC1. *Telex:* 21792, ref. 2564. Song books for children.

Boosey & Hawkes Music Publishers, Ltd., 295 Regent Street, London, W1R 8JH *T.* 01-580 2060. General and educational.

Bosworth & Co., Ltd. (1889), 14–18 Heddon Street, London, W1R 8DP *T.* 01-734 4961, 0475. Orchestral, church, educational, piano, violin and partsongs.

Bourne Music Ltd., 34–36 Maddox Street, London, W1R 9PD *T.* 01-493 6412, 6583. Popular and educational music.

Breitkopf & Härtel (London), Ltd., 8 Horse and Dolphin Yard, London, W1V 7LG *T.* 01-437 3342. Agents for Fenette Music London, Fentone Music London. Breitkopf & Härtel, Friedrich Hofmeister, Deutscher Verlag für Musik, Pro Musica Verlag, Edition Tonos, all of Germany. Alexander Broude Inc., Columbia Music Co., Washington, D.C., Musica Sacra et Profana, Continuo Music Press, Tetra Music Corporation, all of USA. Edizioni Bèrben, Ancona, Italy.

Campbell, Connelly & Co., Ltd. 10 Denmark Street, London, WC2H 8LU *T.* 01-836 1653. General and popular.

Chappell & Co., Ltd., 50 New Bond Street, London, W1A 2BR *T.* 01-629 7600. New York, Toronto, Sydney, Wellington (N.Z.), Paris, Hamburg, Brussels, Milan, Zurich, Stockholm, Madrid, Bussum, Johannesburg. Classical, standard and popular music.

Chester (J. & W.)/Edition Wilhelm Hansen London Ltd. (1860), Eagle Court, London, EC1M 5QD *T.* 01-253 6947–8. *T.A.* Guarnerius, London, EC1. Concert and educational works.

Cramer (J.B.) & Co., Ltd. (1824), 99 St. Martin's Lane, London, WC2N 4AZ *T.* 01-240 1612. General and educational.

Curwen (J.) & Sons, Ltd., 140 Strand, London, WC2R 1HG *T.* 01-836 4011. Music for schools. Educational music. English songs, choral, instrumental and orchestral.

Dash Music Co., Ltd., 10 Denmark Street, London, WC2H 8LU *T.* 01-836 1653. Popular music.

De Wolfe, Ltd., 80–88 Wardour Street, London, W1V 3LF *T.* 01-437 4933–4. Symphonic recorded orchestral (English and foreign). Comprehensive library of recorded music on disc and tape. Original film scores. Recording studio.

Dix, Ltd. (1922), 138–140 Charing Cross Road, London, WC2H 0LD *T.* 01-836 6699. Principally light music.

EMI Music Publishing Ltd., 138–140 Charing Cross Road, London, WC2H 0LD *T.* 01-836 6699. *Telex:* 269189. *T.A.* and *Cables:* Emimus London WC2. Incorporating KPM Music Ltd. (background library), Feldman & Co. Ltd., Robbins Music Corp. Ltd., Peter Maurice Music Co. Ltd., KPM Music Group, Francis, Day & Hunter Ltd., Screen Gems-EMI Music Ltd.

Faber Music, Ltd. (1966), 3 Queen Square, London, WC1N 3AU (Subsidiary of **Faber & Faber, Ltd.** (1929). *T.* 01-278 6881. *T.A.* Fabbaf, London, WC1. A general list of the highest quality, comprising both old and new music.

Fairfield Music Co., Ltd., Borough Green, Sevenoaks, Kent. *T.* Borough Green (0732) 883261. London Showroom: 38A Beak Street, London, W1. *T.* 01-734 8080. Contemporary orchestral, instrumental, chamber and film music.

Feldman (B.) & Co., Ltd., 138–140 Charing Cross Road, London, WC2H 0LD *T.* 01-836 6699. *T.A.* and *Cables:* Humfriv, London, WC2. Popular and semi-classical.

Forsyth Bros., Ltd. (1873), 126 Deansgate, Manchester, M3 2GR *T.* 061-834 3281. Educational piano and instrumental music. Modern teaching material.

Francis, Day & Hunter, Ltd., (1877), 138–140 Charing Cross Road, London, WC2H 0LD *T.* 01-836 6699. Publishers of popular songs, semi-classical works, tutors, orchestral compositions, music plays and standards.

Freeman, H. & Co., 138–140 Charing Cross Road, London, WC2H 0LD *T.* 01-836 6699. Educational piano music.

Galliard Limited imprint of **Stainer & Bell Ltd.,** *q.v.*

Glocken Verlag, Ltd. (1946), 10–16 Rathbone Street, London, W1P 2BJ *T.* 01-580 2827. *Cables:* Operetta, London, W1. *Directors:* Otto Blau, Francis P. Lehár, R. M. Toeman, S. Buchman (Alt.). Musical works by Franz Lehár.

Gwynn (The) Publishing Co. (1937), Llangollen, North Wales, LL20 8SN *T.* 0978-860209. Publishers of Welsh Educational and International Choral Music. Official music publishers to The Welsh Folk Song Society, The Welsh Folk Dance Society, the Court of the Welsh National Eisteddfod and the Council of the Llangollen International Musical Eisteddfod.

†**Harris, The (Frederick) Music Co., Ltd.** Sole Agents: Alfred Lengnick & Co., Ltd., Purley Oaks Studios, 421A Brighton Road, South Croydon, CR2 6YR *T.* 01-660 7646; and at Oakville, Ontario. Speciality, artistic songs, piano and educational music.

Hughes & Son, Publishers, Ltd. (1820), 4–5 Thomas Row, Swansea SA1 1NJ *T.* 0792-52168. Welsh music, educational publications.

Inter-Art Music Publishers (1933), 10–16 Rathbone Street, London, W1P 2BJ *T.* 01-580 2827. *Cables:* Operetta, London, W1. *Directors:* R. M. Toeman, S. Buchman.

Kalmus, Alfred, A., Ltd., 2–3 Fareham Street, Dean Street, London, W1V 4DU *T.* 01-437 5203–4–5. *Trade:* 38 Eldon Way, Paddock Wood, Tonbridge, Kent, TN12 6BE *T.* 089-283 3422. Sole representatives of Universal Edition A. G., Vienna, Universal Edition (London) Ltd, Universal Edition, A. G. Zurich, Universal Edition S.P.A., Milan, Palestrina Complete Edition, Theodore Presser Co., U.S.A., Lea Pocket Scores, U.S.A., Doblinger Edition, Vienna, Hargail Music Inc., U.S.A., International Music Co., U.S.A., Polish Editions, Cracow (complete Chopin-Paderewski), Supraphon, Prague, Harmonia Uitgrave, Hilversum, Artia, Prague, Boelke-Bomart, Inc., U.S.A. Serious music of all types.

Keith Prowse Music Publishing Co., Ltd., 138–140 Charing Cross Road, London, WC2H 0LD *T.* 01-836 6699. Music by various authors and composers.

Leeds Music, Ltd., 138 Piccadilly, London, W1V 9FH *T.* 01-629 7211.

Lengnick (Alfred) & Co., Ltd. (1892), Purley Oaks Studios, 421A Brighton Road, South Croydon, CR2 6YR *T*. 01-660 7646. Music publishers and importers. Publishers of Brahms' and Dvorak's works. Specialise in educational music, leading publishers of English contemporary music. Always ready to consider MSS. of any type. Agents for CeBeDeM (Brussels); Donemus (Amsterdam), Fredk Harris (Ontario) and Iceland Music Information Centre (Iceland).

Leonard, Gould & Bolttler, 99 St. Martin's Lane, London, WC2N 4AZ *T*. 01-240 1612. General and educational.

Maurice (Peter) Music Co., Ltd., The, 138–140 Charing Cross Road, London, WC2H 0LD *T*. 01-836 6699. Popular music.

Novello & Co., Ltd. (1811), Borough Green, Sevenoaks, Kent. *T*. Borough Green (0732) 883261. London Showroom: 38A Beak Street, London, W1. *T*. 01-734 8080. Classical and modern orchestral, instrumental, vocal and choral music, church music, school and educational music, books and primers.

Novello Hire Library, incorporating **Goodwin & Tabb,** Borough Green, Sevenoaks, Kent. *T*. Borough Green (0732) 883261. Vocal, choral and orchestral hire libraries.

Octava Music Co., Ltd. (1938), 10–16 Rathbone Street, London, W1P 2BJ *T*. 01-580 2827. *Cables:* Operetta, London, W1.

Oxford University Press (Oxford University Press established 1478. Music Dept. constituted 1923). Music Department, 44 Conduit Street, London, W1R 0DE *T*. 01-734 5364–6. Orchestral, instrumental, operatic, choral, vocal works, church and organ music by early and modern composers, educational music, courses, and books on music.

Paterson's Publications, Ltd., 38 Wigmore Street, London, W1H 0EX *T*. 01-935 3551. Pianoforte, vocal, choral, orchestral, instrumental, educational and bagpipe music.

Peters Edition, Ltd. (1938), 10–12 Baches Street, London, N1 6DN *T*. 01-253 1638–9. *T.A.* Musipeters, London. Peters Edition, Hinrichsen Edition, Collection Litolff. Classical and modern (piano, organ, other instrumental, vocal, choir and brass band) music. British representatives of American, Dutch, German and Italian music publishers.

Polyphone Music Co., Ltd., The, P.O. Box 1, Rickmansworth, Herts, WD3 3AZ *T*. 01-584 6671. Light orchestral.

Programme Music, Ltd. (1961), 10–16 Rathbone Street, London, W1P 2BJ *T*. 01-580 2827. *Cables:* Operetta, London, W1. *Directors:* R. M. Toeman, S. Buchman.

Reynolds Music, 138–140 Charing Cross Road, London, WC2H 0LD *T*. 01-836 6699. Songs, musical material and sketches for TV and Stage.

Ricordi (G.) & Co. (London), Ltd. (1808), The Bury, Church Street, Chesham, Bucks, HP5 1JG *T*. Chesham 3311 and 4427. *T.A.* Ricordi, Chesham. Publishers of Italian opera, music for piano, classical and contemporary, operatic arias, songs, choral large scale works and part songs for all voices, orchestral works, classical and contemporary, instrumental, string, woodwind, brass tutors, exercises, etc., guitar music of all types.

Roberton Publications, The Windmill, Wendover, Aylesbury, Bucks, HP22 6JJ *T.* Wendover (0296) 623107. *Partners:* Kenneth Roberton, Margaret Roberton. Choral and educational; also piano and chamber music. Represnt Lawson-Gould Music Publishers Inc., New York; Leslie Music Supply, Oakville, Ontario; Paul Price Publications, New Jersey; Waterloo Music, Waterloo, Ontario.

Saville (J.) & Co., Ltd., Audley House, 9 North Audley Street, London, W1Y 2EU *T.* 01-629 6506. School music.

Schirmer, G., Ltd. (1972), 140 Strand, London, WC2R 1HG *T.* 01-836 4011. Classical, piano and instrumental, choral, contemporary.

Schott & Co., Ltd. (1839), 48 Great Marlborough Street, London, W1V 2BN *T.* 01-437 1246. Music of a serious and educational nature is considered including music for recorders, guitar and orchestra.

Smith, R. & Co., Ltd. (1857), P.O. Box 210, Watford, Herts. *Delivery:* Unit 6, Paramount Industrial Estate, Sandown Road, Watford, Herts. *T.* 34146.

Sphemusations, Gramercy House, 12 Northfield Road, Onehouse, Stowmarket, Suffolk. *T.* Stowmarket 3388. Serious music, brass band, choral, instrumental and educational. Records of modern works. Tapes.

Stainer & Bell, Ltd., 82 High Road, East Finchley, London, N2 9PW *T.* 01-444 9135. Book and music publishers including the imprints of **Augener, Belton Books, Galliard, Stainer & Bell, A. Weekes, Joseph Williams.**

Swan & Co. (Music Publishers), Ltd., P.O. Box 1, Rickmansworth, Herts, WD3 3AZ *T.* 01-584 6671. Light orchestral.

Sylvester Music Co., Ltd., 80–82 Wardour Street, London, W1V 3LF *T.* 01-437 4933–4. Popular and orchestral music. Comprehensive library of recorder music on disc and tape. Specially composed scores. Transfers to tape and film.

Thames Publishing (1970), 14 Barlby Road, London, W10 6AR *T.* 01-969 3579. Serious music of all types, particularly vocal, choral and instrumental. Manuscripts welcome *but should always be preceded by a letter.*

United Music Publishers, Ltd. (1932), 1 Montague Street, Russell Square, London, WC1B 5BS *T.* 01-636 5171–2. *Managing Director:* Peter Dodd. Agents for the principal French music publishing houses and specalise in the sale of French, Spanish and other foreign music. Also contemporary English works.

Universal Edition (London), Ltd., 2–3 Fareham Street, Dean Street, London, W1V 4DU *T.* 01-437 5203–4–5. Serious music of all types.

Warren & Phillips, Ltd. (1906), 126 Deansgate, Manchester, M3 2GR *T.* 061-834 3281. Educational piano and instrumental music. Modern teaching material.

Weinberger (Josef), Ltd. (1885), 10–16 Rathbone Street, London, W1P 2BJ *T.* 01-580 2827 (4 lines). *Cables:* Operetta, London, W1. *Directors:* S. Buchman, R. M. Toeman. *Executive Directors:* S. Lengauer, M. Muller. Theatrical and music publishers.

Workers' Music Association (1936), 236 Westbourne Park Road, London, W11 1EL *T.* 01-727 7005. General music organization with emphasis on the social aspects of music. Publications, music courses.

OVERSEAS MUSIC PUBLISHERS

NEW ZEALAND

Price Milburn Music Ltd., P.O. Box 995, Wellington, *T.* 721542. *Directors:* Peter Zwartz, Roderick Biss. Music and books by New Zealand composers, and music and books about music for use in schools. Distributors of records, cassettes, music and books about music from overseas publishers.

UNITED STATES

American Academy of Music, 16 West 61st Street, New York, N.Y., 10023. *T.* 212-245-1100.

Ankerford Music Corporation, 16 West 61st Street, New York, N.Y., 10023.

Associated Music Publishers, Inc., 866 Third Avenue, New York, N.Y., 10022. *T.* (212) 935-5100.

Belwin-Mills Publishing Corporation, 16 West 61st Street, New York, N.Y., 10023. *T.* 212-245-1100.

Boosey & Hawkes, Inc., 30 West 57th Street, New York, N.Y., 10019. *T.* (212) 757-3332. Symphonic, opera, ballet, concert, and educational music.

Bourne Co., 1212 Avenue of the Americas, New York, N.Y., 10036. *T.* 575-1800. Publishers of popular, standard, educational, production, and photo-play music.

Chappell Music Company, 810 Seventh Avenue, New York, N.Y., 10019. *T.* 212-399-7100.

Church (John) Company, c/o Theodore Presser Co., Bryn Mawr, Pennsylvania, 19010. *T.* 215-525-3636. Established 1854. Considers suitable MSS. from composers. Does not use or buy songs or lyrics unless with a musical setting. Publication at the firm's expense only.

Ditson (Oliver) Company, c/o Theodore Presser Co., Byrn Mawr, Pennsylvania, 19010. *T.* 215-525-3636. Established 1835. Considers suitable MSS. from composers. Does not use or buy songs or lyrics unless with a musical setting. Publication at the firm's expense only.

Elkan-Vogel, Inc., c/o Theodore Presser Co., Bryn Mawr, Pennsylvania, 19010. *T.* 215-525-3636. Considers suitable MSS. from composers. Does not use or buy songs or lyrics unless with a musical setting. Publication at the firm's expense only.

Gray Publications, H. W., division of **Belwin-Mills Publishing Corp.,** Melville, N.Y., 11746. *T.* 516-293-3400. Choral music of all types and arrangements. Organ music, sacred songs.

Heritage Music Press, The, 501 East Third Street, Dayton, Ohio, 45401. *T.* 513-228-6118. Division of **Lorenz Industries,** *q.v.*

Hinrichsen Edition, C. F. Peters Corporation, 373 Park Avenue South, New York, N.Y., 10016. *T.* 212-686-4147. Classical and contemporary music.

Lorenz Industries, 501 East Third Street, Dayton, Ohio, 45401. *T.* 513-228-6118. Considers for purchase anthems and church organ voluntaries.

Marks (Edward B.), Music Corporation (1894), 1790 Broadway, New York City, N.Y., 10019. Accepts only musical material from professional writers of reputation on a royalty basis. Publishes every type of music; classic, standard, popular, orchestral, educational, secular, sacred, bank, organ, piano, etc. Distributors of many foreign publications.

Mercury Music Corporation, c/o Theodore Presser Co., Bryn Mawr, Pennsylvania, 19010. *T.* 215-525-3636. Considers suitable MSS from composers. Does not use or buy songs or lyrics unless with a musical setting. Publication at the firm's expense only.

Merion Music Company, c/o Theodore Presser Co., Bryn Mawr, Pennsylvania, 19010. *T.* 215-525-3636. Established 1953. Considers suitable MSS. from composers. Does not use or buy songs or lyrics unless with a musical setting. Publication at the firm's expense only.

Mills Music Inc., 16 West 61st Street, New York, N.Y., 10023. *T.* 212-245-1100.

Peters, C.F., Corporation, 373 Park Avenue South, New York, N.Y., 10016. *T.* 212-686-4147. (Peters Edition, Hinrichsen Edition, Eulenberg Pocket Scores and other European music publications, in U.S.A.)

Presser (Theodore) Co., Bryn Mawr, Pennsylvania, 19010. *T.* 215-525-3636. Established 1883. Considers suitable MSS. from composers. Does not use or buy songs or lyrics unless with a musical setting. Publication at the firm's expense only.

Sacred Music Press, The, 501 East Third Street, Dayton, Ohio, 45401. *T.* 513-228-6118. *Editor:* Dale Wood. Division of **Lorenz Industries,** *q.v.*

Schirmer, G., Inc., 866 Third Avenue, New York, N.Y., 10022 *T.* (212) 935-5100.

Summy-Birchard Company, 1834 Ridge Ave., Evanston, Illinois, 60204. *T.* 312 869-4700. *President:* David K. Sengstack. Publishers of music textbooks and educational music in the fields of piano, choral, instrumental.

Warner Bros. Music, 9200 Sunset Boulevard, Los Angeles, California, 90069. *T.* 213-273-3323. *Cables:* Wang, Los Angeles. Includes, among others, the following companies: WB Music Corp., Warner-Tamerlane Publishing Corp., Harms Inc., M. Witmark, Remick, Advanced, New World Music Corp., Pepamar Music Corp., Schubert Music Publishing Corp., Weill-Brecht-Harms Company Inc., Viva Music Inc., Zapata Music Inc., Curtom Publishing Co. Inc., Rodart Music Corp., Jalynne Corp.

MECHANICAL-COPYRIGHT PROTECTION SOCIETY LTD.

The Society was formed in 1910 by a group of music publishers in anticipation of the introduction of new legislation which for the first time would provide for the protection of copyright material by mechanical reproduction.

This became effective on the introduction of the Copyright Act 1911 when only the music box, piano roll, cylinder and disc recordings were known.

Since those days the Society has grown with the technical advances into sound film, radio and television recordings, magnetic tape, videocassettes, and now grants licences in all matters affecting recording rights, both in the U.K. and throughout the world by virtue of its affiliation with other similar organisations and agencies.

Membership of the Society is open to all music copyright owners, composers, lyric writers and publishers. There is no entrance fee or subscription.

Enquiries for membership should be addressed to the Membership Department, Elgar House, 380 Streatham High Road, London, SW16 6HR. *T.* 01-769 3181.

THE PERFORMING RIGHT SOCIETY, LTD.

The Performing Right Society is an Association of Composers, Authors and Publishers of copyright musical works, established to collect royalties for the public performance and broadcasting of such works and their use by diffusion services; also to restrain unauthorised use thereof.

Licences are granted which convey the necessary permission for the public performance of any of the works of its members and those of the affiliated national societies of more than 30 other countries. The combined membership thus represented by the Society is about 300,000. Over 100,000 premises where music is publicly performed are covered by the Society's licence in the British Isles alone.

The Society's operations do not extend to the performance of plays, sketches or other works of a non-musical character as such—as distinct from any music used in their production—nor to operas, musical plays or other dramatico-musical works when performed on the stage.

The constitution of the Society is that of a Company limited by guarantee having no share capital. The General Council consists of twelve composers and authors and twelve music publishers elected by the members from among their own number. The Society is not a profit-making organisation, the whole of the royalties it collects being distributed amongst its members and the affiliated societies after deduction of administration expenses and contributions to the P.R.S. Members' Fund, established for the benefit of necessitous members and their dependants.

There are two distributions of general performing fees each year, and two distributions of broadcasting fees. The Annual General Meeting is usually held in June.

Applicants for membership are not required to pay an entrance fee, nor is any membership subscription or agency commission payable. All composers of musical works and authors of lyrics or poems which have been set to music, are eligible for membership.

Authors and composers desiring further information should communicate with the Registrar at the Society's offices, 29–33 Berners Street, London, W1P 4AA *T.* 01-580 5544. *T.A.* Perforight, London, W.1.

LITERARY PRIZES AND AWARDS

IN the past year many special awards and prizes have been offered for novels, short stories and works of non-fiction. Details of these awards, as they are offered, will be found in such journals as *The Author*. The number of permanent literary prizes in Great Britain is small compared with America, where there are scores of literary awards.

The Alexander Prize

Candidates for the Alexander Prize may choose their own subject for an Essay, but they must submit their choice for approval to the Literary Director, Royal Historical Society, University College London, Gower Street, London, WC1E 6BT. *T*. 01-387 7532.

The Hans Christian Andersen Medals

The Hans Christian Andersen Medals are awarded every two years to an author and an illustrator who by the outstanding value of their work are judged to have made a lasting contribution to literature for children and young people. The awards are administered by the International Board on Books for Young People. (British Section, c/o Jenifer Marshall, The National Book League, 7 Albemarle Street, London, W1X 4BB *T*. 01-493 9001.)

Arts Council of Great Britain

Grants to Writers

On the recommendation of independent sponsors (publishers, literary editors, etc.) grants may be awarded by the Arts Council to writers who are British subjects or non-British writers resident in Great Britain on a permanent basis; who have normally had at least one volume published or have had a body of work published in literary magazines; and who are currently engaged in writing. The main purpose of such grants is to enable writers to buy time to complete the projects on which they are engaged. Applications are considered on their individual merit, but as a guide it should be borne in mind that the concern of these grants is with literature as an art, and not with the entire range of subjects dealt with in printed books. The scope of these grants is therefore usually confined to works of fiction, poetry, criticism and biography. Intending sponsors should write to the Literature Director, Arts Council of Great Britain, 105 Piccadilly, London, W1V 0AU, for a sponsorship form which, when completed, should be returned to the Literature Director with two copies of a published work (where available).

Grants to Translators

Arts Council grants are available, on publishers' recommendations, for the translation into English of approved works of foreign fiction, biography and autobiography, travel, poetry, or other kinds of creative writing, which have been proposed for publication. Publishers should write to the Literature Director for an application form, on which they are asked to give details of the translators and of their contractual relationship with them.

Guarantees to Publishers

Guarantees against loss are available to publishers for the production of approved works of fiction, poetry, biography and autobiography, children's literature and other kinds of creative writing (including translations) which have been proposed for publication or for reprinting. These guarantees are intended to meet special expenses incurred in the preparation or publication of such works, or to enable the publisher to reduce the retail price of the book below the figure at which it would otherwise have to be set. Application forms are available from the Literature Department and, when completed, should be returned with a copy of the typescript.

The Author's Awards for Mass Market Writing (administered by the Periodical Distributors of Canada)

The annual awards, of which there are eight, totalled $3,300 in 1978. They were founded in 1977 and are open to Canadian citizens or landed immigrants whose works have been published in mass market paperback books or mass market magazines (except weekend newspaper supplements and free distribution publications) and cover fiction, non-fiction, and cover design paperback books, public affairs, humour, personality feature and cover design magazines. Judging is done by an independent panel of judges who have demonstrated their qualifications within the particular areas of literary endeavour. The awards are administered by Periodical Distributors of Canada, Box 61, Suite 3106, Toronto-Dominion Centre, Toronto, Ontario, M5K 1G5.

Authors' Club First Novel Award

The award was instituted in 1954 and is made to the author of the most promising first novel published in the United Kingdom during each year. The award takes the form of a silver mounted and inscribed quill and is presented to the winner at a dinner held in the Club. Entries for the award are accepted from publishers (up to a maximum of three titles from each publisher), and must be full length novels—short stories are not eligible—written and published in the United Kingdom during the year.

The Alice Hunt Bartlett Prize

The Poetry Society announces that this prize of not less than £200 is awarded annually to the author of a volume of poetry comprising not less than 20 poems or 400 lines published in English and presented in duplicate to the Society's library in the year of publication. The closing date for 1979 is 31st December. In judging the entries the adjudicators give special consideration to newly emerging poets so far as merit warrants. In the event of the poems translated into English the prize is divided equally between the author and the translator. This is the most important award made for poetry during the year.

The David Berry Prize

Candidates for the David Berry Prize of £100 may select any subject dealing with Scottish History within the reigns of James I to James VI inclusive, provided such subject has been previously submitted to and approved by the Council of the Royal Historical Society, University College London, Gower Street, London, WC1E 6BT T. 01-387 7532.

The James Tait Black Memorial Prize

The James Tait Black Memorial Prizes, founded in memory of a partner in the publishing house of A. and C. Black Ltd., were instituted in 1918. Two prizes, of £500 each, are awarded annually: one for the best biography or work of that nature, the other for the best novel, published during the calendar year. The prize winners are announced as soon as possible, normally in February. The adjudicator is the Regius Professor of Rhetoric and English Literature in the University of Edinburgh.

Publishers are invited to submit a copy of any novel or biography that in their judgement may merit consideration for the award. Copies should be sent to the Department of English Literature, David Hume Tower, George Square, Edinburgh, EH8 9JX, marked "James Tait Black Prize". They should be submitted as early as possible, with a note of the exact date of publication. Co-operation on this point is essential to the work of the adjudicators. Books considered will not be limited to those of which copies are submitted; but accessibility is now a vital factor, so that submission must, up to a point, improve the chance of success.

By the terms of the bequest, and by tradition, eligible novels and biographies are those written in English, originating with a British publisher, and first published in Britain in the year of the award; but technical publication elsewhere, simultaneously or even a little earlier, does not disqualify. Both prizes may go to the same author; but neither to the same author a second time. The 1977 award winners were George Painter for his biography *Chateaubriand*, Vol. 1, and John Le Carré for his novel *The Honourable Schoolboy*.

The Booker Prize

This annual prize for fiction of £10,000 is sponsored by Booker McConnell Ltd. and administered by the National Book League. The prize is awarded to the best novel in the opinion of the judges, published each year. The Prize is open to novels written in English by citizens of the British Commonwealth, Eire, Pakistan and South Africa and published for the first time in the U.K. by a British publisher. Entries are to be submitted only by U.K. publishers who may each submit not more than four novels with scheduled publication dates between 1st January and 22nd November, but the judges may also ask for other eligible novels to be submitted to them. Entry forms and further information are available from Miss M. Googan, National Book League, 7 Albemarle Street, London, W1X 4BB *T.* 01-493 9001.

The British Academy Research Awards

These are made annually in support of advanced academic research in any branch of the humanities to scholars normally resident in the U.K. who may apply on their own behalf or on behalf of some British body. The main headings under which an application would be eligible are: (*a*) Travel and maintenance expenses in connection with an approved programme of research; (*b*) Fieldwork; (*c*) Provision of mechanical or photographic aids for research; (*d*) Costs of preparation of research for publication; (*e*) In special cases, aid to the publication of research. Successful applicants are normally expected to publish the results within two years. Further details and application forms from The British Academy, Burlington House, Piccadilly, London, W1V 0NS.

The Jock Campbell–New Statesman Award

This £1,000 award is given every three years to a writer born in Africa or the Caribbean for a book of literary merit, published in English. The panel of three or four judges includes the Literary Editor of the New Statesman. Details from The New Statesman, 10 Great Turnstile, London, WC1V 7HJ.

Canadian Authors Association Awards

The awards consist of a silver medal and $1000 and apply in (i) Prose fiction, (ii) Prose non-fiction, (iii) Poetry, (iv) Drama (for any medium). These annual awards are to honour writing that achieves literary excellence without sacrificing popular appeal and are given to works by Canadian authors. Further details from the Canadian Authors Association, 22 Yorkville Avenue, Toronto, Ontario, M4W 1L4.

The Children's Book Circle Eleanor Farjeon Award

In 1965 the Children's Book Circle instituted an award to be given annually for distinguished services to children's books and to be known as the Children's Book Circle Eleanor Farjeon Award in memory of the much-loved children's writer. The award carries with it a prize of £75 and may be given to a librarian, teacher, author, artist, publisher, reviewer, television producer or any other person working with, or for children through books.

Children's Book of the Year Awards

The Children's Book Council of Australia makes annual awards in three sections. (1) Book of the Year (for literary merit and quality of production also considered); (2) Picture Book of the Year (for younger children); (3) Best Illustrated Book of the Year. Prize money available in the three sections is: (1) $2500 (of which at least $1500 goes to the winner who also receives a medal); (2) No monetary prize but a medal is awarded; (3) $2500 (from the Visual Arts Board). Candidates must be Australian citizens or resident in Australia for five of the last ten years. Details from L. Rees, 50 Booroondara Street, Reid, ACT 2601; M. Sourry, Library Services, 35 Mitchell Street, North Sydney, NSW 2060.

Cholmondeley Awards

In 1965, the Marchioness of Cholmondeley established these non-competitive awards, for which submissions are not required, for the benefit and encouragement of poets of any age, sex or nationality. In 1978 awards totalling £2,000 went to Christopher Hope, Leslie Norris, Peter Reading, D. M. Thomas, R. S. Thomas. The Scheme is administered by the Society of Authors.

Collins Biennial Religious Book Award

This £1000 prize was founded in 1969 to commemorate the 150th Anniversary of the founding of Wm. Collins Sons & Co. Ltd. It is given biennially to a living citizen of the United Kingdom, the Commonwealth, the Republic of Ireland, and South Africa for a book which in the judges' opinion has made the most distinguished contribution to the relevance of Christianity in the modern world on one of the following subjects: Science, Ethics, Sociology, Philosophy, Psychology and other religions. The last award was made to Professor Charles Moule for *The Origin of Christology* (Cambridge University Press). Details from Wm. Collins Sons & Co. Ltd., 14 St. James's Place, London, SW1A 1PS.

Commonwealth Poetry Prize

An annual poetry prize of £250, sponsored by the Commonwealth Institute and the National Book League is awarded for a first book of poetry in English published during the previous twelve months by authors from Commonwealth countries other than Britain. Further details are available from the Librarian, Commonwealth Institute, Kensington High Street, London, W8 6NQ *T.* 01-602 3252.

The Duff Cooper Memorial Prize

Friends and admirers of Duff Cooper, first Viscount Norwich (1890–1954), contributed a sum of money which has been invested in a Trust Fund. The interest is devoted to an annual prize for a literary work in the field of biography, history, politics or poetry published in English or French during the previous twenty-four months. There are two permanent judges (the present Lord Norwich, and the Warden of New College, Oxford) and three others who change every five years. The present judges are Father Peter Levi, Professor Richard Ellmann and Mr. Christopher Hampton with Dr. Anne Barton acting for the Warden of New College.

The Rose Mary Crawshay Prizes

Two Rose Mary Crawshay prizes are available each year. The prize was originally founded in 1888, by Rose Mary Crawshay, for yearly prizes on Byron, Shelley, and Keats. The Prizes may be awarded annually to women of any nationality who, in the judgement of the Council of the British Academy, have written or published within three calendar years next preceding the date of the Award an historical or critical work of sufficient value on any subject connected with English Literature, preference being given to a work regarding one of the poets: Byron, Shelley, or Keats. Communications may be addressed to the Secretary of the British Academy, Burlington House, Piccadilly, London, W1V 0NS.

John Creasey Memorial Award

The award was founded in 1973 following the death of John Creasey, to commemorate his foundation of the Crime Writers Association. It is given annually for a first published crime fiction novel. Given by the Crime Writers Association, c/o The National Book League, 7 Albemarle Street, London, W1X 4BB.

The Isaac Deutscher Memorial Prize

This prize of £100 was founded in 1968 and is awarded each year for an essay or full-scale work, published or in manuscript, which contributes to the development of Marxist thought. The judges are P. Anderson, Professor E. H. Carr, Professor E. Hobsbawm, Tamara Deutscher, M. Johnstone, Professor R. Miliband, Professor István Mészáros. The prize for 1978 was awarded to Professor S. S. Prawer. Material should be submitted before 1st May of the current year to The Isaac Deutscher Memorial Prize, c/o Lloyds Bank, 68 Warwick Square, London, SW1.

Christopher Ewart-Biggs Memorial Prize

This Prize of £1,000 is awarded annually to the writer, of any nationality, whose work contributes most to peace and understanding in Ireland; to closer ties between the peoples of Britain and Ireland; or to co-operation between the partners of the European Community. Eligible works must be published in the 12 months ending 31st May of the year of presentation and can be written in either English or French. Entry forms are available from The National Book League, 7 Albemarle Street, London, W1X 4BB T. 01-493 9001.

The Geoffrey Faber Memorial Prize

As a memorial to the founder and first Chairman of the firm, Messrs. Faber & Faber Limited established in 1963 the Geoffrey Faber Memorial Prize.

This Prize of £250 is awarded annually: and it is given, in alternate years, for a volume of verse and for a volume of prose fiction.

Subject to the qualifications set out below, it is given to that volume of verse or prose fiction first published originally in this country during the two years preceding the year in which the award is given which is, in the opinion of the judges, of the greatest literary merit.

To be eligible for the prize the volume of verse or prose fiction in question must be by a writer who is:

(a) not more than 40 years old at the date of publication of the book;
and
(b) a citizen of the United Kingdom and Colonies, of any other Commonwealth state, of the Republic of Ireland or of the Republic of South Africa.

There are three judges. The judges are reviewers of poetry or of fiction as the case may be; and they are nominated each year by the editors or literary editors of newspapers and magazines which regularly publish such reviews.

Messrs. Faber & Faber invite nominations from such editors and literary editors.

No submissions for the prize are to be made.

Prudence Farmer Poetry Prize

This poetry prize was founded in 1974 and is awarded annually to the best poem printed in the New Statesman. The judges include the Literary Editor, from whom further details may be obtained; 10 Great Turnstile, London, WC1V 7HJ. The 1977 prize was awarded to Peter Redgrove.

Sir Banister Fletcher Prize Trust

The late Sir Banister Fletcher, who was President of the Authors' Club for many years, left the Authors' Club a sum of money to be held upon trust:

"to apply the income thereof in or towards the provision of an annual prize for the book on architecture or the arts which, in the opinion of the Committee . . . shall be most deserving of it, such prize to be known as the Sir Banister Fletcher Prize".

The Committee of the Club decided that the prize be awarded annually for the best book on architecture or the fine arts. The award, which is at present £100, is presented to the winner at a dinner held in the Club.

The John Florio Prize

This prize was established in 1963 for the best translation into English of a twentieth century Italian work of literary merit and general interest, published by a British publisher during the preceding year under the auspices of the Italian Institute and the British-Italian Society, and named after John Florio. Details from the Secretary, The Translators' Association, 84 Drayton Gardens, London, SW10 9SD.

E. M. Forster Award

The distinguished English author, E. M. Forster, bequeathed the American publication rights and royalties of his posthumous novel *Maurice* to Christopher Isherwood, who transferred them to the American Academy and Institute of Arts and Letters for the establishment of an E. M. Forster Award, to be given from time to time to a young English writer for a stay in the United States. In 1977 the award was given to David Cook. Applications for this award are not accepted.

Gay News Book Award

This annual award, consisting of a framed commemorative certificate and a cash prize, was instituted in 1975 and is presented each July to the book published within the twelve month period July to July which is of most lasting relevance to the gay community and which is likely to engender further understanding of homosexuality. Further details from the Literary Editor, *Gay News*, 1A Normand Gardens, Greyhound Road, London, W14 9SB *T.* 01-381 2161.

Gold Dagger Award and Silver Dagger Award

Founded in 1955 and awarded annually for a novel of any crime fiction to a novelist from any country. The panel of judges—usually 9 to 11 persons—are reviewers of crime fiction. Given by the Crime Writers Association, c/o The National Book League, 7 Albemarle Street, London, W1X 4BB.

The Greenwood Prize for 1979

The Poetry Society is empowered by the executors of the late Mrs. Julia Wickham Greenwood to offer the sum of £20 as the Shirley Carter Greenwood Prize for 1979 for the best single poem in open competition addressed "The Greenwood Prize, 21 Earls Court Square, London, SW5", before July 31st 1979, only one poem to be submitted by any one competitor, length not exceeding 250 lines; no previously published poem may be entered. A non-de-plume must be adopted and the name and address of the sender must be given in a closed envelope bearing the pseudonym. Copies should be kept as no poems can be returned. The winning poem shall be printed in THE POETRY REVIEW and may be reprinted at the discretion of the Poetry Society and the adjudicator may reserve near winners for publication in THE POETRY REVIEW. This annual prize is one of high authority and significance.

E. C. Gregory Trust Fund

Awards totalling about £5000 are made annually from this Fund for the encouragement of young poets who can show that they are likely to benefit from an opportunity to give more time to writing. A candidate for an Award must: (a) be a British subject by birth but *not* a national of Eire or any of the British dominions or colonies and be ordinarily resident in the United Kingdom or Northern Ireland; (b) be under the age of thirty at 31st March in the year of the Award; (c) submit for the consideration of the Judges a published or unpublished work of Belles-lettres, poetry or drama poems (not more than 30 poems). Entries for the Award should be sent not later than 31st October to the Society of Authors, 84 Drayton Gardens, London, SW10 9SD.

Guardian Fiction Prize

The *Guardian*'s annual prize for a novel published by a British or Commonwealth writer. The winning novel will be chosen by the Literary Editor in conjunction with the *Guardian*'s regular reviewers of new fiction. In 1977 the prize was awarded to Michael Moorcock for his novel *The Condition of Muzak* (Allison & Busby).

Guardian Award for Children's Fiction

The *Guardian*'s annual prize of £150 for an outstanding work of fiction for children by a British or Commonwealth writer, instituted in 1967. In 1978 the award went to Diana Wynne Jones for her novel *Charmed Life* (Macmillan). Further details from The Literary Editor, The Guardian, 119–141 Farringdon Road, London, EC1.

The Hawthornden Prize

The Hawthornden Prize, for which books do not have to be specially submitted, may be awarded annually to the author of what, in the opinion of the Committee, is the best work of imaginative literature published during the preceding calendar year by a British author under forty-one years of age. The Prize is £100. It was founded by the late Miss Alice Warrender in 1919 and is administered by The Society of Authors.

The Felicia Hemans Prize for Lyrical Poetry

The Felicia Hemans Prize consists of a bronze medal. It is awarded annually for a lyrical poem, the subject of which may be chosen by the competitor. Open to past and present members of the University of Liverpool. The prize shall not be awarded more than once to the same competitor. Poems endorsed "Hemans Prize", must be sent in to the Registrar, The University of Liverpool, P.O. Box 147, Liverpool, L69 3BX *T.* 051-709 6022, on or before May 1st. Competitors may submit either published or unpublished verse, but no competitor may submit more than one poem.

The Henfield Writing Fellowship

The University of East Anglia announces the foundation of the Henfield Writing Fellowship to be awarded annually to a writer of established reputation. The Fellowship is the gift of the Henfield Foundation to the University and is jointly supported by the Eastern Arts Association. They have provided for a Fellowship of the value of £700 with free accommodation in the University, to be held by the Fellow appointed for the duration of the Summer Term in each University Year. Brief details of the Fellowship are as follows.

1. The duration of the Fellowship will be the period of the Summer Term (normally ten weeks) and the Fellowship will be re-awarded annually.
2. The Fellow will be expected to reside in the University for the period stated and accommodation will be provided free by the University in the form of a flat on University Plain (the main University site) comprising two bedrooms, living/dining room, kitchen and bathroom.
3. The duties of the Fellow will be discussed with the person appointed at the time of his selection. It will be assumed that one of his duties will be the pursuit of his own writing. The University's claims on his time would thus deliberately be limited and normally they would involve (a) the Fellow making himself available for a specified period each week to discuss writing with students at the University, and (b) a contribution to the teaching of the University in the form of *either* a formal course in creative writing conducted in collaboration with existing members of the Faculty *or* a series of lectures or readings throughout the term.

Applications for the Fellowship should be lodged with the Establishment Officer, University of East Anglia, University Plain, Norwich, NR4 7TJ, by 31st January of each year in which the Fellowship is to be held.

David Higham Prize for Fiction

This prize of £500 which was founded in 1975 is awarded annually to a citizen of the British Commonwealth, Eire or South Africa for a first novel or book of short stories written in English. Entry forms are available from The National Book League, 7 Albemarle Street, London, W1X 4BB *T.* 01-493 9001. Publishers only may submit books.

Historical Novel Prize

The prize, value £1,500, was founded in 1977 in memory of Georgette Heyer and is awarded annually for an outstanding full-length previously unpublished historical novel. For a copy of the rules and application details write to: The Bodley Head, 9 Bow Street, London, WC2E 7AL or Transworld Publishers, Century House, 61–63 Uxbridge Road, London, W5 5SA.

Winifred Holtby Memorial Prize

The prize will be for the best regional novel of the year written in the English language. The writer must be of British or Irish nationality, or a citizen of the Commonwealth. Translations, unless made by the author himself of his own work, are not eligible for consideration.

Publishers are invited to submit novels published during the current year to The Royal Society of Literature, 1 Hyde Park Gardens, London, W2. The closing date for submissions will be December 31st.

The Irish Arts Council

Bursaries for Creative Writers

In 1978 awards totalling £20,000 were offered to writers in creative work to enable them to concentrate on or complete writing projects.

Denis Devlin Memorial Award for Poetry
This award, value approximately £600, is made triennially for the best book of poetry in the English language by an Irish citizen published in the preceding three years.   The next award will be made in 1979.

Macaulay Foundation
Fellowships value approximately £2,500 are awarded once every three years to writers under 30 years of age (or in exceptional circumstances under 35 years) in order to enable them to further their careers.   The cycle of awards is as follows: Literature (1978), Visual Arts (1979), Music (1980).   Candidates must be Irish-born (Northern Ireland included).

Prize for Poetry in Irish
This prize, value approximately £600, is awarded triennially for the best book of poetry in the Irish language published in the preceding three years.   The next award will be made in 1980.

The Marten Toonder Award
Value £2,500.   This award is made on a rotating cycle of three years, as follows: Literature (1977); Visual Arts (1978); and Music (1979).
Further details may be obtained from The Irish Arts Council, 70 Merrion Square, Dublin 2, T. (01) 764685.

Jewish Chronicle—Harold H. Wingate Awards

Two awards of £1,000 each are made each year, one for a work of fiction, poetry or belles-lettres and the other for a work of non-fiction.   The awards are "to encourage those writers and scholars who are interested in Jewish themes and to stimulate an awareness of these subjects among the reading public."   Works must be published in English in the UK by authors normally resident in Britain or the British Commonwealth, Israel, Eire or South Africa. Details are available from the *Jewish Chronicle*, 25 Furnival Street, London, EC4A 1JT, or The National Book League.

The Jomo Kenyatta Prize for Literature

The £250 prize was founded in 1972 and is awarded annually for a work of literature to an author published in English and/or Swahili who must be a citizen of Kenya, Uganda and/or Tanzania.   Details from The Hon. Secretary, Kenya Publishers Association, P.O. Box 72532, Nairobi, Kenya.   Applications should be made before 30th June each year.

The Martin Luther King Memorial Prize

A prize of £100 is awarded for a literary work reflecting the ideals to which Dr. Martin Luther King dedicated his life: viz. a novel, story, poem, essay, play, TV, radio or motion picture script, first published or performed in the United Kingdom during the calendar year preceding the date of the award. Full details of the award can be obtained from John Brunner, Nat/West Bank Ltd., 7 Fore Street, Chard, Somerset, TA20 1PJ.   No enquiries answered without s.a.e.

Kingstons Limited Rhodesia Literary Award

The premier literary award of Rhodesia was taken over by Kingstons Limited in 1978.   It is awarded as three separate prizes of $500 each, one for writing in English, one for Shona and one for Ndebele.   Kingstons present a trophy to each winner, while P.E.N. Rhodesia Centre receive a book in green leather, in which names of winners will be inscribed as a permanent record. The awards are made on literary merit and popular appeal and may be given for a work published since 1st January of the previous year or for a number of works published over a period of time.   Only individuals and not literary clubs or associations or anthologies will qualify for the awards.   The award winners must be Rhodesian by birth, domicile or by long association. Only published work will be considered for these awards. Anyone may apply—the author, the publisher of the work concerned or interested members of the public. Application forms may be obtained from the Secretary, P.E.N. Centre of Rhodesia, P.O. Box 1900, Salisbury, Rhodesia. Completed form and supporting material must reach the Secretary before 31st March in any year.

Allen Lane Publishing Award, The

The award was initiated in 1973 by the organisers of Bristol Literary Dinners to commemorate the life and achievements of Sir Allen Lane, who was educated in Bristol. The award is open to members and associated members of the Publishers' Association, who must have produced not less than 12 new books during the relevant year (to run from March of one year to the following March). All books, other than technical, will be considered and all aspects of publishing—production, presentation, editorial initiative, promotion—will be taken into consideration by the panel. Further details from John Coe, Eversley, 9 The Drive, Henleaze, Bristol, BS9 4LD. *T.* Bristol 62 6665.

The Library Association Besterman Medal

The Library Association Besterman Medal is awarded annually for an outstanding bibliography or guide to the literature first published in the United Kingdom during the preceding year. Recommendations for the award are invited from members of the Library Association, who are asked to submit a preliminary list of not more than three titles. The following are among the criteria which will be taken into consideration in making an award: (i) the authority of the work and the quality and kind of the articles or entries; (ii) the accessibility and arrangement of the information; (iii) the scope and coverage; (iv) the quality of the indexing; (v) the adequacy of the references; (vi) the up-to-dateness of the information; (vii) the physical presentation; (viii) the originality of the work.

The Library Association Carnegie Medal

The Library Association Carnegie Medal is awarded annually for an outstanding book for children written in English and receiving its first publication in the United Kingdom during the preceding year. It was instituted by the Library Association, whose work owes so much to the benefactors of the Carnegie Trust, to commemorate the centenary of Andrew Carnegie's birth in 1835.

Recommendations for the award are made by members of the Library Association and the decision rests with a Panel of the Youth Libraries Group. Consideration is given not only to the literary quality and suitability of the work, but also to the type, paper, illustrations and binding. It should be added that the award is not necessarily restricted to books of an imaginative nature.

The Library Association Kate Greenaway Medal

The Kate Greenaway Medal is intended to recognise the importance of illustrations in children's books. It is awarded to the artist, who, in the opinion of the Library Association, has produced the most distinguished work in the illustration of children's books first published in the United Kingdom during the preceding year. Books intended for younger as well as older children are included and reproduction will be taken into account. Recommendations are invited from members of the Library Association, who are asked to submit a preliminary list of not more than three titles.

The Library Association McColvin Medal

The Library Association McColvin Medal is awarded annually for an outstanding reference book first published in the United Kingdom during the preceding year. The following types of book are eligible for consideration: (i) encyclopedias, general and special; (ii) dictionaries, general and special; (iii) biographical dictionaries; (iv) annuals, yearbooks and directories; (v) handbooks and compendia of data; (vi) atlases. Recommendations for the award are invited from members of the Library Association, who are asked to submit a preliminary list of not more than three titles. The following are among criteria which will be taken into consideration in making an award: (i) the authority of the work and the quality and kind of the articles or entries; (ii) the accessibility and arrangement of the information; (iii) the scope and coverage; (iv) the style; (v) the relevance and quality of the illustrations; (vi) the quality of the indexing; (vii) the adequacy of the bibliographies and references; (viii) the up-to-dateness of the information; (ix) the physical presentation; (x) the originality of the work.

The Library Association Wheatley Medal

The Library Association Wheatley Medal is awarded annually for an outstanding index published during the preceding three years. Printed indexes to any type of publication may be submitted for consideration. Recommendations for the award are invited from members of the L.A. and the Society of Indexers, publishers and others. The final selection is made by a committee consisting of representatives of the L.A. Cataloguing and Indexing Group and the Society of Indexers, with power to co-opt. The award is made to the compiler of the winning index to a work which must have been published in the United Kingdom.

The Sir William Lyons Award

The Lyons Award of £250 is to encourage young people in automotive journalism, including broadcasting, and to foster interest in motoring and the motor industry through these media. It is awarded to any person of British nationality resident in the United Kingdom under the age of 22 and consists of writing two essays and an interview with the Award Committee. Further details from the General Secretary, Jean Peters, Fairfield, Pyrford Woods, Woking, Surrey, GU22 8QT.

Manchester Odd Fellows Social Concern Annual Book Awards

Prizes of £500 each are awarded for the book, or pamphlet of not less than 10,000 words, which provides the most stimulating impetus for the improvement in living conditions within fields of social concern (to be specified each year). Entries must be published in the 12 months ending on 31st July of the year of presentation; must be written by citizens of Britain, the Commonwealth, Eire, Pakistan or South Africa; and must first have appeared in English. Entry forms are available from The National Book League, 7 Albemarle Street, London, W1X 4BB   *T.* 01-493 9001.

Arthur Markham Memorial Prize

A prize for a short story, essay or poems on a given subject is offered annually as a memorial to the late Sir Arthur Markham. Candidates must be manual workers in or about a coal mine, or have been injured when so employed. Full details can be obtained from The Registrar and Secretary, The University, Sheffield, S10 2TN.

The Somerset Maugham Trust Fund

The purpose of this annual award, which consists approximately of £1,000, is to encourage young writers to travel, to acquaint themselves with the manners and customs of foreign countries, and, by widening their own experience, to extend both the basis and the influence of contemporary English literature. Mr. Maugham urged that in the selection of prize-winners, originality and promise should be the touchstones: he did not wish the judges to "play for safety" in their choice.

A candidate for the award must be a British subject by birth and ordinarily resident in the United Kingdom or Northern Ireland. He or she must, at the time of the award, be under thirty-five years of age, and must submit a published literary work in volume form in the English language, of which he or she is the sole author. The term "literary work" includes poetry, fiction, criticism, history and biography, belles-lettres, or philosophy, but does not include a dramatic work. A candidate who wins an award must undertake to spend not less than three months outside Great Britain and Ireland, and to devote the prize to the expenses of this sojourn.

Any questions relating to the terms of the award should be addressed to The Society of Authors, 84 Drayton Gardens, SW10 9SD, to which candidates should send the literary work they wish to submit for an award. Three copies of one published work (which are non-returnable) should be submitted by a candidate, and it must be accompanied by a statement of his or her age, place of birth, and other published works.

The closing date for the submission of books to be considered is December 31st.

The Mofolo-Plomer Prize

This prize, founded in 1975, is awarded annually for a literary work, written in English, by a South African writer, whether resident in South Africa or abroad. The judges for the first award were Chinua Achebe, Alan Paton, Adam Small. Full details from The Mofolo-Plomer Prize Committee, c/o Ravan Press, P.O. Box 31910, Braamfontein, Johannesburg 2017, South Africa.

National Book Council of Australia Awards

Awarded by the National Book Council of Australia for books of the highest literary merit with a first prize of $3000 ($600 to the publisher). Details from Executive Secretary, 4th Floor, 71 Collins Street, Melbourne, Victoria 3000.

John Newbery Medal

This annual prize which was founded in 1922 is given for children's literature to a citizen or resident of the U.S.A. The judges are the 23 members of the Children's Service Division of the American Library Association (all members change annually) and the prize is given to the author of the most distinguished contribution to American literature for children published in the U.S. during the preceding year. In 1978 the award went to Katherine Paterson for *Bridge to Terabithia* (Crowell).

Further details from The American Library Association, 50 East Huron Street, Chicago, Illinois 60611.

The Frederick Niven Literary Award

In memory of Frederick Niven, the Scottish novelist who died in 1944, his widow has inaugurated a prize of £100 awarded every 3 years, for the most outstanding contribution to the novel by a Scotsman or Scotswoman. The prize will not be awarded more than once to the same person, and if on occasion the judges consider that no work submitted reaches a high enough standard, the award may be withheld. Next award covers years 1977–80.

Inquiries to Miss M. Baxter, Hon. Secretary, P.E.N. Scottish Centre, 18 Crown Terrace, Glasgow, G12 9ES *T.* 041-427 0045.

The Nobel Prize

The Nobel Prize in Literature is one of the awards stipulated in the will of the late Alfred Nobel, the Swedish scientist who invented dynamite. The awarding authority is the Swedish Academy (for Literature), and particulars concerning conditions, etc., can be obtained from Nobelstiftelsen, Sturegatan 14, S-11436 Stockholm. No direct application for a prize will, however, be taken into consideration. For authors writing in English it was bestowed upon Rudyard Kipling in 1907, upon W. B. Yeats in 1923, upon George Bernard Shaw in 1925, upon Sinclair Lewis in 1930, upon John Galsworthy in 1932, upon Eugene O'Neill in 1936, upon Pearl Buck in 1938, upon T. S. Eliot in 1948, upon Willian Faulkner in 1949, upon Bertrand Russell in 1950, upon Sir Winston Churchill in 1953, upon Ernest Hemingway in 1954, upon John Steinbeck in 1962, upon Samuel Beckett in 1969, upon Patrick White in 1973 and upon Saul Bellow in 1976. The Nobel Prizes are understood to be worth about £81,300 each in 1977. They number five: (*a*) Physics, (*b*) Chemistry, (*c*) Physiology or Medicine, (*d*) Literature, and (*e*) the Promotion of Peace.

George Orwell Memorial Prize

This prize, founded in 1975, is awarded annually for an article, essay or series of articles commenting on current cultural, social or political issues anywhere in the world. The work must have been published in the U.K. either in a newspaper, periodical or pamphlet in the preceding year. Full details from Penguin Books Ltd., Harmondsworth, Middlesex, UB7 0DA.

Poetry Lovers' Fellowship

For details of the prize awarded annually by the Fellowship see page 344.

Poetry Review Quarterly Premium

A premium prize is offered for the best poem submitted to the Premium Editor during the quarter (without limitation of subject). Not more than two lyrics or one long poem should be submitted. MSS. should reach "The Premium Editor, THE POETRY SOCIETY, 21 Earls Court Square, London, SW5," typewritten if possible. It is essential that entrants to this competition be members of The Poetry Society and that each poem bears the name and address of the author marked "For Premium Competition," *Entrance fee:* 15p.

Barbara Ramsden Award

The award was founded by public subscription in 1971 to honour Barbara Ramsden, M.B.E., an editor of distinction. This major Australian literary award is made each year to both author and to the publisher's editor of an outstanding work of quality writing. The winners are each presented with a plaque specially designed by Andor Meszaros. There is no restriction of category and more than one work may be submitted. The award is administered by the Victorian fellowship of Victorian Writers, of which Barbara Ramsden was a foundation member, and details are available from The Secretary, Victorian Fellowship of Australian Writers, 1/317 Barkers Road, Kew, Victoria 3101.

The Margaret Rhondda Award

This award, first made in July 1968 on the tenth anniversary of Lady Rhondda's death, and afterwards every three years, is given to a woman writer as a grant-in-aid towards the expenses of a research project in journalism. It is given to women journalists in recognition of the service which they give to the public through journalism. Closing date for next award December 31st, 1980. Further details from The Society of Authors, 84 Drayton Gardens, London, SW10 9SD.

The John Llewelyn Rhys Memorial Prize

The prize of £300, inaugurated by the late Mrs. Rhys in memory of her husband who was killed in 1940, and administered jointly by the trustees and the National Book League, is offered annually to the author of the most memorable literary work of any kind which shall have been published for the first time during *previous* calendar year. The only conditions are that such an author shall be a citizen of this country or the Commonwealth, and shall not have passed his or her thirtieth birthday by the date of the publication of the work submitted. Entry forms and further information are available from the John Llewelyn Rhys Memorial Prize, c/o The National Book League, 7 Albemarle Street, London, W1X 4BB *T.* 01-493 9001. Publishers only may submit books.

The Rogers Prize

This £100 prize is awarded from time to time for an essay or dissertation on some medical or surgical subject which will be named 12 months before the closing date. Only persons whose names appear on the Medical Register of the United Kingdom are eligible for this award. Further details are available from the Scholarships Committee, University of London, Senate House, London, WC1E 7HU.

Romantic Novelists' Association Award

The Annual Award for the best Romantic Novel of the Year is open to non-members as well as members of the Romantic Novelists' Association. The Elizabeth Goudge Historical Award and the Modern Award are also open to non-members as well as members. *Requirements:* Novels must be published between January 1st and December 31st. Authors may obtain entry forms from the *Hon. Treasurer:* Miss B. Taylor, Bell's Farm House, Spurriers Lane, Melling, Liverpool, L31 1BA. Entry fee – £2.00 per novel, members and non-members. The Netta Muskett Award is for unpublished writers in the romantic novel field who must join the Association as Probationary members. MSS. entered for this award must be specially written for it. No Award will be made unless a MSS. is accepted for publication through the Association. Further information from the Hon. Treasurer.

The Royal Society of Literature Award under the W. H. Heinemann Bequest

The purpose of this foundation is to encourage the production of literary works of real worth. The prize shall be deemed a reward for actual achievement. Works in any branch of literature may be submitted by their publishers to the verdict of the Royal Society of Literature which shall be final and without appeal. Prose fiction shall not be excluded from competition, but the Testator's intention is primarily to reward less remunerative classes of literature: poetry, criticism, biography, history, etc. Any work originally written in the English language, shall be eligible. The recipient of a Prize shall not again be eligible for five years. The awards for 1977 were made to C. Hill for his book *Milton and the English Revolution;* N. and J. Mackenzie for their book *The First Fabians*; and to F. S. L. Lyons for his book *Charles Stewart Parnell.*

The Schlegel-Tieck Prize

This prize was established in 1964 under the auspices of the Society of Authors and the Translators Association to be awarded annually for the best translation published by a British publisher during the previous year. Only translations of German twentieth-century works of literary merit and general interest will be considered. The work should be entered by the publisher and not the individual translator. Details may be obtained from the Secretary, The Translators Association, 84 Drayton Gardens, SW10, 9SD.

Scottish Arts Council Book Awards

A limited number of Awards, value £400 each, are made each year by the Scottish Arts Council to published books of literary merit written by Scots or writers resident in Scotland. The Awards fall into two categories: Scottish Arts Council New Writing Awards for first books, and Scottish Arts Council Book Awards for established authors. All types of books are eligible for consideration and the closing date is the 31st October of each year. Books are submitted by the author's publisher, who may receive further information from the Literature Department, The Scottish Arts Council, 19 Charlotte Square, Edinburgh, EH2 4DF *T.* 031-226 6051. Writers bursaries are awarded twice a year to Scottish writers or writers resident in Scotland to enable them to devote more time to their work. Applications should be supported by a responsible referee.

The Scott Moncrieff Prize

This prize was established in 1964 under the auspices of the Society of Authors and the Translators Association to be awarded annually for the best translation published by a British publisher during the previous year. Only translations of French twentieth century works of literary merit and general interest will be considered. The work should be entered by the publisher and not the individual translator. Details from the Secretary, The Translators Association, 84 Drayton Gardens, London, SW10 9SD.

Silver Dagger Award – for details see under Gold Dagger Award.

Ally Sloper Award

Founded in 1976, this is an annual award which is presented at the annual convention of British strip/comic artists, and is given to strip cartoonists only, for work in newspapers and comics. The judges are Denis Gifford and advisors from the Society of Strip Illustration and the Association of Comic Enthusiasts. Full details are available from 80 Silverdale, Sydenham, London, SE26. *T.* 01-699 7725.

The W. H. Smith & Son Annual Literary Award

A prize of £1000 is awarded annually to a Commonwealth author (including a citizen of the United Kingdom) whose book, written in English and published in the United Kingdom, within 12 months ending on December 31st preceding the date of the Award, in the opinion of the judges makes the most outstanding contribution to literature. Further details are available from W. H. Smith, Strand House, 10 New Fetter Lane, London, EC4 1AD.

Society of Authors Awards for Radio

These Awards, founded in 1975 in conjunction with the Radiowriters Association of the Society of Authors, are given annually in various categories of broadcast programmes. Further details from the Organiser, Awards for Radio, Society of Authors, 84 Drayton Gardens, London, SW10 9SD.

South East Arts Literature Prize

Founded in 1975, this annual prize of £250 is to encourage new writing. It is awarded to writers living in the region covered by the South East Arts for a book of new fiction, biography, history, criticism, poetry, etc. Further details are obtainable from South East Arts, 58 London Road, Southborough, Tunbridge Wells, Kent, TN4 0PR.

Winifred Mary Stanford Prize

The prize was founded in 1977 by Mr. Leonard Cutts in memory of his wife who died in 1976. The prize of £1000 is awarded biennially and is open to any book published in the U.K. in the English language which has been inspired in some way by the Christian faith, written by a man or woman 50 years of age and under at the date of publication. The subject of the book may be from a wide range, including poetry, fiction, biography, autobiography, biblical exposition, religious experience and witness. Books must have been published in two years prior to the award which is made at Easter; the first award was made in 1978. Literary merit will be a prime factor in selection. Submission by publishers only to Mr. Edward England, Secretary to the Judges, Winifred Mary Standford Prize, c/o Hodder & Stoughton, Mill Road, Dunton Green, Sevenoaks, Kent, TN13 2YB T. (0732) 50111.

E. Reginald Taylor Essay Competition

A prize of £30.00, in memory of the late E. Reginald Taylor, F.S.A., is awarded annually for the best unpublished essay submitted during the year. The essay, not exceeding 7500 words, should show original research on a subject of archaeological, art-historical or antiquarian interest within the period from the Roman era to A.D. 1830. The successful competitor may be invited to read the essay before the Association and the essay may be published in the *Journal* of the Association if approved by the Editorial Committee.
Competitors are advised to notify the Hon. Editor in advance of the intended subject of their work. The essay should be submitted not later than 31st December to the Hon. Editor, P. Everson, B.A., British Archaeological Association, c/o County Planning Department, County Offices, Newland, Lincoln.

Times Educational Supplement Information Book Awards

There are two annual awards of £100 to the authors of the best information books—one for children up to the age of 9, the other for children aged 10–16. The books must be published in Britain or the Commonwealth. Details from the Times Educational Supplement, P.O. Box 7, New Printing House Square, Gray's Inn Road, London, WC1X 8EZ T. 01-837 1234.

The Tom-Gallon Trust

This Trust was founded by the late Miss Nellie Tom-Gallon and is administered by the Society of Authors. Awards amounting to about £100 a year for two years are made biennially from this Fund to fiction writers of limited means who have had at least one short story accepted for publication. Authors wishing to enter should send to the Secretary of Authors, 84 Drayton Gardens, SW10 9SD: (i) a list of their already published fiction, giving the name of the publisher or periodical in each case and the approximate date of publication; (ii) one published short story; (iii) a brief statement of their financial position; (iv) an undertaking that they intend to devote a substantial amount of time to the writing of fiction as soon as they are financially about to do so; (v) a stamped addressed envelope for the return of the work submitted. The closing date for the next aware is September 16, 1979.

The Travelling Scholarship

This is a non-competitive award, for which submissions are not required (see under The Society of Authors, p. 409).

Wandsworth All London Literary Competition

The competition is open to writers of 16 years and over who live, work or study in the Greater London Area. Awards are made annually in three classes, Poetry, Short Story and Play, the prizes totalling £250 in each class. Entries must be previously unpublished work. The award is sponsored by the Greater London Arts Association, and the judging is under the chairmanship of Martyn Goff, Director of the National Book League. Further details from Assistant Director of Recreation (Libraries and Arts), London Borough of Wandsworth, Battersea District Library, 265 Lavender Hill, London, SW11 1JB.

Sir James Wattie Book of the Year Award

This award, founded in 1968, is given annually to a New Zealand writer for a book on any subject. In 1977 the $1700 first prize was given to James Bertram for his book on *Charles Brasch*.

The Welsh Arts Council's Awards to Writers

Two major annual Prizes of approximately £1000 are awarded to a writer in Welsh and a writer in English for their distinguished contribution to the literatures of Wales. Prizes of approximately £500 each are awarded to the authors of books published during the previous calendar year which, in the Literature Committee's opinion, are of exceptional literary merit. A limited number of bursaries are offered throughout the year to writers resident in Wales who wish to be released from their usual circumstances in order to undertake the writing of specific literary works in Welsh or English. Among other awards are the International Writer's Prize, offered every two years, the Tir na n'Og Prize for children's books, and the Creative Writer's Fellowship in the University of Wales. The Council also organizes competitions from time to time. For further details of the Welsh Arts Council's policies, write to the Literature Department, Welsh Arts Council, Museum Place, Cardiff, CF1 3NX *T.* 394711.

The Whitbread Literary Awards

The awards of £1500 each in three categories, Novel, Biography/Autobiography and Children's Book, are selected from books by writers who have lived in Great Britain and Ireland for five or more years.
Further details may be obtained from The Booksellers Association, 154 Buckingham Palace Road, London, SW1W 9TZ *T.* 01-730 8214.

Francis Williams Book Illustration Award

This award is given every five years to practising book illustrators, professional or student, for any book published in Great Britain in which illustration is a major element, including newly illustrated editions of the classics. Illustrations of a purely technical nature and photographs are excluded. The first Exhibition was held at the Victoria and Albert Museum in 1972. Further details from The Victoria and Albert Museum Library, South Kensington, London, SW7 2RL, or The National Book League, 7 Albemarle Street, London, W1X 4BB.

John Rowan Wilson Award

The prize, founded in 1974, is awarded annually to the writer who has done most to promote wit, style and lucidity in treating medical subjects, or the best piece of writing, not necessarily on a medical subject, produced by a writer who is a qualified doctor. The judges are Dr. Michael O'Donnell and Richard Ollard. The most recent award was made to Polly Toynbee for *Hospital*. Nominations should be sent to *World Medicine*, Clareville House, 26–7 Oxendon Street, London, SW1Y 4EL.

Wolfson Literary Award for History

Founded in 1972 and given annually to authors of published works in history. The 1977 awards were given to (1st): Denis Mack Smith for *Mussolini's Roman Empire*, (2nd) Simon Schama for *Patriots and Liberators*. No application is necessary, but further details from M. Paisner, Messrs. Paisner & Co., 44 Bedford Square, London, WC1B 3DU.

Yorkshire Arts Association Literary Awards

The Yorkshire Arts Association offers biennial prizes totalling £2000 for published works of fiction, poetry, drama or creative non-fiction by authors who live in Yorkshire or who have strong literary connections with the region. The Selection Panel has total discretion as to how the money should be divided though the general intention of the Awards is to offer encouragement to younger as well as more established writers. Further details from The Director, Yorkshire Arts Association, Glyde House, Glydegate, Bradford, BD5 0BQ.

Yorkshire Post Book of the Year

In 1977, the first prize went to Alistair Horne (£350 and scroll) for *A Savage War of Peace* and the fiction award (£200 and scroll) went to Olivia Manning for *The Danger Tree*. The Best First Work Award of £250 went to Max Egremont for *The Cousins*, and the runner-up award of £150 went to John Campbell for *Lloyd George, The Goat in the Wilderness*. Six years ago new annual awards of about £250 each were launched for works which in the opinion of the Panel of Judges have made the greatest contribution to the understanding and appreciation of Music and Art.

Nominations are only accepted from publishers and should arrive (together with one copy of the book) by 1st November in the case of main prizes, by 15th January in the case of Best First Work entries and in the Art and Music Award scheme. Correspondence to Richard Douro, The Yorkshire Post, Wellington Street, Leeds, LS1 1RF   *T.* 32701 ext. 512.

SOCIETIES AND CLUBS OF INTEREST TO AUTHORS, JOURNALISTS, ARTISTS, AND MUSICIANS

Academi Gymreig, Yr. *President:* Dr. Kate Roberts; *Chairman:* Dr. R. M. Jones; *Treasurer:* Gwenlyn Parry; *Secretary:* Dr. Harri Pritchard Jones; *Administrative Secretary:* Ann Benyon, Yr Academi Gymreig, 13 Cilgant Sant Andreas, Caerdydd (Cardiff) CF1 3DB   *T.* 0222 398189.
The Society was founded in 1959 to promote creative writing in the Welsh language.   Existing members elect new members on the basis of their contribution to Welsh literature or criticism.   The society publishes a literary magazine, *Taliesin*, books on Welsh literature, and translations of modern European classics into Welsh.   It is currently engaged in the production of a new English/Welsh Dictionary.   The society's annual Easter Conference, at various centres in Wales, is open to all.

Academi Gymreig, Yr: English Language Section.   *President:* A. G. Prys-Jones; *Chairman:* Roland Mathias; *Secretary:* Mrs. Sue Harries, 13 St. Andrews Crescent, Cardif, CF1 3DB.
This section was founded in 1968 to provide a meeting-point for writers in the English language who are of Welsh origin and/or take Wales as a main theme of their work.   Membership at present is by invitation and members pay an annual subscription.   Although it is an autonomous body, members of the English Language Section co-operate with members of the parent body for joint conferences and similar activities.

Agricultural Journalists, Guild of, Goldfield Mill House, Miswell Lane, Tring, Herts, HP23 4EU   *T.* Tring 2267.   *President:* Alexander Kenworthy; *Chairman:* Angus MacDonald; *Hon. General Secretary:* Peter Bell, M.B.E. Established to promote a high standard among journalists who specialise in agricultural matters and to assist them to increase their sources of information and technical knowledge.   Membership is open to those earning their livelihood wholly or mainly from agricultural journalism.

American Correspondents in London, Association of, *President,* Joseph W. Grigg, c/o United Press International, 8 Bouverie Street, London, EC4Y 8BB   *T.* 01-353 2282–4.

American Publishers, Association of, Inc. (1970), 1 Park Avenue, New York, N.Y., 10016.   *T.* 212-689-8920.   *President:* Townsend Hoopes; *Vice President:* Thomas D. McKee.   The Association of American Publishers is a voluntary confederation of over 320 publishers of books of all types. Members of the Association, which was formed by the consolidation of the American Book Publishers Council and the American Educational Publishers Institute on July 1, 1970, produce the majority of printed materials sold to the nation's schools, colleges and libraries, bookstores, through book clubs and to homes.   All regions of the United States are represented in the AAP membership.   Products include print and audio-visual instructional materials; general trade books; reference books; religious books; scientific, technical and medical books—hard bound and paper bound.   Systems of instruction, classroom periodicals, maps, globes, films and filmstrips, audio and video tapes, records and cassettes, slides, transparencies, tests—all are represented within the AAP.

Art Education, National Society for (1888), Champness Hall, Drake Street, Rochdale, Lancs. *T.* 0706 39342. *President:* M. Terry Satterford; *Secretary:* G. F. Williams, A.T.D., D.A.E. A professional association of principals and lecturers in colleges and schools of art and of specialist art and craft teachers in other schools and colleges. Has representatives on National and Regional Committees which are the concern of those engaged in Art and Design education.

Artists, Federation of British, The Mall Galleries, 17 Carlton House Terrace, London, SW1Y 5BD   *T.* 01-930 6844. *Secretary-General:* Maurice Bradshaw, O.B.E. Administers the affairs of all the societies at this address and arranges exhibitions in this country and abroad.

Artists' League of Great Britain, The (Incorporated) (1909). R.W.S. Galleries, 26 Conduit Street, London, W1R 9TA. *T.* 01-629 8300. *Secretary:* Malcolm Fry. Run by Artists for Artists and renders advice and assistance in every difficulty met with in their professional capacity. *Annual Subscription,* £4.00 (minimum), Life membership £30.00, Entrance Fee £1.00.

Arts (1863), 40 Dover Street, London, W1X 3RB. T. 01-499 8581. *Subs:* £85.00. For men and women connected with or interested in arts, literature, or science.

Arts Council of Great Britain, 105 Piccadilly, London, W1V 0AU   *T.* 01-629 9495. *Chairman:* Rt. Hon. Kenneth Robinson; *Secretary-General:* Roy Shaw. *Literature Director:* Charles Osborne. To develop and improve the knowledge, understanding and practice of the arts, and to increase their accessibility to the public throughout Great Britain. **Scottish Arts Council:** 19 Charlotte Square, Edinburgh, EH2 4DF   *T.* 031-226 6051. **Welsh Arts Council:** Holst House, Museum Place, Cardiff, CF1 3NX   *T.* (0222) 394711.

Arts, Royal Society of, John Adam Street, Adelphi, London, WC2N 6EZ   *T.* 01-839 2366. Founded in 1754. Sir Peter Masefield (*Chairman of the Council*), Christopher Lucas (*Secretary*). Fellowship is open to both men and women. The aims of the Society, as indicated by its full title, are, "The encouragement of Arts, Manufactures and Commerce."

Asian Affairs, Royal Society for, 42 Devonshire Street, London, W1N 1LN. *President:* The Lord Greenhill of Harrow, G.C.M.G., O.B.E.; *Chairman of Council:* Sir Arthur de la Mare, K.C.M.G., K.C.V.O.; *Secretary:* Miss M. Fitz-Simons. For the study of all Asia past and present. Founded 1901. Fortnightly lectures etc. Library. *Publication: Asian Affairs,* three times a year, free to members. *Subscription:* £10.00 London members, £8.00 country or abroad; $17 US, £50 Affiliated.

Aslib (1924), 3 Belgrave Square, London, SW1X 8PL. *T.* 01-235 5050. An association for promoting the effective management and use of information in industry, central and local government, education and the professions. For particulars of membership apply: The Director.

Assistant Librarians, Association of (1895), 109 Lower Regent Street, Beeston, Nottingham NG9 2DL. (Group of The Library Association, *q.v.*) *President:* J. P. S. Luckett, B.A., A.L.A.; *Hon. Secretary:* Mrs. J. G. Bray, A.L.A. Publish library text books and bibliographical aids.

Australia Council, Northside Gardens, 168 Walker Street, North Sydney, New South Wales 2060, Australia. *T.* 922 2122. *Chairman:* Professor Geoffrey Blainey, A.O. *General Manager:* John Cameron. *Chief Executive Officer:* Dr. Jean Battersby.

The Australia Council is a statutory authority which provides a broad range of support for the arts in Australia. Established in 1968 as The Australian Council for the Arts (supporting mainly the performing arts), it was re-structured in 1973 to embrace music, theatre, film/radio/television, litera-ture, visual arts, crafts, Aboriginal arts and community arts. (In June 1976 the activities of the film/radio/television Board were transferred to the Australian Film Commission.) In March 1975, by Act of Parliament, the Australia Council was established as an independent authority.

The Council is involved in the administration of grants, public information services, policy development, research, international activities, and advisory services to many other organisations including government bodies. A wide range of projects and activities, both individual and group, receive Australia Council funds. Support includes grants made to enable artists to study, and living allowances to permit others (notably writers) to 'buy time' to follow their creative pursuits. Some of the major initiatives of the Council in past years, include: negotiation with international bodies for the *touring of exhibitions; a Public Lending Right* scheme for Australian authors; *copyright protection; a Provident Fund for performers; Artist-in-Residence* schemes at tertiary institutions, and increased employment for Australian artists in all fields. Australia Council publications include information booklets and an Annual Report.

Literature Board, The, Australia Council, P.O. Box 302, North Sydney, New South Wales 2060. Because of its size, isolation and the competition its literature meets from two huge English speaking worlds, Australia has always needed to subsidise certain kinds of writing, and subsidies have in-creased greatly in number over the last few years. The Literature Board, one of the seven Boards of the Australia Council, was created early in 1973 from the basis of the earlier Commonwealth Literary Fund, first established in 1908.

The Board's objectives are the support of the writing of all forms of creative literature—novels, short stories, poetry, plays, biographies, history and the humanities in general. The Board also assists with the publication of literary magazines and periodicals. It has a publishing subsidies scheme for Australian-based publishers. And it initiates and supports projects of many kinds designed to promote Australian literature both within Australia and abroad.

About two-thirds of the Board's expenditure in the past five years has gone to writers in the form of direct grants, including fellowships (living allow-ances) and Special Purpose Grants. The fellowships currently range in size from $3,000 over a six-month period for young (28 years old and under) writers to $11,000 per year over three years for major writers. The Board has offered 434 fellowships and half-fellowships over the 4 years 1973–77.

Australian Book Publishers' Association, 163 Clarence Street, Sydney 2000, N.S.W.

The Association aims to foster original or licensed publishing in Australia, to help improve Australian book industry as a whole. There are about 98 member firms.

Australian Independent Publishers Association, P.O.Box 4059, Mail Exchange, Melbourne, Victoria 3001.

Australian Society of Authors, The, 24 Alfred Street, Milsons Point, N.S.W., 2061. *T.* 92-7235. *President:* Manning Clark; *Executive Secretary:* Deirdre Hill.

Australian Writers, The Society of, Australia House, Strand, London, WC2B 4LA. Formed in 1952 to further the cause of Australian writers and Australian writing wherever possible.

Authors (1891), (at the Arts Club). 40 Dover Street, London, W1X 3RB   *T.* 01-499 8581. *Secretary:* Edward Walsh.

Authors' Agents, The Association of (1974), 10 Buckingham Street, London, WC2N 6BU   *T.* 01-839 2556. *President:* Michael Sissons; *Vice-President:* George Greenfield; *Secretary:* Deborah Rogers; *Treasurer:* Elaine Greene. Maintains a code of professional practice and behaviour to which all members of the Association commit themselves; discuss matters of common professional interest; and provides a vehicle for representing the view of authors' agents in discussion of matters of common interest with other professional bodies.

Authors' Guild of Ireland, Ltd., 130 Furry Park Road, Dublin, 5.   *T.* 331189. *Directors:* John McCann, E. J. Duffy, John K. Lyons, Thomas Coffey, John McDonnell, Mrs. Iseult McGuinness. A society for the protection of copyright owned and managed, on a non-profit basis, by Full members who must be owners of copyright in literary or dramatic works by reason of authorship, or who are the personal successors of such authors. Agents for the control of performing rights and collection of royalties in Ireland. *Secretary:* J. K. Lyons.

Authors, The Society of, 84 Drayton Gardens, London, SW10 9SD.   *T.* 01-373 6642. *President:* Sir Victor Pritchett, C.B.E.; *Secretariat:* Philippa MacLiesh, George D. Astley, Victor Bonham-Carter.
The Society was founded in 1884 by Sir Walter Besant with the object of representing, assisting, and protecting authors. Since then its scope has been continuously extended, so that today, within the framework of the Society, specialist associations have been created for translators and radio writers (details of which will be found elsewhere in this issue), also groups for educational and children's writers, and book illustrators. Members are entitled to legal as well as general advice in connection with the marketing of their work, their contracts, their choice of a publisher, etc., and also to have litigation in which their work may involve them conducted by the Society and at the Society's expense provided the Committee of Management is satisfied that the member's case is sound in law and ethics and that the proceedings are justified.
Annual Subscription: £18.00. Entrance fee £10.00. Full particulars of membership may be obtained from the Society's offices. (See also page 408.)

Authors' Representatives, Inc., Society of (1928), 101 Park Avenue, New York, N.Y., 10017. *T.* 212-683 5890.

Aviation Artists, The Guild of, affiliated to the Federation of British Artists, 11 Great Spilmans, London, SE22 8SZ   *T.* 01-693 3033. *President:* Frank Wootten, P.G.AV.A.; *Secretary:* Mrs. Y. C. Bonham. A Guild of painters formed in 1971 to promote all forms of aviation art through the organisation of Exhibitions and Meetings. Annual Exhibition Qantas Gallery June/July. Entrance Fee £6. Annual Subscription (exhibiting) Associate and Full Members £8. Friends Non-Exhibiting £4.

Aviation Artists, Society of, 17 Carlton House Terrace, London, SW1Y 5BD *T.* 01-930 6844. *Secretary:* Maurice Bradshaw. To promote a greater appreciation of the artistic opportunities of flight, etc.

Bibliographical Society (1892), British Academy, Burlington House, Piccadilly, London, W1V 0NS. *President:* A. R. A. Hobson, *Joint Hon. Secretaries:* R. J. Roberts, Mrs. M. M. Foot. Acquisition and dissemination of information upon subjects connected with historical bibliography.

Blackpool and Fylde Art Society The. Founded 1884. *President:* W. Smedley. *Hon. Secretary:* Thomas Helm, 47 Blenheim Avenue, Blackpool, FY1 4ER *T.* Blackpool 22527. *Studio:* Wilkinson Avenue, off Woodland Grove, Blackpool. Summer and Autumn exhibitions (members' work only). Studio meetings, practical, lectures, etc., out-of-door sketching.

Bladon Society of Arts and Crafts, The, Hurstbourne Tarrant, Andover, Hampshire, SP11 0AR *T.* Hurstbourne Tarrant 278. *Trustees:* The Rt. Hon. Viscount Eccles, K.C.V.O., Admiral Sir Henry McCall, K.C.V.O., K.B.E., C.B., D.S.O. *Curator:* Peter Strong. To stimulate interest in the arts and crafts by varied exhibitions in the Bladon Galleries. A 19th century chapel containing two separate picture galleries and a permanent but changing crafts section gallery.
All exhibits on sale.

Book Association of Ireland (1943), 21 Shaw Street, Dublin, 2. *T.* Dublin 778115. Promotion of book-reading and wider distribution of books of all kinds, particularly books in Gaelic, books by Irish writers, books published in Ireland and books of Irish interest published anywhere. Enquiries concerning books answered if possible.

Book Publishers Association of New Zealand, Box 31285, Milford, Auckland 9. *T.* 469-681. *Director:* Ray Richards.

Books Across the Sea, The English-Speaking Union of the Commonwealth, Dartmouth House, 37 Charles Street, London, W1X 8AB *T.* 01-629 0104. The English Speaking Union of the United States, 16 East 69th Street, New York, N.Y., 10021. The English Speaking Union is a leading world voluntary organisation devoted to the promotion of international understanding and friendship. As part of this programme, Books Across the Sea exchanges books with its corresponding BAS Committees in New York, Australia, Canada and New Zealand. The books exchanged are selected to reflect the life and culture of each country and the best of its recent publishing and writing. The books are circulated among members and accredited borrowers, bulk loans are made to affiliated schools and public libraries. New selections are announced by bulletin, *The Ambassador Booklist.*

Booksellers Association of Great Britain and Ireland (1895), 154 Buckingham Palace Road, London, SW1W 9TZ *T.* 01-730 8214–6. *Director:* G. R. Davies, O.B.E. To promote and extend the sale of books and improve educational and technical qualifications of those engaged in it.

Britain in Water-Colours, 17 Carlton House Terrace, London, SW1Y 5BD. *T.* 01-930 6844. *Secretary:* Maurice Bradshaw. An annual exhibition for painters in water-colours illustrating the British character and way of life.

British Academy, Burlington House, Piccadilly, London, W1V 0NS. *T.* 01-734 0457. *President:* Sir Isaiah Berlin, O.M., C.B.E.; *Treasurer:* Professor W. G. Beasley; *Secretary:* J. P. Carswell, C.B.

British Amateur Press Association (1890), BM/BAPA, London, WC1. To promote the Fellowship of Writers, Artists, Editors, Printers and Publishers and other craftsmen, and to encourage them to contribute to, edit and print and publish as a hobby magazines and literary works produced by letterpress and other processes.

British Artists, Royal Society of, 17 Carlton House Terrace, London, SW1Y 5BD *T.* 01-930 6844. *President:* Peter Greenham, R.A. *Keeper:* Carl de Winter. Incorporated by Royal Charter for the purpose of encouraging the study and practice of the arts of painting, sculpture and architectural designs. Annual Open Exhibition.

British Association of Industrial Editors, The (1949). *President:* Kenneth Corfield; *Secretary-General:* 3 Locks Yard, High Street, Sevenoaks, Kent, TN13 1LT *T.* 0732-59331. The objects include development of the qualifications of those engaged in producing house journals in the United Kingdom and the Commonwealth and to work for improved standards in all types of house journals; and to provide a consultancy service on all matters relating to house journals. Membership is open to men and women engaged in, or who have a valid interest in industrial, commercial or organisational communication.

British Colonial Society of Artists, Royal, 17 Carlton House Terrace, London, SW1Y 5BD *T.* 01-930 6844. *Secretary:* Maurice Bradshaw. To unite in one body artists of the Commonwealth for the advancement of the arts.

British Copyright Council, The, Copyright House, 29–33 Berners Street, London, W1P 4AA *T.* 01-930 1911 and 580 5544. *Chairman:* Denis de Freitas; *Vice-Chairmen:* Brigid Brophy, Graham Whettam; *Secretary:* Geoffrey Adams; *Hon. Treasurer:* Eric Waughray. Its purposes are to defend and foster the true principles of creators' copyright and their acceptance throughout the world, to bring together bodies representing all who are interested in the protection of such copyright, and to keep watch on any legal or other changes which may require an amendment of the law.

British Council, The, 10 Spring Gardens, London, SW1A 2BN *T.* 01-930 8466. *Chairman:* Sir Charles Troughton, C.B.E., M.C., T.D.; *Director General:* Sir John Llewellyn, K.C.M.G., D.SC., LL.D., F.R.S.(N.Z.). The British Council was established in 1934. In 1940 it received a Royal Charter, which defines its objects as being to promote a wider knowledge of Britain and the English language abroad and to develop closer cultural relations with other countries. It has staff in about 80 countries, and 25 offices in university towns in Britain. The Council's activities overseas include the promotion of the teaching of English and support for educational development at all levels in the formal and non-formal sectors. Assistance is provided in many forms, including advice and information, training courses in Britain and overseas, feasibility and evaluation studies, project design and management, materials and personnel, usually undertaken in collaboration with the Ministry of Overseas Development or international development agencies (e..g the World Bank) and with the relevant national authorities. In particular, support is given to the introduction of new methods in education and to curriculum development. The Council's resources include staff and training facilities for the application of media in education. British Council Representatives overseas act as Education advisers to HM Diplomatic Missions. The Council fosters contacts between professional people active in education, the sciences and the arts in Britain and other countries. It runs or is associated with some 170 libraries of British books and periodicals in the countries in which it is represented; it makes presentations of books and periodicals to appropriate institutions and organises book and periodical exhibitions overseas (263 in 1977–78); its Overseas Reviews Scheme gets British books reviewed in overseas journals. The Council as O.D.M.'s agent also administers the Books Presentation Programme, the Library Development Scheme and the Low Priced Books Scheme. The latter subsidises the production of tertiary level textbooks for sale in speci-

fied countries at greatly reduced prices under the imprint of the English
Language Book Society.

The British Council's publications include: *British Book News, British Medical Bulletin, British Medicine, Higher Education in the U.K.*, a series of bi-
monthly essays, *Writers and Their Work* and *Educational Broadcasting International* (for complete list see Council's Annual Report). To assist professionals in the English Language Teaching field it maintains an English
Teaching Information Centre and publishes information guides, occasional
papers and a journal published three times a year for *ELT Documents*. In
association with Cambridge University Press and the Centre for Information
on Language Teaching, it produces the quarterly *Language Teaching and
Linguistics Abstracts*. Its Archive is a unique collection of unpublished
material on English Language Teaching. The Council has also produced, in
association with the Argo Record Company, a complete set of recordings of
the works of Shakespeare and a recorded anthology of English poetry from
Chaucer to Yeats and some recordings of modern drama. At home, the
Council arranges placements and professional programmes for overseas
students and visitors, on its own account and for British Government and
international organisations, and advises and gives assistance in the field of
overseas student welfare. The Council administers official funds for grants
to certain types of youth exchange between Britain and the Soviet Union,
countries in Europe, and the Commonwealth. Training courses in the production of educational radio and television programmes as well as audio
visual aids are conducted for overseas trainees in the Council's training
complex in Tavistock House.

It organises exhibitions of British art for showing abroad, and British contributions to international events. It supports overseas tours by dramatic
and musical artists and companies. Musical scores and records are also
provided for loan to musical and educational institutions, radio stations
and individual musicians overseas.

British Directory Publishers, Association of, Imperial House, 17 Kingsway,
London, WC2B 6UN. *Chairman:* J. Hooper. To provide for the exchange
of information between members on the technical, commercial and management problems arising in Directory Publishing. Maintains a code of Professional Practice. All correspondence to Neville House, Eden Street,
Kingston upon Thames, KT1 1BY.

British Film Institute, 127 Charing Cross Road, London, WC2H 0EA *T.* 01-
437 4355. *Telex:* 27624. *Director:* Keith Lucas.

The general object of the British Film Institute is "to encourage the development of the art of the film, to promote its use as a record of contemporary
life and manners, to foster study and appreciation of it from these points of
view, to foster study and appreciation of film for television and television
programmes generally, to encourage the best use of television." Its departments include the National Film Archive and the National Film Theatre on
the South Bank. The Institute has also helped to set up over 40 Regional
Film Theatres outside London. Through its information service, its
Monthly Film Bulletin (which gives credit and reviews of every feature film
released in Britain), its quarterly *Sight and Sound* and its Educational Advisory Services (including lecture and schools service), it is of value to writers
dealing with film matters. The annual subscription for Members £6.20 including *Sight and Sound* and N.F.T. programme (post free), or £9.30 including *Sight and Sound, Monthly Film Bulletin* and programme (post free).
Associateship (National Film Theatre) (London) £4.40 (including programme
post free), £2.20 to full-time students at recognised education establishments.
Senior citizens—free.

British Kinematograph, Sound and Television Society (founded 1931. Incorporated 1946), 110–112 Victoria House, Vernon Place, London, WC1B 4DJ *T.* 01-242 8400. *Secretary:* W. Pay. Aims to encourage technical and scientific progress in the industries of its title. Publishes technical information, arranges lectures and demonstrations, and encourages the exchange of ideas.

British Science Fiction Association, Ltd., The (1958). *Chairman:* Arthur C. Clarke; *Membership Secretary:* David Cobbledick, 245 Rosalind Street, Ashington, Northumberland, NE63 9AZ. For authors, publishers, booksellers and readers of science fiction, fantasy and allied genres. Publishes informal magazine, *Matrix*, of news and information, *Tangent*, an amateur writers' magazine, and bimonthly critical magazine, *Vector*; editor David Wingrove, 4 Holmside Court, Nightingale Lane, London, SW12 8TA *T.* 01-673 2069. Membership fees £5.00 per year.

British Science Writers, Association of, 21 Albemarle Street, London, W1. *Chairman:* Alan Cane; *Secretary:* Eleanor Lawrence. An association of science writers, and of editors, and radio, film, and television producers concerned with the presentation of science. Its aims are to improve the standard of science writing and to assist its members in their work. Visits to research establishments, luncheon meetings for people who are concerned with scientific policy, and receptions for scientific attachés and Parliamentarians are among its activities.

British Sculptors, Royal Society of, 108 Old Brompton Road, London, SW7 3RA *T.* 01-373 5554. *President:* Michael Rizzello; *Hon. Treasurer:* John Ravera; *Secretary:* Mrs. F. McGregor Eadie. Aims to promote and advance the Art of Sculpture. It informs and advises its members on professional matters and provides an advisory service to the general public.

British Theatre Association (formerly **British Drama League**) (1919), 9 Fitzroy Square, London, W1P 6AE. *T.* 01-387 2666. *Director:* Walter Lucas. To assist the development of the art of the theatre. The largest library in the country devoted essentially to plays and theatrical subjects.

Brontë Society, Brontë Parsonage Museum, Haworth, nr. Keighley, BD22 8DR *T.* Haworth 42323. *President:* Miss Margaret Lane, M.A. *Chairman of the Council:* Mrs. J. E. Kellett; *Hon. Secretary:* A. H. Preston. Examination, preservation, illustration of the memoirs and literary remains of the Brontë family; exhibitions of MSS and other subjects. *Publications:* The Transactions of the Brontë Society (Annual).

Bulwer-Lytton Circle, The (1973), High Orchard, 125 Markyate Road, Dagenham, Essex, RM8 2LB. *Secretary:* Eric Ford. Promotion of scholarship and research in the life, work and times of Bulwer-Lytton and his family. Subscription £2.00 p.a.

Canadian Authors' Association, 22 Yorkville Avenue, Toronto, M4W 1L4, Ontario *T.* 1-923 2362. *President:* Dr. Agnes C. Nyland; *National Secretary:* Florence Burns.

Canadian Book Publishers' Council. Consists of 50 educational and trade publishers; maintains offices at Suite 701, 45 Charles Street East, Toronto, Ontario M4Y 1S2 *T.* 416-964-7231. Interested in advancing the cause of the publishing business by co-operative effort and in encouragement of high standards of workmanship and service. Co-operates with other organisations interested in the reading and study of books. Canadian Book Publishers' Council has four divisions, the School Group concerned with primary and secondary school instructional materials, and the College Group, the Trade Publishers' Group and the Paperback Group. *Executive Director:* Jacqueline Nestmann.

Canadian Periodical Publishers Association (1973), 3 Church Street, Suite 407, Toronto, M5E 1M2 *T.* 416 363 2616. *Executive Director:* Sheryl Taylor-Munro. Act as a trade association representing members' interests to provincial and federal government, subscription and advertising promotion, servicing members by (*e.g.*) providing mailing lists, and operating a national distribution system for member periodicals.

Cartoonists Club of Great Britain. *Secretary:* Manny Curtis, 71 Morton Way, Southgate, London, N14 7HN *T.* 01-886 3199. Aims to encourage social contact between members and endeavour to promote the professional standing and prestige of cartoonists. *Annual sub.:* New members £10; Full members £6, Associate £7.

Catholic Writers Guild, 24A Elm Bank Mansions, Elm Bank Gardens, Barnes, London, SW13 0NS *T.* 01-876 4167. For Catholic writers, journalists and those working in public relations and broadcasting. Monthly meetings. Subscription £2.00 p.a.

Children's Writers Group, 84 Drayton Gardens, London, SW10 9SD. *T.* 01-373 6642. *Secretary:* Diana Shine. A specialist unit within the framework of The Society of Authors.

City of London Art Exhibition, 17 Carlton House Terrace, London, SW1Y 5BD *T.* 01-930 6844. *Secretary:* Maurice Bradshaw. Annual exhibition for artists living or working in the City of London.

Civil Service Authors, Society of. *Secretary:* Miss Betty Richards, 16 Palmerston Road, Twickenham, Middlesex, TW2 7QX. Aims of the Society are to encourage authorship both by present and past members of the Civil Service and to provide opportunities for social and cultural relationships between civil servants who are authors or aspirant authors. Literary competitions are held annually for members only. *Subscriptions:* £3.00 per annum for London members and £2.00 for provincial members. S.A.E. for enquiries.

Classical Association. *Secretary (Branches):* Mrs. E. Varney, 30 Drury Lane, Lincoln, LN1 3BN. *Secretary (Council):* Professor C. Collard, Department of Classics and Ancient History, The University, Swansea.

Commonwealth Press Union (1909), Studio House, 184 Fleet Street, London, EC4A 2DU *T.* 01-242 1056. Organisation of newspapers, periodicals, news agencies throughout the Commonwealth. *Secretary:* Lieut.-Colonel Terence Pierce-Goulding, M.B.E., C.D.

Composers' Guild of Great Britain, The, 10 Stratford Place, London, W1N 9AE
T. 01-499 8567.
The Composers' Guild was created in June 1945 under the aegis of The
Incorporated Society of Authors, Playwrights, and Composers. In 1948 it
was formed into an independent body under the title of The Composers'
Guild of Great Britain. Its function is to represent and protect the interests
of composers of music in this country and to advise and assist its members
on problems connected with their work.
Annual subscription: £10.00, Associate membership £8.00. Further particu-
lars may be obtained from the General Secretary of the Guild.

**Confédération Internationale des Sociétés d'Auteurs et Compositeurs-Congrès
Mondial des Auteurs et Compositeurs,** 11 Rue Keppler, 75116 Paris, France.
T. 720-5937. *T.A.* Interauteurs, Paris.

Joseph Conrad Society (U.K.), The (1973). *Chairman:* Mrs. Juliet McLauchlan;
Vice-Chairman: Mr. Philip Conrad; *Secretary:* Miss Margaret Rishworth,
Olinda, Beacon Hill Road, Hindhead, Surrey, GU26 6QA. Maintains
close and friendly links with the Conrad family. Activities include an
Annual Gathering, with lectures and discussions; publication of the
Journal and a series of pamphlets; and maintenance of a study centre in
London.

Contemporary Arts, Institute of, 12 Carlton House Terrace, London, SW1Y
5AH *T.* 01-930 0493. A centre which aims at encouraging collaboration
between the various arts, the promotion of experimental work and the
mutual interchange of ideas. Exhibitions, theatre, music, dance, poetry,
lectures and discussions, all play a part in the programme.

Crime Writers' Association (1953), c/o National Book League, 7 Albemarle
Street, London, W1X 4BB. For professional writers of crime novels, short
stories, plays for stage, television and sound radio, or of serious works on
crime. Full membership £6.00 annually; overseas, associate, and country
£3.00. Monthly meetings at National Book League.

Critics' Circle, The (1913). *President:* 1978, B. A. Young; *Vice-President:*
Derek Malcolm; *Hon. General Secretary:* Matthew Norgate, 7 Lloyd
Square, London, WC1X 9BA *T.* 01-837 4379. *Objects:* To promote the
art of criticism, to uphold its integrity in practice, to foster and safeguard the professional interests of its members, to maintain and disburse
a benevolent fund for necessitous members and their dependants, and to support the advancement of the arts. Membership is by invitation of the
Council. Such invitations are issued only to persons engaged professionally,
regularly and substantially in the writing or broadcasting of criticism of
drama, music, films, or ballet.

Cyngor Llyfrau Cymraeg (Welsh Books Council), Queen's Square, Aberystwyth,
Dyfed *T.* 0970 4151–3. *Director:* Alun Creunant Davies. The Welsh
Books Council was founded in 1963 to encourage and increase the interest
of the public in Welsh literature and to support authors of popular books in
the Welsh language. With the establishment of Publicity, Editorial,
Design and Marketing Departments, the Council now promotes all aspects
of book production in Wales and provides a service for Welsh-language
books and English-language books of Welsh interest.

Designers, Society of Industrial Artists and, *Secretary:* Geoffrey Adams, 12 Carlton House Terrace, London, SW1Y 5AH *T.* 01-930 1911. The S.I.A.D. is the chartered body representing professional designers in some 40 different categories of design. Included in the two dimensional area—apart from textile, wallpaper, rug and carpet design—are general, technical and fashion illustration, cartoons, packaging design, printed publicity, catalogues and educational graphics, book and magazine typography, stationery ranges, trade marks and symbols, corporate identity, film and TV graphics and photography. The Society is concerned with standards of competence, professional conduct and integrity; it makes a significant contribution to the establishment of high standards in design education, and represents the views and interests of professional designers in government and other official bodies. The SIADesign Information Service, which puts members in touch with clients, includes a Visible Record of members' work at the Society's office, and a Staff Vacancy Register. Official publication *The Designer.* The Socety's Code of Conduct is included on pages 275–7. Conditions of Engagement and other documentation is available from the Society's office.

Dickens Fellowship (1902), *Headquarters:* The Dickens House, 48 Doughty Street, London, WC1N 2LF *T.* 01-405 2127. *Hon. Secretary:* Alan Watts. House occupied by Dickens 1837–9. Membership rates and particulars on application. Publication: *The Dickensian.*

Dorman (Sean) Manuscript Society, 4 Union Place, Fowey, Cornwall, PL23 1BY. For mutual help among part-time writers, whether housewives or in the various professions and trades, as well as those fully professional. Circulating manuscript parcels affording constructive criticism, with Remarks Book. Special circulators for advanced writers. Technical discussion circulators. Quarterly magazine *Writing* buys verse and articles on journalism. *Subscription:* U.K. and Eire: £2.00 p.a.; £1.25 six months (after six months' trial period at reduced subscription of £1.00). Further particulars and copy of *Writing* supplied on receipt of 40p. and stamped addressed envelope only.

Dunedin Society, The, Founded 1911 for the encouragement of the Scottish creative Arts. *Hon. Secretary:* William MacLellan, 104 Hill Street, Glasgow, G3 6UA *T.* 041-332 1066. The main object of the Society is to provide a focal point through which the creative artist in Scotland can find an interested audience whether in his native country or abroad. Information on all aspects of Scottish culture available on request.

Early English Text Society (1864), Lady Margaret Hall, Oxford. *Hon. Director:* Professor Norman Davis, F.B.A.; *Executive Secretary:* Dr. Anne Hudson. To bring unprinted early English literature within the reach of students in sound texts. Annual subscription, £7.50.

Edinburgh Bibliographical Society (1890), c/o National Library of Scotland, Edinburgh, EH1 1EW *T.* 031-226 4531 ext. 255. *Secretary:* I. C. Cunningham; *Treasurer:* J. M. Pinkerton.

Educational Writers Group, 84 Drayton Gardens, London, SW10 9SD. *T.* 01-373 6642. *Secretary:* Philippa MacLiesh. A specialist unit within the framework of The Society of Authors.

Edwardian Studies Association (1975), High Orchard, 125 Markyate Road, Dagenham, Essex, RM8 2LB. Promotion of integrated approach to studies of Edwardians—Shaw, Wells, Conrad, etc. Publishes: *Edwardian Studies.*

Eighteen Nineties Society, The, 28 Carlingford Road, Hampstead, London, NW3 1RX. *President:* Brian Reade. *Secretary:* Dr. G. Krishnamurti. Formed in 1963 as The Francis Thompson Society, it widened its scope in 1972 to embrace the entire artistic and literary scene of the eighteen-ninety decade. Its activities include exhibitions, lectures, poetry readings. Publishes biographies of neglected authors and artists of the period; also check lists, bibliographies, etc. Its Journal appears periodically, and includes biographical, bibliographical and critical articles and book reviews. The Journal is free to members, and is not for public sale.

George Eliot Fellowship, The (1930). *President:* Tenniel Evans (great, great nephew of George Eliot). *Secretary:* Mrs. K. M. Adams, 71 Stepping Stones Road, Coventry, CV5 8JT *T.* (0203) 592231. Promotes an interest in the life and work of George Eliot and helps to extend her influence. Monthly meetings are arranged and an annual magazine is produced. Annual subscription £1.00.

Empire Art Loan Exhibitions Society, 17 Carlton House Terrace, London, SW1Y 5BD. *T.* 01-930 6844. *Organising Director:* Maurice Bradshaw. To arrange, from public or private sources, exhibitions for loan within the British Commonwealth.

English Association, 1 Priory Gardens, Bedford Park, London, W4 1TT *T.* 01-995 4236. *President:* Dr. R. W. Burchfield; *Secretary:* Lt.-Col. R. T. Brain, M.C., M.A.

English Speaking Board (International), Ltd., 32 Roe Lane, Southport, Merseyside, PR9 9EA *T* Southport 34587. *President:* Sir Michael Redgrave; *Chairman:* Gerard Meath; *Director:* Christabel Burniston. *Aim:* to foster all activities concerned with English speech. It conducts examinations and training courses for teachers and students where stress is on individual oral expression. The examination auditions include talks, prepared and unprepared. Examinations are also held for those engaged in technical or industrial concerns, and for those using English as an acquired language. Three times a year, in January, May and September, members receive the English Speaking Board Journal, *Spoken English.* Articles are invited by the editor on any special aspect of spoken English. Members can also purchase other publications at reduced rates. Individual membership £4 per annum (£35 Life membership). Residential summer conference held annually, July–August. A.G.M. in London in the spring.

Folklore Society, The (1878), c/o University College, Gower Street, London, WC1E 6BT *T.* 01-387 5894. *Hon Secretary:* Venetia J. Newall, M.A., F.R.G.S., F.R.S.A., F.R.A.I. Collection, recording and study of folklore.

Foreign Press Association in London (1888). *President:* F. Beer, *Hon. Secretary:* S. M. Mustafa. *Registered office:* 11 Carlton House Terrace, London SW1Y 5AJ *T.* 01-930 0445 and 8883. *Objects:* The promotion of the professional interests of its members. Membership open to overseas professional journalists, men or women, residing in the United Kingdom. Entrance fee, £25.00; annual subscription, £25.00.

Freelance Photographers, Bureau of (1965), Focus House, 497 Green Lanes, London, N13 4BP *T.* 01-882 3315. *Head of Administration:* John Tracy. To help the freelance photographer by providing information on markets, and free advisory service. Membership fee £9.50 per annum.

FPS (Free Painters & Sculptors), (1952), 15 Buckingham Gate, London, SW1E 6LB. *Secretary:* Nina Hosali. Open Annual London Exhibition. Provincial Exhibitions for Members. Seeks to exhibit the work of progressive-minded artists, irrespective of their differing points of view; to provide opportunities for members to meet and discuss their work by means of lectures, discussions or other ways appropriate. Loggia Gallery and Sculpture Garden available for members to exhibit. *T.* 01-828 5963. (Weekdays 6–8 p.m., Sat. and Sun. 2–6 p.m.)

Graphic Artists, Society of, (1919), 17 Carlton House Terrace, London, SW1Y 5BD *T.* 01-930 6844. *President:* F. Winter. *Secretary:* Gordon Alexander. Membership open to both men and women. Annual exhibition. Drawings and prints in any medium, including collages and constructions.

Green Room (1877), 8–9 Adam Street, London, WC2N 6AA. *T.* 01-240 2844–5. *Subs:* £35. Country membership £15.00. *Entrance fee:* £10.00. Dramatic, musical, literary, artistic. The Club is instituted to promote the association of members of the dramatic profession.

Greeting Card and Calendar Association, The, 6 Wimpole Street, London, W1M 8AS *T.* 01-580 3121–2.

Hakluyt Society (1846), c/o The Map Library, The British Library: Reference Division, Great Russell Street, London, WC1B 3DG. *President:* Dr. E. S. de Beer C.B.E., F.B.A.; *Hon. Secretaries:* Professor E. M. J. Campbell, M.A., F.S.A., and T. E. Armstrong, M.A., PH.D. Publication of original narratives of voyages, travels, naval expeditions, and other geographical records.

Thomas Hardy Society Ltd., The (1967). *Secretary:* The Revd. J. M. C. Yates, The Vicarage, Haselbury Plucknett, Crewkerne, Somerset, TA18 7PB *T.* Crewkerne 72063. *Subscription:* £3.00 (US $6.00) p.a.

Harleian Society (1896), Ardon House, Mill Lane, Godalming, Surrey, GU7 1HA. *Chairman:* R. O. Dennys, M.V.O., O.B.E., F.S.A., Somerset Herald of Arms; *Secretary:* J. P. Heming, B.A. Instituted for transcribing, printing and publishing the heraldic visitations of Counties, Parish Registers and any manuscripts relating to genealogy, family history and heraldry.

Illustrators, The Association of (1973), 10 Barley Mow Passage, Chiswick, London, W4 4PH *T.* 01-994 6477. To further and promote better relationships between illustrators, agents and clients which will result in the raising of standards and through which individual illustrators can support the common good of illustrators as a whole.

Independent Producers, The Association of (1976), 122 Wardour Street, London, W1V 3LT *T.* 01-437 3549. *Chairman:* Richard Craven, *Administrators:* Clare Downs, Sophie Balhatchet. To encourage production of films and to broaden the base of finance and exhibition beyond that which is currently available for film-makers in the U.K. Membership is largely composed of writers, directors, producers, and also distributors, exhibitors and others involved in film production. Its governing body is the Council of Forty.

Independent Publishers Guild (1962), 120B Pentonville Road, London, N1 9JB *T.* 01-278 8905. Represents the interests of its members—companies who publish and produce books under their own imprint and who are independent of any owning group or consortium—and offers a forum for the exchange of ideas and information on matters of mutual concern. *Annual subscription:* £15.00.

Indexers, The Society of. Objects: (1) to improve the standard of indexing; (2) to maintain a Register of Indexers (for details see p. 448); (3) to act as an advisory body on the qualifications and remuneration of indexers; (4) to publish or communicate books, papers and notes on the subject of indexing; (5) to raise the status of indexers and to safeguard their interests.
Membership is open to those who do indexing of books and periodicals, and others interested in promoting its objects. There is no entrance fee. *Annual subscription:* £5.00. Copies of the Society's journal, *The Indexer,* are sent free to members. *Secretary:* J. Ainsworth Gordon, 28 Johns Avenue, London, NW4 4EN *T.* 01-203 0929.

Industrial Painters' Group, 17 Carlton House Terrace, London, SW1Y 5BD *T.* 01-930 6844. *Secretary:* Maurice Bradshaw. To introduce industrial patrons to artists.

Institute of Incorporated Photographers, Amwell End, Ware, Herts, SG12 9HN *T.* Ware 4011–2. *Director* and *Secretary:* E. I. N. Waughray. (Founded 1901, Incorporated 1921). *Principal Objects:* Professional Qualifying Association; to represent all who practise photography as a profession in any field; to improve the quality of photography; establish recognised examination qualifications and a high standard of conduct; to safeguard the interests of the public and the profession. *Membership:* approx. 4000. Admission can be obtained either via the Institute's examinations, or by submission of work and other information to the appropriate examining board. *Designatory Letters:* F.I.I.P. and A.I.I.P. Fellows, Associates and Licentiates are entitled to the designation Incorporated Photographer or Incorporated Photographic Technician. *Meetings:* The Institute organises numerous meetings and conferences in various parts of the country throughout the year. *Publications:* A monthly journal, *The Photographer* and a bienniel Register of Members and *guide to buyers of photography,* plus various pamphlets and leaflets on professional matters.

International Bureau for Cultural Exchange. *Hon. Secretary:* William Mac-Lellan, 104 Hill Street, Glasgow, G3 6UA *T.* 041-332 1066. The function of the Bureau is to assist artists in travelling abroad on the basis of mutual exchange between artists of different countries. Those working in the arts who wish to present their talents abroad and are prepared to assist in presenting the work of foreign artists in their own country, are invited to write to the Bureau.

Irish Publishers Association, c/o Book Ireland, Kingston House, Ballinteer, Dublin 14.

Richard Jefferies Society, The (1950), 6 Chickerell Road, Swindon, Wilts. *T.* 0793-21512. *President:* Prof. W. J. Keith (Toronto). *Hon. Secretary:* Cyril Wright. Promotes interest in the life, works and associations of Richard Jefferies; helps to preserve buildings and memorials, and co-operates in the development of a Museum in his birthplace. Provides a service to students, lecturers, readers and writers. The Society arranges regular meetings in Swindon, and occasionally elsewhere. Outings and displays are organised. The membership is worldwide. *Annual subscription:* 80p.

Johnson Society of London (1928). *President:* The Very Revd. Dean of Westminster, Dr. Edward Carpenter; *Secretary:* Miss Stella Pigrome, 72 Fairfield Road, East Grinstead, West Sussex, RH19 4HB *T.* 26134. To study the life and works of Doctor Johnson, and to perpetuate his memory in the city of his adoption.

Journalists, The Institute of, R. F. Farmer (*General Secretary*), 1 Whitehall Place, London, SW1A 2HE *T.* 01-930 7441. The senior organisation of the profession, founded in 1883 and incorporated by Royal Charter 1890. Men and women are equally eligible for Fellowship (F.J.I.) and Membership (M.J.I.). Maintains a successful Employment Register and has considerable accumulated funds for the assistance of members; offers a service of free legal advice to members in matters relating to their professional activities. A Free-lance Section maintains close co-operation between editors and publishers and free-lances. A panel of free-lance writers on special subjects is available for the use of editorial publishers. There is also a Special Section for Public Relations Officers. Occasional contributors to the press may be eligible for election as Affiliates. *Subscriptions:* £30.00; Affiliate £20.

Keats-Shelley Memorial Association (1903). *Chairman:* Lord Abinger; *Patron:* H.M. Queen Elizabeth the Queen Mother. *Hon. Secretary:* Mrs. C. M. Gee, Keats House, Wentworth Place, Keats Grove, London, NW3 2RR *T.* 01-435 2062. Occasional meetings; annual *Bulletin* and progress reports. Supports house in Rome where John Keats died, and celebrates the poets Keats, Shelley, Byron, and Leigh Hunt. Subscription to "Friends of the Keats-Shelley Memorial" minimum £5.00 per annum.

Kent and Sussex Poetry Society, centre Tunbridge Wells, formed in 1947 to create a greater interest in Poetry. *President:* Patric Dickinson; *Chairman:* Dr. G. Wallace; *Hon. Secretary:* Mrs. Iris Munns, 40 St. James' Road, Tunbridge Wells, TN1 2JZ *T.* 24098. *Annual Subscription:* adults, £2.00; under 18, 50p. Well-known poets address the society, a Folio of members' work is published, and a full programme of recitals, discussions and readings is provided.

Kipling Society, The. *President:* James Cameron. *Hon. Secretary:* John Shearman, 18 Northumberland Avenue, London, WC2N 5BJ *T.* 01-930 6733. *Aims:* To honour and extend the influence of Kipling, to assist in the study of Kipling's writings, to hold discussion-meetings, to publish a quarter journal and to maintain a Kipling Reference Library. Membership details on application.

Lancashire Authors' Association, The (1909), "for writers and lovers of Lancashire literature." *President:* L. M. Angus-Butterworth, M.A., F.S.A.Scot.; *General Secretary:* Mrs. Celia Harvey, 8 Whitefield Road East, Penwortham, Preston, Lancashire, PR1 0XJ *T.* Preston 45785. *Subscription:* £2.50 p.a. *Publications: The Record.*

Learned and Professional Society Publishers, The Association of (1972), The association aims to promote and develop the publishing activities of learned and professional organisations which produce journals and other publications. Membership is open to professional and learned societies with publishing interests: details are available from the Secretary, Robert J. Millson, Institution of Mechanical Engineers, 1 Birdcage Walk, Westminster, London, SW1H 9JJ *T.* 01-839 1211.

Liaison of Actors, Managements & Playwrights (LAMP). *Director:* Winifred Robi, 86 Elgin Avenue, London, W9 2HD *T.* 01-286 5378. Formed with the aim of producing rehearsed stage-readings of new plays in order to bring actors, managements and playwrights into closer contact. Every first Thursday in the month at Lamb & Flag, Rose Street, off Garrick Street, London, WC2, at 8 p.m.

Library Association, 7 Ridgmount Street, London, WC1E 7AE. *T.* 01-636 7543. *Patron:* H.M. The Queen; *President:* Godfrey Thompson, M.A., F.R.S.A., F.L.A. *Secretary:* R. P. Hilliard, B.SC., FCA. Founded in 1877 to promote bibliographical study and research and the better administration of libraries, and to unite all persons interested in library work. Conferences and meetings are held, publications issued and a library and information department maintained. The monthly journal, *The Library Association Record*, is distributed free to all members. Subscription varies according to income.

Library Association of Australia The, Science Centre, 35 Clarence Street, Sydney, N.S.W., 2000. *T.* 29 7724. *Executive Director:* Gordon Bower. The Association is an Australia-wide organisation incorporated by Royal Charter in 1963, with c.8000 members, of whom c. 5000 are professional members. The objects of the Association are (*a*) to promote, establish and improve libraries and library services; and (*b*) to improve the standard of librarianship and the status of the library profession. It publishes the *Australian Library Journal* twenty times a year, as well as a range of specialist publications to cater for the interests of members in different types of libraries. The governing body of the Association is the General Council, which consists of an Executive Committee elected by the membership-at-large, two Councillors elected by the membership-at-large, one Councillor elected by the membership-at-large of each State and Territory and the Chairman, Board of Education and the Executive Director, ex officio.

Literary Fund, The Royal (1790), 11 Ludgate Hill, London, EC4M 7AE *T.* 01-248 4138. Grants made to necessitous authors of some published work of approved literary merit or their dependants. *President:* Janet Adam Smith; *Secretary:* Victor Bonham-Carter.

Literary Societies, Alliance of. *Secretary:* Mrs. Kathleen Adams, 71 Stepping Stones Road, Coventry, CV5 8JT *T.* (0203) 592231. An informal alliance of a number of Literary Societies formed to give mutual help in preserving particularly properties with literary associations.

Literature, Royal Society of (1823), 1 Hyde Park Gardens, London, W2 2LT. *T.* 01-723 5104. Fellows and Members. Men and women. *President:* The Rt. Hon. Lord Butler, C.H.; *Chairman of Council:* Hon. C. M. Woodhouse, D.S.O., O.B.E., F.R.S.L.; *Secretary:* Mrs. P. M. Schute. For the advancement of literature by the holding of lectures, discussions, readings, and by publications. Administrators of the Dr. Richards' Fund and the Royal Society of Literature Award, under the W. H. Heinemann Bequest and the Winifred Holtby Memorial Prize.

London Writer Circle. For mutual help among writers of all grades. Lectures, study groups, MS. clubs, discussions, competitions. *Subs.:* £4.00 (town); £2.00 (country). Entrance fee: 25p. Full particulars from the *Hon. Secretary,* Miss M. E. Harris, 308 Lewisham Road, London, SE13 7PA.

Marine Artists, Royal Society of, 17 Carlton House Terrace, London, SW1Y 5BD *T.* 01-930 6844. *President:* Keith Shackleton. *Secretary:* Carl de Winter. To promote and encourage marine art. Open Annual Exhibition: October.

Master Photographers Association, 76 Vine Lane, Hillingdon, Middlesex, UB10 0BE *T.* Uxbridge 33372. *Cables:* BPEG, Uxbridge. To promote and protect professional photography in all its applications. *Subscription:* £17.00 a year. Members can qualify for awards of Associateship and Fellowship.

Mechanical-Copyright Protection Society Ltd., Elgar House, 380 Streatham High Road, London, SW16 6HR *T.* 01-769 3181. See also page 306.

Medical Journalists' Association (1966), 81 Woodlands Avenue, London, E11 3RB *T*. 01-989 0961. Formed by doctor-writers and journalist/broadcasters specialising in medicine and the health services. Aims to improve the quality and practice of medical journalism both ethical and lay; to provide the means for discussing subjects of common interest to medical journalists; and to improve relationships and understanding between journalists and the medical profession. Activities include visits, working parties, discussion meetings and joint meetings with other groups. Administers an annual Award for medical journalism. Annual subscription: £3.50. *General Secretary:* Jerry Cowhig.

Miniature Painters, Sculptors and Gravers, Royal Society of (1895), 17 Carlton House Terrace, London, SW1Y 5BD *T*. 01-930 6844. *President:* Raymond Lister. *Secretary:* Carl de Winter. Open Annual Exhibition—November/December.

Miniaturists, Society of (1895), R.W.S. Galleries, 26 Conduit Street, London, W1R 9TA *T*. 01-629 8300. Malcolm Fry (Secretary). Members only (both men and women). Annual Exhibition in August.

Motoring Writers, The Guild of, Fairfield, Pyrford Woods, Woking, Surrey, GU22 8QT *T*. Byfleet 44905. *General Secretary:* Jean Peters. To raise the standard of motoring journalism. For writers, broadcasters, photographers on matters of motoring, but who are not connected with the motor industry.

Mural Painters, Society of, 17 Carlton House Terrace, London, SW1Y 5BD *T*. 01-930 6844. *Secretary:* Maurice Bradshaw. To promote and encourage the art of mural painting.

Musical Association, The Royal, c/o Department of Manuscripts, British Library, Great Russell Street, London, WC1B 3DG *T*. 01-636 1544.

Musicians, Incorporated Society of, 10 Stratford Place, London, W1N 9AE *T*. 01-629 4413. *President:* 1978–9: Sir David Willcocks; *General Secretary:* Susan M. Alcock. Representative body of professional musicians; its objects are the promotion of the art of music and maintenance of the honour and interests of the musical profession. *Subscription:* £15.00 per annum.

National Book League, 7 Albemarle Street, London, W1X 4BB *T*. 01-493 9001–5, 01-493 3501. Founded in 1925 as the National Book Council, and incorporated as an educational charity. *President:* Lord Goodman; *Director:* Martyn Goff; *Deputy Director:* Stanley Jackson. The League's principal aim is to foster the growth of a wider and more discriminating interest in books. The membership now exceeds 4,000. Among the League's services free to its members are a lending library of books about books, and the use of the Book Information Service. Book lists on many subjects are published. The League organises touring exhibitions which are shown in many parts of the country. It also takes part in research projects and administers many literary prizes, including the £1,000 Booker Prize for Fiction; also The New Fiction Society and The School Bookshop Association. The headquarters is a meeting-place for members with a buffet and bar. The League produces a quarterly newsletter, *Book News*, circulated to members. Membership is open to all. Annual subscriptions: £6.50. Special facilities and subscriptions for libraries, schools and other corporate bodies. Full details may be had on application to the League.

National Society of Painters, Sculptors & Printmakers (1930), 17 Carlton House Terrace, London, SW1Y 5BD *T.* 01-930 6844. *President:* Krome Barratt, v.p.r.o.i.; *Secretary:* Carl de Winter. For artists of every creed and outlook for an annual Exhibition representing all aspects of art.

National Union of Journalists. *General Secretary:* Kenneth Ashton. Head Office: Acorn House, 314 Gray's Inn Road, London, WC1X 8DP *T.* 01-278 7916. A trade union for working journalists, with 29,602 members and 188 branches throughout the British Isles and Ireland, and in Paris and Brussels. Its wages and conditions agreements cover the whole of the newspaper press, the major part of periodical and book publishing, the news, publications and public relations departments of radio and T.V. services and a number of public relations departments and consultancies. Administers disputes, unemployment, benevolent, and widow and orphan benefits. N.U.J. Superannuation Fund, a separate society, provide pensions. Official publications: *The Journalist* (contributions are not usually paid for), *Freelance Directory* and several policy pamphlets.

New English Art Club, 17 Carlton House Terrace, London, SW1Y 5BD *T.* 01-930 6844. *Secretary:* Carl de Winter. For persons interested in the art of painting, and the promotion of the fine arts. Open Annual Exhibition.

Newspaper Press Fund, Dickens House, 35 Wathen Road, Dorking, Surrey, RH4 1JY *T.* Dorking 87511. *Secretary:* P. W. Evans. For the relief of necessitous newspaper journalists who are members of the fund, their widows, and other dependants. Limited help is available for non-members.

Newspaper Publishers Association, Ltd., The, 6 Bouverie Street, London, EC4Y 8AY *T.* 01-583 8132.

Newspaper Society, Whitefriars House, Carmelite Street, London, EC4Y 0BL *T.* 01-353 4722. *Director:* Douglas Lowndes.

Oil Painters, Royal Institute of (1883), 17 Carlton House Terrace, London, SW1Y 5BD *T.* 01-930 6844. *President:* Alan Gourley; *Secretary:* Carl de Winter. Membership (R.O.I.) open to both men and women. Annual Exhibition is open to all artists.

P.E.N., International. A world association of writers. *International President:* Mario Vargas Llosa. *International Secretary:* Peter Elstob. *President of English Centre:* Lettice Cooper. *General Secretary of English Centre:* Josephine Pullein-Thompson. *Headquarters:* 7 Dilke Street, London, SW3 4JE *T.* 01-352 9549 and 6303. *Cables:* Lonpenclub—London—SW3. *Membership:* approximately 8000.

P.E.N. was founded in 1921 by C. A. Dawson Scott under the presidency of John Galsworthy, to promote friendship and understanding between writers and defend freedom of expression within and between all nations. The initials P.E.N. stand for Poets, Playwrights, Editors, Essayists, Novelists —but membership is open to all writers of standing (including translators), whether men or women, without distinction of creed or race, who subscribe to these fundamental principles. P.E.N. takes no part in state or party politics; it has given care to, and raised funds for, refugee writers, and also administers the P.E.N. Writers In Prison Committee which works on behalf of writers imprisoned for exercising their right to freedom of expression, a right implicit in the P.E.N. Charter to which all members subscribe. Through the P.E.N.–UNESCO Translations' Scheme the two bodies cooperate to promote the translation of works by writers in the lesser-known languages. International Congresses are held most years. In 1976 the English Centre were hosts to the 41st Congress.

Membership of the English Centre is £8.00 per annum for country members, £10 for London members. Associate membership is available for striving writers and persons connected with literature. There is also a category of Corporate Membership (for schools, bookshops, firms, etc.) with an annual subscription of £25.00. Membership of any one Centre implies membership of all Centres at present 73 autonomous Centres exist throughout the world. The English Centre holds frequent discussions and other meetings, a monthly Club Night and occasional literary weekends, and has organised several large-scale conferences; distinguished writers are entertained.

Publications: P.E.N. Broadsheet; P.E.N. Bulletin of Selected Books (bilingual, Fr-Eng., reviews of books in languages of limited currency; sponsored by UNESCO); News Bulletins published by various Centres; English Centre edited a series of annual anthologies of contemporary poetry; *New Poems*—1952–62; from 1965 the volume appeared biennially and from 1972 to 1977 annually. From 1978 PEN and the Arts Council have combined to publish *New Poems* and *New Stories* annually. A report on the June 1964 Oslo Congress, *The Writer and Semantics—Literature as Concept, Meaning and Expression*, was published in *Arena*. A report on the 1966 New York Congress, *The Writer as Independent Spirit*, was published late in 1968, and reports on the Congress in Seoul (1970), Dublin (1971), and Israel (1974) have also appeared.

Painter-Etchers and Engravers, Royal Society of (1880), 26–27 Conduit Street, London, W1R 9TA *T.* 01-493 5436. *President:* H. N. Eccleston, R.W.S. *Secretary:* Malcolm Fry. Fellows (R.E.) and Associates (A.R.E.) may be either men or women. Annual Exhibition: February/March, normally open to non-members. Particulars from the Secretary.

Painters in Water Colours, Royal Institute of (1831), 17 Carlton House Terrace, London, SW1Y 5BD *T.* 01-930 6844. *President:* Aubrey Sykes; *Secretary General:* Maurice Bradshaw. Membership (R.I.) open to both men and women. Exhibitions are open to all artists.

Painters in Water-Colours, Royal Society of (founded 1804), 26–27 Conduit Street, London, W1R 9TA *T.* 01-629 8300. Ernest Greenwood, A.R.C.A. (*President*); Malcolm Fry (*Secretary*). Membership (R.W.S.) open to both men and women. An election of Associates is held usually in January of each year, and applications for the necessary forms and particulars should be addressed to the Secretary in November. Exhibitions: April/September.

Pantomime Association, British, c/o Department of Drama, University of Manchester, Manchester, M13 9PL. *Founder:* Gyles Brandreth. *Acting Director:* David Mayer. Founded to foster greater interest in the traditions of British pantomime. Reference library, information service. Organises exhibitions, lectures, conferences. *Subscription:* £2.00 p.a.; *overseas* £5.00 p.a.

Pastel Society, The (1899), 17 Carlton House Terrace, London, SW1Y 5BD *T.* 01-930 6844. *President:* Aubrey Sykes, P.R.I. *Secretary:* Gordon Alexander. Membership open to both men and women. Exhibitions are open to all artists. Pastel and drawings in pencil or chalk.

Mervyn Peake Society, The (1975). *Hon. President:* Maeve Gilmore; *Chairman:* John Watney, 36/5 Elm Park Gardens, London, SW10. Aims to promote wider appreciation and understanding of Mervyn Peake's work as novelist, poet, playwright, illustrator and painter. Publishes *The Mervyn Peake Review* (*Editor:* G. Peter Winnington, Les 3 Chasseurs, 1411 Orzens, Vaud, Switzerland) twice a year, containing articles (2000–4000 words) and book reviews (1500–3000 words). *Annual subscription:* £3 (U.K.); £4 (overseas); $10 (U.S.A.).

Penman Club, The, 175 Pall Mall, Leigh-on-Sea, Essex, SS9 1RE *T.* Southend 74438. *President:* Trevor J. Douglas. *General Secretary:* Leonard G. Stubbs, F.R.S.A. Literary Society for writers throughout the World, published and unpublished. Members in almost every country. Benefits of membership include criticism of all MSS. without additional charge. Quarterly Magazine and use of large writers' library. *Subscription:* £3.25 p.a. S.A.E. for Prospectus, available from the General Secretary.

Performing Right Society, Ltd. (1914), 29–33 Berners Street, London, W1P 4AA *T.* 01-580 5544. See also page 306.

Periodical Publishers Association, Imperial House, Kingsway, London, WC2 6UN *T.* 01-836 9204 and 7111. *Executive Director:* Tom Hoosun.

Personal Managers' Association, Ltd., The, c/o Fraser & Dunlop, Ltd., 91 Regent Street, London, W1R 8RU *T.* 01-734 7311. *Chairman:* Peter Dunlop. An association of Personal Managers in the theatre, film and entertainment world generally.

Philosophical Society of England, The (1913). *President:* John Wilson, M.A.; *Chairman of the Council:* Canon J. Holloway, B.D., M.TH., F.PH.S. Membership open to all interested in Philosophy. Associate and Fellowship status by examination and Thesis. Open lectures by leading Philosophers. Study groups. Journals: *The Philosopher.* All details from *General Secretary:* Rev. Dr. Edgar J. Ford, M.A., PH.D., E.PH.S., 14 Thompson Street, The Manor, Willenhall, West Midlands, WV13 1SY. *Branches:* Manchester, London, Glasgow, Edinburgh and U.S.A.

Photographic Society, The Royal (1853), 14 South Audley Street, London, W1Y 5DP *T.* 01-493 3967. Aims to promote the general advancement of photography and its applications. Publish *The Photographic Journal* bi-monthly, £6.00 p.a., overseas £6.65 p.a. and *The Journal of Photographic Science* bi-monthly, £14.00 p.a., overseas £15.00.

Player-Playwrights (1948), 1 Hawthorndene Road, Hayes, Bromley, Kent. Weekly meetings in Central London. A society for the benefit of newcomers to Play and T.V. writing. Members' plays tried out on well-equipped stage, followed by discussion and friendly criticism. Annual subscription £2.00. Meetings: 30p. each .

Playwrights Workshop (1949). A meeting place where those people in the Manchester Area interested in drama can meet to discuss playwriting in general and their own plays in particular. Details of places and times of meetings from *Hon. Secretary:* Albert Dobson, 15 Sealand Road, Wythenshawe, Manchester, M23 0JF *T.* 061-998 7284.

Poetry Lovers' Fellowship. *President:* D. M. Gibbons Turner. *Hon. Sec. General:* Marjorie Dawson, M.A. *Hon. Sec. North Region* and *Acting Hon. Sec.:* Lucy Carter, 16 Bocking Lane, Beauchief, Sheffield, S8 7BH. In connection with its campaign against the debasement of English manners, morals, ethics, language and speech by sound-film, wireless, press, state schools and public libraries, it runs examinations in (1) Reading Aloud, (2) Dramatic Speech, (3) Poetry-Speaking, (4) Choral Speaking, (5) Public Speaking, (6) Mime, (7) Storytelling, (8) Shakespeare, (9) Handwriting, etc.; and issues handbooks of technical instruction. The Fellowship also awards an annual prize of £5 for the best essay of 5000 words (general subject: Our Struggle against the Cad).

Poetry Society, The (1909) Incorporated, 21 Earls Court Square, London, SW5. *T.* 01-373 7861 and 2551. *Chairman:* Paddy Kitchen; *General Secretary:* Michael Beckerman; *Treasurer:* Vicky Allen. This Society is the national Society for the encouragement of the art. It provides a forum for all poets and poetry lovers. It has information and library services and competitions. It conducts verse speaking examinations leading to the Society's Gold Medal. Its Centres and Affiliations cover the United Kingdom and other countries. The official organ of the Society is *The Poetry Review.*

Poet's Workshop, The, *Secretary:* James Sutherland-Smith, 21 Earl's Court Square, London, SW5 9BY. The Workshop is a discussion group consisting of poets, both published and unpublished, critics, and people with a serious interest in poetry. Members meet fortnightly in Central London to discuss new unpublished work by a fellow member which is circulated in book form before the meeting. The aim is to help a poet to judge the effectiveness of his work from detailed discussion by an informed and sympathetic audience. Enquiries and visitors welcome.

Portrait Painters, Royal Society of (1891), 17 Carlton House Terrace, London, SW1Y 5BD *T.* 01-930 6844. *President:* Edward Halliday, C.B.E., P.P.R.B.A. *Secretary:* Maurice Bradshaw. Annual Exhibition is arranged in the Galleries, when work may be submitted by non-members with a view to exhibition.

Portrait Sculptors, Society of (1952), 17 Carlton House Terrace, London, SW1Y 5BD *T.* 01-930 6844. ' *President:* Sheila Mitchell; *Secretary:* Maurice Bradshaw. Membership open to men and women. Open Exhibition held annually.

Press Club (1882), 76 Shoe Lane, London, EC4A 3JB *T.* 01-353 2644. Lord Barnetson (*President*), Ron Lawrence (*Secretary*). *Subs.:* £36.00 plus VAT town, £15.00 plus VAT country and £5.00 plus 40p VAT overseas. Entrance fees £20, £10 and £5 respectively. *Eligibility:* men and women in journalism, publishing and allied occupations.

Press Council, The (1953), Independent. *Chairman:* Patrick Neill, Q.C.; *Director:* Noël S. Paul, 1 Salisbury Square, London, EC4Y 8AE *T.* 01-353 1248.

Private Libraries Association (1956), Ravelston, South View Road, Pinner, Middlesex. *President:* Douglas Cleverdon; *Hon. Editor:* John Cotton. *Subscriptions:* £8.00 per annum. International society of book collectors and private libraries. Publications include the quarterly *Private Library*, annual *Private Press Books*, and other books on book collecting. Associated with The Book Plate Society.

Publishers Association, 19 Bedford Square, London, WC1B 3HJ. Established 1896. *T.* 01-580 6321–5. *President:* Graham C. Greene: *Chief Executive and Secretary:* Clive Bradley; *Deputy Secretary:* Peter Phelan; *Education Secretary:* John Davies; *International Secretary:* Malcolm Rowland. The national association of British publishers, incorporating the Book Development Council and the Educational Publishers Council, whose over-all membership represents some 360 firms (starred in the list of British Publishers given earlier in this book).

Radiowriters Association, The (1947), 84 Drayton Gardens, London, SW10 9SD *T.* 01-373 6642. A specialist unit within the general framework of the Society of Authors exclusively concerned with the interests and special problems of radiowriters. Members are entitled to advice on all questions connected with their work for broadcasting, and free access to the Secretariat of the Society should they require legal advice. The annual subscription is £18.00 which includes membership of the Society of Authors. Full particulars may be obtained from the offices of the Association.

Regional Arts Associations. The Arts Council of Great Britain, as well as local authorities, local education authorities, industry, charitable trusts and private patrons, provides funds for Regional Arts Associations which promote the arts in their region.

With their grasp of regional needs and demands they are well equipped to provide a service of information, help and guidance to all kinds of arts organisations in their area, and in many cases can provide financial assistance. They can take the initiative in promoting activities themselves and in planning and co-ordinating regional tours. Most of them issue periodically a magazine or broadsheet containing a calendar of forthcoming events. They can offer transport subsidies to parties travelling to various kinds of performances, etc.

Representatives of all the associations meet as the Standing Conference of Regional Arts Associations.

The subsidy responsibility for many activities in England and Wales has been transferred from the Arts Council of Great Britain to the Regional Arts Associations, but the Arts Council retains as direct beneficiaries a considerable number of the larger organisations, including certain regional theatre companies and major festivals.

Annual subscriptions for Full Membership (Organisations) and Associate Membership (Individuals) vary between the Associations and details may be obtained from the addresses listed below. Membership entitles one to the periodicals and broadsheets and to other benefits.

There are at present no regional arts associations in Scotland and all enquiries should be addressed to The Scottish Arts Council, 19 Charlotte Square, Edinburgh, EH2 4DF *T.* 031-226 0651.

ENGLAND

Eastern Arts Association (1971), 30 Station Road, Cambridge, CB1 2JH *T.* 0223 67707. *Director:* Christopher Rye. Bedfordshire, Cambridgeshire, Essex, Hertfordshire, Norfolk and Suffolk.

East Midlands Arts (1969), Mountfields House, Forest Road, Loughborough, Leicestershire, LE11 3HU *T.* 0509 218292. *Director:* Robert Smith. Derbyshire (excluding High Peak District), Leicestershire, Northamptonshire, Milton Keynes District of Buckinghamshire, Nottinghamshire.

Greater London Art Association (1968), 25–31 Tavistock Place, London, WC1H 9SF *T.* 01-387 9541–5. *Director:* David Pratley. The area of the 32 London Boroughs and the City of London.

Lincolnshire and Humberside Arts (1964), Beaumont Lodge, Beaumont Fee, Lincoln, LN1 1UN *T.* 0522 33555. *Director:* Clive Fox. Lincolnshire and Humberside.

Merseyside Arts Association (1968), Bluecoat Chambers, School Lane, Liverpool, L1 3BX *T.* 051-709 0671–2–3. *Director:* Peter Bevan. Metropolitan County of Merseyside, District of West Lancashire, Ellesmere Port and Neston and Halton Districts of Cheshire.

Northern Arts (1961), 31 New Bridge Street, Newcastle-upon-Tyne, NE1 8JY *T.* 0632 610446. *Director:* David Dougan. Cumbria, Cleveland, Metropolitan County of Tyne and Wear, Northumberland and Durham.

North West Arts (1966), 52 King Street, Manchester, M2 4LY *T.* 061-833 9471. *Director:* Raphael Gonley. Greater Manchester, High Peak District of Derbyshire, Lancashire (except District of West Lancashire), Cheshire (except Ellesmere Port and Halton Districts).

Southern Arts Association (1968), 19 Southgate Street, Winchester, Hants, SO23 9EB *T.* 0962 69422. *Director:* Bill Dufton. Berkshire, Hampshire, Isle of Wight, Oxfordshire, West Sussex, Wiltshire, Districts of Bournemouth, Christchurch and Poole.

South East Arts Association (1973), 58 London Road, Southborough, Tunbridge Wells, Kent, TN4 0PR *T.* 0892 38743. *Director:* Peter Carpenter. Kent, Surrey and East Sussex.

South West Arts (1956), 23 Southernhay East, Exeter, Devon, EX1 1QL *T.* 0392 70338--9. *Director:* Ian Watson. Avon, Cornwall, Devon, Dorset (except Districts of Bournemouth, Christchurch and Poole), Gloucestershire, Somerset.

West Midlands Arts (1971), Lloyds Bank Chambers, Market Street, Stafford, ST16 2AP *T.* 0785 59231–5. *Director:* Geoffrey Sims. County of Hereford and Worcester, Metropolitan County of West Midlands, Salop, Staffordshire, Warwickshire.

Yorkshire Arts Association (1969), Glyde House, Glydegate, Bradford, West Yorkshire, BD5 0BQ *T.* 0274 23051. *Director:* Michael Dawson. North Yorkshire, South Yorkshire, West Yorkshire.

WALES

North Wales Arts Association (1967), 10 Wellfield House, Bangor, Gwynedd, LL57 1ER *T.* 0248 53248. *Director:* D. Llion Williams, Clwyd, Gwynedd and District of Montgomery in the County of Powys.

South East Wales Arts Association (1973), Victoria Street, Cwmbran, Gwent, NP4 3JP *T.* 063-33 67530. *Director:* Peter Booth. South Glamorgan, Mid-Glamorgan, Gwent, Districts of Radnor and Brecknock in the County of Powys, and the City of Cardiff.

West Wales Association for the Arts (1971), Dark Gate, Red Street, Carmarthen, Dyfed, SA31 1QL *T.* 0267 4248. *Director:* T. D. Scourfield. Dyfed, West Glamorgan.

Romantic Novelists' Association, The. *Chairman:* Elizabeth Harrison, 30 Langham House Close, Ham Common, Richmond, Surrey. *Hon. Secretary:* Beatrice Taylor, Bell's Farm House, Spurriers Lane, Melling, Liverpool, L31 1BA. To raise the prestige of Romantic Authorship. Open to romantic and historical novelists.
See also under Literary Awards.

Royal Academy of Arts, Piccadilly, London, W1V 0DS *T.* 01-734 9052. Academicians (R.A.) and Associates (A.R.A.) are elected from the most distinguished artists in the United Kingdom. Major loan exhibitions throughout the year with the Annual Summer Exhibition, May to July. Also runs art schools for 80 students, mainly post-graduate, in painting and sculpture.

Royal Birmingham Society of Artists, 69A New Street, Birmingham, 2. *T.* 643 3768. *President:* Joan Woollard, R.B.S.A., F.R.B.S.; *Hon. Secretary:* Graham Stokes, R.B.S.A. The Society has its own galleries and rooms prominently placed in the city centre. Members (R.B.S.A.) and Associates (A.R.B.S.A.) are elected annually. There are two annual Spring Exhibitions open to all artists and an Autumn Exhibition of Members' and Associates' works. *Annual Subscription* (Friends of the R.B.S.A.): £2.00 entitles subscribers to season ticket for exhibitions and lectures organised by the Society. Further details from the Hon. Secretary.

Royal Society, The (1660), 6 Carlton House Terrace, London, SW1Y 5AG. *T.* 01-839 5561. *President:* Lord Todd; *Secretaries:* Sir Harrie Massey, Professor D. C. Phillips. Promoting natural knowledge (natural science).

Dorothy L. Sayers Historical and Literary Society, The (1976), *Chairman and Secretary:* R. L. Clarke, Roslyn House, Witham, Essex, CM8 2AQ *T.* Witham 512025. To promote and encourage the study of the works of Dorothy L. Sayers; to collect relics and reminiscences about her and make them available to students and biographers. *Annual subscription:* £1.50.

Scientific and Technical Communicators Ltd., The Institute of (1972), 17 Bluebridge Avenue, Brookmans Park, Hatfield, Herts, AL9 7RY *T.* Potters Bar 55392. *President:* R. G. Martyr, A.R.P.S., F.I.S.T.C.; *Hon. Secretary:* Mrs. Eileen Parkinson; *Press and P.R.O.:* M. Austin. A professional body for those engaged in the communication of scientific and technical information. *Objects:* to establish and maintain professional standards, to encourage and co-operate in professional training and to provide a source of information on, and to encourage research and development in, all aspects of scientific and technical communication. *The Communicator of Scientific and Technical Information* is the official quarterly journal of the Institute, and *The Communicator—News Supplement*, a newsletter, is circulated to members.

Scottish Academy, Royal (1826), Princes Street, Edinburgh, EH2 2EL *T.* 031-225 6671. *President:* Sir Robin Philipson, P.R.S.A., H.R.A., A.R.A.; *Secretary:* James Cumming, R.S.A.; *Treasurer:* H. Anthony Wheeler, O.B.E., R.S.A., P.P.R.I.A.S., F.R.I.B.A.; *Administrative Secretary:* F. K. B. Murdoch, C.V.O., M.B.E., T.D. Academicians (R.S.A.) and Associates (A.R.S.A.) and nonmembers may exhibit in the Annual Exhibition of Painting, Sculpture and Architecture. Annual Exhibition dates approximately mid April to early August, Festival Exhibition August/September. Royal Scottish Academy Diploma Collection, normally between October and January. Royal Scottish Academy Competition held in March.

Scottish Arts, 24 Rutland Square, Edinburgh, EH1 2BW *T.* 031-229 1076. *Secretary:* W. J. Merson. *Entrance fee:* £5.67. *Subs.:* £72.00 and £36.00. Art, literature, music.

Scottish Arts Council, The—see Arts Council of Great Britain.

Scottish History Society (1886), Department of History, Taylor Building, King's College, Old Aberdeen, AB9 2UB. *Hon. Secretary:* D. Stevenson, PH.D. The Society exists to discover and print unpublished documents illustrating the history of Scotland.

Scottish Newspaper Proprietors Association, 10 York Place, Edinburgh, EH1 3ET *T.* 031-556 6787. *President and Chairman:* J. L. M. Cotter. *Director:* W. Barrie Abbott, B.L., C.A. To promote and safeguard newspaper interests, and to assist members who are involved in legal proceedings arising out of matter published in their newspapers.

Senefelder Group of Lithographers, 17 Carlton House Terrace, London, SW1Y 5BD *T.* 01-930 6844. *Secretary:* Maurice Bradshaw. To display original work of lithographers.

Sesame Club, 49 Grosvenor Street, London, W1X 0DN *T.* 01-629 4473. *Subs.:* Town £28.00; Country £22. Literary, social and residential. Men and women.

Shakespearean Authorship Society. *President:* The Duke of St. Albans, O.B.E.: *Hon. Secretary:* Dr. D. W. Thomson Vessey, 10 Uphill Grove, Mill Hill, London, NW7 4NJ *T.* 01-959 3483. *Hon. Treasurer:* John Silberrad, 11 Old Square, Lincoln's Inn, London, WC2A 3TS. Object of the Society is to seek, and if possible establish the truth concerning the authorship of the "Shakespeare" plays and poems. *Annual Subscription:* London £5.00, country and overseas £3.00, students £2.00, library £3.00. Members receive *The Bard* published twice yearly by the Society, and are entitled to use the Society's library.

Bernard Shaw Society, 125 Markyate Road, Dagenham, Essex, RM8 2LB. *Secretary-General:* Eric Ford. *Subscription:* £1.50 p.a.

Sherlock Holmes Society of London, The (1951). *President:* Lord Gore-Booth, G.C.M.G., K.C.V.O.; *Chairman:* Colin Prestige, M.A.(Oxon); *Hon. Secretary:* Capt. W. R. Michell, R.N., J.P., 5 Manor Close, Warlingham, Surrey, CR3 9SF. *Objects:* to bring together those who have a common interest as readers and students of the literature of Sherlock Holmes: to encourage the pursuit of knowledge of the public and private lives of Sherlock Holmes and Dr. Watson: to organize meetings and lectures for the discussion of these topics; to co-operate with other bodies at home and abroad that are in sympathy with the aims and activities of the Society. Membership £5.00 p.a. within 50 miles of Baker Street, £4.00 p.a. outside this radius, including two issues of *The Sherlock Holmes Journal.*

Singapore Book Publishers Association, c/o Angus & Robertson (S.E. Asia) Pty. Ltd., 159 Block 2, Ground Floor, Boon Keng Road, Singapore, 12. *T.* 2582889 and 2582663. *President:* Mr. Koh Hock Seng. *Hon. Secretary:* Tony Poh.

Society of Authors—see **Authors, The Society of.**

South Africa Publishers Association, P.O. Box 123, Kenwyn 7790, South Africa.

SPREd—Society of Picture Research and Editors, c/o National Westminster Bank Ltd., 110 Wardour Street, London, W1V 3LD. A professional organisation whose purpose is to bring picture researchers and editors together, to meet, compare views, pool experience, resolve problems and in general, improve the professional status of picture people.

Strip Illustration, Society of, 28 Ladbroke Grove, London, W11. Founded in 1977 by a group of professionals, the Society is open to artists, writers, editors, and anyone professionally concerned with comics, newspaper strips, and strip illustration. Monthly Newsletter, monthly meetings, and an annual convention.

Sussex Playwrights' Club. Founded in 1935 by a group of playwrights to encourage the art of playwriting and an interest in the theatre. Annual subscription: £1.00. Further particulars from the *Hon. Secretary:* Miss Ethel Bale, 41 Norfolk Road, Brighton, BN1 3AB *T.* 735443.

Syndicat des Representants Litteraires Français, 117 Boulevard St. Germain, Paris VI.

Syndicat National de l'Edition (the French publishers' association), 117 Boulevard St. Germain, Paris 75279. *T.* 329 21-01.

Theatre Research, The Society for. *Hon. Secretaries:* Kathleen Barker and Jack Reading, 14 Woronzow Road, London, NW8 6QE. Publishes annual volumes and journal *Theatre Notebook.*

Francis Thompson Society, The, now incorporated in **The Eighteen Nineties Society,** *q.v.*

Translators Association, The (1958), 84 Drayton Gardens, London, SW10 9SD *T.* 01-373 6642. *Secretary:* George Astley. A specialist unit within the framework of the Society of Authors, exclusively concerned with the interests and special problems of writers who translate foreign literary, dramatic or technical work into English for publication or performance in Great Britain or English-speaking countries overseas. Members are entitled to general and legal advice on all questions connected with the marketing of their work, such as rates of remuneration, contractual arrangements with publishers, editors, broadcasting organisations, etc. The annual subscription is £18.00 and includes membership of the Society of Authors. Full particulars may be obtained from the offices of the Association.

Translators' Guild, of The Institute of Linguists, 24A Highbury Grove, London, N5 2EA *T.* 01-359 7445. All correspondence to be addressed to the *Secretary.* The Translators' Guild is the specialist body within the Institute comprising those members of the Institute who have satisfied the requirements as to experience and competence in particular fields of technical, scientific, commercial and literary translation work. Members of the Guild, with full particulars of their languages and the subjects they can handle, appear in the Translators' Index which is kept up to date by means of quarterly supplements.

Travel Writers, The Guild of, 8–10 Parkway, London, NW1 7AA *T.* 01-267 1128. Home: 28 Oakfield Road, Finchley, London, N3 2HT *T.* 01-346 3772. *Hon. Secretary and Information Officer:* Robin Mead. To assist members by arranging meetings and discussions to extend the range of their knowledge and experience and by writing seriously and conscientiously about travel to contribute to the growth of public interest in and knowledge of the subject. Entrance fee £2, annual subscription £7.

Typographic Designers, Society of, *President:* David Plumb, F.S.T.D.; *Hon. Secretary* and *Membership Secretary:* John Slee-Smith, M.S.T.D., 33 Lord Street, Hoddesdon, Herts, EN11 8NA. A body of typographers and designers engaged in visual communications. The Society endeavours to maintain the highest standards of typography and graphic design and to further developments in this sphere. Through full membership to I.C.O.G.R.A.D.A. it participates actively in international typography and design and participates in higher education. Lectures and discussions to exchange views of common interest are held, open to all members and students of typography and graphic design. Membership is open to all typographers, graphic designers and others engaged in the field of visual communications who submit to the Council of the Society, through the Examining Committee, evidence of their competence. and who agree to accept the aims and principles of the Society. Sustaining members subscription by arrangement. Fellows £18; Members £12; Associates £8.

United Society for Christian Literature (1799), Luke House, Farnham Road, Guildford, Surrey, GU1 4XD *T.* Guildford 77536. *President:* Lord Luke. *Chairman:* The Hon. H. Lawson Johnston. *General Secretary:* Rev. Alec Gilmore, M.A., B.D. To aid and undertake Christian publishing at home and overseas.

United Society of Artists, 17 Carlton House Terrace, London, SW1Y 5BD *T.* 01-930 6844. *President:* Gordon Gunn. *Secretary:* Carl de Winter. An exhibiting Society open to all artists.

Jules Verne Circle, The (1978), High Orchard, 125 Markyate Road, Dagenham, Essex, RM8 2LB. *Secretary:* Eric Ford. Promotion of scholarship and research in the life work and times of Jules Verne. *Subscription:* £2.00 p.a.

H. G. Wells Society, The (1960), 24 Wellin Lane, Edwalton, Nottingham. *T.* 0602 231721. *Secretary:* J. R. Hammond. Promotion of an active interest in, and encouragement of an appreciation of the life, work and thought of H. G. Wells. Publishes *The Wellsian* (annually) and *The Newsletter* (quarterly). Subscription: £2.00 per annum.

Welsh Arts Council, The—see **Arts Council of Great Britain.**

Welsh Books Council—see **Cyngor Llyfrau Cymraeg.**

West Country Writers' Association, The. *President:* Christopher Fry, F.R.S.L.; *Chairman:* Bryan Little; *Hon. Secretary:* Doris Hodges, 5 St. Andrews Road, Backwell, Bristol. *T.* Flax Bourton 2293. Founded in 1951 by Waveney Girvan for the purpose of fostering the love of literature in the West Country. An Annual Week-end Congress is held in a West Country city. There are Regional Meetings of Members, a Newsletter-cum-magazine, and correspondence between members. Membership is by invitation of the Committee. Annual subscription: £3.

Wildlife Artists, Society of, 17 Carlton House Terrace, London, SW1Y 5BD *T.* 01-930 6844. *President:* Sir Peter Scott, C.B.E., D.S.O. *Secretary:* Maurice Bradshaw. To promote and encourage the art of Wildlife painting and sculpture. Open Annual Exhibition.

Women Artists, Society of (1855), 17 Carlton House Terrace, London, SW1Y 5BD. *President:* Miss A. R. Kendall. *Secretary:* Maurice Bradshaw. Annual Exhibition, pictures, sculpture and crafts. Open to all women.

Women Writers and Journalists, Society of, c/o 45 Basildon Court, Devonshire Street, London, W1N 1RH. Founded in 1894 for women writers and artists. Lectures, monthly lunch-time meetings. Free literary advice for members. Quarterly journal: *The Woman Journalist.* Subscription: Town £4.00; Country £3.00; Overseas £2.50.

Worshipful Company of Musicians (1500), 4 St. Paul's Churchyard, London, EC4M 8BA *T.* 01-236 2333. *Clerk:* W. R. I. Crewdson.

Worshipful Company of Stationers and Newspaper Makers (1403), Stationers' Hall, London, EC4M 7DD *T.* 01-248 2934. Master: E. Glanvill Benn; *Clerk:* Colonel R. A. Rubens. One of the Livery Companies of the City of London. Connected with the printing, publishing, bookselling and allied trades.

Writers' Guild of Great Britain, The, 430 Edgware Road, London, W2 1EH *T.* 01-723 8074-5-6. See also page 411.

Writers' Luncheon Club, The. *Chairman:* Lord Willis. *Secretary:* Malcolm Hulke, 45 Parliament Hill, London, NW3 2TA *T.* 01-435 9941. Meets quarterly in London. Always a celebrated guest-of-honour present. No formal membership. Send a stamped addressed envelop to the secretary for further details.

Writers' Union of Canada The, 86 Bloor Street West, Suite 514, Toronto, Ontario, M5S 1M5 *T.* 416-961-7373. *Natonal Chairman:* Charles Taylor.

Yorkshire Dialect Society, The (1897). The aims of the Society are to encourage interest in: (1) Dialect speech; (2) the writing of dialect verse, prose and drama; (3) the publication and circulation of dialect literature and the performance of dialect plays; (4) the study of the origins and the history of dialect and kindred subjects—all dialects, not only of Yorkshire origin. *Annual subscription:* £1.00: life membership, £21.00. *Meetings:* the Society organises a number of meetings during the year—details from the Hon. Secretary. *Annual Publications: Transactions* and *The Summer Bulletin* free to members, list of other publications on request. *Hon. Secretary:* Gerald Williams, Fieldhead House, West Street, Hoyland, Barnsley, S74 9AG.

copyright
tax, services

BRITISH COPYRIGHT

E. P. SKONE JAMES, M.A.

GENERALLY

It is not possible, in a short article such as this must be, to examine the law of British copyright in detail. The general principles are explained, and attention is drawn to many points of special interest. Expert legal advice should be sought in difficult cases.

The Copyright Act, 1956 ("the Act") which substantially replaces the Copyright Act, 1911 ("the Act of 1911"), received the Royal Assent on November 5, 1956, and came into operation on the 1st June 1957. The Act has been amended by the Design Copyright Act 1968, which came into operation on the 25th October 1968, and which deals with the relationship between copyright under the Act and copyright under the Registered Designs Act 1949. Also by the Copyright (Amendment) Act 1971, which came into operation on the 17th February 1971 and which permits applications to the Performing Right Tribunal to review its orders under Section 27.

The Act, though more complicated, will not, it is thought, be found to have made substantial changes affecting the rights of writers and artists. The Act provides (Section 45(5)) that no copyright shall subsist otherwise than by virtue thereof, and the Seventh Schedule to the Act contains lengthy transitional provisions which assume that the provisions of the Act have always been in force, but then proceed to modify its provisions in respect of works which were in existence before its commencement. Thus, devolutions of title to copyright works valid under the Act of 1911 are to be treated as remaining valid, and, in general, copyright which subsisted in works under the Act of 1911, will continue to subsist under the Act. Again, the proviso to Section 3, and Section 4 of the Act of 1911, which dealt respectively with the right, 25 years after the death of the author of a published work, to reproduce the work without infringement of the copyright therein if the necessary notice had been given, and, the right to apply to the Judicial Committee of the Privy Council for a compulsory licence in certain circumstances, and the proviso to Section 5(2) of the Act of 1911 are repealed by the Act: but, if the necessary notice has been given under such proviso before Section 3 is repealed, then, as respects reproductions of that work by the person who gave the notice, after the repeal of Section 3, such proviso is to have effect as if re-enacted in the Act (Paragraph 9, 7th Schedule of the Act), and in the case of an assignment or licence before 1957 under the Act of 1911 there will still be a reverter to the personal representatives of the author at the end of twenty-five years from his death.

The Act also made the necessary changes in the law to enable this country to ratify the Brussels Convention and the Universal Copyright Convention.

In March 1977 the Report of the Whitford Committee to consider the law of copyright and designs was presented to Parliament; Cmmd. 6732. It contains a large number of recommendations for revising the law of copyright and recommends the abolition of registered design protection under the Registered Designs Act 1949. Two of the major recommendations were, first that there should be a system of blanket licensing to cater for all user requirements for facsimile copies; secondly that a levy system should be introduced to apply to the sale of all equipment of a type suitable for private recording, with an additional annual licence fee in the case of educational recording payable under a blanket licensing scheme. These recommendations arise because of the problems created by the increased availability and use of reprographic machines, such as photo copiers and of audio and visual recording equipment, such as tape recorders.

NATURE OF COPYRIGHT

Copyright protection is not given to ideas or systems, plots or themes, however original; it is aimed solely to prevent the copying of literary, musical, dramatic or artistic works, sound recordings, films, television and sound broadcasts and published editions of works. The idea, theme or plot must therefore be reduced into material form before protection can be claimed, and then the protection given is to the form and not to the idea. If the idea is reproduced in a quite different form, this is not an infringement of copyright.

Another basic principle of copyright law is that it does not give a monopoly even to the form selected, since it is directed to preventing copying, and not to giving an absolute title to any particular form of words, or of artistic production. Copyright protection is given to dictionaries and directories and to photographs, but this does not mean that another may not lawfully produce independently an almost identical work; he is only guilty of infringement if he copies the earlier work.

A further important matter in regard to copyright protection is that, in the United Kingdom and most European countries at least (see *post* "Works protected abroad"), no formalities are required. Copyright protection is afforded as soon as the page of manuscript is written, the sketch is drawn or the melody is composed. The work does not need to be printed or published, no form of registration is needed, no "copyright reserved" or other copyright notice is required. Publishers are required to deliver certain copies of published books to certain prescribed libraries (Section 15 of the Act of 1911 as amended, which is not repealed by the Act), but failure to do this does not affect the copyright, though it may give rise to liability for penalties (sub-section (6)). Copies of scripts of certain new plays are required to be delivered to the British Museum under the Theatres Act 1968.

KIND OF WORKS PROTECTED

Literary, dramatic and artistic works are defined in the Act (Sections 48(1) and 3(1); see also definitions of "sculpture", "engraving", "photograph", "building", "construction", "drawing", "manuscript", "writing").

It has been decided that the expression "literary" does not involve any qualification of style, but covers any work expressed in print or writing, so long as it is substantial enough to involve some literary skill and labour of composition. And a similarly slight degree of skill and labour is imposed in regard to other classes of works.

Thus selections of poems, abridgements, notes to school textbooks, arrangements of music, football championship fixtures list and other compilations are protected, provided that it is established that the production has involved a certain amount of intellectual endeavour, and is not merely mechanical. Again in *British Northcrop Ltd* v. *Texteam Blackburn Ltd*. 1973 F.S.R. 241 drawings of such items as screws and bolts were held not too simple to lack originality. But it has been decided that copyright does not subsist in prototypes of chairs and settees as works of artistic craftsmanship: *George Hensher Ltd*. v. *Restawhile Upholstery (Lancs) Ltd*. 1974 2 W.L.R. 700 (H.L.).

Under the Act of 1911 (Section 22), artistic works intended for use as industrial designs were not protected under such Act, but could be protected under the Patents and Designs Acts, 1907–31. If the author of such a work failed to register the work as a design he lost both his artistic and designs copyright. Under the Act (Section 10) the author was not required to register his design until it was actually about to be licensed for industrial use, and, even if so licensed without registration, its artistic copyright was preserved, except in regard to industrial use (see *Dorling* v. *Honnor Marine Ltd.* 1964, 2 W.L.R. 195). On the other hand, the protection against industrial use would endure only for the period of fifteen years provided by its registration. This position has been changed by the Design Copyright Act 1968 in respect of works created after its coming into force. The 1968 Act amends section 10 of the Act in such a way that industrial use will not affect copyright under the Act except to limit the period of protection against industrial use. The position as to pre-1968 works is not made clear by the 1968 Act.

Protection under the Registered Designs Act, 1949, requires certain formalities of registration, and a Patent Agent should be consulted.

Sound recordings, films, television and sound broadcasts are defined in the Act (Sections 12 (9), 13 (10) and 14 (10); and see *post* "Sound recordings", "Films", "Broadcasting and Television", "Published Editions").

PUBLISHED EDITIONS

The Act provides for the first time that a separate copyright is to subsist in every published edition of any literary, dramatic or musical work first published in the United Kingdom, or of which the publisher was a qualified person at the date of first publication. The publisher is entitled to such copyright (Section 15 of the Act).

Copyright in published editions subsists until the end of the period of twenty-five years from the end of the calendar year in which the edition was first published, and such copyright is infringed by making, by any photographic or similar process, a reproduction of the typographical arrangement of the edition.

TITLES AND PSEUDONYMS

The title of a book or story is normally not protected under the Act since it is too short to be treated as a literary work. If, however, a title is taken and used in such a way as to cause confusion, a "passing off" action can often be brought successfully.

A similar cause of action arises if an author's pseudonym is used by another in such a way as to cause the public to believe that the second work is by the first author.

Apart from agreement, if an author has been writing for a periodical under a particular pen name, and ceases to contribute, he is entitled to use the pen name elsewhere, and the periodical is not entitled to continue to use it (and see *post* "Anonymous and Pseudonymous works").

TO WHOM COPYRIGHT PROTECTION IS GIVEN

In general the person to be protected is the author. This means the person who has actually written the book or drawn the picture; in the case of a photograph it means the person who, when the photograph is taken, is the owner of the material on which it is taken. A person who has merely suggested a theme, or supplied information, is not an author. This follows from the general principle stated above that protection is given to form and not ideas; it is the author of a form with whom copyright law is concerned.

However, where a literary, dramatic or artistic work is made by an author in the cause of his employment by the proprietor of a newspaper, magazine or similar periodical under a contract of service or apprenticeship, and is so made for the purpose of publication in a newspaper, etc., such proprietor is entitled to the copyright in the work, but only in so far as the copyright relates to such publication: the remainder of the copyright remains in the author (Section 4 (2) of the Act). Subject to this, in the case of photographs and portraits, engravings and sound recordings (Section 4 (3) and 12 (4) of the Act), if the original is ordered, and paid for, the copyright vests in the client, and not in the artist, photographer or maker.

But, if in a case not falling within either Section 4 (2) or Section 4 (3), a work is made in the course of the author's employment by another person under a contract of service or apprenticeship, that other person, and not the author, is entitled to the copyright in the work (Section 4 (4) of the Act). As to the difficulties in deciding whether a contract is a contract of service or a contract for services see *Beloff* v. *Pressdram Ltd.* 1973 F.S.R. 33. In the case of a full-time employee, work done for the employer out of hours will remain the copyright of the servant.

ANONYMOUS AND PSEUDONYMOUS WORKS

Copyright in published literary, dramatic or musical works, and artistic works other than photographs, which are anonymous or pseudonymous, subsists until the end of the period of fifty years from the end of the calendar year in which the work was first published, unless, at any time before the end of that period, it is possible for a person, without previous knowledge of the facts, to ascertain the identity of the author (or one or more of the authors in the case of joint works), by reasonable enquiry (Second Schedule to the Act). However, publication of a work under two or more names is not pseudonymous unless all the names are pseudonyms.

The normal period of copyright is fifty years from the end of the calendar year in which the author died. In certain circumstances, therefore, a shorter period of protection only is obtained (see also "Duration of copyright protection" *post*).

JOINT AUTHORS

Joint authorship involves that two or more persons must have collaborated to produce a single work. Each must have taken some part in producing jointly the work protected; as has been seen, a man who merely suggests the idea or theme is not an author at all. Again, if the parts produced by each are easily separable, it is not a case of joint authorship, but each owns a separate copyright in each part (Section 11 (3) of the Act). The Act provides that, with certain exceptions, references therein to the author of a work are to be construed in relation to a work of joint authorship as a reference to all the authors of the work (Third Schedule to the Act). The more important exceptions are that, for the purposes of establishing copyright in literary, dramatic, musical and artistic works, it is sufficient if only one of the joint authors satisfies the necessary conditions. Further, if one or more of the joint authors does not satisfy the necessary conditions to establish copyright in the joint work, then the remaining author or authors are to be considered the person or persons entitled to the copyright in such work. In the case of a work of joint authorship, neither can deal with the copyright without the consent of the other or others, but, on the other hand, each can bring actions against the other or third parties for any infringement. Other matters of importance to joint authors are referred to under "Duration of copyright protection" *post*.

ASSIGNMENT OF COPYRIGHT

An assignment of copyright must be in writing and signed by or on behalf of the assignor (Section 36 (3) of the Act), but no other formality is required. If signed on behalf of the assignor, the person signing must have the authority of the assignor to sign; see *Beloff* v. *Pressdram Ltd.* 1973 F.S.R. 33. Copyright may be assigned for certain areas, or for a certain period, or the right may be assigned to do certain of the acts which the copyright owner has the exclusive right to do (e.g. the right to make adaptations, the right to perform, and publishing rights). The right to do acts not separately mentioned in the Act may now be assigned separately.

Future copyright (that is, copyright which will, or may, come into existence in respect of any future work, or on the coming into operation of any of the provisions of the Act, or in any other future event), will vest, on the coming into existence of the copyright, in the assignee under a purported assignment of such copyright, without any further document: such assignment must, however, be in writing, and signed by or on behalf of the prospective owner of such copyright (Section 37 (1) of the Act). In drafting publishing agreements and other transactions, authors will therefore have carefully to consider these provisions.

LICENCES

A mere licence to publish or perform or to do other acts which the copyright owner has the exclusive right to do, does not require to be in writing (unless exclusive, and then only to enable the licensee to sue), but may be implied from conduct (see *Solar Thomson Engineering Co. Ltd.* v. *Barton* 1977 R.P.C. 537 licence implied from wording of patent). Licences in writing may be granted by a prospective owner of copyright in relation to his prospective interest therein (Section 37 (3) of the Act). The principal distinction between the position of an assignee and a licensee is that the former can, but the latter cannot, except in the case of an exclusive licence in writing, sue third parties for the infringement of the right. Other distinctions are referred to under "Publishing Agreements" *post*. However, if a licence (in the Act called an "exclusive licence") is made in writing, and signed by or on behalf of the owner or prospective owner of copyright, authorising the licensee exclusively to do any of the acts which the copyright owner has the exclusive right to do, then the licensee has (except against the owner of the copyright) the same remedies for damages, etc., as if the licence had been an assignment, subject to the owner of the copyright, either being joined as Plaintiff or added as Defendant in certain circumstances (Section 19 of the Act). A licensee, like an assignee, may make alterations in the work unless the terms of the licence expressly or impliedly forbid alterations being made and the courts will readily imply such a term (*Frisby* v. *BBC* 1967 2 W.L.R. 1204). Two cases have considered the extent of an implied licence to use an architect's plans, namely *Blair* v. *Osborne & Tomkins* 1971 2 W.L.R. 503 and *Stovin-Bradford* v. *Volpoint Properties, Ltd.*, 1971 3 W.L.R. 256.

No copyright licence is required in respect of out of copyright works, though it is not always easy to ascertain whether or not a work is still in copyright. Art galleries, for instance, often charge a fee for the right to enter the gallery and to take a photograph of a work of art there, but this is normally a condition of entry into the gallery and has nothing to do with copyright. In many cases the work of art will be out of copyright or, if in copyright, the gallery will probably not be the owner of such copyright and should not permit the photograph to be taken. In either of which cases the gallery would not be entitled to charge a fee in respect of copyright.

WHAT CONSTITUTES INFRINGEMENT

Copyright is infringed by the doing or the authorising of the doing of certain restricted acts, referred to as direct infringements, without the licence of the copyright owner. Authority means "sanction, approve or countenance"; see *Moorhouse* v. *University of New South Wales* 1976 R.P.C. 151. Thus copyright is infringed by the reproduction of any substantial part of a copyright work without permission. Such infringements are proved by a detailed comparison of similarities, and proof is often difficult in the case of compilations which, of necessity, resemble one another; in such cases, copying may be proved from the coincidence of trifling errors. In considering whether the part taken is substantial, more regard is had to the importance than to the quantity of what is taken; *Ladbroke (Football), Ltd.* v. *William Hill (Football), Ltd.* 1964

1 W.L.R. 273. Thus, to take a few bars of the essential melody of a tune may constitute an infringement. An infringement is committed whether the copying has been directly from the original, or through an intervening copy, and may be committed where the copying is from memory; *Francis Day & Hunter, Ltd.* v. *Bron* 1963 2 W.L.R. 868. See solar supra as to the risks of infringing, even where an independent designer is used, because of the instructions which he has to be given to produce the work by a person with knowledge of the copyright work or of an object made therefrom.

Other modes of infringement are: to publish an unpublished work, to make an adaptation of a work, which latter includes making a version of the work in which the story or action is conveyed wholly, or mainly, by means of pictures in a form suitable for reproduction in a book or newspaper, magazine or similar periodical, making a translation, dramatising a book and making a novel of a play. (See also "Performance," "Films," "Records," "Broadcasting and Television" *post*, and "Published Editions" *ante*.) It is to be noted that to parody a work, such as a picture or a play, may not be an infringement if the parody amounts to an original work (*Joy Music, Ltd.* v. *Sunday Pictorial Newspapers* (1920), *Ltd.* 1960 2 W.L.R. 645). Further, to copy an idea or concept as against the form in which it is expressed, is not an infringement; *L.B. (Plastics) Ltd.* v *Swish Products Ltd.* 1978 F.S.R. 32.

In addition to the direct infringements above described, an infringement is committed by anyone who knowingly sells, exhibits in public, distributes or imports (otherwise than for private and domestic use) copies unlawfully made (Section 5 of the Act). It is to be noted that in these cases proof of knowledge is essential, and, in practice, it may be difficult to establish these offences, except by giving express notice, and taking action if the offence is committed thereafter. On the other hand proof of knowledge is not necessary where a claim for conversion is made. A converter need not be an infringer; *WEA Records Ltd.* v. *Benson King (Sales) Ltd.*, 1975 1 W.L.R. 44.

PERFORMANCE IN PUBLIC

It is an infringement to perform any substantial part of a literary, dramatic or musical work in public, and to permit a place of public entertainment to be used for private profit for such a performance. Whether a performance is "in public" is a question of fact in each case. It is not necessary that every member of the public shall have access, or that a charge shall be made for admission. Performances at clubs or institutes with limited membership are therefore generally in public for this purpose (see *P.R.S. Limited* v. *Rangers F.C. Supporters Club Greenock*, 1975 R.P.C. 626, held performance at such Club in "public"). A place of public entertainment is defined by the Act (Section 5 (6)), as including any premises which are occupied mainly for other purposes, but are from time to time made available for hire to persons desiring to hire them for purposes of public entertainment (see also "Sound Recordings" and "Broadcasting and Television" *post*).

EXCEPTIONS TO LIABILITY FOR INFRINGEMENT

It cannot of course be an infringement if the consent of the owner of the copyright has been given expressly or is to be implied.

No fair dealing with literary, dramatic, musical and artistic works for purposes of research or private study is an infringement of the copyright therein. Nor is a fair dealing with such works an infringement if it is for the purposes of criticism or review of the work itself or another work, if accompanied by a sufficient acknowledgment. "Sufficient acknowledgment" is defined by the Act (Section 6 (10)). (As to the test of "fair dealing" see *post* article **Subsidiary Rights).**

Some other exceptions in Section 6 of the Act are: reporting current events in newspapers, etc., if accompanied by a sufficient acknowledgement, or by means of broadcasting, or in a film; reproduction for the purposes of judicial proceedings (this applies equally to films and sound and television broadcasts); reading or reciting in public extracts of works, if accompanied by a sufficient acknowledgement; including passages in collections intended for schools, if accompanied by a sufficient acknowledgement. In Section 9 of the Act: copying works of artistic craftsmanship and sculptures exhibited in public, copying works of architecture; including artistic works as backgrounds to films or television broadcasts; reconstructing buildings which are works of architecture. In Section 15 of the Act, making reproductions by or on behalf of librarians of the typographical arrangement of a published edition. In Section 41 of the Act, reproducing the work, or an adaptation thereof, in the course of instruction for schools, or as part of examination questions and answers. In Section 42 of the Act, making or supplying reproductions of public records.

Section 7 of the Act provides that the making or supplying of copies of articles contained in periodical publications, and of parts of published literary, dramatic, and musical works (not being such articles), and any illustrations thereof, by, or on behalf of, the librarian of a library of a class prescribed by Board of Trade Regulations, is not an infringement. (1957, S.I. No. 868).

It should be observed, however, that ignorance was no defence even if reasonable in the circumstances; printers ran considerable risks in this connection since they had often no means of knowing that an infringement was being committed but they were nevertheless liable. However, now, in proceedings for conversion of infringing copies, damages cannot be recovered from an innocent defendant.

WHO IS LIABLE FOR INFRINGEMENT

In the case of an infringement by the publication of a copy, the author, publisher and printer of the infringing work are equally liable.

Where an infringement is committed by performance in public, not only the actual performers, but the firm or company by whom they are employed are liable.

Greater difficulty arises in the determination of the liability of hirers of films, owners of halls, and other persons who have not infringed either personally or by their actual servants. It is an infringement, however, to "authorise" any infringing act so that, if it is proved that any person, by supplying the material or otherwise, made the infringement possible, he will generally be held liable; see "What Constitutes Infringement" *ante*. Section 5 (5) of the Act, however, provides that a person who permits a place of public entertainment to be used for a performance in public of a work, does not infringe the copyright in the work, if he was not aware, and had no reasonable grounds for suspecting, that the performance would be an infringement or, if he gave his permission gratuitously, or for a nominal consideration, or for a consideration not exceeding his estimated expenses consequential from the use of the place for the performance.

THE REMEDIES FOR INFRINGEMENT

A copyright owner whose right is infringed is, in general, entitled as of right to an injunction, i.e. an Order of the Court restraining the Defendant from repeating the infringement, and can insist upon such an Order, although offered a personal undertaking first. It is to be noted, however, that such an Order will be directed only to repetition of the actual infringement; i.e. an Order cannot be obtained to restrain copying of future parts of a serial story because earlier parts have been copied.

A second remedy is damages for infringement. These are usually based upon evidence of loss suffered by the Plaintiff, i.e. that if the infringing book had not been published, he would have been able to publish more copies of his own book or that he otherwise has lost a market for his material. Damages for infringement, may, however, be increased, in effect, by way of an award of exemplary damages if the Court, having regard to the flagrancy of the infringement, and any benefit shown to have accrued to the Defendant by reason of the infringement, is satisfied that effective relief is not otherwise available to the Plaintiff (Section 17 (3) of the Act and see *Beloff* v. *Pressdram Ltd.* 1973 FSR 33). It is permissible, in assessing damages, to have regard to the sort of fee which would have been asked if a licence had been requested. However, if it is proved or admitted that, at the time of infringement, the Defendant was not aware, and had no reasonable grounds for suspecting, that copyright subsisted in the work, the Plaintiff cannot recover infringement damages from the Defendant (Section 17 (2) of the Act). In view of the fact that every work enjoys copyright without formality, such ignorance is difficult to establish, except in special circumstances such as where it might be reasonably thought that the work was out of copyright, or not protected in this country.

Damages, however, can also be based upon a claim for conversion, upon the principle that the infringing material is deemed the property of the copyright owner. Under this head, regard is had, not to the loss to the copyright owner, but to the value of the infringing work. Where only a portion of the work containing the infringement represents infringing material, it is necessary, first to assess the value of the infringing work as a whole by reference to the sale price of each copy multiplied by the number of copies disposed of, and then to assess the damages at that fraction of this figure which the infringing material bears to the whole. Where the portion of the whole which is infringing is relatively slight, e.g. in the case of an infringing article in a newspaper, this calculation is difficult. However, a plaintiff is not entitled to damages for conversion if it is proved or admitted that, at the time of conversion, either that the defendant was not aware and had no reasonable grounds for suspecting that copyright subsisted in the work, or that the defendant believed, and had reasonable grounds for believing, that the articles converted were not infringing copies (Section 18 (2) of the Act, and see "What Constitutes Infringement" *ante*).

An alternative remedy is an account of profits. Here the claim is based, not upon the value of the infringing material, but upon the amount of profit made by the defendant in respect of the infringement, and the plaintiff is entitled to this relief even where the defendant's ignorance of the subsistence of copyright in the work is proved or admitted.

In addition to the foregoing remedies a successful plaintiff is entitled to have delivered up to him all infringing material in the defendant's possession.

The Act, unlike the Act of 1911, does not specifically provide for any period during which a copyright action may be brought, so that, presumably, the Limitation Act of 1939 will apply (see Section 18 (1) proviso of the Act). Therefore the period for bringing actions in respect of infringements of copyright will be six years from the infringement, and, in respect of actions for conversion of infringing copies, will be six years from the conversion whether there is only one conversion, or a succession of conversions. Under the Act of 1911 the period in each case was three years.

There are further restrictions on the remedies obtainable in the case of exclusive licensees (Section 19 of the Act) and in relation to buildings (Section 17 (4) of the Act).

Section 20 of the Act provides for various presumptions of facts in copyright actions. These deal with the subsistence of copyright in a work, the owner of the copyright, the author of the work, the originality of the work, the first publication of the work, and the maker and date and place of first publication of records. These presumptions can greatly simplify the evidence which would be required in a copyright action.

The above remedies are enforceable by civil action.

OTHER REMEDIES

In addition to the remedies above mentioned there are certain special forms of procedure open to persons whose rights are infringed.

Certain infringements of copyright constitute a criminal offence rendering the offender liable to fines or imprisonment (Section 21 of the Act); as to a conspiracy to contravene Section 21 of the Act see *Scott* v. *Metropolitan Police Commissioner* 1974 3 W.L.R. 741. It should be noted, however, that proof of knowledge that an infringement is being committed is essential in all these cases.

It is breach of statutory duty, but not a criminal offence, in relation to literary, dramatic, musical and artistic works without licence: (1) to affix another person's name on a work of which that person is not the author, so as to imply that the other person is the author; (2) to publish, or sell, a work, or reproductions thereof, on which the other person's name has been affixed, knowing that person is not the author; (3) to perform in public, or broadcast, a work, as being a work of which another person is the author, knowing that other person is not the author; (4) to publish or sell an altered artistic work, or reproduction of the altered artistic work, as being the unaltered work, or a reproduction of the unaltered work, knowing that is not the case, and (5) to publish, sell, or distribute reproductions of an artistic work as reproductions made by the author, knowing that is not the case (Section 43 of the Act). Damages are recoverable where such an offence has been committed. "Name" includes initials or a monogram. The right of action under Section 43 is not limited to professional authors and, where the claim under Section 43 is linked to another cause of action, such as defamation, a separate. award of damages can be given as respects Section 43 if the other cause of action does not cover the injury caused by the false attribution of authorship; *Moore* v. *News of the World Ltd.* 1972 2 W.L.R. 419.

Provision is also made (Section 22 of the Act), for the detention by the Customs authorities of infringing copies of copyright works made abroad to be imported into the United Kingdom.

THE DURATION OF COPYRIGHT PROTECTION

The normal period of copyright protection is during the life of the author and fifty years from the end of the calendar year in which he died (Sections 2 (3) and 3 (4) of the Act). In the case of a work of joint authorship, the protection, if it has not expired before the commencement of the Act (see below), extends during the life of the author who dies last and fifty years from the end of the calendar year in which he died (paragraph 2, Third Schedule to the Act).

The Act contains special provisions for determining the period of copyright in relation to works of joint authorship, which are first published under two or more names, of which one or more of the names, or all the names, are pseudonyms (paragraph 3, Third Schedule to the Act).

In the case of literary, dramatic or musical works which have not been published, performed in public, or broadcast before the death of the author, the period is fifty years from the end of the calendar year which includes the earliest occasion on which one of these acts is done (Section 2 (3) of the Act). In the case of engravings not published before the death of the author, the period is fifty years from the end of the calendar year in which they are first published (Section 3 (4) of the Act). For photographs, except those made before the commencement of the Act (see below), the period is fifty years from the end of the calendar year in which the photograph is first published (Section 3 (4) of the Act). For Government publications the period for literary, dramatic and musical works, if published, is until fifty years from the end of the calendar year in which it is first published, and for artistic works fifty years from the end of the calendar year in which the work was made; but, if the artistic work is an engraving or photograph, the period is fifty years from the end of the calendar year in which the engraving or photograph is first published (Section 39 (3) and (4) of the Act). (See as to duration of copyright in "Published Editions" and "Anonymous and Pseudonymous works" *ante* and in "Films", "Sound Recordings" and "Television and Sound Broadcasts" *post*).

In the case of works which were in existence before the commencement of the Act of 1911 (July 1, 1912) the terms of copyright above described apply if the work enjoyed copyright at such date (paragraph 35, Seventh Schedule to the Act).

This involves an examination of the terms of copyright subsisting under the various Acts in force before 1912. In general, protection under these Acts was the life of the author and seven years, or forty-two years from publication (whichever was the longer), but different terms of copyright were given by the various Acts dealing with artistic works.

Where the copyright in a pre-Act of 1911 work has been assigned before 1912, and copyright subsists therein by virtue of any provisions of the Act, such copyright reverts to the author or his assigns at the expiration of the old term of copyright applicable to the work (paragraph 38, Seventh Schedule to the Act), but subject to various options in favour of the assignee.

In the case of records and photographs coming into existence after July 1, 1912, but before the commencement of the Act, the Seventh Schedule to the Act provides that the period of copyright under the Act of 1911 shall apply; further, copright is not to subsist under the Act in a joint work first published after July 1, 1912, but before the commencement of the Act, if the period of copyright under the Act of 1911 in that work expired before the commencement of the Act. This is because the Act provides different periods for these works from those under the Act of 1911. (See as to assignments before 1957 under the Act of 1911 "Generally" *ante*.)

FILMS

(1) Under the Act copyright now subsists in films as such (Section 13 of the Act), but without prejudice to the copyright in any literary, dramatic, musical or artistic works from which the subject-matter is derived (Section 16 (6) of the Act). Thus, there is now copyright in the film itself, and a separate copyright in its subject-matter, whereas, under the Act of 1911, films were protected only as to their constituent parts such as photographs, and, in most cases, as dramatic works. The new film copyright is not to subsist in films made before the commencement of the Act, but the Act provides for the protection of such films if they were dramatic works, and of the photographs forming part of such films (paragraphs 14–16, Seventh Schedule to the Act).

(2) "Film" is defined by the Act (Section 13 (10)), and includes the sounds embodied in any sound track associated with the film. The definition is considered to cover video tapes. Copyright subsists in every film of which the maker was a qualified person for the whole, or a substantial part, of the period during which the film was made, or which is first published in the United Kingdom. The "maker" of a film is defined as the person by whom the arrangements necessary for the making of the film are undertaken, and he is entitled to the copyright in the film. Film copyright subsists, if the film is registrable under Part II of the Films Act, 1960, until registration, and thereafter until fifty years from the end of the calendar year in which it is so registered. If not so registrable, then until the film is published and fifty years from the end of the year in which it is first published; if copyright only subsists in such a film by virtue of its place of publication, then until fifty years from the end of the calendar year in which it was first published.

A form of infringement peculiar to film copyright is to cause the film, in so far as it consists of visual images, to be seen in public, or, in so far as it consists of sounds, to be heard in public, except in the case of newsreel films where fifty years have elapsed from the end of the calendar year in which the principal events depicted in the film occurred.

(3) It is an infringement of the copyright in a novel, or story, to convert it into a film, whether the actual language of the literary work is taken or not. But something more than a mere plot or idea must be taken; it must be proved that the film adopts a substantial part of the incidents used in the story to work out the plot.

There is no copyright in a scene in actual life, e.g. sporting events, so that the organiser has no remedy in the case of the filming of such events provided that the film can be taken without trespass, and the passer-by cannot complain if he is filmed in the street.

(4) Under the Act of 1911, the making of a film involved the creation of an artistic work, i.e. a series of photographs, and, unless it was merely a record of passing events, the creation of a dramatic work. The first owner of the artistic copyright was the owner of the negative at the time it was made, whereas the first owner of the dramatic work might have been difficult to determine. In fact a commercial film used to involve the exercise of a number of separate copyrights since, at each stage of its inception, a separate copyright work might have been produced, e.g. story, screen dialogue and the film as finally cut, and the ownership of copyright would depend upon the agreements of the various parties concerned with the film company.

SOUND RECORDINGS

The Act provides that copyright subsists in every sound recording of which the maker was a qualified person at the time the recording was made, or which has been first published in the United Kingdom (Section 12 of the Act). "Sound recording" is defined by the Act as meaning the aggregate of the sounds embodied in, and capable of being produced by means of, a record of any description other than a film sound track.

The maker of the sound recording is entitled to the copyright therein, except where sound recordings are commissioned, and the "maker" is defined as the person who owns the first record at the time the recording is made. Copyright in sound recordings subsists for a period of fifty years from the end of the calendar year in which the record is first published.

Such copyright can be infringed by making a record of the recording or causing the recording to be heard in public, but it is not an infringement to allow the recording to be heard in public (i) as part of the amenities for the residents of any premises where persons reside or sleep unless a special charge for admission is made, or (ii) as part of the activities of a club or other non-profit-making organisation whose main objects are charitable unless a charge is made for admission, and any of the proceeds are not applied for the purposes of the organisation. In *Phonographic Performance Ltd.* v. *Pontins Ltd.*, 1967 3 W.L.R. 1622 it was held that the holiday camp there in question constituted premises where persons reside or sleep and that, on the facts of that case, records were caused to be heard in public as part of the amenities provided exclusively or mainly for residents or inmates of that camp. If a record of music is performed in public, a licence to perform is required in respect of the record as well as in respect of the music itself. But see below as to broadcast performances.

The Seventh Schedule to the Act contains provisions relating to the subsistence of copyright under the Act in records made before July 1, 1912.

A literary, dramatic or musical work is infringed by making a record of it or including it in the sound track of a film (Sections 2 (5)(a) and 48 (1) of the Act). The right to record such a work is therefore a valuable right and is quite distinct from the publishing right and performing right.

There are, however, a complicated series of provisions (Section 8 of the Act) under which, when a musical work has been once recorded with the consent of the copyright owner, it can be recorded thereafter by anyone else on payment of a fixed royalty, the payment whereof is in general secured by the issue of adhesive stamps to be attached to the record. The normal royalty is $6\frac{1}{4}$ per cent of the ordinary retail selling price of the record with the minimum of .313p for each work reproduced on a single record. In December 1976 a public enquiry was held to consider whether the royalty rates should be varied; the result is "no change." Where the retail selling price was partly cash and partly three chocolate wrappers, it was held by the House of Lords in *Chappell & Co. Ltd.* v *The Nestle Co. Ltd.*, 1953 3 W.L.R. 168 that the section did not apply.

BROADCASTING AND TELEVISION

(1) The Act for the first time establishes copyright in television and sound broadcasts as such, if made by the B.B.C. or the I.B.A., and from a place in the United Kingdom (Section 14 of the Act). This right is therefore limited in this

country to broadcasts by these two bodies and the copyright in their broadcasts vests in them. Further, copyright does not so subsist by virtue of the Act in television and sound broadcasts made before the commencement of the Act. "Television broadcast" means visual images broadcast by way of television together with any sounds broadcast for reception with those images, and "sound broadcast" means sounds broadcast otherwise than as part of a television broadcast. "Broadcasting" is defined by the Act (Section 48(2)). By reason of 1959 S.I. No. 2215 1960 S.I. No. 847 1961 S.I. Nos. 60, 2460, 2462 and 2463 1962 S.I. Nos. 1642, 1643, 2184 and 2185 1963 S.I. Nos. 1037, 1038, 1039 and 1147 1964 S.I. No. 689 1965 S.I. Nos. 1858, 1859, 2009, 2010, and 2158, 1966 S.I. Nos. 79 and 685, 1967 S.I. No. 974 and 1972 S.I. No. 1724 copyright now subsists in broadcasts made in the Isle of Man, Sarawak, Gibraltar, Fiji, Uganda, Zanzibar, Bermuda, North Borneo, Bahamas, Virgin Islands, Falkland Islands, St. Helena, Seychelles, Kenya, Mauritius, Montserrat, St. Lucia, Botswana, Cayman Islands, Grenada, Guyana, British Honduras, St. Vincent and Hong Kong. By reason of 1972 S.I. No. 673 (as amended) copyright now subsists in sound broadcasts made in Austria, Brazil, Chile, Colombia, Congo (People's Republic), Costa Rica, Czechoslovakia, Denmark, Ecuador, Federal Republic of Germany & Berlin (West), Fiji, Guatemala, Italy, Luxembourg, Mexico, Niger, Paraguay, Sweden and Uruguay, and in television broadcasts made in Austria, Belgium, Brazil, Chile, Colombia, Congo (People's Republic), Costa Rica, Cyprus, Czechoslovakia, Denmark, Ecuador, Federal Republic of Germany and Berlin (West), Fiji, France, Guatemala, Italy, Luxembourg, Mexico, Niger, Norway, Paraguay, Spain, Sweden and Uruguay; see as to protection in Gibraltar and in Bermuda (*inter alia*) 1972 S.I. No. 673 (as amended).

Copyright in television and sound broadcasts subsists until the end of fifty years from the end of the calendar year in which the broadcast is made. Such copyright is infringed *inter alia* (a) in the case of television broadcasts in so far as it consists of visual images, by making a film of it otherwise than for private purposes, or by causing it to be seen in public by a paying audience: in so far as it consists of sounds, by making a record of it otherwise than for private purposes, or by causing it to be heard in public by a paying audience, and (*b*) in the case of a sound broadcast, by making a record of it otherwise than for private purposes. Where the alleged infringement is of the visual images of a television broadcast, it is only necessary to prove that the act in question extended to a sequence of images sufficient to be seen as a moving picture. Further, the Act provides that television broadcasts are seen or heard by a paying audience, if seen or heard by persons who either (i) have been admitted for payment to the place where the broadcast is seen or heard and are not (a) residents of such place nor (b) members of a club or society where the payment is only for membership and the provision of facilities for seeing or hearing television broadcasts is only incidental to the main purposes of the club or society, or (ii) have been admitted to such place in circumstances where goods or services are supplied at prices which exceed the price usually charged at that place, and are partly attributable to the facilities afforded for seeing or hearing the broadcasts.

(2) Literary, dramatic and musical works, records and films are infringed by broadcasting them, and artistic works are infringed by including such works in a television broadcast: since this right to broadcast is now additional to the right to perform in public, authors will need to consider this when drafting agreements. If broadcast performances, for instance, in the case of sound broadcasts, are played from a loud-speaker in a public place, this in general involves a separate public performance not covered by any licence to perform given to the broadcasting body, but if the broadcast is from a record, the performance of the broadcast does not, as under the Act of 1911, infringe the copyright in the record as well (Section 40 (1) of the Act). And, dramatising a literary work for the purposes of a broadcast would infringe the right to make adaptations thereof, unless the necessary licence had been given.

PERFORMING RIGHT TRIBUNAL

The Act (Sections 23–30), as amended by the Copyright (Amendment) Act 1971 which added a new section, Section 27A, for the first time establishes a Tribunal, in particular to control licence fees, but it is concerned only with disputes between licensing bodies and persons, or organisations, concerned in the public performance of works. See as to the Isle of Man 1971 S.I. No. 1848. By definition, licensing body excludes organisations whose objects only include negotiation or granting of individual licences each relating to a single work, or works of a single author, where such licences are to do acts with which a writer is most concerned, e.g. licences to perform in public, or broadcast, literary, dramatic and musical works, or adaptations thereof. Writers, other than perhaps songwriters, are not likely therefore to be concerned with the Tribunal, and, where necessary, expert advice should be taken.

The Tribunal consists of a chairman, who can be either a barrister or solicitor, or a person who has held judicial office, and not less than two, nor more than four other members appointed by the Board of Trade. The Fourth Schedule to the Act contains provisions relative to the functions of the Tribunal. Questions of law may be referred to the High Court before, and in some circumstances, after, the Tribunal has given its decision. Rules relating to the Tribunal came into operation on 1st June 1957 (1957 S.I. No. 924 as amended) and have been revoked and replaced by other rules (1965 S.I. No. 1506 as amended by 1971 S.I. No. 636). Upon a reference to the Tribunal under Section 25 of the Act by the Scottish Ballroom Association, the Tribunal varied a 1957 fee tariff and upon an application under Section 27 of the Act by Southern Television Limited the Tribunal held that a clause in a draft licence to perform was unreasonable. During 1960 references were made to the Tribunal in respect of the *Juke Box* tariffs both of the P.R.S. for music and the P.P. Ltd. for records, in each case the tariffs were in substance confirmed. In 1965 the Tribunal determined the terms and charges on which the Isle of Man Broadcasting Company Limited could broadcast records. In 1967, and again in 1972, the Tribunal determined the terms and charges on which the BBC could broadcast music. Decisions of the Tribunal are referred to in *Current Law*.

PUBLISHING AGREEMENTS

The simplest form of publishing agreement is a mere licence to publish in a newspaper or periodical for a single payment. The terms of such agreements usually depend upon implication, or trade custom. Where an article is sent to a periodical without a covering letter, there will be implied, on the one hand a licence to publish, and on the other, an agreement to pay such remuneration as is normal and reasonable. If the article is kept, and the author is sent a proof for revision, the author is entitled to a fee, even if the work is not actually published.

Where a work is to be published on royalty terms, it is important from the point of view of the author that he does not assign his copyright, but only grants a licence. If he assigns, he will not be able to prevent the publisher from selling the rights in the work. He may be seriously prejudiced if the publisher gets into financial difficulties. Some protection is given to authors under Section 60 of the Bankruptcy Act 1914, but this is not available where the publisher is a limited company. A licence, however, is generally personal to the publisher, even if this is not expressly stated, and provision can be made to protect the author in the case of insolvency of the publisher. A difficult question concerns the extent to which works may be altered, the most important consideration being whether the author has assigned his copyright, or merely granted a licence to publish. If the former, then the assignee may freely alter, subject to possible proceedings by the author for defamation, malicious falsehood or under section 43 of the Act. If the latter, then alterations may be freely made by the publisher unless the licence expressly or implicitly forbids it, but subject to defamation and so on as before. However the courts will be very willing to imply a term limiting the right to make alterations: *Frisby v. BBC* 1967 2 W.L.R. 1204. There may be cases, however, where it could be established to the satisfaction of the court that custom permits reasonable alterations, at least of unsigned articles.

It is often difficult to determine whether the words used involve an assignment, or a licence, and this should be clearly expressed. However, an exclusive licensee now has, under the Act, the same rights of action and remedies as if the licence has been an assignment (see "Licences," *ante*).

The publishing agreement, in the interests of the author, should require publication within some fixed time, should deal with the style and price of publication, the method of advertising, the number of free copies allowed, and provide for proper accounts.

Publishing agreements often provide options to the publisher to acquire other rights in a work such as rights to make adaptations, including translations and dramatisation rights and rights to broadcast (see "Broadcasting and Television," *ante*), film rights, and rights to publish abroad. From the author's point of view it is usually preferable that such rights should be granted on royalty terms rather than for a single payment. In view of the provisions of the Act as to future copyright, care should be taken when drafting an agreement (see "Assignment of Copyright", *ante*).

Apart from express agreement a publisher is entitled to dispose of stock in hand after the licence is determined, since such stock, having been lawfully made, does not constitute infringing copies.

WORKS ORIGINATING ABROAD

The Act, except as extended by Order in Council, applies only within the United Kingdom, including Northern Ireland (Sections 31, 32 and 51 of the Act), whereas the Act of 1911, in practice, applied throughout the British Commonwealth. Therefore, there will now be one code for the United Kingdom and other codes for other parts of the Commonwealth, unless the Act, or similar legislation, is in force there. This may not necessarily occur.

Orders in Council under the Act may direct that any of the provisions of the Act shall (*a*) extend to the Channel Islands, the Colonies and Dependencies and (*b*) apply to any other countries to which those provisions do not extend. By an Order (1957 S.I. No. 1523), which came into operation on the 27th September, 1957 (the date at which the Universal Copyright Convention came into effect between the U.K. and other members), as amended, the Act was applied to works originating in Universal Copyright or Berne Convention countries. At that time this included most of the world except the U.S.S.R. This Order for the first time protected works first published in the U.S.A. which was not a member of the Berne Union. This Order and its ancillary orders were largely revoked and replaced by a further Order (1964, S.I. No. 690), which was itself amended and now revoked and replaced by another Order 1972 S.I. No. 673 as amended. By one amendment this Act has been applied to works originating in the U.S.S.R.; 1973 S.I. No. 963. By an Order (1959 S.I. No. 861), which came into operation on 31st May, 1959, the Act was extended to the Isle of Man; such order was amended by 1970 S.I. No. 1437 which came into operation on 12th October 1970; see 1971 S.I. No. 1848 which came into operation on 1st December 1971. By further Orders 1959 S.I. No. 2215, 1960 S.I. No. 847, 1961 S.I. Nos. 60, 2462 and 2463, 1962 S.I. Nos. 629, 1642, 2184 and 2185, 1963 S.I. Nos. 1037, 1038, 1039 and 1147, 1964 S.I. No. 689, 1965 S.I. Nos. 1858, 1859, 2009, 2010 and 2158, 1966 S.I. Nos. 79 and 685, 1967 S.I. No. 974 and 1972 S.I. No. 1724 which came into operation on 1st January, 1960, 1st June, 1960, 1st February, 1961, 1st January, 1962, 1st January, 1962, 1st May, 1962, 6th August, 1962, 11th October, 1962, 11th October, 1962, 10th June, 1963, 10th June, 1963, 10th June, 1963, 4th July, 1963, 21st May, 1964 5th November 1965, 5th November, 1965, 4th December, 1965, 4th December 1965, 1st January, 1966, 5th February, 1966, 16th June, 1966, 5th July, 1967 and 12th December, 1972, respectively, the Act was extended to Sarawak, Gibraltar, Fiji, Uganda, Zanzibar, Bermuda, North Borneo, Virgin Islands, Falkland Islands, St Helena, Seychelles, Kenya, Mauritius, Monserrat, St Lucia, Botswana, Cayman Islands, Grenada, Guyana, British Honduras, St Vincent and Hong Kong, respectively. Works originating in British Colonies other than Sarawak, Gibraltar, Fiji, Uganda, Zanzibar, Bermuda, North Borneo, Virgin Islands, Falkland Islands, St Helena, Seychelles, Kenya, Mauritius, Monserrat, St Lucia, Botswana, Cayman Islands, Grenada, Guyana, British Honduras, St Vincent and Hong Kong, are still protected under the old law as no new Orders have yet been made, as are existing works of foreign origin. In those cases the place of first publication remains of substantial importance. A work is deemed first published within the United Kingdom, or in any other country, if published there within thirty days (or 14 days in the case of existing works) after first publication elsewhere (Section 49 (2)(d) of the Act), and a work is published if reproductions are issued to the public in such quantities as are reasonably necessary to meet the public demand.

Copyright throughout the British Empire extended, prior to the commencement of the Act, to works first published in countries of the Copyright Union, and unpublished works of authors who were nationals of, or resident at the time of the making of the work in, such countries.

HOW FAR BRITISH WORKS ARE PROTECTED ABROAD

Works first published in the United Kingdom, and unpublished works of British subjects, are protected in all Berne and Universal Copyright Convention countries though it should be noted that "first publication" in this case has not necessarily quite the same meaning in all countries. Some countries do not accept the mere issue of copies as constituting publication in a country, and require that copies shall be issued from a distributing centre in the nature of a publishing house in the country, and the simultaneous publication period which, under the Act, will be thirty days, is not universal.

As regards other foreign countries, copyright can only be secured by complying with the formalities prescribed by the law of the country. In the U.S.A. copyright, prior to the 27th September, 1957, was secured by registration and deposit of copies. Copyright could not be acquired unless a "Copyright Reserved" notice was affixed to all copies sold in the U.S.A. Application for registration had to be made promptly or the right to protection was lost, but an interim protection could be obtained which enabled the position to be preserved pending publication in the U.S.A. Books, or periodicals, in the English language, could not secure permanent protection in the U.S.A. unless an edition was printed in the U.S.A. from type set up there. However, after the 27th September, 1957, British authors are relieved of most of the formalities connected with obtaining U.S.A. copyright in published works, including the "Copyright Reserved" notice, registration, deposit of copies, and printing of editions from type set up in the U.S.A. The only formality required is that, from first publication, all copies of the work, whether sold in the U.S.A. or elsewhere, will have to bear the symbol ©, together with the name of the copyright proprietor, and the year of first publication. There is now a new American Copyright Act 1976 which came into force on 1st January 1978 (see p. 369 *post* "U.S. Copyright").

In some South American countries copyright can only be secured by some form of local registration.

THE COPYRIGHT ACTS 1956* AND 1911†

A SELECTION OF CLAUSES OF INTEREST TO WRITERS AND ARTISTS

THE COPYRIGHT ACT 1956

Nature of Copyright (Section 1), *Copyright in Literary, Dramatic, Musical and Artistic Works* (Sections 2, 3 and 4); *Infringement of Copyright in Literary, Dramatic Musical and Artistic Works* (Sections 5, 6, 7, 8 and 9); *Provisions as to Designs* (Section 10), *Copyright in Sound Recordings, Films, Broadcasts and Published Editions* (Sections 12, 13, 14, 15 and 16); *Remedies for Infringement* (Sections 17, 18, 19, 20, 21 and 22); *The Performing Right Tribunal* (Sections 23, 24 and 30); *Application of the Act to other Countries* (Sections 31, 32, 34 and 35); *Assignments and Licences* (Sections 36, 37 and 38); *Crown Copyright* (Section 39); *Educational Material and Public Records* (Sections 41 and 42); *False Attribution of Authorship* (Section 43); *Savings* (Section 46); *Interpretation* (Sections 48 and 49); *General* (Section 51); *Anonymous and Pseudonymous* (the Second Schedule); *Joint Works* (the Third Schedule).

* Published by H.M. Stationery Office, price £1.50 net
† Published by H.M. Stationery Office, price 14p net

THE COPYRIGHT ACT 1911

(Note: the following Section is not repealed by the Act of 1956)—
Section 15

U.S. COPYRIGHT

GAVIN McFARLANE, LL.B., LL.M., PH.D.
Barrister

A. THE SYSTEM OF INTERNATIONAL COPYRIGHT

1. The International Copyright Conventions

There is no general principle of international copyright which provides a uniform code for the protection of right owners throughout the world. There are however two major international copyright conventions which lay down certain minimum standards for member states, in particular requiring members to accord to right owners of other members the same protection which is granted to their own nationals. One is the higher standard Berne Convention of 1886, the most recent revision of which was signed in Paris in 1971, to which the United States does not at present adhere, although it is hoped that as a result of the new domestic American law of copyright she will feel able to join in the near future. The other is the Universal Copyright Convention signed in 1952 with lower minimum standards, and sponsored by Unesco. This also was most recently revised in Paris in 1971, jointly with the Berne Convention. To this latter Convention the United States belongs.

2. Summary of the Universal Copyright Convention

(i) The fundamental intent is to accord reciprocally in each member state to nationals of all other member states the same protection as that member grants to its own nationals.

(ii) The minimum term of protection is the life of the author and twenty-five years after his death (by contrast with the Berne Convention which demands a term of the life of the author and a post-mortem period of fifty years).

(iii) Any national requirement as a condition of copyright of such formalities as deposit, registration, notice, payment, or manufacture or publication within that state shall be satisfied for all works first published outside its territory and of which the author is not one of its nationals if all copies bear the symbol © accompanied by the name of the copyright owner and the year of first publication.

(iv) Publication for the purposes of the Universal Convention means the reproduction in tangible form and the general distribution to the public of copies of a work from which it can be read or otherwise visually perceived.

(v) The effect of American ratification of the Universal Copyright Convention on 16 September 1955 was to alter completely the nature of the protection granted by the United States to copyright works originating abroad. The previous policy of American domestic law had been extremely restrictive for foreign authors, particularly those writing in the English language. But in consequence of ratification American law was amended to exempt from many of these restrictions works published in other member states, or by nationals of other member states. Recent amendments have relaxed the position even further.

3. Effect on British Copyright Owners

The copyright statute of the United States having been brought into line with the requirements of the Universal Copyright Convention, compliance with the formalities required by American law is all that is needed to acquire protection for the work of a British author first published outside the United States.

B. SUMMARY OF UNITED STATES COPYRIGHT LAW

1. Introduction of new Law

After many years of debate, the new Copyright Statute of the United States was passed on 19 October 1976. The greater part of its relevant provisions came into force on 1 January 1978. It has extended the range of copyright protection, and further eased the requirements whereby British authors can obtain copyright protection in America.

2. Works protected in American Law

Works of authorship include the following categories:
- (i) literary works;
- (ii) musical works, including any accompanying words;
- (iii) dramatic works, including any accompanying music;
- (iv) pantomimes and choreographic works;
- (v) pictorial, graphic and sculptural works;
- (vi) motion pictures and other audiovisual works;
- (vii) sound recordings, but copyright in sound recordings is not to include a right of public performance.

3. The rights of a copyright owner

(i) To reproduce the copyrighted work in copies or phonorecords;

(ii) to prepare derivative works based upon the copyrighted work;

(iii) to distribute copies or phonorecords of the copyrighted work to the public by sale or other transfer of ownership, or by rental, lease, or lending.

(iv) in the case of literary, musical, dramatic and choreographic works, pantomimes, and motion pictures and other audiovisual works, but NOT sound recordings, to perform the copyrighted work publicly;

(v) in the case of literary, musical, dramatic, and choreographic works, pantomimes, and pictorial, graphic, or sculptural works, including the individual images of a motion picture or other audiovisual work, to display the copyrighted work publicly.

4. Manufacturing Requirements

These are being phased out, and after 1 July 1982, will cease to have effect. Prior to 1 July 1982, the importation into or public distribution in the United States of a work consisting preponderantly of non-dramatic literary material that is in the English language and protected under American law is prohibited unless the portions consisting of such material have been manufactured in the United States or Canada. This provision does not apply where, on the date when importation is sought or public distribution in the United States is made, the author of any substantial part of such material is neither a national of the United States or, if a national, has been domiciled outside the United States for a continuous period of at least one year immediately preceding that date.

Thus even until 1 July 1982, there is effectively no manufacturing requirement in respect of works of British authors, but the requirements of the copyright notice, deposit and registration must be met.

5. Formalities: Notice, Deposit and Registration

(i) Notice of copyright.

Whenever a work protected by the American Copyright Statute is published in the United States or elsewhere by authority of the copyright owner, a notice of copyright shall be placed on all publicly distributed copies. This shall consist of (1) Either the symbol © or the word "Copyright", or the abbreviation "Copr."

plus (2) the year of first publication of the work, plus (3) the name of the copyright owner.

(ii) Deposit.

Unless exempted by the Register of Copyrights, the owner of copyright or the exclusive right of publication in a work published with notice of copyright in the United States shall within three months of such publication deposit in the Copyright Office for the use or disposition of the Library of Congress two complete copies of the best edition of the work (or two records, if the work is a sound recording). Penalties are provided for failure to comply with the requirement of deposit.

(iii) Registration.

While deposit is mandatory, registration for copyright in the United States is optional. However, any owner of copyright in a work first published outside the United States may register a work by making application to the Copyright Office with the appropriate fee, and by depositing one complete copy of the work. This requirement of deposit may be satisfied by using copies deposited for the Library of Congress. But it is vital to note that no action may be brought for infringement of copyright in the United States until registration of the claim to copyright has been made according to the statutory provisions.

6. Duration of Copyright

An important change in the new American law is that in general, copyright in a work created on or after 1 January 1978 endures for a term of the life of the author, and a period of fifty years after the author's death. This brings the United States into line with most other advanced countries, and will enable her government to ratify the higher standard Berne Convention in due course. Copyright in a work created before 1 January 1978, but not published or copyrighted before then, subsists from 1 January 1978, and lasts for the life of the author and a post-mortem period of fifty years.

Any copyright, the first term of which under the previous law was still subsisting on 1 January 1978, shall endure for twenty-eight years from the date when it was originally secured, and the copyright proprietor or his representative may apply for a further term of forty-seven years within one year prior to the expiry of the original term. In default of such application for renewal and extension, the copyright shall end at the expiration of twenty-eight years from the date copyright was originally secured.

The duration of any copyright, the renewal term of which was subsisting at any time between 31 December 1976 and 31 December 1977, or for which renewal registration was made between those dates, is extended to endure for a term of seventy-five years from the date copyright was originally secured.

These alterations are of great importance for owners of existing American copyrights.

All terms of copyright provided for by the sections referred to above run to the end of the calendar year in which they would otherwise expire.

7. Public Performance

Under the previous American law the provisions relating to performance in public were less generous to right owners than those existing in the copyright law of the United Kingdom. In particular, performance of a musical work was formerly only an infringement if it was "for profit". Moreover, the considerable American coin operated record playing machine industry (juke boxes), had obtained an exemption from being regarded as instruments of profit, and accordingly their owners did not have to pay royalties for the use of copyright musical works.

Now by the new law one of the exclusive rights of the copyright owner is, in the case of literary, musical, dramatic and choreographic works, pantomimes, and motion pictures and other audiovisual works, to perform the work publicly, without any requirement of such performance being "for profit". By Section 114 however, the exclusive rights of the owner of copyright in a sound recording are specifically stated not to include any right of public performance.

While coin operated record players are now brought within the net of public performance, the liability of their operators is fulfilled by obtaining a compulsory licence on application to the Copyright Office, and payment of the fee of $8 per year per machine. This royalty is subject to review by the Copyright Royalty Tribunal.

These extensions of the scope of the right of public performance should augment the royalty income of authors, composers and publishers of musical works widely performed in the United States. All such right owners should ensure that their American interests are properly taken care of.

8. Mechanical Right-Alteration of the rate of royalty.

Where sound recordings of a nondramatic musical work have been distributed to the public in the United States with the authority of the copyright owner, any other person may, by following the provisions of the law, obtain a compulsory licence to make and distribute sound recordings of the work. This right is known in the United Kingdom as "the mechanical right". Notice must be served on the copyright owner, who is entitled to a royalty in respect of each of his works recorded of either two and three fourths cents, or one half of one cent per minute of playing time or fraction thereof, whichever amount is the larger. Failure to serve or file the required notice forecloses the possibility of a compulsory licence, and in the absence of a negotiated licence, renders the making and distribution of such records actionable as acts of infringement.

9. Transfer of Copyright

Under the previous American law copyright was regarded as indivisible, which meant that on the transfer of copyright, where it was intended that only film rights or some other such limited right be transferred, the entire copyright nevertheless had to be passed. This led to a cumbersome procedure whereby the author would assign the whole copyright to his publisher, who would return to the author by means of an exclusive licence those rights which it was not meant to transfer.

Now it is provided by Section 201(d) of the Copyright Statute that (1) the ownership of a copyright may be transferred in whole or in part by any means of conveyance or by operation of law, and may be bequeathed by will or pass as personal property by the applicable laws of intestate succession and (2) any of the exclusive rights comprised in a copyright, (including any subdivision of any of the rights set out in Paragraph B3 above) may be transferred as provided in (1) above and owned separately. The owner of any particular exclusive right is entitled, to the extent of that right, to all the protection and remedies accorded to the copyright owner by that Statute. This removes the difficulties which existed under the previous law, and brings the position much closer to that existing in the copyright law of the United Kingdom.

10. Copyright Royalty Tribunal

A feature of the new United States law is the establishment of a Copyright Royalty Tribunal, with the purpose of making adjustments of reasonable copyright royalty rates in respect of the exercise of certain rights, mainly affecting the musical interests. The Tribunal is to consist of five commissioners appointed by the President with the advice and consent of the Senate for a term of seven years each. This body will perform in the United States a function similar to the Performing Right Tribunal in the United Kingdom.

The new American law spells out the economic objectives which the Copyright Tribunal is to apply in calculating the applicable rates. These are:

(i) to maximise the availability of creative works to the public;

(ii) to afford the copyright owner a fair return for his creative work and the copyright user a fair income under existing economic conditions;

(iii) to reflect the relative roles of the copyright owner and the copyright user in the product made available to the public with respect to relative creative contribution, technological contribution, capital investment, cost, risk, and contribution to the opening of new markets for creative expression and media for their communication;

(iv) to minimise any disruptive impact on the structure of the industries involved and on generally prevailing industry practices.

Every final determination of the Tribunal shall be published in the Federal Register. It shall state in detail the criteria that the Tribunal determined to be applicable to the particular proceeding, the various facts that it found relevant to its determination in that proceeding, and the specific reasons for its determination. Any final decision of the Tribunal in a proceeding may be appealed to the United States Court of Appeals by an aggrieved party, within thirty days after its publication in the Federal Register.

11. Fair Use

One of the most controversial factors which held up the introduction of the new American copyright law for at least a decade was the extent to which a balance should be struck between the desire of copyright owners to benefit from their works by extending copyright protection as far as possible, and the pressure from users of copyright to obtain access to copyright material as cheaply as possible—if not completely freely.

The new law provides by Section 107 that the fair use of a copyright work, including such use by reproduction in copies or on records, for purposes such as criticism, comment, news reporting, teaching (including multiple copies for classroom use), scholarship or research is not an infringement of copyright. In determining whether the use made of a work in any particular case is a fair use, the factors to be considered shall include:

(i) the purpose and character of the use, including whether such use is of a commercial nature or is for non-profit educational purposes;

(ii) the nature of the copyrighted work;

(iii) the amount and substantiality of the portion used in relation to the copyrighted work as a whole; and

(iv) the effect of the use upon the potential market for or value of the copyrighted work.

It is not an infringement of copyright for a library or archive, or any of its employees acting within the scope of their employment, to reproduce or distribute no more than one copy of a work, if:

(i) the reproduction or distribution is made without any purpose of direct, or indirect commercial advantage;

(ii) the collections of the library or archive are either open to the public or available not only to researchers affiliated with the library or archive or with the institution of which it is a part, but also to other persons doing research in a specialised field, and

(iii) the reproduction or distribution of the work includes a notice of copyright.

It is not generally an infringement of copyright if a performance or display of a work is given by instructors or pupils in the course of face to face teaching activities of a non-profit educational institution, in a classroom or similar place devoted to instruction.

Nor is it an infringement of copyright to give a performance of a non-dramatic literary or musical work or a dramatico-musical work of a religious nature in the course of services at a place of worship or other religious assembly.

It is also not an infringement of copyright to give a performance of a non-dramatic literary or musical work other than in a transmission to the public, without any purpose of direct or indirect commercial advantage and without payment of any fee for the performance to any of the performing artists, promoters or organisers if either (i) there is no direct or indirect admission charge or (ii) the proceeds, after deducting the reasonable costs of producing the performance, are used exclusively for educational, religious or charitable purposes and not for private financial gain. In this case the copyright owner has the right to serve notice of objection to the performance in a prescribed form.

C. REMEDIES FOR COPYRIGHT OWNERS

1. Infringement of Copyright

Copyright is infringed by anyone who violates any of the exclusive rights referred to in B.3. above, or who imports copies or records into the United States in violation of the law. The owner of copyright is entitled to institute an action for infringement so long as that infringement is committed while he or she is the owner of the right infringed. *It is vital to note that by virtue of Section 411 of the new law, no action for infringement of copyright can be instituted until registration of the copyright claim has been made.*

2. Injunctions

Any court having civil jurisdiction under the copyright law may grant interim and final injunctions on such terms as it may deem reasonable to prevent or restrain infringement of copyright. Such injunction may be served anywhere in the United States on the person named. An injunction is operative throughout the whole of the United States, and can be enforced by proceedings in contempt or otherwise by any American court which has jurisdiction over the infringer.

3. Impounding and disposition of infringing articles

At any time while a copyright action under American law is pending, the court may order the impounding on such terms as it considers reasonable, of all copies or records claimed to have been made or used in violation of the copyright owner's exclusive rights; it may also order the impounding of all plates, moulds, matrices, masters, tapes, film negatives or other articles by means of which infringing copies or records may be reproduced. A court may order as part of a final judgement or decree the destruction or other disposition of all copies or records found to have been made or used in violation of the copyright owner's exclusive rights. It also has the power to order the destruction of all articles by means of which infringing copies or records were reproduced.

4. Damages and profits

An infringer of copyright is generally liable either for the copyright owner's actual damages and any additional profits made by the infringer, or for statutory damages.

(i) The copyright owner is entitled to recover the actual damages suffered by him as a result of the infringement, and in addition any profits of the infringer which are attributable to the infringement and are not taken into account in computing the actual damages. In establishing the infringer's profits, the copyright owner is only required to present proof of the infringer's gross revenue, and it is for the infringer to prove his or her deductible expenses and the elements of profit attributable to factors other than the copyright work.

(ii) Except where copyright owner has persuaded the court that the infringement was committed wilfully, the copyright owner may elect, at any time before final judgement is given, to recover, instead of actual damages and profits, an award of statutory damages for all infringements involved in the action in respect of any one work, which may be between $250 and $10,000 according to what the court considers justified.

(iii) However, where the copyright owner satisfies the court that the infringement was committed wilfully, the court has the discretion to increase the award of statutory damages to not more than $50,000. Where the infringer succeeds in proving that he was not aware that and had no reason to believe that his acts constituted an infringement of copyright, the court has the discretion to reduce the award of statutory damages to not less than $100.

5. Costs: Time Limits

In any civil proceedings under American copyright law, the court has the discretion to allow the recovery of full costs by or against any party except the Government of the United States. It may also award a reasonable sum in respect of an attorney's fee.

No civil or criminal proceedings in respect of copyright law shall be permitted unless begun within three years after the claim or cause of action arose.

6. Criminal Proceedings in respect of Copyright

(i) Anyone who infringes a copyright wilfully and for purposes of commercial advantage and private financial gain shall be fined not more than $10,000 or imprisoned for not more than one year, or both. However, if the infringement relates to copyright in a sound recording or a film, the infringer is liable to a fine of not more than $25,000 or imprisonment for not more than one year or both on a first offence, which can be increased to a fine of up to $50,000 or imprisonment for not more than two years or both for a subsequent offence.

(ii) Following a conviction for criminal infringement a court may in addition to these penalties order the forfeiture and destruction of all infringing copies and records, together with implements and equipment used in their manufacture.

(iii) It is also an offence knowingly and with fradulent intent to place on any article a notice of copyright or words of the same purport, or to import or distribute such copies. A fine is provided for this offence of not more than $2500. The fraudulent removal of a copyright notice also attracts the same maximum fine, as does the false representation of a material particular on an application for copyright representation.

D. GENERAL OBSERVATIONS

The copyright law of the United States has been very greatly improved as a result of the new statute passed by Congress on 19 October 1976. (Title 17, United States Code.) Apart from lifting the general standards of protection for copyright owners to a much higher level than that which previously existed, it has on the whole shifted the balance of copyright protection in favour of the copyright owner and away from the copyright user in many of the areas where controversy existed. But most important for British and other non-American authors and publishers, it has gone a long way towards bringing American copyright law up to the same standards of international protection for non-national copyright proprietors which have long been offered by the United Kingdom and the other major countries, both in Europe and elsewhere in the English speaking world.

SUBSIDIARY RIGHTS

E. P. SKONE JAMES, M.A.

GENERALLY

The Copyright Act 1956 ("the Act") in Section 1(1) defines "copyright" in relation to a work as the exclusive right to do, and to authorise other persons to do, certain acts in relation to that work in the United Kingdom or in any other country to which the relevant provisions of the Act extend. Such acts in relation to a work of any description, being those acts which in the relevant provision of the Act are designated as the acts restricted by the copyright in a work of that description.

The "copyright" in respect of any work therefore consists of several different "restricted acts," or rights, which are not the same in respect of all works, and each of which may be the subject of a separate licence. It follows, therefore, that great care should be taken in drafting and signing agreements concerned with copyright, that such an agreement expressly refers to the rights in respect of which a licence is intended to be granted. For instance, an agreement to print and publish would not normally vest in the publisher any other rights of the author such as film rights, nor would an agreement granting a publisher the right to convert a literary work into a dramatic work vest in the publisher the film or broadcasting rights. However, such an agreement could expressly give a publisher an option to acquire additional rights, or specify who was to exploit such other rights, and, if the publisher, then specifying whether the author was to receive a percentage of the publisher's receipts. If the author is to receive a percentage, then such percentage should vary with the different rights since some rights will be obviously more valuable than others.

It should be noted also that, since, under the Act, it is now possible to assign future copyright (e.g. copyright which will, or may come into existence in respect of any future work or class of works or other subject-matter), care should be taken that any such agreement expressly excludes future copyright if so desired.

The Act contains special provisions as to libraries, permitting copying for special purposes unless the librarian knows the name and address of a person entitled to authorise the making of the copy, or could, by reasonable enquiry, ascertain the name and address of such a person. For this reason, an author should give his publisher power to grant such authorisation so that the publisher may be entitled to demand a fee, a percentage of which should be payable to the author.

It is not possible in this article to deal with all the rights restricted by copyright in a work but some of those of the greatest importance to writers and artists will be considered, either because they are rights conferred by the Act, or because they form part of such rights. It should be noted that a parody of a work such as a painting or a song is not an infringement if the parody amounts to an original work and no licence need be asked for or given (*Joy Music Ltd.* v *Sunday Pictorial Newspapers (1920) Ltd.* 1960 2 W.L.R. (645).

RIGHT TO REPRODUCE THE WORK BY RECORDS OR FILMS

It is a restricted act in relation to literary, dramatic, musical and artistic works (*inter alia*), to make a record or film thereof. Separate licences for each of these acts would therefore be necessary, though not in the case of a film of an artistic work if such work was included in the film only by way of background or was otherwise only incidental to the principal matters represented in the film.

Film companies will usually require to have the right to broadcast the film of the work but this is not, of course, the same as the right to broadcast the work itself using live actors, which right an author should be sure to retain.

RIGHT TO BROADCAST THE WORK

The Act for the first time makes "broadcasting" (e.g. by sound or television), a separate right in respect of literary, dramatic and musical works, and "including the work in a television broadcast" a separate right in the case of an artistic work, so that a separate licence to broadcast by sound or to broadcast by television is required, except where an artistic work is included in a television broadcast, if its inclusion therein was only by way of background, etc., as mentioned above in respect of a film.

RIGHT TO MAKE ADAPTATIONS OF THE WORK

An "adaptation" is a new expression in the Act the making of which is a restricted act applicable only to literary, dramatic and musical works. An "adaptation" is defined by the Act and means (i) An arrangement or transcription of a musical work, (ii) Converting a non-dramatic work into a dramatic work or vice versa, (iii) Translations of literary or dramatic works. The person making a translation will acquire a copyright in his work if he had a right to translate. (iv) Versions of literary or dramatic works in which the story or action is conveyed wholly or mainly by means of pictures in a form suitable for reproduction in a book or in a newspaper, magazine or similar periodical, e.g. comic strips. This is a new right granted by the Act.

The Copyright Act 1911 contained certain similar rights, but not classed under the one heading, and care should be taken to limit a licence to the particular "adaptation" intended as a licence to make "adaptations" would confer all such rights.

RIGHT TO SERIALISE

The Act does not define "serial rights" though, by reason of common usage, its meaning is well known. In the case of *Jonathan Cape, Ltd.* v. *Consolidated Press, Ltd.*, 1954 1 W.L.R. 3013, by Clause 1 of an Agreement between the author of an original work and the plaintiff publishers, the author agreed to grant to the publishers the exclusive right to print and publish the work "in volume form". Clause 12 of the Agreement referred, *inter alia*, to the first serial rights in the work in the terms "publication of instalments in several issues of a newspaper, magazine or periodical prior to publication in volume form", and Clause 13 referred, *inter alia*, to "all rights of serialisation subsequent to publication in volume form". It was held that Clauses 12 and 13 of the Agreement were concerned with serial rights in regard to the work, and they indicated that the transfer of rights effected by the Agreement was not to include, in the terms contained in Clause 1, the rights as regards the publication of the work in serial form. Further, looking at the Agreement, the real point was that the distinction was made between the publication of the work as a whole, which was meant by the word "volume", and the publication of the work by instalments, which was publication in a serial form, and was dealt with by the Agreement in a separate way. In that case, the defendants published a story in a single edition of a periodical, and it was held that there was an infringement of the plaintiffs' rights to publish in volume form. It would, of course, be possible to licence specifically publication in a single edition of a periodical.

It must be noted that serial rights are not limited to one serialisation since there can be first, second and third, etc., serial rights. Thus the licence should specify in respect of which serial rights it is granted.

Other matters which the licence should specify are: (i) the price to be paid; (ii) the date of payment; (iii) the date of publication; (iv) the place of publication. The last two are most important. The date of publication is important because the article may be a topical article: therefore, in order to preserve the value of the first serial rights, these should be sold on terms that they will be published by a prescribed date. The place of publication is important, and should always be stipulated, because serial rights, like other rights, may be separately sold for publication in different countries.

RIGHT TO HAVE THE WORK, OR PART THEREOF, INCLUDED IN AN ANTHOLOGY

An anthology, strictly a collection of poems, but also extended to include collections of short passages from various authors, is itself the subject of copyright protection. This was decided in an Indian case dealing with Palgrave's *The Golden Treasury of Songs and Lyrics*. The inclusion of a work, or part of it, in an anthology would be an infringement of the author's right to reproduce the work and to publish it, if unpublished, and would require a separate licence. Such a licence would not normally be included in a licence to print and publish (see also "Quotations" below).

RIGHT TO HAVE THE WORK ABRIDGED

The usual form of abridgement, or digest, of a work consists of a statement designed to be complete and accurate of the thoughts, opinions and ideas expressed in the work by the author but set forth much more concisely in the compressed language of the abridger (per Lord Atkinson in *Macmillan & Co., Ltd.* v. *Cooper*, 1923, 40 T.L.R. 186), and is itself the subject of copyright protection. Again, to make a digest of a work would be an infringement of the author's right to reproduce the work and to publish it would also be an infringement. A digest which consisted merely of a synopsis of the plot of a work might not be an infringement of that work, though an offence might be committed if the name of the original author was put on such digest in such a way as to imply that the original author was the author of the digest (Section 43 of the Act).

RIGHT TO HAVE THE WORK QUOTED

Quotation in the wide sense, by including part of the work in an anthology, has been referred to above, and, as a general rule, quotations from works are only permissible if licensed. But it is generally more convenient if the publisher is given a right to license quotations so that the author does not have to be sought on each occasion.

However, the Act provides exceptions to this rule. Thus, no fair dealing with the work for the purposes of research, private study, criticism or review is an infringement of the copyright therein, if, in the last two cases, the work and the author are identified. What is "fair dealing" is a matter of degree and involves a consideration of the number and extent of the quotations and extracts and of the use made of them. It applies to unpublished as well as to published works. "Fair dealing" for the purpose of criticism covers, not only criticsm of the literary style of the work, but also of the doctrine or philosophy expounded in the work; *Hubbard* v. *Vosper* 1972 2 W.L.R. 389. The publication of information known to have been "leaked" will not be a "fair dealing"; *Beloff* v. *Pressdram Ltd.* 1973 F.S.R. 33.

Similarly no fair dealing with the work for the purpose of reporting current events in newspapers, etc., or by broadcasting, or in a film, is an infringement if, in the last two cases, the work and author are identified.

Further, the reading or recitation in public (other than for the purposes of broadcasting), by one person of any reasonable extract from a published, literary or dramatic work, is not an infringement if the work and author are identified. Again, in certain circumstances, the inclusion of a short passage from a published literary or dramatic work in a collection intended for the use of schools is not an infringement.

All these exceptions apply to adaptations of the work as well as to the work itself (as to the meaning of "adaptation" see above).

RIGHT TO HAVE THE WORK REPRINTED

A licence to print and publish may be expressly confined to one edition only, with a right for the author to require further editions to be published when the first edition has gone out of print. If the publisher, on receipt of a notice from the author requesting the publication of a further edition, will not do so, the author should be entitled to go to another publisher.

RIGHT TO HAVE THE WORK PRINTED BY BOOK CLUBS

Book Clubs normally produce a special edition of the work at a cheaper price, and therefore the author's licence to the publisher should contain express provisions as to whether, and on what terms, such editions may be printed.

LIBEL

JAMES EVANS

WHAT follows is an outline of the main principles of the law of Libel, with special reference to points which appear most frequently to be misunderstood. But it is no more than that and specific legal advice should be taken when practical problems arise. The law discussed is the law of England and Wales. Scotland has its own, albeit somewhat similar, rules.

LIBEL: LIABILITY TO PAY DAMAGES

English Law draws a distinction between defamation published in permanent form and that which is not. The former is Libel, the latter Slander. "Permanent form" includes writing, printing, drawings and photographs and radio and television broadcasts. It follows that it is the law of Libel rather than Slander which most concerns writers and artists professionally, and the slightly differing rules applicable to Slander will not be mentioned in this article.

Publication of a libel can result in a civil action for damages and/or in certain cases a criminal prosecution against those responsible, who include the writer (or artist or photographer), the printers, the publishers, and the editor, if any, of the publication in which the libel appeared. Prosecutions are rare. Certain special rules apply to them and these will be explained below after a discussion of the question of civil liability, which in practice arises much more frequently.

In an action for damages for libel, it is for the plaintiff to establish that the matter he complains of (1) has been published by the defendant, (2) refers to himself, (3) is defamatory. If he does so, the plaintiff establishes a *prima facie* case. However, the defendant will escape liability if he can show he has a good defence. There are five defences to a libel action. They are (*a*) Justification, (*b*) Fair Comment, (*c*) Privilege, (*d*) S.4 of the Defamation Act, 1952, (*e*) Apology, etc., under the Libel Acts, 1843 and 1845. These matters must now be examined in detail.

THE PLAINTIFF'S CASE

(1) "Published" in the legal sense means communicated to a person other than the plaintiff. Thus the legal sense is wider than the lay sense but includes it. It follows that the contents of a book is published in the legal sense when the manuscript is first sent to the publishing firm just as much as it is when the book is later placed on sale to the public. Both types of publication are sufficient for the purpose of establishing liability for libel, but the law differentiates between them, since the scope of publication can properly be taken into account by the jury in considering the actual amount of damages to award. On this point, it should be noted that it is not necessary for the plaintiff in a libel action to prove that he has actually suffered any loss. The law presumes damage.

(2) The plaintiff must also establish that the matter complained of refers to himself. It is of course by no means necessary to mention a person's name before it is clear that he is referred to. Nicknames by which he is known or corruptions of his name are just two ways in which his identity can be indicated. There are more subtle methods. The sole question is whether the plaintiff is indicated to those who read the matter complained of. In some cases he will not be unless it is read in the light of facts known to the reader from other sources, but this is sufficient for the plaintiff's purpose. The test is purely

objective and does not depend at all on whether the writer intended to refer to the plaintiff.

It is because it is impossible to establish reference to any individual that generalisations, broadly speaking, are not successfully actionable. To say boldy "All lawyers are crooks" does not give any single lawyer a cause of action, because the statement does not point a finger at any individual. However, if anyone is named in conjunction with a generalisation, then it may lose its general character and become particular from the context. Again if one says "One of the X Committee has been convicted of murder" and the X Committee consists of, say, four persons, it cannot be said that the statement is not actionable because no individual is indicated and it could be referring to any of the committee. This is precisely why it is actionable at the suit of each of them as suspicion has been cast on all.

(3) It is for the plaintiff to show that the matter complained of is defamatory. What is defamatory is decided by the jury except in the extreme cases where the judge rules that the words cannot bear a defamatory meaning. Various tests have been laid down for determining this. It is sufficient that any one test is satisfied. The basic tests are: (i) Does the matter complained of tend to lower the plaintiff in the estimation of society? (ii) Does it tend to bring him into hatred, ridicule, contempt, dislike or disesteem with society? (iii) Does it tend to make him shunned or avoided or cut off from society?

"Society" means right-thinking members of society generally. It is by reference to such people that the above tests must be applied. A libel action against a newspaper which had stated that the police had taken a statement from the plaintiff failed, notwithstanding that the plaintiff gave evidence that his apparent assistance to the police (which he denied) had brought him into grave disrepute with the underworld. It was not by their wrongheaded standards that the matter fell to be judged.

Further, it is not necessary to imply that the plaintiff is at fault in some way in order to defame him. To say of a woman that she has been raped or of someone that he is insane imputes to them no degree of blame but nonetheless both statements are defamatory.

Sometimes a defamatory meaning is conveyed by words which on the face of them have no such meaning. "But Brutus is an honourable man" is an example. If a jury finds that words are meant ironically they will consider this ironical sense when determining whether the words are defamatory. In deciding therefore whether or not words are defamatory, the jury seek to discover what, without straining the words or putting a perverse construction on them, they will be understood to mean. In some cases this may differ substantially from their literal meaning.

Matter may also be defamatory by innuendo. Strictly so called, an innuendo is a meaning that words acquire by virtue of facts known to the reader but not stated in the passage complained of. Words, quite innocent on the face of them, may acquire a defamatory meaning when read in the light of these facts. For example, where a newspaper published a photograph of a man and a woman, with the caption that they had just announced their engagement, it was held to be defamatory of the man's wife since those who knew that she had cohabited with him were led to the belief that she had done so only as his mistress. The newspaper was unaware that the man was already married, but some of its readers were not.

DEFENCES TO A LIBEL ACTION

(a) Justification:

English law does not protect the reputation that a person either does not or should not possess. Stating the truth therefore does not incur liability and the plea of justification namely, that what is complained of is true in substance and in fact, is a complete answer to an action for damages. However, this defence is by no means to be undertaken lightly. For instance, to prove one instance of using bad language will be insufficient to justify the allegation that a person is "foulmouthed". It would be necessary to prove several instances and the defendant is obliged in most cases to particularise in his pleadings giving details, dates and places. However, if there are two or more distinct charges against the plaintiff the defence will not fail by reason only that the truth of every charge is not proved, if the words not proved to be true do not materially injure the plaintiff's reputation having regard to the truth of the remaining charges. It is for the defendant to prove that what he has published is true, not for the plaintiff to disprove it, though if he can do so, so much the better for him.

One point requires special mention. It is insufficient for the defendant to prove that he has accurately repeated what a third person has written or said or that such statements have gone uncontradicted when made on occasions in the past. If X writes "Y told me that Z is a liar", it is no defence to an action against X merely to prove that Y did say that. X has given currency to a defamatory statement concerning Z and has so made it his own. His only defence is to prove that Z is a liar by establishing a number of instances of Z's untruthfulness. Nor is it a defence to prove that the defendant genuinely believed what he published to be true. This might well be a complete answer in an action, other than a libel action, based on a false but non-defamatory statement. For such statements do not incur liability in the absence of fraud or malice, which, in this context, means a dishonest or otherwise improper motive. Bona fide belief, however, may be relevant to the assessment of damages, even in a libel action.

Special care should be taken in relation to references to a person's convictions however accurately described. Since the Rehabilitation of Offenders Act, 1974, a person's convictions may become "spent" and thereafter it may involve liability to refer to them. Reference to the Act and orders thereunder must be made in order to determine the position in any particular case.

(b) Fair Comment:

It is a defence to prove that what is complained of is fair comment made in good faith and without malice on a matter of public interest.

"Fair" in this context means "honest". "Fair comment" means therefore the expression of the writer's genuinely held opinion. It does not necessarily mean opinion with which the jury agree. Comment may therefore be quite extreme and still be "fair" in the legal sense. However, if it is utterly perverse the jury may be led to think that no one could have genuinely held such views. In such a case the defence would fail, for the comment could not be honest. "Malice" here includes the popular sense of personal spite, but covers any dishonest or improper motive.

The defence only applies when what is complained of is comment as distinct from a statement of fact. The line between comment and fact is notoriously difficult to draw in some cases. Comment means a statement of opinion. The facts on which comment is made must be stated together with the comment or be sufficiently indicated with it. This is merely another way of saying that it must be clear that the defamatory statement is one of opinion and not of fact, for which the only defence would be the onerous one of justification. The exact extent to which the facts commented on must be stated or referred to is a difficult question but some help may be derived in answering it by considering the purpose of the rule, which is to enable the reader to exercise his own judgement and to agree or disagree with the comment. It is quite plain that it is not necessary to state every single detail of the facts. In one case it was sufficient merely to mention the name of one of the Press lords in an article about a newspaper though not one owned by him. He was so well known that to mention his name indicated the substratum of fact commented upon, namely his control of his group of newspapers. No general rule can be laid down, save that, in general, the fuller the facts set out or referred to with the comment the better. These facts must always be true, except that in an action for libel partly in respect of allegations of fact and partly of expressions of opinion, a defence of fair comment will not fail by reason only that the truth of every allegation of fact is not proved, if the expression of opinion is fair comment, having regard to such of the facts alleged or referred to in the matter complained of as are proved.

The defence only applies where the matters commented on are of public interest, i.e. of legitimate concern to the public or a substantial section of it. Thus the conduct of national and local government, international affairs, the administration of justice, etc., are all matters of public interest, whereas other people's private affairs may very well not be, although they undoubtedly interest the public.

In addition matters of which criticism has been expressly or impliedly invited, such as publicly performed plays and published books, are a legitimate subject of comment. Criticism need not be confined merely to their artistic merit but equally may deal with the attitudes to life and the opinions therein expressed.

It is sometimes said that a man's moral character is never a proper subject of comment for the purpose of this defence. This is certainly true where it is a private individual who is concerned and some authorities say it is the same in the case of a public figure even though his character may be relevant to his public life. Again, it may in some cases be exceeding the bounds of Fair Comment to impute a dishonourable motive to a person, as is frequently done by way of inference from facts. In general, the imputation is a dangerous and potentially expensive practice.

(c) Privilege:

In the public interest, certain occasions are privileged so that to make defamatory statements upon them does not incur liability. The following are privileged in any event: (i) Fair, accurate and contemporaneous reports of public judicial proceedings in England published in a newspaper, (ii) Parliamentary papers published by the direction of either House, or full republications thereof. The following are privileged provided publication is made only for the reason that the privilege is given and not for some wrongful or indirect motive: (i) Fair and accurate but non-contemporaneous reports of public judicial proceedings in England, whether in a newspaper or not, (ii) Extracts of Parliamentary papers, (iii) Fair and accurate reports of Parliamentary proceedings, (iv) A fair and accurate report in a newspaper of the proceedings at any public meeting held in the United Kingdom. The meeting must be bona fide and lawfully held for a lawful purpose and for the furtherance or discussion of any matter of public concern. Admission to the meeting may be general or restricted. In the case of public meetings, the defence is not available, if it is proved that the defendant has been requested by the plaintiff to publish in the newspaper in which the original publication was made a reasonable letter or statement by way of explanation or contradiction, and has refused or neglected to do so, or has done so in a manner not adequate or not reasonable having regard to all the circumstances. This list of privileged occasions is by no means exhaustive, but they are those most commonly utilised.

(d) S.4 of the Defamation Act, 1952:

The defence provided by the above section is only available where the defamation is "innocent". As has been seen, liability for libel is in no way dependent on the existence of an intention to defame on the part of the defendant and the absence of such an intention does not mean that the defamation is "innocent".

Defamation is innocent if the publisher did not intend to publish the matter complained of about the plaintiff and did not know of circumstances by virtue of which it might be understood to refer to him, or, if the matter published was not defamatory on the face of it, if the publisher did not know of circumstances by virtue of which it might be understood to be defamatory. Further the publisher must have exercised all reasonable care in relation to the publication. If the publisher has published matter innocently, he should make an "offer of amends" to the party aggrieved. This consists of an offer to publish a correction and apology and as far as practicable to inform others to whom the alleged libel has been distributed that the matter is said to be defamatory. If the offer of amends is accepted, it is a bar to further proceedings against the person making the offer. If rejected, the making of the offer affords a defence provided the defendant can prove that he did publish innocently and made the offer as soon as practicable after learning that the matter published was or might be defamatory. The offer must not have been withdrawn and must have been expressed to be for the purposes of the defence under S.4 and have been accompanied by an affidavit. It is vital that the offer should be made swiftly, but it is inadvisable to make it without professional advice owing to its technicality. An example of the first type of innocent publication is where a reference to a person by name has been understood to refer to another person of the same name and this could not reasonably have been foreseen.

An example of the other type of innocent publication is the case referred to earlier in this article of the man pictured with "his fiancée". The publishers did not know that he was already married and that accordingly the picture and caption could be understood to be defamatory of his wife.

In practice all the conditions for a successful defence under this section are infrequently fulfilled.

(e) Apology under the Libel Acts, 1843 and 1845:
This defence is rarely utilised, since if any condition of it is not fulfilled, the plaintiff must succeed and the only question is the actual amount of damages. It only applies to actions in respect of libels in newspapers and periodicals. The defendant pleads that the libel was inserted without actual malice and without gross negligence and that before the action commenced or as soon afterwards as possible he inserted a full apology in the same newspaper, etc., or had offered to publish it in a newspaper, etc., of the plaintiff's choice, where the orginal newspaper is published at intervals greater than a week. Further a sum must be paid into court with this defence to compensate the plaintiff.

CRIMINAL LIBEL

Whereas the object of a civil action is to obtain compensation for the wrong done, the object of criminal proceedings is to punish the wrongdoer by fine or imprisonment or both. There are four main types of writing which may provoke a prosecution and can be collectively described as "Criminal Libels". They are:—

> (i) Defamatory Libel;
> (ii) Obscene Libel;
> (iii) Seditious Libel;
> (iv) Blasphemous Libel

(i) The publication of defamatory matter is in certain circumstances a crime as well as a civil wrong. But whereas the principal object of civil proceedings will normally be to obtain compensation, the principal object of a criminal prosecution will be to secure punishment of the accused, for example by way of a fine. Prosecutions are not frequent but there have been signs of late of a revival of interest. There are important differences between the rules applicable to criminal libel and its civil counterpart. For example, a criminal libel may be "published" even though only communicated to the person defamed and may be found to have occurred even where the person defamed is dead, or where only a group of persons but no particular individual has been maligned.

(ii) It is an offence to publish obscene matter. By the Obscene Publications Act, 1959, matter is obscene if its effect is such as to tend to deprave and corrupt persons who are likely, having regard to all relevant circumstances, to read, see or hear it. "To deprave and corrupt" is to be distinguished from "to shock and disgust". It is a defence to a prosecution to prove that publication of the matter in question is justified as being for the public good, on the ground that it is in the interests of science, literature, art or learning, or of other objects of general concern. Expert evidence may be given as to its literary, artistic, scientific or other merits. Playwrights, in particular, should note the Theatres Act, 1968.

(iii) Writings which tend to destroy the peace of the Realm are seditious and may be the subject of a prosecution. Seditious writings include those which advocate reform by unconstitutional or violent means or incite contempt or hatred for the Monarch or Parliament. These institutions may be criticised stringently, but not in a manner which is likely to lead to insurrection or civil commotion or indeed any physical force. Prosecutions are a rarity, but it should be remembered that writers of matter contemptuous of the House of Commons, though not prosecuted for seditious libel, are, from time to time, punished by that House for breach of its Privileges, although, if a full apology is made, it is often an end of the matter.

(iv) Blasphemous libel consists in the vilification of the Christian religion or its ceremonies. The offence lies not so much in what is said concerning, for instance, God, Christ, the Bible, the Book of Common Prayer, etc., but how it is said. Temperate and sober writings on religious topics however anti-Christian in sentiment will not involve liability. But if the discussion is "so scurrilous and offensive as to pass the limit of decent controversy and to outrage any Christian feeling," it will.

INCOME TAX FOR WRITERS AND ARTISTS

PETER VAINES, A.C.A., A.T.H.

THIS article is intended to explain the impact of taxation on writers and others engaged in similar projects. Despite attempts by many Governments to simplify our taxation system, the subject has become increasingly complicated and the following is an attempt to give a broad outline of the position.

HOW INCOME IS TAXED

a) *Generally*

Authors are usually treated for tax purposes as carrying on a profession and are taxed in a similar fashion to other professional persons, i.e. as self-employed persons assessable under Schedule "D". This article is directed to self-employed persons only, because if a writer is "employed" he will be subject to the rules of Schedule "E" where different considerations apply—substantially to his disadvantage. Attempts are often made by employed persons to shake off the status of "employee" and to attain "freelance" status so as to qualify for the advantages of Schedule "D", such attempts meeting with varying degrees of success. The problems involved in making this transition are considerable and space does not permit a detailed explanation to be made here—proper advice is necessary if the difficulties are to be avoided.

b) *Income*

For income to be taxable it need not be substantial, nor need it be the author's only source of income; earnings from casual writing are also taxable but this can be an advantage, because occasional writers do not often make a profit from their writing. The expenses incurred in connection with writing may well exceed any income receivable and the resultant loss may then be used to reclaim tax paid on other income. This feature has not escaped the Inland Revenue, who sometimes attempt to treat casual work as being a hobby so that any losses incurred cannot be relieved; however, by the same token, any income receivable would not be taxable. This treatment should be resisted vigorously because the Inland Revenue do not hesitate to change their mind when profits begin to arise. From the income receivable there may be deducted certain allowable expenses; in addition, expenditure on capital items such as typewriters, cameras, any recording or other equipment, books, etc., used for business purposes may qualify for valuable capital allowances. Both types of expenditure are dealt with later.

c) *Royalties*

A series of cases has laid down a clear principle that sales of copyright are taxable as income and not as capital receipts if the recipient is carrying on the profession of an author. Similarly, lump sums on account of, or in advance of royalties are also taxable as income in the year of receipt, subject to a claim for spreading relief (see below).

Copyright royalties are generally paid without deduction of Income Tax. However, if royalties are paid to an author who normally lives abroad, tax must be deducted by the payer or his agent at the time the payment is made.

d) *Arts Council Grants*

At the time of writing there is considerable uncertainty regarding the tax position of persons receiving grants from the Arts Council and similar bodies.

The Inland Revenue are refining their attitude towards such grants, treating many of them as income fully taxable in the hands of the recipient. The subject is currently under detailed scrutiny by the Arts Council and a number of other interested parties (including the Inland Revenue) and when the matter has been determined no doubt it will be given wide publicity. In the meantime no general guidance can be given, other than to say that these grants are not always taxable—much will depend on the individual circumstances of the recipient.

ALLOWABLE EXPENSES

To qualify as an allowable business expense, expenditure has to be laid out wholly and exclusively for business purposes. Strictly there must be no "duality of purpose", which means that expenditure cannot be apportioned to reflect the private and business usage, e.g. food, clothing, telephone, travelling expenses, etc. However, the Inland Revenue do not usually interpret this principle strictly and are prepared to allow all reasonable expenses (including apportioned sums) where the amounts can be commercially justified. It should be noted carefully that the expenditure does not have to be "necessary", it merely has to be incurred "wholly and exclusively" for business purposes; naturally however, expenditure of an outrageous and wholly unnecessary character might well give rise to a presumption that it was not really for business purposes. As with all things, some expenses are unquestionably allowable and some expenses are equally unquestionably not allowable—it is the grey area in between which gives rise to all the difficulties and the outcome invariably depends on negotiation with the Inland Revenue.

Great care should be taken when claiming a deduction for items where there is a "duality of purpose" and negotiations should be conducted with more than usual care and courtesy—if provoked the Inspector of Taxes may well choose to allow nothing. An appeal is always possible, but is unlikely to succeed as a string of cases in the Courts has clearly demonstrated. An example is the case of *Caillebotte* v. *Quinn* where the taxpayer (who normally had lunch at home) sought to claim the excess cost of meals incurred because he was working a long way from his home. The taxpayer's arguments failed because he did not eat only in order to work, one of the reasons for him eating was in order to sustain his life; a duality of purpose therefore existed and no tax relief was due. Other cases have shown that expenditure on clothing can also be disallowed if it is the kind of clothing which is in everyday use, because clothing is worn not only to assist the pursuit of one's profession but also to accord with public decency. This duality of purpose may be sufficient to deny relief—even where the particular type of clothing is not the kind otherwise worn by the taxpayer.

Despite the above Inspectors of Taxes are not usually inflexible and the following expenses are among those generally allowed:

a) Cost of all materials used up in the course of preparation of the work.

b) Cost of typewriting and secretarial assistance, etc.; if this or other help is obtained from one's spouse then it is entirely proper for a deduction to be claimed for the amounts paid for the work. The amounts claimed must actually be paid to the spouse and should be at the market rate although some uplift can be made for unsocial hours, etc. Payments to a wife (or husband) are of course taxable in her (or his) hands and may also give rise to a liability to additional National Insurance contributions.

c) All expenditure on normal business items such as postage, stationery, agent's fees, accountancy charges, photography, subscriptions, periodicals, magazines, etc., may be claimed. The cost of daily papers should not be overlooked if these form part of research material. Visits to theatres, cinemas, etc., for research purposes may also be permissible (but not of course the cost relating to guests).

d) If work is conducted at home, a deduction for "use of home" is usually allowed providing the amount claimed is not unreasonable. If the claim is based on an appropriate proportion of the total costs of rent and rates, light and heat, cleaning and maintenance, insurance, etc. then care should be taken to ensure that no single room is used *"exclusively"* for business purposes, because this may result in the Capital Gains Tax exemption on the house as a principal private residence being partially forfeited. However, it would be a strange household where one room was in fact used exclusively for business purposes and for no other purpose whatsoever (e.g. storing personal bank statements and other private papers); therefore the usual formula is to claim a deduction on the basis that most or all of the rooms in the house are used at one time or another for business purposes, thereby avoiding any suggestion that any part was used exclusively for business purposes.

e) The appropriate business proportion of motor running expenses may also be claimed although what is the appropriate proportion will naturally depend on the particular circumstances in each case; it should be mentioned that the well publicised "private motoring benefits" legislation whereby one is taxed accordingly to the size and cost of the car does not apply to self-employed persons.

f) It has been clearly established that the cost of travelling to and from home to one's place of work (whether employed or self-employed) is not an allowable expense. However, if home is one's place of work then no expenditure under this heading is likely to be incurred and no difficulties are likely to arise.

g) Travelling and hotel expenses incurred for business purposes will normally be allowed but if any part could be construed as disguised holiday or pleasure expenditure, considerable thought would need to be given to the commercial reasons for the journey in order to justify the claim. The principle of "duality of purpose" will always be a difficult hurdle in this connection—although not insurmountable.

h) If a separate business bank account is maintained, any overdraft, interest thereon will be an allowable expense. This is the *only* circumstance in which overdraft interest is allowed for tax purposes and care should be taken to avoid overdrafts in all other circumstances.

i) Where capital allowances (see below) are claimed for a television, record or tape player, etc., used for business purposes an appropriate proportion of the costs of maintenance and repair of the equipment may also be claimed.

Clearly many other allowable items may be claimed in addition to those mentioned above. Wherever there is any reasonable business motive for some expenditure it should be claimed as a deduction although one should avoid an excess of imagination as this would naturally cause the Inspector of Taxes to doubt the genuineness of other expenses claimed.

The question is often raised whether the whole amount of an expense may be deducted or whether the V.A.T. content must be excluded. The position is that where V.A.T. is reclaimed from the Customs and Excise (one the quarterly V.A.T. returns by a person who is registered for V.A.T.), that V.A.T. cannot be treated as an allowable deduction. Where the V.A.T. is not reclaimed, the whole expense (including the V.A.T. content) is allowable for Income Tax purposes.

CAPITAL ALLOWANCES

a) *Allowances*

Where expenditure of a capital nature is incurred, it cannot be deducted from income as an expense—a separate and often more valuable capital allowance being available instead. Capital allowances are given for many different types of expenditure, but authors and similar professional people are likely to claim only for "plant and machinery"; this is a very wide expression which may include motor cars, typewriters and other business machines, televisions, record and cassette players used for business purposes, books—and even a horse! Plant and machinery (other than motor cars) qualifies for a first year allowance of 100% which means that the whole cost may be allowed in the year of purchase; motor cars qualify for an allowance of only 25% per annum.

The reason these allowances can be more valuable than allowable expenses is that they may be wholly or partly disclaimed in any year that full benefit cannot be obtained—ordinary business expenses cannot be similarly disclaimed. Where, for example, the income of an author does not exceed his personal allowances, he would not be liable to tax and a claim for capital allowances would be wasted. If the capital allowances were to be disclaimed their benefit would be carried forward for use in subsequent years. (One cannot, however, claim the full 100% allowance in the following year; only the writing down allowance of 25% can be claimed on the reducing balance each year until relief has been obtained for full cost.)

Careful planning with claims for capital allowances is essential if maximum benefit is to be obtained, especially where the spouse also has income chargeable to tax.

Prior to the introduction of the 100% first year allowance, claims could be made on the "renewals" basis whereby all renewals were treated as allowable expenses; no allowance was obtained for the initial purchase, but the cost of replacement (excluding any improvement element) was allowed in full. This basis is no longer widely used, as it is considerably less advantageous than claiming capital allowances as described above.

b) *Books*

The question of whether the cost of books is eligible for tax relief has long been a source of difficulty. The annual cost of replacing books used for the purposes of one's professional activities has always been an allowable expense; the difficulty arose because the initial cost of reference books etc. (for example when commencing one's profession) was treated as capital expenditure and no allowances were due as the books were not considered to be "plant". However, the matter has now been clarified by the case of *Munby* v. *Furlong* in which the Court of Appeal decided that the initial cost of law books purchased by a barrister was expenditure on "plant" and eligible for the 100% first year allowance: This is clearly a most important decision, particularly relevant to any person who uses expensive books in the course of exercising his profession.

PENSION CONTRIBUTIONS

a) *Self employed retirement annuities*

Where a self employed person pays annual premiums under an approved retirement annuity policy, tax relief may be obtained each year for an amount up to 15% of earnings (as reduced by capital allowances) with a maximum premium of £3,000. (This figure of £3,000 applies for 1978/79 and will doubtless be increased in subsequent years.)

These arrangements can be extremely advantageous in providing pensions as premiums are usually paid when the income is high (and the tax relief is also high) and the pension (taxed as earned income when received) usually arises when the income is low and little tax is payable.

b) *Class 4 National Insurance Contributions*

Allied to pensions is the payment of Class 4 National Insurance contributions, although no pension or other benefit is obtained by the contributions; the Class 4 contributions are designed solely to extract additional amounts of National Insurance from self-employed persons and are payable in addition to the normal Class 2 (self-employed) contributions. The rates have been reduced from 6th April 1978 and self-employed persons will be obliged to contribute 5% of their earnings between the range £2,000–£6,250 per annum, a maximum liability of £212.50 for 1978–79. This amount is collected in conjunction with the Schedule "D" Income Tax liability and appears on the same assessment; the comments below regarding assessments, appeals and postponement apply equally to Class 4 contributions although interest does not accrue on their late payment. Tax relief is not available for any National Insurance contributions paid.

SPREADING RELIEF

a) *Relief for Copyright Payments*

Special provisions enable authors and similar persons who have been engaged on a literary, dramatic, musical or artistic work for a period of more than twelve months, to spread certain amounts received over two or three years depending on the time spent in preparing the work. If the author was engaged on the work for a period exceeding twelve months, the receipt may be spread backwards over two years; if the author was engaged on the work for more than 24 months, the receipt may be spread backwards over three years. (Analogous provisions apply to sums received for the sale of a painting, sculpture or other work of art.)

The relief applies to:
   a. lump sums received on the assignment of copyright, in whole or in part;
   b. sums received on the grant of any interest in the copyright by licence;
   c. non-returnable advances on account of royalties;
   d. any receipts of or on account of royalties or any periodical sums received within two years of first publication.

A claim for spreading relief has to be made within eight years from the 5th April following the date of first publication.

b) *Relief where copyright sold after ten years*

Where copyright is assigned (or a licence in it is granted) more than ten years after the first publication of the work, then the amounts received can qualify for a different spreading relief. The assignment (or licence) must be for a period of more than two years and the receipt will be spread forward over the number of years for which the assignment (or licence) is granted—but with a maximum of six years. The relief is terminated by death, but there are provisions enabling the deceased's author's personal representatives to re-spread the amounts if it is to the beneficiaries' advantage.

COLLECTION OF TAX

a) *Assessments*

In order to collect the tax which is due on the profits of authorship the Inland Revenue issue an assessment based on the income for the relevant period. Normally the income to be assessed will be that for the previous year (e.g. the 1978/79 assessment will be based on the accounts made up to some date in 1977/78—perhaps 31st December 1977 or 5th April 1978). However, there are complicated rules for determining the income to be assessed in the years immediately after commencement, and in the years immediately prior to the discontinuance of the profession, and if for any reason there is a change in the date to which accounts are made up.

For those starting in business or commencing work on a freelance basis the Inland Revenue produce a very useful booklet entitled "Starting in Business (IR28)", which is available from any tax office.

When an assessment is received it should be examined carefully and if it is correct, the tax should be paid on the dates specified. Usually the tax is payable in two equal instalments, on 1st January in the year of assessment and on the following 1st July. If payment is delayed then interest may arise—see below.

b) If the assessment is incorrect (for example, if it is estimated), then prompt action is required. An appeal must be lodged within thirty days of the date of issue of the assessment specifying the grounds of the appeal. An appeal form usually accompanies the notice of assessment. (If for some reason an appeal cannot be lodged within the thirty days the Inland Revenue are often prepared to accept a late appeal , but this is at their discretion and acceptance cannot be guaranteed.) If there is any tax charged on an incorrect assessment it cannot simply be forgotten, because it will become payable despite any appeal, unless an application for "postponement" is also made. (This may be done by completing the bottom half of the appeal form.) Tax can be postponed only where there are grounds for believing that too much tax has been charged, and the Inspector of Taxes will agree to postpone tax only if these grounds are reasonable. The tax which is not postponed will usually be payable on the normal due dates . It is necessary to consider claims for postponement most carefully to ensure that approximately the correct amount of tax remains payable; otherwise an unfortunate (and expensive) charge to interest could arise. It is important to recognise that "postponement" does not mean elimination; it simply means that payment of tax may be postponed—usually for only six months. After that period has expired interest will start to run on any tax which has been postponed but which is ultimately found to be payable. As agreement of the final liability may take a long time, a large amount of interest can arise unless a reasonably accurate amount has been paid on time. (Of course if *all* the tax charged on an assessment is paid on time no interest can arise; if the final liability is later found to be higher than that originally assessed a further assessment will be issued, interest on which will not start to run until a further period of thirty days has expired.)

c) *Interest*

Interest is chargeable on overdue tax at a rate of 9% per annum and does not rank for any tax relief which makes the Inland Revenue a very expensive source of credit. Where the amount of interest is less than £10 it is not usually collected but should the interest exceed £10 the full amount will be payable and it is extraordinarily difficult to persuade the Inland Revenue to withdraw a charge to interest—even where the delay is their fault.

However, the Inland Revenue can also be obliged to pay interest (known as repayment supplement) at 9% tax-free where repayments are delayed. The rules relating to repayment supplement are naturally less beneficial and even more complicated than the rules for interest payable but they do exist and can be very profitable if a large repayment has been delayed for a long time.

d) *Example:*

Authors' accounts made up to 30th April 1977 showing profits of £2,000 giving rise to tax of (say) £200.

Assessment issued in September 1978 for 1978/79 in an estimated figure of £5,000—tax charged £1,500.

Appeal must be made within 30 days of issue.

Application for postponement must also be made within 30 days to postpone £1,300 of the tax charged.

Tax therefore becomes payable thus:

1st Jan. 1979	£100
1st July 1979	£100

(if no application for postponement were to be made £750 would become payable on each of these dates. When the final liability is agreed the excess of £1,300 would be refunded but that could take some time, and repayment supplement might not apply.)

Unfortunately life is never as simple as the above illustration would suggest, but it serves to demonstrate the principle.

VALUE ADDED TAX

The activities of writers, painters, composers, etc., are all "taxable supplies" within the scope of V.A.T. and chargeable at the standard rate. (Zero rating which applies to publishers, booksellers, etc., on the supply of books does not extend to the work performed by writers unless the writing falls within the category of news; the position is less clear with regard to authors writing for foreign persons. Changes were made in the V.A.T. rules from 1st January 1978 with the effect that zero rating does not always apply. Proper advice should be sought if there is any doubt regarding the correct treatment.) Accordingly, authors are obliged to register for V.A.T. if their income exceeds certain limits; the annual limit has recently been increased to £10,000 per annum with effect from 12th April 1978, but there are quarterly limits, as under, which if exceeded may render the author liable to registration:

£3,500	in the last calendar quarter
£6,000	in the last two calendar quarters
£8,500	in the last three calendar quarters
£10,000	in the last four calendar quarters

Delay in registering can be a most serious matter because if registration is not effected at the proper time, the Customs and Excise can (and invariably do) claim V.A.T. from all the income received since the date on which registration should have been made. As no V.A.T. would have been included in the amounts received during this period the amount claimed by the Customs and Excise must inevitably come straight from the pocket of the author—and he is unlikely to be able to claim reimbursement from all those whom he ought to have charged V.A.T. in the interregnum.

(This difficulty can give rise to considerable injustice and has done so on a number of occasions; the appeal tribunals concerned have often expressed sympathy for the taxpayer's predicament but have been unable to provide any relief.)

Nevertheless it is possible to regard V.A.T. registration as a privilege and not a penalty, because only V.A.T. registered persons can reclaim V.A.T. paid on such expenditure as stationery, telephone, professional fees, etc., even type-writers and other plant and machinery (excluding cars). However, many find that the administrative inconvenience, the cost of maintaining the necessary records and completing the necessary forms, more than outweighs the benefits to be gained from registration and prefer to stay outside the scope of V.A.T. for as long as possible.

OVERSEAS MATTERS

The self-employed do not (yet) enjoy the privileges relating to working abroad afforded to employed persons—the well publicised 25% and 100% deductions from salary apply only to employees, although proposals are contained in this year's Finance Bill to give similar relief to the self-employed. The self-employed are not well treated in regard to overseas work as they are generally taxed on their world-wide professional income if they are resident in the United Kingdom (which is usually their intention). The point cannot be made too strongly that if fees are earned abroad, no tax saving can be achieved merely by keeping the money outside the country. Exchange Control regulations require foreign earnings to be repatriated to the Schedule Territories (unless special permission is granted) and whether the income is repatriated or not, it remains taxable in the U.K.—and so does any income arising from its investment. Accordingly whenever foreign earnings are likely to become substantial, prompt and effective action is required to limit the impact of U.K. and foreign taxation.

The United Kingdom has double taxation agreements with many other coun-tries (including Eire which is a popular place of emigration for many writers and artists because of special tax provisions which exist in that country), and these agreements are designed to ensure that income arising in a foreign country is taxed either in that country, or in the United Kingdom. Where a withholding tax is deducted from payments received from another country, (or where tax is paid in full in the absence of a double taxation agreement) the amount of foreign tax paid can usually be set off against the related U.K. tax liability.

COMPANIES

When an author becomes successful the prospect of paying tax at alarmingly high rates often drives him to take hasty action such as the formation of companies etc., which may not always be to his advantage. Indeed some authors seeing the exodus into tax exile of their more successful colleagues even form companies in low tax areas in the naive expectation of saving large amounts of tax. Unfortunately such action is just as likely to *increase* their tax liabilities and generate other costs and should never be contemplated without expert advice; some very expensive mistakes are often made in this area which are not always able to be remedied.

To conduct one's business through the medium of a company can be a most effective method of mitigating tax liabilities; however, it is essential to take the utmost care—for example, the company's business must be genuine and conducted properly with regard to the realities of the situation. If the author continues his activities unchanged, simply paying all the receipts from his work into a company's bank account, he cannot expect to persuade the Inland Revenue that it is the company and not himself who is entitled to, and should be assessed to tax on, that income.

No mention has been made above of personal reliefs and allowances (for example the single and married persons allowances, child allowances, life assurance relief, etc.); this is because these allowances and the rates of tax are subject to constant change and are always set out in detail in the explanatory notes which accompany the Tax Return. The annual Tax Return is an important document and should not be ignored because it is crucial to one's tax position. If filling in the Return is a source of difficulty and anxiety, much comfort may be found in the Consumer Association's *Tax Saving Guide*; this is published in March of each year and includes much which is likely to be of interest and assistance.

NATIONAL INSURANCE AND SOCIAL SECURITY

The law and the rules relating to Social Security Insurance embracing the numerous types of cover, benefits, liability and rules for rates of contributions, pensions and other factors are very many and in some cases difficult to understand and no less so to keep up to date in an annual article. Information can be out of date, superseded, amended, added to and varied even before it gets in print in a year book. At the outset of an article such as this, touching problems of National Social Security, it is well to remember these facts. Included in this matter are questions relating to phases as diverse as rates of contributions (employers' and employees'), unemployment benefits, sickness benefits, maternity benefits, widows' benefits, guardians' allowances, child benefit, local rates relief, hospital treatment, prescription charges, dental and optical treatment, pensions for the old, the retired and the not-so-old, supplementary allowances, death grants to the bereaved and a great number of problems arising within each of these as well as borderline cases, and so the writer strongly advises all whether or not they know or feel there is a possibility of their being within the range of any of them to apply to their local post offices for copies of the latest pamphlets dealing with the matters and, where practical, to seek personal advice from officials at Social Security offices. New and increased existing benefits (and sometimes charges) are frequently made known by this method.

From 6 April 1978 the Social Security Pensions Act 1975 introduced earnings-related retirement, invalidity and widow's pensions for Class 1 employees (*q.v.*).

OUTLINE OF THE NEW EARNINGS-RELATED SCHEME

All persons must contribute to the National Social Security Scheme unless they are non-employed or self-employed and can show that their total income, taking cash and kind together (i.e. including the value of board, lodging, free meals, etc.) is under the currently prescribed figure, in which case they *may apply* for exemption from liability to pay contributions. The necessary form on which to make the application can be obtained from the local Social Security Office. Entitlement to benefits is affected by the number of conditions and circumstances.

For the purposes of raising contributions to the new scheme, the insured population is divided into four classes as follows:

CLASS 1

These are payable by persons who work for an employer under a contract of service or who are office-holders with emoluments chargeable to Schedule E income tax. An employee's national insurance contribution liability depends on whether he is in contracted out or not-contracted-out employment. The not-contracted-out employee pays $6\frac{1}{2}\%$ on all earnings up to £120 a week. The employers' rate is $13\frac{1}{2}\%$ (including a $3\frac{1}{2}\%$ National Insurance Surcharge) of the same earnings.

An employee's contracted-out contribution is $6\frac{1}{2}\%$ of the first £17.50 a week of earnings and 4% of earnings between £17.50 and £120 a week. The employer's contribution is 10% (and the $3\frac{1}{2}\%$ surcharge) of the first £17.50 of weekly earnings and $5\frac{1}{2}\%$ (and the $3\frac{1}{2}\%$ surcharge) of earnings up to £120 a week.

Women who have chosen to pay the reduced rate of contributions will pay 2% on all earnings whether not contracted out or contracted out.

Men and women who reach pensionable age (65 for men, 60 for women) pay no contributions even if they work after that age, though employers continue to pay national insurance contributions after the employee's pensionable age at the not-contracted-out rate regardless of the employee's liability position prior to that age.

There is no liability for employer or employee if earnings do not reach the lower earnings limit of £17.50 a week. Class 1 contributions are collected by the Inland Revenue with the PAYE income tax arrangements.

CLASS 2

These are persons engaged in business on their own account. They are responsible for stamping their own cards by purchasing Class 2 national insurance stamps from Post Offices or by a system of direct debit of a Bank or Giro account. The rate of contribution from April 1978 is £1.90 for both men and women and there is no liability to pay contributions after they reach pensionable age (65 for men and 60 for women).

Class 2 contributions are payable in addition to any Class 1 contributions for which a person may be liable, but he can apply for deferment of Class 2 liability if the combination of Class 1 and Class 2 (and, where applicable, Class 4) contributions is liable to exceed a specified maximum. If earnings are expected to be less than £950 p.a. net of a certain expenses a contributor may apply for exception from liability to pay Class 2 contributions for that year.

CLASS 3

Persons falling in neither of the first two categories are regarded as non employed. Class 3 contributions are voluntary and are paid to provide a limited range of benefits, principally the basic retirement pension. The rate for both men and women is £1.80 a week and can be paid in the same way as Class 2 contributions.

CLASS 4

Self-employed contributors are liable to pay Class 4 contributions at a rate of 5% from April 6 1978 on annual profits or gains chargeable to tax under Schedule D between £2000 and £6250. These are collected by the Inland Revenue along with Schedule D income tax.

Reduced Contributions liability

Certain married women and widows retain the right to reduced contributions liability paying Class 1 contributions at the reduced rate of 2% when employed and paying no Class 2 contributions when self employed. This reduced liability is being phased out and retained only by those who were entitled to it at 5 April 1978.

The employers contribution is not affected by the reduced liability.

Reduced contributions do not count for benefit purposes.

An author or artist who is insurable may have some difficulty in determining in which class he comes. He knows, of course, whether he is in salaried (or other form of remunerated) employment, or if he is a free-lance without any control as to how and when he does his writing. But that is not the extent of the test to be applied. If he is free-lance, he is *self-employed.*

A writer's classification can change from week to week; for instance, if an otherwise self-employed person performs eight or more hours' work for an employer under a contract of service in any week, for that week he ranks as an employed person. His employer must stamp the card at the higher rate; the writer is not liable to do it himself.

An employed person is one who is employed under a "contract of service" which would be distinguishable from a "contract for services" which latter does not make one an employed person. The former embodies an element of relationship of master and servant, the one having power to control the way in which the other performs his tasks. Those under "contract for services" are regarded as self-employed persons whereas those under a "contract of service" are deemed to be employed persons. Careful distinction should be made as to the category in which one should rightly be placed, bearing in mind what was once stated by a Master of Rolls when he remarked that "it would be absurd to hold that a skilled music master who gives lessons to a pupil . . . is to be regarded as the 'workman' and the pupil as the employer." That illustrates what is a "contract for services" and there may be circumstances, similar in principle, in which an author may be treated as self-employed rather than employed, as, for instance if he contracted with a pupil to teach authorship. Employment of an author under a contract of service by his wife is treated as self-employment. Employment of a woman by her husband is also treated as self-employment provided the employment is in a "trade or business" and she ordinarily works therein for not fewer than a stated number of hours per week, earning not less than the stated minimum per week; otherwise the employment is disregarded for insurance purposes.

BENEFITS

The following information sets out briefly and in a form easy for reference the main benefits at present obtainable from National Insurance.

Sickness Benefit

To qualify for sickness benefit a claimant must satisfy two contribution conditions. The first condition is that Class 1 (employed earner) and Class 2 (self-employed earner) contributions, amounting to at least 25 times the amount of the contribution payable on earnings at the weekly level earnings limit in force for that year, must have actually been paid in any one income tax year since 6 April 1975. A weekly contribution stamp paid by a self-employed earner is equivalent to the weekly contribution paid as earnings at the lower weekly earnings limit.

Before 6 April 1975 the equivalent condition was payment of 26 flat-rate Class 1 or 2 contributions since entry into insurance.

A claimant who met this condition would be treated as meeting the new one.

The second condition is that the claimant must have paid or been credited in the relevant tax year with Class 1 or 2 contributions equivalent to the Class 1 contributions paid in 50 weeks by someone at the lower earnings limit. The relevant tax year is normally the last complete tax year before the calendar year which includes the first day of the sickness benefit claim. However, if the illness occurs 13 weeks after a previous spell of incapacity or unemployment the tax year used in calculating entitlement in the previous spell will still apply. Each credited contribution is treated as equivalent to a contribution on earnings at the weekly lower earnings limit. If the total of contributions and credits amounts to less than 50 but not less than 25 benefit may be payable at a reduced rate. Increases of benefit may be paid for the claimant's dependants.

In addition to flat-rate benefit, an earnings-related supplement may be payable if the claimant had paid Class 1 (employed earner) contributions on earnings in excess of 50 times the weekly lower earnings limit for the relevant tax year. The supplement is payable after 12 waiting days for a maximum of 156 days (six months not counting Sundays) in a period of interruption of employment. The supplement can also be paid which includes unemployment benefit and maternity allowance.

A person in receipt of a Social Security retirement pension must if admitted to hospital as an in-patient hand in his or her retirement pension book to the hospital authorities as the pension receivable may be reduced after eight weeks stay therein. (See also later in this article relative to other reductions in time of sickness.)

Invalidity Benefit

Sickness benefit may be paid for up to 28 weeks, after which, if incapacity for work continues, it is replaced by invalidity benefit.

This consists of a basic invalidity pension payable at the same rate as retirement pension, and in certain circumstances, of an invalidity allowance paid in addition to the pension at one of three rates depending on the claimants age when he first became unfit for work. Increases for dependants are payable at a higher rate than those for sickness benefit.

Maternity Benefit

1. Maternity grant payable up to nine weeks before the expected week of confinement. If two or more children are born a grant is payable for each additional child.

2. Maternity allowance (while not working) for 18 weeks commencing 11 weeks before the expected week of confinement, payable to women who have paid full contributions as employed or self-employed persons in the relevant income tax year.

An earnings-related supplement may also be payable—see conditions under Sickness Benefit.

Widow's Benefit

1. The relevant contribution conditions must be satisfied on the late husband's insurance.

2. Widow's allowance which is at a higher rate than other widow's benefits is payable for the first 26 weeks of widowhood if the husband was not entitled to a retirement pension or the widow is under 60 years of age. An earnings-related addition may also be payable for the same period if the husband had paid Class 1 (employed earner) contributions on earnings in excess of 50 times the weekly lower earnings limit in the tax year before the benefit year (running from the first Sunday in January each year) in which he died.

3. After first 26 weeks:
   (a) if the widow has one or more children under the age of 19 years she will usually become entitled to a widowed mother's allowance which can continue in payment until the child or youngest child reaches 19.
   (b) When the widowed mother's allowance ends, a widow's pension will be payable if the widow is then over 50 but under 65 years of age.
   (c) If there is no title to widowed mother's allowance a widow's pension will be payable if at the date of her husband's death the widow was over 50 but under 65.
   (d) Special arrangements give immediate cover for sickness and unemployment benefits for the widow who is unable to qualify for a widow's pension under (b) or (c) and is either unable to work because of ill-health or finds difficulty in obtaining employment when her widow's allowance or widowed mother's allowance ends.
   (e) A widow between the ages of 40 and 50 when widowed or when her entitlement to widowed mother's allowance ends, is able to qualify for a widow's pension, scaled down according to her age at that time.

Guardian's Allowance

A weekly allowance payable to a person who is entitled to child benefit for an orphan child normally both the child's parents must be dead and one of them must have satisfied a residence condition. Under special circumstances the allowance may be paid when only one parent is dead.

Child Benefit

This benefit is payable to a person responsible for a child under age 16 or under age 19 if the child is in full time education which is not generally above 'A' level. Normally both the claimant and child must be living in Great Britain. A higher rate of benefit is paid for the first or only child of certain love parents.

Retirement Pension (under old basic scheme)

To qualify for the State (i.e. the basic) pension a man who has reached 65 years or will attain that age (woman 60 years) on or after 6th April 1975 there are two contribution conditions based on one's own contributions. These are—

(1) He or she must have actually paid either 50 flat rate contributions at any time before 6th April 1975 or enough contributions of any class in any one tax year from 6th April 1975 for that year to be a reckonable year for the purpose of calculating the pension.

(2) To qualify at the standard (100 per cent.) rate he or she must have the necessary number of reckonable years in the working life. A reckonable year is one in which one has paid or been credited with enough contributions of any class to reach the qualifying level. Such level is the amount of Class 1 contributions payable on fifty times the weekly lower-earnings limit, that is the weekly earnings below which an employee not liable to pay Class 1 contributions, contributors of Class 2 (self-employed) or Class 3 (voluntary), are treated for this purpose as Class (1) contributors, on earnings at the weekly lower-earnings limit.

Length of working life is in reckonable years by taking one's working life minus 3, in the case of persons of 27 to 30 years of age; minus 4 for those of 31 to 40 and minus 5 for those of 41 and over.

The total number of flat-rate contributions paid or credited for weeks in one's working life between April 1961 when the graduated scheme began up to 5th April 1975 when it ended. This is convertible into a reckonable number of working years by dividing that number by 50 and rounding up any remainder but it must not exceed that number of tax years in one's tax life up to 5th April 1975.

The amount of graduated pension depends on the total amount of graduated contributions paid. For a man, the graduated part of his pension will be 2½p a week for each unit of £7.50 of graduated contributions he paid; for a woman, she will receive 2½p for each unit of £9 she paid. An odd half unit or more in the final total is treated as a whole unit. Graduated pension may also be paid on its own if a person is not entitled to a retirement pension.

Retirement pensions under the old basic scheme are revised periodically and are payable ordinarily at so much per week for life from 65 years of age (if man) or 60 (if woman) if sufficient contributions have been paid and there are an average yearly number of contributions or credits in respect of each year of insurance. People who were of the age of 16 or over on 5th July 1948 and entered insurance then or later, have their yearly contribution average for pension purposes calculated as from 1948. Increased rate of pension may be had by deferring retirement (see leaflet NI 15 obtainable from local Social Security offices). The amounts of the benefits are amended from time to time. Persons of 80 and upward have received an additional 25p per week from 20th September 1971.

Those already retired at 6th April 1978 are not affected by the new earnings-related pension scheme. For details of the new pension provisions see under the Social Security Pension Act 1975 at the end of this article.

Supplementary Pensions and Allowances

Supplementary benefit can be claimed by anyone in Great Britain who has reached the age of 16 years, who is not in full-time employment, and whose income, including National Insurance pensions and benefits is below the minimum level laid down by Parliament. For persons under pension age benefit is usually payable on condition of registration for employment at the Unemployment Benefit Office (unless they are sick). In working out entitlement the value of an owner-occupied house is ignored and a stated portion of one's savings can normally be disregarded. Certain other forms of income may be ignored, e.g. charitable payments for items not covered by supplementary benefit scale rate, and the first part of part-time earnings. Explanatory leaflets (S1 for persons under pension age and SB8 for persons over pension age) and SB9 (with claim form attached) are obtainable from local offices of the Department of Health and Social Security and at Post Offices. These should be obtained and studied. See also new pension provisions later in this article under the Social Security Pension Act 1977 scheduled to operate sometime in 1978.

Claimant or dependent in hospital: Benefits may be affected (reduced or even discontinued) if and while a person is in receipt of social security benefits and is an in-patient in hospital.

Benefits above alluded to include supplementary benefits. These may be discontinued immediately on admission to hospital, some others may be reduced after a stay of four or eight weeks therein.

The following is a summary of benefits affected:

1. *Immediately:*
Supplementary benefits in most cases but not in all.

2. *After four weeks in hospital:*
Attendance allowance is withdrawn.

3. *After eight weeks in hospital:*
Sickness benefit (but not earnings-related supplement), invalidity benefit, non-contributory invalidity pension, widow's benefit and allowances but not earnings-related additional benefit, retirement pension and non-contributory retirement pension in the case of people over 80 years of age, industrial injury benefit and unemployment supplement, industrial widows' and widowers' pensions, invalid care allowance may be affected but some may be continued for up to twelve weeks after being admitted to hospital.

4. *After fifty-two weeks in hospital:*
War widow's pension is reduced.

5. *Generally:*
Where a person is in receipt of *any* social security benefit (including supplementary benefits) his or her social security office should be informed immediately the recipient is admitted to hospital. Similarly one's discharge should be immediately notified.

If additional expense is incurred in visiting a person in hospital supplementary benefit may be *increased*.

When seeking information on any matter herein, one's local office of the Department of Health and Social Security should be contacted and whether in person or in writing one's National Insurance or pension number (or that of the person inquired about) should be quoted.

Death Grant

A lump sum is payable on the death of an insured person or of the wife, husband or child of an insured person. The amount depends both on the age of the deceased person and on the extent to which the contribution conditions are satisfied. No grant is payable for the death of a person who was over pension age at 5th July 1948.

Miscellaneous Points

1. Amounts receivable as benefits are obtainable by cashing Giro Orders at the Post Office.

2. Treatment under the Health Service is available for all persons normally resident in the United Kingdom whether insured or not.

3. As a general rule only Retirement Pensions and Widow's Benefit can be paid abroad, but there are reciprocal agreements on Social Security with a number of countries which may modify the general conditions. Details can be obtained from the local office of the Department of Health and Social Security. Application, therefor should be made in sufficient time if it is desired to draw one's retirement allowance abroad.

4. In his capacity of employer of others an author's or artist's contributions are allowable in full for income tax purposes as a business expense, but a contributor's own payments to the Graduated Pension Scheme are not so allowable as deductions.

5. Title to benefit and relative matters are decided by independent statutory authorities, the first of these is the Insurance Officer. A claimant who disagrees with a decision can appeal to a Local Tribunal. The decision of such Tribunal can be the subject of a further appeal by either the claimant or the Insurance Officer, to the Commissioner. Disputes as to classification of insured persons, contribution records, etc. are questions for decision by the Secretary of State.

6. A self-employed or non-employed person whose income is small (see the first paragraph of this article) can claim exception from payment of National Insurance Contributions.

7. Employed or self-employed persons who do not retire at 65 (men) or 60 (women) can increase their ultimate rate of pension on retirement by continuing to pay contributions until their retirement.

8. A person who retires from employment or self-employment before reaching retirement pension age, 65 (men) or 60 (women), will normally have to continue to pay contributions as a non-employed person until such age is reached. Provided sufficient contributions were paid before retirement there would be entitlement to Sickness Benefit for the relevant benefit year following such retirement.

9. Under the Collection of Contributions Regulations an insured person in Class 2 (self-employed) or Class 3 (non-employed) is required to stamp his or her card in respect of each week for which a contribution is *due*; failure to stamp for any such week is an offence under the Act.

10. When applying for a Retirement Pension one is required to obtain and to fill in and send to the local office of the Department of Health and Social Security, the necessary form, not earlier than four months before the date on which one becomes entitled to receive the pension and not later than one month after the date of retirement. If only a day too soon the form may be returned and if much less than four months in advance, delay in receiving the money and perhaps loss may be caused. A pension cannot be paid for any period which is more than one month before the date of retirement specified in the application unless the person shows that there was good cause for the delay in giving notice of retirement. Separate notice is required in respect of one's wife, if she, too, claims a Retirement Pension. Notices must state that the claimant has retired or is to retire on the specified date, is of the prescribed age and claims his or her pension.

Pensions for the Older and the Not-insured Persons

What the Department of Health and Social Security describe as "New Pensions for Old People" are allowances to those who were too old to contribute to the normal scheme which began in 1948 and for certain of their dependants. To qualify one must:

1. not be receiving a National Insurance Pension *or* be receiving one of less than a prescribed figure;
2. on 5th July 1970 have been 87 (man) or over, (82 woman);
3. be a married woman under 82 but not less than 60 on 2nd November 1970 whose husband qualifies for the new pension;
4. be a widow under 82 whose husband was alive and 65 or over on 5th July 1948 and herself was over 50 when her husband died;
5. be a woman under 82 whose marriage to a man who was alive and 65 or over on 5th July 1948 ended in divorce or annulment after she was 60;
6. be subject to certain residential conditions.

If one is receiving any other pension from public funds, the new pension figures (for old people) may be affected. (There is a (free) leaflet NI 177.)

Widow's Annuities

The Finance Act 1971 introduced into the approved schemes for self-employed persons what is termed a Widow's Annuity Contract under which a taxpayer may contribute a portion of his net relevant earnings (subject to a stated maximum). Any such contributions must be regarded as part of the maximum governing all retirement schemes. The object is to permit self-employed persons to achieve (for their widows) some of the benefits obtainable by those in occupational pension schemes. It is necessary to comply with several conditions. Particulars should be obtained from the Pensions Office by those interested.

New Benefits for the Old, Sick and Disabled

A taxable non-contributory mobility allowance was introduced from 1st January 1976 for severely disabled people who are unable or virtually unable to walk due to physical disablement. It is being introduced gradually by age groups and when fully phased-in by the end of 1979, it will be available to persons aged 5 to pensionable age (60 for a woman, 65 for a man). By the end of 1978, people aged 5 to 58 will be covered and announcements will be made in the Press from time to time as the remaining age groups are brought in. The allowance can be had in addition to supplementary and other cash benefits.

A leaflet (NI 211) can be obtained from one's local office of the Department of Health and Social Security and from the Department's Mobility Allowance Unit at Norcross, Blackpool, FY5 3TA.

A tax-free, attendance allowance as from the 6th December 1971 was introduced for the severely disabled, whether the disablement is due to the effects of old age, illness, physical or mental (or other) condition. It is available in respect of adults and children aged two years and upwards. Certain conditions are specified. These embrace inapplicability to people receiving free treatment under the National Health Service as hospital in-patients, and those in certain residential accommodation such as local authority "homes". The benefit can be had in addition to supplementary and other cash benefits. A leaflet (SPI) can be obtained (free) from one's local office of the Department of Health and Social Security.

A tax-free non-contributory invalidity pension is payable as of right to persons who have not paid sufficient National Insurance contributions to qualify for the ordinary contributory sickness and invalidity benefits. It has been available to men and single women—subject to satisfying the qualifying conditions (see leaflet NI 210)—since November 1975. In November 1977 the benefit was extended to include married women who satisfy the qualifying conditions and who are also incapable of performing normal household duties (see leaflet NI 214). Copies of both leaflets are available (free) from local offices of the Department of Health and Social Security.

Family Income Supplement for Families with Children (FIS)

This is a benefit available to low income families with dependent children where the head of the family is in full-time work. FIS is payable where the family's normal gross weekly income falls below a prescribed amount. Full-time work is defined as 30 or more hours per week and in the case of a couple it is the man who has to satisfy this requirement. Single parents and the self-employed can claim. All children under 16 and those over 16 who are still undergoing secondary education are included in the family if they live in the household. Families receiving FIS are automatically entitled to certain other benefits including free school meals, exemption from prescription charges, free dental and optical treatment under the NHS and free milk and vitamins for expectant mothers and for children under school age. An explanatory leaflet and claim form FIS 1 is available from Post Offices and Social Security offices.

Taxable and Tax-free Benefits

Benefits which are taxable include: Child's special allowance, guardian's allowance, invalid care allowance, widow's benefits, mobility allowance. Benefits *not* taxable include attendance allowance, *all* benefits paid to injured persons under the Industrial Injuries provisions of the Social Security Act except death benefit, death grants, family income supplements, invalidity benefit, maternity benefit, sickness benefit, supplementary benefits under the Ministry of Social Security Act or the Supplementary Benefits, etc. Act (Northern Ireland) and unemployment benefit.

Some Further Possible Benefits

Though most of the additional benefits which, in certain circumstances may be claimable, have been named earlier in this article it may be that certain others have not been clearly indicated and so the following are mentioned since they may be available to some readers. These are:—

industrial injuries benefits; and

attendance allowance for severely disabled people; and

invalid care allowance for those who care for relatives receiving an attendance allowance; and

war pensions for those disabled as a result of service in the armed forces, including other allowances where appropriate, for example, unemployability supplement or constant attendance allowance pensions are also payable to widows and orphans where the deceased husband's or father's death was due to service. Leaflet MPL 151 may be obtained from War Pensions Offices.

War pensions and supplementary allowances thereunder have not normally been included in this article as they are not under the National Insurance Acts but are additional thereto.

NEW PENSIONS PROVISIONS under the SOCIAL SECURITY PENSIONS ACT 1975

The main points of the new earnings- related retirement scheme can be summarised as follows:

1. Relating pensions to earnings means that the higher the pay—up to the scheme's top level—the bigger the pension will be when a person retires, is widowed or becomes an invalid.

2. Pensions in payment will also rise at least in line with the cost of living so that they are protected against inflation.

3. The additional state pension will be worked out on the 20 years after 1978 in which a person earned most and rights from those earnings will be revalued up to pension age at the same rate as national average earnings.

4. For those retiring within the next 20 years the additional pension will still be earned, the amount of which will depend on how long contributions have been paid to the new scheme.

5. Employees who change jobs will not lose any of the new pension rights.

6. Women will still get their pension at 60 but they will have the same rates of benefit and the same contributions as men with the same earnings.

7. Widows will be given all their husband's pension rights if they are widowed over 50, or any age while they have a young family to support.

8. Parents will keep their basic pension rights while away from work bringing up children.

9. Employees who are members of good occupational pension schemes can be contracted-out of part of the state scheme—their additional pension will come from their employer instead of the state.

10. Graduated pension rights earned under the 1961–75 scheme will be increased each year—which will benefit many existing pensioners as well.

The pensions will be in two parts:

1. **A basic pension,** similar to the present flat-rate national insurance pension, currently £17.50 a week for a single person.

2. **An additional pension** related to earnings between a "floor" and a "ceiling". The floor level will be the same as the basic pension (£17.50 in April 1978) and the upper limit, or ceiling, about seven times that amount (£120 in April 1978). This part of the pension will be worked out as 1/80 of pay between the basic pension rate and the upper limit for each year.

The scheme started in April 1978 and a man will contribute until his 65th birthday, a woman until her 60th. If a person contributes for more than 20 years the pension will be worked out on the 20 years that give the best pension.

This means that the **maximum additional** pension a person can earn is 20/80 (one quarter) of earnings between the basic pension level and the upper limit. If pension age (65 for a man, 60 for a woman) is reached before having contributed to the new scheme for the full 20 years the additional pension will be related to the number of complete tax years during which contributions have been made to the new scheme.

Below is an example of how the pensions will be worked out:

Assume the scheme has been in operation for 20 years. A man with a full contribution record, and whose earnings over the last 20 years have been equivalent to £77.50 a week in today's terms would, if he were retiring now, get a pension of £32.50 a week, made up in this way:

1. Basic pension £17.50
2. Additional pension representing
   one-quarter of the remainder of
   his weekly pay above the basic
   pension level, i.e. one quarter
   of £60 (£77.50–£17.50) £15.00
                                             £32.50

If his wife had to rely on his contributions for her pension she would receive £10.50 making their combined pension £43 a week. This compares with the present married couple's pension of £28 a week.

For full details of the new pension scheme see leaflet NP34 obtainable from Social Security Offices.

There are factors which cause the State scheme to be inferior to private employers' "old-fashioned" schemes. These embrace the absence of a lump sum payable on death before retirement, nor is there a tax-free cash sum payable to the pensioner at the time of retirement. Also there are no provisions for earlier retirement than specified (i.e. 65 for men and 60 for women) and widows. Pension figures are mainly less adequate for a woman when compared with her late husband's earnings in the years immediately prior to his death. It will readily be observed that private occupational schemes can be preferable to the State scheme and can embody all the better features of the latter.

Under the provisions of the State scheme there can be a reduction of scheme contributions in the case of contracted-out employers equivalent to about 8 per cent of second-tier earnings.

A word to one changing jobs between the time of the change and 6th April 1980 and if now aged at least 26 years and has been in his present scheme for at least 5 years. In such circumstances, under the Social Security Act 1973, an occupational pension scheme is required to preserve a person's pension benefits for payment at the normal pension age for the scheme. As an alternative, with the member's consent, pension rights may be transferred to a new employers scheme. A refund of contributions may be possible, if scheme rules allow, for at least part of a person's service prior to April 1980 but after that date refunds will only be possible in respect of service prior to April 1975.

Membership of a scheme must be open to both men and women on terms which are the same as to age and length of service needed for becoming a member, and as to whether membership is voluntary or obligatory. Incidentally, discrimination in retirement ages were not introduced into our retirement schemes until 1940 when the age was changed from 65 for both sexes. In regard to this problem many factors were taken into consideration including personal desires of the womenfolk.

Between the date when the above 1975 Act provision came on the Statute book and the time this article appears in this *Yearbook* three years will have elapsed. The new Act was passed by Parliament in order to provide for the supplementation of the flat rate of pensions and other retirement benefits concurrently payable, by earnings-related contributory schemes available to pensioners. A new guide to contributions (NP 23) has been issued by the Social Security Department for those concerned.

Three courses are available to employers concerning the coming into effect of the 1975 Statute. For example, they may contract-out; alter their existing schemes to give their members benefits equivalent to what are considered currently appropriate; or they may abandon existing provisions and modify their own schemes to provide additional benefits or at such figures as they consider would be provided under the 1975 Pensions Act.

The Social Security Pensions Act 1975 brings a new dimension into pensions legislation and planning and in consequence employers must consult with Trade Union representatives on this matter. These facts employers cannot ignore since they embody legal obligations and therefore must be interpreted and applied aright.

AGREEMENTS

PUBLISHERS' AGREEMENTS

Royalty Agreements

The royalty agreement is now the most usual arrangement between author and publisher, and almost invariably the most satisfactory for the author. It provides for the payment to the author of a royalty of an agreed percentage on the published price of all copies of his book which are sold. The rate of royalty varies with circumstances: for general books it often commences at ten per cent and provision is usually made for it to increase after the sale of a certain number of copies. An established author of proved selling-power will command a higher commencing royalty and a more attractive rising scale. Similarly, most authors can secure in their contracts provision for an advance from the publisher in anticipation and on account of the specified royalties, and the amount of this advance will depend largely upon the publisher's estimate of the book's prospect of sales.

Because many publishers' accounts are now computerised there is a trend towards paying royalties on the price received—which can easily be read from a computer printout—rather than on the published price. Appropriate adjustments are of course made to the royalty figure and the arrangement is of no disadvantage to the author.

Most publishing houses nowadays have printed agreement forms in which blanks are left for the insertion of the proposed royalty rates, the sum payable in advance, and so on. The terms are usually agreed between author and publisher before the form is completed, but the fact that a printed form has been signed by the publisher does not mean that an author, before signing it himself, cannot discuss any of its clauses with the publisher. The majority of publishers value the establishment of confidence and understanding between themselves and their authors and are willing to make reasonable amendments.

It is impossible to set out in detail here the numerous provisions of publishing agreements or to comment on the differing effects of these upon different sorts of book. Every sensible author will scrutinise his agreement carefully before signing it, will not hesitate to ask his publisher to explain any point in it which is not clear to him, and if he still has doubts will seek professional advice from a reliable literary agent, or the Society of Authors, or one of the few firms of solicitors who specialise in authors' business.

The careful author will look for a comprehensive clause setting out the contingencies in which the contract is to terminate, what happens if the publisher goes out of business or is taken over, and whether the publisher can sell his rights in the book to a third party without consulting the author.

He will expect the agreement to specify the respective responsibilities of himself and the publisher in the provision of illustrations, indexes, etc. Unexpected fees for reproducing illustrations can swiftly eat up an advance.

He will examine the clauses covering the handling of overseas sales, American rights and subsidiary rights (film, serial, broadcasting, etc.) which for some books may well bring in more than the book publication rights.

He will look for clauses giving the publisher an option to publish his future work and for clauses which may restrict a specialist author's future output by preventing him from writing other books on the same subject. The author should also satisfy himself that he understands what the contract proposes in relation to cheap editions, "remainders", sheet sales, reprints and new editions.

Outright Sale

Outright sale of copyright for an agreed sum is rarely suggested by a publisher, and hardly ever to be recommended, though it may be justified in special cases, as when an author is commissioned to supply a small amount of text as commentary for a book which consists primarily of illustrations. It is a survival from the days when copyright meant for all practical purposes, merely the exclusive right of publication in book form. So long as it was possible to gauge approximately a book's potential sales and the profit to be anticipated, the value of a copyright could be fairly accurately estimated. But to-day, anything from 1,000 to a million copies of a book may be sold and when the various subsidiary rights—the film rights in particular—may prove either valueless or worth thousands of pounds, any arrangement for an outright sale of copyright must be a gamble in which the author is likely to be the loser.

Profit-Sharing and Commission Agreements

Under a profit-sharing agreement the publisher bears the cost of production, but the author makes no money until the book shows a profit, at which point the profit is divided in agreed proportions between author and publisher. In theory this sounds fair, but it is rarely satisfactory in practice. Such agreements can lend themselves readily to abuse, largely because of the difficulty of defining the term "profit".

Under a commision agreement the author bears the cost of production and pays the publisher a commission for marketing the book. If no publisher is prepared to publish a work on the normal royalty basis, the chances are that if the author finances the publication himself he will lose most, if not all, of his outlay. In consequence commission agreements, save in exceptional circumstances, are to be discouraged. Many good publishers refuse to handle books on commission in any circumstances whatsoever; others confine their commission publishing to authoritative books of a highly specialised or scholarly nature. The specialist author who decides that commission publishing is justified by special circumstances should make sure that the firm with which he is negotiating is reputable and able to market his book efficiently.

No firm of standing will publish fiction on commission and publishers offering to do so should be given a wide berth. There are quite a few firms ready to exploit the vanity of a would-be author. Such firms ask the author for a large sum as "a contribution towards the cost" of producing his book. Too often in fact it more than covers the cost of bringing out a small and shoddy edition, which the "publisher" makes no effort to distribute.

Publishing agreements are lucidly discussed at considerable length in Sir Stanley Unwin's *The Truth About Publishing* (Eighth Edition) (George Allen and Unwin, Ltd.).

THE FLORENCE AGREEMENT

This Agreement, on the Importation of Educational, Scientific and Cultural Materials, generally known as the Florence Agreement, sponsored by Unesco, was adopted by the Unesco General Conference in Florence in 1950 and came into effect on 21 May 1952. It is concerned with the free flow of books and the removal of tariff and trade obstacles. The principal undertaking of the signatories is the exemption of books and other educational, scientific and cultural imports from customs duties, and the granting of licences and foreign exchange as far as possible for their importation.

Books of every sort are included in the Agreement, not exempting those printed abroad from the work of an author in the importing country. Unbound sheets do not come under the Agreement.

The following is an up-to-date list of the States adhering to the Agreement: Afghanistan, Austria, Barbados, Belgium, Bolivia, Cameroon, Congo (People's Republic of the), Cuba, Cyprus, Denmark, Egypt (Arab Republic of), El Salvador, Fiji, Finland, France, Gabon, Germany (Federal Republic of), Ghana, Greece, Guatemala, Haiti, Iran, Iraq, Israel, Italy, Ivory Coast, Japan, Jordan, Kenya, Khmer Republic, Laos, Libyan Arab Republic, Luxembourg, Madagascar, Malawi, Malaysia, Malta, Mauritius, Monaco, Morocco, Netherlands, New Zealand, Nicaragua, Niger, Nigeria, Norway, Pakistan, Philippines, Poland, Romania, Rwanda, Sierra Leone, Singapore, Spain, Sri Lanka (Republic of), Sweden, Switzerland, Tanzania (United Republic of), Thailand, Trinidad and Tobago, Tunisia, Uganda, United Kingdom, United States of America, Upper Volta, Viet-Nam (Republic of), Yugoslavia, Zaire (Republic of), Zambia.

NET BOOK AGREEMENT

The Net Book Agreement is an undertaking signed by all members of the Publishers Association, which represents some 95 per cent of all book publishing in the United Kingdom, by which they agree to sell their net-priced books to booksellers on the strict condition that they may not offer them to the public at less than the price fixed by the publisher. Booksellers may, under licence from the Publishers Association, supply public libraries at a ten per cent discount. There is an identical Agreement between publishers not in membership of the Publishers Association who publish at net prices, who nominate the Association as their agent.

The Agreement was referred to the Restrictive Practices Court in 1962 under the Restrictive Trade Practices Act of 1956, and was successfully defended as being not contrary to the public interest, and necessary for the maintenance of a healthy book trade able to meet the public's needs. The Agreement was also vindicated in 1967 under the Resale Prices Act of 1964.

The vast majority of school books are published at non-net prices so that booksellers and school contractors may sell them at a discount because they are bought in class sets.

THE SOCIETY OF AUTHORS

AIMS

The Society exists to promote the interests of authors and defend their rights whenever and wherever they are challenged. Founded by Sir Walter Besant in 1884, it has had a long history of devoted service by leading writers of the day including such men as Shaw, Galsworthy, Hardy, Wells, Barrie, Ian Hay, Eliot, Masefield, Forster, A. P. Herbert and Francis Williams. Their work is continued by their successors on the Society's Council and Management Committee and by all those members who serve on the committees for specialised writers and awards.

WHAT THE SOCIETY DOES

Over 3,000 members are served by an experienced staff under the direction of a Secretariat backed by lawyers, tax and insurance consultants, who all have special knowledge of authors' problems.

The Society provides its services in the following ways:

Individually: It gives members legal and business advice in all matters affecting their rights as authors, including the detailed vetting of contracts. *This is a personal service unequalled by any other organisation representing writers.* Many enquiries relate to the marketing of literary work in all media in this country and overseas. The Society has contacts and close links with allied organisations in the U.K. and abroad; and thus has a fund of information at its disposal not readily available elsewhere. In addition, at a risk which may be considered as beyond the resources of most members, the Society is prepared to take up legal cases concerned with breach of contract, infringement of copyright and claims in liquidation or bankruptcy—when such cases involve matters of principle, and action is authorised by the Committee of Management.

Specially: It has set up subsidiary organisations within the membership having their own rules of admission. These are the *Translators Association,* the *Radio-writers Association,* the *Educational Writers Group* and the *Children's Writers Group.* No extra subscription is required to belong to any of these organisations, details of which are available from the Society's offices (see also entries under "Societies of Interest"). The Society also holds meetings of poets, book illustrators, freelance journalists and dramatists and other specialised writers, and it is always ready to take up matters which are of concern only to a section of the membership. Recently it played an active part in the discussions for a Press Charter under the chairmanship of Lord Pearce. By identifying the problems of specialised writers in this way, the Society has frequently been able to secure much improved conditions and payments.

In the past, many authors made a living entirely from writing, but nowadays only a few can do so. Surveys have confirmed that the majority have to rely on other sources of income. The consequences of this situation may be unexpectedly serious: for instance, a school or university teacher writing an occasional book to expound a method of teaching rather than as a source of income, tends to be careless about publication arrangements. Acceptance of a bad contract or too low a royalty rate may not seem important to him, but it can damage his fellow-authors and undermine the Society's power to secure fair treatment.

Generally: It advances the interests of authors through discussion with Government departments: or organisations such as the Arts Council, BBC, IBA, Publishers Association, Booksellers Association, NUJ, the various teachers' unions, the Open University and other educational institutions; at committees such as the British Copyright Council—on which the Society is represented with other organisations with interests in copyright; the Radio and Television Safeguards Committee; the Theatres' Advisory Council; the Association of Authors' Agents; and the Personal Managers' Association. Also there have always been members of both Houses of Parliament, willing to air publicly in debate and privately with Ministers issues raised by the Society. Direct contact is maintained with equivalent organisations throughout the world through the Society's membership of the International Confederation of Societies of Authors and Composers (CISAC). It is active in promoting legislation benefiting the profession, e.g. the Copyright Acts of 1911 and 1956, the Defamation Act of 1952, the Obscene Publications Act of 1959, taxation concessions under the Finance Acts of 1944, 1953, 1956 and 1967 and improvements to the Social Security Act 1973.

It campaigns ceaselessly for such projects as *Public Lending Right*, exposing the injustice suffered by authors who receive no payment whatever for the use of their books in public and other kinds of libraries—where the scale of lending runs into millions of issues a year. The Society has been intimately involved at every stage, and has been promised legislation by both major political parties. The Society is also currently engaged in negotiations to set up a Collecting Society: the purpose being to collect and distribute fees from reprography and other methods whereby copyright material is exploited without payment to the originators. It sponsors surveys of the economics of authorship and the conditions of the writer; and publishes a quarterly journal, *The Author*, edited by Richard Findlater, in which current questions affecting authorship are explained and ventilated (50p per copy, or £2 a year post free, but free to members). It also issues leaflets on special subjects, e.g. a series of QUICK GUIDES on *Copyright, Libel, VAT, Income Tax, Publishing Contracts, etc.*

AWARDS AND FACILITIES

The Society is also responsible for a number of awards, grants and literary prizes, viz. The Somerset Maugham Award to enable authors under 35 to travel, and the Travelling Scholarship, which has no age restriction: the Tom-Gallon award for short story writers; the Crompton Bequest for aiding the publication of original work of high quality; the Eric Gregory Award for poets under 30; the Margaret Rhondda Award for women journalists; the Hawthornden Prize for a work of imaginative literature by a British author under 41; the Society of Authors Awards for Radio; and three prizes for translations. It helped found and now administers the Phoenix Trust for the support of literary and artistic effort and research. From its Contingency Fund "first-aid" assistance is given and from its Pension Fund small life pensions (there are now twelve) are granted. Lately it has taken charge of the Francis Head Award for assisting authors who, through a physical mishap, are temporarily unable to maintain themselves or their families. The Society has also established a Retirement Benefits Scheme with flexible premium arrangements to suit authors with fluctuating incomes. Contributions now exceed £500,000. The top-income authors have been quick to see the scheme's tax and pension advantages, but any author who can put by even £50–£60 a year should not fail to join the scheme. Particulars of this scheme, and of a Hospital Cash Benefit Scheme operated for the Society, can be obtained from Hartley Cooper Life & Pensions (Brokers) Ltd., Cliffords Inn, Fetter Lane, London, EC4A 1BU. The Society also has a BUPA Group Insurance Scheme for general provision against the cost of illness. This is handled direct from BUPA, Kett House, Station Road, Cambridge, CB1 2JP.

HOW TO JOIN THE SOCIETY

Admission to membership is at the discretion of the Committee of Management, but normally an author will be made a full member if he has had a full-length work published in this country. Associate membership is open to those, for example, who have had radio scripts broadcast or articles published, but no full length work to their credit. The annual subscription is £18.00, with special terms for quarterly payments, and for husband and wife joint membership. Entrance fee £10.00. Further information from The Society of Authors, 84 Drayton Gardens, London, SW10 9SD. Telephone number: 01-373 6642.

THE WRITERS' GUILD OF GREAT BRITAIN

The Writers' Guild of Great Britain is the writers' trade union, affiliated to the TUC, and representing writers' interests in film, radio, television, the theatre and publishing. Formed in 1959 as the Screenwriters' Guild, the union gradually extended its guardianship into all areas of freelance writing activity and copyright protection. In 1974 when book authors and stage dramatists became eligible for membership substantial numbers joined, and their interests are now strongly represented on the Executive Council. Apart from necessary dealings with Government and policies on legislative matters affecting writers, the Guild is, by constitution, non-political, has no involvement with any political party, and pays no political levy. The Guild employs a permanent secretariat and staff and is administered by an Executive Council of twenty-nine members. There are also Regional Committees representing Scotland, Wales, the North and West of England.

The Guild comprises practising professional writers in all media, united in common concern for one another and regulating the conditions under which they work.

WHAT IT DOES

a) *Television*.

The Guild has national agreements with the BBC and the Commercial companies regulating minimum fees and going rates, copyright licence, credits, terms and conditions for television plays, series and serials, dramatisations and adaptations. The important and potentially remunerative areas of cassettes and video-disc exploitation have been conserved and subjected to Guild agreement, and most children's and educational drama has been similarly protected. In 1975 the Guild achieved from the ITV companies a company-contributing pension scheme for free-lance writers and in 1978 the BBC agreed to a similar pension scheme. These schemes apply only to Guild members, however.

b) *Films*.

The Guild has established higher minimum fees (£5,000 for a full-length feature film) with the Film Producers Association and the Children's Film Foundation. A respected voice in the industry, the Writers' Guild was concerned in promoting the Film Development Fund.

c) *Radio*.

The Guild has fought for and obtained a standard agreement with the BBC, establishing a fee-structure which is constantly under review.

d) *Books*.

The Guild is fully committed to the campaign for the loans-based Public Lending Right, and has vigorously lobbied for the scheme, which has all-party support in Parliament. It has drawn up and is negotiating a standard contract between the Guild and publishing houses to provide authors with improved minimum royalties, a better share of all subsidiary rights and a greater say in the production of their books. The particular problems facing the authors of children's books, school text-books, and audio-visual aids are currently receiving special attention. A register of non-fictional titles currently in preparation has been set up, as has the establishment of a structure of professional fees for talks, lectures and readings.

e) *Theatre*.

The Guild is negotiating with both the Society of West End Managers and the major subsidised theatres; fairer advances, a better involvement in all aspects of production, and paid attendance at rehearsals are regarded as particularly important. A register will be compiled of theatre managements which will guarantee to return or accept plays within a reasonable time of manuscript receipt. The Guild has been protesting vigorously at the closure of so many of our major provincial touring theatres.

f) *Miscellaneous*.

The Guild is equally concerned with the fast-developing areas of mechanical photocopying and reprography by audio and video cassettes and similar systems. It has campaigned in the TUC and in Parliament against the unfair discrimination by the social services against the freelance writer. It made submissions to the Annan Commission on the Future of Broadcasting and the Whitford Committee on Copyright.

Regular meetings between the membership and the executive council are held, and a monthly journal *Writers News* is published.

The Guild also fights on behalf of individual members, advises on contracts, protests against unnecessary censorship, helps with VAT and other tax problems.

MEMBERSHIP

Membership is by a points system. One major piece of work (a full-length book, an hour-long television or radio play, a feature film, etc.) entitles the author to full membership; lesser work helps to accumulate enough points for full membership, while associate membership may be enjoyed in the meantime. Affiliate membership is enjoyed by agents and publishers.

The subscription is 1% of that part of an author's income earned in the areas in which the Guild operates. There is a minimum annual subscription of £10 and a maximum of £200.

IN CONCLUSION

The writer is an isolated individual in a world in which individual voices are not always heard. A good agent can provide protection for his clients, but there are many vitally important matters which are susceptible to influence only from the position of collective strength which the Guild enjoys. The writer properly cherishes his or her individuality; it will not be lost within a union run by other writers.

The Writers' Guild of Great Britain, 430 Edgware Road, London, W2 1EH *T.* 01-723 8074. *President:* Lord Willis; *Co-Chairpersons:* John Tully and Maureen Duffy; *General Secretary:* Elaine Steel.

PUBLIC LENDING RIGHT

THE campaign to secure for authors fair payment for the use of their books in libraries dates from 1951 when John Brophy, novelist and poet, proposed that borrowers should pay a penny (1d.) every time they took out a book. Public librarians resisted this proposal mainly on the grounds that it conflicted with the principle of the free library service, and that the cost of administration would absorb too high a proportion of the funds available. The Society of Authors then took up the cudgels, and under the leadership of Sir Alan Herbert (APH), later their President, conducted a vigorous campaign 1960–65: first to legislate for PLR; secondly, to finance the scheme by means of libraries charging borrowers an annual subscription; which would yield a total sum sufficient both to improve the library service and to meet the dues on lending. These moves were blocked, although APH—in his inimitable style—succeeded in making the general public fully aware of the authors' case. After 1965 the campaign was sustained by representatives of the Society of Authors, Publishers Association, and Arts Council, acting together. On advice from Miss Jennie Lee, then Minister for the Arts, it was however decided to ask for State funds to finance PLR, instead of charging the borrower.

In 1971 Lord Eccles (Miss Lee's successor) set up a Working Party representative of all the interests involved, under the general aegis of the Department of Education and Science. Its report published in May 1972 was unanimous, but was framed within the terms of reference set by the Minister: namely to consider how an amendment to the Copyright Act 1956, which added lending to the public to the acts restricted by copyright, might be implemented. As the report was essentially a fact-finding document, it investigated various alternatives for operating PLR, among them loan sampling (as in Sweden) and stock sampling (as in Denmark), and suggested two further possibilities—surcharging (adding a charge to the published price of each copyright book purchased by libraries) and blanket licensing, whereby libraries would be licensed to lend copyright works on payment of one annual licence fee per library: the resulting revenue to be distributed as a percentage of each copyright work purchased. An author would thus receive a second or "lending" royalty in addition to his normal "sale" royalty.

Although the Society of Authors gave guarded welcome to the report and the alternative of blanket licensing, a number of authors (who later formed themselves into the Writers Action Group) expressed dissatisfaction with it, because the rapid progress in the computerisation of library routines promised to make possible the operation of loan sampling, which all agreed was the fairest system, if the technical problems could in fact be overcome. During this debate, prospects brightened in Parliament. During 1973 269 MPs of all parties signed an Early Day Motion supporting the introduction of PLR, while the replacement of Lord Eccles by Norman St. John-Stevas, who publicly approved the cause, and the sponsorship of a Private Member's Bill by Ernle Money, gave hopes of early legislation, which were not dashed by the change of Government early in 1974. On the contrary the new Minister, Hugh Jenkins, displayed great energy, promising legislation by the end of the year, while accelerating the technical evaluation of the loan sampling system favoured by the authors.

The Technical Investigation Group he had set up did valuable work, and in March 1975 published a report which indicated that loan sampling was feasible; but the Minister was not able to bring in a Bill. Authors held a rally in Belgrave Square on St. George's Day to express their frustration. Lord Willis introduced a private PLR Bill in the Lords which was withdrawn on 4 July, at second reading, after a Government assurance that it intended to legislate as soon as possible after technical tests were complete in the autumn 1975.

The final report of the TIG ready in October, confirmed the earlier findings and demonstrated that loans sampling was by now the cheapest as well as the fairest method of implementation. However, the Government did not bring in a Bill until the spring of 1976, when a loans based Bill was introduced in the Lords and the TIG Report was published. The Bill passed through all its stages with two important amendments by Lord Willis and was sent to the Commons in May. It hung fire, two debates on the second reading being adjourned without a vote. Meanwhile Lord Donaldson had taken over from Mr. Jenkins as Minister for the Arts and at the third attempt on 14 October the Bill finally passed its Second Reading.

It had become increasingly clear, however, that a few MPs from both main Parties were determined to talk out the Bill at some stage. The Bill passed through the Committee Stage by 9 November having survived some determined filibustering.

The Report Stage and Third Reading began shortly before four o'clock on 16 November. This time eight MPs joined in the filibustering with such effect that by early in the morning of the 17th the Bill had to be abandoned. The Government's plans were not immediately apparent but once it had been established that a new Government Bill would not be immediately forthcoming, Lord Willis introduced a Private Members Bill in the Lords in January 1977. This Bill ostensibly the same as the Government's own unsuccessful Bill, quickly passed through all stages in the Lords.

On 12 May 1977, during a meeting at No. 10 between the Prime Minister and a representative from the Society of Authors, P.E.N. and the Writers Guild of Great Britain, Mr. Callaghan re-stated his Government's commitment to PLR. No assurance could be given however, that the filibusterers would not recommence their wrecking tactics if a Bill was reintroduced. Lord Willis's Bill was consequently not adopted in the Commons.

However, there arose a suggestion that the Arts Council might operate a non-statutory scheme. It was not immediately clear that the Arts Council could legally operate a PLR scheme and, in the meantime Mr. St. John-Stevas, drawn number 13 in the list of Private Members Bills, declared his intention to introduce a new PLR Bill. This Bill failed to attract enough support to pass its second reading, but, in 1978, the Arts Council and the DES continued to explore the possibilities of a non-statutory scheme. While it was generally accepted that PLR was an inevitability, few would predict how and when it would come about.

BOOKS FOR THE WRITER

The following select, classified and annotated list of books of interest to the writer and all concerned with the book trade has been compiled by Miss Robin Myers. Most of the books included are in print, and are to be found in the library of the National Book League (see p. 341) and in most public libraries. The addition of price at time of going to press, and number of pages should do no more than help assess relative cost and size.

SECTION I: HISTORY AND BIBLIOGRAPHY OF THE BOOKTRADE

Astbury, Ray. *Bibliography and Book Production*. Pergamon, 1967. o.p. 258 pp. Describes the structure of the publishing trade today, copyright, book production and booktrade bibliography.

Bingley, C. *Book Publishing Practice* (with bibliography). New Librarianship Society, Crosby Lockwood, 1966. o.p. The editorial, production, sales and rights departments of publishing are briefly described.

E.P.C. *Publishing for Schools*. Educational Publishers Council, 1977. 95p. 56 pp. A business-like, racily illustrated handbook of practical advice and information, a must for the bookshelf of all authors and publishers of educational books.

Mumby, F. A., and Norrie, Ian. *Publishing and Bookselling*. Cape, 5th ed. rev. 1974 (bibliography). £12.00. 685 pp. Still the only general history of the British book trade, now taking the story to 1970.

Myers, Robin. *The British Book Trade from Caxton to the Present*. Deutsch, 1973 (illus.). £8.50. 404 pp. A bibliographical guide to the trade's history and workings, with introductions to each section and lists of relevant organisations. Includes works on authorship history and practice.

Steinberg, S. H. *500 Years of Printing*. Penguin, 1975. 75p and Faber, 1959. o.p. An excellent, not too technical history of the effects of the spread of printing in Europe.

Publishers' Association: *Introduction to Book Publishing*, ed. Mary Perry, Publishers Association and Printing and Publishing Industry Training Board, 1977. £1.00. 62pp. A symposium of articles, by members of the trade on such aspects as finance, rights, type of publishing, useful, though one is bound to say, thrown together.

Unwin, Philip. *Book Publishing as a Career*. Hamish Hamilton, 1965 (bibliography). o.p. 200 pp. This is the only good British book (there are one or two American ones), describing the work of the various departments of a publishing office.

SECTION II: COPYRIGHT, PUBLIC LENDING RIGHT, AND CENSORSHIP

Carter-Ruck, P. F., and Hickson, Oswald, S. *The Law of Libel and Slander*. Faber, rev. ed. 1972. £12.00. 478 pp. This is slightly less dry than the lawyer's compendium. J. C. C. Gatley, *Libel and Slander*, 7th ed. rev. Sweet and Maxwell, 1973.

Carter-Ruck, P. F., and Skone James, E. P. and F. E. *Copyright, Modern Law and Practice*. Faber, 1965. £7.35. 639 pp. A legal textbook that is intelligible to the non-lawyer and is also comprehensive for the general lawyer. Better for the writer's bookshelf than the lawyer's bible, *Copyright*, by Copinger and Skone James (11th ed. 1971).

Cavendish, J. M. *A Handbook of Copyright in British Publishing Practice.* Cassell, 1974 (bibliography). £6.50. 224 pp. This has the advantage over M. Nicholson (*q.v.*) of having a bibliography, but it is more a publisher's than an author's book.

Ewart, K. *Copyright.* Cambridge University Press, 1952. (Cambridge and Authors' and Printers' Guide No. 5). o.p. A good quick guide.

Findlater, Richard (ed.). *Public Lending Right: A Matter of Justice.* Deutsch and Penguin Books, 1971. £1.50. 112 pp. A symposium by 10 eminent members of the world of books.

Nicholson, Margaret. *Manual of Copyright Practice for Writers, Publishers and Agents.* Oxford University Press, rev. 1970. £3.45. 288 pp. To be recommended for the author's bookshelf.

Publishers' Association. *A Guide to Royalty Agreements*, 5th ed. 1972. £3.00 to non-members. 80pp. Intended as guidance to publishers in drawing up contracts, but it is useful for the writer too. The Society of Authors also issues a leaflet for its members, *Publishing Contracts.* 50p. A memorandum on *Permissions.* 10p. 1970

Society of Authors. *Public Lending Right, A Short History*, bulletin No. 3, 1967. Issued to S.O.A. members.

Society of Authors. *Your Pocket Brief for P.L.R.* 1968. Issued to S.O.A. members. 4 pp. of summary of the proposals, now slightly overtaken by events for Public Lending Right. (See pages 413–14.)

Thomas, Donald. *A Long Time Burning: The History of Literary Censorship in England.* Routledge, 1969. Illus. Bibliography. £7.50. 558 pp. Both scholarly and readable.

Whale, R. F. *Copyright.* Longman, 1971. £5.75. 218 pp. This is a less technical survey of the field than Carter-Ruck and Skone James (*q.v.*), excellent for the writer's bookshelf. Or there is Whale's outline version *Comment on Copyright*, 1969. 17½p.

SECTION III: PREPARING MANUSCRIPTS AND CORRECTING PROOFS

Berry, W. Turner, Johnson, A. F., and Jaspert, W. P. *An Encyclopaedia of Typefaces*, 4th ed. rev. Blandford Press, 1970. £6.90. 384 pp. A useful guide to the typefaces available for letterpress printing.

Butcher, Judith. *Copy-Editing; the Cambridge Handbook.* Cambridge University Press, 1975. £10.50. 339 pp. Intended for publishers, editors, particularly those at the Cambridge Press. But invaluable for authors preparing their final manuscript as well. It is not, however, a real novice's book.

Cambridge Authors' and Printers' Guides. Cambridge University Press. 40p each. 39 pp.
> Anderson, M. D. *Book Indexing.* 1971. o.p.
> Burbidge, P. G. *Notes and References.* 1952. o.p.
> Burbidge, P. G. *Prelims and End-Pages*, 2nd ed. 1969. 60p.
> Carey, G. V. *Punctuation.* 1957. o.p.
> Crutchley, B. *Preparation of Manuscripts and Correction of Proofs*, 6th ed. 1970. 60p.

Only two of these excellent booklets can now be bought new for the writer's bookshelf.

Hart, Horace. *Rules for Compositors and Readers at the University Press*, 37th ed. Oxford University Press, 1967. £2.00. 156 pp. Widely used by printers and editors throughout the trade. Every writer should possess *Hart's Rules* for his own guidance on spelling, punctuation, style, etc., in preparing copy for press.

Mackays. *Type for Books; a Designer's Manual.* Bodley Head, new ed. 1976. £6.00. 280 pp. The specimen book of one major book printer, it is meant for the designer's use, but will also help the writer wishing to envisage what his book could look like.

Rowe, Brenda. *Type it Yourself.* Pitman, 1976. £1.95. Well worth the outlay for the author who wants to produce a presentable manuscript at minimal cost.

University of Chicago Press. *A Manual of Style,* 12th ed. rev. 1973. £7.00 approx. This is one of the fullest and best of the publishers' guides to house style; useful for writers on both sides of the Atlantic.

Westwood, John. *Typing for Print: A Manual for Typists and Authors.* Pitman, 1976. £1.10. 66 pp. This is the first guide on the economical conversion of typescript into print, which is likely to become more and more widely used by publishers. This booklet therefore deserves a place on the author's bookshelf. It is based on *Recommendations for Preparation of Typescript Copy for Printing.* B.S.5261. Pt. I: 1975.

SECTION IV: REFERENCE WORKS—GUIDE TO SOURCES, DICTIONARIES, DIRECTORIES, ETC.

Aids in the Selection of British Books. British Council and National Book League. 1974. 50p. A brief guide, mainly intended for the would-be bookbuyer; a feature is the address list of organisations who have a publishing programme and information service.

Anderson, I. G. *Councils, Committees and Boards; a Handbook of Advisory, Consultative, Executive and Similar Bodies in British Public Life.* C. B. D. Research Ltd., 3rd ed. 1977. £22.50. 420 pp. A companion volume to the *Directory of British Associations* (q.v.) and just as good.

Aslib Directory. 2 vols., 3rd ed. Aslib. 1968–70. £9.00 to non-members. 90+849 pp. (see also *Walford* below). Volume I *Science, Technology and Commerce* lists some 5200 specialist libraries and societies; Volume II covers the humanities in similar manner; a superb, easy to use work, unfortunately not too up to date.

Benét, W. R. *Reader's Encyclopaedia,* 2nd ed. Black, 1967. £6.50. 1128 pp. (See also *Oxford Companion,* below). A useful "companion" with brief notes on authors, literary movements, terminologies, etc.

B.F.M.P. *Authors' Alterations Cost Money.* British Federation of Master Printers. 25p. 8pp. A salutory publication for all authors.

Books in Print. Bowker. New York and London. Annual. Annual list of American books in print; the American equivalent of the Whitaker British volumes.

Brewer, E. C. *Dictionary of Phrase and Fable:* Cassell, 11th ed. 1970. £4.50. 1168 pp. A "must" for the browser and useful for all writers.

Brink, A. and D. Watkins. *The Libraries, Museums and Art Galleries Yearbook.* J. Clarke. 1976. £15.00. 694 pp. Each section has its own index on different coloured paper for ease of use. A less bulky, and slightly more up to date alternative to the *Aslib Directory* (q.v.).

British National Bibliography. (B.N.B.) first issued 1950. Issued weekly, 4 monthly, annually and 5 yearly. Arranged by the Dewey Decimal system and thus can be used as a subject guide. Available for reference (if asked for) in every public library.

British Theatre Directory, Offord. 6th ed. 1977. £2.25. 500 pp. Gives details, under 4 sections of British theatres etc.; theatrical suppliers, and agents including literary agents.

Cassell's Directory of Publishing 1976–77. Cassell, biennial, 1976. £7.50. 608 pp. (See also *L.M.P.* below.) Part I lists book publishers with specialities, and other details. Part II representatives and such services as press cutting agencies, literary agents, prizes, etc.

Collins, T. H. *Author's and Printer's Dictionary; A Guide for Authors, Editors, Printers, Correctors of the Press, Compositors and Typists.* Oxford University Press, 1st ed. 1905, 11th ed. rev. 1973. £3.00. 496 pp.

Concise Cambridge Bibliography of English Literature, ed. G. Watson. 2nd ed. Cambridge University Press, 1965. Hard £5.50 and pbk. £2.20. (See also *Hart's Rules*, above.) A serviceable, cheap substitute for the N.C.B.E.L. A third revised edition is on the way.

Contemporary Authors. a bibliographical guide to current authors and their works. 68 vols. Gale Research Co. 1962—£17.50 approx. per vol. Available in most public libraries; a mine of information, reasonably accurate, on the life and writings of a very odd assortment of living writers.

Dealers in Books: A Directory of Dealers in Secondhand and Antiquarian Books in the British Isles. 9th ed. Sheppard Press. 1978. £6.00. 354 pp. Despite its inaccuracies and deficiencies, it is the best there is, and useful for the book-hunter.

Dictionary of National Biography from earliest times to 1960. 24 vols., £200.00 the set, concise to 1900; concise 1901–50; concise 1951–60. Compact edition with magnifying glass, 2 vols. 1975. £45.00. The full edition available for reference in all public libraries; despite gaps and uneven coverage, a marvellous work.

Encyclopaedia Britannica. 11th ed. 1910–11; 29th ed. 1929; latest ed. 1976 (latest printing 1977) £415.00. The 11th is a classic, still the best for many literary articles; the 29th is the last English edition; since then it has been largely American in slant and now is wholly so. There is, however, no comparable British encyclopaedia.

Henderson, G. P. and S. P. A. *Directory of British Associations and Associations in Ireland*. 8th ed. C. B. D. Research Ltd. 1977. £21.00. 430 pp. Very complete and easy to use—in short, invaluable; includes a subject index, a feature seldom found in directories.

Herbert, John. *Techniques of Radio Journalism*. Black, 1976. £4.50. 123 pp. An experienced journalist tells how to gather, edit and present material for broadcasting.

Hoffman, Ann. *Research: A Handbook for Writers and Journalists 1975/6*. Midas. 1975. Hard £2.95; pbk £1.95. A brief, up-to-date guide to sources; an aid-memoire for the experienced researcher and easy for the beginner to use too.

Hulke, Malcolm. *Writing for Television in the Seventies*. Black. 1974; latest reprint 1976. £4.75. 263 pp. One of the very few writers' manuals of instruction that is worth bothering with.

Industrial Research in Britain, 8th ed. Francis Hodgson. 1976. 884 pp. 200 Swiss francs. Covers the whole field of science and industry; invaluable for tracking down publications that elude the more usual reference works.

International Yearbook and Statesman's Who's Who. Kelly's Directories, 1977. £25.00. 821 pp. To be found in all public libraries.

Literary and Library Prizes, 9th ed. Bowker. 1976. £10.00 approx. 1137 pp. Can be consulted in most public libraries; pretty comprehensive.

Literary Market Place. Bowker annual, latest ed. 1975/76. The American equivalent of *Cassell's Directory* for British publishers.

New Cambridge Bibliography of English Literature. 600–1950. N.C.B.E.L. 5 vols. Cambridge University Press. 1969–74. Plus index. £25.00 per vol. approx. Supersedes the old "C.B.E.L." There are sections on background studies such as education, book production, etc., as well as author-bibliographies, trade catalogues and, in vol. IV, periodicals relating to current and forthcoming books. Available for reference in public libraries.

Oxford Companion to English Literature. Ed. Sir Paul Harvey. 1932, rev. ed. Dorothy Eagle. Oxford University Press. 1967. £6.75. 975 pp. (See also Benét, above.) Indispensable for the literary author and interesting for any. Includes articles on classical and foreign literature where this impinges on English.

Oxford Companion to American Literature. 4th ed. rev. James D. Hart. 1975. £8.00. 1004 pp. On the same lines as O.C.E.L. (*q.v.*) but more narrowly national by the nature of the material.

Oxford English Dictionary (O.E.D.). Oxford University Press. 13 vols. £125.00+supplement A–G £20.00. Compact ed. 2 vols. £40.00. (See also Webster below.) The classic English dictionary on historical principles, with quotations of usages through the ages *The Shorter Oxford English Dictionary* (S.O.E.D.) has further progeny in; the *Concise*, which is all that those who wish to check meanings and spellings will need. There are even more abbreviated versions in the *Pocket* and the *Little* Oxford dictionaries.

Pascoe, L. C. (ed.) *Encyclopaedia of Dates and Events.* (Teach Yourself Books), English Universities Press. 1974. £1.75. 840 pp. Worth the writer's shelf-space. Both a potted encyclopaedia of history and a quick reference for journalists who write on anniversaries.

Paxton, John. *Everyman's Dictionary of Abbreviations.* Dent. 1974. £3.95. 416 pp. The most suitable of the many such dictionaries for the writer's bookshelf, being fairly comprehensive, compact and modestly priced.

Penguin Dictionary of Modern Quotations. Ed. J. M. and M. J. Cohen. Penguin. 1971. £1.00. 368 pp. A useful companion to the *Oxford Dictionary of Quotations*; for those who need modern, rather than classical quotations.

Roget, P. M. *Thesaurus of English Words and Phrases.* 1st ed. 1852, latest editions, Longmans £4.75 and Penguin o.p. A unique work and one that every writer should possess.

Times Atlas of the World. 1977. £29.00. 560 pp. For those who have no favourite of their own, we recommend this or, for those who want something smaller and cheaper, *The Times Concise Atlas of the World.* 1975. £12.50. 264 pp.

Titles and Forms of Address, A Guide to their Correct Use. 15th ed. Black. 1976. £2.50. 188 pp.

Walford, A. J., and others. *A Guide to Reference Material.* 3 vols. 3rd ed. Library Association. Vol. I Science and Technology. 1973. Vols. II and III covering social and historical sciences, philosophy and religion, the arts and literature are expected soon. 2nd ed. 1968–70. £7.20 per vol. to non-members. (See also *Aslib Directory* above.) Never to be forgotten in the search for subject bibliographies. The annotations are brief and excellent. Available for reference in all public libraries.

Webster, Noah. *Third International Dictionary of the English Language.* Bell. £50.00. For those wanting a dictionary of American English. Webster is for America what the O.E.D. (*q.v.*) is for British English and has equally diverse editions; we list the full one.

Whitaker's Almanack. Whitaker annual. 1977. £5.20. 1240 pp. An essential reference tool. A classic of its kind.

Whitaker. *British Books in Print.* Annual since 1957. £18.00. Records all British books in print in April of each year; available in all public libraries; alphabetical under author and title, and has a comprehensive list of British publishers with addresses and telephone numbers. Very easy to use.

Whitaker. *Children's Books in Print.* Annual since 1969.

Whitaker. *Paperbacks in Print.* 1st ed. 1960. Now issued quarterly. It does an impossible job of recording all paperbacks as satisfactorily as can be expected.

Whitaker. *Religious Books in Print.* 1st ed. 1974. Omits religious books for children since they appear in *Children's Books in Print* (*q.v.*).

Whitaker, J. *Publishers in the United Kingdom and their Addresses.* Annual. £1.20. 64 pp. This handy list has one side of the page blank for notes and amendations.

Who Was Who. 6 vols. 1897–1970 continuing. £11.50 per vol. An essential companion to the D.N.B. (*q.v.*) in the overlap period (1897–1960). A cumulation of the annual *Who's Who* vols.
Who's Who. Black. Annual. Latest ed. 1978. £22.50. 2688 pp.

The World of Learning. 1977–78. 2 vols. Europa. 1977. £24.00. 2036 pp. Some 25,000 universities, museums, libraries and the like are listed under country with names of professors, librarians and others. Not an easy work to find one's way about in, but there is nothing else quite like it. For those who do not need world coverage, *The Commonwealth Universities Yearbook* is much easier to use, and just as reliable.

Willing's Press Guide. 103rd ed. 1977. £8.00. 746 pp. Lists some 8000 British and 5000 overseas newspapers, periodicals and annuals. As a quick guide, it is unbeatable.

Writing for the BBC. BBC Publications. 6th ed. 75p. Full of useful information of what the BBC requires and what they pay free-lance contributors.

JOURNALISTS' CALENDAR

1979

ANNIVERSARIES AND CENTENARIES

429 Vandals ravaged North Africa.
529 Monastery of Monte Cassino founded.
    Justinian Code of Civil Law.
779 Charlemagne's campaigns in Saxony.
1079 William the Conqueror created the New Forest.
    Rebuilding of Winchester Cathedral in progress.
    Pierre Abélard, b.
1129 First Pipe Roll in England.
1229 Toulouse University founded.
    Tosa Tsunetaka, Japanese artist, b.
1279 Statute of Mortmain.
1379 England regained Berwick-on-Tweed.
    Feast of Visitation of BVM instituted.
    New College, Oxford, founded by William of Wykeham.
1479 Copenhagen University founded.
    Johann Busch, German church reformer, d.
1529 Name "Protestant" adopted at Diet of Spires.
    Pope opposed annulment of Henry VIII's marriage.
    Reformation Parliament.
1579 Eastland Company established.
    Guido Bentivoglio, historian, b.
    Poor Law in Scotland.
    Luis Vélez de Guevara, Spanish writer, b.
1629 Massachusetts Bay Company chartered.
    Worshipful Company of Spectacle Makers incorporated.
1679 Licensing Act expired.
    Terms "Whig" and "Tory" came into use.
1729 *St. Matthew Passion:* Bach.
    John Wesley became leader of the Methodists at Oxford.
1779 Crompton's Spinning Mule.
    Countess of Huntingdon built Spa

Fields Chapel, London.
Iphigenia in Tauris: Gluck.
Amadis de Gaule: Bach.
First Epsom Oaks.
War against Mahrattas, India.
Siege of Gibraltar began.
1829 *William Tell:* Rossini.
    Mouth organ invented by Damian; concertina by Wheatstone.
    Oil first discovered in USA.
    Invention of braille.
    Rosas came to power in Argentina.
    Jean Baptiste Regnault, French artist, d.
    King's College School founded.
1879 Margaret Wintringham, educationist and politician, b.
    Scandium discovered by L. F. Nilson.
    First telephone exchange in London.
    6th Symphony: Bruckner.
    Dorothea Katherine Chambers, tennis player, b.
    Wu Lien-teh, Oriental physician, b.
    Aleksandr Tsankov, Bulgarian statesman, b.
    War of Chile with Peru and Bolivia.
    Royal University of Ireland founded.
    1st Church of Christ Scientist established, Boston.
    Vanessa Bell, artist, b.
1929 Term "apartheid" first used.
    Colonial Development Fund started.
    New Tilbury Dock, London.
    Museum of Modern Art, New York, founded.
    Viola Concerto: William Walton.
    Sir John in Love: Vaughan Williams.
    Iron lung invented.
    Jigme Dorji, Prime Minister of Bhutan, b.
    Union of Church of Scotland and United Free Church of Scotland.

PUBLICATIONS (Books)

1379 c. *Complaint of Mars:* Chaucer.
1479 *Book of Courtesy:* Caxton.
1529 c. *The Complaint:* Lindsay.
1579 *Travels of Marco Polo* (trans.):

Frampton.
Schoole of Abuse: Gosson.
Defence of Poetry, Music and Stage Plays: Lodge.

Mirrour of Mutabilitie: Munday.
Plutarch's Lives (trans.): North.
1629 *Mélite:* Corneille.
Lover's Melancholy: Ford.
Roman Actor (prod.): Massinger.
The Wedding (pub.): Shirley.
1679 *Fifty Comedies and Tragedies* (pub.): Beaumont and Fletcher.
History of the Reformation in England Vol. I: Burnet.
Troilus and Cressida: Dryden.
1729 *Poems on Several Occasions,* 3rd ed.: Carey.
Damon and Phillida: Cibber.
Polly: Gay.
The Wanderer: Savage.
Britannia (pub.): Thomson.
Sophonisba (prod.): Thomson.
1779 *Olney Hymns:* Cowper and Newton.
Iphigenie auf Tauris: Goethe.
Dialogues concerning Natural Religion: Hume.
Lives of the Poets: Johnson.
Nathan der Weise: Lessing.
The Mirror: Mackenzie.
Bengal Atlas: Rennell.
1829 *Comédie Humaine* (begun): Balzac.
Advice to Young Men: Cobbett.
Contes d'Espagne et d'Italie: de Musset.
The Young Duke: Disraeli.
The Shepherd's Calendar: Hogg.
Eugene Aram's Dream: Hood.
Les Orientales: Hugo.
Black-eyed Susan: Jerrold.
Library of Entertaining Knowledge: Knight.
Imaginary Conversations, 2nd series: Landor.
Devereux: Lytton.
The Disowned: Lytton.
Frank Mildmay: Marryat.
Analysis of the Human Mind: James Mill.
History of the Jews: Milman.
Misfortunes of Elphin: Peacock.
Joseph Delorme: Sainte-Beuve.
Tom Cringle's Log (begun): Michael Scott.
Anne of Geierstein: Walter Scott.
Tales of a Grandfather, 2nd series: Walter Scott.
Sir Thomas More: Southey.
1879 *Shakespeare Key:* Cowden Clarke.
The Impressions of Theophrastus

Such: George Eliot.
Progress and Poverty: Henry George.
A Doll's House: Ibsen.
Study of Psychology: Lewes.
The Egoist: Meredith.
Etymological Dictionary of the English Language (begun): Skeat.
Principles of Ethics: Spencer.
Travels with a Donkey: Stevenson.
The Red Room: Strindberg.
The Lover's Tale: Tennyson.
Doña Luz: Valera.
L'Assommoir: Zola.
1929 *Near and Far:* Blunden.
The Testament of Beauty: Bridges.
The Stricken Deer: Cecil.
The Gothic Revival: Clark.
Les Enfants Terribles: Cocteau.
Bitter Sweet: Coward.
The Quest for Certainty: Dewey.
The Sound and the Fury: Faulkner.
Amphitryon 38: Giraudoux.
Goodbye to all that: Graves.
The Man Within: Greene.
The Missing Muse: Guedalla.
Rope: Hamilton.
The Midnight Bell: Hamilton.
A Farewell to Arms: Hemingway.
What is Philosophy?: Heidegger.
A High Wind in Jamaica: Hughes.
The Universe around us: Jeans.
Dodsworth: Lewis.
Poet's Pub: Linklater.
Preface to Morals: Lippmann.
Blind Fireworks: MacNeice.
The Hawbucks: Masefield.
The Sacred Flame: Maugham.
Portrait in a Mirror: Morgan.
Oxford History of Music (begun).
Paper Houses: Plomer.
The Literary Career of James Boswell: Pottle.
The Good Companions: Priestley.
All Quiet on the Western Front: Remarque.
Street Scene: Rice.
Marriage and Morals: Russell.
The Apple Cart: Shaw.
Journey's End: Sherriff.
The Outcast: Stephens.
Medieval Latin Lyrics: Waddell.
Look Homeward, Angel: Wolfe.
A Room of One's Own: Woolfe.
The Winding Stair: Yeats.

PUBLICATIONS (Journals)

1729 *Salisbury and Winchester Journal.*
1779 *Irish Racing Calendar.*
1829 *Falmouth Packet.*
Londonderry Sentinel.
Perthshire Advertiser.
South Wales Weekly Argus.
Welshman.

1879 *Annual Report of Church Benefit Society.*
Batley News.
Bicester Advertiser.
Boy's Own Paper.
Cambridge Review.
Catholic Fireside.

Chart and Compass.
Churchman.
Contract Journal.
Dentists Register.
Directory of Directors.
Dyer, Textile Printer, Bleacher, and
    Finisher.
Evening Express (Aberdeen).
Good Templars' Watchword.
Henley and South Oxfordshire
    Standard.
Hornsey Journal.
Journal of Conchology.
Journal of Institute of Bankers.
Life of Faith.
Littleport Gazette.
Liverpool Echo.
Machinery Market.
Marine Engineer and Naval Archi-
    tect.
New Ross Standard.
North Bucks Times and Bletchley
    Observer.
Penarth Times.
Plumber and Journal of Heating.
Prophetic News.
Sale and Stretford Guardian.
Salford City Reporter.
Shire Horse Stud Book.
Surrey Mirror and County Post.
Vaccination Inquirer.
Watchtower.
World's Paper Trade Review.
1929 Acton Chamber of Commerce
    Bulletin.
Aircraft Engineering.
Books.
Bristol Evening World.
British Journal of Urology.
British Plastics.
Bus and Coach.
Confectionery and Baking Craft.
Council Fire.
Dairy Farmer.
Dental Magazine.
District Courier (Manchester).
Evangelical Quarterly.
Football Echo (Weymouth).
Fur Record.
Harper's Bazaar.
Hayes, Harlington, Hillingdon and
    District Chronicle.
Highway Engineer and Local Gov-
    ernment Surveyor.
Horse.
Hosiery Times.
Hospital.
Journal of Dairy Research.
Leader (Dromore).
Liberal Jewish Monthly.
Light Steam Power.
Listener.
Liturgy (as Music and Liturgy).
Lourdes Messenger.
Machinery Lloyd.
Manningtree and Mistley Standard.
Metallurgia.

Music Journal.
News of Salvation.
Oversea Education.
Plebs.
Rayon Record.
Red Star Weekly.
Sailplane and Glider.
Trading Post.
Water Engineer's Handbook.
World's Press News and Adver-
    tisers' Review.
Young Farmer.

JANUARY
— George Ferrers, poet and politician,
    d. 1579.
1 William Clowes, the elder, printer, b.
    1779.
    Bishop Stanley of Norwich, b. 1779.
    Tommaso Salvini, Italian tragedian,
    b. 1829.
    Ernest Jones, psychoanalyst, b. 1879.
    E. M. Forster, novelist, b. 1879.
    Holt Thomas, aircraft pioneer, d.
    1929.
2 Caleb Cushing, American statesman,
    d. 1879.
4 F. P. Plowden, author, d. 1829.
5 Stephen Decatur, American naval
    officer, b. 1779.
    Zebulon Montgomery Pike, explorer,
    b. 1779.
    Alexander I of Yugoslavia assumed
    dictatorial powers, 1929.
6 Haxey Hood Game, Lincolnshire.
    Julia Glover, actress, b. 1779.
7 Plough Sunday.
    Henry Arthur Jones, dramatist, d.
    1929.
9 T. W. Robertson, actor and dramatist,
    b. 1829.
10 Sir David Tennant, South African
    politician, b. 1829.
11 Friedrich von Schlegel, German poet,
    d. 1829.
12 Edmund Burke, b. 1729.
    Lazaro Spallanzani, Italian scientist,
    b. 1729.
    British Zulu War, 1879.
13 Sir William Reid Dick, b. 1879.
14 Abdication of King Amanullah of
    Afghanistan, 1929.
    H. O. Walker, American artist, d.
    1929.
15 Edward Matthew Ward, artist, d.
    1879.
    Ernest Thesiger, actor, b. 1879.
    Martin Luther King, b. 1929.
17 Catherine Booth, "mother of the Sal-
    vation Army," b. 1829.
18 Peter Mark Roget, ("Thesaurus"), b.
    1779.
19 Theodosius the Great became Em-
    peror, 379.
    William Congreve, playwright, d.
    1729.

20 David Garrick, d. 1779.
Clifford Douglas, founder of theory of Social Credit, b. 1879.
22 Gotthold Lessing, German writer, b. 1729.
Isandhlwana disaster, Zulu War, 1879.
23 Union of Utrecht, 1579.
Frederic Wood Jones, anthropologist, b. 1879.
24 Dissolution of Cavalier Parliament, 1679.
25 Conversion of St. Paul.
Burns Night.
William Shield, musician, d. 1829.
George Chaworth Musters, "King of Patagonia," d. 1879.
26 Republic Day, India.
Julia Margaret Cameron, photographer, d. 1879.
28 William Gerard ("Single-Speech") Hamilton, b. 1729.
William Burke, criminal, executed, 1829.
30 Commemoration of execution of Charles I (1649).
31 Rudolf Ludwig Mössbauer, German scientist, b. 1929.
Trotsky expelled from Russia, 1929.

FEBRUARY
— Ewen Cameron, highland chief, b. 1629.
1 Henri Chrétien, French scientist, b. 1879.
2 Candlemas.
Jedburgh Ball Game (also on Shrove Tuesday).
3 Jan Steen, Dutch artist, d. 1679.
Sir Frederick John Jackson, explorer, d. 1929.
4 Independence Day, Sri Lanka.
James Nasmyth, botanist, d. 1779.
5 Joost van den Vondel, Dutch poet, d. 1679.
6 National Day, New Zealand.
Edwin Samuel Montagu, politician, b. 1879.
Germany agreed to Kellogg Pact, 1929.
7 Castiglione, Italian diplomat and author, d. 1529.
William Boyce, composer, d. 1779.
9 George V began convalescence at Bognor, Sussex, 1929.
Litvinov Protocol (Eastern Pact), 1929.
10 Pope Leo XII, d. 1829.
Admiral Sir Edmund Fremantle, d. 1929.
11 Admiral Keppel acquitted after court martial, 1779.
Francis Henry Egerton, 8th Earl of Bridgewater, d. 1829.
Honoré Daumier, French artist, d. 1879.

Lateran Treaty established independent Vatican City, 1929.
12 Lily Langtry, actress, d. 1929.
13 Jonathan Peel, politician and patron of horse racing, d. 1879.
Omar Torrijos Herrera, Panamanian statesman, b. 1929.
Commissioner Higgins became General of Salvation Army, 1929.
14 Captain James Cook, explorer, killed in Hawaii, 1779.
15 Graham Hill, racing driver, b. 1929.
James Rodney Schlesinger, American administrator, b. 1929.
17 Charles Jeremiah Wells, poet, d. 1879.
Sir Francis Bridgeman, admiral, d. 1929.
Yasir Arafat, leader of Al Fatah, b. 1929.
18 End of Sixth Crusade, 1229.
J. R. Stephens, chartist, d. 1879.
20 Sir Nicholas Bacon, Lord Keeper, d. 1579.
Sir Augustus Wall Callcott, artist, b. 1779.
Joseph Jefferson, American actor, b. 1829.
21 Friedrich Karl von Savigny, German jurist, b. 1779.
Sir Mountstuart Elphinstone Grant Duff, statesman and author, b. 1829.
Gertie Millar, actress, b. 1879.
General Sir John Maxwell, d. 1929.
23 Lord Denman, lord chief justice, b. 1779.
Agnes Arber, botanist, b. 1879.
Marshall Hall, lawyer, d. 1929.
25 Capture of Vincennes, Indianapolis, by Colonel George Rogers Clark, 1779.
Sir Nathaniel Barnaby, naval architect, b. 1829.
26 Frank Bridge, composer, b. 1879.
28 James, Duke of York, banished, 1679.

MARCH
— Helen Alexander, Scottish covenanting heroine, d. 1729.
— First production of Eugen Onegin, Tschaikovsky, 1879.
1 St. David's Day.
Thomas Earnshaw, watchmaker, d. 1829.
2 Parliament dissolved following scenes involving the Speaker, 1629.
Hermann Vezin, actor, b. 1829.
Carl Schurz, American soldier and statesman, b. 1829.
Sir Edward Seymour, admiral, d. 1929.
3 Sir James Fitzjames Stephen, judge, b. 1829.
W. K. Clifford, mathematician, d. 1879.

4 Samuel Noble, minister of the "New Church," b. 1779.
S. R. Gardiner, historian, b. 1829.
Andrew Jackson became President, USA, 1829.

5 Roman Catholic Relief Bill passed House of Commons, 1829.
Lord Beveridge, economist, b. 1879.
Erik Hilding Carlsson, Swedish rally driver, b. 1929.

6 Edict of Restitution, 1629.
Third Parliament of Charles II, 1679.
Sir Arthur William Blomfield, architect, b. 1829.

8 Otto Hahn, German nuclear scientist, b. 1879.
Keith Lucas, scientist, b. 1879.
Viscount Finlay, lord chancellor, d. 1929.

10 Daniel Sedgwick, hymnologist, d. 1879.

12 Lee Bible, racing driver, killed, 1929.
William T. Dannat, American artist, d. 1929.

13 William Broadhead, agitator, d. 1879.
H. S. Tuke, artist, d. 1929.
Baron Phillimore, judge, d. 1929.

14 James Ley, Earl of Marlborough, judge, d. 1629.
F. C. Lewis, artist, b. 1779.
H. E. Monro, poet, b. 1879.
Einstein, b. 1879.

15 William Lamb, Viscount Melbourne, statesman, b. 1779.
Lord Catto, Governor of Bank of England, b. 1879.

16 Sir Mark Sykes, traveller and politician, b. 1879.

17 St. Patrick's Day.

19 Clara Clairmont, Byron's "Claire," mother of Allegra, d. 1879.

20 E. H. Young, Baron Kennet, politician and author, b. 1879.
Marshal Foch, d. 1929.

21 John Law, controller-general of French finance, d. 1729.
Wellington challenged Earl of Winchelsea to duel, 1829.

23 Sir Roger Bannister, b. 1929.

25 Lady Day.
Tichborne Dole, Hampshire.

27 Jorge Manrique, Spanish poet, d. 1479.
Edward Jean Steichen, American photographer, b. 1879.

28 Rev. F. B. Meyer, Baptist preacher, d. 1929.

30 England–India air service began, 1929.
Lord Montagu of Beaulieu, motoring pioneer, d. 1929.

31 Pius VIII became Pope, 1829.
Maria Susan Rye, social reformer, b. 1829.

APRIL

— Queen Victoria's visit to Italy, 1879.

1 John Langhorne, poet, translator of Plutarch, d. 1779.
Robert Surtees, antiquary, b. 1779.

2 Marcellus Laroon, the younger, artist, b. 1679.

3 Karl Benz, German engineer, d. 1929.

4 William Palmer, theologian and archaeologist, d. 1879.

5 Income Tax year ends in Britain.
Count Nikolaus zu Dohna-Schlodien, German naval commander, b. 1879.
Francis Neil Gasquet, Dom Aidan, cardinal, d. 1929.

6 André Previn, conductor, b. 1929.

7 William Shrubsole, divine, b. 1729.
Martha Ray shot by James Hackman (executed April 19), 1779.

8 Sir Anthony Panizzi, British Museum librarian, d. 1879.

9 Sir Gerald Kelly, artist, b. 1879.

10 General William Booth, Salvation Army, b. 1829.
R. W. Sibthorpe, divine, d. 1879.
Mike Hawthorne, racing driver, b. 1929.

11 First horse buses in Paris, 1829.
Alexander Buchan, meteorologist, b. 1829.

12 Flora Annie Steel, novelist, d. 1929.

13 Thomas Percy, bishop and anthologist, b. 1729.
Roman Catholic Relief Bill passed in House of Lords, 1829.

14 Christiaan Huygens, physicist, b. 1629.
James Branch Cabell, American writer, b. 1879.

16 Henry Duncan McLaren, 2nd Baron Aberconway, industrialist, b. 1879.
Sir John Morris-Jones, Welsh poet and scholar, d. 1929.
J. Havelock Wilson, founder of National Union of Seamen, d. 1929.

20 Henry Cope Colles, musicologist, b. 1879.
Robert Lynd, essayist, b. 1879.

21 Impeachment of Danby, 1679.
William Knyvett, composer, b. 1779.

23 St. George's Day.
St. George's Court, Lichfield.
Shakespeare's birthday celebrations.

24 St. Egbert, d. 729.

25 Charles Tennyson Turner, poet, d. 1879.

26 Sir Owen Richardson, scientist, b. 1879.
Felix Eugen Fritsch, botanist, b. 1879.

29 Richard Cheyney, Bishop of Gloucester, d. 1579.
Sir Thomas Beecham, conductor, b. 1879.
Sir George Younger, Baron Younger, d. 1929.
Jeremy Thorpe, Liberal politician, b. 1929.

MAY

1 English College established in Rome, 1579.
   Frederick Sandys (or Sands), Pre-Raphaelite artist, b. 1829.

2 Catherine II, Empress of Russia, b. 1729.
   John Galt, novelist, b. 1779.
   James Francis Byrnes, American statesman, b. 1879.

3 James Sharp, Archbishop of St. Andrews, murdered, 1679.

4 John Finnie, artist, b. 1829.
   Earl of Surrey, first Roman Catholic M.P. (for Horsham) elected, 1829.
   William Froude, engineer, d. 1879.
   Sir Frederick Stopford, general, d. 1929.
   Audrey Hepburn, b. 1929.

5 Isaac Butt, Irish politician, d. 1879.
   Charles Grafly, American sculptor, d. 1929.

7 Joan of Arc raised siege of Orleans, 1429.
   Charles Abbot, Lord Colchester, Speaker, d. 1829.

8 Helston Furry Dance, Cornwall.

9 Ceolwulf became King of Northumbria, 729.
   Greeks captured Lepanto, 1829.

10 Lady Dorothy Pakington, author, d. 1679.
   Thomas Young, doctor, scientist and Egyptologist, d. 1829.

12 Burt Bacharach, modern composer, b. 1929.

13 Peace of Teschen, end of War of Bavarian Succession, 1779.
   Jabez Bunting, nonconformist minister, b. 1779.
   George Ernest Hicks, trade unionist, b. 1879.

14 Henry Sewell, first Premier of New Zealand, d. 1879.
   Baron Lindsay of Birker, educationalist, b. 1879.

17 National Day, Norway.
   Samuel Clarke, divine, d. 1729.
   John Jay, American diplomat and justice, d. 1829.

19 Viscountess Nancy Astor, b. 1879.
   2nd Viscount Astor, b. 1879.
   Sir William Joseph Jordan, New Zealand politician, b. 1879.

21 Earl of Rosebery, d. 1929.

22 Giuseppe Parini, Italian poet, b. 1729.

24 W. L. Garrison, abolitionist, d. 1879.

25 Lord Beaverbrook, b. 1879.

27 Habeas Corpus Act, 1679.

28 Thomas Moore, Irish poet, b. 1779.
   Mrs. Stopford Green, historian, d. 1929.

29 Garland Day, Castleton, Derbyshire.
   Grovely Forest Rights, Wiltshire.
   William Dodd, counterfeiter, b. 1729.
   Sir Humphry Davy, d. 1829.

30 Mark Hambourg, pianist, b. 1879.
   Election in Great Britain, Labour returned, 1929.

31 Union Day, South Africa (1910).
   Albertino Mussato, chronicler and poet, d. 1329.

JUNE

— Daniel Terry, actor, d. 1829.

— Swan River Settlement (Western Australia) established, Perth capital, 1829.

— Tennyson's *Timbuctoo* published, 1829.

1 Glorious First of June, Battle of Ushant, 1794.
   C. S. Parker, politician and writer, b. 1829.
   Prince Imperial killed in Zululand, 1879.

2 A. S. M. Hutchinson, novelist, b. 1879.

3 Sir Charles Anthony Brooke, rajah of Sarawak, b. 1829.
   Francis Ridley Havergal, hymnwriter, d. 1879.
   Lionel Nathan Rothschild, banker, d. 1879.

4 Mabel Lucie Attwell, illustrator, b. 1879.

5 Constitution Day, Denmark.
   Baron Mount Stephen, philanthropist, b. 1829.
   Admiral Sir Cecil Burney, d. 1929.
   Formation of MacDonald ministry, 1929.

6 Sir Leslie Patrick Abercrombie, architect, b. 1879.

7 Robert Bruce, d., David II succeeded, 1329.
   Bishop William Warburton of Gloucester, d. 1779.

8 Young Plan for reparations, 1929.
   J. E. Millais, artist, b. 1829.
   Bliss Carman, poet, d. 1929.
   Margaret Bondfield became first woman Cabinet Minister, 1929.

9 Friedrich Wolfgang Adler, Austrian politician, b. 1879.

10 First Oxford–Cambridge boat race, Henley, 1829.

11 Professor Alfred Newton, zoologist, b. 1829.
   Sir Edward Braddon, Premier of Tasmania, b. 1829.

15 Magna Carta commemorations.

16 Spain declared war on Great Britain in league with France, 1779.
   Sir Maurice Powicke, historian, b. 1879.
   William Bramwell Booth, Salvation Army leader, d. 1929.

17 Drake proclaimed British sovereignty over California, 1579.
   G. W. M. Reynolds, writer and politician, d. 1879.

18 France took St. Vincent, West Indies, 1779.
19 Act of Parliament for formation of Metropolitan Police, 1829.
21 John Skelton, poet, d. 1529.
1st Baron Geddes, administrator, b. 1879.
Leonard Hobhouse, philosopher, d. 1929.
22 Battle of Bothwell Bridge, Covenanters defeated by Monmouth, 1679.
Ellen Thorneycroft Fowler, novelist, d. 1929.
23 St. John's Eve. Chain of bonfires, Cornwall.
Viscount Camrose, newspaper proprietor, b. 1879.
24 Midsummer Day.
Wall pulpit sermon, Magdalen College, Oxford.
25 Dion Boucicault, the younger, actor-manager, d. 1929.
26 J. B. Manson, painter, b. 1879.
27 James Smithson, founder of Smithsonian Institution, d. 1829.
John Laird Main Lawrence, Governor-General of India, d. 1879.
28 Peace of Alais ends Huguenot wars, 1629.
Alexander Keith Johnston the younger, geographer, d. 1879.
Edward Carpenter, sociology writer, d. 1929.
29 James Fitzmaurice Fitzgerald slain, 1579.
Anton Raphael Mengs, artist, d. 1779.

JULY
— Matthew Sutcliffe, Dean of Exeter, d. 1629.
— First botanical expedition organised from Britain, 1629.
1 Dominion Day, Canada (1867).
Guy John Fenton Knowles, art connoisseur, b. 1879.
2 Elizabeth Claypole, Cromwell's daughter, b. 1629.
Sir Horace Rumbold, diplomat, b. 1829.
4 Independence Day, USA.
French took Grenada, West Indies, 1779.
Pioneer omnibus service, Paddington to Bank, 1829.
Zulus defeated at Ulundi, 1879.
5 Tynwald Day, Isle of Man.
Field-Marshal Sir Hew Dalrymple Ross, b. 1779.
Tony Lock, England cricketer, b. 1929.
6 Lady Frances Waldegrave, d. 1879.
7 Peter James Kenney, Irish divine, b. 1779.

9 Sir Harry Poland, lawyer, b. 1829.
Respighi, Italian composer, b. 1879.
Hassan II, King of Morocco, b. 1929.
13 William Hedley, inventor, b. 1779.
14 Bastille Day, France.
Richard de Lucy, "the loyal," chief justiciar, d. 1179.
Richard Langhorne executed, 1679.
Archbishop E. W. Benson, b. 1829.
15 Hugo von Hofmannsthal, Austrian poet, d. 1929.
17 Charles VII crowned at Rheims, 1429.
James Duport, theologian, d. 1679.
18 George Wakeman brought to trial, 1679.
20 Sir Henry Sidney, Lord Deputy of Ireland, b. 1529.
21 National Day, Belgium.
23 Vespasian, d. 79.
William Shrubsole, musician and theologian, d. 1829.
24 Kellogg Pact came into force, 1929.
27 Briand succeeded Poincaré as Premier of France, 1929.
28 John Speed, map-maker, d. 1629.
29 Annual pilgrimage to Hastings Castle.
30 Robert Wild, puritan divine, buried, 1679.

AUGUST
— Thomas Newcomen, inventor, d. 1729.
— Robert Barclay Allardice (Captain Barclay), pedestrian, b. 1779.
1 Lammas.
Lorenz Oken, German naturalist, b. 1779.
Bernhard Baron, tobacco manufacturer, d. 1929.
3 Viscount Peel, Speaker, b. 1829.
4 Feast of St. Wilfrid celebrations, Ripon, Yorkshire.
Papal encyclical against modern metaphysics, 1879.
Adelaide Kemble (Mrs. Sartoris), singer, d. 1879.
5 Antony Bek, Bishop of Norwich, b. 1279.
Charles Fechter, actor, d. 1879.
Dame Millicent (Mrs. Henry) Fawcette, suffragette, d. 1929.
6 Johann von Lamont, astronomer, d. 1879.
Germany accepted Young Plan; Allies agreed to evacuate Rhineland, 1929.
7 Maximilian defeated French at Guinegatte, 1479.
Karl Ritter, geographer, b. 1779.
8 First steam locomotive in USA, Baltimore to Ohio, 1829.
Graf Zeppelin airship began round the world flight, 1929.
10 Viscount Howe, general, b. 1729.
George Long, classicist, d. 1879.
11 David Landsborough, naturalist, b. 1779.

13 John Ireland, composer, b. 1879.
15 Ethel Barrymore, actress, b. 1879.
  Sir Edwin Lankester, zoologist, d. 1929.
16 Clifton Brown, Viscount Ruffside, Speaker, b. 1879.
19 Edward Moran, artist, b. 1829.
  A. S. Peake, biblical scholar, d. 1929.
  Sergei Diaghilev, d. 1929.
20 Jöns Jakob Berzelius, Swedish chemist, b. 1779.
  Henry Parry Liddon, divine, b. 1829.
  R. W. Seton-Watson, historian, b. 1879.
21 Otto Goldschmidt, pianist and composer, b. 1829.
  Henry Ainley, actor, b. 1879.
  Claude Grahame-White, aviator, b. 1879.
22 Charles Clerke, circumnavigator, d. 1779.
24 Eruption of Vesuvius; Pliny the elder, d. 79.
  Cardinal de Retz, d. 1679.
25 St. Ebba, d. *c.* 679.
26 Sir Ernest Satow, diplomat and historian, d. 1929.
27 Sir Rowland Hill, postal reformer, d. 1879.
28 Basil Mathews, writer and ecumenist, b. 1879.
29 Samuel Curtis, botanist, b. 1779.
30 Thomas Longman, publisher, d. 1879.

SEPTEMBER
1 Richard Steele, writer, d. 1729.
  Peace treaty signed with Zulu chiefs, 1879.
2 Sir Thomas Modyford, governor of Jamaica, buried 1679.
  Edward Sonnenschein, philologist, d. 1929.
3 Judge Bigham, Viscount Mersey, d. 1929.
4 Sir Wilfrid Lawson, politician, b. 1829.
5 Briand proposed European federal union, 1929.
6 Karl Joseph Wirth, German politician, b. 1879.
  Sir Barry Jackson, theatre director, b. 1879.
7 John Armstrong, Scottish writer, d. 1779.
  Friedrich August Kekulé, b. 1829.
8 Edward Grigg, Baron Altrincham, politician, b. 1879.
10 Arnold Palmer, golfer, b. 1929.
11 Archbishop Robert Kilwardby, d. 1279.
12 John William Fletcher, divine, b. 1729.
  Richard Temple Grenville, statesman, d. 1779.
13 Henry Stacy Marks, artist, b. 1829.
  Annie Kenney, suffragette, b. 1879.
  Sir Robert Lorimer, architect, d. 1929.

14 Treaty of Adrianople, 1829.
15 Charles Stanhope, 3rd Earl of Harrington, d. 1829.
  Joseph Lyons, Prime Minister of Australia, b. 1879.
  Murray Gell-Mann, scientist, b. 1929.
16 James Hamilton, language teaching experimentalist, d. 1829.
17 Don John of Austria, the younger, d. 1679.
  John Campbell, lord chancellor and legal biographer, b. 1779.
  Karl Hillebrand, German author, b. 1829.
  Robert Herdman, artist, b. 1829.
  William Henry Perkin, scientist, d. 1929.
  Stirling Moss, b. 1929.
18 Joseph Story, American legal writer, b. 1779.
19 George Ambrose Lloyd, Baron Lloyd, statesman, b. 1879.
20 Victor Sjöström, Swedish actor and film director, b. 1879.
  Admiral Sir Hedworth Meux, d. 1929.
21 Philip Thomas Howard, the Cardinal of Norfolk, b. 1629.
22 Robert Wilson, miscellaneous writer, baptised, 1579.
  Sir Norman Warren Fisher, civil servant, b. 1879.
23 John Paul Jones' victory in naval battle between American and British ships in the North Sea, 1779.
  Francis Kilvert, diarist, d. 1879.
  John Freeman, poet, d. 1929.
25 W. M. Rossetti, man of letters, b. 1829.
26 Moses Mendelssohn, philosopher and critic, b. 1729.
28 Admission of Sheriffs of London.
  St. Wenceslaus, King of Bohemia, murdered, 929.
29 Michaelmas Day.
  Election of Lord Mayor of London, Guildhall.
  William Quarrier, founder of Orphan Homes of Scotland, b. 1829.
  Edmund Falconer (O'Rourke), actor, d. 1879.

OCTOBER
— Sir Edwin Sandys, statesman, d. 1629.
— Stephenson's *Rocket* won Liverpool–Manchester competition, 1829.
— Sir John Weir, physician, b. 1879.
— National Land League formed in Ireland, 1879.
— Firth College (later University of Sheffield) opened 1879.
— USA suspended loans to Europe, 1929.
1 Nigeria National Day.
  Disputation between Luther and Zwingli, 1529.
2 Sir Idris Bell, Welsh scholar, b. 1879.

3 John Banister, composer, d. 1679.
André Brunot, French actor, b. 1879.
Stresemann, d. 1929.
Britain resumed relations with USSR, 1929.
Name "Yugoslavia" adopted, 1929.

4 Lesotho National Day.
Jacques Blumenthal, composer, b. 1829.
W. E. Davies, "Leviathan" of the race-track, d. 1879.

5 Francis Peyton Rous, Nobel Prize winner for Physiology, b. 1879.

6 Mountstuart Elphinstone, governor of Bombay, b. 1779.

7 Charles II prorogued Parliament, 1679.
British troops invaded Afghanistan, 1879.

8 Isaac Penington, the younger, quaker, d. 1679.

9 Sir Richard Blackmore, physician and author, d. 1729.
Baron Simon of Wythenshawe, industrialist, b. 1879.
Felix von Laue, German scientist, b. 1879.

10 John of Bridlington, saint, d. 1379.

11 Grand Vizier Mehmed Sokollu, d. 1579.
Lord Brabazon, 12th Earl of Meath, d. 1929.

12 Lionel Cust, art historian, d. 1929.
Robert Coles, psychiatrist, b. 1929.
Airship R101 launched, 1929.

15 Nadir Khan, King of Afghanistan, 1929.

17 Cardinal Wolsey dismissed, 1529.
A. H. Garrod, zoologist, d. 1879.

21 Trafalgar Day ceremonies.
Edison produced successful light bulb, 1879.

22 Sir Matthew Smith, artist, b. 1879.
Sir Ignatius Valentine Chirol, traveller and writer, d. 1929.

23 Habibullah executed in Afghanistan, 1929.
Thomas Tout, historian, d. 1929.

24 Wall Street crisis, USA, 1929.

25 Sir Thomas More became Lord Chancellor, 1529.

26 National Day in Austria and Iran.
Roger Boyle, Earl of Orrery, d. 1679.
Lord Cockburn, Scottish judge, b. 1779.

28 Prince von Bülow, German statesman, d. 1929.

29 Sheridan's *The Critic* first produced, 1779.
Franz von Papen, German statesman, b. 1879.
John Blackwood, publisher and editor, d. 1879.

30 John Rogers, American sculptor, b. 1829.

NOVEMBER

— Joseph Trapp, miscellaneous writer, b. 1679.

— Dual control, Great Britain and France, established in Egypt, 1879.

1 C. L. Gruneisen, journalist, d. 1879.
Lord Francis Scott, soldier and politician, b. 1879.

3 Field-Marshal Sir Hugh Gough, b. 1779.
Vilhjalmur Stefansson, explorer, b. 1879.

4 London–Brighton Veteran Car Run.
Will Rogers, American humorist, b. 1879.
Tardieu became Premier of France, 1929.

5 Washington Allston, American artist, b. 1779.
James Clerk Maxwell, British physicist, d. 1879.
Sir Edmund Craster, Bodleian librarian, b. 1879.

6 Henry VI crowned, 1429.
Joseph Train, Scottish antiquary, b. 1779.

7 Leon Trotsky, b. 1879.

9 Treaty of Seville, 1729.

10 Lord Mayor's Show, London.
Helen Angeli, authoress, b. 1879.
Nicholas Vachel Lindsay, American writer, b. 1879.

13 Thomas Chippendale, furniture maker, buried, 1779.
S. S. Laurie, educationist, b. 1829.
Basle Bank for International Settlements founded, 1929.

14 Birthday of HRH Prince of Wales.
Adam Öhlenschläger, Danish poet, b. 1779.

15 Sir John Paston, courtier and letter writer d. 1479.
Jonathan Cape, publisher, b. 1879.

18 Arthur Cohen, lawyer, b. 1829.
T. P. O'Connor, journalist and politician, d. 1929.

19 Arthur Henry Mann, musician, d. 1929.

20 Charles Halpin ("Miles O'Reilley"), writer, b. 1829.

21 Sir Thomas Gresham, d. 1579.

22 John T. Delane, editor of *The Times* newspaper, d. 1879.
J. A. Broun, meteorologist, d. 1879.
Sir Thomas Wentworth (Pasha) Russell, administrator in Egypt, b. 1879.

24 Gladstone began his Midlothian campaign, 1879.
Clemenceau, d. 1929.

26 Arthur Charles Hamilton-Gordon, Baron Stanmore, colonial governor, b. 1829.

27 Sir Archibald Primrose, Lord Carrington, Scottish judge, d. 1679.
French Chamber moved from Versailles to Paris, 1879.

28 Anton Rubinstein, pianist and com-
    poser, b. 1829.
29 Commander Byrd flew to South Pole
    and back, 1929.
30 St. Andrew's Day.
    J. A. Roebuck, politician, d. 1879.
    Second Rhineland zone evacuated,
    1929.

DECEMBER
— John Fletcher, dramatist, b. 1579.
— Praisegod Barebones, d. 1679.
— Viceroy and Indian princes began
    Roundtable Conference on Domin-
    ion status for India, 1929.
1   R. W. Dale, nonconformist divine,
    b. 1829.
2   Advent.
3   Marchioness of Londonderry, b.
    1879.
4   Thomas Hobbes, d. 1679.
    Suttee abolished in India, 1829.
    Sir Hamilton Harty, conductor, b.
    1879.
5   Spenser's *Shepheardes Calender*
    licensed, 1579.
    Sir Henry Joly de Lotbinière, Canad-
    ian politician, b. 1829.
6   St. Nicholas.
7   Sir Patience Ward, Lord Mayor of
    London, b. 1629.
    Rudolf Friml, composer, b. 1879.
    General Sir Charles Monro, d. 1929.
9   Seyyid Khalifa bin Harub, Sultan of
    Zanzibar, b. 1879.

10 Ernest Shepard, artist, b. 1879.
11 Henry Fowler, hymn-writer, b. 1779.
    Sir Henry Clinton, the younger, gen-
    eral, d. 1829.
    Sir David Dale, ironmaster, b. 1829.
    Kenneth MacMillan, choreographer,
    b. 1929.
12 John Osborne, playwright, b. 1929.
    First performance, *The Rio Grande*,
    Lambert, 1929.
13 Anthony Collins, deist, d. 1729.
14 Admiral Sir Henry Jackson, radio
    pioneer, d. 1929.
16 Closing the Gates, Londonderry.
    Proclamation of Transvaal Republic,
    1879.
18 Attack by hired men on Dryden in
    London, 1679.
    Joseph Grimaldi, actor, b. 1779.
    Jean Baptiste de Lamarck, d. 1829.
    Paul Klee, Swiss artist, b. 1879.
21 Stalin, b. 1879.
22 Michel Baron, French actor, d. 1729.
    General Edward Bulwer, b. 1829.
    Referendum in Germany on Young
    Plan which is upheld, 1929.
27 W. H. Dixon, traveller and historian,
    d. 1879.
28 Tay Bridge disaster, 1879.
29 Edward King, Bishop of Lincoln, b.
    1829.
31 Hogmanay and New Year's Eve
    ceremonies.
    Paisley cinema disaster, 1929.
    Peter May, cricketer, b. 1929.

MAKING A BOOK

PREPARATION OF TYPESCRIPT

Neatness

The first impression made on a publisher and a publisher's reader may be vital. They will try to discount the physical appearance of your typescript, but a tatty typescript covered with handwritten corrections, on different sizes of paper and with inadequate margins and spacing, will perhaps not receive benign consideration first thing on a Monday morning.

The printer

Even if you have followed the advice below, have a signed contract in your pocket, and the publisher is awaiting the final manuscript with impatience, there is another reason for neatness. The manuscript has to go to a printer for setting. The printer's compositor is basically a copy typist, working a complicated and expensive set of keyboards. He must be able to read your typescript quickly and accurately, and at the same time he must interpret a code of marks which the copy editor will make all over it.

Typing

Many publishers refuse even to consider handwritten manuscripts. No publisher will accept them as final copy. If you cannot afford to have the whole script typed before acceptance, there are ways round the problem. See below under "preliminary letter".

The paper used should be uniform in size, preferably the standard size A4, which has replaced the old foolscap and quarto sizes. Neither flimsy paper nor very thick paper should be used. If in doubt, ask the stationer for a standard A4 typewriter paper. Use one side of the paper only. It is helpful but not essential if manuscripts are typed to a width of 60 characters per line. For this makes it easier for printers and publishers to calculate the extent of a work and so—using copyfitting tables—to work out the space occupied when it is printed.

For ordinary typescripts, use the black ribbon. For plays, use red for names of characters, stage directions, etc., and black for dialogue. If a two-colour ribbon is not available use capitals for character names and underline stage directions in red by hand. Keep a fairly new ribbon in the typewriter so that it is black but not splodgy. Remember that type-writer maintenance is a tax-deductible expense!

Margins

Good margins are essential, especially on the left hand side. This enables the copy editor to include instructions to the printer. On A4 paper a left-hand margin of 1½–2 inches allows sufficient space.

Double spacing

This is necessary if you are to make any corrections to the typescript, and there are always some improvements which you will want to make; they can only be made clear to the printer if there is space available between the lines. The copy editor too needs this extra space.

Corrections to typescript

Corrections to the final typescript should be kept to a minimum. Often the publisher's editor will want to suggest a few additional changes—this happens even to the best authors—and once all or some of these are included, the typescript may have become very messy. If the publisher then feels it is not in a fit state for the printer he may well ask you to have it retyped.

Consistency

Be as consistent as possible in your choice of variant spellings, use of sub-headings, etc.

Numbering

Pages (or folios as publishers prefer to call them to distinguish them from the pages of the final book) should be numbered throughout. If you need to include an extra folio after say folio 27, call it 27a, and write at the foot of folio 27: "Folio 27a follows". Then write at the foot of 27a: "Folio 28 follows". Don't do this too often or you will confuse and irritate your readers.

Binding

Printers prefer to handle each folio separately, so do not use a binder which will make this impossible. Ring binders are very acceptable. Alternatively you can use a cardboard envelope folder. In this case it will help if you can clip the pages of each chapter together, but never staple them.

Protection of typescripts

This can be achieved by placing a stiffer piece of paper at front and back. On the first folio of the typescript itself, give the title, your name and, most important of all, your address. It is worth including your address elsewhere also, just in case the first folio becomes detached.

SUBMISSION OF MANUSCRIPTS

Publishers use the word manuscript when they mean typescript, so in dealings with publishers this is the word to use.

Choosing your publisher

It will save you time and postage if you check first that you are sending your manuscript to a firm that will consider it. Publishers specialise. It is no use sending a work of romantic fiction to a firm that specialises in high-brow novels translated from obscure languages just because they are described in this book as fiction-publishers. It is still less use to send it to a firm which publishes no fiction at all.

The way to avoid the more obvious mistakes is to look in your library or bookshop for books which are in some way similar to yours, and find out who publishes them. Remember, though, that paperbacks are usually editions of books published first in cased editions. Paperback publishers will not be interested in a first novel, for instance.

Preliminary letter

This again will save you time, money and probably frustration. The letter by itself will tell the publisher very little; what he would in most cases prefer to see is a brief preliminary letter together with a synopsis of the book and a few specimen pages from it. This will enable him to judge whether it might fit into his list, and whether he wants to see more. This is one way of avoiding paying a typing bill until it looks as though the investment in the manuscript may be worthwhile.

There is no point whatsoever in asking for a personal interview. The publisher will prefer to consider the manuscript on its own merits, and will not want to be influenced by a personal meeting.

Postage of manuscripts

Always send postage to cover the return of your manuscript, or explain that you will arrange to pick it up from the publisher's office if you prefer. (Again, if your manuscript has been rejected the publisher will not be willing to discuss the reasons in person.)

Manuscripts can be sent by the compensation fee service, registered post, or by recorded delivery. Further details are available from the Post Office. Recorded delivery is useful because you can check that the publisher has received the manuscript. Whether you send it first or second class depends entirely on how fast you want it to arrive. A properly packed parcel almost always arrives by either rate.

Packing is important. It is not enough to put the manuscript in an envelope. Padded bags are a good idea and are available in several sizes from many stationers.

At all costs, *keep a duplicate*, with all the latest changes to the text included on it.

Your own records

It may be worth keeping a record of all manuscripts sent out. One suggested layout is given below.

Date	Name of Ms	Where sent	Accepted/Rejected	Date

Estimating

To estimate the length or *extent* of a manuscript, calculate the average number of words per page over say eight pages. Multiply the average by the number of pages in the manuscript, making allowances for half-pages at the end of chapters, etc.

What is the publisher doing with your manuscript?

Whether or not the publisher finally accepts or rejects the manuscript, there is usually a considerable interval between submission and the publisher's decision. Most publishers acknowledge receipt of manuscript, and if you do not receive an acknowledgement it is advisable to check that the manuscript has arrived. Apart from that, it is not worth chasing the publisher for a quick decision: if pressed, the publisher will probably reject, purely because this is the safer decision.

You should hear from the publisher within about two months. During this time he will either have had the manuscript read "in the house" or will have sent it to one or more advisers whose opinion he respects. Favourable readers' reports may mean that the publisher will immediately accept the manuscript, particularly if it fits easily into his current publishing programme.

On the other hand, a reader's report may be glowing, but the publisher may still hesitate. He knows he has a good book, but he wants to be sure he will be able to sell it. He is, after all, considering an investment of at least £3000 and frequently more. He may need time to obtain further opinions, and also to obtain estimates from printers, to judge whether the book could be produced at a reasonable price. The worst delays occur when the publisher is attracted to a manuscript but cannot see how he can publish it successfully.

If you have not had a decision after two months, write either a tactful letter saying 'I don't want to rush you, but . . .' or alternatively request an immediate decision and be prepared to start again with another publisher.

If your book is topical you have a right to a speedy decision, but it is as well to establish this early on.

Illustrations

If illustrations form a large part of your proposed book, and you expect to provide them yourself, then they should be included with the manuscript. If you are sending specimen pages you should include also some sample illustrations. This applies largely to children's picture books and to travel books. It is prudent to send duplicate photographs, photocopies of line drawings and so on so that little harm is done if illustrations go astray. In the case of a children's book, then obviously one finished piece of artwork is essential plus photocopies of roughs for the rest (one must bear in mind that the final artwork may have to be drawn to a particular size and the number of illustrations fixed according to the format chosen). If you have written a children's story, or the text for a picture book, do *not* ask a friend to provide the illustrations. If the publisher likes your story he may well not like your friend's artwork: you will have considerably lengthened the odds against the story being accepted. Of course this does not apply when an artist and author work closely together to develop an idea, but in that case it is best to start by finding a publisher who likes the artist's work before submitting the story.

Travel manuscripts should be accompanied by a sketch map to show which area you are writing about. The publisher will have an atlas in his reference shelves, but it may not have sufficient detail for him to follow your manuscript. Irreplaceable material should not be sent on speculation.

Many illustrated books these days have illustrations collected by the publishers. If your proposed book is to be illustrated, it is best to establish early on who is responsible for the illustration costs: an attractive royalty offer might be less attractive if you have to gather the pictures, obtain permission for use, and foot the bills.

Quotations

It is normally the author's responsibility to obtain (and pay for) permission to quote written material which is still in copyright. Permission should always be sought from the publisher of the quoted work, not from the author. Fees for quotation vary enormously: for fashionable modern writers permission may be costly, but in other cases only a nominal fee of a few pounds is charged. There is no standard scale of fees. It is permissible to quote up to about 200 words for the purpose of criticism or review, but this does not apply to use in anthologies, nor does it apply to poetry. And it is a concession, not a right. Even though this is your area of responsibility, your publisher may be able to give you some advice.

AFTER ACCEPTANCE

There are many ways of producing books, especially with the advent of modern printing processes but they all have certain points in common from the author's point of view, and it is as well to be forewarned.

As author you will see either one or two stages of proofs. Sometimes you will be shown the finalised copy of the typescript immediately before it goes to press. If so, this is really your last chance to make changes which will not tend to sour relations with your publisher! Take the opportunity to comb through the manuscript, and if there are changes which you suspect you will want to make in proof, make them now.

Corrections to proofs

There was a time when authors could virtually rewrite their books in galley proof, and revise them again at page. Do not be seduced by biographies of Victorian writers into thinking that this is the way the professional writer works!

Modern printing is highly mechanised, but corrections involve extensive hand-work. This makes corrections far more costly than the original setting. You will probably have signed a contract undertaking to pay the cost of corrections (other than printer's errors) over say 10 per cent or 15 per cent of the cost of composition. This does not mean that you can change ten or fifteen lines in every hundred.

The cost of adding a comma at galley stage, in modern processes, may be £1.00. If you add a word in one line of a paragraph, it will probably mean resetting down to the end of the paragraph. If you add a word at page stage, and this results in the paragraph being longer, many pages may have to be adjusted by one line until the end of the chapter is reached. The cost of adding that one word could be as much as £10 in an extreme case. What to you seemed a simple improvement may take an hour's work on expensive equipment.

Stages of proofs

Increasingly often only one stage of proofs is used in book production, and there is rarely any need for the author to see more than one stage. The proofs may be in several forms. Ask your editor how many stages of proofs you will see. It could be that, in the not too distant future, you will be asked to check computer print-outs which bear no resemblance to the finished book but which do contain everything that will appear in that book!

Galley or 'slip' proofs hold columns of text about two feet long. They may be either a rough print taken from metal type, or photographic proofs called *ozalids* if the text has been set by filmsetting.

Page proofs have been made up into pages, including page numbers, headlines, and so on. It is prohibitively expensive to make corrections at this stage, except to the printer's own errors.

Page-on-galley proofs are an intermediate stage, used mainly for books without illustrations. Corrections which result in extra lines are nearly as expensive as in full page proofs.

It is worth noting that during the production of some books which have illustrations in the text, such as children's or travel books, the editor or designer has to do a scissors and paste job to put the whole thing together and this may require some minor modifications to make the final result come together happily.

Authors who want to know more about the technicalities of preparing a manuscript for the press should consult *Copy-Editing* by Judith Butcher, Cambridge University Press, 1975, £10.50. Much of this is outside the author's scope, but dipping into this book would make him aware of points of style and consistency, particularly with reference to the use of inverted commas, roman and arabic numerals, italic and roman, rendering of foreign words, etc.

For details of other books concerning the preparation of typescripts and manuscripts see BOOKS FOR THE WRITER, Section III.

CORRECTING PROOFS

The following notes and table are extracted from BS 5261: Part 2: 1976 and are reproduced by permission of the British Standards Institution, 2 Park Street, London, W1A 2BS, from whom copies of the complete Standard may be obtained.

NOTES ON COPY PREPARATION AND PROOF CORRECTION

The marks to be used for marking-up copy for composition and for the correction of printers' proofs shall be as shown in table 1.

The marks in table 1 are classified in three groups as follows,

(a) Group A: general.
(b) Group B: deletion, insertion, and substitution.
(c) Group C: positioning and spacing.

Each item in table 1 is given a simple alpha-numeric serial number denoting the classification group to which it belongs and its position within the group.

The marks have been drawn keeping the shapes as simple as possible and using sizes which relate to normal practice. The shapes of the marks should be followed exactly by all who make use of them.

For each marking-up or proof correction instruction a distinct mark is to be made:

(a) in the text: to indicate the exact place to which the instruction refers;
(b) in the margin: to signify or amplify the meaning of the instruction.

It should be noted that some instructions have a combined textual and marginal mark.

Where a number of instructions occur in one line, the marginal marks are to be divided between the left and right margins where possible, the order being from left to right in both margins.

Specification details, comments, and instructions may be written on the copy or proof to complement the textual and marginal marks. Such written matter is to be clearly distinguishable from the copy and from any corrections made to the proof. Normally this is done by encircling the matter and/or by the appropriate use of colour (see below).

Proof corrections shall be made in coloured ink thus:

(a) printer's literal errors marked by the printer for correction: green;
(b) printer's literal errors marked by the customer and his agents for correction: red;
(c) alterations and instructions made by the customer and his agents: black or dark blue.

Table 1. Classified list of marks

NOTE. The letters M and P in the notes column indicate marks for marking-up copy and for correcting proofs respectively.

Group A General

Number	Instruction	Textual mark	Marginal mark	Notes
A1	Correction is concluded	None	/	P Make after each correction
A2	Leave unchanged	------- under characters to remain	Ⓙ	M P
A3	Remove extraneous marks	Encircle marks to be removed	✕	P e.g. film or paper edges visible between lines on bromide or diazo proofs
A3.1	Push down risen spacing material	Encircle blemish	⊥	P
A4	Refer to appropriate authority anything of doubtful accuracy	Encircle word(s) affected	(?)	P

Group B Deletion, insertion and substitution

Number	Instruction	Textual mark	Marginal mark	Notes
B1	Insert in text the matter indicated in the margin	⋏	New matter followed by ⋏	M P Indentical to B2
B2	Insert additional matter identified by a letter in a diamond	⋏	⋏ Followed by for example ◇Ⓐ	M P The relevant section of the copy should be supplied with the corresponding encircled letter marked on it e.g. ◇Ⓐ
B3	Delete	/ through character(s) or ⊢─────┤ through words to be deleted	♂	M P
B4	Delete and close up	⌒/ through character or ⊢──⌣──⊣ through characters e.g. charaⓐcter charaaacter	⌒♂	M P

Table 1 *(continued)*

Number	Instruction	Textual mark	Marginal mark	Notes
B5	Substitute character or substitute part of one or more word(s)	/ through character or ⊢———⊣ through word(s)	New character or new word(s)	M P
B6	Wrong fount. Replace by character(s) of correct fount	Encircle character(s) to be changed	⊗	P
B6.1	Change damaged character(s)	Encircle character(s) to be changed	✕	P This mark is identical to A3
B7	Set in or change to italic	——— under character(s) to be set or changed	⊔	M P Where space does not permit textual marks encircle the affected area instead
B8	Set in or change to capital letters	═══ under character(s) to be set or changed	≡	
B9	Set in or change to small capital letters	═══ under character(s) to be set or changed	=	
B9.1	Set in or change to capital letters for initial letters and small capital letters for the rest of the words	≡ under initial letters and ═══ under rest of the word(s)	≡⁼	
B10	Set in or change to bold type	∿∿∿∿ under character(s) to be set or changed	∿	
B11	Set in or change to bold italic type	∿∿∿∿ under character(s) to be set or changed	⊔∿	
B12	Change capital letters to lower case letters	Encircle character(s) to be changed	≢	P For use when B5 is inappropriate

Table 1 *(continued)*

Number	Instruction	Textual mark	Marginal mark	Notes
B12.1	Change small capital letters to lower case letters	Encircle character(s) to be changed	⧸	P For use when B5 is inappropriate
B13	Change italic to upright type	Encircle character(s) to be changed	⫪	P
B14	Invert type	Encircle character to be inverted	↻	P
B15	Substitute or insert character in 'superior' position	/ through character or ∧ where required	under character e.g.	P
B16	Substitute or insert character in 'inferior' position	/ through character or ∧ where required	over character e.g.	P
B17	Substitute ligature e.g. ffi for separate letters	⊢━━━⊣ through characters affected	⌣ e.g. ffi	P
B17.1	Substitute separate letters for ligature	⊢━━━⊣	Write out separate letters	P
B18	Substitute or insert full stop or decimal point	/ through character or ∧ where required	⊙	M P
B18.1	Substitute or insert colon	/ through character or ∧ where required	⊙⋮	M P
B18.2	Substitute or insert semi-colon	/ through character or ∧ where required	⁏	M P

Table 1 *(continued)*

Number	Instruction	Textual mark	Marginal mark	Notes
B18.3	Substitute or insert comma	/ through character or ∧ where required	,	M P
B18.4	Substitute or insert apostrophe	/ through character or ∧ where required	'̓	M P
B18.5	Substitute or insert single quotation marks	/ through character or ∧ where required	'̓ and/or '̓	M P
B18.6	Substitute or insert double quotation marks	/ through character or ∧ where required	"̓ and/or "̓	M P
B19	Substitute or insert ellipsis	/ through character or ∧ where required	• • •	M P
B20	Substitute or insert leader dots	/ through character or ∧ where required	⊙⊙⊙	M P Give the measure of the leader when necessary
B21	Substitute or insert hyphen	/ through character or ∧ where required	⊢–⊣	M P
B22	Substitute or insert rule	/ through character ∧ where required	⊢–⊣	M P Give the size of the rule in the marginal mark e.g. ⊢1 em⊣ ⊢4 mm⊣

Table 1 *(continued)*

Number	Instruction	Textual mark	Marginal mark	Notes
B23	Substitute or insert oblique	/ through character or ⅄ where required	(/)	M P
Group C Positioning and spacing				
C1	Start new paragraph			M P
C2	Run on (no new paragraph)			M P
C3	Transpose characters or words	between characters or words, numbered when necessary		M P
C4	Transpose a number of characters or words	3 2 1	1 2 3	M P To be used when the sequence cannot be clearly indicated by the use of C3. The vertical strokes are made through the characters or words to be transposed and numbered in the correct sequence
C5	Transpose lines			M P
C6	Transpose a number of lines		——— 3 ——— 2 ——— 1	P To be used when the sequence cannot be clearly indicated by C5. Rules extend from the margin into the text with each line to be transplanted numbered in the correct sequence
C7	Centre	⌈enclosing matter to be centred⌋	⌈ ⌋	M P
C8	Indent			P Give the amount of the indent in the marginal mark

Table 1 *(continued)*

Number	Instruction	Textual mark	Marginal mark	Notes
C9	Cancel indent			P
C10	Set line justified to specified measure	and/or		P Give the exact dimensions when necessary
C11	Set column justified to specified measure			M P Give the exact dimensions when necessary
C12	Move matter specified distance to the right	enclosing matter to be moved to the right		P Give the exact dimensions when necessary
C13	Move matter specified distance to the left	enclosing matter to be moved to the left		P Give the exact dimensions when necessary
C14	Take over character(s), word(s) or line to next line, column or page			P The textual mark surrounds the matter to be taken over and extends into the margin
C15	Take back character(s), word(s), or line to previous line, column or page			P The textual mark surrounds the matter to be taken back and extends into the margin
C16	Raise matter	over matter to be raised under matter to be raised		P Give the exact dimensions when necessary. (Use C28 for insertion of space between lines or paragraphs in text)
C17	Lower matter	over matter to be lowered under matter to be lowered		P Give the exact dimensions when necessary. (Use C29 for reduction of space between lines or paragraphs in text)
C18	Move matter to position indicated	Enclose matter to be moved and indicate new position		P Give the exact dimensions when necessary

Table 1 *(continued)*

Number	Instruction	Textual mark	Marginal mark	Notes
C19	Correct vertical alignment								P
C20	Correct horizontal alignment	Single line above and below misaligned matter e.g. mi₍s₎aligned		P The marginal mark is placed level with the head and foot of the relevant line
C21	Close up. Delete space between characters or words	linking ⌒ characters	⌒	M P
C22	Insert space between characters	| between each word requiring spacing	Y	M P Give the size of the space to be inserted when necessary
C23	Insert space between words	Y between each word requiring spacing	Y	M P Give the size of the space to be inserted when necessary
C24	Reduce space between characters	| between characters affected	⋔	M P Give the amount by which the space is to be reduced when necessary
C25	Reduce space between words	⋔ between words affected	⋔	M P Give amount by which the space is to be reduced when necessary
C26	Make space appear equal between characters or words	| between characters or words affected	Y	M P
C27	Close up to normal interline spacing	(each side of column linking lines)		M P The textual marks extend into the margin

Table 1 *(continued)*

Number	Instruction	Textual mark	Marginal mark	Notes
C28	Insert space between lines or paragraphs			M P The marginal mark extends between the lines of text. Give the size of the space to be inserted when necessary
C29	Reduce space between lines or paragraphs			M P The marginal mark extends between the lines of text. Give the amount by which the space is to be reduced when necessary

The Life and Work of William Caxton, by H W Larken

[An Extract]

Few people, even in the field of printing, have any clear
conception of what William Caxton did or, indeed, of
what he was. Much of this lack of knowledge is due to the
absence of information that can be counted as factual
and the consequent tendency to vague generalization.

Though it is well known that Caxton was born in the
county of Kent, there is no information as to the precise
place. In his prologue to the *History of Troy*, William Caxton
wrote "for in France I was never and was born and
learned my English in Kent in the Weald where I doubt
not is spoken as broad and rude English as in any place
of England." During the fifteenth century there were a
great number of Flemish cloth weavers in Kent; most
of them had come to England at the instigation of
Edward III with the object of teaching their craft to the
English. So successful was this venture that the English
cloth trade flourished and the agents who sold the cloth
(the mercers) became very wealthy people. There have been
There have been many speculations concerning the origin
of the Caxton family and much research has been carried
out. It is often assumed that Caxton's family must have
been connected with the wool trade in order to have
secured his apprenticeship to an influential merchant.

W. Blyth Crotch (Prologues and Epilogues of William
Caxton) suggests that the origin of the name Caxton (of
which there are several variations in spelling) may be
traced to Cambridgeshire but notes that many writers
have suggested that Caxton was connected with a family
at Hadlow or alternatively a family in Canterbury.

Of the Canterbury connection a William Caxton
became freeman of the City in 1431 and William Pratt,
a mercer who was the printer's friend, was born there.
H. R. Plomer suggests that Pratt and Caxton might possibly
have been schoolboys together, perhaps at the school St.
Alphege. In this parish there lived a John Caxton who
used as his mark three cakes over a barrel or tun, and
who is mentioned in an inscription on a monument in
the church of St. Alphege.

In 1941, Alan Keen (an authority on manuscripts)
secured some documents concerning Caxton; these are
now in the British Museum. Discovered in the library of
Earl Winterton at Shillinglee Park by Richard Holworthy,
the documents cover the period 1420 to 1467. One of
Winterton's ancestors purchased the manor of West
Wratting from a family named Caxton, the property
being situated in the Weald of Kent.

There is also record of a property mentioning Philip
Caxton and his wife Dennis who had two sons, Philip
(born in 1413) and William.

Particularly interesting in these documents is one
recording that Philip Caxton junior sold the manor of
Little Wratting to John Christemasse of London in 1436,
the deed having been witnessed by two aldermen, one of
whom was Robert Large, the printer's employer.
Further, in 1439 the other son, William Caxton, con-
Wratting to John Christemasse, and an indenture of 1457
concerning this property mentions one William Caxton
veyed his rights in the manor Bluntes Hall at Little
alias Causton. It is an interesting coincidence to note that
the lord of the manor of Little Wratting was the father of
Margaret, Duchess of Burgundy.

In 1420, a Thomas Caxton of Tenterden witnessed the
will of a fellow townsman; he owned property in Kent and
appears to have been a person of some importance.

---

[1] See 'William Caxton'.

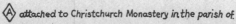
Ⓐ attached to Christchurch Monastery in the parish of

AT THE SIGN OF THE RED PALE

The Life and Work of William Caxton, *by H W Larken*.

An Extract

FEW PEOPLE, even in the field of printing, have any clear conception of what William Caxton did or, indeed, of what he was. Much of this lack of knowledge is due to the absence of information that can be counted as factual and the consequent tendency to vague generalisation.

Though it is well known that Caxton was born in the county of Kent, there is no information as to the precise place. In his prologue to the *History of Troy*, William Caxton wrote '. . . for in France I was never and was born and learned my English in Kent in the Weald where I doubt not is spoken as broad and rude English as in any place of England.'

During the fifteenth century there were a great number of Flemish cloth weavers in Kent; most of them had come to England at the instigation of Edward III with the object of teaching their craft to the English. So successful was this venture that the English cloth trade flourished and the agents who sold the cloth (the mercers) became very wealthy people.

There have been many speculations concerning the origin of the Caxton family and much research has been carried out. It is often assumed that Caxton's family must have been connected with the wool trade in order to have secured his apprenticeship to an influential merchant.

W. Blyth Crotch (*Prologues and Epilogues of William Caxton*) suggests that the origin of the name Caxton (of which there are several variations in spelling) may be traced to Cambridgeshire but notes that many writers have suggested that Caxton was connected with a family at Hadlow or alternatively a family in Canterbury.

Of the Canterbury connection: a William Caxton became freeman of the City in 1431 and William Pratt, a mercer who was the printer's friend, was born there. H. R. Plomer[1] suggests that Pratt and Caxton might possibly have been schoolboys together, perhaps at the school attached to Christchurch Monastery in the parish of St. Alphege. In this parish there lived a John Caxton who used as his mark three cakes over a barrel (or tun) and who is mentioned in an inscription on a monument in the church of St. Alphege.

In 1941, Alan Keen (an authority on manuscripts) secured some documents concerning Caxton; these are now in the British Museum. Discovered in the library of Earl Winterton at Shillinglee Park by Richard Holworthy, the documents cover the period 1420 to 1467. One of Winterton's ancestors purchased the manor of West Wratting from a family named Caxton, the property being situated in the Weald of Kent. There is also record of a property mentioning Philip Caxton and his wife Dennis who had two sons, Philip (born in 1413) and William.

Particularly interesting in these documents is one recording that Philip Caxton junior sold the manor of Little Wratting to John Christemasse of London in 1436— the deed having been witnessed by two aldermen, one of whom was Robert Large, the printer's employer. Further, in 1439, the other son, William Caxton, conveyed his rights in the manor Bluntes Hall at Little Wratting to John Christemasse, and an indenture of 1457 concerning this property mentions one William Caxton alias Causton. It is an interesting coincidence to note that the lord of the manor of Little Wratting was the father of Margaret, Duchess of Burgundy.

In 1420, a Thomas Caxton of Tenterden witnessed the will of a fellow townsman; he owned property in Kent and appears to have been a person of some importance.

[1] See 'William Caxton'.

INDEXING

The Society of Indexers maintains a Register of members whose practical competence in compiling indexes has been tested and approved by its Board of Assessors. There are over a hundred Registered Indexers, including qualified specialists in virtually all academic and professional fields. Introductions are freely available to authors, publishers, and others responsible for commissioning indexes, by contacting the Society's Registrar, Mrs. Elizabeth Wallis, 25 Leyborne Park, Kew Gardens, Surrey, TW9 3HB   *T.* 01-940 4771.

For other details of the Society of Indexers, and the address for all other enquiries, see the entry under "Societies of Interest to Authors, etc.".

TRANSLATION

THE role of the translator in enabling literature to pass beyond its national frontiers is receiving growing recognition. In view of the general increase of activity in this field, it is not surprising that many people with literary interests and a knowledge of languages should think of adopting free-lance translating as a full- or part-time occupation. Some advice may be usefully given to such would-be translators.

The first difficulty the beginner will encounter is the unwillingness of publishers to entrust a translation to anyone who has not already established a reputation for sound work. The least the publisher will demand before commissioning a translation is a fairly lengthy specimen of the applicants' work, even if unpublished. The publisher cannot be expected to pay for a specimen sent in by a translator seeking work. If, on the other hand, a publisher specifically asks for a lengthy specimen of a commissioned book the firm will usually pay for this specimen at the current rate. Perhaps the best way the would-be translator can begin is to select some book of the type which he feels competent and anxious to translate, ascertain from the foreign author or publisher that the English-language rights are still free, translate a substantial section of the book and then submit the book and his specimen translation to an appropriate publisher. If he is extremely lucky, this may result in a commission to translate the book. More probably, however—since publishers are generally very well informed about foreign books likely to interest them and rarely open to a chance introduction—the publisher will reject the book as such. But if he is favourably impressed by the translation, he may very possibly commission some other book of a similar nature which he already has in mind.

In this connection it is important to stress that the translator should confine himself to subjects of which he possesses an expert knowledge. In the case of non-fiction, he may have to cope with technical expressions not to be found in the dictionary and disaster may ensue if he is not fully conversant with the subject. The translation of fiction, on the other hand, demands skills (e.g. in the writing of dialogue) and the translator would be wise to ask himself whether he possesses these skills before taking steps to secure work of this nature.

Having obtained a commission to translate a book, the translator will be faced with the question of fees. These vary considerably from publisher to publisher but for the commoner European languages they range from £10.00 upwards per thousand words. Sometimes translators are able to obtain, in addition to the initial fee, a royalty of $2\frac{1}{2}\%$ after a sale of five thousand copies of the first edition of their work. More usually, however, publishers will consent to pay royalties of this nature, if at all, only on second editions and reprints. In the past it was common practice for a translator to assign his copyright to the publisher outright, but this is no longer the rule. Most reputable publishers will now sign agreements specifying the rights they require in the translation and leaving the copyright in the translator's hands. In the case of plays a proportion of the author's royalties (up to 50%) is the usual method of payment.

Advice regarding fees, copyright and other matters may be obtained from the Translators' Association of the Society of Authors (see page 350).

Technical translators are catered for by the Translators' Guild of the Institute of Linguists (see page 350). Annual prizes are awarded for tranlations from the German, the Italian and the French languages (see LITERARY PRIZES AND AWARDS).

EDITORIAL, LITERARY AND PRODUCTION
SERVICES

Academic Authors, P. J. Edmonds and Associates, 39 Western Road, Little-hampton, West Sussex, BN17 5PG *T.* 090 64 21786. Advisory and editorial work for publishers and authors: especially science, industry, topography; maps.

Authors' Research Services (1966), Ann Hoffmann, Forest Lodge, Broadwater Forest, Eridge, Tunbridge Wells, Kent, TN3 9JP *T.* Tunbridge Wells 34655. Offers comprehensive research service to writers, proof reading, indexing, photo-copying and secretarial assistance.

Berkeley Publishers Ltd. (1969), 9 Warwick Court, London, WC1R 5DJ *T.* 01-405 1549. *Directors:* Charles Stainsby (Managing), Richard Buehrlen, M.A., F.C.A., Simon Goodenough, M.A., Gillian Cormode. Editorial and design unit producing original as well as commissioned books on service contracts for worldwide market. Now also preparing complete printed books for international co-editions. Available also as editorial and design consultants for books, magazines and newspapers, and as consultants for sponsored books.

Bridgeman, Harriet, Ltd., 51 Sloane Gardens, London, SW1W 8ED *T.* 01-730 1345. Specialists in fine art book production and design.

Cagney, Peter, Associates (1952), 2nd Floor, 17 Second Avenue, Hove, Sussex, BN3 2LL *T.* 0273 778007. Press writing, publishing and print-design services. Editorial service for printers, publishers and advertising agencies, using specialised humorous approach. Complete editorial and production services for books, magazines, house journals, promotional literature, etc., at home and abroad, using new cost-cutting techniques. Script Centre writes original material for stage, radio and television.

Central Office of Information, Hercules Road, London, SE1 7DU *T.* 01-928 2345. Commissions feature articles on British science, industry and way of life for publication in overseas newspapers, magazines and trade press. Also 500–600 word radio scripts on popular science topics.

Colwell, Morris A., & Associates (1974), 282 Hatfield Road, St. Albans, Herts, AL1 4UN. *T.* 56535. *Proprietors:* Morris A. Colwell, M.I.E.E.E., HON. M.I.P.R.E., M.J.I., J. M. Colwell. Technical editorial consultants, manuscript preparation, technical artwork for books and journals, MSS assessment (all types), books designed and prepared for press; specialist in electronics, electro-mechanics, travel, do-it-yourself.

Copplestone, Trewin, Publishing Ltd. (1972), Advance House, 101–109 Ladbroke Grove, London, W11 1PG *T.* 01-229 8861. *Telex:* 25766. *T.A.* Trewcop, London, W11. *Directors:* Trewin Copplestone, Audrey Levy, Walter H. Spreckley. Illustrated books on all subjects; editorial, design and production service for publishers; specialist reprints.

Crisp, Alistair and Christine, First Floor Flat Eastholm, Parton Road, Church-down, Gloucestershire GL3 2JJ. Editorial, proof reading, research, transcription and advisory service on all musical matters (books and printed music).

Dineen, Jacqueline (1976) Flat 4, 70A Holmesdale Road, Reigate, Surrey RH2 0BJ *T.* 073–72 48593. Writing, rewriting, updating and revision; copyediting; literary and picture research: proof reading.

ELB Languages Group Ltd., comprising Trade & Industrial Translation Centre Ltd. and Eastern Languages Bureau Ltd. (1958), 61 Carey Street, London, WC2A 2JG *T.* 01-242 9276. *Telex:* 24224. *Directors:* A. C. W. Crane, M.B.E., F.I.L. (Chairman), D. E. Lee (Managing), T. P. E. Beglan, B.A., M.I.L., L. Viney. Comprehensive book translation service, including translation, research, checking, typing, editing and proof-reading, at competitive prices. Available in all the languages of world trade including rarer languages (i.e. East European, Middle Eastern and Oriental).

Ford, Brian J., Mill Park House, 57 Westville Road, Cardiff, CF2 5DF *T.* Cardiff (0222) 27222. Consultant adviser to international bodies on scientic matters, author, producer/director and editor of specialist publications including film, radio and television in addition to science magazines, books and journals. Presenter of several major BBC programmes.

Freelance Press Services (1967), Forestry Chambers, 67 Bridge Street, Manchester, M3 3BQ *T.* 061-832 5079. A Market Research Department for the freelance writer and photographer. Issues a monthly Market News service the *Contributor's Bulletin*; also *Freelance Writing and Photography* (Q.); £1.75 p.a. A good rate of pay made for news of editorial requirements. (Small amounts are credited until a worthwhile payment is reached.) Sole Agents for the U.K. for the books of the American Writer Inc., including *The Writers Handbook*; also the American *Writers Market.*

Free-lance Report Market Research, John Liggins Limited, 2 Park Street, Fleckney, Leicester, LE8 0BB. *T.* Leicester (0533) 402579, and BCM/ Buildings, London, WC1. An old-established firm offering a comprehensive information and research service for journalists, writers, publishers, photographers and artists. Issues the *Free-lance Report*, founded 1931, quarterly as a subscription rate of £8.50 p.a., supplements extra, providing information on new publications, on their requirements, etc.

Freelance Services (Joan Wilkins Associates Ltd.), 37 Maida Vale, London, W9 1TP *T.* 01-2866 0115. (24 hours answer service). Comprehensive editorial, literary and production services. Book design. Brochure artwork and typography. Specialists in production of short run camera ready books from MSS to binding. Picture, literary and technical research and abstracting.

Gay, Jean (1965), Fox Cottage, Ansty, Salisbury, Wiltshire, SP3 5QD *T.* 07-4787 593. *Director:* Mrs. Jean Gay. Copy-editing, proof reading, indexing, index-refolioing.

Geoslides, 4 Christian Fields, London, SW16 3JZ *T.* 01-764 6292. Visual aid production services: slide packs; filmstrips; packaging. Photo library. Commission photography. Specialist work for educational publishing.

Hassell, John (1973), Mayfield House, Wootton Rivers, Marlborough, Wiltshire, SN8 4NT *T.* Burbage 810 384. *Director:* John Hassell. Advisory and editorial work for authors and publishers. Complete design, production, distribution and publishing service.

Holland-Ford Associates (Robert), 103 Lydyett Lane, Barnton, Northwich, Cheshire, CW8 4JT *T.* 0606 76960. *Director:* Robert Holland-Ford. Impresarios, Concert/Lecture Agents.

Illustration Research Service, Mrs. Stuart Rose, 25 Balcombe Street, London, NW1 6HE *Telephone Answering Service:* 01-251 0101. Representatives in Paris, Rome, Madrid, Washington and Amsterdam. A research service for authors, publishers, art editors and T.V. producers.

Indexers, The Society of, 28 Johns Avenue, London, NW4 4EN *T.* 01-203 0929 see p. 338 and p. 448 for further details).

Indexing, R. and R. Haig-Brown, Lambrook House, Wootton Grove, Sherborne, Dorset, DT9 4DL *T.* Sherborne (Dorset) 2804. Registered member of the Indexers' Society. Most subjects, including legal titles, business books and social welfare. Full details on application.

Jade Literary Services (1974), 20 Braeside Avenue, London, SW19 3PT *T.* 01-542 7654 and Weybridge 43476. Jacqueline Dyck. *Consultant:* M. M. Akkouh. Copy editing, proof reading, typing final drafts. Special interests: humanities, fiction, African and Middle East affairs.

Lynton Literary Services, Rosebank, Sinai Hill, Lynton, Devon, EX35 6AR *T.* 05985-2282. *Partners:* Norman Hillyer, Ruth Hillyer. Editing, preparing for press, proof reading, copy-editing, indexing, Member of the Society of Indexers. Any subject especially religious studies, theology, sociology, philosophy, social history, biography. European agent for Religious and Theological Abstracts Inc, Myerstown, Pa. USA.

Morley Adams, Ltd. (1917), Oldebourne House, 46–47 Chancery Lane, London, WC2A 1JB *T.* 01-242 8638–9. *Directors:* L. W. Burgess, H. R. Dickinson, W. J. M. Grimshaw. Specialists in the production of crosswords and other puzzles, quizzes, etc. Experts in handling advertisers' competitions.

Moseley, James (1972), 5 Tollhouse Road, Crossgate Moor, Durham DH1 4HU *T.* 0385-68665. Technical illustration.

Niekirk, Paul H. (1976), 40 Rectory Avenue, High Wycombe, Buckinghamshire, HP13 6HW *T.* 0494–27200. Text editing for works of reference and professional and management publications, particularly texts on law. Freelance writing. Editorial consultancy and training. Marketing consultancy and research.

Oriental Languages Bureau, Lakshmi Building, Sir P. Mehta Road, Fort, Bombay 1, India. *T.* 263451. *T.A.* Orientclip. *Partner:* Rajan K. Shah. Undertakes translations and printing in all Indian languages.

Parrish (Walter) International Ltd. (1970), 49 Great Marlborough Street, London, W1V 1DB *T.* 01-437 9176. *T.A.* Primedia, London, W1. *Telex:* 8812120. *Directors:* W. Parrish, T. Auger. Designers and producers of illustrated books.

Penman Literary Service, The (1950), 175 Pall Mall, Leigh-on-Sea, Essex, SS9 1RE *T.* 01-0702 74438. Preparation of authors' MSS. for submission—from typing, with any necessary attention to punctuation, spelling and general lay-out, to full revision and re-typing if requested. Charges depend upon work recommended and/or desired in the particular case. Also stencil cutting and duplicating.

Pick, Christopher, Flat 2, 172 Clive Road, London, SE21. *T.* 01-761 2585. Editor, writer and researcher on political, historical, literary topics. Specialist in illustrated books and children's information books. Series planning and development work undertaken.

Picture Research Agency, Pat Hodgson, 6 Lancaster Cottages, Richmond, Surrey, TW10 6AE *T.* 01-940 5986. Illustrations found for books, films and television. Written research also undertaken particularly on historical subjects, including photographic and film history.

Piggott, Reginald and Marjorie, 81 Larchfield Avenue, Newton Mearns, Glasgow, G77 5QW *T.* 041-639 4042. Cartographers to University presses and academic publishers in Britain and overseas.

Press Editorial Syndicate (1964), 27A Arterberry Road, Wimbledon, London, SW20. *T.* 01-947 5482. *T.A.* Bakerbook, London. *Director:* W. Howard Baker. Specialist editorial services for book publishers. Fiction and nonfiction produced to order, from synopsis stage to copy ready for press.

Procaudio Ltd. (1962), 4A Queen Anne's Gardens, London, W4 1TU *T.* 01-994 0853. *Directors:* Rose-Mary Sands, David Wade, Pan Wade. Creative scripting, full studio production and manufacture of discs (sleeves and labels), cassettes, tapes, slides and film strips, either separately or combined in complete A–V programmes. Educational and promotional. We like research—picture research is our speciality; also archive work, talking with children, verse production, drama, handling music.

Queen Anne Press, Division of **Macdonald & Jane's Publishers Ltd.,** Paulton House, 8 Shepherdess Walk, London, N1 7LW *T.* 01-251 1666. An associate company of **B.P.C. Publishing Ltd.**

Rainbird, George, Ltd., 36 Park Street, London, W1Y 4DE *T.* 01-491 4777. *Directors:* Michael Rainbird (Managing), Peter Phillips (Deputy Managing), Ib Bellew, James Fairweather, John Hadfield, Michael O'Mara (USA), Valerie Reuben. Specialists in colour reproduction, fine book design and printing. Editorial services. Free-lance artists' and designers' work used.

Roger Smithells Ltd., Editorial and Publishing Services, 6 Balfour Road, London, N5 2HB *T.* 01-226 4345. An editorial unit which handles the production of periodical and other publications. Journalistic specialists in everything relating to travel and holidays; newspaper and magazine articles; compilers of travel books. Producers of "Sebastian Cash" travel and holiday features and Reader Information Service.

Roth-Mills (1974), Threeways, Vicarage Lane, Nonington, Dover, Kent, CT15 4LA *T.* 0304 840985. *Directors:* Ernest Roth, Sonya Mills. Publishers' editorial service, copy-editing, anglicising, proof reading.

Rutland, Jonathan, Windword, Plain Road, Marden, Kent. *T.* Maidstone 831307. Editorial service, design and layout of illustrated books, especially in the educational field. Photographic work on a wide range of subjects.

Science Unit, Mill Park House, 57 Westville Road, Penylan, Cardiff, CF2 5DF *T.* Cardiff (0222) 27222. Independent scientific consultancy specialising in microscopical matters. Advises on programmes and publications in general scientific field. Activities are world-wide, with publications in many overseas and foreign-language editions.

Seminar Cassettes Ltd. (1973), 218 Sussex Gardens, London, W2 3UD *T.* 01-262 7357. *Directors:* Rose-Mary Sands, Sunday Wilshin. Spoken word cassettes on current affairs, psychology, metaphysics, ecology and interviews with literary and artistic figures. Widely used in English language teaching and in universities, polytechnics, school libraries and bookshops as unique and authentic source material. Sole European agent for *Psychology To-day* USA library of spoken-word cassettes.

Shaw Maclean Services, 114 Blinco Grove, Cambridge, CB1 4TT *T.* 0223 44414. Vernon Robinson (*Technical Director*). Editorial production of educational books: copy-editing, proof reading, indexing, typing service (+ sci./math for camera ready copy). Advisory service for technical authors.

Songhurst, Robert and Jane (1976), 3 Yew Tree Cottages, Sandling, near Maidstone, Kent. *T.* Maidstone 57635. Literary consultants, authors' works advised upon, literary and historical research, feature writing, reviewing.

Technical Art Services Ltd. (1968), 10A Baldock Street, Ware, Herts. *T.* Ware 4816. *Directors:* D. A. Hoxley, R. Travis. The preparation of finished artwork for all types of educational publications. Technical illustration and graphic design and printers.

Tecmedia Ltd. (1972), 3–5 Granby Street, Loughborough, LE11 3DU *T.* 0509 30248 and 216735. *Telex:* 342244. *London Office:* Stukeley Street, Drury Lane, London, WC2. *T.* 01-405 3136. *Directors:* J. G. Barker, M.B.I.M., M.Inst.M., J. Glassman, B.SC., F.R.I.C., L. Shenfield, B. Watkiss. Complete camera-ready artwork for technical and educational books working from raw copy, sketches, etc., to final printed job. Multi-media resource packages for education and training.

Trewin Copplestone Publishing Ltd.—see Copplestone, Trewin, Publishing Ltd.

Vickers, John, 27 Shorrolds Road, London, SW6 7TR *T.* 01-385 5774. Archives of British Theatre from 1939–1960.

Wainwright, Gordon R., 22 Hawes Court, Sunderland, SR6 8NU *T.* 59180. Criticism, advice, revision and all other editorial work for publishers and authors, especially those concerned with educational books. Public relations and publicity. Preparation, planning, editing, writing and publication of books, pamphlets, house journals, company histories, brochures, reports, promotional literature, etc. Articles on education and training matters supplied to newspapers, journals and magazines. Training in report writing, rapid reading and non-verbal communication. Lecture service. Consultancy service in all aspects of communication.

Walbrook Consultants Limited, Walbrook Court, 42A Bow Lane, London, EC4M 9EU *T.* 01-236 1887. *Managing Director:* Alan J. Kennard. Publishers for industrial clients. Complete editorial, design and production of shareholder publications, annual reports, employee reports, house journals, reviews, brochures, catalogues and company histories.

Webb & Bower Ltd. (1975), 21 Southernhay West, Exeter, Devon, EX1 1PR *T.* 0392 35362. *T.A.* Webbower Exeter. *Telex:* 21792 (844). *Directors:* Richard Webb (Managing), Delian Bower (Editorial). Book production, editorial and design unit specialising in the preparation of illustrated books for the U.K., U.S.A. and international co-edition markets.

Writer's & Speaker's Research (1954), Joan St. George Saunders and Joan Bright Astley, 56 Brunswick Gardens, London, W.8. *T.* 01-727 2289. Provides a research service for writers, broadcasters and public speakers.

TYPEWRITING SERVICES

A NUMBER of the agencies listed below do not state their terms because these vary for the many different varieties of work which they undertake. They are willing to quote their terms for work submitted to them or to give a professional indication of their rates on receiving a description of MS to be submitted.

It is wise to enclose a stamped, addressed envelope when making a preliminary enquiry.

London

MRS. SYLVIA SILKOFF, 178 Hampden Way, Southgate, N14. *T.* 01-368 3924. £1.50 per hour, includes one carbon copy.

MRS. B. SLANEY, 36b Stanmore Road, N15 3PS *T.* 01-889 2954. £1.30 per 1000 words, carbon copy included.

MRS. M. N. JIVANJEE, 51 Burmarsh, Marsden Street, NW5 3JA *T.* 01-267 3295. £1.25 per 1000 words.

JOAN LIPKIN-EDWARDS and UNIQUE FREELANCE SECRETARIES, 4 Hill Top, NW11 6EE *T.* 01-455 8187 and 1266. £1.50 to £3 per 1000 words; up to £3.50 per hour—depending on legibility.

SUSAN M. BACCINO, 19 Lovelace Road, SE21 8JY *T.* 01-670 3487. £1.60 per 1000 words, including 1 carbon copy, 5p. each per extra carbon.

BETTY NUNN (OFFICE SERVICES), 14 Grecian Crescent, Upper Norwood, SE19 3HH *T.* 01-670 0922. 50p per 1000 words, 2p per page per carbon copy. 50p per copy for binding.

MISS G. E. L. CONSENTIUS, 47 Gloucester Street, SW1V 2DB *T.* 01-821 7372. Translations German–English–German, MSS literary subjects charges according to subject-matter and by arrangement.

PETER COXSON TYPING SERVICE, THE, 31 Delmerend House, Ixworth Place, Chelsea, London, SW3 3SB *T.* 01-584 0198 (Mrs. Walker) or 01-876 5306. Please phone or write before calling. From 72p per 1000 words plus 6p per carbon per 1000 words.

MISS DORIS E. GREGORY, 42 Triangle Place, SW4 7HX *T.* 01-720 2838. 60p per 1000 words, plays 20p per quarto page, including one carbon copy. Additional carbon copies 5p per 1000 words. Postage and paper extra.

PETER JOHN, 67 Sedlescombe Road, SW6. *T.* 01-385 6093. Scripts from 70p per 1000 words. Tape-recording and cassette transcription £1.25 per hour; speeds, 1, 3 and 7, single, double-track and four-track. Postage extra at cost.

MAUREEN MARRS SECRETARIAL SERVICES, 89–90 Turnmill Street, EC1M 5QU *T.* 01-253 8318. MSS £1.00 per 1000 words. Carbon copies 1p per page. Plays 22p per quarto page, 25p per foolscap page, carbon copies 1p per page.

SCOTT'S, 80 Queensway, London, W2. *T.* 01-727 5828. IBM typewriters, transcription, duplicating, photo-copying. Rates on application.

JANE ADDISON, 221 Hamlet Gardens, Hammersmith, W6 0TS *T.* 01-748 1231. £1.00 per hour.

VERBATIM, 31 Kensington Church Street, W8 4LL *T.* 01-957 3745. £3.50 per hour.

FREELANCE SERVICES (Joan Wilkins Assocs. Ltd.), 37 Maida Vale, London, W9 ITP *T.* 01-286 0115 (24 hours answer service). Comprehensive secretarial and typing service Selectric typewriters. Manuscripts, scripts, theses, technical specifications, reports, tape transcriptions, etc. Printing, binding. Rates on application.

MRS. AUDREY TESTER, 72 Berrylands, Surbiton, Surrey, KT5 8JY *T.* 01-399 6990. Work collected in London.

Avon
MRS. H. P. HOBBS, 6 Lansdown Road, Bath, BA1 5EE *T.* 318125.

MRS. M. ROBERTS, 11 North Meadows, Peasedown St. John, nr. Bath, BA2 8PS 50p per 1000 words, plus 5p per carbon copy. Paper, postage, etc., extra.

MRS. D. M. NEWTON, 19 Ridgeway Road, Long Ashton, Bristol, BS18 9EY *T.* Long Ashton 3216. £1.00 per 1000 words, plus 10p per 1000 carbon copy.

MRS. JANE WELSMAN, 67 Alma Vale Road, Clifton, Bristol, BS8 2HR *T.* Bristol 38882. 45p per 1000 words, manual; 3p per carbon copy.

Bedfordshire
MRS. E. M. PICKERING, 121 Highbury Grove, Clapham, Bedford, MK41 6DU 85p per 1000 words including 1 carbon. Extra carbons 1p each. Also duplicating. Postage extra.

MRS. S. GORDON, 23 Mowbray Crescent, Stotfold, Hitchin, Herts, SG5 4DY *T.* Hitchin 730963.

Berkshire
G. B. LAMB, 154 Clewer Hill Road, Windsor, SL4 4DB *T.* 53447. £1.75 per hour. IBM typewriter.

Buckinghamshire
MISS O. BARROW, 8 Alham Road, Walton Court Farm, Aylesbury. 50p per 1000 words, plus one carbon copy; 2p each additional carbon.

BUCKINGHAM SECRETARIAL SERVICES, Chatham House, Stowe, Buckingham, MK18 5DF *T.* Buckingham 2215. M/S copying £1.20 per 1000 words and up to 3 carbons. T/S copying £1.00 per 1000 words and up to 3 carbons.

MRS. I. TURNBULL, 8 Furlong Road, Bourne End, SL8 5DG *T.* Bourne End 27526. Secretarial and Printing Services.

MRS. V. M. TAGGART, Old Orchard, Bull Lane, Gerrards Cross, SL9 8RZ *T.* 82869. Audio/copy IBM typing/composing. Rates on application.

Cambridgeshire
MRS. HILARY BAKER, Kirkley House, 143 London Road, Chatteris, PE16 6LU *T.* 3118. £1.25 per hour.

MISS P. M. O'CALLAGHAN, 3 Sandford, Ravensthorpe, Peterborough, PE3 7LH *T.* 0733-264447. 75p per hour; 2p per carbon copy.

Cheshire
TEMPLE STAFF BUREAU, 5 Temple Chambers, Frodsham Street, Chester, CH1 3LE *T.* 313221. 70p per hour inclusive of one carbon copy.

MRS. B. A. THORNE, Trevaylor, Kingsley Road, Crowton, Nr. Northwich, CW8 2RW *T.* Kingsbury 88018. £1.00 per 1000 words, carbon copy included.

Mrs. Gwen M. Budden, Aigh Vie, Daleford Lane, Whitegate, nr. Northwich, CW8 2BW *T.* Sandiway 882030.

Mrs. J. M. Claydon, 28 Cambridge Street, Heaviley, Stockport, SK2 6PY Rates on application.

Mrs. Veronica O'Neill, f.s.c.t., 14 Wordsworth Close, Wistaston, Crewe, CW2 8DF. 45p per 1000 words including one carbon copy, postage extra.

Cornwall
Ruth D. Parker, 5a Fore Street, Troon, Camborne, TR14 9EF *T.* Camborne 713103. 40p per 1000 words, 4p per carbon copy.

Protemps Agency Services (Cornwall) Ltd., 1st Floor, Lloyds Bank Chambers, 28 Commercial Street, Camborne *T.* 715375. Terms by arrangement. Also duplicating and photocopying.

Mrs. V. Peters, 7 Higher Boskerris, Carbis Bay, St. Ives. *T.* St. Ives 5110. 35p per 1000 words, 4p per carbon copy. Minimum charge £1.00.

Cumbria
Betty Cuthbertson, Flat No. 2, Devonshire Chambers, Penrith *T.* (0768) 5490. Rates on application.

Derbyshire
Mrs. Maude Wallace, 15 Bowden Road, The Heath, Glossop, SK13 8AA *T.* 61081. Rates on application.

Mrs. P. Pickering, RSA Teach. Cert., Home Farm, Ireton Wood, Idridgehay, DE4 4JD *T.* Cowers Lane 548. 60p per 1000 words including 2 carbon copies. Quotations given for plays/verse/scientific and technical work. Electric typewriter.

Devon
W. Corneck, 3 Higher Penn, Brixham, TQ5 9PA *T.* Brixham 3658. 30p per 1000 words.

Miss Olive Jones, Stables South, Trehill, Kenn, Exeter, EX6 7XJ *T.* Kennford 832495. 45p per 1000 words, inclusive of stationery and one carbon copy, plus postage. Extra carbons at 2p per A4 sheet. Quotations for novels, plays, TV scripts, etc.

Mrs. M. Maxwell, 21 Brinkburn Court, Manor Road, Sidmouth, EX10 8RP *T.* Sidmouth 6520. Authors' and other MSS, theses and all types of work including secretarial, professional and commercial. Terms by arrangement.

Mrs. A. Hebbard, 45 Outland Road, Milehouse, Plymouth, PL2 3DA *T.* Plymouth 54129. Quotations on request.

Dorset
Miss I. H. Andrade, 4 Southwood Avenue, West Southbourne, Bournemouth, BH6 3QA *T.* Bournemouth 426135. Terms by arrangement.

Joan Maynard, 22 Maxwell Road, Winton, Bournemouth, BH9 1DL 40p per 1000 words including 1 carbon, 2p per extra carbons.

Joan Prain, Stanjoby, Eype, nr. Bridport, DT6 6AP *T.* Bridport 22555. 40p per 1000 words, 5p per 1000 words per carbon copy.

Miss Jean E. Bellamy, 19 Links Road, Parkstone, Poole. *T.* Canford Cliffs 709468. Terms by arrangement. MSS, theses, duplicating, tapes.

Fox Business Aids Ltd., 3 Frederick Place, St. Thomas Street, Weymouth, DT4 8HQ *T.* 73338. £3.00 per hour.

Durham

Mrs. J. McArthur, 26 Kingsmere, Chester-le-Street, DH3 4DB *T.* Chester-le-Street 883622. Rates on application.

East Sussex

Mrs. Christine Padmore, Sycamore Cottage, 52 Gorham Avenue, Rottingdean, Brighton, BN2 7DP *T.* Brighton 35079. Terms by arrangement.

Mrs. Q. Smith, 20 Beckets Way, Framfield, Nr. Uckfield, TN22 5PE *T.* Framfield 288. From 45p per 1000 words. For theses from 50p per 1000 words. Audio work.

Mrs. Peggy Taylor, 23 Belgrave Crescent, Seaford, BN25 3AU *T.* Seaford 891633. Rates on application.

Essex

Miss M. F. Bruce, 15 Mount Crescent, Brentwood, CM14 5DB *T.* Brentwood 227986 (not Tuesdays). 50p per 1000 words, 5p per 1000 words carbon copy. Stationery included but postage extra.

Mrs. B. Perridge, 8 Duke's Close, North Weald, Epping. *T.* North Weald 2534. Quotations on request.

Mrs. E. Williams, 29 Selbourne Road, Hockley. *T.* Hockley 2472. 50p per 1000 words including 1 carbon copy. Stationery and postage extra.

Penman Literary Service, The (1950), 175 Pall Mall, Leigh-on-Sea, Essex, SS9 1RE *T.* 01-0702 74438. 20p per quarto page, inclusive of stationery. Postage extra.

Irene Cox, 30 Tennyson Road, Romford. 60p per 1000 words; 4p per carbon copy.

South Office Services, Osborne Cottage, Little Chesterford, Saffron Walden. *T.* Great Chesterford (079-983) 462. From 50p per 1000. Also duplicating, tape transcripts, shorthand notes, editing and indexing.

Ashwell Office Services, 51 Southchurch Boulevard, Southend-on-Sea, SS2 4UL *T.* 0702 65318. 50p per 1000 words, including 1 carbon, paper extra. MSS., theses; also duplicating.

Mrs. M. E. Ransome, Harbour, 160 Elm Tree Avenue, Walton-on-Naze, CO14 8TF *T.* Frinton 3442. MS., Plays, tapes, etc. (Charges vary according to technicality of work.)

Mrs. J. Hebden, 19 St. Helen's Road, Westcliff-on-Sea, SS0 7LA *T.* Southend 40014. From 35p per 1000 words including 1 carbon. Also revision if required.

Gloucestershire

Mrs. Doreen Sammels, Thika, Oakley Road, Battledown, Cheltenham, GL52 6PA *T.* Cheltenham 53614. 75p per 1000 words, plus 2½p per page for carbon copies.

Mrs. M. Morgan, 20 Orchard Way, Huntley, GL19 3EL *T.* Longhope 590. 45p per 1000 words plus 1p per carbon copy; or 80p per hour.

Hampshire

Jackman Business Services, Beaulieu Road, Christchurch, BH23 2EA *T.* Christchurch 77303. Rates on application.

Mrs. M. Musslewhite, 8 Penryn Close, Woodlands, Boyatt Wood, Eastleigh. *T*. Eastleigh 611594. 70p per 1000 words, 5p per carbon copy.

Mrs. M. J. Slipper, 8 Ashdown Road, Fawley, Southampton, SO4 1EF *T*. Fawley 891026. 50p per 1000 words, carbon copies 5p per 1000 words. Quotations for plays and verse.

Coxson's Country Typing (Literary and Academic), Pococks Cottage, Hawkley, Nr. Liss. Rates on application.

Jobways, 13 Bournemouth Road, Chandlers Ford, Eastleigh, SO5 3DA *T*. Chandlers Ford 68080 or 3246. Full range of secretarial services, including I.B.M. electric typewriters and Xerox photocopier.

Mrs C. A. Chalk, 55 Eastfield Lane, Ringwood *T*. 6431. 50p per 1000 words, including 1 carbon copy.

Mrs. M. Westmore, 9 Meadowside, Pan Estate, Newport, Isle of Wight, PO30 2BQ 40p per 1000 words, including 1 carbon copy; extra copies 2p per sheet.

Herefordshire
Mrs. M. Storer, dip.soc., Bel Air, Llangrove, Ross-on-Wye, HR9 6EY *T*. Llangarron 414. Rates on application.

Hertfordshire
Hirasec, Stonycroft, 32 Blacketts Wood Drive, Chorleywood, WD3 5QH *T*. Chorleywood 3851. From 60p per 1000 words.

Mrs. Eileene M. Barham, 44 Spring Gardens, Garston, Watford, WD2 6JJ *T*. Garston 76277. From 50p per 1000 words. Carbon copies, stationery and postage extra.

Mrs. Irene Way, 49 Spring Gardens, Garston, Watford, WD2 6JJ *T*. Garston 72750. From 50p per 1000 words, stationery and postage extra.

Rickmansworth Typing Service, 74 High Street, Rickmansworth. *T*. Rickmansworth 76991.

Kent
D. E. Brand, 62 St. Stephen's Road, Canterbury, CT2 7HU *T*. 60716. 70p per 1000 words including carbon copy.

Georgina Mayell, 18 Tichbourne Close, Allington Park, Maidstone. *T*. 670173. All types of work including secretarial. Terms by arrangement.

Mrs. C. Gilbey, 3 Sycamore House, Rose Street, Sheerness, ME12 1AR *T*. Sheerness 4183. Comprehensive typing service. IBM electric typewriter. Terms on application.

Beryl Baker, 16 Upper Grosvenor Road, Tunbridge Wells, TN1 2EP £2.00 per hour; 40p per copy for binding.

Lancashire
Mrs. I. Harrison, m.f.t.comm., 81 Horncliffe Road, South Shore, Blackpool, FY4 1LL *T*. 42467. 50p per 1000 words, including 1 carbon copy. Paper, postage extra. Quotations for plays.

Mrs. Hilary Denmead, Underhill, Piccadilly, Lancaster, LA1 4PX *T*. 65831. 75p per 1000 words plus 1p per carbon copy. Paper and postage extra.

B. and E. Carvell, 32 Sunbury Avenue, Penwortham, Preston, PR1 9HR *T*. Preston 43954. 20p per A4 includingg 1 carbon copy; extra carbons 1p each. Cassette transcription. Postage extra.

MRS. K. TAYLOR, 15 Rossall Road, Rochdale.   T. Rochdale 47185.   Details and rates on application.

Leicestershire

MRS. M. AUSTIN, 16 Beaumont Leys Close, Beaumont Leys Lane, Leicester, LE4 2ED   T. 355754.   50p per 1000 words; carbon copies 4p each per 1000 words.   Packing, paper and postage extra.   Quotations for plays, poetry, etc.

Lincolnshire

JONES BLAKEY, 14 Monteith Crescent, Boston, PE21 9AX   T. Boston (0205) 63437.

MRS. A. M. BARRY, Ash Cottage, Keal Coates, Nr. Spilsby, PE23 4AG   T. East Kirkby 358.   70p per 1000 words, plus 1 carbon, A4; General typing and MSS.

MRS. R. SCUPHOLME, 17 Axholme Road, Scunthorpe, South Humberside, DN15 7HL

Manchester

MRS. C. I. HOLBROOK, M.F.T.COMM., 22 Peacock Grove, Hyde Road, Gorton, Manchester, MI8 7FL   T. 061-223 2356.   Novels, etc. 50p per 1000 words, including 1 copy, extra copies 5p per 1000 words, paper, postage, packing extra.   Quotations for plays, etc.

Merseyside

MISS MARGARET SMITH, 6 Alton Court, Alton Road, Oxton, Birkenhead, L43 1XN   T. 051-652 8301.   £1.00 per 1000 words including 2 carbon copies. Electric typewriter.   MSS, theses, fiction.

MISS SHEILA WATSON, 7 Rockside Road, Liverpool, L18 4PL   T. 051-724 5309. £1.00 per 1000 words, 6p per carbon copy.   Cassette transcribing of interviews, etc., undertaken.

Middlesex

MRS. R. BARNETT, 22 Monastery Gardens, Enfield.   T. 01-363 8677.   £1.15 per 1000 words, including carbon copies.

EDNA HARRISON, 3 The Vale, Feltham, TW14 0JZ   T. 01-751 2369.   Terms by arrangement.

STAR SECRETARIAL SERVICE, Mrs. E. Bogan, 12 Broadmead Close, Hatch End, Pinner.   T. 01-428 1680.   £1.00 per 1000 words, or £1.25 per hour from handwriting, including carbon copy.

MRS. E. COLLIER, 26 Renfrew Road, Hounslow West, TW4 7RN   T. 01-570 9928.   Electric typewriter.   Rates on application.

MRS. DOREEN AUMONIER, 54 Albury Drive, Pinner, HA5 3RE   T. 01-866 3418. 60p per 1000 words, plus 5p per 1000 words carbon copy, plus cost of materials.

MRS. KATHLEEN BAWDEN, 4 Westfield Way, Ruislip, HA4 6HN   T. Ruislip 34167. From £1.00 per hour, plus cost of materials.

Norfolk

MISS D. I. BROWN, 23 St. Andrew's Close, Holme Hale, Thetford, IP25 7EH   T. Holme Hale 440 374.   70p per 1000 words, including 1 carbon copy.

TYPING CENTRE, THE, 35 Surrey Street, Norwich, NR1 3NX *T.* (0603) 614677 and 58164. £2.00 per hour. IBM Selectric.

MRS. D. GRAY, 2 Crofton Flats, East Runton, Cromer. 30p per 1000 words, carbons 3p per 1000 words. Plays 20p per quarto page. Quotations for theses, editing, verse.

THELMA M. THERESE, 14 Cullum Close, Swanton Morley, Dereham. 60p per 1000 words plus 2p per 1000 words carbon copy. Tape/Cassette transcription. Indexing, editing, binding, proof reading. Electric typewriter.

MRS. F. MEADOWCROFT, 48 Charles Close, Wroxham, NR12 8TU *T.* 060-53 2825. 75p per 1000 words plus 1 carbon copy.

North Yorkshire
MRS. VAL SMITH, 38 Meadlands, Appletree Village, York, YO3 0PB *T.* York 26407. 80p per 1000 words, 1p per carbon copy.

Nottinghamshire
MRS. J. A. MITSON, 35 Humberston Road, Wollaton, Nottingham. *T.* 285003. From 70p per 1000 words.

MRS. BARBARA STURGESS, 47 Ordsall Road, Retford, DN22 7PW From 75p per 1000 words, one carbon included. Postage extra.

Oxford
MRS. B. ROPER, Heathercroft, Upperton, Brightwell Baldwin, Oxford, OX9 5PB *T.* Watlington 2689. 90p per 1000 words, 1p per carbon copy.

MRS. R. A. WILSON, Buscot Lock, Buscot, Nr. Faringdon. *T.* Lechlade 52434. 45p per 1000 words, 3p per carbon copy; stationery, postage extra.

MISS R. M. SMYTH, Orchard Cottage, The Holloway, Harwell. *T.* 243. £1.00 per 1000 words, 3p per carbon copy.

MRS. JOYCE P. HEWITT, 311 London Road, Headington, Oxford, OX3 9EJ *T.* Oxford 67165. From 65p per 1000 words, also cassettes and stenorettes.

Shropshire
MRS JOAN LANE, 1 Boulton Grange, Randlay, Telford *T.* Telford 591044. £1.20 per 1000 words including 1 carbon copy.

MISS HEATHER STRANGE, 5 Hampton Beach, Worthen. *T.* Worthen 434. £1.50 per 1000 words including 1 carbon copy.

Somerset
MRS. YVONNE J. HAGGETT, B.A., 14 Stockland, Bridgwater, TA5 2PY *T.* Combwich (0278) 652 686. From 66p per 1000 words, including 1 carbon copy, stationery; extra carbons 1p per page. Plays from 19p per page. Translations from French; typing from French and German.

South Yorkshire
MRS. L. LEE, 45 Rowan Tree Dell, Totley, Sheffield, S17 4FL *T.* Sheffield 369413 (after 4 p.m.). Rates on application.

JOAN SMITH, 40 Balmoral Crescent, Gosforth Valley, Sheffield, S18 5ZY *T.* 0246-416656. Secretarial, academic and literary typing service. Est. 1968. Rates on application.

MRS. P. GRAYSON, 58 Mowson Crescent, Worrall, Sheffield, S30 3AG *T.* Oughtibridge 2450. 50p per 1000 words, 1p per carbon copy.

MRS. H. WAY, 10 Lennox Drive, Horbury Road, Wakefield, WF2 8LN *T.* 75967. 35p per A4 page, inclusive of paper and 1 carbon copy.

Staffordshire

MRS. GILLIAN BAILLIE, 36 Hartlands Road, Eccleshall, Stafford, ST21 6DW *T.* 850068.   £1.00 per 1000 words, 3p per sheet.

MRS. L. J. REED, 63 Maythorne Road, Blurton, Stoke-on-Trent, ST3 3AE *T.* 0782 314532.   £1.00 per 1000 words.

MRS. MARIE W. WHITE, 258 Ash Bank Road, Bucknall, Stoke-on-Trent, ST2 9EB *T.* Ash Bank (0782) 730 2835.   £1.00 per 1000 words, 1p per carbon copy.

Suffolk

MRS. IRENE HONE, 65 Normanston Drive, Lowestoft. *T.* 0502-65082 (after 6 p.m.).   Charges by arrangement.

RAMSDENS, 22 Beach Road, Lowestoft, NR32 1EA *T.* 0502-62819.   All kinds of typing work undertaken.   Electric typewriters, carbon ribbons.

MRS. M. INGS, 3 Cotswold Drive, Long Melford, Sudbury. *T.* Sudbury 71163.   Manuscripts 40p per 1000 words; other work 10p per page.   1½p per carbon copy.

Surrey

MRS. B. E. CHAVASSE, Spion Kop, Grove Road, Hindhead, GU26 6QR *T.* 5512.   80p per 1000 words including 1 carbon copy.

MAUREEN CLARKE, 97 Bradmore Way, Old Coulsdon, CR3 1PE *T.* Downland 55412.   £1.00 per 1000 words, including 1 carbon copy.

SECRETARY BIRD, 69 Sheen Road, Richmond, TW9 1YJ *T.* 01-948 3831.   £1.50 per hour.   Electric typewriter, carbon ribbon.

MRS. CHERRY JONES, 3 The Roystons, Berrylands, Surbiton, KT5 3HJ *T.* 01-390 2833.   £1.00 per 1000 words, including 1 carbon copy.

TITIAN SECRETARIAL SERVICE, 10 Watts Road, Thames Ditton, KT7 0DE *T.* 01-398 0130.   Quotations on request.   Philips tapes transcribed; Xerox copy service.

Warwickshire

MRS. S. R. GALLIMORE, Fosse View, Ashorne, Nr. Warwick, CV35 9DU *T.* Moreton Horrell 385.   70p per 1000 words including carbon copy.

West Midlands

MRS. C. SPINDLER, 67 Howard Road, Kings Heath, Birmingham, B14 7PG *T.* 021-444 8776.   45p per 1000 words, including one carbon copy.

MRS. M. P. BOLTON, Oakford, 44 South Road, Handsworth, Birmingham, B18 5LD   35p per 1000 words, plus 5p per 1000 words each carbon copy, plus postage.

MRS. S. GASKELL, 24 Melford Hall Road, Solihull, B91 2ES *T.* 021-705 2509.   From 50p per 1000 words; interested in musical subjects.

MRS. KATHLEEN M. HUGHES, 51a Hill Street, Stourbridge, DY8 1AR *T.* 5867.   £1.00 per hour.

MISS HARRIS, 17 The Crescent, Tettenhall Wood, Wolverhampton, WV6 8LA *T.* Wolverhampton 756674.   Business, literary, scientific.   Rates on application.

West Sussex

MRS. MARIE STEVENS, 4 Savernake Walk, Furnace Green, Crawley, RH10 6LZ *T.* 20697.   Terms on application; electric typewriter.

Mrs. S. Webb, 39 Northgate Road, Crawley, RH10 1YA *T.* Crawley 514839. 70p per 1000 words.

Mrs. P. A. Thomas, 50 Northgate Road, Northgate, Crawley, RH10 1YA *T.* Crawley 36134. From 70p per 1000 words including 1 carbon copy.

Granlee Typewriting and Duplicating Service, 92 The Street, Rustington. BN16 3NJ *T.* 5540. From 65p per page.

Multijob Enterprises, 30 Seamill Park Crescent, Worthing, BN11 2PN *T.* 34788. Authors' manuscripts; from typescript, 60p; manuscript, 70p, and technical 80p, all per 1000 words including one carbon. Editing and indexing, illustrations, tail-drawings to order. Postage extra.

West Yorkshire

Mrs. D. Marczinke, Sunnyside, Burras Avenue, Otley, LS21 3ER 50p per 1000 words, plus 1p per carbon copy.

Secretarial Services (Aireborough & Otley), 6 Manor Square, Otley, LS21 3AP *T.* Otley 3567. Rates on application. Specialists in novels, plays, technical theses, etc.

Skipton Office Services (Duplicating and Typing), Central Chambers, 2 Otley Street, Skipton, BD23 1DZ *T.* Skipton 3153. 50p per 1000 words including 1 original and 1 copy. Extra copies 1½p each. Tape transcription.

Mrs. P. King, 7 Foss Avenue, Wetherby, LS22 4YL *T.* 4918. 40p per 1000 words, carbon copies 2p per 1000 words. Plays 12p per page.

Wiltshire

Jakki Becker, 17 Water Lane, Salisbury, SP2 7TE *T.* 5762. 85p per 1000 words, 15p per carbon copy.

Worcestershire

Carter Typing & Secretarial Service, Mary Carter, 62 High Street, Evesham, Worcestershire, WR11 4HG *T.* Evesham 3018. Manuscripts, theses, Rates negotiable.

Mrs. C. M. Allan, 8 Wise Grove, Rugby. *T.* 76683. 20p per 100 words including 1 carbon copy.

Wales
Caernarvonshire

S. Masterson, 1 Boston Terrace, Port Dinorwic. *T.* 670 457. 10p per quarto page, with one carbon copy, additional copies, 1p per page. A4 size 15p per page, plus one carbon copy.

Dyfed

Nan Morgan, 7 The Slade, Fishguard, SA65 9PD *T.* Fishguard 87-2334. Rates on application.

J. R. Ladd, 6 Danlan Road, Pembrey, SA16 0UL 50p per 1000 words; 60p per hour for poetry and technical work; 1p per carbon copy.

Gwent

Miss Eileen Harris, 100 Gaer Park Avenue, Newport, NPT 3NW *T.* 0633 62486. 50p per 1000 words including 1 carbon copy; extra copies 2p per 1000 words. Postage extra. Knowledge of medical terminology. Will collect within 20 miles radius.

Gwynedd

Miss N. M. Frood, 42 Hawes Drive, Deganwy Conwy, LL31 9BW *T.* 0492 81931. 75p per 1000 words including 1 carbon copy; 25p each additional copy. Postage extra.

Powys

MRS. E. H. OWEN-JOHN, Bryncyn Green, Churchstoke, SY15 6EN   *T*. Churchstoke (058-85) 300.   Terms on application.

Scotland

JOAN BIGGAR, 15 Parkhouse Gardens, Ardrossan, Ayrshire, KA22 8BG   *T*. 0294-65726.   70p to £1.00 per 1000 words, including carbon copies.   Research service on all subjects, rates by arrangement.

ELECTRIC TYPING AND PHOTOCOPYING SERVICE, Grace Young, 3 Cherry Tree Park, Edinburgh, EH14 5AQ   *T*. 031-449 3782.   Rates on application.

MRS. M. M. BROWN, Top Flat, 18 Montague Street, Glasgow, G4 9HX   *T*. 041-339 4118.

MRS. J. KERNACHAN, 19 Camphill Avenue, Langside, Glasgow, G41 3AU   *T*. 041-632 4419.   From 50p per 1000 words including 1 carbon copy. Quotations for modern languages.

MRS J. M. LEGGAT, 19 Deveron Road, Calderwood, East Kilbride, Glasgow, G74 2HR   *T*. East Kilbride 21713.   70p per 1000 words including carbon copy.

MRS. JOAN LISTER, 15 Torrington Crescent, Mount Vernon, Glasgow, E2.   50p per 1000 words, plus 1 carbon copy.

MRS. GRACE R. ANDERSON, 12 Dirleton Gate, Bearsden, Glasgow, G61 1NP   *T*. 041-942 3218.   Charges on request.

MRS. E. YOUNG, 43 Maple Drive, Johnstone, Renfrewshire, PA5 9RS   *T*. Johnstone 21672.   From 65p per 1000 words including carbon copy; extra carbon copies 6p per 1000 words.   Quotations for plays and verse.

GOVERNMENT OFFICES AND PUBLIC SERVICES

Enquiries, accompanied by a stamped addressed envelope, should be sent to the Public Relations Officer.

Agriculture, Fisheries and Food, Ministry of, Whitehall Place, London, SW1A 2HH *T.* 01-839 7711.

Ancient and Historical Monuments of Scotland, Royal Commission on, 54 Melville Street, Edinburgh, EH3 7HF *T.* 031-225 5994.

Ancient and Historical Monuments in Wales, Royal Commission on, Edleston House, Queens Road, Aberystwyth, Dyfed SY23 2HP *T.* Aberystwyth 4381-2.

Arts Council of Great Britain, 105 Piccadilly, London, W1V 0AU *T.* 01-629 9495.

Australia, High Commissioner for Commonwealth of, Australia House, Strand, London, WC2B 4LA *T.* 01-438 8000, also Canberra House, Maltravers Street, Strand, London, WC2R 3EH *T.* 01-438 8000.

Barbados High Commission, 6 Upper Belgrave Street, London, SW1X 8AZ *T.* 01-235 8686-9.

Bodleian Library, Oxford, OX1 3BG *T.* Oxford (0865) 44675.

Botswana High Commission, 162 Buckingham Palace Road, London, SW1W 9TJ *T.* 01-730 5216.

British Airways. Head Office, Speedbird House, P.O. Box 10, Heathrow Airport (London), Hounslow, Middlesex, TW6 2JA *T.* 01-759 5511; Victoria Terminal, P.O. Box 13, London, SW1W 9SR *T.* 01-834 2323. West London Terminal, Cromwell Road, London, SW7. *T.* 01-370 4255; Bealine House, Ruislip, Middlesex. *T.* 01-845 1234; 75 Regent Street, London, W1A 2HX *T.* 01-828 9711; 107 New Bond Street, London, W1Y 9AA *T.* 01-828 9711; 101-102 Cheapside, London, EC2V 6DT *T.* 01-828 9711.

British Broadcasting Corporation, Broadcasting House, London, W1A 1AA *T.* 01-580 4468.

British Council, The, 10 Spring Gardens, London, SW1A 2BN *T.* 01-930 8466.

British Film Institute, 127 Charing Cross Road, London, WC2H 0EA *T.* 01-437 4355. *Telex:* 27624.

British Gas Corporation, 59 Bryanston Street, Marble Arch, London, W1A 2AZ *T.* 01-723 7030.

British Library Lending Division, Boston Spa, Wetherby, West Yorkshire, LS23 7BQ *T.* Boston Spa (0937) 843434. *Telex:* 557381.

British Library Newspaper Library, Colindale Avenue, London, NW9 5HE *T.* 01-200 5515.

British Museum, Great Russell Street, London, WC1B 3DG *T.* 01-636 1555.

British Railways Board, 222 Marylebone Road, London, NW1 6JJ *T.* 01-262 3232.

British Standards Institution, British Standards House, 2 Park Street, London, W1A 2BS *T.* 01-629 9000.

British Theatre Centre, 9 Fitzroy Square, London, W1P 6AE

British Tourist Authority, 64 St. James's Street, London, SW1A 1NF *T.* 01-629 9191.

Canada, High Commissioner for, Canada House, Trafalgar Square, London, SW1Y 5BJ *T.* 01-629 9492.

Central Electricity Generating Board, Sudbury House, 15 Newgate Street, London, EC1A 7AU *T.* 01-248 1202.

Central Office of Information, Hercules Road, London, SE1 7DU *T.* 01-928 2345. Projects official British policy overseas through supplies of press, radio and television material, books, films, exhibitions, photography and display material to British information posts abroad. In the UK it conducts government campaigns explaining new laws and health and safety measures, assists armed forces recruitment, and publicises rights and duties of the public.

College of Arms or Heralds' College, Queen Victoria Street, London, EC4V 4BT *T.* 01-248 2762.

Commonwealth Institute, Kensington High Street, London, W8 6NQ *T.* 01-602 3252–6. Educational publicity about the Commonwealth. Exhibition galleries, cinema, art gallery, licensed restaurant, bookstall, film strips, etc. Contemporary reference library for use by general public, of books and periodicals.

Copyright Receipt Office, The, The British Library, Store Street, London, WC1E 7DG *T.* 01-636 1544.

Countryside Commission, John Dower House, Crescent Place, Cheltenham, Gloucestershire, GL50 3RA *T.* 0242-21381 ext. 298.

Court of the Lord Lyon, HM New Register House, Edinburgh EH1 3YT *T.* 031-556 7255.

Cyprus High Commission, 93 Park Street, London, W1Y 4ET *T.* 01-499 8272.

Defence, Ministry of, (Press and P.R. Depts.) (General, Navy, Army and Air Force Departments), Main Building, Whitehall, London, SW1A 2HB *T.* 01-218 9000.

Design Council, The Design Centre, 28 Haymarket, London, SW1Y 4SU *T.* 01-839 8000.

Education and Science, Department of, Elizabeth House, York Road, London, SE1 7PH *T.* 01-928 9222.

Electricity Council, 30 Millbank, London, SW1P 4RD *T.* 01-834 2333.

Employment, Department of, 8 St. James's Square, London, SW1Y 4JB *T.* 01-214 6000.

Energy, Department of, Thames House South, Millbank, London, SW1P 4QJ *T.* 01-211 3000. *Telex:* 918777.

English Tourist Board, 4 Grosvenor Gardens, London, SW1W 0DU   *T.* 01-730 3400.

Environment, Department of the, 2 Marsham Street, London, SW1P 3EB   *T.* 01-212 3434.

Foreign and Commonwealth Office, Downing Street, London, SW1A 2AL   *T.* 01-233 3000.   *Telex:* 263563/4/5 (a/b Prodrome London).

Forestry Commission, 231 Corstorphine Road, Edinburgh, EH12 7AT   *T.* 031-334 0303.

Gambia High Commission, 60 Ennismore Gardens, London, SW7 1NH   *T.* 01-584 1242–3.

General Register Office, now part of the **Office of Population Censuses and Surveys,** *q.v.*

Ghana, High Commissioner for, 13 Belgrave Square, London, SW1X 8PR   *T.* 01-235 4142–5.

Guyana High Commission, 3 Palace Court, Bayswater Road, London, W2 4LP   *T.* 01-229 7684–8.

Hayward Gallery (Arts Council), South Bank, Belvedere Road, London, SE1 8XZ   *T.* 01-928 3144.

Health and Social Security, Department of, Alexander Fleming House, Elephant and Castle, London, SE1 6BY   *T.* 01-407 5522.

Historic Buildings Councils
   England: 25 Savile Row, London, W1X 2BT   *T.* 01-734 6010.
   Wales: Welsh Office, Pearl Assurance House, Greyfriars Road, Cardiff, CF1 3RT   *T.* 0222 44151, ext. 441.
   Scotland: 25 Drumsheugh Gardens, Edinburgh, EH3 7RN   *T.* 031-226 3611.

Historical Manuscripts, Royal Commission on, Quality House, Quality Court, Chancery Lane, London, WC2A 1HP   *T.* 01-242 1198.

Historical Monuments (England), Royal Commission on, Fortress House, 23 Savile Row, London, W1X 1AB   *T.* 01-734 6010.

Home Office, Queen Anne's Gate, London, SW1H 9AT   *T.* 01-213 3000.
   Public Relations Branch: Director of Information Services: D. D. Grant.

Independent Broadcasting Authority, 70 Brompton Road, London, SW3 1EY   *T.* 01-584 7011.

India, Information Service of, India House, Aldwych, London, WC2B 4NA   *T.* 01-836 8484 ext. 102.

Industry, Department of, 1 Victoria Street, London, SW1H 0ET   *T.* 01-215 7877.   *Telex:* 8811074.

Inland Revenue, Board of, Somerset House, London, WC2R 1LB   *T.* 01-438 6622.

Ireland, Ambassador of, 17 Grosvenor Place, London, SW1X 7HR   *T.* 01-235 2171.

Jamaican High Commission, 50 St. James's Street, London, SW1A 1JS.

Kenya High Commissioner, 45 Portland Place, London, W1N 4AS   *T.* 01-636 2371.

Lesotho, High Commission of the Kingdom of, 16A St. James's Street, London, SW1A 1EU *T.* 01-839 1154–5.

London Museum—see Museum of London.

London Records Office, Corporation of, Guildhall, London, EC2P 2EJ *T.* 01-606 3030.

London Transport Executive, 55 Broadway, SW1H 0BD *T.* 01-222 5600.

Malawi High Commission, 33 Grosvenor Street, London, W1X 0HS *T.* 01-491 4172–7.

Malaysian High Commission, 45 Belgrave Square, London, SW1X 8QT *T.* 01-245 9221. Tourism: 17 Curzon Street, London, W1. *T.* 01-499 7388.

Malta High Commission, 24 Haymarket, London, SW1Y 4DJ *T.* 01-930 9851–5.

Mauritius High Commission, 32–3 Elvaston Place, London, SW7 *T.* 01-581 0294.

Metrication Board, Millbank Tower, Millbank, London, SW1 4QJ *T.* 01-211 3000.

Museum of London, London Wall, EC2Y 5HN *T.* 01-600 3699. Amalgamating the collections of the London Museum and the Guildhall Museum.

Museum of Mankind (Ethnography Department of the British Museum), 6 Burlington Gardens, London, W1X 2EX *T.* 01-437 2224–8.

National Coal Board, Hobart House, Grosvenor Place, London, SW1X 7AE *T.* 01-235 2020.

National Economic Development Office, Millbank Tower, Millbank, London, SW1P 4QX *T.* 01-211 3000.

National Maritime Museum, Greenwich, London, SE10 9NF, including the Old Royal Observatory *T.* 01-858 4422.

National Savings, Department for, Publicity Division, 4th Floor, Charles House, 375 Kensington High Street, London, W14 8SD *T.* 01-603 2000, ext. 173.

National Trust, The, 42 Queen Anne's Gate, Westminster, London, SW1H 9AS *T.* 01-930 1841 and 0211.

National Trust for Scotland, The, 5 Charlotte Square, Edinburgh, EH2 4DU *T.* 031-226 5922.

Natural Environmental Research Council, Polaris House, North Star Avenue, Swindon, SN2 1EU *T.* Swindon (0793) 40101.

New Zealand, High Commissioner for, New Zealand House, Haymarket, London, SW1Y 4TQ *T.* 01-930 8422.

Nigerian High Commission, Nigeria House, 9 Northumberland Avenue, London, WC2N 5BX *T.* 01-839 1244.

Northern Ireland Tourist Board, River House, High Street, Belfast, BT1 2DS *T.* Belfast 31221.

Office of Population Censuses and Surveys, St. Catherines House, 10 Kingsway, London, WC2B 6JP *T.* 01-242 0262.

Patent Office (Department of Trade), 25 Southampton Buildings, London, WC2A 1AY *T.* 01-405 8721. *Sale Branch* (for information retrieval services), Patent Office, Block C, Station Square House, St. Mary Cray, Orpington, Kent, BR5 3RD *T.* Orpington (66) 32111.

Post Office Central Headquarters, 23 Howland Street, London, W1P 6HQ *T.* 01-631 2345.

Prices and Consumer Protection, Department of, Millbank Tower, Millbank, London, SW1P 4QU *T.* 01-211 3000. *Telex:* 918829.

Public Record Office. *Head Office:* Ruskin Avenue, Kew, Richmond, Surrey, TW9 4DU *T.* 01-876 3444. *Branch Office:* Chancery Lane, London, WC2A 1LR *T.* 01-405 0741.

Public Trustee Office, Kingsway, London, WC2B 6JX *T.* 01-405 4300.

Racial Equality, Commission for, Elliot House, 10–12 Allington Street, London, SW1E 5EH *T.* 01-828 7022.

Royal Mint, Llantrisant, Pontyclun, Mid-Glamorgan, CF7 8YT *T.* Llantrisant 222111 and Tower Hill, London, EC3N 4DR *T.* 01-488 3424.

Saudi Arabia, Royal Embassy of, Ugandan Interest Section, Uganda House, Trafalgar Square, London, WC2. *T.* 01-839 1963.

Science Museum, South Kensington, London, SW7 2DD *T.* 01-589 3456. Enquiries to Information Office. Ext. 653 and 632.

Scotland, National Library of, George IV Bridge, Edinburgh, EH1 1EW *T.* 031-226 4531. *Telex:* 72638 NLSEDI G.

Scottish Home and Health Department, New St. Andrew's House, St. James Centre, Edinburgh, EH1 3TF *T.* 031-556 8400.

Scottish Office, New St. Andrew's House, Edinburgh, EH1 3SX *T.* 031-556 8400 and Dover House, Whitehall, London, SW1A 2AU *T.* 01-233 3000.

Scottish Record Office, HM General Register House, Edinburgh, EH1 3YY *T.* 031-556 6585.

Scottish Tourist Board, 23 Ravelston Terrace, Edinburgh, EH4 3EU *T.* 031-332 2433.

Serpentine Gallery (Arts Council), Kensington Gardens, London, W2. *T.* 01-402 6075.

Sierra Leone, High Commissioner for, 33 Portland Place, London, W1N 3AG *T.* 01-636 6483–6.

Singapore High Commission, 2 Wilton Crescent, London, SW1X 8RW *T.* 01-235 8315.

South Africa, Republic of, South African Embassy, Trafalgar Square, London, WC2N 5DP *T.* 01-930 4488.

Sri Lanka (Ceylon) High Commissioner for, 13 Hyde Park Gardens, London, W2 2LU *T.* 01-262 1841.

Stationery Office, Her Majesty's, Sovereign House, Botolph Street, Norwich, NR3 1DN *T.* 0603-22211 and Atlantic House, Holborn Viaduct, London, EC1P 1BN *T.* 01-583 9876.

Swaziland High Commission, 58 Pont Street, London, SW1. *T.* 01-589 5447.

Tanzania High Commission, 43 Hertford Street, London, W1Y 8DB *T.* 01-499 8951.

Trade, Department of, 1 Victoria Street, London, SW1H 0ET *T.* 01-215 7877. *Telex:* 8811074.

Transport, Department of, 2 Marsham Street, London, SW1P 3EB *T.* 01-212 3434.

Treasury, HM, Treasury Chambers, Parliament Street, London, SW1P 3AG *T.* 01-233 3000.

Trinidad and Tobago High Commission, 42 Belgrave Square, London, SW1X 8NT *T.* 01-245 9351.

United Kingdom Atomic Energy Authority, 11 Charles II Street, London, SW1Y 4QP *T.* 01-930 5454.

Victoria and Albert Museum, South Kensington, London, SW7 2RL *T.* 01-589 6371. Closed on Fridays.

Wales, The National Library of, Aberystwyth, Dyfed, SY23 3BU *T.* 3816–9. *Telex:* 35165.

Wales Tourist Board, Welcome House, High Street, Llandaff, Cardiff, CF5 2YZ *T.* Cardiff 567701. *Telex:* 497269.

Wellington Museum, Apsley House, 149 Piccadilly, Hyde Park Corner, London, WIV 9FA *T.* 01-499 5676. Closed Mondays and Fridays.

Welsh Office, Gwydyr House, Whitehall, London, SW1A 2ER *T.* 01-233 6066 and 8526.

West India Committee (The West Indies, Belize, British Virgin Islands, Cayman Islands Turks and Caicos Islands), 48 Albemarle Street, London, W1X 4AR *T.* 01-629 6353.

Zambia High Commission, 7–11 Cavendish Place, London, W1M 0HB *T.* 01-580 0691.

In *Whitaker's Almanack* will be found names and addresses of many other public bodies.

RECENT JOURNAL CHANGES

The following changes of title, mergers and terminations of publication of periodicals listed in the *Yearbook* have recently taken place.

Because of the proliferation of technical journals, and the limited market in most of these for freelance contributions, a considerable number of the most specialist of such publications which were previously listed in the Yearbook now no longer appear.

CHANGES OF NAME AND MERGERS

Canoeing Magazine   now incorporated in Canoeing
Ecologist   now the The New Ecologist
Fan   absorbed into Supersonic
Gardeners Chronicle   now GC & HTJ
Health   now Chest, Heart and Stroke Journal
Hi!   merged with O.K.
Journal of the Royal United Services Institute for Defence Studies   now RUSI Journal

Lawn Tennis   now Tennis
New Motorcycling Monthly   now Motorcycling Monthly
Modern Caravanning   incorporated in Caravanning Monthly
New Vegetarian   now Alive
Sewing and Knitting   now Womancraft with Sewing and Knitting
Shop Fitting International   now Shop Fitting and Display
Silhouette   now Slimmer Magazine
Small Boat   incorporated into Yacht and Boat Owner
Sunday Telegraph Magazine   now Telegraph Sunday Magazine
Teachers World   incorporated in Junior Education
Universities Quarterly   now New Universities Quarterly

MAGAZINES CEASED PUBLICATION

Britannia
Children's Book Review
City Press
Diana
Display International
Electrical Age
Hornet
Hospital Life
Industrial Archaeology
Kent
Making Music
New Mirabelle
Parade

Paris-Presse
Prima
Psychic Researcher
Science Fiction Monthly
Sparky
Spearhead
Story World
Sunday
Supersonic
Transport History
Valiant and Lion
Wizard

CLASSIFIED INDEX OF JOURNALS AND MAGAZINES

* Commonwealth, Irish and South African Journals

This Index is necessarily only a broad classification.   It should be regarded as only a pointer to possible markets, and should be used with discrimination.

SHORT STORIES

This list does not include all the women's journals requiring short stories, *see also under*
FEMININE

*Adam (Aus.)
Ambit
Anglo-Welsh Review
*Atlantic Advocate (Can.)
Blackwood's Magazine
*(Bombay) Illustrated
    Weekly (In)
Catholic Fireside
Christian Herald
Contemporary Review
Custom Car
Dalesman
Encounter
Evening News
*Family Radio & TV (S.A.)
*Fiddlehead (Can.)

Good Housekeeping
*Ireland's Own
*Irish Press
*(Johannesburg) Sunday
    Times (S.A.)
*Landfall (N.Z.)
Listener
Love Affair
Loving
*Malahat Review (Can.)
Matrix
New Review
*Onlooker (In.)
*Reality (Ire.)
Red Letter
*Saturday Night (Can.)

Sign
Spectator
Stand
Sunday Post
Sunday Sun
*Sun-Herald (Aus.)
*(Sydney) Bulletin (Aus.)
*(Sydney) Morning Herald
    (Aus.)
Telegraph Sunday
    Magazine
True Romances
Un-common Sense
Weekend
Yachting World

DETECTIVE SHORT STORIES

Catholic Fireside
London Mystery

Reveille

Weekend

THRILLER SHORT STORIES

Catholic Fireside
London Mystery

Reveille

Weekend

LONG COMPLETE STORIES

From 8000 words upwards   *(See also under* FEMININE)

Annabel
Catholic Fireside
Hers
*Landfall (N.Z.)

Love Story Library
My Weekly Story Library
Red Letter

Stand
True
Woman's Weekly Library

SERIALS

(See also entries under FEMININE)

Australian Woman's
  Weekly (Aus.)
*(Bombay) Illustrated
  Weekly (In.)
Catholic Fireside

Christian Herald
*Ireland's Own
People's Friend
People's Journal
*Reality (Ire.)

Red Letter
Secrets
Weekly News

CARTOONS

(See also FOR YOUNG PEOPLE: HUMOROUS AND PICTURE PAPERS)

Accountancy
Anglers Mail
Animal Ways
Annabel
Busy Bees' News
Catholic Pictorial
*Cleo (Aus.)
Countryman
Coventry Evening
  Telegraph
*Cross (Ire.)
Guider
Hi-Fi News
Insurance Brokers
  Monthly

*Ireland's Own
Kent Life
Local Council Review
Morning Star
*Motorman (N.Z.)
New Statesman
Opinion
Parents
Parks & Sports Grounds
*Perth Daily News (Aus.)
Private Eye
Punch
Red Tape
Reveille
Scouting

She
600 Magazine
*Southern Cross (S.A.)
Sunday Post
Swimming Pool Review
Teacher
Today's Guide
Tribune
TV Times
*United Asia (Ind.)
Weekend
Woman and Home
Yorkshire Post
Young Soldier, The

CROSSWORDS

Catholic Pictorial
*Irish Times

*Reality (Ire.)

Sunday Post

HUMOUR

Annabel
*Cross (Ire.)
Custom Car
Cycling
Dundee Evening
  Telegraph and Post

Good Housekeeping
Hi-Fi News
Honey
*Ireland"s Own
Jewish Telegraph
Kent Life

Private Eye
Punch
*Reality (Ire.)
600 Magazine
Sunday Post
Weekend

FEMININE

Fiction, Home, Fashions, Children, Beauty Culture

Annabel
*Australian Women's
  Weekly (Aus.)
*(Bombay) Eve's Weekly
  (In).
*Charmaine (S.A.)
*Chatelaine (Can.)
Cosmopolitan
*Cross (Ire.)
*Darling (S.A.)
Edinburgh Evening News
Family Circle
Good Housekeeping
Harpers and Queen
Hers
Home and Country
Home Words
Homes and Gardens
Honey
*Irish Press
Junior Age
*Keur (S.A.)
Lady

Lancashire Evening
  Telegraph
Living
*Living and Loving (S.A.)
Look Now
Love Story Picture Library
Mother
Mother and Baby
My Weekly
*New Idea (Aus.)
*New Zealand Woman's
  Weekly (N.Z.)
Nursery World
Over 21
People's Friend
People's Journal
Red Letter
Red Star Weekly
*Rooi Rose (S.A.)
Scottish Home and
  Country
Secrets
She

Spare Rib
Sunday Post
Townswoman
True
Vogue
Weekend
Woman
Woman and Home
Womancraft with
  Sewing and Knitting
*Woman's Day (Aus.)
Woman's Journal
Woman's Own
Woman's Realm
Woman's Story Magazine
*Woman's Way (Ire.)
Woman's Weekly
Woman's Weekly Good
  Life
Woman's World
World's Children

MEN

(*See also* AVIATION, SPORT, etc.)

Entomologist's Monthly
  Magazine

Homemaker

Signature

LETTERS TO THE EDITOR

Annabel
Art and Craft in
  Education
*Australian Home
  Beautiful
*Australian Home Journal
*Australian Woman's
  Weekly
Auto Car
Bankers Magazine
British Deaf News
*Caritas (Ire.)
Catholic Fireside
Countryman
Do It Yourself
East-West Digest
Family Circle
Freelance Writing &
  Photography

Garden News
Good Housekeeping
Hers
Homemaker
Honey
Ideal Home
Jewish Telegraph
Living
*Living and Loving (S.A.)
Love Affair
Mother
Mother and Baby
Motorcycling Monthly
19
Over 21
Photoplay Film Monthly
Popular Gardening
Practical Camper
Practical Gardening

Practical Householder
Practical Photography
Red Letter
Red Star Weekly
Reveille
She
Sunday Mail
TAVR Magazine
TV Comic
True Story
Woman
Woman's Own
Woman's Realm
*Woman's Way (Ire.)
Woman's Weekly

GOSSIP PARAGRAPHS

Aberdeen Press and
  Journal
Angler's Mail
Angling
Angling Times
Animal Ways

Architectural Review
Art and Antiques Weekly
*Auckland Star (N.Z.)
Baptist Times
Birmingham Evening Mail
Bristol Evening Post

British Deaf News
British Weekly
*Bulletin (Aus.)
CTN
Camera User Magazine
Campaign

*(Cape Town) Cape Times (SA)
Catholic Herald
Catholic Pictorial
Cheshire Life
Christian Record
Church of England Newspaper
Cosmetic World News
Countryman
Coventry Evening Telegraph
Daily Mail
Daily Mirror
Do It Yourself
Dog News
Drapers' Record
Early Music
Eastern Evening News
Edinburgh Evening News
Education and Training
Engineering
Evening Chronicle
Evening Standard
Fashion Weekly
Field
Freelance Writing & Photography
Garden News
Gas World
Gay News
Gem Craft

Gems
Golf Monthly
Guider
Hi-Fi News and Record Review
Homemaker
Horse & Pony
Insurance Brokers' Monthly
Jewish Telegraph
Justice of the Peace
Lancashire Evening Telegraph
Melody Maker
*Melbourne Australasian Post
Mother
Motor Cycle
Motor Cycle Racing
New Musical Express
*New Zealand Yachting and Power Boating
Opinion
Over 21
Paperback Buyer
Parents
Poultry World
Power Farming
Printing World
Private Eye
Radio Times
Scottish Field

*Southern Cross (S.A.)
Stage and Television Today
Studio International
Sunday Express
Sunday Times
TAVR Magazine
Teacher
Tennis
*Timaru Herald (N.Z.)
The Times
Times Educational Supplement
Times Educational Supplement Scotland
Times Higher Educational Supplement
The Universe
Vole
West Africa
Western Mail
Western Morning News
Woman's Realm
*Woman's Way (Ire.)
Woman's Weekly Good Life
World Bowls
Yachts and Yachting
Yorkshire Life
Yorkshire Post

BRIEF FILLER PARAGRAPHS

Aberdeen Press and Journal
Aeroplane Monthly
Air Pictorial
Angler's Mail
Angling
Angling Times
Animal Ways
Annabel
Architectural Design
Architectural Review
*Auckland Star (N.Z.)
*Australian Home Beautiful
Autocar
Balance
Baptist Times
Birmingham Evening Mail
British Deaf News
British Weekly
Building
*Bulletin (Aus.)
Busy Bees News
CTN
Camera User Magazine
*(Cape Town) Cape Times (SA)
*Caritas (Ire.)
Catering Times
Catholic Herald
Catholic Pictorial
Cheshire Life

Christian Record
Church of England Newspaper
Computer Weekly
Cosmetic World News
Countryman
Daily Telegraph
Dairy Industries
Dog News
Do It Yourself
Drapers' Record
Early Music
Eastern Evening News
Edinburgh Evening News
Education and Training
Electrical Review
*Electronics Australia
Engineering
Evening Standard
*Farmer's Weekly (SA)
Fashion Forecast
Fashion Weekly
Freelance Writing & Photography
Garden News
Gas World
Gay News
GC & HTJ
Gem Craft
Gems
Golf Illustrated

Golf Monthly
Guideposts
Guider
Hi-Fi News and Record Review
Homes and Gardens
Homemaker
Horse World
Jewish Telegraph
Lancashire Evening Telegraph
Liverpool Echo
Local Government Chronicle
*Makara (Can.)
Manx Life
Masonic Square
Melody Maker
Model Engineer
Mother and Baby
Motor Boat and Yachting
Motor Cycle
Nautical Magazine
New Musical Express
*New Zealand Gardener
*New Zealand Outdoor
*New Zealand Yachting and Power-Boating
Nursing Mirror
Over 21
Petfish Monthly

Pony
Popular Hi-Fi
Popular Motoring
Poultry World
Printing World
Private Eye
Radio Times
Reader's Digest
Reveille
Safety Education
She
Ship and Boat
  International
*Southern Cross (S.A.)
Spare Rib

Stamp Collecting
Sunday Express
Sunday Sun
Sunday Times
Swimming Pool Review
TAVR Magazine
Teacher
Tennis World
*Timaru Herald (N.Z.)
Times Educational
  Supplement
Times Educational
  Supplement Scotland
Times Higher Educational
  Supplement

Town and Country
  Planning
Universe
Vole
Waterways World
Woman's Realm
Woman's Weekly Good
  Life
World Bowls
World Fishing
Yachting Monthly
Yachts and Yachting
Yorkshire Post

FOR YOUNG PEOPLE
PERIODICALS

Boys and Girls
Animal Ways
Beezer
Blue Jeans
Brownie
Bullet
Bunty
Bunty Library
Busy Bees News

Commando
Cross
Fab 208
Hotspur
Junior Bookshelf
Living
Magic Comic
Pink
Pippin

Pony
Railway World
Scouting
Star Love Stories
Tiger and Scorcher
Today's Guide
Topper
TV Comic
Victor

HUMOROUS AND PICTURE PAPERS

Beano, The
Beezer
Bunty
Buster
Commando
Dandy, The
Debbie
Debbie Library

Emma
Hotspur
Judy
Magic Comic
Mandy
Mandy Library
Misty
Pink

Scoop
Star Love Stories
Tammy
Tiger and Scorcher
Today's Guide
TV Comic
Twinkle
Warlord

SOME JOURNALS WHICH CONTAIN A CHILDREN'S PAGE
OR COLUMN

Birmingham Evening Mail
Church Times
Coventry Evening
  Telegraph

*Ireland's Own
Jewish Chronicle
*Melbourne Age (Aus.)
Morning Telegraph

Nursery World
People's Friend
Sunday Post
Woman

SUBJECT ARTICLES
ADMINISTRATION AND LAW

Bankers Magazine
Contemporary Review
Country Gentleman's
  Magazine
Criminologist
Data Systems
Education
Family Law
Hotel, Catering, and
  Institutional
  Management
  Association Journal
Industrial Safety

Insurance Brokers
  Monthly
Journal of Park and
  Recreation
  Administration
Justice of the Peace
Local Council Review
Local Government
  Chronicle
Local Government Review
*Management (N.Z.)
Millennium
Municipal Review

New Society
Opinion
Personnel Management
Police Journal
Political Quarterly
Post
Professional
  Administration
Round Table
Social Service
Sociological Review
Solicitors' Journal
Work Study

ADVERTISING AND SALESMANSHIP

Campaign
Design
Display International

Insurance Brokers
  Monthly

Selling Today

AGRICULTURE AND GARDENING

Amateur Gardening
Big Farm Management
British Farmer and
  Stockbreeder
Country Gentlemen's
  Magazine
Country Life
Countryman
*Countryman (Aus.)
Country-side
Dairy Farmer

Farmer's Weekly
*Farmer's Weekly (S.A.)
Field
Fruit Trades' Journal
*Garden and Home (S.A.)
Garden News
GC & HTJ
Grower
Horticulture Industry
Journal of Park
  Administration

*New Zealand Farmer
*New Zealand Gardener
Pig Farming
Popular Gardening
Power Farming
Practical Gardening
*Rhodesian Farmer
Scottish Farmer
*Studies (Ire.)
Town and Country
  Planning

ANIMALS, ETC.

Animal Ways
Animal World
Birds and Country
  Magazine
British Racehorse
Cage and Aviary Birds
Countryman
Country Quest
Country-side

Dog News
Entomologists Monthly
  Magazine
Gamekeeper
Heredity
Horse and Pony
Horse and Hound
Light Horse
Petfish Monthly

Pig Farming
Pony
Poultry World
Riding
Shooting Times and
  Country Magazine
Stud and Stable
Wildlife

ARCHITECTURE AND BUILDING

Architect
Architects' Journal
Architectural Design
Architectural Review
Building
Building Societies'
  Gazette
Built Environment
Burlington Magazine
Clergy Review

Contemporary Review
Design
Education
Homes and Gardens
House Builder and Estate
  Developer
Ideal Home
In Britain
Industrial Safety
International Construction

Lancashire Life
Local Historian
Middle East Construction
Municipal Review
Museums Journal
National Builder
Shop Fitting and Display
Studio International
Town and Country
  Planning

ART AND COLLECTING

Antique Collector
Antique Dealer and
  Collectors Guide
Antiques
Apollo
Art & Antiques Weekly
Art and Artists
Artist
Arts Review
Burlington Magazine

Coins
Connoisseur
Contemporary Review
Country Life
Creative Camera
Design
Gems
Homes and Gardens
Illustrated London News
*Irelands Own (Ire.)

Lancashire Life
Museums Journal
Numismatic Chronicle
Philately
Stamp Magazine
Stand
Studio International
Tribune
Un-common Sense

AVIATION

Aeromodeller
Aeroplane Monthly
Air Pictorial
*Australian Flying
*Canadian Aviation (Can.)

Flight International
Popular Flying
Royal Air Forces
  Quarterly
Spaceflight

Town and Country
  Planning
*Wings over Africa (SA)

BLIND AND DEAF-BLIND
(Published by the Royal National Institute for the Blind, see page 172)

Braille Chess Magazine
Braille Digest
Braille Journal of
  Physiotherapy
Braille Musical Magazine
Braille News Summary
Braille Radio Times
Braille Rainbow
Channels of Blessing
Crusade Messenger
Daily Bread
Diane
Fleur de Lys

Gleanings
"Law Notes" Extracts
Light of the Moon
Monthly Announcements
Moon Magazine
Moon Messenger
Moon Newspaper
Moon Rainbow
National Braille Mail
New Beacon (in Braille
  and letterpress)
Nuggets
Physiotherapists' Quarterly

Piano Tuners' Quarterly
Portland Magazine
Progress
Roundabout
School Magazine
Scripture Union Daily
  Notes
Tape Record
Theological Times
Torch
Trefoil Trail

CINEMA AND FILMS

Campaign
Films and Filming
Gambit
International Broadcast
  Engineer

Movie Maker
New Statesman
Photoplay Film Monthly
Screen International
Sight and Sound

Speech and Drama
Stand
Studio Sound
Tribune
Un-Common Sense

ECONOMICS, ACCOUNTANCY AND FINANCE

Accountancy
Administrative
  Accounting
*Australian Financial
  Review (Aus.)
Banker
Bankers' Magazine
Building Societies Gazette
Business Scotland
*(Calcutta) Capital (In.)
Certified Accountant
City Press
Commerce International
*Commerce (In.)

Contemporary Review
Dairy Industries
Data Processing
  Practitioner
Economic Journal
Economica
Economist
Far East Week by Week
Financial Times
Grower
Hotel, Catering, and
  Institutional
  Management
  Association Journal

Insurance Brokers
  Monthly
Investors Chronicle and
  Stock Exchange Gazette
Local Government
  Chronicle
New Statesman
Round Table
*Studies (Ire.)
Time and Tide
Tribune
West Africa
World Survey

EDUCATION

A.M.A.
Amateur Stage
ARELS Journal
Art and Craft in
  Education
British Esperantist
Catholic Education To-day
Centre Point
Child Education

Education
Education and Training
English
Esperanto Teacher
Guider
Health Education Journal
Housecraft
Industrial Society
Junior Bookshelf

Junior Education
Local Historian
Modern Language Review
Modern Languages
Month
Mother
Municipal Review
Museums Journal
Music Teacher

New Blackfriars
New Era
New Humanist
New Statesman
New Universities Quarterly
Nursery World
Outposts
Parents Voice
Pictorial Education
PNEU Journal
Preparatory Schools
    Review

Question
*Reality (Ire.)
Safety Education
School Librarian
Scottish Educational
    Journal
Special Education
Speech and Drama
Spoken English
*Studies (Ire.)
Teacher
Theology

Times Educational
    Supplement
Together
Tribune
Unesco Courier
Use of English
Visual Education
World's Children

ENGINEERING AND MECHANICS

(See also under AGRICULTURE, ARCHITECTURE, AVIATION, MOTORING, NAUTICAL, RADIO,
SCIENCE, TRADE AND COMMERCE)

*Australian Mining
Buses
Car Mechanics
Civil Engineering
Computer Survey
Computer Weekly
Control and
    Instrumentation
Design
Electric Living
*Electrical Engineer (Aus.)

Electrical Review
Electrical Times
Engineer
Engineering
Engineering Materials
    and Design
Gas World
Industrial Safety
*Industrial Management
    (Aus.)
International Construction

Model Engineer
Model Railway
    Constructor
*N.Z. Energy Journal
*N.Z. Engineering
*N.Z. Engineering News
Practical Woodworking
Railway Gazette
Railway Magazine
Railway World
Spaceflight

HEALTH, MEDICINE AND NURSING

Balance
British Deaf News
British Medical Journal
British Naturism
*Caritas (Ire.)
Chest, Heart and Stroke
    Journal
Community Care
Contemporary Review
Health Education Journal
Here's Health

Hers
Industrial Safety
*Irish Journal of Medical
    Science
Lancet
Mother
Mother and Baby
New Humanist
New Statesman
New Vegetarian
Nursery World

Nursing Mirror
Nursing Times
Parents
Pharmaceutical Journal
Physiotherapy
Practitioner, The
Pulse
Quarterly Journal of
    Medicine
Slimmer Magazine
World Medicine

HISTORY AND ARCHAEOLOGY

Antiquity
Bedfordshire Magazine
Coins
Contemporary Review
Country Quest
English Historical Review
Geographical Magazine
Heythrop Journal

History
History Today
Illustrated London News
In Britain
Lancashire Life
Local Historian
Midland History
Museums Journal

New Blackfriars
Round Table
Scotland's Magazine
Scottish Historical Review
*Studies (Ire.)
World Survey

HOME
(See also FEMININE)

*Australian Home
    Beautiful (Aus.)
*Caritas (Ire.)
Design
Do It Yourself
Electrical Living
Embroidery
*Garden and Home (S.A.)

Homemaker
Home Science
Homes and Gardens
House & Garden
Housecraft
Ideal Home
Jewish Telegraph
Mother

Mother and Baby
Parents
Practical Householder
Safety Education
*Your Family (S.A.)
Womancraft with Sewing
    and Knitting

LITERARY

Anglo-Welsh Review
Author
Blackwood's Magazine
Book Collector
Books and Bookmen
Bookseller
*Canadian Author (Can.)
*Canadian Forum
*Canadian Literature
Contemporary Review
Critical Quarterly
*Dalhousie Review (Can.)
Delta
Dickensian
Encounter
English

Freelance Writer &
    Photography
Frontier
Illustrated London News
Indexer
Index on Censorship
Journalist
Junior Bookshelf
*Landfall (N.Z.)
Library
Library Review
London Magazine
*Malahat Review (Can.)
*Meanjin Quarterly (Aus.)
New Library World
New Review
New Statesman

Paperback Buyer
Outposts
Question
*Quill & Pen (Can.)
*Reality (Ire.)
Scottish Review
Spectator
Stand
*Studies (Ire.)
Theology
Times Literary
    Supplement
Tribune
Use of English
Woman Journalist
Writing

MOTORING

Autocar
Car
Car Mechanics
Caravan
Caravanning Monthly
Commercial Motor
Custom Car

Good Motoring
Hot Rod & Custom UK
Motor
Motor Cycle
Motor Cycle News
Motor Cycle Racing
Motorcycling Monthly

Popular Motoring
Practical Motorist
*Revs (Aus.)
Thoroughbred and
    Classic Car
*Wheels (Aus.)

MUSIC AND RECORDING

Early Music
Gramophone
Hi-Fi News
Jazz Journal International
Melody Maker
Music and Letters
Music and Musicians

Music in Education
Music Review
Music Teacher
Music Week
Musical Opinion
Musical Times
New Musical Express

Organ
Popular Hi-Fi & Sound
Radio & Record News
Records and Recording
Studio Sound
Tempo
Tribune

NATURAL HISTORY

Aquarist and Pondkeeper
Birds and Country
    Magazine
Blackwoods Magazine
Cage and Aviary Birds
Country Life
Countryman
Country Quest
Country-side
Dalesman

Ecologist Quarterly
Entomologists' Magazine
Essex Countryside
Gamekeeper and
    Countryside
Geological Magazine
Grower
Guider
Lancashire Life
Museums Journal

Naturalist
Nature
New Ecologist
Petfish Monthly
Scotland's Magazine
Scottish Field
Shooting Times
Vole
Whole Earth Magazine
Wildlife

NAUTICAL OR MARINE

Blackwoods Magazine
Canoeing Magazine
Industrial Safety
Marine Week
Motor Boat
Nautical Magazine
Navy International

*New Zealand Yachting
    and Power Boating
Port of London
Practical Boat Owner
Sea Breezes
*Seacraft (Aus.)
Ship & Boat International

Ships Monthly
Yacht and Boat Owner
Yachting Monthly
Yachting World
Yachts and Yachting

PHILATELY

*Irelands Own
Philatelic Magazine
Philately

Stamp Collecting
Stamp Lover
Stamp Magazine

Stamp Monthly

PHOTOGRAPHY

Amateur Photographer
British Journal of
  Photography
Camera User Magazine

Creative Camera
  Forensic Photography
*Irelands Own
Movie Maker

Photography
Practical Photography
Studio International

POLITICS

*Australian Quarterly
British Weekly
Candour
China Quarterly
Contemporary Review
*Current Affairs Bulletin
  (Aus)
*Current Events (In.)
East-West Digest
Illustrated London News
International Affairs
Justice of the Peace

Labour Monthly
Labour Weekly
Liberal News
*National Times (Aus)
New Blackfriars
New Statesman
Peace News
Political Quarterly
Question
Round Table
*Studies (Ire.)
*Thought (In.)

Town and Country
  Planning
Tribune
Ulsterman
Un-Common Sense
Unesco Courier
West Africa
*Winnipeg Free Press
  (Can.)
World Development
World Survey
World Today

RADIO AND TELEVISION

Broadcast
Campaign
Gramophone
Hi-Fi News
Intermedia
International Broadcast
  Engineer
Listener

Media Reporter
New Statesman
Practical Wireless
Radio & Record News
Radio Times
Short-Wave Magazine
Stage and Television
  Today

Studio Sound
Television
Tribune
TV Times
*TV Times (Aus.)
Video

RELIGION AND PHILOSOPHY

*Aryan Path (In.)
Baptist Times
British Weekly
Catholic Education Today
Catholic Fireside
Catholic Herald
Catholic Pictorial
*Catholic Weekly (Aus.)
Christian Herald
Christian Record
Church News
Church of England
  Newspaper
Church of Ireland Gazette
Church Times
Churchman
Clergy Review
Contemporary Review
*Cross, The (Ire.)
Crusade
Downside Review
Evangelical Quarterly

Faith and Freedom
Friend
Guideposts
Heythrop Journal
Home Words
Inquirer
Jewish Telegraph
Labour Monthly
Life and Work
Mankind Quarterly
Methodist Recorder
Mind
Modern Churchman
Month
New Blackfriars
New Humanist
New Outlook
News Extra
News Plus
Pax
Quaker Monthly
Question

*Reality (Ire.)
Reform
Sign
*Southern Cross (S.A.)
Spiritualist Gazette
*Studies (Ire.)
Studies in Comparative
  Religion
Tablet
Theology
Third Way
Together
Tribune
Un-Common Sense
Universe
War Cry
West Africa
*Word (Ire.)
World Outlook
Young Soldier

SCIENCE

(See also under AGRICULTURE, AVIATION, CINEMA, ENGINEERING, HEALTH, HISTORY, MOTORING, NATURAL HISTORY, NAUTICAL, PHOTOGRAPHY, RADIO, SPORTS, TRAVEL)

Computer Weekly
Contemporary Review
Criminologist
Data Processing
Design
Fire
Geological Magazine
Heredity

Illustrated London News
Impact of Science on
    Society
*Irish Press
Mankind Quarterly
Mind
Nature
New Blackfriars

New Humanist
New Scientist
Practical Electronics
Psychologist Magazine
Science Progress
West Africa

SERVICES: NAVAL, MILITARY, AIR, AND CIVIL

Air Pictorial
Army Quarterly
Battle
Blackwoods Magazine
Opinion

Red Tape
Round Table
Royal Air Forces
    Quarterly

Royal British Legion
    Journal
RUSI Journal
TAVR

SPORT, GAMES, HOBBIES AND PASTIMES

(See also under AGRICULTURE, ANIMALS, ART, AVIATION, CINEMA, FEMININE, HOME, MEN, MOTORING, MUSIC, PHILATELY, PHOTOGRAPHY, RADIO, THEATRE, TRAVEL)

Aeromodeller
Anglers' Mail
Angling
Angling Times
*Australasian Dirt Bike
*Australian Angler
*Australian Outdoors
    (Aus.)
*Australian Sporting
    Shooter
British Chess Magazine
Camping
Canoeing Magazine
Climber and Rambler
Club Secretary
Cricketer
Cycling
Edinburgh Evening
    News
Field, The
Gamekeeper and
    Countryside

Games & Puzzles
Gem Craft
Gems
Golf Illustrated
Golf International
Golf Monthly
Golf World
Great Outdoors
Guider
Horse and Hound
In Britain
Karate
Light Horse
Model Engineer
Model Railway
    Constructor
Model Railways
*New Zealand Outdoor
*Outdoor Canada Magazine
Parks & Sports Grounds
Practical Camper
Railway World

Scottish Field
Scouting
Sea Angler
Shooting Times
Skier
Small Boat
*South African Yachting,
    Power Waterski & Sail
Sport and Recreation
Sporting Life
Tennis
Tennis World
*Top Sport (S.A.)
Trout and Salmon
Woodworker
*Word (Ire.)
World Bowls
World Fishing
Yachting Monthly
Yachting World
Yachts and Yachting

THEATRE, DRAMA AND DANCING
(See also under CINEMA, MUSIC)

Amateur Stage
Ballroom Dancing Times
Contemporary Review
Dance and Dancers
Dancing Times
Drama
Gambit
Illustrated London News

In Britain
Karate
*Landfall (N.Z.)
New Statesman
*Performing Arts in
    Canada
Plays and Players
Radio Times

*Reality (Ire.)
Speech and Drama
Stage and Television
    Today
Theatre Quarterly
Tribune
TV Times

TOPOGRAPHY

Bedfordshire Magazine
Buckinghamshire and
  Berkshire Countryside
Cheshire Life
Country Life
Country Quest
Coventry Evening
  Telegraph
Cumbria
Dalesman
Derbyshire Life and
  Countryside
Dorset

Eastern Daily Press
Essex Countryside
Gloucestershire and Avon
  Life
Hampshire
Hertfordshire
  Countryside
In Britain
Inverness Courier
Kent Life
Lancashire Evening Post
Lancashire Life
Local Historian

Manx Life
Mid-Kent Gazette
Scottish Field
Scottish Tatler
Sussex Life
This England
Town and Country
  Planning
Warwickshire and
  Worcestershire Life
Yorkshire Life
Yorkshire Ridings

TRADE AND COMMERCE

(See also under ARCHITECTURE, ADVERTISING, AGRICULTURE, CINEMA, ECONOMICS,
ENGINEERING, MOTORING*)*

Achievement
Bookseller
Brewing & Distilling
  International
British Printer
Business Credit
Catering & Hotel
  Management
Catering Times
Cosmetic World News

CTN
Data Processing
Data Systems
Draper's Record
European Plastics News
Far East Week by Week
Fashion Forecast
Fashion Weekly
Games and Toys
Gifts

Grocer
Industrial Participation
Industrial Safety
Industrial Society
Marine Week
Printing World
Swimming Pool Review
Woodworker
World Development

TRAVEL AND GEOGRAPHY

Blackwood's Magazine
British Esperantist
British-Soviet Friendship
Bulletin of Hispanic
  Studies
*Canadian Geographical
  Journal (Can.)
Caravan, The
Catholic Fireside
Contemporary Review

Expedition
Geographical Journal
Geographical Magazine
*Hibernia (Ire.)
Illustrated London News
In Britain
*Ireland of the Welcomes
Local Historian
*Natal Witness (S.A.)

*New Zealand Holiday
  (N.Z.)
Northern Scotland
Railway World
Town and Country
  Planning
*United Asia (In.)
Voyager
Waterways World
World Survey

UNITED KINGDOM PRESS-CUTTING AGENCIES

Note.—In the following section it should be noted that no agency can check every periodical, local paper, etc., and that some agencies cover more than others. Special attention should be given to the time limit specified by certain agencies.

International Press-Cutting Bureau (1920), 70 Newington Causeway, London, SE1 6DF   *T.* 01-403 0608.   *T.A.* Adverburo, London, SE1.   *Subscription rates:* On application.   *Representatives:* Brussels, Copenhagen, Geneva, Madrid, Milan, Paris, Lisbon, Stockholm, Berlin, Helsinki, The Hague.

Newsclip (incorporating **Apcut, Ltd.**), 69 Fleet Street, London, EC4Y 1NS   *T.* 01-353 7191.   *Subscription rates:* On application.

Press Information (Scotland), Ltd., Virginia House, 62 Virginia Street, Glasgow, G1 1TX   *T.* 041-552 6767.   Comprehensive Scottish cuttings service. *Subscription rates:* On application.

OVERSEAS PRESS-CUTTING AGENCIES

AUSTRALIA
Australian Press Cuttings Agency Reg., Stalbridge Chambers, 443 Little Collins Street, Melbourne, C.1, Victoria, 3000. $16 per 100 cuttings.

Barrow, Ivo, P.O. Box 49, Carnegie, Victoria, 3163.   Rates on application.

CANADA
Canadian Press Clipping Services, 481 University Avenue, Toronto, M5W 1A7 *T.* 595-1811.

INDIA
International Clipping Service, Lakshmi Building, Sir P. Mehta Road, Fort, Bombay, 1.   *T.* 263451 (Telegrams: Orientclip).   *Partner:* Rajan K. Shah. Supplies Press Cuttings of news, editorials, articles, advertisements, press releases, etc., from all India, Pakistan, Ceylon, Burma and Goa papers. Undertakes compilation of statistical reports on competitive Press advertising pertaining to all products.

IRELAND
PR Services, Old Bawn Way, Tallaght, Co. Dublin.   *T.* Dublin 511242.   Covering all Republic of Ireland, and Northern Ireland newspapers and periodicals.

NEW ZEALAND
Chong's Press Cutting Bureau, P.O. Box 8143, Newton, Auckland.   All New Zealand Publications covered.   Normal review charge $8.00 per month (up to 10 books) plus 20c. per cutting.   (Also accepted $5.00 per book plus 20c. per cutting).

SOUTH AFRICA
S.A. Press Cutting Agency, 2nd Floor, Lionel House, Pickering Street, Durban, Natal.   *T.* 370403.   *T.A.* Newscut, Durban.   English and Afrikaans newspapers and trade journals from Zambia to the Cape.   *Minimum rates:* R17.00 per 100 cuttings.

SRI LANKA
International Press Cutting Service, 63/21 Bowala, Kandy, Sri Lanka (Ceylon).
   Representatives: Brussels, Geneva, Berlin, Paris, Stockholm, Helsinki, Calcutta, Karachi, Singapore, Wellington. Undertakes other investigations.
   Subscription rates: 100 cuttings—£5; 300 cuttings—£12.50 : 500—£19.50;
   1000 cuttings—£35.
   Subscription expires after 12 months.

UNITED STATES
Burrelle's Press Clipping Bureau (1888), 75 East Northfield Avenue, Livingston,
   New Jersey 07039.   *T.* 201-992-6600.

Luce Press Clippings, Inc., 420 Lexington Avenue, New York, N.Y., 10017.

New England Newsclip Agency, Inc., 5 Auburn Street, Framingham, Mass.
   01701.   *T.* 617-742 4200 and 617-879 4460.

Reviews on File, Walton, N.Y., 13856.   *T.* 607-865-4226.   *Owner:* Dorothy M.
   Brandt.   Back clippings on authors.

index

This sentence contains "five wor